NATURALISM

———— and ————

RELIGION

NATURALISM
—— and ——
RELIGION

—— k a i ——
NIELSEN

 Prometheus Books
59 John Glenn Drive
Amherst, New York 14228-2197

Published 2001 by Prometheus Books

Inquiries should be addressed to
Prometheus Books
59 John Glenn Drive
Amherst, New York 14228–2197
VOICE: 716–691–0133, ext. 207
FAX: 716–564–2711
WWW.PROMETHEUSBOOKS.COM

05 04 03 02 01   5 4 3 2 1

Library of Congress Cataloging-in-Publication Data

Nielsen, Kai, 1926–
    Naturalism and religion / Kai Nielsen.
        p. cm.
    Includes bibliographical references and index.
    ISBN 1–57392–853–4
    1. Naturalism—Religious aspects. 2. Atheism. I. Title.

BL2747.3 .N487 2000
211'.6—dc21   00–045841

Printed in the United States of America on acid-free paper

For Gertrude, Tziporah, Adel,
Chandra, Shabbir, and Isaac
Steadfast Friends and Good Philosophers

CONTENTS

PART TWO: AN EXAMINATION OF SOME ACCOUNTS OF NATURALISM: FOR AND AGAINST

PART THREE: THE CHALLENGE OF WITTGENSTEIN

ACKNOWLEDGMENTS

I would like to thank Murray Clarke, Jocelyne Couture, Stanley French, Christopher Gray, Andrew Lugg, Hugo Meynell, Jack Ornstein, Andrew Wayne, and Vladmir Zeman for their conversations and criticisms of some of the ideas expressed here. I have learned from them. I would particularly like to thank Andrew Lugg and Stanley French for their penetrating remarks concerning the long and difficult chapter on Wittgenstein. They have saved me from some false steps.

I would also like to thank Merlette Schnell for the speedy and accurate word processing. The same goes for Brenda Roberts's speedy but still conscientious reading of the proofs. They both made my life much easier.

INTRODUCTION

I

W hat I want most to achieve in *Naturalism and Religion* is to give a perspicuous articulation and soundly reasoned account of a thoroughly secular and as well a thoroughly humanist way of looking at things and of living in our world—our modern, or, if you will, post-modern world. I want to give an articulation and defense of such a way of looking at our world and a way of responding to it that will answer to our expectations of what a truly human life would be. This, of course, involves getting some grip on what "a truly human life" could come to, including, of course, coming to have some reasonable sense of what we are talking about when we use that in some ways perplexing phrase.

Our world is a world of vast flux with whole populations on the move; a world which is, at least in a de facto sense, becoming more multicultural and more pluralistic and in which objectified human relations are almost a matter of course—where people (if they ever were) are not seen as being ends in themselves, even where lip service is paid to that idea—and in which alienation is very deep and very pervasive (Hobsbaum 1994, 1995). We have to face this when we try to come to grips with the questions posed in the first paragraph.

A thoroughly secular view will be atheistic and naturalistic, but, if humanistic as well (after all, Stalin and Pol Pot were atheists), it will be a distinctive kind of atheism and naturalism. For a humanist atheism, human beings—all human beings—count. Indeed in an important way, it will be egalitarian; that is, it will be the view that the life of everyone matters and matters equally. It will tie its social hopes, as Richard Rorty does, and as John Dewey did before him, to the achievement of the most extensive approximation possible of "a global, cosmopolitan, democratic; egalitarian, classless, casteless society" (Rorty 1999, xii; Nielsen 1985). For us secular humanists this egalitarian social hope can be an almost despairing hope, given the ugly, brutish, uncaring, vastly inegalitarian world in which we live and which appears to be firmly with us for the foreseeable future. Still it remains a social hope worth fighting for. We need in our circumstances repeatedly to remind ourselves of Antonio Gramsci's remark about the pessimism of the intellect and the optimism of the will.

Secular humanists among themselves, and nonsecular humanists as well, will differ over how such an egalitarian world might be achieved or approximated and over just how it is to be articulated—what exactly we will take a proper equality to be—but they will make it, though differing about its exact articulation, a central ideal among their ideals—their hopes for the kind of world we should seek to make a reality, namely a world of social equals where the life of everyone matters equally; we seek a classless, genderless, nonracist, casteless world—a world where, as George Orwell put it, there will be no bowing and scraping.

This is the kind of secularist and atheist a secular humanist atheist will be, though let me remind you again that not all atheists and not all naturalists have been, even in aspiration or in idealized conception, such atheists or naturalists. There have been Fascist naturalists and atheists and ruggedly individualist ones committed to egoism or something very like it and there have been, and still are, religious humanists.

This book, except for a few asides, will focus on the atheist and naturalist side of the notion of "atheist humanism" or "naturalistic humanism." But in the case I make for atheism and naturalism, humanism, as I gestured at a characterization above, will be there as a crucial background assumption. And I have argued for it elsewhere and extensively. It is not for me a promissory note or an article of faith (Nielsen 1985, 1996, 207–89). Moreover, the very kind of naturalism I argue for, namely a social naturalism and a thoroughly nonscientistic naturalism, is designed to allow a conceptual place for normative matters, centrally, but not exclusively, for moral and political normative matters. (See chapter 2.) My naturalism is not a Skinnerian "value-free" naturalism. Without reenchanting the world, it is a naturalism which has a place—an objective place—in a nonreified sense of that term—for norms and values in a disenchanted world. There is nothing reductive about it.

However, as we shall see, the notion of naturalism is more problematic then it at first may seem. In the first chapter I shall give a characterization of it that I think for most purposes is adequate. But in chapters 5 and 6 we shall see that something more, though building on what I say in chapter 1, should be said. And I shall bring out in doing that how naturalism can plausibly be said to come under challenge and something of what needs to be said by way of response to this challenge to gain a compelling and attractive conception of naturalism.

In fine, *Naturalism and Religion* seeks clearly to articulate and render plausible naturalism and, what ineluctably goes with it, atheism. It seeks, that is, not only to articulate and explicate—to perspicuously display—naturalism, but as well to give a sound and rounded defense of naturalism. It seeks to provide a narrative, replete with argument and with a vision of things, that makes being a naturalist something desirable to be.

This book is structured in the following way. In Part One I characterize naturalism and atheism and provide a naturalistic explanation of the functions of religion, attempting to show that what underlies religious symbols are facts about human beings and societies, facts about their needs, fears, and aspirations in turn reflecting the conditions in which they live. I further argue, against the grain, that there is an important and correct way in which understanding religion is incompatible with believing in it. That notwithstanding, I seek to make clear what there is about religion, even in our cultural environment, that really grips some sensitive, knowledgeable, and reflective people. I then go on to argue that these needs—this sense of life—can and should be answered to by an utterly secular orientation. Seeing without evasion the consequences of a consistent atheism does not (*pace* the early Sartre) rob life of its significance or make social and political commitment arbitrary. We need not be forced to religion, against our reason—against what we reasonably believe about the world—to make sense of our lives.

In Part Two I examine some accounts for and against naturalism and some demands for a greater clarification of what it is. First, stepping back to a generation just before our own, I look at the now unfortunately neglected articulations and defenses of naturalism and atheistic humanism made by Sidney Hook and Ernest Nagel and the responses of a selected range of their critics (among them a Wittgensteinian one). After giving an account of Hook and Nagel and their critics, I then critically examine their naturalism, as well as that of Antony Flew, in the light of where we stand now philosophically and culturally. This includes an exchange between Sidney Hook and myself where, under the umbrella of a common secular humanism, the old and new (to put it somewhat tendentiously) pragmatic naturalism and atheism confront each other. I also explain and then assess the forceful and rigorously analytical case made by Jean Hampton that naturalism stands for nothing clear or compelling and may even be incoherent. These chapters, taken together, further clarify what it is to be a naturalist and an atheist and the substantial and methodological grounds for naturalism and atheism.

In Part Three I seek to make both clearly available and to assess what I take to be the strongest intellectual challenge to secularism and naturalism—to the very idea of the desirability of a postreligious culture—namely that of Wittgenstein himself and of some Wittgensteinians. I have in mind O. K. Bouwsma, Norman Malcolm, D. Z. Phillips, Hilary Putnam, Rush Rhees, and Peter Winch. I try to set out these Wittgensteinian views, as well as Wittgenstein's own way of viewing religion, in their most compelling forms and then argue that, significant as they are, they do not undermine, or even render fragile, a through and through atheistic and secular orientation. And they do not shield religion from the wolves of disbelief (if that is what they are).

II

Critiquing such sophisticated articulations of religion, some fellow secular humanists may believe, is not where it is at vis-à-vis religion today, at least in the United States and to a somewhat lesser extent in the rest of North America and in Latin America. In the United States religion is rampant and massively, though, of course, not exclusively, Neanderthal. In a recent survey taken in the United States, 88 percent of the population (if the sample taken was accurate) maintained that they had never had any doubts about the existence of God. Even if this survey is inaccurate and this is true of only 40 percent of the population, it is still an intellectual and moral disgrace—a disgrace that should be a scandal in the United States. And that it is a disgrace is something with which many, if not all, of the religious persons whose views I will be concerned to critique would agree, though some very orthodox Christian philosophers such as Alvin Plantinga, J. P. Moreland, and William Lane Craig might welcome it. Given, for example, the account of religion that Plantinga gives, I should think that he should welcome it, but being a philosopher of integrity it is also unclear that he would. It is difficult to believe that any genuine philosopher—and he surely is one—would. But such speculations aside, the social fact is that in the United States there is a cultural climate where there is strong imput from a fanatical and puritanical religious right—from the likes of Pat Buchanan. It has pushed the political agenda in the United States to the right. We have anti-abortion, anti-euthanasia, pro-death penalty platforms fiercely defended; we have stiffer prison sentences being handed out, more prisons being built (including private ones run as businesses), until by now the United States has more people in jail than any other country in the world and in these jails, 75 percent are blacks though they are 25 percent of the whole population. The number of people imprisoned recently has reached two million. And the above hardly completes the list of reactionary social practices that have become part of the very fabric of American society.

This very right-wing, religiously inspired agenda forces politicians, who wish to survive politically (and what politician doesn't), to say publicly perfectly ridiculous things about religion, things that in all likelihood the better educated among them (Clinton and *perhaps* both Bush father and Bush son, for example) must know to be moonshine. Moreover, the power of the religious right-wing political and religious agenda forces these politicians not only to mouth pious nonsense, but to favor very retrograde and unenlightened social measures and programs as well.

It is here, some of my secular-humanist colleagues will tell me, that the battle over religion must be fought and not over such arcane issues as those I discuss.[1] Wittgensteinian or Kierkegaardian fideism, right or wrong, counts for nothing, socially speaking, in our struggles over religion. And my fellow secular-humanist colleagues might add (perhaps a little uneasily) that my naturalism, indeed our naturalism, counts for little more in such struggles.

In an important way they are right. It is from such crude forms of religiosity—a religiosity that is little better than superstition—that the political and social danger of religion arises in our midst and it is in this form that religion is a driving social force to be reckoned with in the United States and similar societies (e.g., Australia, Canada, and Quebec).[2]

Such religiosity proceeds with zeal, as if the Enlightenment had never existed. And if the Pat Buchanans of the world should triumph, we would be led into utter darkness where life would indeed be nasty, brutish, and perhaps even short or at least shorter, but nasty and brutish, certainly. I am very glad that I have secular-humanist colleagues who take up this good fight and that there are journals such as *Free Inquiry* that take on such Neanderthals. I should think for an intellectual that would be a very wearisome and boring Sisyphean task indeed, but still a task that must be done.

I do not think, however, that philosophy can have much effect here. These fundamentalists do have their philosophical spokespersons (more likely spokesmen), e.g., William Lane Craig and J. P. Moreland. They have learned techniques of the contemporary philosophical trade and deploy them to defend fundamentalism. They will read the critiques secular humanists make of religion and of their own accounts—remember Lenin said "Know your enemy"—and they will respond in predictable ways.[3] But rank-and-file fundamentalists will not read us. I speak of people who would close down abortion clinics, make the death penalty freely available and availed of (remember Bush's record in Texas), make sure evolution is not taught in the schools, make "creation science" a regular part of the science curriculum, ban the inclusion of "evil books" from public school curricula and from public libraries, shut gays and lesbians down (get them, since they always will be with us, firmly back in the closet), and halt the influence of liberals (to saying nothing of socialists) on our cultural life. They, of course, will be glad to hear that there are those great philosophers out there—J. P. Moreland and William Lane Craig—who have utterly refuted those evil atheists with their barnyard moralities. But they will not, to any considerable extent, read Moreland or Craig, let alone us. They will just go on in their Neanderthalish and oppressive ways. Only occasionally when some individuals out of their own inner turmoil with religion come to have some reasonably persistent doubts, doubts which touch their personal lives, will they read us. And for that reason it is important that there be secular humanists who write in ways that speak to where they are.[4] But that will only be a drop in the bucket. Most believers are not so stressed. They just think of us (if they think of us at all) unquestionably and unambivalently as part of the evil empire.

What is needed more urgently on our part than such work is for us to think through and then propose ways of turning around—it surely cannot be done overnight—the vast mass of people out there who are so blinkered (so unthinkingly oriented) and who go about acting and seeing things in such reactionary and irrational ways. However, the proper answer to this is not only in giving people a sober education (as Freud once put it) and in having a decent media,[5] but to insure that everyone has sufficient means and security to live a decent life. (I principally have in mind here, given my "barnyard morality," the material conditions of life.) Where people are secure in this and other ways as well and can live such a life and have a reasonable education—a life that gives them some hope and ameliorates their alienation—religion, and particularly such Neanderthal sects, will have a hard sell as they do in the Nordic countries. (Remember not so very many years ago, before the rise in these countries of social democracies, these countries were fiercely, pervasively, and frequently Neantherthalishly religious.[6])

In spite of the power of the religious right, it is paranoid to see the United States as dominated by it, though it is certainly not paranoid to believe that in recent years American society has been to some considerable extent adversely affected by it. Still there are massive and not ineffective counterbalancing forces. There is in the United States not only the people who read the *New York Review of Books*, the *New Yorker*, the *Boston Review of Books*, the *Village Voice*, and the like, but a far greater mass of relatively educated and usually reasonably secure people who read the *New York Times*, the *Los Angeles Times*, and the *Washington Post*. They are a mix of a liberal and a conservative (often a somewhat liberal conservative) population reasonably effective in the public affairs of the United States. They can, rather conservative though many of them are, as are the newspapers they read, still be counted on in normal circumstances to resist the worst forms of fundamentalist and reactionary attack on American cultural life—the tradition whose high points include Jefferson, Emerson, Whitman, and Dewey. We should not forget that there is a difference between the educated conservative population—think of readers of the *Wall Street Journal* and the *Economist*—and the reactionary religious right. If, as it is not unreasonable to hope, this broad spectrum of reasonably educated and typically reasonably secure people could in a few years be persuaded to accept a social agenda which pushes their society to be a little more egalitarian—a little more like the Nordic countries—then the lives of people who are now poor and are living without hope will be significantly changed for the better.[7] This is a conjecture and perhaps nothing like this will happen. But it is not unreasonable to hope that it could.

With this change in the life conditions (including education) the terrible state of religious consciousness that afflicts the United States could in time be reversed.[8] It will not make secular humanists of us all, but it will bring more liberal tolerance and a greater secularizing of attitudes and practices into our world, even with liberal forms of Judaism and Christianity remaining powerful institutions: indeed the dominant religious institutions.[9] With such changes in society reactionary religious movements will not be as influential in setting the agenda of cultural and political life as they are now. With such conditions, with progressive social measures becoming more nearly the norm, we can expect religion slowly to wither away or at least scale down as it has to a considerable extent in the Nordic countries.[10]

Critical intellectuals critiquing religion can, and should, help push these matters along, but the most important forms of critique will be political and economic and not directly, or predominantly, of religion. So when I turn to such matters I turn to politics. Religious realignment in a more secular direction will come if a more progressive politics can gain hegemony. So I think doing political and social theory and critique—particularly critique—is vastly more important than doing the philosophy of religion or religious critique, though I do not deny that it has a place. (After all, I do it.) So when I write about religion, as in this book, I have a different aim than some of my secularist-humanist colleagues. I want to ascertain, if that is at all possible, what stance toward the world—what view of the world—really well-informed, sensitive, and reflective persons, with a good education and a good philosophical understanding (and some understanding of science), would be likely to and, as well, should make theirs where they care about themselves and their fellows, and where they are seeking to live a genuinely human life.[11] An important part of that task will be to come to understand what that is: to understand what a really human life comes to and, as well, to live it. Presumably it could be many things. But presumably there is also some unity here. But then, what unity?

As important as these questions are to us, we must also realize that they are desperately vague. But that is not to say that they cannot be made less so or that, standing there vague as they are, we have no understanding of them at all. With the unfolding of the Enlightenment, it has come to seem to not a few of us that we should be secularizers, through and through and all the way down. Those who think that, unless they are very *parti pris*, will not think that that is the only way to live a human life, but they do think it could be a considerable facilitator for a lot of people in our cultural contexts who would otherwise be deeply alienated, guilty, confused about what humans can be and achieve, and the like. Some, a not inconsiderable "some," have thought that for anyone so situated religious options are becoming dead options. Indeed for some they already are (Levine 1996, 346–50). However, there are reflective, informed, and sensitive others who are also so situated, for whom religion is a very live option. I speak of people sometimes tortured by doubts, aware of the evils that religion has brought and is still bringing upon us (the pope's apology notwithstanding), aware as well of religion's considerable implausibilities and at least seeming incoherencies, and yet people for whom religion is a live option. Indeed sometimes even a compellingly live option. Some of them, as Pascal did long ago, even believe that it is the only really live option for a human being who would not be evasive with herself. Think of Kierkegaard or of Karl Barth or of Simone Weil or of Alasdair MacIntyre during his fideist phase (MacIntyre 1956, 1957). I want to ascertain, if I can, whether there is anything like a right answer here or a more adequate answer or at least a more reasonable answer or whether it is all a matter of some probably unscrambled combination of how you have been brought up and of your particular wiring (Nielsen 1985, 119–87).[12] It seems to me that this is an important issue, even when it is nearly drowned out by the honking of fundamentalist geese.

III

I try with my attention to Wittgensteinians and fideists to consider the strongest account that we have directed (in part) toward the attempt to make it evident to us (if that can be done) that and how religion is, and indeed should, be a live option even for—perhaps most particularly for—the sort of persons I have just described. And indeed more widely as well. But there will be those who will deny that such accounts are that: namely the really significant and interesting accounts of, and at least in effect defenses of, the deep significance of a religious life. What is really significant, they will say, mind-bogglingly it seems to me, is the recent development of systematic analytic philosophy of religion after the demise of positivism and of Oxford linguistic philosophy with its trivialities. Systematic analytic philosophy of religion returns—and this is being taken as a positive thing by those making the above challenge—to the traditional metaphysical problems concerning religion. Such philosophers try to solve them, using the techniques of contemporary analytic philosophy, rather than regarding them as pseudoproblems with their characteristic metaphysical pseudo-propositions up for dissolution as houses of cards. The work of Richard Swinburne, James F. Ross, Marilyn McCord Adams, Robert Merrihew Adams, and Philip L. Quinn is typical of such an approach. And this is the underlying metaphilosophical position advocated by Michael Dummett (Dummett 1978, 437–58). These systematic analytical philosophers of religion simply uncritically adopt a basically Dummettian metaphilosophy.

It is true that such work is almost invariably carefully argued and responsibly researched. It is also true that it appears unblushingly in full metaphysical attire with none of the shyness about metaphysics of earlier analytic philosophy of religion. But there is the rub. These writers want to turn the clock back. They write as if Wittgenstein, Quine, Davidson, Kuhn, Cavell, Putnam, and Rorty had never written. The logical positivists and the Hägerströmians may have created, without seeing it as such, another metaphysics in attacking metaphysics. But it would be very hard to make that claim stick (Quine somewhat aside) with the philosophers mentioned above. But their critiques of metaphysics are probing and make a strong claim to being sound.[13] Moreover, they provide alternative ways of proceeding in philosophy which are brilliantly articulated. Notwithstanding that, this new brand of analytical philosophy of religion bypasses them and proceeds as if we could, in metaphysical, methodological, and metaphilosophical innocence, just go on with business as usual, though now using sharper analytical tools.[14] Until (if ever this can be achieved) they have given us good reasons to think that there is something in metaphysical enterprises, there is little of significance or interest in their often erudite, intricate, and careful work. I suppose we could analytically reconstruct and conceptually clarify Mary Baker Eddy's metaphysical tract too, but that would hardly enhance interest in it or further our understanding of the significance of religion. These analytical philosopher-theologians need first, against the antimetaphysical arguments of Wittgenstein, Davidson, Rorty, and Putnam, to give us some reason to think that there is in the sorts of things they are doing something significant.

Even if we do think (mistakenly I believe) that these antimetaphysical critiques are in some important ways off mark and that there is some point in taking a metaphysical turn and constructing a First Philosophy, the naturalist (metaphysical realist, physicalist) accounts of David Armstrong, J. J. C. Smart, and David Lewis seem far more plausible than ones that postulate very problematic "supernatural realities" which appear at least not to be compatible within a scientific perspective (Armstrong 1973, 1995, 1999; Smart 1995; Lewis 1984).[15] This naturalist metaphysical realist road is not a road I would take, but perhaps I am too *parti-pris* and the Wittgenstein-Putnam-Rorty antimetaphysical critiques may not have, after all, been all that compelling. So, for the nonce riding the metaphysical horse, the naturalistic ones, on that assumption, seem clearly to win out over other metaphysical accounts. If we must do metaphysics, what we need to recognize is that physicalism or something close to it is the only metaphysical game in town, if there are any metaphysical games in town. Riding the metaphysical horse, for the sake of the argument, we should say that on grounds of simplicity and coherence alone, it would seem that we should stick with the naturalistic accounts (Armstrong's rather systematic and straightforward one, for example) if we go in for any metaphysics at all. But the more important thing is to get off the horse and to challenge the very metaphysical enterprise itself as something without any coherent point or place in our trying to gain an understanding of ourselves and our world.

Reflect, in particular and for our purposes, on these systematic analytical metaphysical accounts of religion. What have they accomplished? Their analytical refinements have not resulted in the establishment of the soundness of any of the versions of the ontological argument, the cosmological argument, design arguments, or the establishment that religious experience yields evidence for the existence of God. Nor have they shown or given us sound reasons for believing there are miracles the existence of which make it irrational not to believe in God or—a rather weaker claim—even rational to believe in Him. And they have not shown that morality requires belief in God or that a theistic morality—or something more specific such as a Jewish morality or a Christian morality or an Islamic morality—is the most adequate morality available to human beings (Nielsen 1996, 79–113, 427–56, 557–97).

We are essentially here where Hume and Kant left us. If we are religious, we at best have nothing to rely on other than our faith—and then just one among many conflicting faiths (take your pick)—and even that, as Hume powerfully argued, is very problematic. These systematic analytic philosophers of religion have done very little, if anything, to advance matters here, even by their own lights, or to show how metaphysics, and particularly a theistic metaphysics, is a plausible option or even a coherent notion.

Moreover, their approach is a very rationalistic approach to religion. They do not take a proper regard for what it is that makes religion so important to people and why some of them stick to it in the face of daunting intellectual impediments and strong secular challenges, seeing it, as they do, as something essential to make sense of their and our tangled lives: to give us a sense of how life is not just one goddamned thing after another until we die and rot (if the crematorium doesn't get there first). Such religious people see religion as rooted in our emotions and reflective endorsements—reflective endorsements that they see as running against the grain of a pervasive secular culture. Sometimes they even take that culture to be a culture that has a deep rational secular rationale—something that is almost irresistibly reasonable. It surely looks like from a rational point of view to be the only game in town.[16] They feel this to the full, and sometimes face it nonevasively, but all the same they contend that without religious commitment human life will be gravely impoverished. It is with such matters, I argue, that we should come to grips and not with whether we can somehow, against all odds, tease out a sound cosmological argument or any argument or any evidence for the existence of God.[17] That is an old game that has come a cropper again and again. The history of philosophy since the Enlightenment has made that plain. New developments in physical cosmology and biology are not going to help one whit. Only some of the terminology changes. It is high time we stop playing that game—put that old horse out to pasture.

The dialectic of the Enlightenment has so worked itself out that going back to natural theology should be seen for what it is, i.e., something that is utterly pointless. What is crucial to face instead is whether we need a belief, however overwhelmed with intellectual impediments, in a Jewish, Christian, or Islamic God to make sense of our lives and to live really human lives. Fideists and some Wittgensteinians have argued that we do while most atheists have denied it as this atheist does. What is to be believed here? Are there anything like decent answers to such questions? This is what I wish to face as honestly and carefully as I can. Doing so will require considerable voyaging, but a voyaging that will always be in the service of answering that question, if indeed it can be answered.

NOTES

1. That is where the battle over religion is to be fought in our circumstances. But what I am talking about is not a matter of "a battle" at all. Rather in the context that I address in this book, we have two or more sides—a certain secular side and a certain religious side (each hopefully at their best) and sometimes "a side" somewhere in between—all with various articulations and all with integrity, honesty, with a reasonable store of information, and without trying to repress anyone, arguing for their own perspective. (Again they argue fallibilistically. That is to say, they are willing to change or alter their position if something else, all things considered, seems, on careful reflection, to be the more reasonable, where the sense of "reasonable" is taken very broadly. They do not expect or seek certainty.) This, of course, is an idealization. Things are a little more rough and tumble than that in actual discourses among intellectuals. We all know that partisanship, wittingly, but more frequently unwittingly, is something which often obtains. But, given what we take to be "the vocation of an intellectual" (Max Weber's sense of "vocation"), we will have intellectuals trying to figure out and to give us a sense of how it is best to orient our lives. They are trying impartially to seek the reflective endorsement of honest searchers. "Battle" is not at all the right word or conception here.

2. Though it is also correct to say that the disease is not so virulent in either present-day Canada or present-day Quebec.

3. The same thing might be said of us, i.e., us secular humanists. What we must make as sure of as we can, so as not to make that true, is that we respond as genuinely critical intellectuals not stereotypically but as people trying to think through the matter at hand as honestly as we can without assuming that a certain position must just be right. I hope *Naturalism and Religion* exemplifies that. But self-deception is common in such contexts. I only hope that I have been able to maintain that integrity and clarity about myself.

4. Probably the ones who will be most effective here will be those secular humanists who were once fundamentalists and know that situation from the inside.

5. If the English translation of the French monthly *Le Monde Diplomatic* were widely read across the United States—say as widely read as the *New York Times*—and a shorter, somewhat simpler version existed and was also widely available and widely read by people whose attention span is a little shorter, I would think that it in a relatively short period of time would do a lot to turn around many of the reactionary attitudes so prevalent in the United States, particularly if, along with it, there were rather more critically intelligent television programs than those now available showing at prime time and on major networks.

6. The decline of religion in Quebec, though not nearly so deep as it is in the Nordic countries, has occurred and is continuing to occur. The social transformation in other respects has not been as great either and no doubt these two phenomena are causally connected. There are, to be sure, social-democratic tendencies in Quebec, but they are only tendencies. Still secularization and a turn away from religion in Quebec has been extensive since the Quiet Revolution and the causes of that turn are much like the causes of the change in the Nordic countries.

Increased wealth somewhat more widely distributed and a better education made for a modern world helps a lot.

7. This assumes extensive change coming from the pressure of the middle strata of society. But they, though there has been a minority within it who have fought for progressive change, have not usually been a source of progressive social change. See the next note for a discussion of this issue.

8. There is one thing that casts a pall of gloom over this happy scenario. The Nordic countries did not achieve social democracy from above or from the middle, but via the militant struggles of a socialistically oriented working class. They had allies, of course, but they were the principal agents. There seems at present at least to be nothing like this in the United States or in the rest of North America. My above scenario rests on its being the case that an enlightened reasonably well-off middle and even upper strata of the population of the United States would come to see that rather more egalitarian and progressive social measures are the right way to go morally speaking and/or are in their interests as well as in the interests of the poor. It is not difficult to be skeptical about their coming to so react. Still perhaps we should not be too cynical about the effectiveness of such moral motivations particularly when they do not cost a lot. People may not be wired for decency, but they can be decent. Why isn't it possible that people with a sober education and securely placed would not come to see that more egalitarian arrangements would be the decent thing to have, reasonable and pretty much cost-free? Though it is still possible to surmise that some of the more thoughtful of them might believe that an educated and politically aware population might very well be a threat to the established social order—that is to the privileges and power of the upper and better-off middle strata. But again Sweden has those more progressive social arrangements and the capitalist order *seems* to be as intact there as it is in the United States. But they also built strong militant working-class parties, when the capitalist order was not so secure, in the way the United States never succeeded in doing. When there arose militant parties in Sweden, there also arose militant parties in the United States. But in Sweden, though somewhat toned down, they became a majority party or, with the split between the Left and the still more Left, a majority party and a large minority party (i.e., the communists). Nothing very close to that happened in the United States. See Richard Rorty on how top-down leftist initiatives and bottom-up leftist initiatives tend to reinforce one another and how it is possible reasonably to believe that both are important and that it is not the case that everything which is effective must come just from bottom-up initiatives (Rorty 1998, 53–54). Yet without a large, organized, united, militant mass of people who are faring badly or somewhat badly and are determined to do something about it, nothing is very likely to change to any considerable extent. I do not think that it is just Marxist dogma to give priority to bottom-up initiatives and to think that without them nothing much will happen. The pall of gloom remark with which this note starts is principally rooted in the fact that no such critical mass of militant people exists at present in the United States and that it is unclear how one might be brought into existence. What is crucial for us to consider is how one could be brought into existence in the United States, the linchpin country in the capitalist chain.

9. Note that people who are not secularists can still recognize the importance and desirability of some secularizing tendencies. Think, for example, of the
way Iran (2000) is going now.

10. This may be a too Whiggish scenario, but it does give us an empirical
possibility which we can work to make more than a possibility. Again we should
see how struggle is so crucial in attaining anything decent.

11. That is to ask a lot of us and perhaps few of us can attain that understanding. But we can approximate it and recognize that it is ideally the standpoint
from which we should make such judgments.

12. What the comparative weight of each imput may be is something that is
impossible to ascertain. See Nielsen 1985, 148–87.

13. I do not mean to give to understand that they are all the same. They by
no means are identical. But there are family resemblances and they make a
common thrust against the viability and point of metaphysics.

14. We should, as Rorty has well argued, be very careful in talking of our
"sharp analytical tools." In the history of analytic philosophy, what has at one
time been taken to be a new sharp analytical tool has later come to seem an old
dogma of no use. Think, for example, of the appeal to a sharp analytic/synthetic
distinction, to conceptual analysis, and even (though for the nonce more controversially) to conceptual schemes (Rorty 1982, 211–30).

15. We will see in chapter 6 Jean Hampton challenging the claim that we
have good grounds for believing that we know or even should believe that science shows that belief in such entities is incompatible with a scientific attitude.
But see my response there.

16. But what is this rational point of view? Do we have any clear sense of
what we are talking about here? Isn't it almost as much of a reification as God? Is
it not another obscure crutch or can we give it a reasonable demythologization?
(See here Nielsen 1996, 432–49.)

17. I am not against analytic philosophy. In fact I see myself as being both a
pragmatist-Marxian and an analytic philosopher. Indeed I think of myself as an
analytical Marxian. But I am against systematic analytic philosophy of religion à
la Swinburne, etc.

BIBLIOGRAPHY

Armstrong, D. M. 1973. "Continuity and Change in Philosophy." *Quadrant* 17,
    nos. 5–6: 19–23.
———. 1995. "Naturalism, Materialism and First Philosophy." In *Contemporary
    Materialism: A Reader*, edited by Paul K Moser and J. D. Trout, 35–51. New
    York: Routledge.
———. 1999. "A Naturalist Program: Epistemology and Ontology." *Proceedings
    and Addresses of the American Philosophical Association* 73, no. 2: 77–89.
Dummett, Michael. 1978. *Truth and Other Enigmas*. Cambridge, Mass.: Harvard
    University Press.
Hobsbawm, Eric. 1994. *Age of Extremes: The Short Twentieth Century*. London:
    Abacus.

———. 1995. "Ethnicity, Migration and the Validity of the Nation-State." In *Toward a Global Civil Society*, edited by Michael Walzer, 235–40. Providence, R.I.: Berghahn Books.

Levine, Andrew. 1996. "Just Nationalism: The Future of an Illusion." In *Rethinking Nationalism*, edited by Jocelyne Couture et al., 345–63. Calgary, Alberta: The University of Calgary Press.

Lewis, David. 1984. "Putnam's Paradox." *The Australasian Journal of Philosophy* 62: 221–36.

MacIntyre, Alasdair. 1956. *Difficulties in Christian Belief*. London: SCM Press.

———. 1957. "The Logical Status of Religious Belief." In *Metaphysical Beliefs*, edited by Ronald W. Hepburn, 168–205. London: SCM Press.

Nielsen, Kai. 1985. *Equality and Liberty: A Defense of Radical Egalitarianism*. Totowa, N.J.: Rowman and Allanheld.

———. 1995. *On Transforming Philosophy*. Boulder, Colo.: Westview Press.

———. 1996. *Naturalism without Foundations*. Amherst, N.Y.: Prometheus Books.

Rorty, Richard. 1982. *Consequences of Pragmatism*. Minneapolis, Minn.: University of Minnesota Press.

———. 1998. *Achieving Our Country*. Cambridge, Mass.: Harvard University Press

———. 1999. *Philosophy and Social Hope*. London: Penguin Books.

Part One

ARTICULATING NATURALISM

—————— 1 ——————

NATURALISTIC EXPLANATIONS OF RELIGION

I

Naturalism denies that there are any spiritual or supernatural realities. There are, that is, no purely mental substances and there are no supernatural realities transcendent to the world or at least we have no sound grounds for believing that there are such realities or perhaps even for believing that there could be such realities. Naturalism sometimes has been reductionistic (claiming that all talk of the mental can be translated into purely physicalist terms) or scientistic (claiming that what science cannot tell us humankind cannot know). The more plausible forms of naturalism are neither across the board reductionistic nor scientistic. Most claims that we make are not scientific claims, yet they can, for all of that, be true or false. Many of them are quite plainly and uncontroversially in place. That it snows in Ontario in winter, that people very frequently fear

From *Studies in Religion/Sciences Religieuses* 26, no. 4 (1977): 441–66.

death, that keeping promises is, generally speaking, a desirable thing are some unproblematic examples. And very frequently mentalistic talk in terms of intentions, thoughts, beliefs, feelings, and the like is not only useful, but indispensable if we are to make sense of human life and of the interactions between people. And such remarks are typically true or false and, again, sometimes unproblematically so. But it is, for the most part, hardly scientific talk, though from this, of course, it does not follow that it is antiscientific talk. It is just nonscientific. But there we are still talking about, under different descriptions, the same physical realities as we are when we give macroscopic descriptions of bodily movements, though in using mental terms we are usually talking for a different purpose. These descriptions are different, and usefully so, but, all the same, only one kind of reality is being described, namely, physical realities. There are no purely mental realities—realities independent of physical realities—in a naturalistic account of the world.

Religions, whether theisms or not, are belief-systems (though this is not all they are) which involve belief in spiritual realities.[1] Even Buddhism, which has neither God nor worship, has a belief in what Buddhists take to be spiritual realities and this is incompatible with naturalism as is theism as well, which, at least as usually understood, is a form of supernaturalism. Naturalism, where consistent, is an atheism. It need not be a militant atheism and it should not be dogmatic: it should not claim that it is certain that theism is either false or incoherent. Yet a naturalist, if she is consistent, will not be an agnostic, but will be an atheist arguing, or at least presupposing, that theism is either false or incoherent or in some other way unbelievable. Naturalism, that is, is incompatible with belief in God or a belief that God exists; so naturalists cannot be agnostics, saying, as agnostics do, that we do not know, or perhaps even cannot know, whether or not God does or does not exist. In accepting naturalism, a naturalist is also accepting that there is no God. But naturalists, if they are reasonable, will argue for atheism in a fallibilistic, and sometimes even in a moderately skeptical, manner: a manner that is characteristic of modernity including that peculiar form of modernity that some call postmodernity. A naturalist need not be a skeptic (indeed cannot be a skeptic through and through) though she can be, as Hume was, a limited and moderate skeptic. It should also be noted that a skeptic, limited or otherwise, need not be a naturalist, atheist, or even an agnostic as the fideistic stances of Pascal and Kierkegaard brilliantly exemplify. But, whether a limited skeptic or not, a naturalist, if she is reasonable, will be a fallibilist, but, that notwithstanding, still an atheist. "Dogmatic atheism" is not a pleonasm and "fallibilistic atheism" is not an oxymoron.[2]

Atheism has a critical side and an explanatory side. The critical side is exemplified in the works of d'Holbach and classically most profoundly in Hume and in our period by (among others) Axel Hägerström, Bertrand Russell, Paul Edwards, J. L. Mackie, Wallace Matson, Paul Kurtz, Richard Robinson, Antony Flew, Ingemar Hedenius, Kai Nielsen, and Michael Martin. Such an atheism gives grounds, in one way or another, for the rejection of all belief in supernatural or spiritual beings and with that, of course, Judaism, Christianity, and Islam with their common belief in God who created the universe out of nothing and has absolute sovereignty over creation.

Most naturalists also reject the conception, common to such theisms where they are even remotely orthodox, that human beings are sinful, utterly dependent on God, and can only make adequate sense of their lives by accepting without question God's ordinances for them. Naturalists reject that conception of human beings as well as the distinctive morality that goes with it. They believe that people can make sense of their lives and reasonably order their lives as moral beings without any belief in God or any other spiritual realities.

Critique and explanation are distinct and naturalists characteristically engage in both. But some kinds of explanation, as we shall see, if successful, are also critiques of religious belief and practice. People who, as Robin Horton puts it, see the world through Judeo-Christian spectacles are inclined to believe that naturalistic explanations of theistic belief explain religion by explaining religion away and are superficial to boot (Hortin 1993, 101–93). Some of them, not unsurprisingly, are (Baron d'Holbach's and Bertrand Russell's, for example), but others are not (Ludwig Feuerbach's and Émile Durkheim's, for example).

A naturalistic conception of religion will explain religion as a function of human needs and of the conditions of life which give rise to those needs. But it should be asked what (if anything) would constitute an adequate naturalistic explanation of religion? Here Marx Wartofsky well remarks that a "viable conception of religion is one which doesn't explain religion away, but rather explains its origins, its distinctive cultural and historical forms, its persistence in various institutions, its changing contexts and development, its continuing and present existence in the modes of belief and action of individuals" (Wartofsky 1982). To this it should be added that it needs, as well, to explain its extensive resilience in a deeply secularized world where, in Max Weber's phrase, the disenchantment of the world has, and for some time now, cut deeply and pervasively into our lives.

Some will say that no naturalistic conception can be fully adequate, for we cannot understand the reality of religion in such a neutral spectator's way. Only those who have actually experienced the reality of God, have felt for themselves the awe and dread of God's presence, can understand the reality of what is being talked about. But this is false or at the very least question-begging. Rudolph Otto, Friedrich Schleiermacher, and Martin Buber give us, from within a theistic perspective, deep and compelling accounts of religious *experience*—of the sense of the presence of God—but, after all, what we actually have here are psychological descriptions of the experiential life of some human beings. Moreover, two naturalistic philosophers, Axel Hägerström and Ronald Hepburn, have, turning to those accounts and extending them in a sensitive way, given us explicitly naturalistic accounts of religious experience and religious sensibilities (Hägerström 1949, 1964; Hepburn 1958). Just as it is not necessary to be neurotic to understand neurotics, so it is not necessary to be religious to understand religious experience, though it may be true that someone who has never felt the power of a neurotic response will not be likely to understand very deeply neuroses and that someone who has never been caught up in a religious life, as both Hägerström and Hepburn once were, will not be very likely to have a deep understanding of religious experience or sentiment. Without that experience and without having been deeply involved in a religious life, they are likely to have a tin ear for religious experience. But there are plenty of religiously sensitive exreligious believers who once were deeply committed religiously who understand religious experience perfectly well. Not all naturalists have a tin ear for religion.

It will also be the case that naturalistic explanations will become of paramount interest only when the critique of theism has been thought to have done its work. Marx's, Freud's, and Durkheim's accounts of religion, as they were themselves well aware, become most significant for religion, and more generally most normatively and critically significant, after we have come to believe, if we have come to believe, that the Enlightenment critiques of religion by Bayle and Hume, perhaps with a little contemporary rational reconstruction, are sound and even fairly unproblematically so. But it is not implausible to think that in our situation, coming down to us from the Enlightenment, there is, and best set in a historical narrative, what in effect is a cumulative argument (more literally a cluster of arguments with many strands and a complex development) against theism that has with time increased in force. Starting with the early Enlightenment figures, finding acute and more fully developed critiques in Hume and Kant, and carried through by their contemporary rational reconstructers (e.g., Mackie and Martin), the various arguments for the existence of God (including appeals to religious experience) have been so thoroughly refuted that few would try to defend them today and even those few that do so do so in increasingly attenuated forms. The move has increasingly been in religious apologetic to an appeal to faith and to arguments that claim that without belief in God life would be meaningless and morality groundless: that naturalism leads to nihilism or despair (Penelhum 1997; Hyman 1997). That fideistic reaction was in the century before ours—to take a key example—a very prominent phenomenon in Russian social life of certain leisured and educated strata, deeply alienated in their useless lives. This is forcefully depicted in the writings of Dostoevsky, Turgenev, and Chekhov.

Naturalists in turn point to the fact that such theistic responses do not face the fact that a perfectly reasonable and morally compelling secular sense can be made of morality, that alleged revelations and faiths are many and not infrequently conflicting and moreover, and distinctively, that the very concept of God is not unproblematical. Where, to turn to the latter, the theisms are plainly anthropomorphic, where we have something like a belief in a Zeus-like God, then religious claims are plainly false. Where theisms are more theologically ramified and the religion, at least in that sense, is more developed, theistic religions move away from animism to a more spiritualistic conception of God, e.g., "God is Pure Spirit," "God is not a being but Being as such," "God is the mysterious ground of the universe." But with this turn (an understandable turn for theism to take given the pressure of science and secular outlooks) religious claims, though becoming thereby not so clearly, or perhaps not even at all, falsifiable, are threatened with incoherence (Martin 1997).

As we move away from anthropomorphism to claims that God is Unlimited, the Ultimate Being transcendent to the universe, we no longer understand to whom or to what the term "God" refers. If we try to think literally here we have no hold on the idea of "a being or Being that is transcendent to the universe." And to try to treat it metaphorically is (a) to provoke the question what is it a metaphor of and (b) to lose the putatively substantive nature of the claim. God, in evolved forms of theism, is said to be an infinite individual who created the universe out of nothing and who is distinct from the universe. But such a notion is so problematical as to be at least arguably incoherent.[3] So construed, there could be no standing in the presence of God, no divine encounters, and no experiencing God in our lives. With anthropomorphism we get falsification and superstition—God is taken to be some mysterious and elusive entity or existent; without anthropomorphism, where God is said not to exist, i.e., to not be an existent, but to be eternal Ultimate Being, we get at least apparent incoherence.

Some theists have responded that the word "God" (and, of course, cognates in other languages) can be taught—can be given sense—by the use of definite descriptions such as "the first cause," "the sole ultimate reality," and the like. But these alleged descriptions are as problematical as the term "God" itself, for the key terms in such *putative* descriptions are themselves very good candidates for incoherence. We neither know what "self-caused being," "eternal utterly independent being," "maker of the universe," or "first cause" refer to nor do we in any other way understand what they *mean*. We do not know how to use them in sentences which make claims which have either truth-conditions or assertability-conditions.[4] They are just as puzzling as "God" or "eternal Ultimate Being" and appeal to them will not help us to come to understand what we are talking about when we speak of God. They are, many naturalists argue, grand but empty phrases without a determinate meaning (Hägerström 1964). To say that they refer to an ultimate mystery is just an evasive way of saying that we do not understand them. It in reality is just arm waving.

At the core of theistic belief there is a metaphysical belief in a reality that is alleged to transcend the empirical world. It is the metaphysical belief that there is an eternal, ever-present, creative source and sustainer of the universe. The problem is how it is possible to know or even reasonably to believe that such a reality exists or even to understand what such talk is about ("empirical world" may well be a redundancy). Naturalists believe that if we continue to try to see through Judeo-Christian spectacles that there is nothing to understand here. We are faced with the hopeless task of trying to make sense out of an incoherent something we know not what. Yet religious belief, much of which, in some way or other, is theistic belief, is culturally speaking pervasive even with the continuing disenchantment of the world.

The response of Reformed Philosophers—philosophers such as Alvin Plantinga and Nicholas Wolterstorff—philosophizing out of a Calvinist tradition, is that these alleged difficulties can legitimately be set aside. Believers have just as much right to believe in God without grounds or philosophical articulation as naturalistic philosophers (or for that matter anyone else) have a right to believe in the external world or in other minds, matters which, Reformed Philosophers claim, cannot be evidentially or argumentatively established either (Plantinga 1997; Wolterstorff 1997). But such a response, currently popular though it be in some circles, is, for at least three reasons, off the mark. Belief in God is not pervasively accepted across cultures in the way that belief in other-minds and the external world is; there can be no just relying on some putative revelation for they are many and frequently conflicting and we have no basis for picking out the real thing from the merely putative. Moreover, the appeal to such a basis paradoxically takes us away, if we think about it a little, from a straight appeal to revelation as the basis for belief. For we need criteria, independently of the alleged revelation, to judge whether a putative revelation is a genuine revelation. Finally, and thirdly, as we have already seen, there are questions about the very intelligibility of talk of God in a way that there is not about the external world or about other-minds. The idea that anthropologists might, and indeed actually do, come across cultures without a belief in God is a commonplace; the idea that anthropologists might come across a culture that does not believe that there is an external world or other minds is a patent absurdity (Nielsen 1996, 79–89, 119–39, 153–54, 445).

II

So with the critical work (the critique of the truth-claims of theism) essentially done by Hume, we should set both metaphysical speculation and fideistic *angst* aside and turn to naturalistic explanations of religious belief. The main players here from the nineteenth century are Ludwig Feuerbach, Friedrich Engels, Karl Marx, Max Stirner, and Friedrich Nietzsche and, from the twentieth century, Émile Durkheim, Max Weber, Axel Hägerström, Sigmund Freud, Bronislaw Malinowski, and Antonio Gramsci. Their accounts, varied though they are, are all thoroughly naturalistic.

These naturalists assume that by now it has been well established that there are no sound reasons for religious belief: there is no reasonable possibility of establishing religious beliefs to be true; there is no such thing as religious knowledge or sound religious belief. But, when there are no good reasons for religious belief and that that is so is, as well, tolerably plain to informed and impartial persons not crippled by ideology or neurosis, and yet religious belief, belief that is both widespread and tenacious, persists in our cultural life, then it is time to look for the *causes* of religious beliefs: causes which are not also reasons justifying religious belief. And indeed, given the importance of religious beliefs in the lives of most human beings, it is of crucial importance to look for such causes and indeed to find them, if we can. Here questions about the origin and functions of religion become central, along (though somewhat less centrally) with questions about the logical or conceptual status of religious beliefs.

Let us see how some of this goes by starting with Feuerbach and then, going to our century, moving on to Freud. (We will later turn to other such naturalists.) For Feuerbach, religion is the projected image of humanity's essential nature. To understand what religion properly is requires that explanation and elucidation be taken out of the hands of theology and turned over to anthropology. Even more iconoclastically, Feuerbach boldly asserts that theology must be reduced to anthropology. Feuerbach sees himself, vis-à-vis religion, as engaged in changing in a profound way the very way things are viewed, changing religion's very object, as it is in the believer's imagination, into a conception of the object as it is in reality, namely, that God is really the species-being (the idealized essence) of human beings rather than some utterly mysterious supernatural power. To talk about God, for him, is to talk about human beings so *idealized.*

Freud also discusses religion in psychological and anthropological terms. Religion in reality is a kind of mass obsessional delusion, though for understandable, and often very emotionally compelling reasons, it is, of course, not recognized as such by believers or at least not clearly and unwaveringly so. That would be altogether too threatening. What religious beliefs and practices in reality do, according to Freud, is to depress the value of life and distort "the picture of the real world in a delusional manner"—which, Freud had it, comes to "an intimidation of the intelligence." By so functioning, religion has succeeded in "sparing many people an individual neurosis. But hardly anything more" (Freud 1930, 31–32). Religion, on Freud's account, is the universal obsessional neurosis of humanity. It emerges out of the Oedipus complex—out of the helpless child's relation to what seems to the child an all-powerful father. "God," Freud tells us, "is the exalted father and the longing for the father is the root of the need for religion" (Freud 1957). Religious beliefs and doctrines "are not the residue of experience or the final result of reflection; they are illusions, fulfilments of the oldest, strongest and most insistent wishes of mankind; the secret of their strength is the strength of these wishes" (Freud 1957, 51).

In many circumstances in life we are battered and helpless. Faced with this helplessness, we unconsciously revert to how we felt and reacted as infants and as very young children where quite unavoidably we were subject to a long period of infantile dependence—a period where we are utterly helpless—and, given the sense of security we need because of this helplessness, we develop a father-longing. We need at that tender age someone who will protect us. Freud believes that human beings initially come to believe that this is what the father does. We come to recognize in later life that our fathers are by no means perfect protectors, nor could they be, even with the best motivations. In a world replete with threatening circumstances that we cannot control and not infrequently only imperfectly understand, we, "unconsciously reverting to our infantile attitudes, create the gods (Freud 1957, 27)." Thus religion functions to exorcise the terrors of nature, to reconcile us to the "cruelty of fate, particularly as shown in death," and to "make amends for the sufferings and privations that communal life of culture has imposed on man" (Freud 1957, 27). To speak of God is in reality not to speak, as believers believe, of a supernatural creator and sustainer of the world—there are no such spiritual realities—but of an imagined, idealized father, all knowing, all powerful, and all good, who deeply cares for us, and who can and will protect us.

For Feuerbach and Freud religious ideas are about psychological-anthropological realities. There is a stylized, and I believe a misleading, difference (alleged difference) characteristically thought to obtain between them and Engels, Marx and Durkheim. For the latter, by contrast with Feuerbach and Freud, religion is taken instead to be about *society*—about social realities. For Marx, all precommunist "historical" societies are class societies, driven by class struggles, where the class structures are epoch-specific and rooted in the material conditions of production. Religion, on his conception, and Engels's conception of things as well, functions principally to aid the dominant class or classes in mystifying and, through such mystification, helping to control the dominated classes in the interests of the dominant class or classes. Religion, as ideology, serves to reconcile the dominated to their condition and to give them an illusory hope of a better, purely spiritual world to come after they depart this vale of tears. This typically works in the interests of the dominant class or classes as a device to pacify what otherwise might be a rebellious dominated class, while at the same time "legitimating" the wealth and other privileges of the dominating class or classes. In this peculiar way—definitely an ideological way—religion works to "unify" class society, while at the same time giving expression to distinctive class interests. It serves both to "unify" class society and to sanctify class domination, while giving the dominated class an illusory hope—though, of course, not one seen by them to be illusory—of a better life to come after the grave (Marx and Engels 1958; Nielsen 1996, 467–507).

Durkheim, though in a rather different way, also saw religion as unifying society. In his view, however, it *genuinely* unified society. As Steven Lukes put it, Durkheim "saw religion as social in at least three broad ways: as socially determined, as embodying representations of social realities, and as having functional social consequences" (Lukes 1985, 462). In all these ways, talk of God is in reality talk about society, but they are different ways and only the part about embodying representations of social realities, as E. P. Evans-Pritchard, among others, noted, is *necessarily* naturalistic (Evans-Pritchard 1965). However, if a naturalistic turn is taken, questions about social determination and the social function of religion, rather than questions about the truth of religious beliefs, come to the forefront where they gain a pertinence that they did not have before. Still, questions about (a) what are the causes of religious beliefs and practices and what sustains them, (b) questions about the role they play in the life of human beings, and (c) questions about their truth should be kept apart, though admittedly (a) and (b) are intertwined. But at least initially, they should be held apart, as they can be conceptually in our thinking about them, and examined separately. Durkheim, like Marx and Freud, and like Feuerbach before them, believed, as we have already remarked, that earlier thinkers of the Enlightenment had established that religious beliefs make no sound truth-claims. Against this background, with his distinctive account of how religion embodies representations of social realities, Durkheim sought to give an utterly naturalistic account of what we are talking about, since we cannot, he has it, reasonably take religious beliefs at face value. But, with his distinctive account of how religion embodied representations of social realities, Durkheim sought to give an utterly naturalistic account of what we are talking about when we speak of God. God and the other religious beings of other religious systems "are aspects of society" (Durkheim 1912, 1915). Religion, for him, was a mode of comprehending social realities. As Lukes well put it, Durkheim saw religion "as a sort of mythological sociology" (Lukes 1985).

To put matters in a stylized way once more, while for Freud religious realities were psychological realities and for Feuerbach they were anthropological, for Durkheim they were sociological realities. Two points are relevant here, both made by Evans-Pritchard, among others: (1) all of these accounts are *reductionistic* and (2) for Durkheim, in reality, his sociological notions about religion were suffused with psychological notions. There is no keeping these matters apart in the way Durkheim wished and as his conception of sociology required. (Here his practice was better than his beliefs about his practice.) However, it goes the other way as well. Freud's "psychology of religion" and Feuerbach's anthropological account were also sociological accounts. So with all the figures discussed above (Marx and Engels included) we have a social psychological, socioeconomic account of the origin of religion, the status of religious ideas, and the functions of religion. They, of course, differently emphasize this and that, but they have an underlying common conception of religion. What Lukes says of Durkheim was common to all the above naturalistic theoreticians of religion. They refused to take religious symbols at what orthodox believers would take to be their face value; they refused to see, in the case of the theisms, the world through Judeo-Christian spectacles. They sought instead "to go 'underneath' the symbol to the reality which it represents and which gives it its 'true meaning' and (they sought to show as well) that all religions 'answer, though in different ways, to the given conditions of human existence' " (Lukes 1985, 482).

Religious believers of the monotheistic sort as part of their religious life sometimes utter utterances like the following: (1) "God is my creator and sustainer upon whom I am utterly dependent," (2) "God is an awesome and fearsome judge," (3) "God is the ineffable Holy One who alone is worthy of worship," or (4) "God is the supreme source of goodness." In trying to give a naturalistic account of the meaning of these utterances and of the referents of their key terms, a naturalistic intellectualist cognitive account will not do. A naturalistic rendition of (2), for example, as "I feel as if an imaginary and fearsome father were judging me" is not going to do as an account of the meaning or use of (2), for "I feel as if an imaginary and fearsome father were judging me but all the same I know there is no God" is neither a deviation from a linguistic regularity nor is it a contradiction. In that rather straightforward way without such "translations" or renderings it, like a lot of other bits of religious-talk, makes sense: makes sense, that is, if we do not think, rather carefully, about what we are trying to say. Still, coherent or not, such talk has a use (a function) in the language. Similarly with (1) "I feel utterly dependent but there is no God upon whom I can depend" makes sense, in that minimal sense, i.e., it has a use in the language, but it would not meet religious expectations (deep and pervasive religious expectations) if "God" were taken to be equivalent to "the believer has feelings of utter dependence." Indeed, it would not even make the minimal sense that (1) has, for on that naturalistic understanding of "God," (1) would be "translated" as "I feel utterly dependent, but I do not feel utterly dependent." Such naturalistic "translations" or "renderings" are not even remotely plausible for the standard Moorean naturalistic fallacy reasons, i.e., Moore's open-question argument and his noncontradiction argument, deployed in his attack on what he took to be ethical naturalism (Moore 1901; see also Couture and Nielsen 1995, 1–30).

Recognition of this has led to what among anthropologists has been called a symbolist account of religious-talk (Horton 1993) and what has been called noncognitive (expressive-evocative or performatory) accounts by philosophers. According to such accounts, in uttering such utterances as (1) to (4) above, religious believers, whether they realize it or not, are doing something performative: they are expressing certain of their deepest feelings, feelings connected with certain life orientations, and, in the very uttering of these utterances, tending, as well, to evoke similar emotions, reaffirming or leading to similar life orientations in others. This expressive-evocative approach is more plausible than a purely intellectualistic naturalism, yet it also leaves out something vital that intellectualist accounts try unsuccessfully to capture, namely, the alleged (intended) cognitive cosmological claim—the putatively factual assertions with their mysterious alleged propositional content—that many religious believers believe obtains when they utter certain key religious utterances. "My Lord and my God" may very well be purely expressive-evocative, but the sample religious utterances quoted above are thought by believers and by some nonbelievers to do something else as well; "God created the heavens and the earth" and "God providentially orders the world" are also so thought of by such persons. Expressive-evocative they are, but they also are *taken* to be cognitive claims (truth-claims or assertability-claims allegedly with truth-conditions or assertability-conditions) about a mysterious, scarcely understandable power allegedly external to the world (Nielsen 1962). But this, in reality, is a mystification. But, all the same, that claim cannot be given up by religious believers without radically transforming our understanding of such religious utterances from something they have been taken to be throughout their history into something very different. Some religious persons may want to make that radical rupture. But then it is vital to see exactly what is being done: to see, that is, how very deep the rupture is and how far it departs from the core tradition of our theistic religions.[5]

Such considerations lead, if thought through, to what I shall call the error-theory of religious discourse, an account parallel to what J. L. Mackie called an error-theory of moral discourse (Mackie 1946, 1977). Edward Westermarck and Mackie have developed it for morals and Mackie argues that Hume, in effect, had such an account as well. It also has been extensively developed for morality, law, and religion, though not under that label, by the Swedish philosopher Axel Hägerström (as well as by other Scandinavian theorists extensively influenced by him) and is, I believe, *implicit* in Feuerbach, Durkheim, and Freud.

For moral discourse it goes like this: in uttering (sincerely avowing) moral utterances orthodox believers in morals try to assert, indeed *think* they are asserting, the existence of distinctively prescriptive (normative) properties as well as expressing and evoking emotions (principally approbations and disapprobations). But in reality there are, and indeed can be, no such properties, no such objective and categorical prescriptivities. There are only natural (nonnormative) properties and the attitudes we take to them and to certain states of affairs of which these natural properties are properties and to the actions these attitudes generate. Believers in morals have a metaphysical belief *about* their moral beliefs, and thus a metaethical belief, as well, that is literally incoherent. They believe that there is some mysterious categorical prescriptivity somehow inherent in things (including human actions) or that, supervening natural properties, there are nonnatural properties that are inherently or intrinsically prescriptive. But such metaphysical conceptions are themselves incoherent.[6] There are only natural properties (actually a pleonasm) and events, actions, states of affairs, and the like, toward which human beings have certain attitudes and take certain stances. The normativity that gives life to morality—that makes morality possible—comes in through our emotions or attitudes and is expressed linguistically by the expressive-evocative nature of moral language. Normativity in reality, though not in the beliefs *about* normativity of many people, is a matter of feelings and attitudes. It is not something there to be discovered as a property of actions or things. What we actually have are states of affairs (purely empirical matters), attitudes toward those states of affairs, and the actions generated by these attitudes. There is no metaphysical-normative-something we know not what. There is no categorical prescriptivity just somehow inherent either in the world or in "the supernatural world." To believe that there is, error-theorists have it, is the pervasive error of orthodox "believers in morals," which error-theorists take to be most of humankind and not just a few metaphysically inclined philosophers (Mackie 1946).

We have those states of affairs, attitudes, and actions, plus, for many people (standard believers in morals), a mistaken metabelief *about* morality, namely, that there are some mysterious nonnatural "objective" properties which give moral beliefs an objectivity and authority that is not captured by even the most informed reflective intersubjectivity that could be gained by getting our beliefs, attitudes, and commitments to act in certain ways into wide and general reflective equilibrium: in short, into the most coherent, consistently related, and complete patterning that we can for a time forge of our various beliefs, attitudes, principles, the factual information available and generally accepted scientific (including social scientific) theories available to us at a given time. This comes to the most complete holistic explanation and justification that we can for a time garner (Rawls 1995; Daniels 1996; Nielsen 1996). However, the starkly contrasting orthodox nonintersubjective, or at least allegedly somehow "more than intersubjective" in effect metaphysical conception of objectivity is what standard (if you will, orthodox) believers in morals just *assume*. It is this, they believe, that is "real objectivity" (what I would take to be a *reified* conception of objectivity), a conception of objectivity that is very different than the coherentist, intersubjective consensus gained in even a very wide and general reflective equilibrium. But such a reified conception of objectivity with its linked conception about norms and their justifiability is in error, albeit a powerful and gripping error, an error unwittingly made, Mackie believes, by the vast majority of people. Our very common sense, Mackie claims, contains this incoherent, or at least false, metaphysical belief. Indeed our common sense concerning such matters is suffused with this mystification. He sees it as an error pervasive among human beings that has become built into many very entrenched expectations about our very first-order moral discourse and belief. But, however psychologically understandable it is, it is still an incoherence or at least a false belief *about* morality. But, since the incoherence or falsity is in the metabelief, it does not, at least where the incoherence or falsity is not noted, normally impede the smooth, or allegedly smooth, functioning of moral discourse.[7]

A similar error-theory argument for religious discourse and belief can be articulated. Consider the somewhat long-winded utterance, "God is my redeemer, before whose awesome and fearsome presence I stand in fear and trembling, and upon whom I am utterly dependent, a being whom I love and before whom I also stand in longing for a transformative communion with him, the source of all goodness, holiness, and, as well, a mysterious ultimate reality beyond my sinful understanding." This mouthful is a rather clumsy expressive-evocative utterance, but it contains, as well, an abundance of putative cosmological claims: putative knowledge claims about what the universe is like, about what the human condition is in this universe, and about what "lies beyond" the universe. The utterance does express feelings of awe, fear, dependency, love, longing for communion, and a *sense* of mystery, holiness, righteousness, and goodness, with the feelings these conceptions are expressive and evocative of, and, with it being the case as well, that the utterance tends to function to evoke similar feelings in others, if they are attuned to religion. But in addition to that, the believer who sincerely utters this utterance also has a strange belief *about* the source of these feelings, namely, that it is a mysterious supernatural power, somehow purely spiritual in nature, yet all-powerful, all-knowing, and all-good, who is the creator and sustainer of the universe. But it is this belief *about* what the believer utters that is incoherent. This metabelief, if you will, makes no sense at all.

Just as believers in morals, to remain reasonably orthodox believers in morals, must have some incoherent conception of a categorical prescriptivity inherent in the world to give them the sense of unconsciously reified objectivity they so much—though not under that description—desire, so the believers in God must have an incoherent metabelief in a supernatural something somehow beyond and independent of the universe to give them a similar sense of "religious objectivity," when in reality all that is being talked about are the conditions of human existence: Feuerbach's anthropology and Durkheim's mythical sociology. For Jewish, Christian, and Islamic discourse successfully to function expressively and evocatively, believers must have this incoherent belief in a supernatural power. (They must, of course, not recognize that it is incoherent.) That mystified, and mystifying, belief is absolutely essential for religious believing. If religious believers give it up, given what these religions have been, they cease to be Jewish, Christian, or Islamic believers.[8] Hence, the persistent and, it seems to me, rather desperately ineffective attacks by Reformed epistemologists and other orthodox religious theoreticians on claims made by some naturalists concerning the incoherence of theistic conceptions. This is a point on which believers, if they are even within a country mile of orthodoxy, cannot yield. For, if they yield that, their faith becomes plainly irrational. So we need both to account for that incoherence and to explain what the believer's belief is really about in an utterly naturalistic manner. An error-theory of religion, parallel to the error-theory of morality, does just that. (For nontheistic religions it would have to take a somewhat different form.)

This error-theory of religion comports very well with the following key remark of Durkheim: "As long as science has not come to explain it to them, men know very well that they are acted upon, but they do not know by what. So they must invent by themselves the idea of these powers with which they feel themselves in connection" (Durkheim 1912, 278–79). Religion, Durkheim also claimed, should be seen not simply as a system of beliefs but primarily as a system of forces. People caught up in and with a religious life will not just be persons who see the world in a certain way—though they will do that too—and who, with what they take to be their religious insight, know what others do not know; they are, as well, people who feel within themselves an extraordinary power. They feel, as Durkheim put it himself, a "force which dominates him [*sic*], but which, at the same time, sustains him and raises him above himself" (Durkheim 1912, 98). And, Durkheim added, "for the believer, the essence of religion is not a plausible or seductive hypothesis about man or his destiny. He sticks to his faith because he cannot renounce it, so he thinks, without losing something of himself, without being cast down, without a diminution of his vitality, a lowering of his moral temperature" (Durkheim 1912, 101). Without, Durkheim believed, an empathetic feeling for and sensitivity to religion, there is no understanding it. Without that, we would be, vis-à-vis religious sensibilities, like a tone-deaf piano tuner toward sounds. But, as we have observed earlier, non-believers can have, and sometimes do have, the requisite sensibilities. Most are not at all like people from Mars vis-à-vis Judaism, Christianity, or Islam or at least one or another of these religions.

An error-theory, without departing from an utterly naturalistic basis, acknowledges the importance of the pervasive and persistent affective side of religion, while still accounting for the ersatz-cognitive side, which is so necessary for its continued successful functioning, though, of course, it cannot be recognized to be ersatz-cognitive by the person sustained in belief. It shows us how religion, with its claims to a mysterious "higher truth," is so rooted in error that we can have no sound reasons for believing that religious claims even could be true. But it also shows how these are necessary illusions if the religious life is to remain intact. And it explains, as well, the strong hold that the religious life has on people. Though keeping some modern societies in mind (usually the wealthier societies with higher average levels of education), we should qualify this by saying "some people." The disenchantment of the world and the resistance to re-enchantment in such societies (Sweden and Denmark, for example) has gone very deep.

III

If such a naturalistic account of religious representations is sound, or at least on its way to being sound via some more sophisticated restatement, we can then (forgetting about its alleged claim to truth) appropriately turn our attention to the social and psychological functions of religion: the roles it plays in the lives of human beings. These are things that naturalists have characteristically taken to be at the very heart of the matter in thinking about religion.[9] That is, our attention turns now not to questions concerning the truth or coherence of religious beliefs or to their logical status or to what sense they have, but to an attempt to understand their role in life, whether the beliefs themselves are coherent or not.

Religion answers to various human needs.

1. It functions to provide the bonds that unite a society; it functions to provide a society with its sense of moral unity. It functions to uphold and reaffirm at regular intervals the collective sentiments and ideas which make up its unity and distinctive nature. (Durkheim)

2. It functions to reinvigorate and in that way uphold the authority of the social group. In this way it functions to help sustain and keep stable the social order. (Durkheim)

3. It functions ideologically to induce the dominated class or classes to accept the harsh social order in which they are oppressed and, not infrequently, brutalized. But it also, and connectedly, affords them, living as they do in a heartless and often hopeless world, a hope (in reality an illusory hope) for recompense for their sufferings and deprivations in what will be a life of bliss in heaven, after their bodily death, if only now they will trust in God and patiently accept their station and its duties, harsh though such a life may be. In that way religion is the opiate of the people. Religion is in this, and similar ways, an instrument of social control in the interests of the exploiting classes and source of illusory hope for the exploited classes. (Marx)

4. It functions to enable people to cope with life: to face death, estrangement, the defeat of hopes, moral failure, loss of loved ones, prolonged illness, and the like. In short, it has a coping function vis-à-vis the various ailments to which we are heir. (Malinowski)

5. Given the fact that human beings are intensely afraid of death, religion functions to instill the belief, illusory though it be, that we can escape utter annihilation. With their funerary ritual functions, religions help people face the final crisis of life. The need is very great to provide us with assurances that we will preserve our personal identities after death. Religion provides us with such assurances and thereby has an essential function for human beings. (Malinowski)

6. Given our long infantile dependency and helplessness, and with the resultant father-longing that human beings have, religion functions to provide us with a sense of security, to "exorcise the terrors of nature . . . to reconcile one to the cruelty of fate, particu-

larly as shown in death . . . [and to] make amends for the sufferings and privations that the communal life has imposed on us." (Freud 1957, 27)

7. Religion functions even among adults as an unconscious wish-fulfilment to provide people (the great mass of people), so driven by their unconscious, with an imaginary substitute for a protecting and caring father. "God," as we have seen Freud putting it, "is the exalted father, and the longing for the father" with the sense of security this illusory belief can afford. Such is, Freud has it, "the root of the need for religion" (Freud 1957, 36). Religion is intimately linked with the father complex and our helplessness gives the characteristic features to the adult's reaction to his own sense of helplessness, i.e., the formation of religion. (Freud 1957, 38)

8. Religion functions, in virtue of its being a system of ideas and practices, to provide human beings with a way of comprehending what goes on in their world and some sense of control of some of the events in their lives. (Horton)

The Durkheimian and Marxian functions (1) to (4) stress the social role of religion as do (7) and (8) (though less clearly). The other functions of religion noted have more to do with how religion impacts on individuals. However, as we have previously remarked, the line of demarcation is not sharp. After all, all individuals are necessarily social individuals living in different societies with different social systems. These functions point to different things religion, intentionally or unintentionally, does in society.

It is a mistake to say of any one of these functions that it is the *really genuine function* or the *true function* of religion and the others are not really functions at all or are, comparatively, minor functions (Hallden 1960). It is even a mistake to rank them in terms of their alleged basicality. Even when we restrict ourselves to theisms (monotheisms or otherwise), religions have been rather different things at different times and even, as Max Weber shows, different for different strata in the same society at the same time. Sometimes one of these features is more prominent than the others and at other times others are. In modern societies where science has had a very deep impact (8) has not much of a role or perhaps even (in some societies among some strata) no role. That (8) has not much of a place is particularly so for the relatively educated strata of such societies and for the religious denominations with which they tend to have, if they have any religious affiliation at all, an affiliation. The function specified in (8) is in such societies now more and more taken over by science. But, as Robin Horton convincingly shows, (8) is prominent in many African religions and in earlier forms of Christianity and, in the less sophisticated forms of Christianity, it still continues to have that function (Horton 1993, 147–258). Similarly in complex pluralistic modern societies, Durkheim's social-bonding, moral-unity role arguably drops out or is very much attenuated. Religion, if anything, becomes in such societies socially divisive. Similarly, the Freudian conception, taken just as we have it, works better for males than for females and arguably better in patrilineal societies than in matrilineal ones. Still, all of these diverse functions are functions, of greater or lesser prominence, for religion at various times and at various places and for various peoples. There is no *essence* of religion, *essence* of theism or even *essence* of Judaism, Christianity, or Islam, requiring some function to be the one true function of religion, theisms, or (becoming still more specific) Christianity and the like (Halldén 1960).

Do any of these eight functions of religion at work in a society preclude the working of any of the others? I do not believe so. Some, of course, make stresses that others do not and some ignore things that others press. Durkheim, in seeing religion only in its function in establishing and reaffirming group solidarity, never seems to consider the Marxian claim that "religious beliefs have ideological functions legitimating the domination of one group or class over another" (Morris 1987, 122). But a Marxian could, and should, claim that very often, when class conflict is not overt or very prominent, religion does provide most people in the society with a sense (no doubt an illusory sense) of moral unity shielding people from a strong sense within the society in question of "them and us" and providing a sense of social cohesion and, in this convenient ideological way, helping to sustain the extant class-structured social order. And indeed this is exactly what the Marxian claims give to understand. Only the sense of moral unity for the Marxian is ideological—class societies are in reality conflictual—but this sense of moral unity is still an important and necessary illusion that helps to sustain the smooth, or relatively smooth, functioning of a class society, something that sometimes obtains when there is no sharp incompatibility between the forces and relations of production. And religion yielding this illusory sense of moral unity is indeed very useful for the dominant classes in sustaining their hegemony. Moreover, this illusory sense of moral unity generated by ideology will normally not be seen as ideological by the people affected by it. Indeed, for the ideology properly to work that usually must be so. Ideology, that is, often serves to disguise the class nature of society. Religion, as does ideology generally, often functions in a society to give people a sense, albeit an illusory sense, of social cohesion, a heightened sense of having collective sentiments and ideas which unite them, affording them a sense of having close social bonds in spite of different and (in reality) conflicting conditions of life along with the different interests that go with them. So religion could have exactly the functions that Durkheim specifies, and in addition have a mystificatory ideological function leading people into believing and acting as if their society is homogeneous and unified when actually it is not. This is an excellent device for social control in class society.

IV

Where we come to accept such a naturalistic functional picture of religion, the question then arises whether religion is something which will always be with us. In a modern, deeply secularized world where the disenchantment of the world is pervasively felt, will people continue, as this solidifies, to have religious commitments? The question also forces itself on us, as it was forced on Freud and Durkheim, whether it is *desirable* to hope that religion will gradually wither away and that its functions will incrementally, though slowly, be taken over by utterly secular substitutes?

As a matter of present anthropological fact, all cultures have religions (though not all of them are theisms), but what is not clear is (a) what the future will be like and (b) what, if we are to have any choice in the matter, it should be like. Engels and Marx thought that with the changes in the forces of production that were coming into being, classless societies would come into existence and that in such societies religion would gradually wither away. Freud thought, though certainly with a considerable amount of skepticism, that religion might, just might, wither away; he thought, as well, that if it did it would be a good thing. But he also thought that this conviction of his was complex and challengeable. The contrast between Freud's nuanced, though still utterly atheistical, reflections and Lenin's dogmatism concerning the desirability of the end of religion is instructive here. Freud's sense of how complex things are comes out powerfully in his discussion of the matter in the final sections of his *The Future of an Illusion.* About such matters Durkheim was even more intellectually ambivalent than Freud, but, as functionally compelling for most people as he took religion to be, he also thought that as a scientific culture became ever more pervasive, a sociological understanding and orientation toward the world might come to take over the functions now played by religion. And, as he saw it, the very having of such a sociological understanding and orientation toward the world is tantamount to having a secular understanding and orientation toward the world. Some later secular thinkers have come to believe that Freud and Durkheim were still too caught up in nineteenth-century beliefs about progress and about how human beings can come to master their world (Bell 1979). Both Freud and Durkheim, it is now not infrequently believed, were, in this respect, far too optimistic. Others think, frequently incurring the charge of being too optimistic themselves, that the question about the social viability of an utterly secular outlook and orientation to life in time coming to replace a religious one cannot, and should not, so easily be turned aside, as it usually is, as empirically infeasible whatever its intellectual rationale (Nielsen 1996).

I have set out a range of naturalistic explanations of religion. It is frequently argued, or sometimes just rather uncritically assumed, as I noted initially, that naturalistic explanations of religion in effect and unavoidably destroy the very subject matter they are designed to explain. Religion, it is frequently claimed, *must be believed to be properly understood.* Durkheim's own belief that "whoever does not bring to the study of religion a sort of religious sentiment has no right to speak about it" shows, some believe, that neither his own naturalistic analysis nor any other naturalistic account could be adequate.[10] No matter how we cut it, religious beliefs, on such an account, are in error and religious beliefs could have no sound claim to being true. His very explanation (as all naturalistic explanations) is incompatible, where accepted, with the person who accepts it, continuing to be a religious believer, if he would be at all consistent. If this is so, and on the not implausible assumption that people have some minimal concern for consistency, naturalist explanations of religion would, if widely accepted, destroy religion itself, the very phenomena it purports to explain. A philosopher (Gustave Belot) asked Durkheim, putting forth what Belot took to be a *reductio,* "who would continue to pray if he knew he was praying to no one, but merely addressing a collectivity that was not listening?" Where is the person, Belot continued, who would continue to take part in "communion if he believed that it was no more than a mere symbol and that there was nothing real underlying it?" Explanation, given Durkheim's way of going about things, involves critique—a thoroughly secular critique—here and that very fact, the claim goes, reveals its explanatory inadequacy.

The naturalist should respond—and here is one of the places where what I have called an error-theory should come into play—that it is false to say that on such a conception there is nothing real underlying religious symbols. There is something very real indeed—facts about human beings and society—only the reality is not what the *believer* takes it to be. Rather than its being the case that understanding religion requires belief, understanding religion in a genuine way is incompatible with believing it. Here the naturalist turns the believer's familiar argument around. Moreover, this secular understanding can be a sensitive, empathetic understanding attuned (as Durkheim thought it must be) to the realities of religious experience and sentiment. This is shown most forcefully in the accounts of religious experience and sentiment given by Feuerbach, Hägerström, and Hepburn. Having a feel for religion does not require having the related belief, but it does require having a sense of what it is that makes religion so compelling, and so psychologically necessary, for so many people, indeed historically speaking, for most people. And to have that sense, as error-theorists stress, is to see, among other things, how religious beliefs are inescapably objectifying (reifying) beliefs committed to an incoherent conception of objectivity.

Naturalistic explanations are, of course, incompatible with religious belief. But they are not thereby inadequate explanations. They do not explain religion away in explaining that religious claims could not be true, for the account explains religion's origins, explains its claim to truth, explains how this very claim is something the believer cannot abandon, explains how, that notwithstanding, that very claim to truth is in error, the depth of that error, its persistence in spite of that in various institutional contexts and in the personal lives of human beings. The naturalistic explanations of the type we have discussed explain, as well, religion's various cultural and historical forms, how and why they change and develop as they do, and their continuing persistence and appeal in one or another form (Wartofsky 1982, 154–73).[11] An account which does these things well is a good candidate for a sound conception of religion, yielding an adequate range of explanations of the phenomena of religion. The naturalistic explanations we have discussed, particularly when taken together, do just that.

APPENDIX

This strange objectifying (reifying) belief about religion (the belief that there is a mysterious supernatural reality that is Ultimate Reality), this metabelief, this metaphysical metabelief, is also, or at least appears to be, a first-order religious belief. This is so because it says that there is a mysterious supernatural power, utterly spiritual in nature, all powerful, all knowing, all good, who created and sustains the universe. A sentence expressing this belief at least appears to be a first-order sentence used to try to assert something very baffling indeed. Perhaps we have here what the logical positivists called "word-magic." Perhaps what is expressed by the sentence is what Rudolf Carnap called a pseudoproposition misleadingly put, as pseudopropositions characteristically are, in the material mode. But such a way of putting things may make for more difficulties than it solves. What can be less controversially said is that we have something here which appears at least to be first-order, but it also involves a metabelief about there being a strange metaphysical reality—a supernatural something we know not what—somehow, in ways we do not understand, distinct from the natural order, just as on the error-theory of morality "pleasure is the sole intrinsic good" involves the metabelief that "intrinsic good" refers to or connotes a nonnatural property, intrinsic goodness, a property which is somehow also mysteriously distinct from the natural order.

Both orthodox "believers in morals" and religious believers have, error-theorists claim, an incoherent, or at least a thoroughly mistaken, conception of objectivity, a conception that, such believers believe, must somehow just go with the sincere avowal of their moral and religious beliefs. (This is not to deny what is frequently the case, namely, that one might be such a "believer in morals"—even an orthodox one, as G. E. Moore and C. D. Broad were—without being a religious believer.) But for both sets of orthodox believers, their moral and religious utterances, when made seriously, are avowals, though both sets of believers think, concerning their own respective avowals, that they are, as well, somehow mysteriously something more than avowals. In both cases, error-theorists claim, the metabeliefs, crucial in the eyes of both sets of believers, are incoherent or at least incontrovertibly false. (I think that they should have insisted on incoherence here, but Mackie opts, for reasons which seem to me inexplicable, for saying they are false beliefs: beliefs rooted in massive error. See note 6.)

There is, however, a crucial difference between moral and religious utterances as there is a parallel crucial difference in the beliefs that go with them. The moral beliefs the moral utterances express can be demythologized away from such an assumption of objectivism—from such an objectivistic (reifying) metaethics at least implicitly assumed—so that these moral beliefs can, freed of incoherence, continue to have a role in our lives even with the demise of such orthodox "believing in morals" (a believing that has been a common-enough philosophical disease from Plato to Moore). There is, however, nothing like such a demythologizing for "believing in God." (To demythologize the Gospels is one thing, to demythologize the very concept of God, emptying the world of a belief in the supernatural, is another. Rudolf Bultmann attempted the former, but never the latter.) Belief in God just is inescapably broadly Platonic in background assumption. Remember, as well, that objectivism is one thing and objectivity is another. Objectivity in moral domains, and perhaps in all domains, comes to the intersubjectivity of wide and general reflective equilibrium. Objectivism is an incoherent reification of that. (See here the second part of my preface to *Naturalism without Foundations*, as well as chapters 2 and 5 and the introduction to Part Four.)

NOTES

1. I do not say, or give to understand, that religion is essentially doctrine. Indeed, there is an important difference between living a religious life and

believing a religious doctrine. The former is plainly much more important than the latter. Still, we cannot have the former without something of the latter. In some religions doctrine is more important than in others. But there are no "doctrineless religions"—not even Zen Buddhism—even though the crucial point of religious doctrine is to help structure and facilitate the religious life. But, all the same, what is most fundamental in being religious is to live a religious life. Doctrine is in service of that and sometimes it fails and in reality gets in the way. Still, there is no religious life without religious doctrine. (See also note 3.) Naturalistic accounts need not, and indeed should not, deny the reality and the import of the fact that what is most fundamental in religion is the religious life. Where naturalistic accounts run deep, as in Feuerbach and Hägerström, they look closely at how the religious life grips, or at least deeply affects, people: how it, not infrequently, powerfully takes hold of their lives. This was exactly what Marx, Gramsci, Durkheim, and Malinowski did. The thrust of the latter part of this chapter is to show that naturalism, neither by definition nor in any other way, tries to rule out the significance of religious life as found in religious ceremonies and other practices and otherwise, and sometimes very intensely, in the very personal lives of people. It does, however, see them in a different way than they are seen from inside religion. It is, however, question-begging and tendentious to assume that the participant's point of view is always the more adequate point of view. It may be where we start, but it need not be our end point.

2. See my "Atheism without Anger or Tears" (Nielsen 1994). For a fuller statement see my *Naturalism without Foundations* (Nielsen 1996).

3. A reader has objected that I just dogmatically assert that religious beliefs are incoherent and that I compound that error by just assuming incorrectly that what is coherent and what is not is context-independent. But in Part One, I *argue*, perhaps both unconvincingly and incorrectly, for the incoherence of nonanthropomorphic religious conceptions, though I do assume it in Parts Two, Three, and Four. But they build on what I argue in Part One. Moreover, I have argued in detail, again perhaps unconvincingly and incorrectly, for this incoherency thesis in a series of books. See Nielsen 1971, 1973, 1982, 1989, 1996, and Nielsen and Hart 1990. I also explicitly stress there the context-dependence of concepts of incoherence, but argue against the balkanization of religious concepts and religious language-games. We should start, in analyzing religious beliefs, with religious practices and the use of religious utterances as they stand in such religious contexts. But religious discourse is intertwined with other uses of language. When we see how they are related, how they fit together, and reflect carefully on the uses of religious terms and sentences in their live contexts in religious practices and as part of some natural language (e.g., French or English), they seem at least to be incoherent. Referring expressions such as "God" or "heaven" occur in them, but we have no idea of how to specify, even taking them in context, their referents; some key religious utterances appear to be in some sense factual cosmological (itself a pleonasm) assertions—at least in their surface grammar—but we cannot specify their truth-conditions or their assertability-conditions; there are key religious utterances that some say we must understand metaphorically or symbolically, but we cannot say what they are metaphors or symbols of. But there is no just *only* understanding

them metaphorically or symbolically. To be either a metaphor or a symbol they must be a metaphor or a symbol of something, metaphorical and symbolic use is logically parasitic on literal use. And do not say there are no literal uses to be contrasted with metaphorical uses. There is a big difference between "Hitler had a black moustache" and "Hitler had a black soul." In fine, religious-talk is *so short on sense* that the claim of incoherence seems at least to be apposite. Stated so succinctly these claims may seem dogmatic. I hope *seems* is not *is* here. I have argued these points in detail and with care in the books mentioned earlier in this note, hoping at the very least to have avoided dogmatism and sheer assertion. In *Naturalism without Foundations* (Nielsen 1996) I argue most fully the point about contextuality.

4. Naturalism—or at least my naturalism and the naturalisms of other pragmatists—does not use "language police." It does not set forth (like Rudolf Carnap or Alfred Tarski) a model of an ideal language, but takes language as it comes, including, of course, its practice-embedded religious-talk. It does not require that defenders of religious life put their experiences, practices, and sense of life into some prescribed narrow "empirical language" or "scientific language"—something that in reality does not exist and there is no good reason to think that it could be constructed. Nothing even remotely like that is involved in my account. I mention this because a reviewer of this essay somehow thought, in a way that utterly baffles me, that this was what I was doing or at least assuming.

5. One reviewer comments: to be sure religion has been all of the things naturalists claim, from being a psychological crutch to supporting a class system of a particular economic era. But what naturalists fail to see, he also asserts, is that there is more to religion than what this allows. Its spiritual practices are sometimes transformational, enabling *some* religious persons to live more authentic and more complete lives than *some* people who are not religious. But many naturalists, including this naturalist, acknowledge this and some (Durkheim, Malinowski, Gramsci, and Fromm) stress it, explain it, and show its rationale in utterly naturalistic terms. Moreover, the opposite is also true. The ways of living and conceiving of things of *some* atheistical people enable them to live more authentic and complete lives than *some* people who are religious. Utterly secular practices can be transformational too. The more crucial question is whether we can say with any objectivity which practices at their best are the most adequate transformations. (It is a separate question whether we have adequate criteria for "best" or "most adequate" practices in such domains or any domain. I argue that we do. See chapters 9 and 10 and the Postscript.) And again, and again distinctly, we should reflect on the fact (or at least the putative fact), stressed at the end of the first note, that the participant's point of view is not necessarily the superior point of view.

6. Mackie would say false. However, since we have no idea of what it would be like to use such conceptions to make true statements and thus, keeping in mind the necessity of a nonvacuous contrast here, we have no idea of what it would be like for them to make false statements either. This being so, it is better to speak of incoherence here. See Antony Flew, "The Burden of Proof" (Flew 1985).

7. Perhaps it would be better to speak of the alleged and hoped-for coherence. There is a lot of cognitive and other dissonance in moral talk and conception.

8. Some have argued that I put too much stress on reflective activity and take

it as the primary thing in our lives. But I have never done that. It is not, I agree, the primary thing, though it is not nothing either. To think that it is the primary thing would be an absurd rationalistic prejudice. Consider the Zen saying "If one is truly religious one has no need for religion." I am, the argument goes, with my philosopher's preconceptions, blind to a fact that many who are themselves believers miss, as Kierkegaard among others so perceptively saw, namely, *the religious life*. Some of them, if they are a certain kind of intellectual, even construct great philosophical mansions (e.g., Hegel and Schelling) while living in a religious shack. And many who are in fact—or so it is said—deeply religious do not claim to be. They have no religious doctrine. There is both truth and falsity here. Truth in that there are people who are not believers (do not believe in God or any of the other religious entities or accept any religious conceptions, or, in some instances, they cannot even make coherent sense of them) who still have some of the key *attitudes* of people who are religious. They have what Paul Tillich called ultimate commitments and concerns and, as Kierkegaard stressed, a certain sort of inwardness, while still having no belief at all in "the ground of being and meaning" which is supposed to be for theologians like Tillich the proper object of ultimate concern and commitment. Indeed, such secularist "believers" may not—and perhaps with good reason—have any understanding of such talk. In *that* sense Spinoza, Feuerbach, Marx, Freud, Russell, and Einstein were religious. I would very much prize being thought to be religious, and actually to be religious, in *that* sense.

And indeed I hope, and even think, I am *in that sense* religious. It is important, I say moralistically but I think rightly, speaking in my own voice, to have the inwardness of which Kierkegaard spoke and to have a strong sense of commitment and concern. (I would rather not qualify these notions with "ultimate," for I do not understand what such a notion comes to. I expect that, *if* it comes to anything very intelligible at all, it must be tied up with some strong form of foundationalism: itself a conception that is very problematical. For the point about foundationalism see my *On Transforming Philosophy: A Metaphilosophical Inquiry* [Boulder, Colo.: Westview Press, 1995], Part 2.) We are lucky if we have such commitment and concern. Indeed that is something to which I aspire. But in *that sense* to be religious is just to have that inwardness and to be a deeply concerned and committed person. But those things—vital as they are to our very humanness— are as open to an atheist as to anyone else. All that notwithstanding, though some atheists, if they are lucky, may themselves be such people, it is not all of what it is to be a Christian, a Jew, a Moslem, a Hindu, or a Buddhist of any kind or to accept a religion or to engage in religious practices or to live a religious life. In *the sense in question* one can be deeply religious without any of that. People stressing that sense take what may be a necessary condition for being religious and treat it as if it were also sufficient. But this is, as Sidney Hook once observed, conversion by stipulative redefinition. We will—to shift ground a little—not flourish as human beings if we are not reflective to some extent. But, Aristotle to the contrary notwithstanding, that is not the point in or of living. Indeed, there is no one thing that constitutes the point in or of living. There are many and diverse ways of living that can be partially constitutive of human flourishing. Some reflectiveness, though sometimes of a rather minimal sort, plays a part in all of them. But to take reflectiveness or (what is not the same thing) rationality to be the key thing in a good life is surely very *parti-pris*. It is little more than a rationalistic philosophical prejudice. No one thing captures the point in or of living, for there is no "*the* point in or of living," though this is not at all to say that, this being so, our lives are, let alone must be, without point. Such Dostoevskyanism is just hyperbolic rhetoric. See Kurt Baier, "The Meaning of Life" (Baier 1981) and Kai Nielsen, "Linguistic Philosophy and 'The Meaning of Life'" (Nielsen 1981). See also chapter 4.

9. Some have thought that morality is the real truth of religion and that this we can have without the encrusted beliefs with which the centuries have surrounded religion. This, of course, is naturalist-friendly, but would hardly suffice from a religious point of view, for the very distinctive moralities that are *religious* moralities cannot set aside, without a radical change in their very moral import, all, or even most, of those encrusted beliefs. See Terence Penelhum, "Ethics with God and Ethics Without" (Penelhum 1991) and the last two chapters of Nielsen 1996.

10. See notes 1, 5, and 8.

11. See notes 1, 5 and 8.

BIBLIOGRAPHY

Baier, Kurt. 1981. "The Meaning of Life." In *The Meaning of Life*, edited by E. D. Klemke, 81–117. Oxford: Oxford University Press.

Bell, Daniel. 1979. "The Return of the Sacred: The Argument about the Future of Religion." In *Progress and Its Discontents*, edited by G. A. Almond, M. Chodorow, and R. H. Pearce, 501–23. Berkeley: University of California Press.

Couture, Jocelyne, and Nielsen, Kai. 1995. "Introduction: The Ages of Metaethics." In *New Essays on Metaethics*, edited by Jocelyne Couture and Kai Nielsen, 1–30. Calgary, Alb.: University of Calgary Press.

Daniels, Norman. 1996. *Justice and Justification: Reflective Equilibrium in Theory and Practice*. Cambridge: Cambridge University Press.

Durkheim, Émile. 1912. *Les formes élémentaires de la vie religieuse*. Paris: Alcan.

———. 1915. *The Elementary Forms of Religious Life*. Translated by J. A. Swain. London: Allen & Unwin.

Evans-Pritchard, E. E. 1965. *Theories of Primitive Religion*. Oxford: Clarendon Press.

Flew, Antony. 1985. "The Burden of Proof." In *Knowing Religiously*, edited by L. S. Rouner, 103–15. Notre Dame, Ind.: University of Notre Dame Press.

Freud, Sigmund. 1930. *Civilization and Its Discontents*. Translated by W. D. Robson-Scott. London: Hogarth Press.

———. 1957. *The Future of an Illusion*. Translated by W. D. Robson-Scott. Garden City, N.Y.: Doubleday.

Hägerström, Axel. 1949. *Religionsfilosofi*. Stockholm: Natur och Kultur.

———. 1964. *Philosophy and Religion*. Translated by P. T Sandin. London: Allen & Unwin.

Halldén, Soren. 1960. *True Love, True Humour and True Religion: A Semantic Study*. Lund, Sweden: W. K. Gleerup.

Hepburn, Ronald. 1958. *Christianity and Paradox*. London: Watts.

Hortin, Robin. 1993. *Patterns of Thought in Africa and the West.* Cambridge: Cambridge University Press.

Hyman, John. 1997. "Wittgensteinianism." In *A Companion to the Philosophy of Religion*, edited by P. L. Quinn and C. Taliaferro. Oxford: Blackwell.

Lukes, Steven. 1985. *Emile Durkheim.* London: Penguin Press.

Mackie, J. L. 1946. "A Refutation of Morals." *Australasian Journal of Psychology and Philosophy* 24: 77–90.

———. 1977. *Ethics: Inventing Right and Wrong.* Harmondsworth: Penguin Books.

Martin, Michael. 1997. "The Verificationist Challenge." In *A Companion to the Philosophy of Religion*, edited by P. L. Quinn and C. Taliaferro. Oxford: Blackwell.

Marx, Karl, and Engels, Friedrich. 1958. *On Religion.* London: Lawrence and Wishart.

Moore, G. E. 1901. "The Value of Religion." *Ethics* 12, no. 1: 81–98.

Morris, Brian. 1987. *Anthropological Studies of Religion: An Introductory Text.* Cambridge: Cambridge University Press.

Nielsen, Kai. 1962. "On Speaking of God." *Theoria* 28: 110–37.

———. 1971. *Contemporary Critiques of Religion.* New York: Herder and Herder.

———. 1973. *Skepticism.* New York: St. Martin's Press.

———. 1981. "Linguistic Philosophy and 'The Meaning of Life.'" In *The Meaning of Life*, edited by E. D. Klemke, 177–204. Oxford: Oxford University Press.

———. 1982. *An Introduction to the Philosophy of Religion.* New York: Macmillan.

———. 1989. *God, Scepticism and Modernity.* Ottawa: University of Ottawa Press.

———. 1994. "Atheism without Anger or Tears." *Studies in Religion/Sciences Religieuses* 23: 193–209.

———. 1995. *On Transforming Philosophy: A Metaphilosophical Inquiry.* Boulder, Colo.: Westview Press.

———. 1996. *Naturalism without Foundations.* Amherst, N.Y.: Prometheus Books.

Nielsen, Kai, and Hart, Hendrick. 1990. *Search for Community in a Withering Tradition: Conversations between a Marxian Atheist and a Calvinist Christian.* Lanham, Md.: University Press of America.

Penelhum, Terence. 1991. "Ethics with God and Ethics Without." In *On the Track of Reason: Essays in Honour of Kai Nielsen*, edited by Rodger Beehler, David Copp, and Béla Szabados, 107–18. Boulder, Colo.: Westview Press.

———. 1997. "Fideism." In *A Companion to the Philosophy of Religion*, edited by P. L. Quinn and C. Taliaferro. Oxford: Blackwell.

Plantinga, Alvin. 1997. "Reformed Epistemology." In *A Companion to the Philosophy of Religion*, edited by P. L. Quinn and C. Taliaferro. Oxford: Blackwell.

Rawls, John. 1995. "Reply to Habermas." *Journal of Philosophy* 92, no. 3 (March): 132–80.

Wartofsky, Marx. "Homo Homini Deus Est: Feuerbach's Religious Materialism." In *Meaning, Truth, and God*, edited by L. S. Rouner, 154–73. Notre Dame, Ind.: University of Notre Dame Press.

Wolterstorff, N. 1997. "The Reformed Tradition." In *A Companion to the Philosophy of Religion*, edited by P. L. Quinn and C. Taliaferro. Oxford: Blackwell.

---------- 2 ----------

ON BEING A SECULARIST
ALL THE WAY DOWN

I

I shall argue for being a through and through secularist in all domains
of life and belief. This comes to being either an atheist or an agnostic,
though ideally an agnostic who is not anguished over the possibility that
God does not exist and that there are no other purely spiritual realities.[1]
And, since fallibilism is by now the name of the game for all reasonable
belief, the dividing line between atheism and agnosticism is not sharp. In
speaking of an atheist, I refer to someone who rejects belief in God either
(a) because she believes that it is false or highly unlikely that God exists,
(b) believes that the concept of God is incoherent or so problematic as to
make such belief impossible or irrational, or (c) because she believes that
the term "God" is being used in such a manner that it is so devoid of substance as to make religious belief, rhetorical effects aside, indistinguishable from purely secular beliefs except for the fact that religious beliefs

From *Philo* 1, no. 2 (fall/winter 1998): 6–21.

are associated with certain religiously distinctive stories which in turn are stories which (on such an account) the religious believer, though she must entertain them in a vivid and lively way, may or may not believe. On which basis the rejection is made by an atheist depends on how "God" is being construed by religious people. The kind of atheist I am rejects (i) anthropomorphic conceptions of God on the basis of (a), (ii) belief in the God of developed Judaism, Christianity, or Islam on the basis of (b), and (iii) purely symbolic conceptions of God such as Richard Braithwaite's and R. M. Hare's on the basis of (c) (Nielsen 1985, 9–31).

The atheism I articulate and defend is a naturalism in that it rejects all forms of supernaturalism. But it is a social naturalism that rejects physicalism, even the moderate nonreductive physicalism of Richard Rorty, Donald Davidson, and Daniel Dennett.[2] It does so not because it embraces any form of dualism or epiphenomenalism except perhaps some form of property dualism, but because such an atheist regards human beings as not being just biological beings, let alone machinelike beings, but instead takes human beings to be irreducibly social beings and the human animal as being a self-interpreting animal (see Taylor 1985, 45–76; Sauer-Thompson 1998). Social relations are partly constitutive of what it is to be a human being.[3] They are not just danglers that might be snipped off to reveal the purely biological nature of what it is to be human. But that does not at all mean that I believe that there is some ghost in the organism.

This social naturalism is also a *nonscientistic* naturalism. It rejects, as a piece of incoherent metaphysics, the Quinean, Smartian, Armstrongian belief—the belief of metaphysical or "scientific" realists—that physics, or natural science more generally, yields our best approximation of the one true description of the world and that any further filling in of that must be done by physics or a science based on physics (see Couture and Nielsen 1993, 30–55). I think that that is nothing more than a scientistic metaphysical dogma. By contrast I argue that there is no one vocabulary—or for that matter several vocabularies taken in conjunction—that can tell it like it is and that science is not privileged here such that what science cannot tell us humankind cannot know (see Nielsen 1996, 25–55). Our knowing and conceptualization is inescapably perspectival. We have different social practices with their different language-games that exist for different purposes. We cannot coherently say that one of them, say, the discourses of physics, is "closer to reality" than, say, the discourses of biology, social anthropology, literature, politics, or the give and take of our common life (see Rorty 1991). They all have different rationales and they can do their jobs well or ill in helping us to cope with different problems, but none of them is closer to "the truth" or more adequately tells us what reality really is like in itself (e.g., Putnam 1990). Poetry is no more or no less distant than chemistry from "the truth" or closer or less close to revealing what reality is really like in itself. Physics and chemistry do, of course, tell us more about structures in the world than poetry. Indeed poetry is not concerned with that at all. But these sciences do not tell us more about what reality is like or about what "ultimate" reality is like or about what reality in itself is like than poetry.

We do not know what we are talking about in speaking of "ultimate reality" or of "reality in itself" or even about just plain old reality full stop. Both these sciences and poetry as well help us cope with reality though in quite different ways and for very different purposes. We learn from reading poetry about human sensibilities, feelings, and conceptions of life. These tell us about realities, but about different realities, realities we can be interested in for different reasons than the realities chemistry and physics tell us about. But there is no sense in saying that one reality rather than the other is "really reality." Both tell us about things that are "equally real" but answer to very different human interests. To think the contrary—to think physics or biology or anything else tells us what reality is like in itself—is without coherent meaning. There is no sense in talking about how reality is in itself or of the uniquely correct description of the world. And to claim this is not to give voice to or to assume some form of idealism in disguise or even an antirealism, but just a thorough-going form of perspectivism (e.g., Rorty 1991, 1998). It is incompatible with scientific or metaphysical realism but not with common-sense realism, a perfectly nonmetaphysical view (see Putnam 1994).

My social naturalism is also a form of historicism (Nielsen 1996, chapter 1). I mean by that, in Hegel's famous phrase, that there is no over-leaping history: our conceptions, attitudes, and beliefs are embedded in, indeed are a part of, social practices and forms of life that are historically and in considerable measure culturally distinctive and determinate. Our very identities and conceptions of ourselves and of the world, our convictions about how we should relate to others, live our lives, and how the political order should be ordered, cannot stand free of these social practices, forms of life, and the traditions of which they are a part. But we are not culturally or conceptually imprisoned by this nor is this a form of cultural relativism or indeed any form of relativism. We are not culturally/conceptually imprisoned because, in Otto Neurath's by now over-worked but still illuminating phrase (what was once a metaphor), we can and do repair and rebuild the ship at sea. We alter our social practices in the light of new situations: sometimes as a result of their contact with other social practices including sometimes the rather different social practices of other cultures. Certain social practices even sometimes get abandoned or transformed, typically slowly, but sometimes rapidly, and sometimes almost beyond recognition. Moreover, though always by operating with social practices, we have the ability to reflect on our social practices and critically to assess them though surely not all of them at once. We operate *with* them, but, while still operating with some, we can operate *on* our own social practices as well, though not, of course, on all of them at once. We, that is, can always critically examine a social practice or clusters of social practices using still other social practices (Rorty 1998, 122–37). We never, however, stand free of all social practices and view the world from the point of view of the universe or the point of view of nowhere. There is no ahistorical perspective—no "perspectiveless perspective" or God's-eye perspective—from which we can view things. But we are not conceptually imprisoned for all of that. We, to repeat, repair and rebuild the ship at sea.

This historicism is not a cultural or conceptual relativism for, wherever it is we stand, we can look back at previous ways of life or look sideways at other extant ways of life, and sometimes see how we have now come to have either a more adequate or less adequate cluster of social practices than these other ways of life (Taylor 1985, 116–33). And in so reflectively assessing things (in so making these comparisons) we can sometimes come to see—though we always start from there (that is, from our own social practices, or at least from some of them)—that they (though here taken individually or in clusters) are the less adequate practices. This reflective ability to look back or to look sideways is perhaps most easily seen with traditions: we can recognize, though usually with difficulty, when they have developed and when they have degenerated. Perhaps to a very limited extent, we can even conjecture how the trajectory of our social practices might better develop. This is always a very risky business and self-deception and wish fulfillment is an ever present possibility—a possibility that not infrequently turns into a reality. And our understanding here is not merely theoretical, we need a practical understanding of these practices as well. We gain this either through past or present involvement with them (from their being our practices) or through a reading of literature, history, or ethnographies that vividly take us, so to say, inside them. They give us, that is, where we are not actual participants, the closest approximation we can get to a *knowledge by practice*. But it is clear enough that we can, and upon occasion do, sometimes without—or virtually without—ethnocentrism take evaluative stances toward our own social practices as well as other social practices. We are not limited to saying "Well this is just what we do in our tribe" (Taylor 1985). The salient historicist point is that we do this without ever being able to attain some God's eye or cultureless view of the world. We can never stand thoroughly free of our culture. But this need not be blinkering. Cultures are not bounded systems. There is repeated cross-fertilization between cultures and we can, and sometimes are, free in certain respects from some aspects of our culture without ever having the ability—the very thing makes no sense—to stand completely outside our culture and to view things in utter independence of it.

This social naturalism, which is nonscientistic and nonutterly biological, is not only social but, as well, a contextual-historicist naturalism. And it escapes the frequent, and I think, well-taken critique of some other naturalisms (e.g., the "scientific realism" of Smart, Armstrong, and Quine) that they make something like a religion, or at least an ideology, out of the natural sciences, taking them, without justification, to be what will tell us what the world (human and nonhuman) is really like and that all other perspectives are, except perhaps as sometimes useful expedients, illusory (Sauer-Thompson 1998). That kind of scientistic naturalism claims to be continuous with science and indeed to be scientific itself. But "scientific realism" is ersatz science. It is indeed free of an appeal to the spiritual entities of theistic metaphysics. But it no more fixes belief by what Peirce and Dewey called the scientific method than does Thomistic-Aristotelianism. In both cases we have metaphysical theories whose claims are so problematical as to be arguably incoherent or at least best set aside as yielding very little, if anything, in the way of understanding. At best we learn something *second-order* about our concepts (Couture and Nielsen 1993, 30–53). My social naturalism is not metaphysical and is not held hostage to such difficulties. Scientific naturalism and theistic metaphysics take in each other's dirty linen.

II

Let us now turn to religion. A social naturalism cannot coherently take the road of J. L. Mackie and Bernard Williams and argue that since (a) core elements of religion conflict with scientific realism (bald naturalism or physicalism, if you will) and since (b) physics (more generally natural science) gives the best approximation we can have at any given time after the rise of science of the one true description of the world, we then should conclude that religious beliefs are either false or very probably false (Mackie 1982; Williams 1990). Put more simply, but more crudely, physics and only physics—the scientistic claim goes—tells it approximately like it is as far as the furniture of the universe, human and otherwise, is concerned. But religion, the claim continues, at least where it is a theism, conflicts with physics—conflicts in its account of the universe—so religious belief systems and religious cosmological beliefs must be at best false. Such a frequently traveled atheistic path is closed to a social naturalism for social naturalism is a thoroughgoing *perspectivism* which holds that the very idea of the one true description of the world is without sense. Talk of the one correct explanation of the world or of science (or anything else) telling us what "ultimate reality" is like or what human beings really are—to say nothing of providing a "final theory"—is scientific mythology and not a rational activity continuous with science.[4] Reductionist, eliminativist, or functionalist physicalism is not a part of science or even continuous with science. Rather we have with them an activity coming up with metaphysical pictures that are without rational warrant. We are just trading a materialist metaphysics for a theistic metaphysics, an idealist metaphysics or a dualist metaphysics (the last two, of course, may also be a theistic metaphysics). The point is that none of these metaphysical schemes make sense and none of them, even if (contrary to what I have just said) they can somehow be seen to make some sense, are helpful in our understanding of life and society or in coming to have a reflective orientation concerning our lives (Sauer-Thompson 1998). We learn nothing more about what is sometimes portentously called "the human condition" from studying them. But social naturalism is not a skepticism any more than Ludwig Wittgenstein's and Hilary Putnam's way of seeing things are skeptical views. It, like Wittgenstein's and Putnam's way of seeing things, and Isaiah Berlin's as well, is indeed deeply skeptical of metaphysics and foundationalist epistemology, but that is another matter entirely. That does not imply or in any way warrant general skepticism (Nielsen 1995, Berlin 1998).

III

Yet social naturalism, as I initially remarked, is an atheism or at least an agnosticism, though a thoroughly fallibilistic atheism or agnosticism. There is no more some secular certainty than there is religious certainty. So why, given this fallibilism, an atheism? Why be secularists all the way down, or even indeed at all, if our condition is that of such a thorough perspectivism and contextualism? Even some of the reformed philosopher-theologians are perspectivists.[5] I will come at that indirectly. Fideists and friends of fideism, such as Wittgenstein and Putnam, do not deny, where the form of fideism is sophisticated, that a religion will have a belief-system. Talk of commitment, trust, and faith without such background beliefs makes no sense. Moreover (*pace* Norman Malcolm) there can be no *belief-in* without *belief-that*. But fideists stress that being a belief-system is not the crucial thing about religion.[6] That is not what makes religious belief so important to so many people. We are creatures—sometimes anguished creatures—who, self-interpreting beings that we are, are trying to make sense of our lives and our world. Religion intervenes here. For some of us—perhaps for many of us, particularly if we have something like an advanced education—as modernity or (if you will) postmodernity sinks in, we, in our very way of responding and living, will come to recognize that religion is already for us what William James called a dead option (see Levine 1996; Nielsen 1997). But for others it is not. It is for many—and among them sometimes intellectuals—an option that they are passionate about. For them it is anything but dead. It is tied up with making sense of their lives, making sense of their world (of what life between human beings can be and what kind of civil society or political order we should try to create or sustain). Put otherwise, it is a consideration which, as things turn out, and turn out variously for us, may or may not be decisive in our attempts to find our way in the moral wilderness (e.g., Putnam 1997).

But it is vital to see that we are not all of the same mind or heart here. It is another feature of the intractable pluralism of our societies. And it is here where religion as well as secularism have their bite. We can be rather bemused and not very interested in J. L. Mackie and Richard Swinburne going toe-to-toe over which belief-system, a secular one or a theistic one, has the better claim to having "the true cosmology." Even if Mackie delivers a KO to Swinburne, a Kierkegaardian or Wittgensteinian fideism remains. A religious believer could be deeply skeptical, even cynically skeptical, concerning such moves in natural theology and metaphysics—indeed so skeptical, as to be either bored or mildly amused by such controversies—and still be thoroughly convinced that religion is necessary to make sense of one's life and of morality.[7] Kierkegaard was such a fideist. It is there, such a fideist believes, where religiously speaking it is at and not essentially over competing belief-systems, metaphysical worldviews and competing epistemologies. If we accept that, as this social naturalist does, what should we say concerning religion and what should we say about being a secularist all the way down?

To begin to get a purchase on that, first note that there is some common ground between utter secularizers such as myself and some religious believers. Both of us, if we are even remotely attentive readers of a tolerably good newspaper, and even somewhat reflective, will realize that we live in a moral wilderness: thousands of people—and unnecessarily—starve each year, many more are so malnourished as infants that in the few years that they can be expected to live they will not be able to function properly. Great masses of people, most of them children and most of them people of color, suffer from easily and cheaply curable diseases. And what is more—and this is as plain as plain can be—these things do not need to obtain (see Nielsen 1984, 1997a; Pogge 1994, 1996). It is also the case, and relatedly, that a quarter of the world's population live in conditions of dire poverty, live, to not put too fine a word on it, in conditions that are swinish. Again it is anything but evident that this is necessary. And in the face of this, the wealthy countries of the world continue to get wealthier and the poor countries poorer (Brittain and Elliott

1998). And within the rich capitalist democracies themselves, the disparity of wealth between the wealthier strata of the society and the poorer continues to grow and increasingly the strata in the middle gets in one way or another squeezed. Insecurity in employment grows and for the most part the conditions of work become less and less pleasant. We university professors are a comparatively well-off and comparatively secure and privileged segment of society. Yet it should be evident at least to those of us who have been around for a while how the quality of life in universities, including security of employment for newly minted Ph.D.s, rather steadily deteriorates.

Moreover, and now again speaking generally, not only our social environment continues to deteriorate, but, as Greens and other environmentalists graphically detail, our natural environment is going down the tubes as well, in some instances perhaps irreversibly. Yet our governments do next to nothing about it and, generally speaking, not out of ignorance either. Add to this the fact that the social world we live in becomes increasingly ugly and unpleasant; brutality is widespread and indifference to others even more widespread; child labor flourishes in certain parts of the world as does slavery (literal slavery and not just wage slavery). Racism in one form or another is pervasive. In the United States, for example, it is rampant. It differs from some not too distant times past in that it is, to some considerable extent, disguised. But all the same it is there and viciously so (see Mills 1997). The litany of our ills— the horrors that are part of the daily lives of many people—could readily be continued. But the above is enough to indicate the moral wilderness in which we live. (I am not giving to understand that these are the only kinds of things that make it a moral wilderness.) But these matters are common knowledge among us and standardly a matter of common concern for many secularists and religious believers alike. Moreover, it is not (*pace* Alasdair MacIntyre) a moral wilderness because we are *conceptually* at sea about our modern morality having only fragments of past moralities now largely opaque to us.

Some religious believers—believers not very well anchored in the world—might try to blame our ills here principally on secularism and the Enlightenment or post-Enlightenment. But there is little merit in that. *Perhaps* scientistic attitudes, from Holbach to Quine, are in some very minor way responsible for our situation by in effect blunting our understanding of what social critique and moral reflectiveness could come to. The ideology of contemporary "scientific realists" may contribute to the obliterating (if only by rather contemptuous neglect) of the cultural space needed for the very existence of an institutionally acknowledged and respectful role for critical intellectuals, including that of philosophers so conceiving of themselves.[8] Such activities, it is frequently thought by such scientistic philosophers, just aren't philosophy or even any kind of serious intellectual endeavor. They are good for common room chat but not for much else.

But, all that notwithstanding, the main culprit is industrial society. And the extant and recently demised versions of industrial societies are either capitalist societies (still very much with us) or those, now for the most part defunct, authoritarian noncapitalist Statist societies that vainly tried to compete with capitalist societies (see Fehér, Heller, and Markus 1983). We have other *models* of industrial society, but no other *exemplifications*. This being so, it seems to me evident that we should lay the blame for the ills I have listed principally on capitalism and most firmly on globalizing capitalism.[9] But, if that seems too *parti-pris* to you, let it pass and consider the fact that it would really and uncontroversially be *parti-pris* to lay the blame for these ills on secularism. Our industrial societies have been, and still are, massively religious societies.[10] Indeed theistically religious societies. Moreover, Enlightenment thought need not be scientistic. Two of the great exemplars of Enlightenment thought, David Hume and John Dewey, were secularists all the way down without being scientistic with the blunting of the critical thrust of normative inquiry that goes with scientism (Habermas 1970, 81–122). And the same is true of the social naturalism I have articulated.

There is another important common point of departure between at least some secularists (including this secularist) and some religious intellectuals that is relevant here. John Rawls and Thomas Scanlon instance it well on the secular side and Alasdair MacIntyre and Charles Taylor on the religious side. It is the common recognition that in moral and normative political reflection and inquiry we must start from, and in some sense return to, the social practices in our common social life, including the considered convictions which are deeply embedded in them: the, as Rawls puts it, at least provisional fixed points of our moral life. I have called them moral truisms and Jeffrey Stout has called them moral platitudes (Nielsen 1995, 1996; Stout 1988, 1992). Some have misleadingly and portentously called them natural laws. But, at least for people in modern cultures, they could not even begin moral inquiry or reflection without their being assumed and, to use Wittgenstein's way of putting it, we could not find our feet with anyone who did not acknowledge them as normative for their lives. Whatever else we may say about the sources of normativity we need to acknowledge that. A person without them and the social practices that go with them would be without what by now we understand as a morality.

These moral truisms include prominently such things as truthfulness being a virtue, promises being something to be kept, integrity being something to be cultivated, human well-being being desirable, an understanding of one's situation being a good thing, human suffering or pain being bad, caring about others and for oneself good, cooperation on fair terms being essential to a decent human life, mutual respect and recognition being essential for human flourishing, and the care for children being something which is morally obligatory. These are just as available to, and as fully acknowledgeable, and acknowledged, by atheists as by religious believers. They may have their *origin* in religion, but validity is independent of origin and by now, vis-à-vis religion, they are normatively speaking *free standing*. These moral truisms—and I do not, of course, take the list to be exhaustive—need not be taken as foundational for the moral life. (It may very well be that nothing need be so taken.) Rather they come as a cluster of beliefs with none of them, or some more precise rational reconstruction of them, standing in any sort of hierarchy as first principles or as basic beliefs foundational for the moral life. The force any one of them has is effected by the others. Indeed we will not even properly understand them if we try to take them in isolation. Sometimes some of them conflict and it needs to be seen (if this can be pulled off) which of them, in *some specific problematic situation*, has pride of place. (Here we see, as Dewey so well stressed, how important context is. I have built contextualism into the very structure of my social naturalism [Nielsen 1996, 25–77].)

All of these moral truisms are *defeasible*; any of them (taken one or a few at a time) can be overridden by other moral considerations, including other moral truisms, coming to have greater force in some specific situation. (It is important, however, to recognize that our moral truisms do not come to us in anything like a *lexical* order.) None of them are certainly true or in any other way certainly established nor are they always to be acted on, nor are they "properly basic." That very vocabulary and the way of thinking that goes with it is eschewed. But they always have some *prima facie* or presumptive force. Someone who just sets them aside in her "moral reasoning" is not reasoning morally at all (Nielsen 1996, 26–72). However, we only get something for some of these moral truisms *sounding* like moral certainties when they are transformed in the direction of conceptual remarks and have shed their substantive content, as when we go from the genuinely substantive moral truism "to cause pain is bad" to "to cause pain without point or reason is evil."

The appeal to moral truisms is not a backhanded way of claiming certitude and it is not to turn one's back on fallibilism. Moreover, it need not be at all to espouse foundationalism. But it is also important to recognize that religious believers, at least if they are even remotely orthodox, *at some point*, and in some way (though sometimes obliquely) will claim certainty. They may be shockingly skeptical in all sorts of ways, trumping in some ways Hume, but tucked away in some corner will be some kind of claim to certitude. This is as true of Pascal, Hamann, and Kierkegaard as it is of any other religious believer. It is just that with them the claim to certitude is not so up front. Religious people will not, perhaps cannot, accept the full force of fallibilism and remain Jews, Christians, or Moslems.[11] But, by contrast, secularists frequently do not claim certainty. Moreover—and this is the normatively vital point here—a secularist need not, nor should she, claim or seek certainty. Here we can see a crucial difference between a religious stance and an utterly secular one, and again we find good reasons here for being secularists. It is a cultural accomplishment to be able to abandon the quest for certainty, to live comfortably with fallibilism and, all the same, not to be at all caught up by skepticism, nihilism, or cynicism. And in some of the more fortunate parts of the world we are stumbling along in that direction.

It is also true that these moral truisms are vague and indeterminate in their application, though neither so vague nor so indeterminate as to lose substantive content and to fail to be action-guiding. Take, for example, truthfulness is a good thing. That is perfectly compatible with considerable differences about what truthfulness requires. *Some* Christians—Kant and MacIntyre, for example (MacIntyre 1990)—believe that it is never right to lie while I, and not a few others, including some Christians, think that while lying is always *prima facie* wrong that we sometimes not only should lie but that sometimes we have an obligation to lie if nothing else is likely to prevent a certain very harmful result. (This is the "terrible consequentialism" that Anscombe so detested. She, in a fine fit of fanaticism, said she did not want to talk with anyone with such views [Anscombe 1981].) It is not that lying should come trippingly on the tongue, but that in certain circumstances we must—morally must—lie. And we can believe this, I remark in passing, without being utilitarians. If I, to use a well worn example, am living under Nazi occupation, and the Gestapo is at my door asking if there are any Jews in there, I have, if I am hiding Jews, an obligation to lie, even if in doing so I put myself at some considerable risk. So while some think (usually Christians) that it is never right to lie—thinking perhaps that everything is in God's hands and that we may never do evil that good may come—others (usually secularists) think that it is not only sometimes right to lie, but also that it is sometimes morally required. Both accept the moral truism that truthfulness is a good thing; again to speak portentously, they are both likely to believe that care for truth is a standard of rectitude in life, but they differ, and differ deeply, concerning application of the requirement of truthfulness.

People will differ over the scope of truthfulness, just what it commits one to and even over what it means to be truthful.[12] To consider only the latter here, suppose that I, a Quebec sovereignist, am at a table in Alberta with a group of people who have no reason at all to believe that of me and they begin to speak in a dinner table conversation rather vehemently against what they call "Quebec separatism." Suppose I say nothing. Have I been untruthful and (to boot) shown lack of integrity? People will strongly disagree about whether I have. There will be similar differences over the scope of truthfulness, when (if ever) to lie, how important the moral maxim "Do not lie" is, and over what it exactly (or even inexactly) commits one to. The other moral truisms are similarly vague and indeterminate.

Such considerations have led some theists—though not only them— to say that to have anything like an adequate conception of the good and the right we need either to turn to Scripture and Revelation or to some full-blown metaphysical-cum-moral theory such as Thomistic-Aristotelianism or, of course, to both. But all these are nonstarters. There are different and sometimes conflicting putative Scriptures and putative Revelations. Indeed, if we go genuinely anthropological with the putative Revelations, we will have to acknowledge that there are thousands of them: almost as many as there once were different cultures. So there is plainly the problem of ascertaining which, if any, is the genuine article. To just take one of the putative Scriptures or Revelations—say the Christian one—as binding and authoritative is question-begging and flatly ethnocentric. But appealing to something outside the putative Divine Scripture or putative Revelation such as miracles (alleged miracles) or to the *magisterium* of the Catholic Church or the authority of any other church is to rely on some other ground than that of Scripture (putative) or Revelation (putative) and thereby to lose the force of that appeal (Nielsen 1985, 1996). Moreover, an appeal to a magisterium as authoritative is just dogmatically and uncritically to appeal to one tradition among others. Perhaps something like that would be plausible in a world *without* knowledge of other traditions or perhaps *without* a knowledge of a competing long-standing secular tradition without the religious anchorage of any of the religious traditions. But that is not our world.

We have plainly and irretrievably lost our innocence. And an appeal to the Thomistic-Aristotelian tradition is, standing where we are now, an appeal to a spent tradition. The idea that the universe is teleologically ordered, as it claims, is at best without warrant and at worst incoherent. And there is no sound argument for the existence of God or the immortality of the soul or for a belief in miracles. And this is widely, though not quite universally, recognized. The whole Thomistic-Aristotelian apparatus is a relic of the past undermined by the tradition of critical philosophical thought.

Must we continue to redo (perhaps with a little rational reconstruction here and there) the work that Hume and Kant did so well before us? Should we continue to play the role of Philo? Standing where we stand now to do any of these things seems to be extremely Quixotic. It is to return to considerations that we have very good reasons to believe have been thrashed out sufficiently already. A claim that some miracles have really been established to be true or that we have a new perfectly sound argument for the existence of God is more likely to be met with a yawn rather than with philosophical interest. We have been over these grounds too many times already. It is not that we can stand free of traditions, but that working from within (from within the broad confines of the Western tradition), the secular tradition wins at least on these counts. Recall also that for a long time now we have lived in a world in which various religious traditions compete and that Christian, Jewish, and Islamic traditions, or more accurately some articulations of them, are all thoroughly embedded in a broader Western tradition.[13] And to appeal to a metaphysical moral theory such as Thomistic-Aristotelianism is (a) to have in tow all the very problematic features of metaphysics and particularly of such a supernaturalistic metaphysics and (b) it is, as well, to appeal to one of the religious traditions among the various traditions as authoritative in the face of other traditions (religious and secular). Just making an appeal to authority like that has all the appearances of an utterly arbitrary move. Why accept claims taken as just appeals to tradition which seem at least to have as much or as little warrant as the others? It comes down, however embellished it is with scholarship, to making a bald dogmatic claim to authority.

I agree, however, with the claim sometimes made by some theistic philosophers that while an appeal to moral truisms is a necessary starting point in moral inquiry and moral reflection, it is not enough to yield a satisfactory account of morality. It is here where what has been called wide and general reflective equilibrium comes into play (see Nielsen 1996; Daniels 1996; Rawls 1971, 1993, 1995; Scanlon 1992). We start, and inescapably, with our considered convictions, including our moral truisms, and we seek to get them into wide and general reflective equilibrium not only by forging them into a coherent package, typically by making adjustments as we proceed to get a better fit of our considered convictions at various levels of abstraction as well as with our other moral beliefs, but also by seeking the most coherent assemblage we can obtain of both of them together and with, as well, while doing some sifting here, our various moral theories, theories of human nature, theories of social structure and social organization. We will also, in using the method of wide reflective equilibrium, consider the import of what we reasonably believe to be facts about the world, including facts about human society and various psychological facts about individuals. We will seek, as well, to get them into a coherent fit with our other beliefs, including, of course, our considered convictions. Using this holistic coherentist method—and always using it fallibilistically and in line with historicism—we will seek for a time and for a culture or cluster of related cultures in our particular world, or ideally, and probably unrealistically, the assemblage of cultures in the modern world, for the most coherent conception of how things hang together we can for a time get, including essentially, in trying to see how things hang together, seeing how our lives as moral persons hang together. We can, however, never reasonably expect firm closure; we will at best get something that for a time obtains, knowing full well that this will always be only for a time. The reflective equilibrium will, sooner or later, be upset and another will need to be forged. But this is just what it is to live with fallibilism.

In this way, in forging such a wide reflective equilibrium, we can make our moral truisms somewhat more determinate—make them, that is, into something more than moral truisms. And while we have here a fallibilism, a historicism, and a contextualism, our views are neither relativist nor ethnocentric. They are not ethnocentric because, while we start with our considered convictions, we have a method for criticizing the views and practices with which we start by either correcting them, in accordance with our goal of coherence, by modifying them or in some instances even by abandoning them for other principles, views, and practices, always with the same goal of coherence in mind. We are not stuck with just saying that these are our considered judgments and that they are the ones we must stick with or at least that we, utilizing the method of tenacity, are just going to stick with through thick and thin. It is not relativistic either for it is not saying, absurdly and incoherently, that there are many sets of considered judgments (including sometimes conflicting or perhaps—if that notion makes sense—incommensurable sets) and that they are "all equally valid" (whatever that could mean). Rather, wide reflective equilibrium yields grounds for assessing in terms of coherent overall fit clusters of considered judgments embedded in different social practices. It will not, at least in many situations, say that we have no grounds for favoring one cluster of social practices over another or claiming, absurdly and incoherently, that they are all "equally true" or "equally sound" or even "equally valid." And, where for a time, after we have applied conscientiously the method of wide reflective equilibrium and we still have what at least looks like a tie, we can reasonably, if ever this actually obtains, go back to the drawing board, and, using the method of wide reflective equilibrium, try again to *forge* a reflective equilibrium that will not have that untoward result. There is no justified or acceptable principle of sufficient reason that says we, at least in the fullness of time, must succeed, but there is nothing that tells us that we must, or even will, or probably will, fail.

So here we have a method—a way of fixing belief—available to someone who is a secularist all the way down to make sense of her moral and political life without any of the obscurities and *inescapably* ethnocentricizing factors that are unavoidable for the religious believer. There is nothing for the secularist like "Christ is the truth and the way." In that way, knowing they have no need of such a skyhook, secularists can, if they will hold onto their brains, take seriously and to heart their considered judgments, and put them together with other things they have good reasons for believing, take themselves out of the moral wilderness understood here as an incoherence *about*, or perhaps even *in*, moral belief and commitment. In another way—the way I described when I listed some of the horrors of our world—they, and religious believers as well, will remain in it. But that is because of *capitalism* and not because of a secular orientation or a religious orientation or because of the presence of or the absence of some metaphysics or epistemology. And capitalism is something they can in good conscience both fight together whatever their religious, nonreligious, or antireligious orientations and whatever metaphysical or antimetaphysical or epistemological or antiepistemological views they may, or may not, espouse. It is tempting, at least for me, to think *positive* metaphysical or epistemological views are free-spinning wheels that turn no machinery and have little relevance, except sometimes as encumbrances, to moral and political life and that *negative* antimetaphysical or antiepistemological views are only important as bits of philosophical therapy. With the demise of the positive views we could forget about the negative ones.[14]

NOTES

1. In the following quotation Andrew Levine gives expression to an attitude that is very pervasive among secularists: ". . . a broadly secular worldview has become part of the common-sense of many of us. There are even sizeable numbers of people who, like myself, are unable to identify with religious sensibilities experientially. For us, the world of the faithful seems both exotic and ridiculous. It is accessible to us only in the way that, say, Greek mythology is; from the *outside*. We know that religions have millions of adherents, many of whom are ardent believers, just as we know that belief in the exploits of Zeus was once fervent and widespread. But in neither case can we understand the phenomenon empathically. Before the Enlightenment, most people experienced nonbelief as a failing to be overcome. Nowadays, many nonbelievers experience the inability to understand belief empathically as a triumph. We consider ourselves *beyond* theism" (Levine 1996). For careful delineations of what agnosticism and atheism come to, see Ronald Hepburn, "Agnosticism" (Hepburn 1967), and my *Philosophy and Atheism: In Defense of Atheism* (Nielsen 1985, 9–28, 55–106).

2. This is a change from my *Naturalism without Foundations* (Nielsen 1996) where I advocated a form of nonreductive physicalism.

3. Even a wolf-child, if there ever were any, in being nurtured by wolves,

in a weak and extended way, enters into social relations. But that there have ever been any such children is not very likely.

4. It could be responded that we should not saddle Mackie and Williams with such exuberant metaphysical claims. Why cannot they simply say that science, in contrast with religion, is our best bet to the truth, not that it tells us about "ultimate reality"? That is better, but it still ends up claiming that something is our best bet to the truth as if we had a nonparticular language-game-independent or form-of-life-independent understanding of the truth or indeed any clear understanding of *the truth* period, so that we could coherently say that science is a better bet to the truth than literature: that molecular biology puts us into a closer relation with the truth than naturalistic novels. What I am arguing is that such talk is incoherent and that there is no reason—indeed no coherent possibility—of thinking anything like that. We do, of course, understand (though perhaps we do not have any very perspicuous *analysis* of it) what it is for a particular statement to be true or false, but that is a different matter. See also Stephen Toulmin, "Contemporary Scientific Mythology" (Toulmin 1957).

5. My metaphor about being secularists all the way down has misled some. Andrew Lugg has responded that being secularists all the way down is clearly compatible with the idea that there is a place for religion. A theist could argue "Yes, we can be secularists, but we don't have to be, and why after all should we be?" My metaphor apart, I *argue* that we should be secularists (atheists) because it is a more reasonable and humanly desirable thing to be than to be a theist or any other kind of religious believer. The import of the metaphor is that we could and should, in showing the preferability of a secular view to a religious one, go all the way down to the very attempt to make sense of our lives, to find something worth being committed to in our moral and political responses. The sense of "going all the way down" is that in concerning ourselves with the choice between a secularist response or a religious response, we do not merely, or perhaps even at all, concern ourselves with cosmology and similar theoretical issues, but with issues that are at the core of our lives. See also Nicholas Wolterstorff, "The Reformed Tradition" (Wolterstorff 1997).

6. See Hendrik Hart and Kai Nielsen, *Search for Community in a Withering Tradition* (Hart and Nielsen 1990), for Hart's response.

7. Terence Penelhum in his often illuminating discussions of fideism still remains too rationalistic about fideism and misses the depth of Kierkegaard's (or for that matter Pascal's) probing and the force and significance of a faith that may come with deep intellectual skepticism about religion. This is shown when he concludes an essay on fideism by remarking "The caricature of faith as a passionate and wholehearted certainty about matters that are uncertain is a deeply mistaken one. Fideism, unfortunately, has helped to create and perpetuate it" (Penelhum 1997, 381 ff.). There is faith, and one very significant thing about fideism is its depiction and elucidation of a faith that can go—and reasonably—with utter intellectual skepticism about religion. Its significance is further enhanced by its characterization of human life and particularly for those people who will not make an idol of reason.

8. For further discussion, see Jürgen Habermas, *Toward a Rational Society* (Habermas 1970).

9. Hendrik Hart, who counts himself as a thoroughgoing opponent of capitalism, thinks I demonize capitalism. By this he means I "give it the counterrole of God, namely the devil." He adds "If in your [my] thinking you have both a specific location for keeping us on track (wide reflective equilibrium) you display some very classic qualities of religion" (from a personal communication). Well, perhaps, but I do not demonize capitalism. I certainly do not think it is the source of all our ills. But I do think that it is the source of some very important ones and I try to say what some of them are. And I do argue that they are sufficient to turn our social world into a moral wilderness (e.g., Brittain and Elliott 1998). Similarly, reflective equilibrium is not a secular source of salvation. It hardly, for example, answers to what for some may be a very personal and private sense of despair and meaninglessness. But in many contexts it shows us how to see morality as more than a rather chaotic and arbitrary jumble of beliefs and sentiments.

10. Unless, like Kierkegaard, we use such strict criteria for "being religious" that we end up saying, as he did, that there are no Christians in the Christian Kingdom of Denmark.

11. Both Robert Audi and Hendrik Hart have argued that not all religious believers need be on a quest for certainty and that they need not reject fallibilism. Claims to certainty are even dismissed by some religious thinkers as misplaced Cartesian anxiety. I take this point. But I think that it should be added that this is a very recent phenomenon, probably in some considerable measure a response to the persuasiveness of pragmatist secular fallibilism. What has historically given religion much of its power is its claim in one way or another, cognitively or effectively or both, to hold out the hope of some certitude in our groping to make some sense of our tangled lives. Moreover, and distinctly, once fallibilism is let in and becomes persuasive religion it becomes increasingly vulnerable to secular alternatives.

12. Alasdair MacIntyre has insightfully discussed these matters and he has drawn a very different conclusion than I have. He argues against Jeffrey Stout's appeal to a consensus concerning what Stout calls moral platitudes and, in effect, against what I have called moral truisms. MacIntyre argues that, though Stout is "indeed right in thinking there is a consensus of platitudes in our moral culture," this does not have the significance that Stout attaches to it. (Presumably the same argument would apply to me.) This consensus rooted in moral platitudes, MacIntyre contends, "belongs to the rhetorical surface of that culture and not to its substance. The rhetoric of shared values is of great ideological importance, but it disguises the truth about how action is guided and directed. For what we genuinely share in the way of moral maxims, precepts, and principles is insufficiently determinate to guide action and what is sufficiently determinate to guide action is not shared" (MacIntyre 1990, 349). MacIntyre indeed brings out very clearly as an illustration of the thesis that many of the ways in which the maxim "Never tell a lie" is indeterminate and how within our societies both in theory and in practice there is much disagreement, uncertainty, and ambivalence about truth telling. But he fails to note that, this dissensus notwithstanding, there is also a wide substantive consensus both in theory and in practice about truth telling and lying. There is massive agreement that people who simply routinely lie or are careless about the truth or lie whenever it is convenient behave wrongly. Clinton is simply a prominent example.

Moreover, people do not utterly disagree about what counts as "routinely," "careless," and "convenient" here. We can easily give clear paradigms. There is also wide agreement about the wrongness of some (some considerable some) specific cases of lying. The following are all taken to be plainly wrong in standard situations and *ceteris paribus*. A stranger in a city asks for directions and he is deliberately lied to; a used car salesman extensively lies about the condition of a car he is selling; a professor gives a grade to a paper and tells the student he has read it when he hasn't; a person who has AIDS lies about it and has unprotected intercourse with someone who doesn't have AIDS; police lie about torturing someone with no criminal record whom they have arrested for a trivial offense where they have no reason to believe that that person has committed a serious crime; a biker gang blows up the car of a rival gang, killing several children playing in the street nearby, and then lies about it in court under oath. Obviously this list could be easily expanded.

What we see here is that there are plenty of plain paradigms of lying that are massively and unambivalently believed to be lying that is completely unacceptable. We also can easily recognize that prohibitions against these things guide action. Moreover, as is argued in the text, cases that are more problematic—sometimes very much more problematic—can sometimes be rendered less so by careful moral argument. And it is reasonable to believe that there would sometimes be widespread agreement concerning such cases where the method of wide reflective equilibrium is in place and people are attending to such arguments. (Wide reflective equilibrium, it should be remarked, is an extension of common-sense ways of reasoning.) I argue in the text that that is so for MacIntyre's case of lying when an innocent human life is immediately at stake. It is here where the rigidity of Aristotelian-Thomism gets in MacIntyre's way. (See MacIntyre 1990, 356–67.)

The use of wide reflective equilibrium—a method that is compatible with a number of substantive ethical theories or with having no such ethical theory at all—can reduce, but not utterly eliminate, the indeterminacies of truth telling as it can for many, perhaps all, of the other moral platitudes. But if we conclude with MacIntyre "that a necessary precondition for a political community's possession of adequately determinate shared rationally founded moral rules is the shared possession of a rationally justifiable conception of human good," we will wait until hell freezes over, for we will never in our intractably pluralist societies—societies which are here to stay—come to have such a shared conception. (MacIntyre 1990, 351.) Rawls is a better guide here. The drive to affirm certainty runs deep in religion and in religious thinkers. MacIntyre, for all his sensitivity to history and to different cultures, is no exception. He requires more certainty—stronger, more determinate action-guides—for morality than can be had or that we need to have to have a reasonable morality (MacIntyre 1990, 348–57). MacIntyre critiques, unsuccessfully I have argued, Stout (e.g., Stout, *Ethics after Babel*). Stout's subtle and compelling "Truth, Natural Law and Ethical Theory," (1992) written after MacIntyre's essay, should also be studied in this context.

13. Only small isolated sects like the Amish or the Hutterites can—and then only partially—escape this.

14. See my *On Transforming Philosophy*. I want to thank Jocelyne Couture, Hendrik Hart, Andrew Lugg, and Jack Ornstein for their critical examination of my

arguments here. Ornstein raised the question, *contra* my fallibilism, "Are there not some things, including some empirical things, that we are certain of and does this not refute fallibilism?" I will acknowledge that there are some certainties, including some empirical certainties, but contend that that does not refute or even count against fallibilism. But isn't this just the philosopher's not infrequent gambit of first saying it and then taking it all back? No, as I will explain, it is not. Empirical certainties are statements such as "it gets dark earlier in December in Ontario than in June," "People eventually die," "Some birds migrate," "Sometimes some people get angry." They are of course not a priori true and in that sense they are not certain. But that only means that it is not self-contradictory to deny them. But for people situated as we are, we are as confident that they are true as we can be that any statement we believe to be a priori true is actually a priori true. (Remember the fate of the law of excluded middle.) To say that this shows that nothing is certain is just to say that we can in some sense think that any statement might be false even if we are in circumstances in which we are at a loss to say what that would be like. But for us situated as we are the examples of empirical certainties given above are things we are perfectly confident about, haven't the slightest reason to doubt, and even believe that anyone in our situation who tried to doubt them would be mad. So in that perfectly ordinary sense some things are certain. But fallibilists are not concerned to deny that, but to contend that any interesting considerations that people have reasonably disputed are less than certain and that in the history of human thought many things that for a time were ubiquitously taken to be certain have later been found to be false or at least actually doubtful. For further discussion, see Norman Malcolm, "The Verification Argument" (Malcolm 1950).

BIBLIOGRAPHY

Anscombe, G. E. M. 1981. *Ethics, Religion and Politics*. Minneapolis: University of Minnesota Press.

Berlin, Isaiah. 1998. "My Intellectual Path." *New York Review of Books* 45, no. 8: 53–60.

Brittain, Victoria, and Elliott, Larry. 1998. "The Rich and Poor Are Growing Further Apart." *Guardian Weekly* (20 September): 19.

Couture, Jocelyne and Nielsen, Kai. 1993. "On Construing Philosophy." In *Métaphilosophie/Reconstructing Philosophy?*, edited by Jocelyne Couture and Kai Neilsein, 30–55. Calgary, Alb.: University of Calgary Press.

Daniels, Norman. 1996. *Justice and Justification: Reflective Equilibrium in Theory and Practice*. Cambridge: Cambridge University Press.

Fehér, Ferenc, Heller, Agnes, and Márkus, György. 1983. *Dictatorship Over Needs: An Analysis of Soviet Societies*. Oxford: Basil Blackwell.

Habermas, Jürgen. 1970. *Toward a Rational Society*. Translated by Jeremy J. Shapiro. Boston: Beacon Press.

Hart, Hendrik, and Nielsen, Kai. 1990. *Search for Community in a Withering Tradition*. Lanham, Md.: University Press of America.

Hepburn, Ronald. 1967. "Agnosticism." In *Encyclopedia of Philosophy*, vol. 1, edited by Paul Edwards, 56–59. New York: Macmillan and The Free Press.

Levine, Andrew. 1996. "Just Nationalism: The Future of an Illusion." In *Rethinking Nationalism*, edited by Jocelyne Couture, Kai Nielsen, and Michel Seymour, 345–63. Calgary, Alb.: University of Calgary Press.
MacIntyre, Alasdair. 1990. "The Privatization of Good: An Inaugural Lecture." *Review of Politics* 52, no. 4: 356–67.
Mackie, J. L. 1982. *The Miracle of Theism*. Oxford: Clarendon Press.
Malcolm, Norman. 1950. "The Verification Argument." In *Philosophical Analysis: A Collection of Essays*, edited by Max Black, 244–95. Ithaca, N.Y.: Cornell University Press.
Mills, Charles. 1997. *The Racial Contract*. Ithaca, N.Y.: Cornell University Press.
Nielsen, Kai. 1984. "Global Justice, Capitalism and the Third World." *Journal of Applied Philosophy* 1, no. 2: 175–86.
———. 1985. *Philosophy and Atheism: In Defense of Atheism*. Amherst, N.Y.: Prometheus Books.
———. 1995. *On Transforming Philosophy: A Metaphilosophical Inquiry*. Boulder, Colo.: Westview Press.
———. 1996. *Naturalism without Foundations*. Amherst, N.Y.: Prometheus Books.
———. 1997a. "Is Global Justice Impossible?" In *Global Justice, Global Democracy*, edited by Jay Drydyk and Peter Penz, 19–54. Winnipeg and Halifax: Fernwood Publishing.
———. 1997b. "Naturalistic Explanations of Religion." *Studies in Religion* 26, no. 4: 441–66.
Penelhum, Terence. 1997. "Fideism." In *A Companion to the Philosophy of Religion*, edited by Philip L. Quinn and Charles Taliaferro, 381ff. Oxford: Blackwell.
Pogge, Thomas W. 1994. "An Egalitarian Law of Peoples." *Philosophy and Public Affairs* 23, no. 3: 195–224.
———. 1996. "The Bounds of Nationalism." In *Rethinking Nationalism*, edited by Jocelyne Couture et al., 463–504. Calgary, Alb.: University of Calgary Press.
Putnam, Hilary. 1990. *Realism with a Human Face*. Cambridge, Mass.: Harvard University Press.
———. 1994. *Words and Life*. Cambridge, Mass.: Harvard University Press.
———. 1994. "Sense, Nonsense and the Senses: An Inquiry into the Powers of the Human Mind." *Journal of Philosophy* 41, no. 9: 445–517.
———. 1997. "God and the Philosophers." *Midwest Studies in Philosophy* 21: 175–87.
Rawls, John. 1971. *A Theory of Justice*. Cambridge, Mass.: Belknap Press of Harvard University Press.
———. 1993. *Political Liberalism*. New York: Columbia University Press.
———. 1995. "Reply to Habermas." *Journal of Philosophy* 92, no. 3: 132–80.
Rorty, Richard. 1991. *Objectivity, Relativism and Truth*. Cambridge: Cambridge University Press.
———. 1998. *Truth and Progress*. Cambridge: Cambridge University Press.
Sauer-Thompson, Gary. 1998. "Dancing in the Dark: Postmodernism, the Renewal of Philosophy, and the End of the Analytic Enlightenment." Ph.D. diss., Flinders University.
Scanlon, T. M. 1992. "The Aims and Authority of Moral Theory." *Oxford Journal of Legal Studies* 12, no. 1: 1–23.

Stout, Jeffrey. 1988. *Ethics after Babel*. Boston: Beacon Press.

———. 1992. "Truth, Natural Law and Ethical Theory." In *Natural Law Theory*, edited by Robert P. George, 71–97. Oxford: Clarendon Press.

Taylor, Charles. 1985. *Human Agency and Language*. Cambridge: Cambridge University Press.

Toulmin, Stephen. 1957. "Contemporary Scientific Mythology." In *Metaphysical Beliefs*, edited by Stephen Toulmin et al. London: SCM Press.

Williams, Bernard. "Review of Charles Taylor's Sources of the Self." *New York Review of Books* 37 (8 November): 44–48.

Wolterstorff, Nicholas. 1997. "The Reformed Tradition." In *A Companion to the Philosophy of Religion*, edited by Philip L. Quinn and Charles Taliaferro, 165–70. Oxford: Blackwell.

3

THE FACES OF IMMORTALITY

I s there an afterlife or any reasonable possibility of an afterlife, or is belief in an afterlife—of a postmortem existence—somehow incoherent, or is it instead merely a false belief? Given the new philosophical dispensation in the aftermath of the undermining of foundationalism, it is better for secularists such as myself to "split the difference" and contend that conceptions of the afterlife are so problematical that it is unreasonable for a philosophical and scientifically sophisticated person living in the West in the twentieth century to believe in life eternal, to believe that we shall survive the rotting or the burning or the mummification of our "present bodies." There are questions of fact here, questions of interpretation of fact, and questions of what it makes sense to say which come as part of a package, and it may well be that in some instances it is not so easy to divide these questions so neatly. In a good Quinean manner I will let philosophy range over all these considerations.

If immortality is taken, as I shall take it, in a reasonably robust way and not simply as the sentimentalism that we shall live in the thoughts of others, belief in the afterlife—or so I shall argue—is so problematical that it should not be something to be believed. It is a belief, depending on how exactly the afterlife is construed, that is either fantastically unlikely to be true, or is instead an incoherent belief which could not possibly be true. Bodily resurrection, one of the reigning conceptions of the afterlife, may well, on some of its formulations, be a coherent belief (at least on some readings of "coherent"), but it is a belief which is very unlikely indeed to be true. Its unlikelihood rests, as I shall show, on a number of grounds. One of them is, of course, the nonexistence of God. If there were a God and he was what, say, Orthodox Christianity takes him to be, we might take bodily resurrection to be a straight matter of faith (Vesey 1977, 306). Even so, I will argue, there will still be extraordinary difficulties, difficulties so great that not a few believers in God have turned away from any such conception. They have, that is, opted for belief in God without belief in immortality. In this context we should keep firmly in mind that if the grounds for believing in God are scant the grounds for believing in bodily resurrection are doubly scant. Belief in it is a considerable scandal to the intellect.

I shall, after some preliminaries, start with a discussion of bodily resurrection, go on to a discussion of disembodied existence, and finally turn to a last cluster of considerations of broadly moral and human rationales for having a concern for immortality and having a hope that it may, after all, be a reality. This last consideration will be linked to the claim made by some that belief in immortality is necessary to make life in an otherwise intolerable world have some sense in the face of what, some argue, would otherwise be human despair, a despair that is inescapable where human beings come to escape double-mindedness and face nonevasively the bleakness of their lives without God and the possibility of eternal life (Kierkegaard 1954).

II

In speaking of immortality we are speaking of the endless existence of a person after what we call her "death" or at least the death of her body. What is agreed on all sides, and what is an inconvertible fact, is that after a time for all of us our bodies cease to be energized, and left alone they will simply rot, and no matter how they are manipulated, when they are thoroughly in that state—there is no evidence of their ever being reenergized. (In that respect we are not like batteries.) Believers in immortality believe that, all this to the contrary notwithstanding, we, as human beings, persons, selves, somehow do not really die but have instead an endless existence after such a deenergization and disintegration of our bodies or (if you will) our "earthly bodies."

Jewish, Christian, and Islamic defenders of immortality take two fundamentally different positions in their characterization of the afterlife. The first position I shall characterize is probably the more religiously orthodox position and the second position, until rather recently, would more likely appeal to philosophers and perhaps even to common sense since the time of Descartes, and in certain strata of society extending down to our own time. Since I believe both views are fundamentally defective, I shall not be concerned to take sides with respect to them, but to be, after a characterization of them, concerned to critique them both. The two views are, respectively, bodily resurrection by God to eternal life, and Cartesian dualism with its belief in an indestructible, immaterial individual self distinct from the body in which this self is said to be housed. This self is also thought to be capable, without any body in which it must be housed, of existing as a disembodied individual who is also a person.

Belief in bodily resurrection is clearly something deeply embedded in the orthodox Judeo-Christian-Islamic traditions. Unless we take seriously the idea that there could be, and indeed there actually is, a God and that he, being omnipotent, could do whatever is logically possible, bodily resurrection is a very difficult thing in which to believe on empirical grounds. On those grounds it just seems utterly fantastic and no doubt is something whose reality is very unlikely indeed. However, it appears at least not to be an incoherent notion, at least if we take an incoherent notion to be a notion which is logically impossible, for example, "a round square," or not understandable (comprehensible), for example, "Reagan sleeps faster than Thatcher." People on such an account, when resurrected, do not have to be radically different from those men and women we meet on the street, including ourselves, where as Antony Flew once put it, "People are what you meet. We do not meet only the sinewy containers in which other people are kept, and they do not encounter only the fleshy houses that we ourselves inhabit" (Flew 1967, 142). Rather the people we meet are flesh and blood individuals: energized, purposively acting bodies through and through a part of the physical world (if that isn't a pleonasm).

What bodily resurrection teaches us is that we embodied beings will survive the death of our present bodies and that our postmortem existence, though in certain respects it will be very different, will be, ontologically speaking, in a manner essentially similar to our premortem existence. We will come to have, when resurrected, an energized physical body essentially like that of our present body except that it will be a better one, though better along familiar lines, and differing from our present bodies in that it cannot ever wear out or become deenergized. It must, and will, last forever. (It is like the suit in *The Man in the White Suit*.) We have an energized body, and, as we go along the history of our life trajectory, that body at some time ceases to be energized and then, perhaps after considerable decay or even disintegration, gets, according to the bodily resurrection story, a refurbished or a reconstituted body and, most importantly of all, it gets a reenergized body as a dead battery gets recharged. We are rather like a lake, to switch the analogy, that dries up and then, on the same lakebed, refills again. Peter Geach, a stalwart defender of bodily resurrection, forcefully puts the matter in this way:

> The traditional faith of Christianity, inherited from Judaism, is that at the end of this age the Messiah will come and men will rise from their graves to die no more. That faith is not going to be shaken by inquiries about bodies burned to ashes or eaten by beasts; those who might well suffer just such death in martyrdom were those who were most confident of a glorious reward in the resurrection. One who shares that hope will hardly wish to take out an occultistic or philosophical insurance policy, to guarantee some sort of survival as an annuity, in case God's promise of resurrection should fail. (Geach 1969, 29)

Leaving God out of it, the notions of inert bodies being reenergized or even particles of dust being brought together and formed again into a single body and then reenergized are logical possibilities (in the philosopher's sense of that phrase) and in that sense (a sense familiar to philosophers) these notions are coherent.

Of course, to say that something is logically possible is not to say much. It is logically possible that Geach might sprint from Leeds to London in three seconds or eat a thousand ears of corn in two seconds, though we better not ask for a story about how he will do these things. Similarly, it is logically possible that I might grow an aluminium exoskeleton just as the metamorphosis in the Kafka story is, as the logical positivists used to say, consistently describable. However, that is a kind of low-order coherence if coherence at all. It is in reality no more than a necessary condition for coherence. What it does mean is that we know what it would be like to see a metallic substance spreading all over Nielsen's body and for his bones and the like to turn into something like iron rods. And we can follow the Kafka story. But we do not at all understand how such things are causally possible. They make no sense at all in terms of what we know about the world. (All we have are mental pictures here but still it does not appear that any syntactical rules have been violated.) And it is not even clear that we know what it would be like to see Geach run from Leeds to London in three seconds or even in three minutes. Suppose I were in an airplane at a very high altitude with very powerful binoculars. I could possibly spy out Geach at Leeds in his running shorts starting with the starter's gun and then track him as he ran—now in three seconds—to London, though, if we get specific, what it would be like to carry out such a tracking so rapidly is hard to say. However, I do know or think I know, what it would be like three seconds later —though I would have to move my binoculars awfully fast—to spy out Geach or a Geach-like replica at the outskirts of London. Given, as I remarked, the speed of his alleged running, the tracking (the very idea here) gets more obscure. What, for example, would it be like to see him running at such a speed? (But perhaps I could have a movie camera and replay the whole thing in very slow motion. Still he must have moved his arms and legs with incredible speed. And how did he do that? How is that possible? For God, all things are possible but not for Geach.)

Such stories depend for their intelligibility on their being underdescribed. The more we, remaining stubbornly literal, try to fill them in, the more problematical they become, the less coherent they seem. (Philosophers talk of "the limits of intelligibility" but we have no clear idea of what we are talking about here.[1]) Still, perhaps no contradictions are involved in their characterizations: problematicity and doubtful coherence yes, inconsistency no, or at least perhaps no. (Still, what is or isn't consistent is not always easy to ascertain.) Where no disembodiment assumptions sneak in by the back door to carry the self from one body to the next, bodily resurrection seems at least to be some kind of obscure logical possibility. Still, that is not saying very much at all.

Many logical possibilities are not genuine possibilities. It is totally irrational for me to believe I can levitate, survive in the winter outside in my swimming trunks at the North Pole, or that this body of mine will go on functioning in good order indefinitely. Is it not just as irrational to believe in bodily resurrection? Well certainly it is *without* a belief in the God of Judaism, Christianity, or Islam. But with it, it is not so clear. Recall that for those religions God has promised such a resurrection and for God everything is possible. God, that is, is conceived of as omnipotent which entails that he can do anything that it is logically possible to do. (But he cannot create a round square—a clear logical impossibility.) So if you can come to believe in the God of these three sister religions—and continue to conceive of him in a fairly orthodox way—you can come, readily enough, to believe in immortality in the sense of bodily resurrection though it also may cut the other way too, for some may feel that if to believe in God one must believe in bodily resurrection then one can hardly believe in God. (Perhaps we need something like reflective equilibrium here.) If our faith commits us to things like that, it is not unnatural to believe, then it is hard to be a person of faith.

However, again an extreme fideist, remembering his James Joyce, may believe that if it is logically possible, and indeed humanly speaking necessary, to believe in one absurdity, that is, God, it is easy enough to believe in another, that is, bodily resurrection. Still, I think that it is reasonable enough to say that, if there is a God, and if he is as he is portrayed in the orthodox Judaic, Christian, and Islamic traditions, then it is not unreasonable (scandal to the intellect that it is) to believe in survival through bodily resurrection. Theologians may debate over exactly what is the least imperspicuous representation of this, but that it will occur is itself reasonable to expect *given such background beliefs*. (But we should not forget how arcane and implausible these background beliefs are, beliefs which include the idea of there being an infinite disembodied individual who is both an individual and omnipresent, and is an individual, and a person as well, that is transcendent to the world.)

It is, I believe, for reasons such as this that Godfrey Vesey, after arguing that bodily resurrection; is a coherent notion, remarks that "bodily resurrection is a matter of faith, not of philosophy" (Vesey 1977, 306). If one has the faith of a Jew, Christian, or Moslem, one can reasonably believe in bodily resurrection, if not, not. However, philosophy, or at least reflective deliberation, need not stop just where Vesey thinks it must, for we can, and should, ask whether this faith is reasonable or indeed, for us (that is we intelligentsia), standing where we are now, knowing what we know, not irrational (viewed from a purely cognitive perspective). We should also ask, irrational or not, whether we should, everything considered, crucify our intellects and believe in God and bodily resurrection even if such beliefs are irrational. (There may be a case—a reasonable case—as we shall see later, for sometimes, if we can bring it off, having, in certain very constrained circumstances, irrational beliefs [Parfit 1984, 12–13].)

It is because of such considerations that I, in several books, have labored hard and long over questions about the necessity of faith and over whether belief in God is reasonable, if we have a good understanding of what our situation is (Nielsen 1971, 1973, 1982, 1985). I have argued, as has Antony Flew in a rather parallel way, that belief in an anthropomorphic god is little better than a superstition, and that belief in God, when conceptualized in the nonanthropomorphic way, is incoherent (Flew 1966, 1976). The nonanthropomorphic conceptualization is where God has come to be conceptualized, in developed Judaic, Christian, and Islamic traditions, as an infinite immaterial individual, omnipresent, but still a person transcendent to the world (to the whole universe). It is this conceptualization that we are maintaining that is incoherent. It is a conception, incoherent as it is, that is beyond reasonable belief for a person in the twentieth century with a good philosophical and scientific training. (For those who are not in a good position to be cognizant of its incoherency it is another matter.)

I hasten to add, lest I seem both unreasonable and arrogant in making the above claim, that reasonable people can have, and perhaps are likely to have, *some* unreasonable beliefs. I am not saying, let me repeat, that educated religious believers are unreasonable, while I am plainly reasonable. That would be gross hubris and silliness to boot. But I am saying that their belief in God, and with that, their belief in bodily resurrection, is unreasonable. However, I am also saying that *if* it were reasonable to believe in the God of our orthodox traditions, it would not be unreasonable to believe in bodily resurrection. So I have, in my work, concentrated on belief in God, and not on immortality, taking the former belief to be the central thing on which to concentrate.

It is hardly in place for me to repeat my arguments here or to try to develop new ones. However, if, on the one hand, they, or some more sophisticated rational reconstruction of them, are sound, or, if, on the other hand, arguments against the existence of God like those of Wallace Matson or J. L. Mackie are sound, or by some rational reconstruction could be made so, then belief in bodily resurrection is unjustified. (For the same conceptualization of God, they cannot, of course, both be sound.) I should add here that both Matson and Mackie profess (strangely it seems to me as it does to Flew as well) to have no difficulties with the intelligibility or coherence of God-talk (Flew 1985, 11–14). (They are the atheist counterparts or alter egos of Swinburne and Penelhum.) We say that belief in the God of developed forms of these traditions is incoherent; they say, by contrast, that the belief is merely false or at least on careful scrutiny clearly appears to be false. The Matson-Mackie arguments, that is, are arguments claiming to establish that belief in God, though coherent, is unjustified, and that it is more reasonable to believe that God exists is false than to believe in God or to remain agnostic. But in either eventuality, it is unreasonable to believe in bodily resurrection. If either the Flew-Nielsen coherence arguments, or the Matson-Mackie arguments about justifying belief in God, or an appeal to faith are sound, then, given the radical diversity of putative revelations, belief in God for philosophically informed people is unreasonable. And if belief in God is unreasonable, it is surely not reasonable to believe in bodily resurrection. But if one or another of these skeptical arguments are not sound or cannot be made so with a little fiddling, and if we are justified in believing in God or perhaps justified in accepting such a belief as an article of faith, then belief in bodily resurrection seems to be reasonable if God is what the orthodox say he is. (I say "seems" for, as it does to Reinhold Niebuhr and Paul Tillich, such talk might still seem to be such an intellectual affront that it would be more reasonable and, morally more desirable, to somehow construe the whole matter symbolically as do Niebuhr and Tillich.)

Before I leave the topic of bodily resurrection I should note that there is a felt difficulty concerning it that some, in a way that baffles me, find naggingly worrisome (Penelhum 1976, 1982). Suppose Sven dies and rots and eventually turns to dust and indeed further suppose his grave gets upturned and the dust, which is all that he is now, is spread randomly by the wind. God, being omnipotent, at the Last Judgment gathers these specks of dust together and reconstitutes them into an energized body that looks exactly like Sven and has all the memories Sven had, but, the objection goes, what appears is not Sven,

> the very same person that died previously but merely a replica or simu-
> lacrum of him: for, since there is a time-gap between death and resur-
> rection, during which the original body may very well have been
> destroyed altogether, the connecting link that would make it unambigu-
> ously the same person and not a replica will have disappeared.
> (Penelhum 1982, 47)

There are a number of things that should be said here. First, there is no reason, unless we gratuitously assume some very strange physics, to believe that the connecting link is broken: that there is not a bodily continuity. Those specks of dust scattered about and mixed with a lot of other dust are still the specks of dust of Sven, and God, being omnipotent, can readily gather up all the specks of dust and only those specks of dust that are Sven and reconstitute Sven and reenergize Sven's reconstituted corpse. For a while we have bits of Sven and then we have Sven all together again. That should not be difficult at all for God, given his intelligence and omnipotence. There is nothing there that should be conceptually puzzling. First we had Friday's *Globe and Mail* and then we had bits of paper scattered all over and then we had them all gathered up and pasted together into *The Globe and Mail*.

We no more need to speak of a gap-inclusive entity here than we need to speak of a gap-inclusive entity between my old battery which had gone dead and the same battery reenergized. There is no more a gap in identity between the human being first energized and then in turn deenergized and then reenergized again, than there is between the live battery, the dead battery, and the battery charged up again. In both cases we maintain bodily continuity. The ashes of my pet canary, in a container on my desk, are still the ashes of my pet canary. The same physical entity transformed. God has a little more work cut out for him in putting Sven back together again than the garage mechanic who charges my battery. (God, unlike the king's men, would have no trouble with Humpty-Dumpty.) But then again, God would not be God if he could not do it. There surely are no logical impossibilities here that omnipotence could not overcome unless perhaps omnipotence is itself an incoherent notion. (I shall assume here it is not.)

Second, certainly it could—and perhaps just as well—be a replica and perhaps there would be no verifiable difference between a situation describing the real Sven and a situation describing his replica. But this by now should not be in the least surprising. It is just the old story of theory being *undetermined* by data. Both descriptions make verifiable claims but perhaps there is no further verifiable claim that will enable us to decide between them, but post-Quinean philosophy of science has taught us to be neither surprised nor disturbed by that. There will often be a proliferation of theories all equally, or at least apparently equally, compatible with the same observed and perhaps even the same observable data. We must choose between theories on other grounds, and if Jews, Christians, or Moslems have independent reason for accepting the God-centered narrative, then they can safely and reasonably ignore replica possibilities. They are not going to get certainty but then, as fallibilism has taught us, we never do in any interesting cases and, after all, why must they have certainty? They can instead be sturdy knights of faith confident that they have deflected philosophical arguments designed to show that talk of bodily resurrection is incoherent. Defeating such rationalism, they can live as persons of faith in their trust in God's promised resurrection: a promise that human beings will rise from their graves and die no more. (I do not want to deny what I argued in the previous chapter, that the quest for certainty is very strong in believers. I only mean to point out here that *in certain ways* believers, like everyone else, can live with uncertainty.)

III

Let us now turn to an examination of a defense of immortality rooted in Cartesian dualism. That is, we will turn to claims to disembodied existence. There are Christians (Geach, for example) who vehemently reject such a conception of immortality as a philosophical myth which they take to be intellectually unsupportable and religiously unnecessary. There are other Christian philosophers who fervently wish that it would be true but are not even convinced that the very idea of disembodied personal survival is not nonsense (Penelhum 1982, 53). Believers often see the claim to disembodied personal existence as a conception of Greek origin, refurbished and streamlined by Descartes. Many of them claim that it is in reality foreign to a genuinely biblical worldview. Whatever may be the larger truth here, we should note that in contrast with the biblical worldview, which is more communitarian in spirit, the Cartesian view nicely meshes with the intense individualism of the modern period (Hollis 1985, 119–20).

However, as has been pointed out, Jesus' own sayings about the afterlife are ambiguous as between the resurrection of a material body and a "spiritual body" (whatever that means [Hick 1976, see also

Penelhum 1979]).Later Christian thought has also waffled here. It has tended to teach the ultimate resurrection of our earthly bodies, no matter how long dead or in what state of decomposition, while permitting the average believer to expect an immediate transition of her soul at the moment of death (Hick 1976). Yet, a not inconsiderable number of believers, particularly some Protestant Christians, and, among them some philosophers, have opted (even in the age of Ryle, Wittgenstein, and Dennett) for a disembodied self and the form of immortality that goes with it. Moreover, it should not be forgotten that even some atheists have believed in this form of immortality (for example, McTaggart). However, it is only against the background of a biblical worldview that such a purely speculative conception, at least *prima facie* implausible, is of much interest. Christians, understandably, long for life eternal in the fellowship of God and it has come to seem to a not inconsiderable number of them that the best face that can be put on this is to see ourselves, if this can be justifiably done, as disembodied selves: spiritual continuants whose very spirituality (thinking, willing, feeling nonmaterially) is what makes us what we are. It is this that is our essence. This Cartesianism seems too much untutored common sense in many modern Christian environments (more likely so in Orange County than in Scarsdale) to be a clear enough notion, but many philosophers and theologians have found it very baffling indeed. Can we actually attach sense to the thesis that persons can exist disembodied? Can we be disembodied continuants who are also individuals who are, as well, persons? (Even if somehow we can attach some sense to the notion, we have a long way to go to the making of it a belief that can plausibly be thought to be true.)

Hywel Lewis is just such a Christian philosopher. Lewis does not think "that any case for immortality can begin to get off the ground if we fail to make a case for dualism" (Lewis 1977, 282). He is fully aware that many able philosophers think a belief in disembodied personal existence or in disembodied persons is an incoherent belief, devoid of any intelligible sense, and he is concerned to make a case for rejecting that (among philosophers) widely held belief. He attempts, that is, to defend a belief in disembodied personal survival. In its classical Cartesian form it maintains that persons are real selves or souls, namely particular immaterial conscious things (continuants) which have feelings and thoughts, are capable of willing and acting and which are only contingently connected with the bodies ("physical bodies," if you will) in which they are sometimes housed.

It is this self—a self by which each person is what he is—which each of us, in our own direct, immediate experience, realizes is distinct from his body and is capable of being what it is even if there is no body at all. We, the story goes, just experience ourselves as distinct from our bodies. Lewis thinks that this is just a *datum of experience*. Our sense of self-identity, which is prior to any conception we have of personal identity, just tells us that this is so. We are each directly aware of ourselves as we are directly aware of being in pain or of having a sudden thought.

A standard problem for any belief in an immaterial self is over how it is possible to individuate this self (distinguish it from other selves) since it does not have a body. Lewis in defending his view that a knowledge of an immaterial self is just a datum of awareness remarks,

> There must, then, I agree, be individuation. But how is this possible if the immaterial substances in question cannot, as the thought of them would seem to imply, "be individuated by spatial relations"? This problem, I must now add, does not worry me a great deal, and it never has. It has always seemed evident to me that everyone knows himself to be the being that he is in just being so. We identify ourselves to ourselves in that way, and not in the last resort on the basis of what we know about ourselves. The reaction to this is sometimes to retort that we seem to be running out of arguments, and we must surely make our case by argument. This is a trying situation for a philosopher to have to meet; quite clearly he does not want to seem unwilling to argue. But argument is not everything, we have also to reckon with what we just find to be the case, we cannot conjure all existence into being by argument and we cannot, as I hope does not sound pretentious, argue against reality.[3] (Lewis 1977, 289)

It may be, as Terence Penelhum has remarked, "that such a doctrine has no content, and just amounts to an empty assertion that our problem really does have an answer" (Penelhum 1982, 51). It may be, as Godfrey Vesey and Sydney Shoemaker think, that in so reasoning Lewis in effect construes "I" as a proper name when it is not, and when in reality it functions more like "here" such that "I" no more names a person that "here" names a place (Vesey 1977, 301–306; Shoemaker 1977, 307–11). On Lewis's account, even if I suffer amnesia, I do not lose the direct sense of self-identity—my direct awareness of self—of which he speaks. There just is this direct self-awareness. Vesey asserts that such a self-identification is an illusion, and so cannot give meaning to talk of personal immortality (Vesey 1977, 306). There are perfectly nondeviant uses of "here" where "here" does not name a place. As Vesey puts it,

> Suppose that, although I am quite lost, I say to myself "I know where I am, I'm here." This use of "here," although completely uninformative, may nevertheless seem to be a significant, nonempty use. It borrows a facade of meaning from the informative uses. Similarly, an empty, soliloquizing use of "I," may 'borrow a facade of meaning from the informative, interpersonal, uses.' (Vesey 1977, 305)

Suppose I am suffering from amnesia and I remember Lewis's doctrine that "Everyone knows himself to be the being that he is in just being so," so, fortified by that, I know who I am: "I am I." I just find it to be the case in immediate experience that I am I. This is just something, the Cartesian story goes, we find to be so in a self-disclosure or in self-awareness. But if we recall that "I," in standard contexts, is no more used to name a person than "here" names a place, we should recognize the emptiness of Lewis's remark that "Everyone knows himself to be the being he is in just being so." It is like saying "Everyone knows where he is, in that he can say, 'I'm here' and not be wrong" (Vesey 1977, 305; Shoemaker 1977, 311).

Perhaps, as J. L. Mackie thinks, things are not quite that simple (in philosophy they usually are not) (Mackie 1985). However, even if the above arguments about emptiness do not go through there is, I believe, a simpler objection to such an account. Suppose we grant that there is this dumb or brute self-awareness (perhaps "inarticulate" is the better word) giving one some kind of inchoate self-identity. I am directly aware of myself in a manner similar to the way in which I am directly aware that I am thinking—like the having of a sudden thought—or having a pain. But this brute datum (if that is what it is) is just that: it does not itself carry the heavy interpretive weight that Lewis in effect puts on it, namely that the self of which I am aware is immaterial (disembodied). That is clearly an *interpretation* of the experience to which there are alternative interpretations and one would (*pace* Lewis) have to argue for that alternative. (Argument cannot stop where Lewis wants it to.) One could not rightly claim that it is just something found to be true in experience. Indeed to the extent that we do not understand "immaterial thing," "immaterial individual," "disembodied person," we might think that that interpretation is a nonstarter in being only a putative interpretation.

Be that latter point as it may, what we have here, in claiming that we are directly aware of ourselves as not just a self, as something I know not what which has thoughts and feelings and initiates actions, but also as a disembodied agent, is in reality an *interpretation* and not just a datum of experience, just as much as when I say that the pain I feel is the stimulation of my C fibers I do not report my experience but interpret it. Both are interpretations of experience. They are not direct data of experience. And if we say, misleadingly I believe, that all experiences are interpretations, then we must recognize that there are degrees of interpretiveness and grades of theoreticity. There cannot be the direct way to immortality that Lewis seeks, not even as an enabling doctrine. "I am immortal" cannot be a matter of direct awareness in the way "I am tired" is.

It is a rather common belief among many analytical philosophers (A. J. Ayer, Peter Strawson, and Bernard Williams among them) that the very idea of a disembodied person is incoherent, for reference to a body is a necessary condition for establishing the identity of a person and for ascribing identity through time to a changing person. We indeed characteristically appeal to memory as well in determining whether a person at a later time was one and the same person as at some earlier time. But when memory and bodily criteria conflict bodily identity takes pride of place. Suppose, to take an example, Hans dies and it is alleged that his spirit lives on. However, because having a body is a necessary condition for making ascriptions of personhood, we can have no way, even in principle, of ascertaining whether there is really a disembodied Hans who is the same person as the ruddy-cheeked Hans we used to know. The very idea of a "bodiless individual" seems to be unintelligible (Penelhum 1982, 41).

If we try to substitute memory as the *primary* criterion for personal identity we will fail, for we need to be able, for there to be memories at all, to distinguish between real and apparent memories, between Mildred's thinking she remembers cashing the check and her actually remembering it. Only genuine memories guarantee identity, not merely apparent ones. Actually remembering that I was a professor of philosophy at the University of Calgary guarantees my identity, only thinking I remember it does not. But for these to be real memories as distinct from apparent memories the events thought to be remembered must actually have occurred *and* they must have happened to the person remembering them. Memory cannot constitute personal identity or, more plausibly, be the fundamental criterion of personal identity for it presupposes that such identities have been established, that we can determine who it is that has the memories. So memory will not do the fundamental work. The only alternative—or at least the only other alternative argument—for in any fundamental way establishing personal identity is having the same body (bodily continuity).

However, are there not at least conceivable happenings that would loosen our attachment to bodily identity as a necessary condition for establishing personal identity and not only show that people, like Locke's Cobbler and the Prince, could "exchange bodies" but that they could also exist without bodies at all? The following story is designed to show that bodiless existence is a *logical* possibility. Suppose I am a rather credulous fellow and I live in a house with a spouse, two children, my aged mother, and two dogs. The house initially is a perfectly normal house, but then one day strange things, sometimes in front of us all, start happening. Lights inexplicably go on and off, doors open and close, and chairs move in unaccountable ways. The happenings cannot be traced to any member of the family, to the dogs, to neighbors, to friends, or to agents whom we ordinarily would regard as people, or to the wind, or to anything like that. Suppose I, the credulous one, hypothesize that the house is haunted by a poltergeist to the considerable amusement of the more skeptical members of the family. But then suppose my son, age sixteen, begins to receive premonitions of what is going on. He can predict accurately when a door is going to open, a light go on, a chair at the table will move, and the like. He says an invisible person, S, has talked to him. Pressed he retracts "talked"—no one else hears it and no tape recorder catches it. He now says rather that "talked" is a groping way of saying S lets him know like thoughts popping into his head. But this, whatever it is, goes on with considerable accuracy for some time. My son (for example) says S told him that S is going out in the garden and sure enough the back door to the garden opens and closes.

Suppose, after a time, S comes out of the closet, so to say, and gives my son to understand that S is lonely and wants to belong to the family and to be accepted. After dinner, Sarah, as S tells my son she wants to be called, communicates to him that she is going to wash up, take care of the fireplace, and turn the thermostat down in the evening and up in the morning. We see, with no body around making it happen, dishes go from the table to the dishwasher, matches striking against the grate and regularly lighting the fire at the desired time, and just before I get to it I see the thermostat go up in morning and down in the evening set to the required daytime and nighttime temperature with no discernible hand moving the thermostat. Sarah, as we now have started to call S, lets my son know that she is beginning to feel like a member of the family. She lets him know she will be on the watch-out for us and guard us. Subsequently Sarah lets my son know that my daughter is in danger in the backyard, and indeed we rush out and discover she has fallen into the well, and at another time she warns us, again through my son, that my German Shepherd is in danger and again we rush to the backyard and find him confronted by a rattlesnake. The whole family becomes convinced, after such episodes, that Sarah is real, that she is an invisible person and a family friend. She might, if people want to talk that way, be said to have a "subtle invisible body" that neither the family members nor the dogs can see or in any way detect; for example, no one ever bumps into her and she never steps on the dogs' paws. If such conceivable things did actually happen we might be led quite naturally and quite plausibly to use the name "Sarah" and to think of Sarah as a person, indeed to take her to be a person albeit a disembodied person. If such things really happened there would, it is natural to say, be at least one disembodied person.[4]

If things really were so to transpire would we be justified in calling Sarah a person? Well, it would be at least plausible to say Sarah met all of Daniel Dennett's suggested conditions for personhood, namely, rationality, intentionality, propriety as the object of a personal stance, ability to reciprocate such a stance, verbal communication, and a special kind of consciousness (Dennett 1978, 267–85). She shows, to take the elements fitting her most problematically, concern for the well-being of the family, for example, her protection of my daughter and concern for the well-being of my German Shepherd as instanced in the rattlesnake event. This gives rise to gratitude and affection and Sarah reciprocates concern with other acts, for example, at Thanksgiving various mixings mysteriously go on in the kitchen done by none of the regular family members and by no visible hands and a lovely Indian pudding emerges. And we have seen how Sarah communicates, though it is perhaps stretching things a bit to call it verbal communication. Sarah also seems plainly to be aware of herself and her surroundings. We identify Sarah in identifying these happenings.

Could Sarah be identified with a normal human being known to have lived a normal life? Suppose in checking the records I discover that a previous owner several years back had had a shy and retiring daughter, also called Sarah, who had died while living in what is now my house. Suppose it is further discovered from accounts about her that she had a personality very like that of "our Sarah" and that when we ask "our Sarah" about that young woman Sarah says that she is that very woman and leads us in the attic to a hidden box of letters from that Sarah to her parents. Under such circumstances it would be reasonable to believe that our disembodied Sarah was that very woman. So it appears at least we have described what would have to be the case to become acquainted with a disembodied person and indeed a disembodied person who had formerly had a perfectly normal body. We have given verifiable, empirical sense to the concept showing that it makes sense to speak of "bodiless persons" and that such a concept, bizarre as it is, is an intelligible one. It has what used to be called empirical meaning.

The first thing that needs to be said about this is that, conceivable or not, things like this do not happen. Some might say this is irrelevant because, after all, what is at issue is that such talk is intelligible and this only requires that disembodied individuals be consistently describable, not that there actually be the slightest likelihood that there really are such beings. There is not the slightest chance that there are people whose skin is naturally orange and hair naturally purple but the conception, like that of "golden mountain" or "wooden jetliner," is perfectly intelligible. We do have some understanding here in the way we do not have for "Procrastination drinks melancholy," or "Reagan sleeps slower than Trudeau," but then again we must remember that intelligibility, and even more obviously coherence, admits of degrees and perhaps of kinds. When we think concretely about what causally speaking would have to be in place for there to be a wooden jetliner that actually could fly we see that such a conception doesn't fit in with anything else we know. In terms of what we know about the world, it just doesn't make any sense at all and the same is true of Sarah and of Locke's story of the Cobbler and the Prince. In that perfectly standard way these accounts are incoherent. They are just stories we can tell, like certain children's stories or certain science fiction. Part of their charm (where they have any) is that they couldn't happen, and our reason for our confidence that they couldn't happen is not that we have made careful inductive investigations like looking to see if there are magpies in New York State or if the quail are different in the east of North America than in the west. Rather, our source of confidence is that these things actually obtaining just does not fit with what we know or at least reasonably believe about the world. Just how could a wooden jetliner take off or fly at 500 miles an hour at 40,000 feet? How would it stand the stress, and so on and so on? The wood would have to be remarkably hard, very different indeed from anything we know to be wood. Such things just do not make sense and at least in this way Sarah doesn't make sense either. There are indeed more things in heaven and earth, Horatio, than are dreamt of in your philosophy. But in this context that is just empty talk. These things never happen and we would, to put it mildly, be extremely skeptical—and rightly so—of any claim that something like this did happen. People touched by modernity would not accept at face value the claim that my watch just disappeared into thin air as distinct from a claim that I had just lost it and could not find it. There cannot be wooden jetliners, Sarah's, or Locke's phenomenon, any more than there can be, as Evans-Pritchard was perfectly aware, Zande witchcraft substance.

However, the cobbler and the prince and Sarah aside, there are cases of alleged possession and mediumship and there is Sally Beauchamp, Dr. Jekyll and Mr. Hyde, and *The Three Faces of Eve*. Some cases of this sort have actually been said to have happened by noncredulous people of intellectual and moral integrity and the fictional cases have a certain verisimilitude. But in these cases, if we look at them soberly and non-metaphorically, we need not, and indeed should not, say that we have, as for example in the Eve thing, three persons caged in one body. There are not three Eves but the one Eve has a multiple personality. We should speak in these cases of a plurality of *personalities*, not of *persons*. This, as J. L. Mackie points out, is much more guarded and plausible a claim to make than to say there are, mysterious as it may seem, three different persons (Mackie 1985). We need not invoke disembodied existence or even dualism to handle such cases. They are bizarre and puzzling enough anyway, assuming they are not fraudulent, without adding *unnecessarily* ontological puzzlement. Here is a good place to apply the old maxim about not multiplying entities or conceptions of entities beyond need.

More generally, to return to the question about logical possibilities, we should take to heart David Wiggens's point that the concepts we use, and the particulars we identify and describe in using them, are not such that they can range over all at least putative logical possibilities. They are rather constrained by the nomological grounding of the sortal words we use (Wiggens 1986). We must not confuse what we can imagine or conceive with what is possible. We can conceive of an ice-cream cake at the center of the sun, but such a state of affairs is not possible. For it to be possible the ice-cream cake, as the wooden jet, would have to have so changed that it could no longer coherently be called an ice-cream cake. In identifying any particular, say a candy bar melting in my pocket, this ability to identify and reidentify is closely tied up with our concept of what the thing in question is. We expect the bar to melt in my pocket, but the claim that it survived unmelted on the hot stove, let alone in the center of the sun, is not a possibility that the concept allows for any more than our concept of what it is to be a wren allows for the possibility that it might fly at 60,000 feet and at the speed of 2,000 miles an hour. Where we have a sortal concept it is constrained by the physical laws that apply to the exemplifications of those concepts. Copper cannot do just anything; rather it must obey the laws of nature which enable us to distinguish it as a substance. What in fact happens is the basis of all our concepts. It constrains the conceptual connections inherent in our use of language. Iron cannot melt in snow and the flesh and blood Sarah, who used to live in my house long before I lived there, cannot become a disembodied person. It *may* be that the idea of a "disembodied person" is not contradictory—we *may* have (beyond mental pictures) understood my narrative of Sarah—but disembodied persons are neither physically nor, as some people like to talk, metaphysically possible (Gillett 1986, 384). We cannot rely on thought experiments—on various underdescribed fantasies—rather, as Wiggens puts it, we have to work back from the extensions to work out what is essential to something being the thing it is. "For persons this extension is living, embodied, human beings" (Gillett 1986, 384). Person may not be a natural kind, but a human being—a human person—is. For our kind of natural kind, mind and character are dependent for their activities on a body in causal interaction with the world (Gillett 1986; see also Mackie 1985, 1–27). We have no coherent grounds for thinking ourselves to be immaterial substances or disembodied continuants incapable of destruction.

IV

This discussion has been metaphysical, somewhat arcane, and, it seems to me, quaint. It is not the sort of thing that contributes either to the growth of knowledge or to salvation. It is, or so it seems to me, strange that people should be arguing about such things in our epoch. Yet argue they do. I think what fuels such talk is a deep human problem and I want now to turn to that. Such talk, to come at it at first indirectly, is at home against a religio-ethical background, as Pascal and Dostoevsky well saw, otherwise what we have are just some not very interesting metaphysical puzzles. After all, there is over personal identity and the like, as Derek Parfit and Thomas Nagel have shown, far more fascinating metaphysical conundrums than the ones generated by such religious concerns, conundrums that we can, if we like doing that sort of thing, wile away our time with, if we are sufficiently leisured and undriven (Parfit 1984; Nagel 1986). It is not the metaphysical puzzles about immortality but the human side of immortality that can be gripping and it is that, and that alone, that gives these arcane metaphysical investigations whatever point they may have. Given our entangled lives, given the deep frustration of human hopes and aspirations, given the unnecessary hell that is the fate of many (40,000 people simply live on the streets in New York to say nothing of what goes on in Calcutta), it is surely understandable that we humans should ask "Shall I live again?" and, noting the often utterly pointless suffering of the world, ask of those so suffering "Shall they live again? Could there be 'another world' in which they could live in some decency?"

We live in a world where 30,000 people, most of them quite unnecessarily, die of starvation each day, where people are horribly tortured and degraded and where the rich not infrequently live frivolous and expensive lives, living off the backs of the poor, and where in our part of the world Yuppidom reigns supreme. It is hard, given such a world, to just accept the fact of all those people dying in misery who have hardly had a chance to live. It is hard to accept the fact that they should just die and rot and that that is all there is to it. Of course, cognitively speaking it is easy to accept that, for what could be more obvious, but, morally speaking, it is very hard indeed to accept. Our moral sense rebels at such a world.

It is easy enough for someone like myself, surrounded by a caring environment, living in comfort and having interesting work, which I can hope will have some significance, to accept the inevitability of death and my eventual utter destruction. It would be nice if it were not so and I could go on living as I am but that cannot be and others will continue after me. That is not such a hard cluster of facts to accept. Moreover, it is evident enough anyway.

The thing is to make something of the life I have. It can be a good and meaningful life and whether it is or not, in the circumstances in which I live, is not independent of what I do. And I can hope that I'll be lucky enough, without cancer or the like, to have my "allotted time." I would be frustrated if I do not and perhaps irrationally bitter, but, if I happen to be unlucky, it would just be something—and we have here the unforgettable example of Freud—to be, if I am capable of being reasonable under such circumstances, stoically accepted. But with luck nothing like that will happen to me or those close to me and I can live out my life in a meaningful and pleasant way and eventually die. What did Tolstoy get so exercised about?

I think Reinhold Niebuhr was right in turning with contempt from the egoism of healthy individuals, living what would be otherwise normal lives, having obsessive hang-ups about the fact that they will eventually die. For them to be so all important to themselves hardly inspires admiration. For those ageing Yuppies (perhaps former Yuppies is the right phrase), firmly situated in Yuppidom, who have such preoccupations, where there is no suffering or Strindbergian or O'Neillish laceration or self-laceration, their worries are not something to inspire much sympathy or concern. The temptation is to tell them to get on with it and stop snivelling. (Dietrich Bonhoeffer had a good sense of this.)

However, for the suffering, ignorant, and degraded millions, living in hellish conditions, and who have unremittingly, through no fault of their own, lived blighted lives, the inevitability, and at least seemingly evident finality, of death is another thing entirely. This, though plainly there before our eyes, is what is so hard to accept. We do not have something here which is just, or perhaps even at all, a philosopher's puzzle or a neurotic's worry. The matter of blighted lives is a very real one indeed. Five hundred million children and adults suffer from malnutrition and 800 million live, or try to live, in extreme poverty. This remains true while globally $1 trillion is given to military spending, a spending which is astronomically beyond the needs of anything, for the various great powers principally involved, that could even remotely count as defense. Yet the World Food Council concluded in 1984 that $4 billion a year committed internationally until the end of the century would ensure access to food and productive lives for the 500 million people most in need, and set on track a stable world food order where among the poorer nations basket cases would not constantly pop up. However, the brute facts are that a trillion dollars a year goes into doomsday military spending and even a comparatively paltry $4 billion can't be found to save people from starvation and malnutrition. (Here we are reminded of the world of *1984*.)

Thinking of the callousness of it all, the hypocrisy of many great nations, the placid acceptance of this by the masses, even though such a situation is totally unnecessary, is very sickening indeed. It is understandable, given that, that people despair of the world and that there, out of despair with our human lot, arises a hope for and even faith in immortality, an immortality that will give those (along with everyone else) who never have had anything like a decent chance in life another life that is worthwhile. This is not a matter of a kind of grubby individual craving for life eternal but a longing for a morally and humanly worthwhile life for humankind as a whole. (Has our individualism and egoism dug so deep that we cannot really believe that people are genuinely capable of such hopes?)

There is a stance within Christianity, though no doubt there are similar stances within Judaism and Islam as well, often associated with Irenaean universalism, which maintains that human suffering would be irredeemably tragic if our present earthly life were not followed by another in which the suffering of each individual could he made worthwhile for that individual (Hick 1976, 152–66). Suppose, in pursuing this, we ask the famous trio of questions of Kant: "What can I know?," "What ought I to do?" and "What may I hope?" Think particularly of the last one, "What may I hope?" and then think of (to put it gently) the unhappy world that we know—keeping in mind the facts that I have just described, facts which are but some salient members of a set of deeply disquieting facts. Hopes are hard to maintain against the persistence and pervasiveness of such facts. Max Horkheimer, who certainly was no defender of a theistic world perspective, well put it when he remarked "moral conscience . . . rebels against the thought that the present state of reality is final" (Horkheimer 1974, 2). Still, in the struggles of our everyday life, our hopes for a realization, or even approximation, of a truly human society, a society of human brotherhood and sisterhood, a just society or even a rational society, are constantly being defeated. We do not, in fact, given our economic and scientific potential, have something that even remotely approximates a caring society or a just society. (It is pure propaganda for a cabinet minister to speak—boast might be a more accurate word—as one recently did of there being equality and social justice in Canada. But that is standard issue for politicians in our capitalist democracies.)

Such states of affairs led Kant, Lessing, and even Voltaire, to postulate immortality in order to make some match between our hopes and what is achievable in "this world." It is easy to satirize such Kantian postulations of "pure practical reason" and it is utter folly, as J. L. Mackie has well argued, to try to argue from such *hopes* to *any likelihood* at all that such a reality will come to be.[5] However, as we know from Pascal and Dostoevsky, it may be rational in certain circumstances to have a belief or to cause a belief to come to be formed (if we can) which, viewed from a purely intellectual or cognitive perspective, is an irrational belief. If I am lost in the Canadian North, and if a firm belief that I stand a good chance of getting out is, as a matter of fact, essential if I am going to have any chance at all of getting out, though in fact my objective chances are pretty slim, then it is reasonable for me to come to have that false belief if there is some possibility that I can somehow come to have it in that circumstance. (Recall Pascal on holy water and Schelling's answer to armed robbery.)

Is it similarly reasonable, given the human condition, for me to hope for human immortality in the form of universal salvation for humankind even though the objective likelihood of anything like that being the case is extremely low? In responding to this question I am going to assume that the cognitive situation vis-à-vis immortality is as I have claimed and argued it to be. If the situation is not as bad as I argue it is, then we should perhaps, depending on what we believe the situation to be, draw different conclusions. But suppose I have managed to tell it like it is, then should we continue to hope, or at least wish, for immortality?

Let me describe a scenario that understandably might push a person in the direction of Pascalian hope. Imagine this person, as a humane and sensitive person, reflective and reasonable, with a good education, coming of age in the West just after the First World War. Suppose she becomes a Marxist or an anarchist, or some other kind of socialist, and says and feels, given what is then going on in the world, that now there is hope in the world. Now imagine her living through all the times in between up to our time and now, as a rather old person, though still with sound faculties and a humane attitude, she becomes, given the world she has seen and continues to see before her, utterly disillusioned with secular struggle (including, of course, political struggle) being able to bring that hope into the world or even to bring into the world (small isolated pockets apart, for example, Iceland or Denmark) a tolerable amount of decency. It isn't that she now comes to think that religious revival will bring it into the world—a kind of moral rearmament with God in the driver's seat. Nothing, she now believes, will bring such all order of kindliness into the world. There can be, she believes, Brecht to the contrary notwithstanding, no laying the foundations of kindliness. She has simply given up on the world. The caring for humankind and the detestation of human degradation that launched her into political struggle is still there but she has utterly lost the sense that there is hope in the world, that there will be any lasting or large-scale remedy for these ills. She doesn't as a result become a reactionary. She still supports progressive causes, though, unlike a Marxist or an anarchist—an E. P. Thompson or a Noam Chomsky—she will no longer, given her disillusion, throw her whole life into such activities, but, while continuing to support progressive causes, turns more and more to religious concerns and thinks and feels through the issue of immortality again.

Suppose, in thinking immortality through on the cognitive side, she comes to a conclusion very similar to mine. But, unlike me, she, keeping in mind Irenaean universalism, comes passionately to hope for immortality in the form of a hope for universal salvation for humankind. Suppose further, facing nonevasively the odds, it becomes, not so much a hope (the odds are too dismal for that) but a *wish*, but still a wish that persistently remains with her and guides her life. Is this an attitude that it is desirable that we should come to share with her? It is certainly undesirable if it comes to block our struggling in the world, if it leads to a quietism in the face of evil; to being like Martin Luther rather than like Thomas Münzer. If that is the upshot, it is better to develop the set of attitudes that accepts that the human situation is irredeemably tragic and that we, in such a situation, in Camus's metaphor, should relentlessly fight the plague, knowing full well that the plague is always with us, sometimes striking virulently and at other times for a time remaining only latent, but always being something that will return, after an uneasy lull, to strike again in full fury. The thing to do is, acknowledging this, to unyieldingly and relentlessly fight the plague. What we should do is to tackle the most glaring ills or at least the ills we can get a purchase on, taking to heart and accepting the fact that there will be no extensive or permanent successes. We will have neither Christian nor Marxist eschatological hopes, but, like Camus, we will accept stoically an irredeemably tragic vision of the world. Doesn't this tragic sense of life square better with a nonevasive human integrity than the religious turn?

Not necessarily and perhaps not at all if the religious person takes, in a nonevasive way, a kind of Irenaean turn. Suppose she does not stop relentlessly fighting the plague and doesn't fight it because of the hopes/wishes she entertains for the afterlife, but fights the plague to fight evil and does so while still wishing for a salvation for humankind, wishing for a fate which is not irredeemably tragic and where human salvation is a reality. Isn't this way of reacting to life and to the world more desirable than sticking with a bleak Camus-like tragic vision, *if* so wishing does not lead to any self-deception about how astronomically slight the chances for salvation are, and if it doesn't weaken one's resolve to fight the plague or make one, in some other way, less effective in fighting the plague? With some people it might dull the native edge of resolution, but surely it need not. One can doggedly fight the plague and have such eschatological wishes as well. She can, that is, continue to fight and, utterly unblinkered, have the wish that salvation could be our lot as human beings. So held, this attitude seems at least to have everything the Camusian attitude has and something more as well and thus, everything considered, it is a more desirable attitude.

However, these are not the only alternatives. A Marxist, an anarchist, or a revisionist socialist social democratic vision of things are not visions which are the tragic visions of an existentialist humanism or of a Freudian or Weberian view of life. If any of these forms of socialism can become and remain a reality—or can even firmly get on the agenda—and be the forms (different as they are among themselves) that Marx, Bakunin, or Bernstein envisaged, or some rational reconstruction of them, without becoming like the later Stalinist *and* social democratic deformations of socialism (for example, on the social democratic side, the Blair or Schroeder governments), then there could be hope in the world. There would be, in such an eventuality, the reasonable prospect of a decent world, or, more than a decent world order, a truly human world order where human flourishing would be extensive.

The person in our scenario turned away from such hopes because of the terrible historical events since the souring of the Russian Revolution, events such as forced collectivization, the purge trials, the Second World War, the hegemony of Pax Americana, the Vietnam War, the rise of Islamic Fundamentalism (for example, Iran), the rise, both politically and religiously, of reactionary forms of Christianity and Judaism in America and Israel, persistent mass starvation, and the pervasiveness of doomsday war machines. She has seared into her consciousness the realization that though we have modes of production capable of delivering plenty to the world, 30,000 starve each day, and even in the so-called First World many live, though often quite unnecessarily, very blighted lives indeed. The Russian Revolution did not spread to the West and we got instead, as Rosa Luxembourg anticipated, with the failure of its spread, on the one hand bureaucratic and authoritarian forms of statism which, if socialisms at all, are state socialisms of the worst sort and, on the other hand, matched with that we have forms of state capitalism bent on an imperialistic domination and a heartless exploitation of the world. We have, in *most* of the nations of the world, neither capitalism with a human face nor socialism with a human face. We were, that is, caught between two very unsavory social systems indeed. Now we have only one hegemonic social system. The result is that we have, and quite unnecessarily, a pervasiveness of terror, a denial of autonomy and equality, and massive exploitation and poverty. This picture, which *at most* is only slightly over-drawn, turns the person in our scenario, despairingly, to Irenaean universalism, to the hope, which for her, given her estimation of the probabilities, is little more than a wish, that there will, in an afterlife, be a universal salvation in which the sufferings of each individual could somehow be made worthwhile for that individual.[6]

What needs to be said here in response is that—given the turn of things historically, and given certain assumptions about human nature—however unlikely it may be that socialism on the necessary worldwide scale can be anything like the socialism of which Marx and Bakunin dreamt, it is still far more likely to become the case (to put it mildly) than is the religious eschatological dream. That is to say that something like this secular vision of the world could obtain is still vastly more likely than bodily resurrection or disembodied existence and the sustaining of Irenaean universalism. (Remember we might still have one or another of the first two things without having Irenaean universalism.) Neither the kingdom of heaven on earth nor the kingdom of heaven in a "resurrection world" are very likely, but a kingdom of heaven on earth, of the two alternatives, is by far the least unlikely of two unlikely prospects. Moreoever, there is, with the former, though *perhaps* even here the chances are rather slight, some prospect of some *approximation* of it. The other's prospects are close to being nil. This being so, the desirable thing is struggle to make that hope in the world a social reality in all the ramified ways that need to be done. What may be unlikely there is at least much less unlikely than the Irenaean thing. It may be apple pie by and by for everyone but it is at least not in the sky.

However, again there is a response from the religious wisher for immortality somewhat similar to her response to the Camusian. Could one not have the socialist thing through and through without any evasion at all and still have this wish for a universal salvation that need in no way be a replacement for a deflect from the struggle for a classless society united in sisterhood and brotherhood where the conditions for both autonomy and equal liberty are maximized? There are reactionary atheists (for example, A. Rand and A. Flew) and there are religious Marxists or at least quasi-Marxists (for example, Gregory Baum and Dorothee Sölle). The latter have on their agenda the struggle for a classless society as much as those "standard Marxists" who are atheists.

Marx and Bakunin were passionate atheists but there is nothing that is canonical to Marxism or anarchism (libertarian socialism) that requires atheism, however plausible atheism may be on other grounds. Both atheism and socialism can be plausibly said to be part of the Enlightenment project. Still, that project is not such a seamless web that it is evident that one could not have socialism without atheism or atheism without socialism. There is a kind of conservative liberalism that goes well with atheism and some atheists are just plain reactionaries and there can be, and is, a socialism that is also religious. Perhaps the most coherent worldview would have socialism and atheism running tandem, but that that is so is not overwhelmingly evident. There is a lot of *lebensraum* for bracketing such considerations and in practical class struggles they can perhaps be ignored. Why divide comrades over a speculative matter that may not at all effect the struggle for socialism? Religion, of course, has indeed been an opiate of the people and a bastion of reaction, but, again, that is not intrinsic to its nature, though its pervasiveness is understandable ideologically.

I think the answer to my above question is that one could be consistently committed to a socialist transformation of the world and have, as well, Irenaean hopes for the salvation of humankind. One could, as some liberation theologians are, be through and through committed to the class struggle *and* have these wishes for an afterlife of a very distinctive kind. Where this is open-eyed, with an awareness of the fantastic and perhaps even incoherent nature of the belief, and is taken as a wish and not allowed to stand in the way of class struggles and other progressive struggles (struggles around racism and sexism), there is nothing wrong with such a wish.

I *suspect* that as a matter of psychosociological fact such an attitude will, though perhaps only in some rather subtle ways, stand in the way of liberation—solid liberation in the world—but to the extent that it does not and to the extent it neither wittingly nor unwittingly cooks the books as to the evidence, there is no reason for atheists like myself to criticize it as unreasonable or as in anyway morally untoward, though it is not an attitude we will share even though we recognize that even in a classless, nonracist and nonsexist world order there will be human ills: children born horribly deformed, terrible accidents, a loss of partner or child, and the like. It is reasonable to expect that even ills of this sort will be less frequent in such a society with its developed productive forces (including its more developed science) and greater security and greater wealth more evenly distributed. Still, such ills will always be our lot. We can lessen their incidence and surround them with a new environment, but we can never eliminate them. They will always be with us. This being so, in some ways a certain kind of belief in immortality could "answer" to that as no secular *weltbild* could. Atheists should not blink at that fact or try to obscure its force. They should only point out that, given everything we know, it is an idle wish humanly understandable though it be.

So why not add such a hope or at least such a wish to our repertoire? For me, to speak for a moment personally, the astronomical unlikeliness of such a conception answering to anything real, coupled with the equal unlikelihood of there being a God who could ordain a certain kind of immortality, for (as the Greeks and Romans show us) not just any immortality will do, makes such hopes merely idle wishes and as such nothing to make a matter of the fabric of my life. We have better things to do than to dwell on such idle wishes. Hume, I believe, had a remarkably sane and humane mindset here as did Freud. And Hume and Freud, conservatives though they were, as well as Marx and Bakunin, can remain, without any tension at all, heroes of a contemporary intellectual wedded to the emancipatory potential of the Enlightenment project, while being fully cognizant of the dark underside of it that, on the one hand, Adorno and Horkheimer and, on the other, Foucault, have in their different ways so well exposed. There are plenty of things in both Hume and Marx that no intellectually sophisticated and informed person could accept anymore, along with central things which, with a little rational reconstruction, can be seen to be both sound—or at least arguably sound—and important, and which have forged our contemporary understanding of ourselves and our world such that for a person who has taken these things to heart none of the faces of immortality provide live options (Nielsen 1978, 1986).

NOTES

1. Thomas Nagel talks this way in his *The View from Nowhere* (1986).

2. Sydney Shoemaker argues in the same volume that there is a non-Cartesian dualism which is not conceptually incoherent as he believes Cartesian dualism to be. Cartesian dualism, if sound, could support disembodied existence, but, as Shoemaker sees it, it is conceptually incoherent. Non-Cartesian dualism, he argues, is conceptually coherent but it does not support disembodied existence. However, even this battened down dualism with its talk of immaterial substances being related to material substances by a quasispatial relationship seems of doubtful coherence, as Shoemaker half admits in a footnote on p. 268.

3. Thomas Nagel, without embracing dualism, in effect reveals the rational kernel behind such an impulse (Nagel 1986, 13–37).

4. This little tale is adopted from a tale by G. R. Gillett, "Disembodied Persons" (Gillett 1986).

5. J. L. Mackie argues this convincingly in his "Sidgwick's Pessimism" (Mackie 1976, 326–27). For a more detailed argument for this see his *The Miracle of Theism* (Mackie 1984).

6. There is a point I pass by here made forcefully years ago by Alasdair MacIntyre. The point is this: no matter what comes after in an afterlife the sufferings of people here and now are not thereby made worthwhile. Suppose an infant at birth is born with some horrible physical defect that causes him to be wracked constantly with terrible pain. After two years of such hell he dies and goes to heaven. How does the bliss of his afterlife at all make those terrible sufferings worthwhile? They are hardly a necessary condition for this bliss. See Alasdair MacIntyre, *Difficulties in Christian Belief* (1956) and "The Logical Status of Religious Belief" (1957).

BIBLIOGRAPHY

Brown, Stuart C., ed. 1977. *Reason and Religion.* Ithaca, N.Y.: Cornell University Press.

Dennett, Daniel. 1978. *Brainstorms.* Montgomery, Vt.: Bradford Books.

Flew, Antony. 1966. *God and Philosophy.* London: Hutchinson.

————. 1967. "Immortality." In *The Encyclopedia of Philosophy*, vol. 4, edited by Paul Edwards. New York: The Free Press.

————. 1976. *The Presumption of Atheism.* New York: Barnes & Noble.

————. 1985. "The Burden of Proof." In *Knowing Religiously*, edited by Leroy S. Rouner, 110–14. Notre Dame, Ind.: University of Notre Dame Press.

Geach, Peter. 1969. *God and the Soul.* New York: Routledge & Kegan Paul.

Gillett, G. R. 1986. "Disembodied Persons." *Philosophy* 61, no. 237: 377–86.

Hick, John. 1976. *Death and Eternal Life.* London: Collins.

Hollis, Martin. 1985. *Invitation to Philosophy.* Oxford: Basil Blackwell.

Horkheimer, Max. 1974. *Critique of Instrumental Reason.* New York: Seabury Press.

Kierkegaard, Soren. 1954. *The Sickness Unto Death.* Translated by Walter Lowrie. New York: Doubleday Anchor Books.

Lewis, Hywel. 1977. "Immortality and Dualism." In *Reason and Religion,* edited by Stuart Brown, 282–300. Ithaca, N.Y.: Cornell University Press.

MacIntyre, Alasdair. 1956. *Difficulties in Christian Belief.* London: SCM Press.

———. 1957. "The Logical Status of Religious Belief." In *Metaphysical Beliefs,* edited by Ronald Hepburn, 168–205. London: SCM Press.

Mackie, J. L. 1976. "Sidgwick's Pessimism." *Philosophical Quarterly* 26, no. 105: 326–27.

———. 1984. *The Miracle of Theism.* Oxford: Clarendon Press.

———. 1985. *Persons and Values.* Oxford: Clarendon Press.

Nagel, Thomas. 1986. *The View from Nowhere.* New York: Oxford University Press.

Nielsen, Kai. 1971. *Contemporary Critiques of Religion.* New York: Herder and Herder.

———. 1973. *Skepticism.* New York: St. Martin's Press.

———. 1978. "Death and the Meaning of Life." In *The Search for Values in a Changing World,* 483–90. New York: The International Culture Foundation.

———. 1982. *An Introduction to the Philosophy of Religion.* London: Macmillan.

———. 1985a. "God and Coherence." In *Knowing Religiously,* edited by Leroy S. Rouner, 89–102. Notre Dame, Ind.: University of Notre Dame Press.

———. 1985b. *Philosophy and Atheism.* Amherst, N.Y.: Prometheus Books.

Parfit, Derek. 1984. *Reasons and Persons.* Oxford: Clarendon Press.

Penelhum, Terence. 1976. *Survival and Disembodied Existence.* London: Routledge & Kegan Paul.

———. 1979. Critical notice. "John Hick: Death and Eternal Life" *Canadian Journal of Philosophy* 9 (March): 141–62.

———. 1982. "Survival and Identity." In *Analytical Philsophy of Relgion in Canada,* edited by Mostafa Faghfoury, 35–53. Ottawa, Ont.: University of Ottawa Press.

Shoemaker, Sydney. 1977. "Immorality and Dualism" and "Postscript." In *Reason and Religion,* edited by Stuart Brown, 259–81, 307–11. Ithaca, N.Y.: Cornell University Press.

Vesey, Godfrey. 1977. "Remarks." In *Reason and Religion,* edited by Stuart Brown, 301–306. Ithaca, N.Y.: Cornell University Press.

Wiggens, David. 1986. *Sameness and Substance.* Oxford: Basil Blackwell.

---- 4 ----

THE MEANING OF LIFE

Anglo-Saxon philosophy has in various degrees "gone linguistic." From the faithful attention to the niceties of plain English practiced by John Austin, to the use of descriptive linguistics initiated by Paul Ziff in his *Semantic Analysis*, to the deliberately more impressionistic concern with language typical of Isaiah Berlin and Stuart Hampshire, there is a pervasive emphasis by English-speaking philosophers on what can and cannot be said, on what is intelligible, and on what is nonsensical. When linguistic philosophy was first developing, many things were said to be nonsense which were not nonsense. However, this is something of the past, for linguistic philosophy has for a long time been less truculent and more diffident about what it makes sense to say, but only to become—some would say—unbelievably bland, dull, and without a rationale that is of any general interest.[1]

Critics from many quarters have raised their voices to assault linguistic philosophy as useless pedantry remote from the perennial con-

From *Cross Currents* (summer 1964): 233–56.

cerns of philosophy or the problems of belief and life that all people encounter when, in Hesse's terms, they feel to the full "the whole riddle of human destiny." Traditionally the philosophical enterprise sought, among other things, to give us some enlightenment about our human condition, but as philosophy "goes linguistic," it has traitorously and irresponsibly become simply talk about the uses of talk. The philosopher has left his "high calling" to traffic in linguistic trivialities.

Criticism of linguistic philosophy has not always been this crude, but there has typically been at least the implied criticism that linguistic philosophy could not really do justice to the profound problems of human beings with which Plato, Spinoza, or Nietzsche struggled.

It is my conviction that such a charge is unfounded. In linguistic philosophy there are some partially new techniques but no "abdication of philosophy." Surely most linguistic philosophy is dull, as is most philosophy, as is most anything else. Excellence and insight in any field are rare. But at its best linguistic philosophy is not dull and it is not without point; furthermore, though it often is, it need not be remote from the concerns of human beings. It is this last claim—the claim that linguistic philosophy can have nothing of importance to say about the perplexities of belief and life that from time to time bedevil us—that I wish to challenge.

With reference to the concepts of human purpose, religion, and the problematical notion "the meaning of Life," I want to show how in certain crucial respects linguistic philosophy can be relevant to the perplexities about life and conduct that reflective people actually face. "What is the meaning of Life?" has been a standby of both the pulpiteer and the mystagogue. It has not come in for extended analysis by linguistic philosophers, though Ayer, Wisdom, Baier, Edwards, Flew, Hepburn, and Dilman have had some important things to say about this obscure notion which when we are in certain moods perplexes us all and indeed, as it did Tolstoy and Dostoevsky, may even be something that forces itself upon us in thoroughly human terms (Ayer 1963). I want to show how the use of the analytical techniques of linguistic philosophy can help us in coming to grips with the problems of human purpose and the meaning of Life.

Part of the trouble centers around puzzles about the use of the word "meaning" in "What is the meaning of Life?" Since the turn of the century there has been a lot of talk in philosophical circles about "meanings" of "a meaning criterion" and a good measure of attention has been paid to considerations about the meanings of words and sentences. But the mark (token) "meaning" in "What is the meaning of Life?" has a very different use than it has in "What is the meaning of 'obscurantist'?" "What is the meaning of 'table'?" "What is the meaning of 'good'?" "What is the meaning of 'science'?" and "What is the meaning of 'meaning'?" In these other cases we are asking about the meaning or use of the word or words, and we are requesting either a definition of the word or an elucidation or description of the word's use. But in asking "What is the meaning of Life?" we are not asking—or at least this is not our central perplexity—about "What is the meaning of the word 'Life'?" What then are we asking?

Indirection is the better course here. Consider some of the uses of the general formula: "What is the meaning of that?" How, in what contexts, and for what purposes does it get used? Sometimes we may simply not know the meaning of a word, as when we come across a word we do not understand and look it up in a dictionary or ask the person using it in conversation what it means. It is not that he is using the word in an odd sense and we want to know what *he* means by it, but that we want to know what is meant by that word as it is employed in the public domain.

There is the quite different situation in which it is not about words that we are puzzled but about someone's nonlinguistic behavior. A friend gives us a dark look in the middle of a conversation in which several people are taking part and afterwards we ask him "What was the meaning of those dark looks?" We were aware when we noticed his dark look that he was disapproving of something we were doing but we did not and still do not know what. Our "What was the meaning of that?" serves to try to bring out what is the matter. Note that in a way here we are not even puzzled about the meaning of words. The recipient of the dark look may very well know he is being disapproved of; but he wants to know what for. Here "What is the meaning of that?" is a request for the point or the purpose of the action. In this way, as we shall see, it is closer to the question "What is the meaning of Life?" than questions about the meaning of a word or a sentence.

We also ask "What is the meaning of that?" when we want to know how a particular person on a particular occasion intends something. We want to know what *he means* by that. Thus if I say of some author that he writes "chocolate rabbit stories" you may well ask me what I mean by that. Here you are puzzled both about the meaning of the phrase "chocolate rabbit stories," for, as with "the pine cone weeps" or "the rock cogitates," it is a deviant collection of words, and you are puzzled about the point or purpose of making such a remark. After all, the point of making such an utterance may not be evident. Suppose I had said it to a stupid and pompous writer blown up with a false sense of his own importance. I could explain my meaning by saying that I was obliquely giving him to understand that his stories, like chocolate rabbits, were all out of the same mold: change the names and setting and you have the same old thing all over again. And the point of my utterance would also become evidence, i.e., to deflate the pompous windbag. The phrase "chocolate rabbit stories" has no fixed use in human discourse, but language is sufficiently elastic for me to be able to give it a use without generating any linguistic or conceptual shock. To explain my meaning I must make clear the use I am giving it and make evident why I choose to use such an odd phrase.

"What is the meaning of Life?" is in some very significant respects like this last question though it is of course also very different. It is different in being nondeviant and in being a profoundly important question in the way the other question clearly is not. But note the likeness. In the first place when we or other people ask this question we are often not at all sure what we are asking. In this practical context we may in a way even be puzzled about the word "life," though, as I have said, the question does not primarily function as a request for the explanation of the use of a word. There is a sense in which life does and there is a sense in which life does not begin and end in mystery. And when we ask about life here we are not asking Schrodinger's question or J. B. S. Haldane's. We are not in search of some property or set of properties that is common to and distinctive of all those things we call "living things." We are typically concerned with something very different and much vaguer. We are asking: "Is life just one damn thing after another until finally one day we die and start to rot? Or can I sum it up and find or at least give it some point after all? Or is this just a silly illusion born of fear and trembling?" These are desperately vague, amorphous questions, but—as John Wisdom would surely and rightly say—not meaningless for all that. And for some of us, and perhaps for all of us, *sometimes*, they are haunting, edging questions, questions we agonize over, then evade, then again try to come to grips with.

First, I want to say that, like "What is the meaning of calling them chocolate rabbit stories?" "What is the meaning of Life?" does not have a clear use; but that it does *not* have a clear use does not, I repeat, entail or in any way establish that it does not have a use or even that it does not have a supremely important use.[2] Second, "What is the meaning of life?" most typically—though not always—functions as a request for the goals *worth* seeking in life though sometimes it may serve to ask if there are any goals worth seeking in life.[3] We are asking what (if anything) is the point to our lives? What (if anything) could give our lives purpose or point? In anguish we struggle to find the purpose, point, or rationale of our grubby lives. But if this is the nature of the question, what would an answer look like? For this to be a fruitful question, all of us must ask ourselves individually: what would we take as an answer? When we ask this we are apt to come up with a blank; and if we are readers of philosophical literature we may remember that, along with others, a philosopher as persuasive and influential as A. J. Ayer has said that all such questions are unanswerable. But if they are really unanswerable—or so it would seem—then they are hardly genuine questions.

I will concede that *in a sense* such questions are unanswerable, but in a much more important sense they *are* answerable. We can be intelligent about and reason about such questions. Any analysis which does not bring this out and elucidate it is confused and inadequate. In destroying pontifical pseudoanswers the baby has frequently gone down with the bath water. In showing what kind of answers could not be answers to this question, the temptation is to stress that there are no answers at all and that indeed no answers are needed. I want to try to show why this is wrong and what an answer would look like.

II

How then is it possible for our life to have a meaning or a purpose? For a while, oddly enough, Ayer in his "The Claims of Philosophy" is a perfectly sound guide.[4] We do know what it is for a human being to have a purpose. "It is a matter," Ayer remarks, "of his intending, on the basis of a given situation, to bring about some further situation which for some reason or other he conceives to be desirable."

But, Ayer asks, how is it possible for life in general to have a meaning or a purpose?

Well, there is one very simple answer. Life in general has a purpose if all living beings are tending toward a certain specifiable end. To understand the meaning of life or the purpose of existence it is only necessary to discover this end.

As Ayer makes perfectly clear, there are overwhelming difficulties with such an answer. In the first place there is no good reason to believe living beings are tending toward some specifiable end. But even if it were true that they are all tending toward this end such a discovery would not at all answer the question "What is the meaning or purpose of life?" This is so because when we human beings ask this exceedingly vague question we are not just asking for *an explanation* of the facts of existence; we are asking for a *justification* of these facts. In asking this question we are seeking a way of life, trying as suffering, perplexed, and searching creatures to find what the existentialists like to call an "authentic existence." And as Ayer goes on to explain,

> a theory which informs them merely that the course of events is so arranged as to lead inevitably to a certain end does nothing to meet their need. For the end in question will not be one that they themselves have chosen. As far as they are concerned it will be entirely arbitrary; and it will be a no less arbitrary fact that their existence is such as necessarily to lead to its fulfillment. In short, from the point of view of justifying one's existence, there is no essential difference between a teleological

explanation of events and a mechanical explanation. In either case, it is a matter of brute fact that events succeed one another in the ways they do and are explicable in the ways they are.

In the last analysis, an attempt to answer a question of why events are as they are must always resolve itself into saying only *how* they are. Every explanation of why people do such and such and why the world is so and so finally depends on a very general description. And even if it is the case, as Charles Taylor powerfully argues, that teleological explanations of human behavior are irreducible, Ayer's point here is not all weakened, for in explaining, teleologically or otherwise, we are still showing how things are; we are not justifying anything (Taylor 1964).

When we ask: "What is the meaning of life?" we want an answer that is more than just an explanation or description of *how* people behave or *how* events are arranged or *how* the world is constituted. We are asking for *a justification* of our existence. We are asking for a justification for why life is as it is, and not even the most complete explanation and/or description of *how* things are ordered can answer this quite different question. The person who demands that some general description of man and his place in nature should entail a statement that man ought to live and die in a certain way is asking for something that can no more be the case than it can be the case that ice can gossip. To ask about the meaning of our lives involves asking how we should live, or whether any decision to live in one way is more *worthy* of acceptance than any other. Both of these questions are clearly normative questions; yet no statement of *fact* about how we in fact do live can by itself be sufficient to answer such questions. No statement of what ought to be the case can be deduced from a statement of what is the case. If we are demanding such an answer, then Ayer is perfectly right in claiming the question is unanswerable.

Let me illustrate. Suppose, perhaps as a result of some personal crisis, I want to take stock of myself. As Kierkegaard would say, I want to appropriate, take to heart, the knowledge I have or can get about myself and my condition in order to arrive at some decision as to what sort of life would be most meaningful for me, would be the sort of life I would truly want to live if I could act rationally and were fully apprised of my true condition. I might say to myself, though certainly not to others, unless I was a bit of an exhibitionist, "Look Nielsen, you're a little bit on the vain side and you're arrogant to boot. And why do you gossip so and spend so much of your time reading science fiction? And why do you always say what you expect other people want you to say? You don't approve of that in others, do you? And why don't you listen more? And weren't you too quick with Jones and too indulgent with Smith?" In such a context I would put these questions and a host of questions like them to myself. And I might come up with some general explanations, good or bad, like "I act this way because I have some fairly pervasive insecurities." And to my further question, "Well, why do you have these insecurities?" I might dig up something out of my past such as "My parents died when I was two and I never had any real home." To explain why this made me insecure I might finally evoke a whole psychological theory and eventually perhaps even a biological and physiological theory, and these explanations about the nature of the human animal would themselves finally rest, in part at least, on various descriptions of how humans behave. In addition, I might, if I could afford it and were sufficiently bedeviled by these questions, find my way to a psychiatrist's couch and there, after the transference had taken place, I would eventually get more quite personalized explanations of my behavior and attitudes. But none of these things, in themselves, could tell me the meaning of life or even the meaning of my life, though they indeed might help me in this search. I might discover that I was insecure because I could never get over the wound of the loss of my father. I might discover that unconsciously I blamed myself. As a child I wished him dead and then he died so somehow I did it, really. And I would, of course, discover how unreasonable this is. I would come to understand that people generally react this way in those situations. In Tolstoy's phrase, we are all part of the "same old river." And, after rehearsing it, turning it over, taking it to heart, I might well gain control over it and eventually gain control over some of my insecurities. I could see and even live through again what *caused* me to be vain, arrogant, and lazy. But suppose that even after all these discoveries I really didn't want to change. After stocktaking, I found that I was willing to settle for the status quo. Now I gratefully acknowledge that this is very unlikely, but here we are concerned with the logical possibilities. "Yes, there are other ways of doing things," I say to myself, "but after all is said and done I have lived this way a long time and I would rather go on this way than change. This sort of life, is after all, the most meaningful one. This is how I really want to act and this is how I, and others like me, ought to act." What possible facts could anyone appeal to which would prove, in the sense of logically entail, that I was wrong and that the purpose of life or the meaning of life was very different than I thought it was? It is Ayer's contention, and I think he is right, that there are none.

"But you have left out God," someone might say. "You have neglected the possibility that there is a God and that God made us in his image and likeness and that God has a plan for us. Even Sartre, Heidegger, and Camus agree that to ask 'What is the Meaning of Life?' or 'What is the purpose of human existence?' is, in effect, to raise the question of God. If there is a God your conclusion would not follow, and, as Father Copleston has said, if there is no God human existence can have no end or purpose other than that given by man himself."[5]

I would want to say, that the whole question of God or no God, Jesus or no Jesus, is entirely beside the point. Even if there were a God, human existence can, in the relevant sense of "end," "purpose," or "meaning," have no other end, purpose, or meaning than what we as human beings give it by our own deliberate choices and decisions.

Let us see how this is so. Let us suppose that everything happens as it does because God intends that it should. Let us even assume, as we in reality cannot, that we can know the purpose or intentions of God. Now, as Ayer points out, either God's "purpose is sovereign or it is not. If it is sovereign, that is, if everything that happens is necessarily in accordance with it, then it is true also of our behavior. Consequently, there is no point in our deciding to conform to it, for the simple reason that we cannot do otherwise." No matter what, we do God's purpose. There is no sense in saying it is *our* purpose, that it is something we have made our own by our own deliberate choice. I have not *discovered* a meaning for my life and other people have not *discovered* a meaning for their lives. If it were possible for us *not* to fulfill it, the purpose would not be God's *sovereign* purpose and if it is his sovereign purpose, it cannot, in the requisite sense, be *our* purpose, for it will not be something of which it would make sense to say that we chose it. It is just something that necessarily happens to us because of God's intentions. If we are compelled to do it, it is not *our* purpose. It is only our purpose if in some sense we want to do it and if we could have done otherwise.

On the other hand, if God's purpose is not sovereign and we are not inexorably compelled to do what God wills, we have no reason to conform to God's purpose unless we independently judge it to be *good* or by our own independent decision make it our purpose. We cannot derive the statement "*x* is good" from "that Being whom people call 'God' says '*x* is good'" or from "that Being whom people call 'God' wills *x*" unless we *independently* judge that whatever this Being *says* is good *is good* or whatever that Being wills *ought* to be done. Again, as Ayer remarks, this "means that the significance of our behavior depends finally upon our own judgments of value; and the concurrence of a deity then becomes superfluous."[6]

The basic difficulty, as Ayer makes clear, is that in trying to answer the questions as we have above, we have really misunderstood the question. "What-is-the-meaning-of-that?" and "What-is-the-purpose-of-that?" questions can be very different. We have already noted some of the differences among "What-is-the-meaning-of-that?" questions, and we have seen that "What is the meaning of Life?" in many contexts at least can well be treated as a "What-is-the-purpose-of-that?" question. But "What is the purpose of life?" is only very superficially like "What is the purpose of a blotter?" "What is the purpose of brain surgery?" or "What is the purpose of the liver?" The first is a question about a human artifact and in terms of certain assumed ends we can say quite explicitly, independently of whether or not we want blotters, what the purpose of blotters is. Similarly brain surgery is a well-known human activity and has a well-known rationale. Even if we are Christian Scientists and disapprove of surgery altogether, we can understand and agree on what the purpose of brain surgery is, just as we all can say Fearless Fosdick is a good safecracker, even though we disapprove of safecrackers. And again, in terms of the total functioning of the human animal we can say what livers are for, even though the liver is not an artifact like a blotter. If there is a God and God made man, we *might* say the question "What is the purpose of human life?" is very like "What is the purpose of umbrellas?" The human animal then becomes a Divine artifact. But, even if all this were so, we would not—as we have already seen—have an answer to the *justificatory* question we started with when we asked, "What is the meaning of life?" If we knew God's purpose for man, we would know what man was made for. But we would not have an answer to our question about the meaning of life, for we would not know if there was purpose *in* our lives or if we could find a point in acting one way rather than another. We would only know that there was something—which may or may not be of value— that we were constructed, "cut out," to be.

Similarly, if an Aristotelian philosophy is correct, "What is the purpose of life?" would become very like "What is the purpose of the liver?" But here again a discovery of what end humans are as a matter of fact tending toward would not answer the perplexity we started from, that is to say, it would not answer the question, "What is the meaning of life, how should we live and die?" We would only learn that "What is the purpose of life?" could admit of two very different uses. As far as I can see, there are no good reasons to believe either that there is a God or that the human animal has been ordered for some general end: but even if this were so it would not give us an answer to the question "What is the meaning of life?"

This is so because the question has been radically misconstrued. When we ask "What is the meaning of life?" or "What is the purpose of human existence?" we are normally asking, as I have already said, questions of the following types: "What should we seek?" "What ends—if any—are worthy of attainment?" Questions of this sort require a very different answer than any answer to "What is the meaning of 'obscurantism'?" "What is the purpose of the ink-blotter?" and "What is the purpose of the liver?" Ayer is right when he says, "what is required by those who seek to know the purpose of their existence is not a factual description of the way that people actually do conduct themselves, but rather a decision as to how they *should* conduct themselves." Again he is correct in remarking "There is a sense in which it can be said that life does have a meaning. It has for each of us whatever meaning we severally *choose* to give it. The purpose of a man's existence is constituted by the ends to which he, consciously or unconsciously, devotes himself."

Ayer links this with another crucial logical point, a point which the existentialists have dramatized as some kind of worrisome "moral discovery." Ayer points out that "in the last resort . . . each individual has the responsibility of making the choice of how he ought to live and die" and that it is logically impossible that someone else, in some authoritative position, can make that choice for him. If someone gives me moral advice in the nature of the case I must decide whether or not to follow her advice, so again the choice is finally my own. This is true because moral questions are primarily questions about what to do or what to try to become. In asking how I ought to live, I am trying to make up my mind how to act and what kind of life to live. And to say I deliberately acted in a certain way implies that I decided to do it. There is no avoiding personal choice in considering such questions.

But Ayer, still writing in the tradition of logical empiricism, often writes as if it followed from the truth of what we have said so far, that there could be no reasoning about "How ought a person to live?" or "What is the meaning of life?" Thus Ayer says at one point in "The Claims of Philosophy," "He [the moral agent] cannot prove his judgments of value are correct, for the simple reason that no judgment of value is capable of proof." He goes on to argue that people have no way of demonstrating that one judgment of value is superior to another. A decision between people in moral disagreement is a "subject for persuasion and finally a matter of individual choice."

As we have just seen there is a sound point to Ayer's stress on choice vis-à-vis morality, but taken as a whole his remarks are at best misleading. There is reasoning about moral questions and there are arguments and reasoning in morality. There are principles in accordance with which we appraise our actions, and there are more general principles, like the principle of utility or the principles of distributive justice in accordance with which we test our lower-level moral rules. And there is a sense of "being reasonable" which, as Hume and Westermarck were well aware, has distinctive application to moral judgments. Thus, if I say, "I ought to be relieved of my duties, I'm just too ill to go on," I not only must believe I am in fact ill, I must also be prepared to say, of any of my colleagues or anyone else similarly placed, that in like circumstances they too ought to be relieved of their duties if they fall ill. There is a certain *generality* about moral discourse and a person is not reasoning morally or "being reasonable" if she will not allow those inferences. Similarly, if I say "I want x" or "I prefer x" I need not, though I may, be prepared to give reasons why I want it or prefer it, but if I say "x is the right thing to do" or "x is good" or "I ought to do x" or that "x is worthy of attainment," I

must—perhaps with the exception of judgments of intrinsic goodness—
be prepared to give reasons for saying "*x* is the right thing to do," "*x* is
good," "I ought to do *x*," and the like. (Note, this remark has the status of
what Wittgenstein would call a grammatical remark.)

It is indeed true in morals and in reasoning about human conduct
generally that justification must come to an end; but this is also true in
logic, science, and in common-sense empirical reasoning about matters of
fact; but it is also true that the end point in reasoning over good and evil
is different than in science and the like, for in reasoning about how to act,
our judgment finally terminates in a choice—a decision of principle. And
here is the truth in Ayer's remark that moral judgments are *"finally* a
matter of individual choice." But, unless we are to mislead, we must put
the emphasis on "finally," for a dispassionate, neutral analysis of the uses
of the language of human conduct will show, as I have indicated, that
there is reasoning, and in a relevant sense, "objective reasoning," about
moral questions. It is not at all a matter of pure persuasion or goading
someone into sharing your attitudes.

I cannot, of course, even begin to display the full range of the reasoning which has sought to establish this point. But I hope I have said
enough to block the misleading implications of Ayer's otherwise very
fine analysis. Early linguistic philosophy was primarily interested in (1)
the descriptive and explanatory discourse of the sciences, and (2) in
logico-mathematico discourse; the rest was rather carelessly labeled
"expressive or emotive discourse." But the thrust of the work of linguistic
philosophers since the Second World War has corrected that mistaken
emphasis, as recent analytical writing in ethics makes evident. Here I
commend to you R. M. Hare's *The Language of Morals* and his *Freedom and
Reason*, Stephen Toulmin's *An Examination of the Place of Reason in Ethics*,
Kurt Baier's *The Moral Point of View*, Marcus Singer's *Generalization in
Ethics*, P. H. Nowell-Smith's *Ethics*, Bernard Mayo's *Ethics and the Moral
Life*, and George von Wright's *The Varieties of Goodness*. They would also
reinforce the point I tried briefly to make against Ayer, as would an exam-
ination of the work of Philippa Foot or John Rawls.[7]

III

There are, however, other considerations that may be on our minds when
we ask "What is the meaning of life?" or "Does life have a meaning?" In
asking such questions, we may not be asking "What should we seek?" or
"What goals are worth seeking really?" Instead we may be asking "Is anything worth seeking?" "Does it matter finally what we do?" Here, some
may feel, we finally meet the real tormenting "riddle of human existence."

Such a question is not simply a moral question: it is a question concerning human conduct, a question about how to live one's life or about whether to continue to live one's life. Yet when we consider what an answer would look like here we draw a blank. If someone says "Is anything worthwhile?" we gape. We want to reply, "Why, sitting in the sunshine in the mornings, seeing the full moon rise, meeting a close friend one hasn't seen in a long time, sleeping comfortably after a tiring day, all these things and a million more are most assuredly worthwhile. Any life devoid of experiences of this sort would most certainly be impoverished."

Yet this reply is so obvious we feel that something different must be intended by the questioner. The questioner knows that we, and most probably he, ordinarily regard such things as worthwhile, but he is asking if these things or *anything* is worthwhile *really*? These things *seem* worthwhile but are they in really? And here we indeed do not know what to say. If someone queries whether it is really worthwhile leaving New York and going to the beach in August we have some idea of what to say; there are some criteria which will enable us to make at least a controversial answer to this question. But when it is asked, in a philosophical manner, *if anything, ever* is really worthwhile, it is not clear that we have a genuine question before us. The question borrows its form from more garden-variety questions but when we ask it in this general way do we actually understand what we mean? If someone draws a line on the blackboard, a question over the line's straightness can arise only if some criterion for a line's being straight is accepted. Similarly only if some criterion of worthiness is accepted can we intelligibly ask if a specific thing or anything is worthy of attainment.

But if a sensitive and reflective person asks, "Is anything worthwhile, really?" could he not be asking this because, (1) he has a certain vision of human excellence, and (2) his austere criteria for what is worthwhile have developed in terms of that vision? Armed with such criteria, she might find nothing that human beings can in fact attain under their present and foreseeable circumstances *worthy* of attainment. Considerations of this sort seem to be the sort of considerations that led Tolstoy and Schopenhauer to come to such pessimistic views about life. Such a person would be one of those few people, who, as one of Hesse's characters remarks, "demand the utmost of life and yet cannot come to terms with its stupidity and crudeness." In terms of his ideal of human excellence nothing is worthy of attainment.

To this, it is natural to respond, "if this is our major problem about the meaning of life, then this is indeed no intellectual or philosophical riddle about human destiny. We need not like Steppenwolf return to our lodging lonely and disconsolate because life's 'glassy essence' remains forever hidden, for we can well envisage, in making such a judgment, what would be worthwhile. We can say what a meaningful life would look like even though we can't attain it. If such is the question, there is no 'riddle of human existence,' though there is a pathos to human life and there is the social-political pattern problem of how to bring the requisite human order into existence. Yet only if we have some conception of what human life should be can we feel such pathos."

If it is said in response to this that what would really be worthwhile could not possibly be attained, an absurdity has been uttered. To say something is worthy of attainment implies that, everything else being equal, it ought to be attained. But to say that something ought to be attained implies that it *can* be attained. Thus we cannot intelligibly say that something is worthy of attainment but that it *cannot* possibly be attained. So in asking "Is anything worthy of attainment?" we must acknowledge that there are evaluative criteria operative which guarantee that what is sincerely said to be worthy of attainment is at least in principle attainable, And as we have seen in speaking of morality, "*x* is worthy of attainment" does not mean "*x* is preferred," though again, in asserting that something is worthy of attainment, or worthwhile, we imply that we would choose it, everything else being equal, in preference to something else. But we cannot intelligibly speak of a choice if there is no possibility of doing one thing rather than another.

Life is often hard and, practically speaking, the ideals we set our hearts on, those to which we most deeply commit ourselves, may in actual fact be impossible to achieve. A sensitive person may have an ideal of conduct, an ideal of life, that she assents to without reservation. But the facts of human living being what they are, she knows full well that this ideal cannot be realized. Her ideals are intelligible enough, logically their achievement is quite possible, but as a matter of *brute fact* her ideals are beyond her attainment. If this is so, is it worthwhile for her and others like her to go on living or to strive for anything at all? Can life, under such circumstances, be anything more than an ugly habit? For such a person, "What is the meaning of life?" has the force of "What *point* can a life such as mine have under these circumstances?" And in asking whether such a life has a point she is asking the very question we put above, viz. can life be worth living under such conditions.

Again such a question is perfectly intelligible and is in no way unanswerable any more than any other question about how to act, though here too we must realize that the facts of human living *cannot* be sufficient for a person simply to read off an answer without it in any way affecting his life. Here, too, *any* answer will require a decision or some kind of effective involvement on the part of the person involved. A philosopher can be of help here in showing what kind of answers we cannot give, but it is far less obvious that he can provide us with a set of principles that together with empirical facts about the person's condition and prospects, will enable the perplexed person to know what he ought to do. The philosopher or any thoughtful person who sees just what is involved in the question can give some helpful advice. Still the person involved must work out an answer in anguish and soreness of heart.

However, I should remind him that no matter how bad his own life was, there would always remain something he could do to help alleviate the sum total of human suffering. This certainly has value and if he so oriented his life, he could not correctly say that his life was without point. I would also argue that in normal circumstances he could not be sure that his ideals of life would permanently be frustrated, and if he held ideals that would be badly frustrated under almost any circumstances, I would get him to look again at his ideals. Could such ideals really be adequate? Surely man's reach must exceed his grasp, but how far should we go? Should not any ideal worth its salt come into some closer involvement with the realities of human living? And if one deliberately and with self-understanding plays the role of a Don Quixote can one justifiably complain that one's ideals are not realized? Finally, it does not seem to me reasonable to expect that *all* circumstances can have sufficient meaning to make them worthwhile. Under certain circumstances life is not worth living. As a philosopher, I would point out this possibility and block those philosophical-religious claims that would try to show that this could not possibly be so.

Many people who feel the barbs of constant frustration come to feel that their ideals have turned out to be impossible, and ask in anguish—as a consequence—"Does life really have any meaning?" To a person in such anguish I would say all I have said above and much more, though I am painfully aware that such an approach may seem cold and unfeeling. I know that these matters deeply affect us; indeed they can even come to obsess us, and when we are so involved it is hard to be patient with talk about what can and cannot be said. But we need to understand these matters as well; and, after all, what more can be done along this line than to make quite plain what is involved in his question and try to exhibit a range of rational attitudes that could be taken toward it, perhaps stressing the point that though Dr. Rieux lost his wife and his best friend, his life, as he fought the plague, was certainly not without point either for him or for others. But I would also try to make clear that finally an answer to such a question must involve a decision or the having or adopting of a certain attitude on the part of the person involved. This certainly should be stressed and it should also be stressed that the question "Is such a life meaningful?" is a sensible question, which admits of a nonobscurantist, nonmetaphysical treatment.

IV

There are many choices we must make in our lives and some choices are more worthwhile than others, though the criteria for what is worthwhile are in large measure at least context-dependent. "It's worthwhile going to Leningrad to see the Hermitage" is perfectly intelligible to someone who knows and cares about art. Whether such a trip to Leningrad is worthwhile for such people can be determined by these people by a visit to the museum. "It's worthwhile fishing the upper Mainistee" is in exactly the same category, though the criteria for worthwhileness are not the same. Such statements are most assuredly perfectly intelligible; and no adequate grounds have been given to give us reason to think that we should philosophically tinker with the ordinary criteria of "good art museum" or "good trout fishing." And why should we deny that these and other things are really worthwhile? To say "Nothing is worthwhile since all pales and worse still, all is vain because we must die" is to mistakenly assume that because an eternity of even the best trout fishing would be not just a bore but a real chore, that trout fishing is therefore not worthwhile. Death and the fact (if it is a fact) that there is nothing new under the sun need not make all vanity. That something must come to an end can make it all the more precious: to know that love is an old tale does not take the bloom from your beloved's cheek.

Yet some crave a more general answer to "Is anything worthwhile?" This, some would say, is what they are after when they ask about the meaning of life.

As I indicated, the criteria for what is worthwhile are surely in large measure context-dependent, but let us see what more we can say about this need for a more *general* answer.

In asking "Why is anything worthwhile?" if the "why" is a request for *causes*, a more general answer can be given. The answer is that people have preferences, enjoy, admire and approve of certain things and they can and sometimes do reflect. Because of this they find some things worthwhile. This of course, is not what "being worthwhile" *means*, but if people did not have these capacities they would not find anything worthwhile. But, by contrast, *reasons* why certain things are worthwhile are dependent on the thing in question.

If people find x worthwhile they generally prefer x, approve of x, enjoy x, or admire x on reflection. If people did not prefer, approve of, enjoy, or admire things then nothing would be found to be worthwhile. If they did not have these feelings, make these reflective endorsements, the notion of "being worthwhile" would have no role to play in human life; but it does have a role to play and, as in morality, justification of what is worthwhile must finally come to an end with the reflective endorsements and choices we make.

Moral principles, indeed, have a special onerousness about them. If something is a moral obligation, it is something we ought to do through and through. It for most people at least, and from a moral point of view for everyone, overrides all nonmoral considerations about what is worthwhile. If we are moral agents and we are faced with the necessity of choosing either *A* or *B*, where *A*, though very worthwhile, is a nonmoral end and where *B* is a moral one, we must choose *B*. The force of the "must" here is logical. From a moral point of view there is no alternative but to choose *B*. Yet we do not escape the necessity of decision for we still must *agree* to *adopt* a moral point of view, to *try* to act as moral agents. Here, too, we must finally make a decision of principle.[8] There are good Hobbesian reasons for adopting the moral point of view but if one finally would really prefer "a state of nature" in which all were turned against all, rather than a life in which there was a freedom from this and at least a minimum of cooperation among human beings, then these reasons for adopting the moral point of view would not be compelling to such a person. There is, in the last analysis, no escape from making an endorsement or a choice.

In asking "What is the meaning of Life?" we have seen how this question is in reality a question concerning human conduct. It asks either "What should we seek?" or "What ends (if any) are really worthwhile?" I have tried to show in what general ways such questions are answerable. We can give reasons for our moral judgments and moral principles and the whole activity of morality can be seen to have a point, but not all questions concerning what is worthwhile are moral questions. Where moral questions do not enter we must make a decision about what, on reflection, we are going to seek. We must ascertain, if we can, what—all things considered—really answers to our interests or, where there is no question of anything answering to our interests or failing to answer to our interests, we should decide what on reflection we prefer. What do we really want, wish to approve of, or admire? To ask "Is anything worthwhile?" involves our asking "Is there nothing that we, on reflection, upon knowledge of ourselves and others, want, approve of, or admire?" When we say "So-and-so is worthwhile" we are making a normative judgment that cannot be derived from determining what we desire, admire, approve of, or are willing to endorse. That is to say, these statements do not entail statements to the effect that so-and-so is worthwhile. But in determining what is worthwhile this is *finally* all we have to go on. In saying something is worthwhile, we (1) *express* our preference, admiration, or approval; (2) in some sense imply that we are prepared to defend our choice with *reasons*; and (3) in effect, indicate our belief that others like us in the relevant respects and similarly placed, will find it worthwhile too. And the answer to our question is that, of course, there are things we humans desire, prefer, approve of, or admire. This being so, our question is not unanswerable. Again we need not fly to a metaphysical enchanter.

As I said, "Is anything really worthwhile, really worth seeking?" makes us gape. And "atomistic analyses," like the one I have just given, often leave us with a vague but persistent feeling of dissatisfaction, even when we cannot clearly articulate the grounds of our dissatisfaction. "The real question," we want to say, "has slipped away from us amidst the host of distinctions and analogies. We've not touched the deep heart of the matter at all."

Surely, I have not exhausted the question for, literally speaking, it is not one question but a cluster of loosely related questions all concerning "the human condition"—how we are to act and how we are to live our lives even in the face of the bitterest trials and disappointments. Questions here are diverse, and a philosopher, or anyone else, becomes merely pretentious and silly when he tries to come up with some formula that will solve, resolve or dissolve the perplexities of human living. But I have indicated in skeletal fashion how we can approach general questions about "What (if anything) is worth seeking?" And I have tried to show how such questions are neither meaningless nor questions calling for esoteric answers. I have also shown that they do require any metaphysical flight into the transcendental or to the transcendent.

V

We are not out of the woods yet. Suppose someone were to say: "Okay, you've convinced me. Some things are worthwhile and there is a more or less distinct mode of reasoning called moral reasoning and there are canons of validity distinctive of this *sui generis* type reasoning (see here Toulmin 1950). People do reason in the ways that you have described, but it still remains the case that here one's attitudes and final choices are relevant in a way that it isn't necessarily the case in science or an argument over plain matters of fact. But when I ask: 'How ought people act?' 'What is the meaning of life?' and 'What is the meaning of *my* life, how should I live and die?' I want an answer that is logically independent of any human choice or any pro-attitude toward any course of action or any state of affairs. Only if I can have that kind of warrant for my moral judgments and ways-of-life will I be satisfied."

If a person demands this and continues to demand this after dialectical examination we must finally leave him unsatisfied. As linguistic philosophers or indeed as anyone else who would be coherent, there is nothing further we can say to him. In dialectical examination we can again point out to him that he is asking for the logically impossible, but if he recognizes this and persists in asking for that which is impossible there are no further rational arguments that we can use to establish our point. But, prior to this last-ditch stand, there are still some things that we can say. We can, in detail and with care, point out to him, describe fully for him, the rationale of the moral distinctions we do make and the functions of moral discourse. A full description here will usually break this kind of obsessive perplexity. Furthermore, we can make the move Stephen Toulmin makes in the last part of his *The Place of Reason in Ethics*. We can describe for him another use of "Why" that Toulmin has well described as a "limiting question" (Toulmin 1950; see also Nielsen 1979).

Let me briefly explain what this is and how it could be relevant. When we ask a "limiting question" we are not really asking a question at all. We are in a kind of "land of shadows" where there are no clear-cut uses of discourse. If we just look at their grammatical form, "limiting questions" do not appear to be extra-rational in form, but in their depth grammar—their actual function—they clearly are. "What holds the universe up?" looks very much like "What holds the Christmas tree up?" but the former, in common sense contexts at least, is a limiting question while the latter usually admits of a perfectly obvious answer. As Toulmin himself puts it, limiting questions are "questions expressed in a form borrowed from a familiar mode of reasoning, but not doing the job which they normally do within that mode of reasoning" (Toulmin 1950, 205). A direct answer to a limiting question never satisfies the questioners. Attempted "answers" only regenerate the question, though often a small change in the questions themselves or their context will make them straightforward questions. Furthermore, there is no standard interpretation for limiting questions sanctioned in our language. And limiting questions do not present us with any genuine alternatives from which to choose.

Now "limiting questions" get used in two main contexts. Sometimes, they merely express what Ryle, rather misleadingly, called a "category mistake." Thus someone who was learning English might ask: "How hot is blue?" or "Where is anywhere?" And, even a native speaker of English might ask as a *moral* agent, "Why ought I to do what is right?" We "answer" such questions by pointing out that blue cannot be hot, anywhere is not a particular place, and that if something is indeed right, this entails that it ought to be done. Our remarks here are grammatical remarks, though our speaking in the material mode may hide this. And if the questioner's "limiting question" merely signifies that a category mistake has been made, when this is pointed out to the questioner, there is an end to the matter. But more typically and more interestingly, limiting questions do not just or at all indicate category mistakes but express, as well or independently, a *personal predicament*. Limiting questions may express anxiety, fear, hysterical apprehensiveness about the future, hope, despair, and any number of attitudes. Toulmin beautifully illustrates from the writings of Dostoevsky an actual, on-the-spot use, of limiting questions:

> He was driving somewhere in the steppes. . . . Not far off was a village, he could see the black huts, and half the huts were burnt down, there were only the charred beams sticking out. As they drove in, there were peasant women drawn up along the road. . . .
>
> "Why are they crying? Why are they crying?" Mitya [Dmitri] asked, as they dashed gaily by.
>
> "It's the babe," answered the driver, "the babe is weeping."
>
> And Mitya was struck by his saying, in his peasant way, "the babe," and he liked the peasant's calling it a "babe." There seemed more pity in it.
>
> "But why is it weeping?" Mitya persisted stupidly. "Why are its little arms bare? Why don't they wrap it up?"
>
> "The babe's cold, its little clothes are frozen and don't warm it."
>
> "But why is it? Why?" foolish Mitya still persisted.
>
> "Why, they're poor people, burnt out. They've no bread. They're begging because they've been burnt out."
>
> "No, no," Mitya, as it were still did not understand. "Tell me why it is those poor mothers stand there? Why are people poor? Why is the babe poor? Why is the steppe barren? Why don't they hug each other and kiss? Why don't they sing songs of joy? Why are they so dark from black misery? Why don't they feed the babe?"
>
> And he felt that, though his questions were unreasonable, and senseless, yet he wanted to ask just that, and he had to ask it just in that way. And he felt that a passion of pity, such as he had never known before, was rising in his heart, that he wanted to cry, that he wanted to do something for them all, so that the babe should weep no more, so that the dark-faced, dried-up mother should not weep, that no one should shed tears again from that moment. . . .
>
> "I've had a good dream, gentlemen," he said in a strange voice, with a new light, as of joy, in his face. (Toulmin 1950, 210)

It is clear that we need not, may not, from the point of view of analysis, condemn these uses of language as illicit. We can point out that it is a muddle to confuse such questions with literal questions, and that such questions have no fixed *literal* meaning, and that as a result there are and can be no fixed literal ways of answering them, but they are indeed, genuine uses of language, and not the harum-scarum dreams of undisciplined metaphysics. When existentialist philosophers and theologians state them as profound questions about an alleged ontological realm there is room for complaint, but as we see them operating in the passage I quoted from *The Brothers Karamazov*, they seem to be not only linguistically proper but also an extremely important form of discourse. It is a shame and a fraud when philosophers "sing songs" as a substitute for the hard work of philosophizing, but only a damn fool would exclude song-singing, literal or metaphorical, from the life of reason, or look down on it as a somehow inferior activity. Nonliteral "answers" to these nonliteral, figurative questions, when they actually express personal predicaments or indeed more general human predicaments may, in a motivational sense, *goad* people to do one thing or another that they *know* they ought to do or they may comfort them or give them hope in time of turmoil and anxiety. I am not saying this is their only use or that they have no other respectable rationale. I do not at all think that; but I am saying that here is a rationale that even the most hard-nosed positivist should acknowledge.

The person who demands "a more objective answer" than any that can be given within the framework of the modes of moral and normative reasoning to his question, "How ought people to live?" or "What is the meaning of Life?" may not be just muddled. If he is *just* making a "category mistake" and this is pointed out to him, he will desist, but if he persists, his limiting question probably expresses some anxiety. In demanding an answer to an evaluative question that can be answered independently of any attitudes he might have or choices or endorsements he might make, he may be unconsciously expressing his fear of making decisions, his insecurity and confusion about what he really wants, and his desperate desire to have a Father who would make all these decisions for him. And it is well in such a context to bring Weston LaBarre's astute psychological observation to mind. "Values," LaBarre said, "must from emotional necessity be viewed as absolute by those who use values as compulsive defenses against reality, rather than properly as tools for the exploration of reality" (LaBarre 1954). This remark, coming from a Freudian anthropologist, has unfortunately a rather metaphysical ring, but it can be easily enough demythologized. The point is, that someone who persists in these questions persists in a demand for a totally different and "deeper" justification or answer to the question "What is the meaning of Life?" than the answer that such a question admits of, may be just expressing his own insecurity. The heart of rationalism is often irrational. At such a point the only reasoning that will be effective with him, if indeed any reasoning will be effective with him, may be psychoanalytic reasoning. And by then, of course you have left the philosopher and indeed all questions of justification far behind. But again the philosopher can describe the kinds of questions we can ask and the point of these questions. Without advocating anything at all he can make clearer to us the structure of "the life of reason" and the goals we human beings do prize.

VI

There is another move that might be made in asking about this haunting question: "What is the meaning of Life?" Suppose someone were to say: "Yes I see about these 'limiting questions' and I see that moral reasoning and reasoning about human conduct generally are limited modes of reasoning with distinctive criteria of their own. If I am willing to be guided by reason and I can be reasonable there are some answers I can find to the question: 'What is the meaning of Life?' I'm aware that they are not cut and dried and that they are not simple and that they are not even by any means altogether the same for all people, but there are some reasonable answers and touchstones all the same. You and I are in perfect accord on that. But there is one thing I don't see at all, 'Why ought I to be guided by reason anyway?' and if you cannot answer this for me I don't see why I should think that your answer—or rather your schema for an answer—about the meaning of Life is, after all, really any good. It all depends on how you *feel*, finally. There are really no answers here."

But again we have a muddle; let me very briefly indicate why. If someone asks "Why ought I to be guided by reason anyway?" or "Is it really good to be reasonable?" one is tempted to take such a question as a paradigm case of a "limiting question," and a very silly one at that. But as some people like to remind us—without any very clear sense of what they are reminding us of—reason has been challenged. It is something we should return to, be wary of, realize the limits of, or avoid, as the case may be. It will hardly do to take such a short way with the question and rack it up as a category mistake.

In some particular contexts, with some particular people, it is (to be paradoxical, for a moment) reasonable to question whether we ought to follow reason. Thus, if I am a stubborn, penny-pinching old compulsive and I finally take my wife to the "big city" for a holiday, it might be well to say to me "Go on, forget how much the damn tickets cost, buy them anyway. Go on, take a cab even if you can't afford it." But to give or heed such advice clearly is not, in any fundamental sense, to fly in the face of reason, for on a deeper level—the facts of human living being what they are—we are being guided by reason.

It also makes sense to ask, as people like D. H. Lawrence press us to ask, if it really pays to be reasonable. Is the reasonable, clear-thinking, clear-visioned, intellectual animal really the happiest in the long run? And can his life be as rich, as intense, as creative as the life of Lawrence's sort of man? From Socrates to Freud it has been assumed, for the most part, that self-knowledge, knowledge of our world, and rationality will bring happiness, if anything will. But is this really so? The whole Socratic tradition may be wrong at this point. Nor is it obviously true that the reasonable man, the man who sees life clearly and without evasion, will be able to live the richest, the most intense or the most creative life. I hope these things are compatible but they may not be. A too clear understanding may dull emotional involvement. Clear-sightedness may work against the kind of creative intensity that we find in a Lawrence, a Wolfe, or a Dylan Thomas.

But to ask such questions is not in a large sense to refuse to be guided by reason. Theoretically, further knowledge could give us at least some vague answers to such unsettling questions; and, depending on what we learned and what decisions we would be willing to make, we would then know what to do. But clearly, we are not yet flying in the face of reason, refusing to be guided by reason at all. We are still playing the game according to the ground rules of reason.

What is this question, "Why should I be guided by reason?" or "Why be reasonable?" if it isn't any of these questions we have just discussed? If we ask this question and take it in a very general way, the question is a limiting one and it does involve a category mistake. What could be *meant* by asking "Why ought we *ever* use reason at all?" That to ask this question is to commit a logical blunder, is well brought out by Paul Taylor when he says

> it is a question which would never be asked by anyone who thought about what he was saying, since the question, to speak loosely, answers itself. It is admitted that no amount of arguing in the world can make a person who does not want to be reasonable want to be. For to argue would be to give reasons, and to give reasons already assumes that the person to whom you give them is seeking reasons. That is it assumes he is reasonable. A person who did not want to be reasonable in any sense would never ask the question, "Why be reasonable?" For in asking the question, Why? he is seeking reasons, that is, he is being reasonable in asking the question. The question calls for the use of reason to justify *any* use of reason, including the use of reason to answer the question. (Taylor 1956)

In other words, to ask the question, as well as answer it, commits one to the use of reason. To ask "Why be guided by reason at all?" is to ask "Why be reasonable, ever?" As Taylor puts it, "The questioner is thus seeking good reasons for seeking good reasons," and this surely is an absurdity. Anything that would be a satisfactory answer would be a "tautology to the effect that it is reasonable to be reasonable. A negative answer to the question, Is it reasonable to be reasonable? would express a self-contradiction."

If all this is pointed out to someone and he still persists in asking the question in this logically senseless way there is nothing a philosopher *qua* philosopher can do for him, though a recognition of the use of limiting questions in discourse may make this behavior less surprising to the philosopher himself. He might give him all five volumes of *The Life of Reason* or *Vanity Fair* and say, "Here, read this, maybe you will come to see things differently." The philosopher himself might even sing a little song in praise of reason, but there would be nothing further that he could say to him, philosophically; but by now we have come a very long way.

VII

Ronald Hepburn is perceptive in speaking of the conceptual "darkness around the meaning-of-life questions" (Hepburn 1966). We have already seen some of the reasons for this; most generally, we should remark here that people are not always asking the same questions and are not always satisfied by answers of the same scope when they wrestle with meaning-of-life questions. And often, of course, the questioner has no tolerably clear idea of what he is trying to ask. He may have a strong gut reaction about the quality and character of his own life and the life around him without the understanding or ability to conceptualize why he feels the way he does. Faced with this situation, I have tried to chart some of the contexts in which "What is the meaning of Life?" is a coherent question and some of the contexts in which it is not. But there are some further contexts in which "meaning-of-life questions" get asked which I have not examined.

There are philosophers who will agree with me that in a world of people with needs and wants already formed, it can be shown that life in a certain "subjective sense" has meaning, but they will retort that this is not really the central consideration. What is of crucial importance is whether we can show that the universe is better with human life than without it. If this cannot be established then we cannot have good reason to believe that life really has meaning, though in the subjective senses we have discussed, we can still continue to say it has meaning.[9]

If we try to answer this question, we are indeed brought up short, for we are utterly at a loss about what it would be like to ascertain whether it is better for the universe to have human life than no life at all. We may have certain attitudes here but no idea of what it would be like to know or have any reason at all to believe that "It is better that there is life" is either true or false or reasonably asserted or denied. It is quite unlike "It is better to be dead than to live with such a tumor." Concerning this last example, people may disagree about its correctness, but they have some idea of what considerations are relevant to settling the dispute. But with "It is better that there be life" we are at a loss.

We will naturally be led into believing that "What is the meaning of

Life?" is an unanswerable question reflecting "the mystery of existence," if we believe that to answer that question satisfactorily we will have to be able to establish that it is better that there is life on earth than no life at all. What needs to be resisted is the very acceptance of that way of posing the problem. We do not need to establish that it is better that the universe contains human life than not in order to establish that there is a meaning to life. A life without purpose, a life devoid of satisfaction, and an alienated life in which people are not being true to themselves is a meaningless life. The opposite sort of life is a meaningful or significant life. We have some idea of the conditions which must obtain for this to be so, i.e., for a person's life to have significance. We are not lost in an imponderable mystery here and we do not have to answer the question of whether it is better that there be human life at all to answer that question. Moreover, this standard nonmetaphysical reading of "What is the meaning of Life?" is no less objective than the metaphysical reading we have been considering. *There are no good grounds at all for claiming that this metaphysical "question" is the real and objective consideration in "What is the meaning of Life?" and that the more terrestrial interpretations I have been considering are more subjective.* This transcendental metaphysical way of stating the problem utilizes unwittingly and without justification arbitrary persuasive definitions of "subjective" and "objective." And no other grounds have been given for not sticking with the terrestrial readings.

A deeper criticism of the account I have given of purpose and the meaning of life is given by Ronald Hepburn.[10] It is indeed true that life cannot be meaningful without being purposeful in the quite terrestrial sense I have set out, but, as Hepburn shows, it can be purposeful and still be meaningless.

> One may fill one's days with honest, useful and charitable deeds, not doubting them to be of value, but without feeling that these give one's life meaning or purpose. It may be profoundly boring. To seek meaning is not just a matter of seeking justification for one's policies, but of trying to discover how to organize one's vital resources and energies around these policies. To find meaning is not a matter of judging these to be worthy, but of seeing their pursuit as in some sense a fulfillment, as involving self-realization as opposed to self-violation, and as no less opposed to the performance of a dreary task. (Hepburn 1966)

A person's life can have significance even when he does not realize it and even when it is an almost intolerable drudge to him, though for human life generally to have significance this could not almost invariably be true for the human animal. But one's own life could not have significance for oneself if it were such a burden to one. To be meaningful to one, one's life must be purposive and it must be a life that the liver of that life finds fulfilling in the living of it. These conditions sometimes obtain and when it is also true that some reasonable measure of an individual's purposive activity adds to the enhancement of human life, we can say that his life is not only meaningful to him but meaningful *sans phrase* (Hepburn 1966).

This is still not the end of the matter in the struggle to gain a sense of the meaning of life, for, as Hepburn also points out, some will not be satisfied with a purely terrestrial and nonmetaphysical account of the type I have given of "the meaning of Life"[11] (Hepburn 1966). They will claim "that life could be thought of as having meaning only so long as that meaning was believed to be a matter for discovery, not for creation and value-decision" (Hepburn 1966). They will go on to claim that "to be meaningful, life would have to be comprehensively meaningful and its meaning invulnerable to assault. Worthwhile objectives must be ultimately realizable despite appearances" (Hepburn 1966).

However, even if they are not satisfied with my more piecemeal and terrestrial facing of questions concerning the meaning of life, it does not follow that life can only have meaning if it has meaning in the more comprehensive and less contingent way they seek. It may be true that life will only have meaning *for them* if these conditions are met, but this does not establish that life will thus lack meaning unless these conditions are met. That is to say, it may be found significant by the vast majority of people, including most nonevasive and reflective people, when the conditions I have alluded to are met and it may be the case that everyone should find life meaningful under such conditions.

It is not the case that there is some general formula in virtue of which we can say what the meaning of life is, but it still remains true that people can through their purposive activity give their lives meaning and indeed find meaning in life in the living of it. The man with a metaphysical or theological craving will seek "higher standards" than the terrestrial standards I have utilized.

Is it rational to assent to that craving, to demand such "higher standards," if life is really to be meaningful? I want to say both "yes" and "no."

On the one hand, the answer should be "no," if the claim remains that for life to be meaningful at all it must be comprehensively meaningful. Even without such a comprehensive conception of things there can be joy in life, morally, aesthetically, and technically worthwhile activity and a sense of human purpose and community. This is sufficient to give meaning to life. And as Ayer perceptively argues and as I argued earlier in the essay, and as Hepburn argues himself, the man with a metaphysical craving of the transcendental sort will not be able to succeed in finding justification or rationale for claims concerning the significance of life that is any more *authoritative* and any more certain or invulnerable to assault than the nonmetaphysical type of rationale I have adumbrated. In actuality, as we have seen, such a comprehensive account, committed, as it must be, to problematic transcendental metaphysical and/or theological conceptions, is more vulnerable than my purely humanistic reading of this conception.

On the other hand, the answer should be "yes" if the claim is reduced to one asserting that to try to articulate a comprehensive picture of human life is a desirable thing. However, it should be noted that this is quite a reduction in claim. In attempting to make such an articulation, the most crucial thing is not to wrestle with theological considerations about the contingency of the world or eternal life, but to articulate a comprehensive normative social and political philosophy in accordance with which we could set forth at least some of the conditions of a nonalienated life not simply for a privileged few but for humanity generally. We need to show in some general manner what such a life would look like and we need to attempt again, and with a reference to contemporary conditions, what Marx so profoundly attempted, namely, to set out the conditions that could transform our inegalitarian, unjust, vulgar, and—as in countries such as apartheid South Africa and the United States—brutal capitalist societies into truly human societies.[12] Linguistic philosophers and bourgeois philosophers generally have been of little help here, though the clarity they have inculcated into philosophical work and into political and moral argument will be a vital tool in this crucial and yet to be done task.[13] When this task is done, if it is done, then we will have the appropriate comprehensive picture we need, and it is something to be done without any involvement with theology, speculative cosmology, or transcendental metaphysics at all.[14]

NOTES

1. John Passmore remarks in his brief but thoroughly reliable and judicious *Philosophy in the Last Decade* "Philosophy is once again cultivating areas it had declared wasteland, or had transferred without compunction to other owners" (Passmore 1969, 5).

2. John Wisdom has driven home this point with force. In particular see his "The Modes of Thought and the Logic of 'God'" (Wisdom 1965).

3. Ronald Hepburn has correctly stressed that this for some people may not be what is uppermost in their minds when they ask that question. See Hepburn 1966. See also Ilham Dilman's remarks about Hepburn's analysis in "Life and Meaning" (Dillman 1965).

4. See Ayer 1963. The rest of the references to Ayer in the text are from this essay. His brief remarks in his "What I Believe"(Ayer 1966) and in his introduction to *The Humanist Outlook* (Ayer 1968) are also relevant as further brief statements of his central claims about the meaning of life.

5. See his discussion of existentialism in his *Contemporary Philosophy*.

6. While I completely agree with the central thrust of Ayer's argument here, he has, I believe, overstated his case. Even if our behavior finally depends on our own standards of value, it does not follow that the concurrence of the deity, if there is one, is superfluous, for we could still find crucial moral guidance from our grasp of something of God's wisdom.

7. I have discussed these issues in my "Problems of Ethics"(Nielsen 1967b) and "History of Contemporary Ethics" (Nielsen 1967a).

8. I have discussed the central issues involved here at length in my "Why Should I Be Moral?"(Nielson 1963. See also Nielson 1999)

9. See in this context Hans Reiner, *Der Sinn unseres Daseins* (1960). This view has been effectively criticized by Paul Edwards in "Meaning and Value of Life" (Edwards 1967).

10. Hepburn's criticisms are directed toward an earlier version of this essay, which appeared as "Linguistic Philosophy and 'The Meaning of Life'" (Nielsen 1964).

11. For arguments of this type see F. C. Copleston, "Man and Metaphysics I" (Copleston 1960). See in addition his continuation of this article in successive issues of *The Heythrop Review* and his *Positivism and Metaphysics* (Copleston 1965).

12. For a contemporary Marxist account see Adam Schaff, *A Philosophy of Man* (Schaff 1963). But also note the criticism of Schaff's views by Christopher Hollis in "What is the Purpose of Life?" (Hollis 1961).

13. The strength and limitations here of linguistic analysis as it has been practiced are well exhibited in Ayer's little essay "Philosophy and Politics" (Ayer 1967).

14. If what I have argued above is so, many of the esoteric issues raised by Milton Munitz in his *The Mystery of Existence* and in his contribution to *Language, Belief, and Metaphysics*, edited by Kiefer and Milton Munitz, can be bypassed.

BIBLIOGRAPHY

Ayer, A. J. 1963. "The Claims of Philosophy." In *Philosophy of the Social Sciences*, edited by A. Natanson. New York: Random House.

———. 1966. "What I Believe." In *What I Believe*, 15–16. London: George Allen & Unwin, Ltd.

———. 1967. *Philosophy and Politics*. Liverpool: Liverpool University Press.

———. 1968. "Introduction." In *The Humanist Outlook*, edited by A. J. Ayer, 3–10. London: Pemberton.

Copleston, F. C. 1960. "Man and Metaphysics I." *Heythrop Journal* 1, no. 2 (January): 16. For a more extended discussion, see Copleston, F. C. 1974. *Religion and Philosophy*. Dublin: Gill and Macmillan, Ltd.

———. 1965. *Positivism and Metaphysics*.

Dilman, Ilham. 1965. "Life and Meaning." *Philosophy* 40 (October): 35–45.

Edwards, Paul. 1967. "Meaning and Value of Life." In *The Encyclopedia of Philosophy*, vol. 4, edited by Paul Edwards, 474–76. New York: Macmillan.

Hepburn, Ronald. 1966. "Questions about the Meaning of Life." *Religious Studies* 1: 125–40.

Hollis, Christopher. 1961. "What Is the Purpose of Life?" *The Listener* 70: 133–36.

LaBarre, Weston. 1954. *The Human Animal*. Chicago: University of Chicago Press.

Munitz, Milton. 1965. *The Mystery of Existence*. New York: Appleton-Century-Crofts.

———. 1970. "The Concept of the World." In *Language, Belief, and Metaphysics*, edited by Howard E. Kiefer and Milton Munitz. Albany: State University of New York Press.

Nielsen, Kai. 1963. "Why Should I Be Moral?" *Methodos* 15, nos. 59–60: 275–306. This article is reprinted along with a much more extended discussion in Nielsen, Kai. 1989. *Why Be Moral?* Amherst, N.Y.: Prometheus Books.

———. 1964. "Linguistic Philosophy and 'The Meaning of Life.'" *Cross-Currents* 14 (summer): 313–34.

———. 1967a. "History of Contemporary Ethics." In *The Encyclopedia of Philosophy*, vol. 3, edited by Paul Edwards, 100–17. New York: Macmillan.

———. 1967b. "Problems of Ethics." In *The Encyclopedia of Philosophy*, vol. 3, edited by Paul Edwards, 117–34. New York: Macmillan.

———. 1979. "Religion, Science, and Limiting Questions." *Studies in Religion* 8, no. 3 (summer): 259–65.

———. 1999. "Moral Point of View Theories." *Critica* 31, no. 93 (December): 105–116.

Passmore, John. 1969. *Philosophy in the Last Decade*. Sydney: Sydney University Press.

Reiner, Hans. 1960. *Der Sinn unseres Daseins*. Tubingen: M. Niemeyer.

Schaff, Adam. 1963. *A Philosophy of Man*. New York: Monthly Review Press.

Taylor, Charles. 1964. *The Explanation of Behavior*. London: Routledge and Kegan Paul.

Taylor, Paul. 1956. "Four Types of Relativism." *Philosophical Review* 23, no. 3: 265–78.

Toulmin, Stephen. 1950. *An Examination of the Place of Reason in Ethics*. Cambridge: Cambridge University Press.

Wisdom, John. 1965. "The Modes of Thought and the Logic of 'God.'" In *Paradox and Discovery*, 1–22. Oxford: Basil Blackwell.

Part Two

AN EXAMINATION OF SOME ACCOUNTS OF NATURALISM

For and Against

5

CONTEXTUALISTIC NATURALISM:
Hook, Nagel, and a Miscellany of Their Critics

I

I shall expound and critically explore the naturalism of Sidney Hook and Ernest Nagel. In doing so I shall do it both in the light of where we stand now in discussions of naturalism and with reference to some of the critiques of Hook's and Nagel's naturalism by their contemporaries. My aim is not only to set the record straight with respect to their naturalism and its implications for religion but to examine the soundness of their views.

Before embarking on that I want to draw, and then utilize in discussing Hook and Nagel, some distinctions made in some current discussions of naturalism. I want, first to say briefly, and I hope nontendentiously, what naturalism is and in doing so identify and distinguish some species. I will distinguish among *cosmological (worldview) naturalism, methodological naturalism, ethical naturalism,* and *scientistic naturalism* (the last being principally a subspecies of *methodological naturalism* exemplified paradigmatically by Bertrand Russell and W. V. Quine). What is common to all these naturalisms, except *necessarily* to ethical naturalism, is the belief that everything belongs to the world of nature and can be, and indeed should be, studied by the methods appropriate for studying that world. For naturalists that world is the only world there is. Spiritual or supernatural worlds are illusory. The different species of naturalism I shall characterize as follows:

1. *Cosmological (worldview) naturalism* is at least a putatively substantive view which holds that everything is either composed of natural entities or is dependent for its existence on natural entities. In so speaking of naturalism, the aim is to capture the distinction (putative distinction) between the *natural* and the *supernatural*, where "nonnatural" or "supernatural" refers to such things as the objects of many of the distinctive and central beliefs and conceptions of theism, deism, idealism, to *noumena*, the *elan vital*, spirits, and the like.

2. *Methodological naturalism* is a methodological commitment to employing in inquiry *only* the norms and methods of inquiry of the empirical sciences together with their logico-mathematical auxiliaries. This, the claim is, is the only way we legitimately and securely can fix belief.

3. *Ethical naturalism* is the view that ethical beliefs are a subspecies of empirical beliefs, that there are among moral utterances, fundamental utterances which express moral propositions which make empirical cognitive claims, some claims that are either true or false and sometimes are claims that are warrantedly assertable. All ethical terms either stand for natural (empirical) properties (including, of course, relational properties) or for *sui generis* moral properties which *must* asymmetrically supervene on natural properties. All moral understanding is by way of beliefs which are empirically confirmable and disconfirmable (directly or indirectly). There are no synthetic a priori moral propositions. And there is no moral knowledge based on intuition.

4. *Scientistic naturalism* is the view that all knowledge or reasonably held beliefs are scientific, based on scientific beliefs or on commonsensical beliefs whose method of confirmation and disconfirmation is of basically the same type as that of scientific beliefs and that they could not be legitimately held where they are not compatible with scientific beliefs. All acceptable methods of justification are commensurable with science and most paradigmatically with the natural sciences. Sometimes, put more crudely, and partially distinctly from what I have just said above, scientistic naturalism is said to be the belief that what the developed natural sciences, and particularly physics, cannot tell us humankind cannot know. There can be no knowledge that conflicts with or is incommensurable with that of the developed natural sciences. Nothing, the claim goes, can resist explanation by the methods characteristic of the natural sciences.

Hook and Nagel were clearly naturalists in the first three senses and some have argued, problematically I believe, that they were scientistic naturalists as well, though they clearly were not reductionists. They, that is, rejected *reductionist* physicalist or materialist views (Dewey, Hook, and Nagel 1945). I shall be concerned here principally with their *cosmological* naturalism and their *methodological* naturalism though I shall also briefly consider whether they are as well in any plausible sense *scientistic* naturalists and whether that would be a good thing. I shall not, however, consider their ethical naturalism except for some brief and noncommittal remarks concerning a certain criticism of their views. I do this because in considering the bearing of naturalism on religion and on metaphysics (ontology) that issue can be set aside. Some nonnaturalists in ethics (e.g., G. E. Moore and C. D. Broad) were cosmological naturalists and, as well, atheists and some theists (e.g., Jacques Maritain and Richard Neibuhr) were *ethical* naturalists. Both groups could consistently hold those positions (Couture and Nielsen 1995, 5–6; Frankena 1964, 446). More importantly, recall that many distinguished staunch cosmological naturalists and sometimes methodological naturalists as well were noncognitivists or error-theorists (projectivists) firmly rejecting ethical naturalism. In recent times past I refer to Bertrand Russell, Axel Hägerström, Ingemar Hedenius, Richard Robinson, A. J. Ayer, W. R. Dennes, Patrick Nowell-Smith, J. L. Mackie, and Charles Stevenson, and, among our actual contemporaries, to Simon Blackburn, Bernard Williams, and Alan Gibbard. Their *ethical* naturalism-unfriendly-noncognitivism or projectivism is every bit and as thoroughly naturalistic on the cosmological side as that of ethical naturalists such as Hook, Nagel, and Dewey or in our time Peter Railton or Richard Miller. Indeed the deep rationale for their noncognitivism or projectivism is their belief that a naturalistic world-perspective, which they are concerned to uphold, cannot accommodate values as truth claims. Values have more to do with attitudes (crudely, feelings) than with states affairs with their propositional expressions with truth-conditions or assertability-conditions. I rather ambivalently, and only recently, have come down, rather tentatively, on the side of ethical naturalism in the nuanced form it takes in the work of Peter Railton (Couture and Nielsen 1995, 285–96). But I need not and should not espouse that here in defending the cosmological claims of naturalism against religious challenges. I can, and should, in doing this, stand clear of metaethical issues and "the ontology of morals." Rather, traveling metaphysically light, like John Rawls, Norman Daniels, and Thomas Scanlon, I can, sticking with *wide reflective equilibrium*, make sense of the reasonableness and objectivity of morality without any metaethical commitments or commitments in the ontology of morals (Nielsen 1996). In examining the work of Hook and Nagel I shall so restrain myself concerning ethical naturalism, though they plainly, and perhaps correctly, did not. And this move on my part seems fully to be in the spirit of pragmatism and with what Nagel calls contextualist naturalism.

One further preliminary: Jean Hampton, who describes herself as "someone who is committed to being a Christian analytic philosopher," in an acute, powerful, and nuanced way has attacked naturalism in all its forms (Hampton 1998, xii). She argues we have no even nearly adequate understanding of what naturalism is. We have no notion of "natural" that has been precisely defined or clearly characterized such that in speaking as I have above of "natural entities" we have any reasonable understanding of how "natural" qualifies "entities" or what a nonnatural entity or property could be. She also argues, and relatedly, that we have "no commonly accepted statement of what makes a theory scientifically acceptable or unacceptable" (Hampton 1995, 107–34). I shall in the chapter that follows this one bring out succinctly the force of her arguments and consider if (a) in Hook's and Nagel's accounts there are the resources adequate to meet them or (b) whether, Hook and Nagel aside, there are adequate resources to meet them.[1]

II

Hook and Nagel were lifelong close friends. They were roughly of the same age, went as undergraduates to the City University of New York, did their doctoral work at the same time at Columbia University and studied there with such different naturalists as Morris R. Cohen, John Dewey, and F. J. E. Woodbridge. They were part of what has been called Columbia naturalism, a tradition which is represented today by Isaac Levi and Sidney Morgenbesser.

Nagel characterized his naturalism as a contextualistic naturalism and Hook characterized his as an experimental or pragmatic naturalism, though, as we shall see, they come to much the same thing (Nagel 1956, xviii; Hook 1961a, viii). I shall refer in this discussion principally to their canonical statements of naturalism occurring in certain essays in Hook's collections *The Quest for Being* and *Pragmatism and the Tragic Sense of Life* and in Nagel's collections *Logic without Metaphysics* and *Sovereign Reason*.

Writing in 1944 Nagel remarks that "perhaps the sole bond uniting all varieties of naturalists is that temper of mind which seeks to understand the flux of events in terms of the behaviors of identifiable bodies" (Nagel 1956, 55). He seeks to develop a naturalistic account consistent with that temper and the understanding that goes with it. He limits himself, in a good methodological naturalist manner, to obtaining knowledge about the world by employing the methods employed by the various empirical or mathematico-empirical sciences (e.g., social anthropology, on the one hand, and physics, on the other) and rejects claims to having "a priori insight into the most pervasive structure of things" or for that matter into having any such insight or knowledge of any facts or norms (Nagel 1956, 57). It is, in his words, "a naturalism free from speculative vagaries and committed to a wholehearted operational standpoint . . . [expressive of] the temper of modern mathematico-experimental science" (Nagel 1956, 57). Nagel rejects, for what are by now long familiar reasons, early logical empiricist formulations of the verifiability theory of meaning with its phenomenalist stress on direct verification by way of simple sense-constituents (sense-data or *qualia*). Such a restrictive theory of meaning would rule out knowledge of the past and render meaningless much of science such as when we speak of point particles, light waves, electrons, or genes. But in a good Peircean fashion, Nagel accepts "the pragmatic maxim that there is no difference between the objects of beliefs and conceptions where there is no possible difference in observable behavior" (Nagel 1956, 71). But, he quickly adds, with *early* logical empiricism in mind, I will "not therefore insist that all significant statements must be descriptive of what can be directly observed" (Nagel 1956, 71). There is no such conceptual connection between the pragmatic maxim and such a simplistic reductive and atomistic empiricism (Misak 1991, 3–45).

He also stresses—revealing in part what he means by calling his naturalism contextualist—that a "naturalism . . . based on scientific methods . . . must recognize that no formula can be constructed which will express once for all *'the meaning'* of any portion of scientific discourse, and instead of attempting to construct such formulae it must turn seriously to the analysis of specific uses and functions of specific systems of expressions in specific contexts" (Nagel 1956, 70). It is also evident that his naturalism is not only contextualistic, but, like Quine's, it is a holistic naturalism as well. Logical and mathematical concepts and the expressions of them "help to organize the conduct of empirical investigations in the interest of achieving certain specific ends" (Nagel 1956, 91), "statements in the sciences are systematically connected . . . *only systems of beliefs can be put to a definite test*" (Nagel 1956, 92, italics mine). Language is not like a mirror of existence or of nature such that "the articulation of adequate discourse must have a structure identical with the order and connection of things" (Nagel 1956, 92). His contextualist experimental naturalism is neither reductionistic nor atomist or pictorial. Rather like Quine's and Davdison's it is holistic. The "isolated portions of discourse possess significance only in terms of their place and function in the system of language habits" (Nagel 1956, 92). His conception of scientific method reflects that and with it, of course, the manner of his *methodological* naturalism. Keeping these considerations in mind, as we shall see later, is important in assessing some of the criticisms made of his and Hook's naturalism.

This gives us a sense of Nagel's *methodological* naturalism. But it reveals little about his *cosmological* naturalism except that, again like Quine's, it will not make claims that are distinct from scientific claims or a scientific world-perspective (Quine 1969, 26). It is not a *philosophical* naturalism distinct from science and articulating the underlying presuppositions (putative presuppositions) of science in some sort of independent ontology or metaphysics. Nagel, and Hook as well, will have no more truck with this than will Quine or Rorty.

This naturalism is an overall outlook of, or so Nagel has it, a scientific worldview, but a worldview that does not underpin or "stand outside" science. In his 1954 presidential address to the American Philosophical Association, he sought to state "as simply and succinctly" as he could "the substance of those intellectual commitments I like to call 'naturalism'" (Nagel 1956, 5). Like George Santayana, and, as we shall see, like Sidney Hook, that naturalism, as Nagel sees it, "merely formulates what centuries of human experience have repeatedly confirmed" (Nagel 1956, 6). He takes it to be a "sound generalized account of the world encountered in practice and in critical reflection" (Nagel 1956, 6).

What specific substantive cosmological conception does Nagel have? It is a view which goes beyond a purely methodological one, a metholodogical view utilizing in fixing belief what he and Hook—both following Peirce and Dewey—call the method of scientific intelligence. It proffers in addition a substantive view "on things in general" (Nagel 1956, 6). It is "a generalized account of the cosmic scheme and of man's place in it, as well as a logic of inquiry"—so we have in Nagel's account both what I have called a *cosmological* and a *methodological* naturalism (Nagel 1956, 6). And Nagel takes it to be supplying, while *not* being a distinctive philosophical view or a foundation for science, an "inclusive intellectual image of nature and man" which, in its distinctiveness, "sets it off from other comprehensive philosophies" (Nagel 1956, 6). Yet its logical status is rather puzzling for, unlike idealist, realist or Kantian metaphysical views, it does not claim to be a priori true or to be establishable by pure reflection or logical demonstration. It is not something we can provide a transcendental argument for. And, as we have just noted, it resolutely rejects a "general view of nature and man as the product of some special philosophical mode of knowing" (Nagel 1956, 6). Yet his cosmological naturalism is still a putatively substantive view. This is a view, puzzling as it is, that he shares with Hook and which they both share with their mentor, Dewey. It is not a claim of any of the sciences, but still there is no such thing on their view as a special philosophical claim or way of knowing that could yield some knowledge not attainable by science or serve as a ground for a guardianship or a monitoring of science. It has no such Kantian pretensions.

Here we see their cosmological and their methodological naturalism interlocked. But Nagel stresses that his naturalism is also not "a theory in the sense that Newtonian mechanics provides a theory of motion" (Nagel 1956, 6). He goes on to add that naturalism "does not . . . specify a set of substantive principles with the help of which the detailed course of concrete happenings can be explained or understood [or predicted]. Moreover, the principles affirmed by naturalism are not proposed as either competitors or underpinnings (foundations) for any of the special theories which the positive sciences assert." (Nagel 1956, 6) But this makes their logical status and conceptual role somewhat puzzling. They are neither the principles of a First Philosophy giving some distinct knowledge not obtainable by science nor are they very general scientific statements themselves.

The following remark by Nagel is meant to help clear up matters here, but it is not clear to me that it does. Nagel remarks

> The account of things proposed by naturalism is a distillation from knowledge acquired in the usual way in daily encounters with the world or in specialized scientific inquiry. Naturalism articulates features of the world which because they have become so obvious are rarely mentioned in discussions of special subject matter, but which distinguish our actual world from other conceivable worlds. The major affirmations of naturalisms are accordingly meager in content; but the principles affirmed are nevertheless effective guides in responsible criticism and evaluation. (Nagel 1956, 6–7)

In making this distillation Nagel comes up with two theses which he takes to be central to naturalism. The first is what he calls "the existential and causal primacy of organized matter in the executive order of nature" (Nagel 1956, 7). That is rather a mouthful, but Nagel translates it into the concrete as follows:

> This is the assumption that the occurrence of events, qualities and processes, and the characteristic behaviors of various individuals, are contingent on the organization of spatio-temporally located bodies, whose internal structures and external relations determine and limit the appearance and disappearance of everything that happens. (Nagel 1956, 7)

He adds "that this is so is one of the best-tested conclusions of experience" (Nagel 1956, 7).[2]

It is important to recognize that this naturalism is not a reductive materialism or a reductive naturalism (Nagel 1956, 7–9, 19–38). There are things noted in experience—"modes of action, relations of meaning, dreams, joys, plans, aspirations [which] are not as such material bodies or organizations of material bodies" (Nagel 1956, 7). What makes his view a naturalism in spite of being nonreductive is the following:

[What naturalism asserts] as a truth about nature is that though the forms of behavior or *functions of* material systems are indefeasibly parts of nature, forms and functions are not themselves agents in their own realization or in the realization of anything else. In the conception of nature's processes which naturalism affirms, there is no place for the operation of disembodied forces, no place for an immaterial spirit directing the course of events, no place for the survival of personality after the corruption of the body which exhibits it. (Nagel 1956, 7)[3]

The second central substantive thesis of naturalism, Nagel has it, is that of a *pluralism* rather than a *monism*. It is an irreducible feature of the cosmos that there is a variety of things with their different qualities and functions (Nagel 1956, 7–8). There is no homogeneous ground-floor, fundamental stuff, no "homogeneous ultimate reality," no substance that makes up the universe or transempirical substance that underpins or grounds the universe or is constitutive of the universe. The variety of discrete things, sometimes mundane, sometimes less so, are causally linked with each other but there is no substance in which all of them inhere. Nagel's naturalism is neither a monism nor an atomism but a pluralism where the links between the different things that make up the world are contingent and they are constantly changing. Human traits and human beings as well as other animal life and indeed nonanimal things are not everlasting and are "dependent on a balance of forces that doubtless will not endure indefinitely" (Nagel 1956, 8). All things including organisms are as much a part of the "ultimate" furniture of the world as atoms or neutrons or stones, stars or water. None are forever, nor are any of them "the ultimate stuff" (as if we understood what that meant), and all are part of integrated systems of bodies, including ones such as biological organisms "which have the capacity because of their material organization to maintain themselves and the direction of their characteristic activities" (Nagel 1956, 8). Irreducible "variety and logical contingency are fundamental traits of the world we actually inhabit" (Nagel 1956, 9).

It is in such a framework that naturalism envisages the career and destiny of human beings.[4] The emergence and the continuance of human society is "dependent on physical and physiological conditions that have not always obtained and that will not permanently endure" (Nagel 1956, 9). Human beings are biological organisms and as such are forms of organized matter. But there is biological evolution—naturalists follow Peirce and Dewey in taking Darwin seriously—and while human beings possess "characteristics which are shared by everything that exists" they also manifest "traits and capacities that appear to be distinctive" of them (Nagel 1956, 9). But the recognition of this gives us no grounds at all for trying to conceptualize human beings in some supernaturalist way as "intrusions into nature," whatever (if anything) that means (Nagel 1956, 9). While firmly regarding human beings as through and through a part of nature, naturalists "usually stress the emergence of novel forms in physical and biological evolution, thereby emphasizing the fact that human traits are not identical with the traits from which they emerge" (Nagel 1956). There is here no denigration (*pace* T. S. Elliot and C. S. Lewis) of human beings in naturalism or by naturalists. They need not, and most do not (including Hook and Nagel), think of human beings as nasty, clever little animals with unbounded selfishness. (There will be more of this later when I discuss Raphael Demos's critique of naturalism.)

III

Hook's views on naturalism are very similar to Nagel's. He also stresses, with his "experimental or pragmatic naturalism," *methodological* naturalism and he defends a *cosmological* naturalism that is pluralistic and nonreductionist in much the same way as is Nagel's (Hook 1961a, vii and 155). But more so than Nagel, he takes a leaf from ordinary language philosophers (what was once called Oxford philosophy) and attends carefully to ordinary language and to the confusions that result from not paying careful attention to the use of the terms of ordinary language and to the incoherencies that can result when we talk as Thomists do and as Paul Tillich does of Being, the unconditional ground of being, being-itself, being beyond essence and existence, and the like (Hook 1961a, 145–95; Hook 1961b, 59–64). Like Wittgenstein and ordinary language philosophers, he well realizes that language in such employments has gone on a holiday and that philosophers who talk like that have no coherent idea of what they are talking about (Hook 1961a, 148–60). But Hook, following Dewey, and again like Nagel, had what could be called a descriptive metaphysics—a thoroughly naturalistic putatively empirical metaphysics which sought to give a description of the generic traits of the natural world in contradistinction to specific traits of the world which are the subject-matter of the sciences.

However, like Nagel, the logical empiricists and the Classical pragmatists, Hook does not believe that we can establish anything about the nature of reality a priori or by definition. Indeed, for him, as for the classical pragmatists, a priori metaphysics is incoherent. There is no room in their accounts for transcendental arguments. And while he also spends a not inconsiderable amount of time showing that some metaphysical or ontological claims are incoherent, he nevertheless thinks that we can empirically establish what the generic traits of the world are and he believes we can make both true and false ontological statements of the empirical sort just described. They are "those statements or propositions which we believe to be cognitively valid, or which assert something that is true or false, and yet are not found in any particular science" (Hook 1961a, 168). But they are, all the same, Hook has it, empirical statements about our familiar empirical world.

These "ontological statements" are empirical truisms and, as Hook remarks, the facts they state are "ontological only because no science owns them" (Hook 1961a, 168). His examples, much like G. E. Moore's list of common-sense propositions, are these: "There are many colors in the world; Colors have no smell or sound; It is possible to perceive two things at the same time; There are many kinds of processes in the world; Some processes are evolutionary; Thinking creatures inhabit the earth" (Hook 1961a, 168). It should be realized, however, that what is asserted by these sentences is not what we were talking about in the previous paragraph. They do not refer to the generic traits of existence. But, on his account, propositions asserting the generic traits of existence are thought to be logically of the same type as the above empirical truisms.

As distinct from what is going on in descriptive metaphysics in characterizing the generic traits of existence, the role of *these* "ontological statements"—these "commonplaces or truisms"—is philosophically *therapeutic*. We deploy them as reminders when some metaphysician says something which is incompatible with them. Some philosopher says "Time is unreal" and we remind him that butterflies were caterpillars before they were butterflies or that people eventually die. Since these statements are true or at least we can be more confident that they are true than we can of "Time is unreal," we have a very good reason indeed for rejecting the philosopher's ontological claim.

Ontological statements have, for Hook, another use than the therapeutic one of "stocking our arsenals of sanity" (Hook 1961a, 170). We sometimes call attention to certain features of the world because they "have especial relevance to the career of human life on earth" (Hook 1961a, 170). Since they concern matters such as the life and death of human beings, they are anthropocentric, but neither antinaturalist nor unscientific or subjective for all of that. What kind of life can we *expect* to have? What kind of life can we reasonably hope to have? These questions—vague though they be—are deeply significant questions for us. (We saw something of this in chapters 3 and 4.) In thinking about what kind of life would be a flourishing life, given our contingency and our needs, and in thinking about our life and death, we are not, for the most part, or in some instances at all, engaging in a scientific activity or making scientific claims, but we, Hook contends, are not making claims that conflict with science or are incapable of public empirical confirmation. It is hyperbolic to say as Hook does that in doing these things we are articulating a "scientifically grounded *lebensphilosophie.*" But, whether we are or not, we are, Hook has it, making empirically testable claims without at all departing from a naturalistic orientation. Here we can see a facet of naturalism—indeed most particularly of the naturalism of Hook—that is plainly non-scientific, but not antiscientific or unscientific. This aspect of Hook's work should make us loath to apply the label "scientistic" to his philosophy.

The core cosmological claim of naturalism, which Hook believes is established by the scientific method, is "that the occurrence of all qualities or events depends upon the organization of a material system in space-time, and that their emergence, development and disappearance are deter-mined in such organization" (Hook 1961, 185–86; see also 202). Asked how we are to understand "material" here Hook remarks, in a way that Jean Hampton has criticized, that "naturalism as a philosophy takes it [i.e., the word "material"] to refer to the subject matter of the physical sciences" (Hook 1961a, 186; Hampton 1995). What physical sciences—more accu-rately the physical sciences of the time—take as their subject matter is what we will take to be material. Whatever problems we may have with that, we should remember that Hook's account, like Nagel's, is not reductionistic. Human beings are not, for most purposes, to be *described* in terms of physics or chemistry. Social anthropology will talk about human beings in a mentalistic vocabulary and our talking about ourselves as political and moral beings will also go on in those terms (Nielsen 1998a and this volume, chapter 2). But that notwithstanding, and consistently with its antireduc-tionism, "*naturalistic* humanism. . . . regards man as an integral but distinc-tive part of nature. . . . wholly a creature of natural origin and natural end" (Hook 1961a, 197). Moreover, and reasserting the centrality of method-ological naturalism again, Hook remarks that naturalism "does hold that where there is no evidence drawn from observed or observable effects, existence cannot be responsibly attributed. Otherwise the distinction between fact and fantasy disappears" (Hook 1961a, 205). He also makes it very clear that for him *methodological* naturalism rules it over *cosmological* naturalism: which categorial terms are taken to be basic—terms used to characterize the generic traits of nature—is determined, he believes, by the use of scientific method. Different naturalists will take different categories to be basic, but they will all agree on the use of the scientific method as the proper way of fixing belief—including belief concerning which categorial terms to adopt.[5] "The analysis of this method may be made in terms of cat-egories like thing, structure, function, power, act, cause, relation, quantity, and event. The choice of which categories to take as basic in describing a method depends upon the degree to which they render coherent and fruitful what we learn by the use of [scientific] method" (Hook 1961a, 191). With this we can clearly see why Hook calls his naturalism an experimental or pragmatic naturalism.

IV

I now turn to some of their contemporaries who took issue with them. Naturalism for Hook and Nagel was, at least not in intent, a dogma or an a priori truth, but they did think, while remaining resolute fallibilists, that, as Nagel put it, their naturalistic tenets are supported by compelling empirical evidence (Nagel 1956, 12). Indeed they took it to be conclusively established. Is it?

Others, not unsurprisingly, thought otherwise. The critics whose views I shall examine in this chapter—all roughly their contemporaries—are O. K. Bouwsma, Arthur E. Murphy, and Raphael Demos. I choose them not randomly but for the distinctive places on a spectrum of responses to naturalism that they represent. Bouwsma was a kind of laid back Wittgensteinian who, as something of a Woody Allen of philosophy, liked to josh people out of their philosophical positions. In this he was a predecessor of Richard Rorty. (But it is important to remember that they not only josh, they also argue.) That notwithstanding Bouwsma was also a firm Calvinist (showing that all Calvinists need not be dour) though he thought that his religious commitments were rather independent of his distinctively philosophical commitments. Arthur Murphy, though also deeply influenced by Wittgenstein, though hardly a Wittgensteinian, was much more of a systematic philosopher than Bouwsma and perhaps, in contrast to Bouwsma, overly earnest and moralistic. But that notwithstanding he was a careful and perceptive thinker and not just a sweet singer (Nielsen 2001). While sharing the contextualist approach of the pragmatists and (Peirce apart) their rejection of metaphysics, he was in certain respects deeply critical of the pragmatists and this carries over to Hook's and Nagel's pragmatic naturalism and instrumentalism (Murphy 1993, 144–78, 330–68, 688–722; Murphy 1963, 200–14). Raphael Demos, a Harvard philosophy professor, was a traditional Christian philosopher who, not unsurprisingly, took a traditionalist stance, both philosophically and religiously, toward the naturalism of Hook and Nagel. In his criticisms of naturalism we find a traditional metaphysician and orthodox Christian speaking, though with a somewhat distinctive twist (Demos 1945, 1953, 1960). I shall try to do something to sort out what these diverse criticisms come to and to see at least something of where it leaves naturalism.

I will start with Bouwsma. Bouwsma concentrates on what I have called *methodological* naturalism. He in good Wittgensteinian fashion sees it as embodying a nest of conceptual confusions and regards the so-called issue or cluster of issues between naturalists and nonnaturalists as being without issue—as being without rational point. Again, on his view, we have more "houses of cards"—the usual fate, Wittgensteinians have it, of philosophical constructions.

Bouwsma has great fun with the naturalist's claim, as expressed by Hook, that what unites naturalists is "the wholehearted acceptance of scientific method as the *only* reliable way of reaching truth about the world, nature, society, and man. The least common denominator of all historic naturalism, therefore, is not so much a set of specific doctrines as the method of scientific or rational empiricism" (Bouwsma 1965, 71–72, quoting Hook 1944, 45). It is a method which is taken by naturalists to have universal applicability and it is (as Hook put it) "the only reliable way of reaching truth."

Why is this so, if indeed it is so, asks Bouwsma? The answer of pragmatic naturalists, he maintains, is that only scientific method is successful. To this Bouwsma first trots out a standard antinaturalist counter: logic and mathematics are successful; they yield knowledge, and indeed, firmly established knowledge, but these disciplines are not empirical disciplines. So, after all, we have some knowledge that is not established by the scientific method. If the naturalist responds by saying that what they yield is not really "knowledge," he is merely stipulating, and arbitrarily so (Bouwsma 1965, 76–77). But this criticism is plainly beside the point. Nagel makes it quite clear in his "Logic without Ontology" that he, unlike J. S. Mill and W. V. Quine, does not take logic and mathematics to be empirical disciplines and he makes it equally clear that his conception of scientific method includes as integral parts—and indeed as "cognitive parts"—logic and mathematics. They are the analytic and a priori component of science and we could not have science without them (Nagel 1956, 55–92). Hook would say much the same thing. So methodological naturalism is not vulnerable on that count.[6]

A distinct cluster of criticisms made by Bouwsma of naturalism is more indirect, but they also have more force. He begins by asking whether the sentences defining naturalism are exclamatory, empirical, or tautological (Bouwsma 1965, 75). If the naturalist tries to say that his sentence "The scientific method is the only reliable way of reaching truth" is itself an empirical claim, then it could, and should, be responded that though scientific method is often a successful way of fixing belief, still we have no proof or even a confirmation that it is the *only* reliable way of fixing belief or of reaching truth or of what reliably can be taken for truth. As Bouwsma put it, giving it a somewhat different spin than I just have,

> . . . we also know that scientific method has never been justified from a purely intellectual point of view . . . [and] that this request for a justification involves a question which cannot possibly be answered by any such method. If you tried to answer it in this way, your method would, of course, give rise to the same request. Hence, unless we admit that there are altogether reasonable questions, but no method at all for

answering them, there must be at least one method other than scientific method alone for answering questions. And so it is not true that scientific method alone is successful. (Bouwsma 1965, 79)

As Bouwsma well recognizes, the naturalist has a ready response to this. The naturalist's critic in asking for proof here—from "a purely intellectual point of view" (whatever that is)—is simply "assuming that a good argument must be like a syllogism or like a proof in geometry" (Bouwsma 1965, 42, 79). But that is rationalism, not naturalism, running wild. Not everything that is "proved," rationally established, pragmatically vindicated, if you will, can be proved like that (Feigel 1950). To claim that it must be is just arbitrarily persuasively to define "proof." We do not, as Hook has remarked, have to know things such as in nature every event has a cause or that we can give a general proof of induction to come to reliable conclusions using a reliable method concerning bridges, hydrogen, vitamins, earthquakes, or global warming. This knowledge is, of course, fallible and subject to correction, but is all the same generally reliable. And this obtains no matter what we say about the uniformity of nature or the law of the excluded middle or determinism. For the vindication of the scientific method there is no need for anything beyond this. We need no skyhooks that give us necessity or certainty and it is pointless to go around looking for them. But there is success here where there is not with the other methods.

This claim, Bouwsma remarks, for "the success of scientific method is something so modest that it requires no such justification [e.g., geometrical-like proof]. It is justified, if you like, in the same way that your expectations generally are. If you expect to eat at six, and you do eat at six, what more do you want?" (Bouwsma 1965, 79–80). Bouwsma concludes

> This reply is, I take it, sufficient. Refutation [of naturalism] has failed. If you claim for science that its arguments require some necessary propositions about the order of nature, then obviously the justification of these arguments will require them. But the naturalist's account of scientific method need not involve any such necessary propositions. So once again that scientific method is successful does not presuppose that there is besides this some other method. (Bouwsma 1965, 80)

However, Bouwsma thinks, though the naturalist is not refuted nor can he be, the dispute between naturalism and their opponents is perfectly pointless. Indeed, he has it, there is no rational dispute. Both sides are being fervent about different things. But it is all sound and fury signifying nothing. It is as if they had different loves. They use "proof" in different ways and have *different criteria for success*. The nonnaturalist or antinaturalist philosopher has a theory and with it a method—he has a different love—that does not enable him to make predictions either of the weather or anything else, but he has different criteria than the naturalist for success. And he is trying to catch a different cat or, better, a different *kind* of animal.

Moreover, to return to the question about the logical status of a main thesis of naturalism, i.e., that the scientific method is the *sole* reliable way of justifying beliefs. We have seen that it cannot be refuted "by detecting any contradiction, nor by adducing any evidence" (Bouwsma 1965, 81). But—or so Bouwsma has it—here is the rub: "You cannot do this because there is no thesis" (Bouwsma 1965, 81). Why is this so? Because the main thesis of naturalism does not express a basic belief, or indeed any belief, of naturalists or anyone else, because there "is no belief at all. There is no belief because nothing has been said which could be false" (Bouwsma 1965, 82).[7] It is not an analytic truth and thus true by definition or in any other way (if there is another way) an a priori truth. But it cannot, on the other hand, be *contingently* true if it cannot be false. But, Bouwsma has it, we have no idea of what it would be like for it to be false. And this is so, to add insult to injury, according to the very verificationist rules that Hook and Nagel attribute to what Hook calls *scientific empiricism*. What we need to recognize, Bouwsma contends, is that the main naturalist thesis does not make either a true or a false statement either a priori or empirical. It should instead be treated as "an enunciation of policy" as Rudolf Carnap and Carl Hempel came to treat the testability (more crudely the verifiability) theory of cognitive meaning. In the case of the main thesis of naturalism, it should be taken as in effect saying "'Let us be scientific' and negatively 'No more metaphysics'" (Bouwsma 1965, 82).

We need to ask then, "Is methodological naturalism a good policy?" Is it a proposal we should accept? The naturalist could, in the spirit of the early Peirce, reply thus: Philosophers have tried metaphysics; they have tried ways other than scientific for fixing belief, for ascertaining what we might reasonably take to be true or to take for truth or to be warrantedly assertable. But, at least during the modern period with its extensive pluralism, there never has been with these other methods of fixing belief anything but local and temporary agreement with no progress in the direction of a reflective and informed consensus. (The Middle Ages might have been a different matter.) The scientific method, though through and through fallibilistic, works and carries with it a considerable consensus about its working. So if we want to be reasonable we will stick with the scientific method and leave metaphysics to spirit-seers and other crazies.

To this it could in turn be responded that naturalists are assuming that metaphysics and science are aiming at the same thing. And, thinking this, they see that metaphysics fails while science succeeds. But this is like complaining that a good potato peeler is not a good corkscrew. Why should we assume, or even desire, that science and metaphysics aim at the same thing? In turn the naturalist could respond that even if it were true that metaphysics and science do not aim at the same thing, it is clear that "metaphysics fails in whatever it aims at, whereas science succeeds. How foolish, to engage in failure. So in either case naturalism is the best policy" (Bouwsma 1965, 82). So, after all, the naturalist is vindicated.

Bouwsma counsels that this is not the end of the matter. Philosophers will dispute over whether metaphysics and science aim at the same thing and over whether metaphysics is a failure. Moreover, must we, or even should we, say, for example, where we do not have a consensus, that we have a failure? How do we—or do we—know that without consensus there must be failure? These questions are, he grants, obscure but they press down on us all the same. Given what at least appears to be the human significance of these issues, Bouwsma finally chances his arm: "metaphysics and science do not aim at the same thing [he declaims]. Metaphysics arises out of the fact that men come to have a variety of beliefs, beliefs about God, about how they should live, about the material world, about their own other-worldly destiny, etc." (Bouwsma 1965, 82–83). Some people have set aside such beliefs—or nearly all of them. But most people live with them, somehow in some way they make up their minds and hearts about them, or are at least sometimes uneasy. In the face of this some have, understandably enough, tried to prove that certain of these metaphysical beliefs are true. In this, Bouwsma avers, they have failed and naturalists are right to point this out. There is, Bouwsma has it, no criterion of proof or warrant in metaphysics. There is, he remarks, among metaphysicians no agreement upon even one purported proof or warrant. If, then, the purpose of metaphysics is to prove or justify their stances, "metaphysics provides no intelligible account of what this could be" (Bouwsma 1965, 83). Here, Calvinist though he be, he is clearly one with Rudolf Carnap as well as with Hook and Nagel (Carnap 1959, original German publication 1932).

But—there always seems to be a "but" in philosophy and *perhaps* rightly so—the above is not, Bouwsma avers, the whole of the story. Wilfrid Sellars, as firm a naturalist as Hook or Nagel, characterized "philosophy"—taking it in its most general and least contested way—to be "an attempt to see how things, in the broadest possible sense of the term, hang together, in the broadest sense of the term" (Sellars 1963, 1–40). Bouwsma gives, acceptingly, a characterization of metaphysics that has an affinity to Sellars's characterization of philosophy, but in some ways goes beyond it. People, he remarks, in their various perplexities, variously engendered, have tried "to weave together the contents of their beliefs into some coherent pattern, to keep more steadfastly before their minds the scene of their hopes, their aspirations and their fears"

(Bouwsma 1965, 83). The great systems of speculative philosophy and natural theology—metaphysical schemes we have inherited from the tradition of philosophy—presented themselves in turgid, obscure, and often incoherent ways. Indeed they were often not only obscure but obscurantist as well. But this need not be so. Varieties of belief held by people feeling the need, if they can manage anything like this, to make sense of their tangled lives and of their social world, will continue, as Bouwsma puts it with a fine metaphor, to be elaborated and to result in the fashioning of a "crazy or a sane quilt in which to wrap oneself against all temporary weathers" (Bouwsma 1965, 83).

Bouwsma will not, and in my view rightly, turn his back on such endeavors as resting on a mistake, as reflecting *mere* confusions that a rational tough-minded person would free herself from. And in the case of one such scheme—presumably a Christian Calvinist one—Bouwsma will even, as he puts it, love it. But, again like Carnap, but hardly in the spirit of positivism, he thinks, as does Rush Rhees as well, that a "metaphysics with this single aim will, when successful, to be much more like poetry or a novel than like the metaphysics which, with divided and obscure aims, has puzzled and pleased men in the past" and—I would add—has led some of them to turn away from metaphysics with either Carnapian scorn or Rortyan joshing.

So what, in the light of this, is Bouwsma's verdict on naturalism? He succinctly enunciates it in his final paragraph:

> Naturalism, as a policy, is then no mystery. It has seized upon a certain clear notion of proof, and in the light of this clear notion of proof it is easy to see from what defect metaphysics has come to be sick. Metaphysics will walk again only when it surrenders pretension to proof and, as humbly as the Apostles' Creed, begins its words with: I believe! (Bouwsma 1965, 83)

What should we say about this verdict or more generally of this critique of Bouwsma's? If metaphysics is like poetry or a novel it is a very bad likeness. It is, that is, very bad literature. It takes, however turgidly and obscurely, an argumentative form and tries to provide reasons for its claims. And it hardly has the descriptive, interpretive, and narrative style of poetry, drama, or a novel. Bouwsma is on the mark in stressing that it is not science or even very like science. And he is also right to say that, where it understands what it is doing, it does not have such aims. It is also the case that it cannot provide geometry-like proofs—recall Fredrich Waismann's remark that it is salutary and sobering to consider the number of theorems proved in philosophy (Waismann 1968, 1–38). But it neither follows from these considerations nor do they in any way vindicate the claim that it is like poetry, drama, or a novel. There is no either/or here. It, as I remarked, normally takes an argumentative form with "ifs" and "thens" and the like. And this is not incidental to how metaphysicians see their task. They do not just dish out what they take to be their insights. They do (or often do), as some philosophers have recently rightly stressed, place their arguments and accounts in something like a narrative form and they typically have a vision, as William James never tired of telling us, and, as Hook stressed, they articulate a *lebensphilosophie* (Hook 1974, 3–25). This Bouwsma nicely expresses with his sentence about fashioning a crazy or a sane quilt in which to wrap oneself against all temporary weathers. But he should not say that metaphysics is poetry or like poetry or like the novel. It is not even like an anthropologist's just-so stories. Rather *we* should say, coming down on the antimetaphysical side, that we should drop metaphysics. But we still should keep something of the spirit of Bouwsma's account. In weaving together the contents of our beliefs into some coherent pattern to wrap ourselves against temporary weathers and to give coherent and reflective expression to our hopes and aspirations, we should give what is broadly construed a normatively structured (though still argument-supported and empirical evidence–sensitive) narrative account of human life (including, of course, our lives in society and its possibilities). In doing that we do something a little more like, though certainly not identical with, what is often done in novels or drama. It should provide a kind of narrative very different from metaphysics and very *lebensphilosophie*-friendly. That is what is needed. We need something more in the spirit of Shakespeare, George Elliot, or Turgenev than that of Leibniz, Bradley, or McTaggart. Some philosophers, namely Spinoza, Hume, Feuerbach, Marx, Santayana, and Dewey, have given powerful narratives, though hardly on the model of literature, and with this something of the weaving and unweaving and the coherent articulating of beliefs and attitudes, including, and centrally, beliefs about how we should live. In doing this they are doing the sort of thing that Bouwsma to my mind rightly commends.[8] But note the above-mentioned philosophers who have done this are all in the naturalistic tradition of which Hook and Nagel sought to give a succinct programmatic and in some ways canonical articulation. They tried to articulate a sharply delineated conception of what others have done without very much (Hume and Dewey apart) in the way of such a programmatic conceptualization. And only Spinoza and Santayana among these classical naturalists placed their vision of things—their seeing of how things hang together and the human point of their so hanging—in a metaphysical form and it is not unreasonable to believe that Spinoza and Santayana succeed in spite, not because, of their metaphysics.

What Bouwsma has retrieved as "metaphysics as poetry" is neither metaphysics nor poetry but philosophy, as we saw Wilfrid Sellars conceiving it, though hardly practicing it, as something that (a) is compatible with seeing philosophy as something which need not even be tied to a disciplinary matrix and where we can properly see Henry James, Ralph Waldo Emerson, and Henry David Thoreau as much more philosophical than Saul Kripke, Jerry Fodor, or David Lewis, and (b) where we can see philosophy, so conceived, as integral to the ways Hook and Nagel do philosophy and to how James and Dewey did philosophy before them (Rorty 1982; see also section V of chapter 9, this volume).

I would also maintain concerning these matters that we cannot simply—or even not so simply—commend saying "I believe" as Bouwsma does at the end of his essay for, as he also says, a little earlier in his essay and I have cited perhaps *ad nauseam*, it is possible to "fashion a *crazy* or a *sane* quilt in which to wrap oneself against all temporary weathers" (Bouwsma 1965, 83, italics added). Such fashioning indeed requires belief—here involving endorsement—but for the quilt to come out *sane* rather than *crazy* also requires *reflective* and *knowledgeable* endorsement as something that both has those normative effects and as something which actually hangs together. It requires the concentrated effort to be reasonable and to effectively utilize what Dewey called creative intelligence. But this is not all that it requires. It requires imagination and empathy as well and much more. But it does require this commitment to rationality or better reasonability. Rationality or reasonability are, of course, not everything, but they are a very important something in helping to protect us against all temporary weathers (Rawls 1999, 573–615; Nielsen 1998b). But this is no reversion to rationalism or to metaphysics as usually understood. Understood, that is, in such a way that "rationalistic metaphysics" is pleonastic. We can well say goodbye to metaphysics without becoming either scientistic or religiose or foolishly batting our heads against science.

V

I now turn to examining the critique of naturalism made by Arthur E. Murphy. While Bouwsma zeroes in on what I have called Hook's and Nagel's *methodological* naturalism, Murphy zeroes in on both their *methodological* naturalism and their *cosmological* naturalism and on the connection between them. He maintains that their naturalism presents itself as a systematic philosophical claim "rivaling in its pretension to comprehensive and exclusive validity in all areas of human experience the great 'isms' of the past" (Murphy 1963, 213). It seeks in all domains "to distinguish reliable knowledge from speculative imagination"—knowledge from fantasy as Hook puts it—and to articulate a set of basic categories of naturalism which, "if they are taken as a basis of philosophical criticism all theories incompatible with naturalism can be 'critically' eliminated" (Murphy 1963, 213). He thinks such pragmatic naturalists often substitute zeal for reform for sober philosophical analysis and that they, with such reformist zeal, tend to identify philosophers committed to freedom of inquiry with those philosophers who are naturalists forgetting that there are idealists such as Brand Blanshard and E. S. Brightman who are every bit as committed to the freedom of inquiry as are naturalists. Naturalists, Murphy further claims, adopt a method which actually blocks the road to inquiry their contrary intentions notwithstanding.

Whatever may or may not be true of some naturalists Hook and Nagel are not guilty of the first two charges and as for naturalism blocking the road to inquiry, Hook, I believe, has adequately responded to that charge (Hook 1961a, 186–87). I shall without argument set these issues aside. Murphy, however, has deeper critical questions to put to naturalism, and it is those with which I shall be concerned. Murphy claims that for naturalism "to justify the claim of scientific method to exclusive and unlimited cognitive validity, the 'naturalist' needs a *philosophically justifiable philosophy*" and that, Murphy argues, naturalism has not produced (Murphy 1963, 214, italics added).

No reasonable person will dispute that science and the use of its methods gives us reliable knowledge. But it is another thing again to claim, Murphy avers, "that no *other* procedure is philosophically legitimate, that the truth which it [science] achieves is the one type of knowledge and truth, the only truth by which men can live well" (Murphy 1963, 206). Naturalists claim that their being committed to this view is rationally warranted on philosophical grounds and that they are not just cheerleading for science. What is this rational warrant and how good is it?

It is in considering this where Murphy turns to the substantive claims of *cosmological* naturalism. Naturalism sets out to accept only natural categories and to reject all supernatural or transempirical categories and to show how this is justified. The naturalism defended by Hook and Nagel and before them Dewey seeks, as we have seen for Hook and Nagel, to do this while remaining thoroughly antireductionist. Of course, if in its aversion to reductionism, it simply says whatever we encounter in whatever way is natural, then, to put it minimally, little is accomplished. We must have some way of demarcating which categories count as natural and which as supernatural or nonnatural and to show that the former alone are real or nonillusory. Traditionally naturalists simply claimed that their basic category was matter or material substance and that that alone had independent existence. But with the development of physics in the twentieth century such a notion has become, to put it mildly, nonexplanatory (see R. W. Sellars 1944 and 1949 for such a traditionalist naturalist or materialist view). There is only a trace of the old materialism in Nagel's articulation of the *cosmological* claim of naturalism previously quoted, namely the thesis of "the existential and causal primacy of organized matter in the executive order of nature" (Nagel 1956, 7). This, as Nagel avers, partially translated into the concrete and freed of the obscurities of the old materialism, "is the assumption that the occurrence of events, qualities, and processes, and the characteristic behaviors of various individuals are contingent on the organization of spatio-temporally located bodies, whose internal structures and external relations determine and limit the appearance and disappearance of everything that happens" (Nagel 1956, 7). Bringing cosmological naturalism and methodological naturalism together, Nagel avers "that this is so is one of the best-tested conclusions of experience" (Nagel 1956, 7).[9] Hook's position, as we have also seen, is basically the same as Nagel's. Naturalism, he has it, on its substantive side, is the thesis "that the occurrence of all qualities or events depends upon the organization of a material system in space-time and their emergence, development, and disappearance are determined by changes in such organization" (Hook 1961a, 185–86). To square his account with contemporary physics and to avoid nineteenth-century difficulties, Hook takes (as we have seen) "material" to refer to "the subject matter of the physical sciences" (Hook 1961a, 186).[10]

So this is what Hook and Nagel take the categories of naturalism to be. Murphy most centrally on this issue takes the basically similar but somewhat more explicit account of another naturalist, William R. Dennes, as his principal subject for examination and critique; but what he says of Dennes applies as well to Hook and Nagel. Their views are very similar. Dennes takes the basic categories of naturalism to be *event, relation*, and *quality* and it is the factors of process, quality, and relation "which contemporary naturalism takes to be the constituents of all that occurs, of all that exists" (Dennes 1944, 282; see, as well, Dennes 1960). On such an account the explanation of a natural event could not require an extranatural cause or ground. What would be the cause of an event would be, indeed could be, on such an account, only another event, for the constituents of all that is real are events, relations, or qualities and the processes that go with them. (Qualities and relations being qualities and relations of events.) When we ask for a cause we are asking for some stretch of natural processes (a distinctive relation between events) and an explanation of events could only be found in the qualities and relations of such events. This is, Murphy remarks, almost tautologically so *if* events, qualities, and relations are basically, or in the final analysis, the constituents of all there is. If this naturalistic claim is right then nothing else at all could serve as an explanation (Murphy 1963, 207). So the fundamental naturalistic claim, Murphy has it, is the momentous one that "nature is all, that natural processes (including those of human living) do not imply anything beyond themselves and do not require for their existence or for their explanation any grounds but the further stretches of natural processes which we observe or inductively infer to be their contexts, that in the world in which there is one event (that is, in which anything happens) we can distinguish and significantly infer or speculatively suppose nothing but further events and their relations and qualities" (Murphy 1963, 207, quoting Dennes 1944, 288).

How can such a claim be justified or how could, what comes very much to the same thing, Hook's or Nagel's statement of their basic naturalistic cosmological claim be justified, be shown to be something we should take to be true? We certainly cannot, without being arbitrary, just postulate or stipulate it. And a naturalist, of course, does not want to take it as a dogma either. And he certainly does not want to regard it as a synthetic a priori truth that we somehow know by intuition. But to treat such fundamental naturalistic claims as very general empirical hypotheses we would have to be able to say what it would be like for them to be false or at least to be able to say what it would be like to infirm them. But can we do so? Do we even know how to go about trying to do so? We are here back to questions very much like some of those Bouwsma pressed. Murphy puts a related point thus:

> A philosophy that limits you to talking about events, relations, and qualities leaves you free, on scientific evidence, to frame any hypothesis you please about events, relations, and qualities. But it does not leave you free to frame hypotheses about time-transcending substances. That, however, is no real limitation, provided that you are already committed to a metaphysics of events, relation, and quality and have decided that these are the constituents of all that exists. It is indeed a truism to say that the factor of process cannot be excluded from events. But that is because the question of the relation of process to existence has already been settled in the dictum that the only existents are qualified and related events. (Murphy 1963, 209)

But again the question returns, like the return of the repressed, how do we know that the only existents are qualified and related events? We cannot say, if we are naturalists, that we intuit it. Peirce has well blocked such an appeal to what is "agreeable to reason." If we say instead that it is an empirical claim then, as an empirical claim, we must be able to state its test conditions, i.e., its truth-conditions or at least its assertability-conditions. But then it must be possible to say what it would be like for that statement (i.e., that the only existents are qualified and related events) to be false or to at least say what would count as disconfirming or at least infirming instances of it. If we say the observation, direct or indirect, of a spiritual substance would so count naturalists will deny that that could be a genuine falsification or disconfirming instance because such substances are not discoverable or in anyway ascertainable by the use of scientific method—even *in principle* by the use of scientific method. They are not observable or inferable from what is observable. Why not "even in principle"? Because, given our choice of basic categories, namely the categories of event, relation, and quality, no such spiritual substances are recognizable or acceptable or even coherently describable *given such categories*. But isn't such an appeal question-begging? Why accept this naturalistic set of categories or any set of categories similar to it rather than Aristotelian ones or Christian ones? Suppose we say we should do so because that is the way things are and things are as they are whatever we may say of them or think about them. Indeed we must, if we wish to be nonevasive, *select our categories to fit the facts*. And it is our naturalistic categories that fit the facts. But again the question comes trippingly off the tongue, how do we know, or even warrantedly believe, that that is so? Do we just intuit it? Do we *without categories* just observe it to be so? But how could we possibly make *such* observations? Moreover, and perhaps more fundamentally, what do we *mean* when we say a set of categories fits or fails to fit the facts? We have little in the way of lucidity here. Indeed it does not look like we have anything coherent here.

If we say, alternatively, that this choice of categories is just a very fundamental linguistic or conceptual choice, what Carnap would call a choice of framework, a proposal concerning how to talk and how to conceptualize things, we can in turn ask, why make this choice, why accept this proposal, why adopt this framework? We cannot say, if we take this turn, because this proposal tells it like it is, enables us just to ascertain how things are. Because that would be plainly question-begging for it is a proposal concerning how to conceptualize things and, with that conceptual apparatus, to speak and think of how things are. If we say instead, like Carnap and on some readings Peirce, that we judge such proposals on pragmatic terms in terms of their success we are back to what we discussed before. "Success according to what?" Success in enabling us to make accurate predictions and retrodictions or success in gaining surcease from sorrow? Or success according to something altogether different? If we say "Forget about surcease from sorrow and other such coping and stick with successful predictions and retrodictions—stay in 'the cognitive domain,' " it is perfectly relevant to in turn respond that there are, as well, other things we human beings care about and would reflectively continue to care about. There are other endorsements that we could reflectively make. Moreover, we do not want pervasively to play fast and loose with "cognitive." Why are not reflective moral and other evaluational endorsements cognitive? We must not have too narrow a criterion for success if we would be reasonable.

Moreover, and all that aside, naturalists—or so at least it would seem—do not want to take the statement "The only existents are qualified and related events" as a proposal but as a synthetic statement of the way things are. (Note it hardly looks like a proposal.) But we are again back to the question how does, or does, the naturalist know or warrantedly believe that is the way things are? How could such a claim be confirmed or disconfirmed or even infirmed?

Suppose we say that the error is in our trying to think that we can determine what are the facts of the matter—the way things are—independently of a choice of basic categories, independently of the conceptual framework adopted. To think that, we say, is an illusion that naturalism should not succumb to. Naturalists should not take "The only existents are qualified and related events" as a synthetic statement, either empirical or a priori, of the way things are, or worse still of the way things must be, however tempting the former may be, but as a fundamental proposal about how best to describe things at a very basic level and to conceptualize the world. We should not be fooled by its surface grammar into thinking it makes sense to take it as anything other than a *proposal* about how to conceptualize and categorize the world. There are, we should realize, just different ways of talking and coping with things, things, none of which are specifiable or even thinkable independently of some particular conceptual framework with its categories, which are not *found* but just somehow "*chosen*"—perhaps as the result of "historical choices"—choices made, and in return repeatedly modified, over a long period of time which by now are so firmly socialized in us that they do not feel like choices at all.

This "Kantian-historicist" turn—this "historicist-Kantian" turn, if you will—may be more troublesome than many naturalists recognize, including this naturalist. But if it has the clear implication, that it at least *appears* to have, that it entails some form of *linguistic idealism*, then it is *a reductio* forcing us back to the drawing board. It would seem that, like Richard Rorty and Hilary Putnam have attempted to do, we must be able to say and show that it has no such idealist entailments or implications if it is properly understood or alternatively we need to be able to say that we must understand things in some very different ways, thoroughly non-Kantian, nonhistoricist ways (Rorty 1991; Putnam 1992). But then what ways? We seem still to be in search of a proper form of naturalism.

VI

Sidney Hook's "Naturalism and First Principles" is a canonical statement of naturalism (Hook 1961a, 172–95). In it he makes some direct responses to Murphy, and to Demos as well. Indeed his essay could reasonably be read as an extended (albeit indirect) response to Murphy's critique and I shall so read it and examine it for resources adequately to so respond to the critique by Murphy which I stated and extended a bit. This will include a consideration of whether he has an adequate response to the above mentioned problems about linguistic idealism.

Before we look at Hook's counter let me remind you of two central claims made by Murphy: (1) Naturalists, he claims, "have bypassed philosophy in its most important function, which is that of *justifying* philosophical categories as rationally and comprehensively as possible" (Murphy 1963, 210) and (2) Naturalists, "having committed themselves in advance to a position which identifies reasonable procedure with that which does not differ 'sharply' from that of the more fully developed sciences, . . . will limit the scope of reasonable inquiry to what can be settled by the methods these sciences employ" (Murphy 1963, 211). Murphy, as we have seen, regards this as a mistake on the part of naturalists. So how does Hook respond to Murphy's critique and is his response adequate?

Murphy takes it that it is crucial that a sound philosophy be clear about *its own presuppositions* and be able to justify them and with them justified then use them as comprehensively as possible to justify its philosophical categories.[11] This is what, Murphy has it, a sound philosophy must do. Indeed, he even goes so far as to claim that this is the most important function of philosophy. Hook *au contraire* thinks we often should bypass a consideration of our endlessly conflicting first principles and (what may come to the same thing) set aside a search for our underlying presuppositions. Furthermore, we should keep steadfastly in mind that, in spite of the endemic disagreement over fundamentals, "there are working truths on the level of practical affairs which are everywhere recognized and which everywhere determine the pattern of reasonable conduct in secular affairs, viz., the effective use of means to achieve ends" (Hook 1961a, 172).[12] What we have here in its core essentials is not, Hook argues, just a matter of something that our tribe with its developed scientific institutions has, but is something which in at least a rudimentary form is pancultural (Hook 1961a, 189–91).

Hook makes it clear right from the start that he is not claiming that the assumptions of naturalism are necessarily true, but that he is claiming that they are more reasonable than their alternatives (Hook 1961a, 174). Murphy is not looking, any more than Hook is, for necessary truth nor for a strictly logical justification—proof—here. So we can set those things aside. Murphy and Hook do not divide over them, but Murphy would argue that (*pace* Hook) naturalism has not been established as more reasonable than its alternatives. Perhaps it is, but that it is, he avers, has not been shown.

Hook tries to establish contextualist naturalism's greater reasonability by first challenging the necessity or even the prime importance of establishing first principles, naturalistic or otherwise. "That first principles must be justified," he remarks, "before we can achieve assured knowledge is a view seemingly held by some philosophers but rarely by anyone else. Scientists, for example, have satisfactorily solved problem after problem without feeling called upon to solve the problem of justifying their first principles" (Hook 1961a, 174). We do not need to know what the correct principles of scientific reasoning are or what are the basic presuppositions of science or of everyday life to know that a certain germ has more to do with the cause of tuberculosis than the climate or that yellow fever is not contagious but is caused by the bites of certain mosquitoes. Similarly we do not have to have a worked out ethical theory, or even any ethical theory at all, to know that inflicting suffering on dogs or cats just for the fun of it is wrong and that treating people with respect is good. We are more confident of the warrant of those beliefs, scientific and moral, than of any first principles that people might appeal to for their justification (Hook 1961a, 124). Here Hook is one with G. E. Moore, the Moore *not* of *Principia Ethica*, but of his later writings in defense of common sense. But again Murphy would agree (Murphy 1964).

That we need not justify our first principles before having assured knowledge of such common sense matters still allows us reasonably to be agnostic about naturalism or, for that matter, its denial. So that *in itself* will not help the naturalist's case. Indeed it might incline us to be Wittgensteinian or Bouwsmanian about such philosophical beliefs and the need for justification here. Moreover, and distinctly, it would not show that *in addition* the justification of such first principles was *not* itself an important enterprise even though our ordinary beliefs do not hang on such first principles. Justification, if it could be had, of such first principles would still be a *desideratum*. Hook only asserts in a good critical commonsensical manner that we can have justified beliefs in many practical domains without justifying any first principles or even knowing what they are. He does not say that their justification is not important or that they cannot be justified, though he would surely demur, and rightly so, from Murphy's traditionalist claim that it is philosophy's *most important function* to justify such first principles, philosophical categories, or underlying presuppositions (Murphy 1963, 210). His above argument as well as many considerations familiar from Wittgenstein make that evident enough. Murphy in spite of himself is being too much of a metaphysician and traditional philosopher here. But all that does not gainsay Murphy's critique of naturalism, namely that it is important for it to philosophically justify its own basic categories and that the key naturalistic arguments of Hook and Nagel, and people with a similar orientation, e.g., Dennes, fail to do so and are question-begging. However, one thing that counts against Murphy here, and that Wittgensteinians such as Rush Rhees have sensitized us to, is the opaqueness of "philosophically" here. What work, if any, is it doing in such a context (Rhees 1997)?

So we should look further into Hook's case. One consideration to take note of is Hook's claim that in establishing naturalism to be a more reasonable view—a more adequate view than its alternatives—he will not deploy a distinctively philosophical view, a distinctively philosophical position, but will deploy the same general scientific method: a method continuous with the workaday common sense used by "those who do the world's work—the cobblers, the carpenters, and the gardeners—when they are asked to justify one set of procedures rather than alternative ones" (Hook 1961a, 175). In other words he will stick—try to stick—with methodological naturalism in seeking to justify the cosmological claims of naturalism, determining what are the basic categories of naturalism and in settling issues concerning their justification. There is, as he sees it, no justifiable conception of a distinctively *philosophical* method, distinct from the scientific method, that we can follow instead.[13]

Murphy has argued, as have others as well, that here over a very vital matter naturalists are begging the question. To see what is involved here note, as Hook puts it himself, that some of his *critics* claim

> the methods and categories of common day activity and science—upon
> which naturalism relies—are designed to take note of the existence of cer-
> tain things, the existence of other things like immaterial entities, cosmic
> purposes, Gods, and disembodied souls are ruled out a priori. The asser-
> tion of their existence on the naturalist's view must therefore be not merely
> false but meaningless or contradictory. (Hook 1961a, 175–76)

But it is just such a claim—the critique goes—that is a prioristic and question-begging.[14]

Hook's response to this is double-pronged. First he asserts that if such a charge of circularity is valid it holds for *every* philosophical position. "Certainly," Hook remarks, "whatever falls outside the scope of the basic explanatory categories of any philosophical position cannot be recognized [by that position]" (Hook 1961a, 176). We can call it being in the categorial predicament if we like (Hall 1960, 8, 15, 140–42, 162).[15] But the crucial thing to recognize, as Hook stresses, is that his above statement is a tautology (Hook 1961a, 176). He then continues

That these categories are restrictive follows from their claim to be meaningful since a necessary condition of a meaningful statement is that it
should be incompatible with the opposite. (Hook 1961a, 174)[16]

If this was all Murphy was claiming there would be no gainsaying it. It
comes close to being a tautological claim. So, if that is so, he has made no
claim at all; he has claimed nothing. But he asserts more. He claims that
the restrictions naturalism makes are arbitrary, not rationally motivated.
Indeed they are perhaps even partisan. But that, whether justified or not,
cannot be justified on the basis of the above tautology or quasitautology.
What Murphy must establish is that the restrictions of that particular categorial system have such arbitrary and rationally unmotivated and perhaps even partisan features. But that does not follow from their simply
being restrictions, for then all categorial systems would be arbitrary and
could not, no matter what was said for or against them, be more reasonable or more adequate than any other. And that surely is implausible.
Moreover, to say they are all arbitrary—nay, even equally arbitrary—is to
use "arbitrary" in such a way that it has little sense left.

Hook next turns to the second prong of his argument. After the above
argument concerning the restrictions *of all* categorial systems, Hook
makes some remarks specifically concerning the naturalistic ones of the
type we have discussed. He claims that the "only legitimate question here
is whether they are narrowly restrictive, whether there are matters of
knowledge in common experience which they exclude or whose existence they make unintelligible" (Hook 1961a, 176). Hook seems at least to
concede that circularity and categorial-centricity are inescapable, but
what he resists is saying that "these assumptions are mere stipulations or
arbitrary postulations which express nothing but the *resolutions* of
philosophers" (Hook 1961a, 174). There can, he avers, be a more or less
objective interpreting of the facts of experience (Hook 1961a, 174).

So viewed, the central cosmological claims of naturalism—the articulation of its categories—while not *just* being resolutions, are nonetheless
resolutions, though not *just* resolutions of philosophers. They are what
we, in discussing Bouwsma earlier, called proposals. They are not factual
statements true or false, as on the surface they appear to be; they are not
even confirmable or infirmable as being probably true or false. They are
instead like Carnap's framework sentences, proposals about how to conceptualize things whose use is to be justified pragmatically.

If the only pragmatic test is success, then we have already seen the difficulties anyone is in, naturalist and nonnaturalist alike, if she uses success
as a criterion for acceptance. Hook, alternatively, speaks of making his naturalistic assumptions reasonable to reasonable persons (Hook 1961a, 176).
Crucial marks of a reasonable person are a willingness to take responsi-

bility for her actions, to explain why she proceeds to do one thing rather than another, to be prepared to give evidence for her beliefs where giving evidence is relevant and reasonably available, and (where it can be reasonably done) to justify her conduct by giving the grounds for it and/or by articulating its rationale (Nielsen 1998b). Then, taking a jibe at Murphy, Hook remarks that "the naturalist does not speak, as one of its critics does, in large terms of 'justifying philosophical categories as rationally and comprehensively as possible' and then fail to tell us in what specific ways philosophical rationality and comprehensiveness differ from scientific rationality and comprehensiveness" (Hook 1961a, 177). Hook asks, "Are the laws of logic and canons of evidence and relevance any different in philosophy from what they are in science and common sense?" (Hook 1961a, 177). *Perhaps* they are? But the burden of proof is surely on such critics of naturalism to show that they are and to show, if they are, just what they are and how they are to be justified.

Even if, Hook further asserts,

> all philosophical positions are *au fond* question-begging, there would still remain the task, pursued by all philosophers, of determining which of all question-begging positions is more adequate to the facts of experience. Every philosopher who seriously attempts an answer does assume *in fact* that there is some common method of determining when a position is adequate to the facts of experience and when not. The contention of the naturalists is that this common method is in principle continuous with the method which we ordinarily use to hold individuals to responsible utterance about things in the world—a method which is preeminently illustrated in the ways in which men everywhere solve the problem of adaptation of material means to ends. (Hook 1961a, 177–78)

There are two matters that are troubling in Hook's remarks, the first of which would not put him at odds with Murphy who makes the same at least *prima facie* plausible claim, but it would put him in conflict with Quine with his ontological relativity and even more so with such neo-pragmatists as Hilary Putnam, Richard Rorty, and myself. I refer to Hook's innocent sounding but actually conceptually problematic remarks *about positions being more or less adequate to the facts of experience.* What is it to be "adequate or, for that matter, to fail to be adequate, to the facts of experience?"[17] In old, now discredited theories of meaning, knowledge, and of truth, we thought of language as picturing or mirroring the world, of a copy theory of knowledge, of a correspondence theory of truth with sentence-shaped facts to match our atomic sentences. We thought, as with logical atomism, of sentences or propositions corresponding to the world and the like. If we could make sense of such talk, then talk of a philosophical position being adequate or more adequate or less adequate to the facts of experience might have some sense. At least it would be a way to talk and to think, once we got ourselves into such a metaphysical harness, though indeed a deeply puzzling way. But such metaphysical-philosophical endeavors, as those mentioned above, seem at least to be mythical, and opaquely so at that, in a post-Quine, post-Davidson, post-Kuhn philosophical world. That is to say, these ways of looking at things, as diverse as they in some ways are, make it very difficult to make sense of such traditional conceptions. Moreover, as we have seen in setting out Nagel's position, he too rejects any mirroring conception of language and the world. Presumably Hook would too. Perhaps Quine et al. are all out to lunch. But their ways of viewing things have at least a not inconsiderable *prima facie* plausibility and, if they are in the ballpark of being on the mark, we are going to have a lot of trouble (to put it mildly) with making sense of "being adequate to the facts of experience."[18] A fact is what a true statement states, but we have no coherent conception of facts as sentence-like or sentence-shaped entities, natural or nonnatural, which sentences correspond to. And this should—or so at least it seems—be something that a pragmatist, contextualist naturalist, and instrumentalist such as Hook should be saying.

Perhaps with Rorty we should argue instead that naturalistic positions enable us to cope with problematic situations more adequately than do nonnaturalistic and most particularly supernaturalistic ones. But what we should not say is that they are more adequate to the facts of experience than alternative positions (Rorty 1991; Nielsen 1999). We should say that, for we do not understand what we are talking about in so speaking about a position or even of a proposition being more adequate or less adequate to the facts of experience than another. And with that we have no understanding of what it would be like for us to have a method of determining when a position is adequate to the facts of experience and when not. We should just drop this whole way of talking about things and adopt Rorty's nonrepresentationalist language of coping instead. But we should be cautious here and not too quickly foist a representationalism on a pragmatist such as Hook. Perhaps all he means by saying one view is more adequate to the facts of experience than another view is that it enables us to cope more adequately with problematic situations than another? If that is so, as it very well might be, then Hook is home and free here. (Even more strongly given his instrumentalism this is how he should be understood.) That nonrepresentationalist way of speaking may also be metaphorical but (if so) it is a less puzzling and a far more useful metaphor than the old representationalist ones. Some accounts that have pushed us in that direction have resisted Rorty's going whole-hog here and giving up all talk of a fact of the matter and of relying instead on weaving and unweaving of the web of belief (Quine 1990, 117–19; Dennett 1993, 234–35). I am halfway inclined to think against the Quine-Dennett response that Rorty, and I should add Davidson too, have just followed out the logic of the matter more consistently than have Quine and Dennett. But that surely is a very contentious matter concerning which we need to take no sides here. But there are two things that seem hard to deny on even the most conservative assumptions *apres* considerations that are in common to Wittgenstein, Quine, Strawson, and Davidson. We cannot plausibly say, as Hook does, that "every philosopher who seriously attempts an answer [to the question which philosophical positions are more adequate to the facts of experience] does assume in fact that there is some common method of determining when a position is adequate to the facts of experience and when not" (Hook 1961a, 177). If there is anything to what Davidson and Wittgenstein have been saying concerning such matters we cannot say that. We cannot do that for such talk is so problematic that philosophers (or for that matter anyone else) will not understand, or at best only very feebly so, what they are talking about here. But all of that notwithstanding, such considerations do nothing to undermine naturalism. It could, and I believe should, take in the above respect a Rortyan form without abandoning much that was important to Hook and Nagel and in doing so it does not lend support to Murphy's critique of naturalism, for Murphy here makes the same arguably mistaken assumptions that Hook makes. But it does work against Hook's own explicit defense of naturalism unless we read it nonrepresentationally as we very well might. Indeed the principle of interpretive charity should take us in that direction.

I turn now to the second problematic matter concerning Hook's remarks quoted above. Even assuming, what might after all be true, that we can, Quine and Wittgenstein to the contrary notwithstanding, make sense of one philosophical position being more adequate than another to the facts of experience, even assuming that we can make some warranted judgments concerning this, and even assuming that every philosopher who seriously considers the matter "does assume in fact that there is some common method of determining when a position is adequate to the facts of experience and when not," we still have to give some adequate grounds for the pragmatic naturalist's belief—a belief shared by Hook and Nagel and John Dewey before them—"that this common method is in principle continuous with the method which we ordinarily use to hold individuals to responsible utterance about the existence of things in the world, a method which is preeminently illustrated in the ways in which men everywhere solve the problem of adaptation of material means to ends" using instrumental rationality (Hook 1961a, 178). This may work very well "in what broadly speaking we may call the technological aspect of human culture" and for other straightforwardly empirical claims and even for some others that are not so straightforwardly empirical, but how it would or could work for the basic theses of cosmological naturalism, if we try to treat them as very general empirical claims, is anything but evident for the reasons we have already surveyed. In short we do not know their truth-conditions or assertability-conditions or even how to go about ascertaining what they are. We are in the swamp here.

If we instead treat them as proposals—as having the logical status of proposals—of naturalistic philosophers, they also remain problematical. It is not clear that we can show that they are plausible proposals, let alone the most reasonable proposals we can come up with. It does not, at least on the surface, look like we have a *common* reasonably unproblematic method extending from many plain scientific and commonsensical means-ends issues to those about the adequacy of naturalistic categories for how we should conceive of and characterize things to the rather plain moral and aesthetic claims we often make. Consider a cluster of claims of the latter two types: "It is wrong to allow donors of organs to specify their donation of organs along racial, gender, or religious lines"; "The multicultural nature of our societies should be respected and protected"; "The right to have and to express both religious beliefs of various kinds or nonreligious beliefs is to be respected and protected"; "The avoidance of unnecessary suffering should be a central aim of any decent society"; "The life of everyone matters and matters equally"; "The good of self-respect is the most important of our primary goods"; "Expressionism is a deeper art form than impressionism"; or "Though both the English and the Russians had great traditions of novel writing the Russians are generally superior to the English." These and a host of similar normative claims are routinely argued about, *sometimes* there is something approaching a rough consensus in the rich capitalist democracies about what is more reasonable to believe here about some of these utterances but not about others and some of them are widely regarded as being so contested that we can have no reasonable idea where the truth or the normative adequacy lies concerning them. But concerning all of them—the contested, uncontested, or minimally contested ones alike—it is deeply controversial that a form of ethical naturalism can be articulated and defended in which these utterances are taken to be a species of empirical hypothesis subject simply to the constraints of instrumental rationality in the way "Americans like ham and eggs for breakfast" and "Americans take homosexuality to be an evil" can be empirically confirmed or disconfirmed. The expression of the above moral and aesthetic convictions seem at least to have no such straightforward assertability-conditions or perhaps no assertability-conditions at all. Indeed it is unclear (to understate it) how they can be taken to be empirical hypotheses capable of confirmation and disconfirmation (Murphy 1963, 211–12 and 1964, 257–70; Nielsen 2001).

Murphy, who is as contextualistic as Dewey, Hook, and Nagel about moral reasoning and as firmly rejects the morality of ultimate principles à la Kant and Sidgwick as they do, also rejected ethical naturalism and the claim that in practical reasoning (including moral reasoning) we use the scientific method and engage in the same basic patterns of inquiry that we use in science and over common-sense questions about how to bake a cake or to pitch a tent. He rejected, that is, the use in such domains of a method in which we, as Hook put it, following the Dewey formula, "recognize the problem, state the hypotheses, draw the inferences, perform the experiment, and make the observation" (Hook 1961a, 186).

Perhaps we could *redescribe* ethical problems, or at least some of them, so that they could be tackled and resolved in this way. That is what Dewey set out to do and Hook follows him here. But it is far from evident that that can be done or at the very least can be done for many of our moral and other normative convictions. We, as reflective moral agents, will say things like "It is vital for people to develop a sense of self-worth." But that seems more like a matter of reflective endorsement than something based on observation made in the light of an empirical hypotheses about human behavior.

Alternatively we might widen our conception of "scientific method" much beyond what I have taken it to be above. We could take it to mean little more than the reliance on disciplined, fallibilistic, reflective experience, observation, and problem-oriented attempts to coherently place together our considered convictions or judgments in various domains where they are held in the light of our best available articulation of what we reasonably take to be the relevant facts (Nielsen 1998a, 1998b). But, if we do that, we have something more like a Rawlsian wide reflective equilibrium than a naturalistic articulation of the scientific method that Hook calls the method of scientific empiricism. Naturalists, such as Hook and Nagel, as well as Dewey before them, commendably wanted to extend scientific method into new areas including most essentially to morals, politics, and philosophy itself. Where they limited themselves to scientific method rather straightforwardly described their success was very problematical. Were they to extend—broaden still more—this conception of scientific method there would be more plausibility to their claims, but then their method would look less and less like scientific method, though this is not at all to suggest that it would be an unscientific let alone an antiscientific method. Rawls's method of wide reflective equilibrium, to take a crucial case, is neither unscientific, antiscientific, nor antinaturalist. But we also get something that *looks* like a rather more careful articulation of reflective common sense.

Setting normative matters—that is, considerations concerning practical reason—aside, let me from another angle reconsider some of Hook's central claims concerning naturalism. Hook, in good empiricist fashion, and following William James, stresses the importance of seeking verification for one's convictions (Hook 1961a, 175). And like the logical empiricists he holds "that there is no evidence for the assertion of the existence of anything which does not rest upon some observed effects" (Hook 1961a, 186). It is not, of course, the case, Hook remarks, that only what can be observed exists. But he does maintain that there is no justification for believing in the existence of anything that does not rest upon some observed effects. (It should be noted that "rest upon" here is not very clear.) This is a core claim of his pragmatism and scientific empiricism. But what of the categorial claim of naturalism that the occurrence of all qualities or events depends upon organization of a material system in space-time? Or what about the related categorial claim that the only existents are qualified or related events? We can give all of what might be thought to be the confirming or disconfirming evidence we want, but we cannot even in principle cite what would even count as disconfirming or even infirming evidence for those propositions and thus they are not testable propositions. Moreover, it is a mistake to speak of confirming evidence as we did, for if there is no even possible disconfirming or infirming evidence there can be no confirming evidence either for there is no even possible nonvacuous contrast here to give "confirming evidence" sense. It is just something which is mistakenly thought to be "confirming evidence." Should we say then those naturalistic propositions at the center of Hook's and Nagel's account are pseudopropositions? No, we should not say that. We should say instead that their surface grammar is misleading and that we should take them instead as proposals about how best to conceptualize things.

Hook rejects, and not without point, that there is some distinctive type of knowledge of the categorial propositions of naturalism or a method of attaining this knowledge that is distinct from that of empirical knowledge garnered by the use of the scientific experimental method, that is, of scientific method. There is nothing that counts as distinctive "philosophical knowledge or understanding" that is distinct from empirical knowledge. That "puppies are young dogs" is analytically true is itself something we know to be true empirically by knowing the use of our language. (And, *pace* Cavell, that someone knows the use of the language is itself an empirical claim about them and about what that use of language is.) And there is no distinctive philosophical method, but only the scientific method for attaining any knowledge or justified beliefs that we may have or can come to have concerning such matters. Scientific knowledge and knowledge claims using the same kind of method are, he claims, the only kind of knowledge we have. If we are to have philosophical knowledge it must be of that kind. As Hook puts it,

Naturalism makes no assumptions over and above those that have been made every time the borders of our knowledge have been pushed back. It therefore has the cumulative weight of the historic achievements of common sense and science behind it. (Hook 1961a, 186)

It is, Hook claims, only by the use of this hypothetico-deductive-inductive method—what C. S. Peirce called the combined use of abduction, deduction, and induction—that genuine knowledge can be obtained. There is no philosophic knowledge or philosophic wisdom that can be otherwise gained and warranted. To the extent that we have philosophic knowledge at all, it is just this empirical knowledge which alone, Hook, and Nagel as well, have it, warrants belief and yields knowledge. In using this method different naturalists will take different terms to be categorial. They will use terms like "thing", "structure," "function," "power," "cause," "act," "relation," "quantity," and "event." "The choice," Hook argues, "of which categories to take as basic in describing a method depends upon the degree to which they render coherent and fruitful what we learn by the use of the method" (Hook 1961a, 191). But, Hook continues, it is a complete *non sequitur* "to assume that because one asserts that the fundamental categories of description are X and Y and Z, and that they hold universally, one is therefore asserting that the world cannot be significantly described except in terms of X, Y, and Z" (Hook 1961a, 191). It is not even to say that the world consists in nothing but X, Y, and Z. We can use terms A, B, and C, which we take *not* to be categorial and still go on to say, as nonreductionist naturalists will, "that the conditions under which any existing thing is significantly describable in terms of A, B, and C are such that they are describable in terms of X, Y, and Z" (Hook 1961a, 191). I can describe the movement of my pen in terms of intentional actions, but I can also describe it, rather more brutishly, in terms of bodily movements without any reference to intentional acts. We can describe things in our categorial terms, but they need not, without our abandoning our categories, be so described. And no claim need be made by naturalists that everything we will want to say about them will, or perhaps even can, be made in those categorial terms.

However, Hook fails to note something that naturalists also need to insist on to make their position coherently naturalistic. What in addition they need to insist on is that, if X, Y, and Z are the basic naturalistic categories, then, while things can be described in terms, say A, B, and C, they cannot correctly be described in terms which are *incompatible* with X, Y, and Z if naturalism with those categorial terms is warranted. Those categorial terms, if they are indeed the correct categorial terms (assuming such talk makes sense), determine the range of what can in that categorial system be coherently said and thought. But then Murphy's questions remain: how do we know—or indeed can we know—that these are the correct, or, if not correct, the most adequate, categorial terms and how do we know—assuming we can know the above—that we can determine what are the correct or the most adequate set of categorial terms by the use of the scientific method? Is the naturalist, his intentions to the contrary notwithstanding, not just arbitrarily postulating them? Is he not, though no doubt unwittingly, merely expressing his resolve to think in these terms?

To this it might be responded that propositions expressed in terms incompatible with the basic categories X, Y, and Z—say event, relation, and quality—cannot make genuine knowledge claims or express warrantedly assertable beliefs because (a) they do not make empirically testable claims and (b) only empirically testable claims can make genuinely synthetic knowledge claims.

Again we seem at least to be back à la Murphy with the core claims—*perhaps* better called the underlying assumptions or presuppositions—of that form of naturalism that Hook calls *scientific empiricism*. Do we just have to say, à la Bouwsma, if we would stick with it,"I believe"? That certainly would not fit the temper of thought of Hook and Nagel or, for that matter, of Dewey or any naturalist (including this naturalist) except perhaps that of George Santayana. But are naturalists caught with "Here I stand, I can do no other"?

VII

Raphael Demos thinks they are so stuck. Naturalism and Christianity as well as the other religious belief systems are, among other things, philosophical *Weltanschauungen* with unifying views having as essential components *lebensphilosophies* all of which, and equally, rest on faith (Demos 1945, 1961b). He remarks that the "formalization of religious belief is theology; the formalization of natural science is naturalism. We may legitimately call both naturalism and theology exhibitions of philosophical thinking provided we understand that neither goes beyond formalization, that neither attempts to justify its correlative system of belief. They both rest on faith" (Demos 1953, 76; 1961b). There are some minor errors here that need first to be identified and then set aside for they are not essential to his view that both *theology* (e.g., Christian, Jewish, Islamic, etc.) and naturalism, on the one hand, as well as, on the other hand, Christianity, Judaism, Hinduism, and secular humanism are all grounded (if that is the right word) on faith. That is to say, the ways of life and worldviews and the philosophical articulations of them (theology and naturalism) all, Demos has it, rest on faith: on pure trust. The small errors Demos makes are (1) neither theology nor naturalism typically involve *formalization* as distinct from some *systemati-zation*; (2) not all formalization of natural science is naturalistic; (3) natu-ralism is not simply concerned with natural science; and (4) it is false to say that neither theology nor naturalism "attempts to justify its correlative system of belief." They may do a very bad job at it. They may, as Demos like Murphy believes, make question-begging arguments and assump-tions, but they do *try* to justify their respective claims. *Maybe*, when pushed, they reveal that they rest in effect on faith, but still they seek to jus-tify their positions. He thinks naturalists like logical positivists are obliv-ious to this need for "ultimate justification." (It is not even clear that this is true of logical positivists. See Feigl 1950.)

Demos, unlike Bouwsma and Murphy, is a rather traditional Chris-tian *philosopher*. He announces that he speaks "as an advocate of religion" and of Christianity in particular (Demos 1960, 164). And, unlike a fideist, he seeks to give his advocacy a philosophical and indeed a metaphysical basis in spite of his reliance (ultimate reliance?) on faith. Atheism and sec-ular humanism are similarly, he has it, forms of advocacy that mistakenly think of themselves, Demos believes, as scientific views or at least as views embodying "scientific rationality." But what we have here, he claims, is nothing of the kind. Rather we have what in effect are dogmatic articulations of a secular faith rather than something which is either empirically warranted or "grounded in reason" (Demos 1961b). At the deepest level we have with them question-begging claims which assume what needs to be justified and by implicit definitional fiat rule out both all theistic or other religious views and nonnaturalistic (e.g., idealist) views (Demos 1945). Moreover, these naturalisms, their intentions to the contrary notwithstanding, are in effect value-nihilisms which cannot make sense of morality (with its claim to objectivity) or of our commit-ment, including the secular humanist's own sincere commitment, to democracy (Demos 1945, 1960).

Let us have a look at Demos's core claims here. Hook's conceptual-ization of scientific method makes use of the hypothetico-deductive observational method using abduction, deduction, and induction in a Peircean manner. By contrast Demos is in search of ultimate presupposi-tions articulated as premises which are "known by an immediate insight of reason" (Demos 1945)—what Peirce ironically called the appeal to "what is agreeable to reason." (It was something, Peirce thought, that was akin to taste.) For Hook, as for Peirce, induction serves to *test* hypotheses (abductions) but for Demos premises, including ultimate premises, are "obtained by induction from experience" (Demos 1945, 269). Hook and Demos agree on the obvious, namely that induction is distinct from deduction. But while Hook sees induction as a device for *testing* hypotheses Demos sees induction as "what makes deduction possible by furnishing premises for reasoning" (Demos 1945, 269). For Demos the crucial thing is getting premises, and most particularly *ultimate* premises, for knowledge. But in doing this, he stresses, we need to be confident, and indeed rationally so, that we have the *proper ultimate premises*. We need to get premises which convincingly articulate what the nature of knowledge is and we need to ascertain exactly how knowledge claims are validated. That comes, Demos, following Plato and Aristotle, argues, to its being the case that what we need here is a guarantee that rational insight is valid *and* that we have such an immediate rational insight that certain ultimate premises are true. (How this *could* be an *induction* from experience is entirely unclear.) The underlying assumption for Demos is that this direct rational insight is valid, while, by contrast, the underlying assumption for naturalism is that it is sense experience that is valid (Demos 1961b).[19] Moreover, we cannot, Demos believes, take that naturalist assumption as a plain, practically undeniable, common-sense truism, for philosophers of the stature of Plato and Descartes have argued that sense-experience is illusory (Demos 1945, 270). We cannot just assume they are wrong.[20] The central question that needs to be faced in this context, he maintains, is "how premises as to knowledge are to be obtained" (Demos 1945, 270).

We should start, in trying to come to grips with this, by taking to heart the fact that we have *traditions* and that they are often reasonably taken as a valid source of belief. It is a mistake to be, as Demos says Hook is, in any wholesale fashion contemptuous of tradition, taking it to be "inherited confusion" or "primitive folk-ways." (To say this is a very curious thing to say of Hook, for Dewey went out of his way to deny this and Hook usually closely follows Dewey.) Sometimes, of course, it is these things, but not always. And the idea of being able to stand utterly free of all traditions and to assess them for their reasonability has no clear sense. Demos is right in seeing tradition as *a* valid source of plausible belief; it "embodies the trial and error groping of everyday living, extended into the dimension of time" (Demos 1945, 268). But traditions rather typically conflict and oppose each other. "How then," Demos asks himself, "does one choose among them save by the method of reflective inquiry?" (Demos 1945, 268). As important as traditions are as a source of plausible belief, Demos and Hook agree that we cannot reasonably take any of them to be absolute for they not infrequently conflict and at that point, if we would be reasonable, we must use some method of reflective or scientific inquiry to choose between them. We cannot in the end—or even over any extensive examination—just appeal to tradition. But then which method should we choose: the scientific method of the naturalists or a reflective method of the metaphysical tradition relying on rational insight to obtain the appropriate premises or some still distinct method?

Both the naturalist and the rationalist try to get beyond prevailing traditions. But how is this to be done? In our own Western tradition, Demos has it, "our own supreme premise is that truth is arrived at by reflection over experience" (Demos 1945, 270). But he is also quick to point out that other traditions think otherwise. He concludes from this that our ultimate premises can neither be grounded in rational insight nor in sense experience since both such philosophically traditional claims to "ultimate grounding" can be and have been challenged (Demos 1945, 270).[21]

Naturalism is one tradition with its reliance on sense experience and scientific method; rationalism is another with its reliance on insight into synthetic a priori truths achievable by pure reflection; and mysticism is still another. Demos regards them all as faiths opposing other faiths and he asks

> Is there some super-tradition . . . to be used as a standard for all traditions; or is there just plain reason, a universal, native power of the mind, not authoritarian to be sure, but with the function rather to taking all the traditions and all the faiths as data, weighing each against all, and aiming to reconcile them together in an all inclusive scheme? (Demos 1945, 270)

It is, to put it minimally, not unreasonable to be skeptical about such an alleged native power of the human mind. This is what rationalists and traditional philosophers have aspired to, but is not this plainly an illusory quest? Or, if that is too strong, is not such a rationalism very problematic indeed?

Naturalists, such as Hook and Nagel, have, Demos argues, tried to do an end run around this classic issue "by separating doctrine from method"—methodological naturalism from substantive naturalism. "There should [in their view as Demos sees it] be no authority of doctrine," but "there should be an authority of method" (Demos 1945, 270). Demos thinks this view of theirs rests on a mistake for no such separation can be made. "It is no good," he remarks, "trying to refute the mystic by telling him his views are not arrived at by the use of scientific method; he does not accept the premises of science as to what constitutes knowledge" (Demos 1945, 271). Moreover, scientific method rules out by its very way of proceeding any appeal to synthetic a priori principles or any appeal to private experience which cannot be intersubjectively characterized. And if the scientific method adopts the categorial language of naturalism such that "everything has to be an event, then the idea of a timeless God is excluded from the outset and without argument" (Demos 1945, 271). It is excluded, that is, by an implicit *persuasive* definition.

Again we are back to an argument similar to Murphy's, namely that naturalism rests on a question-begging procedure. But by Demos it is used to stress the claim that its substantive doctrine of categories (whatever this substantive doctrine is) constrains what the very use of the scientific method can entertain or can conceptualize. Finally method is seen not to be independent of doctrine because we find naturalists appealing, in the very using of the scientific method, to the belief that it is an essential part of this method, that it have the "rule that principles claiming to be a priori should be subject to the test of reflective experience" (Demos 1945, 271). But there we have substantive doctrine dictating method for this very method commits the methodological naturalist to a rejection of certain forms of rationalism—that is to a rejection of certain substantive doctrines. Any claim to have an a priori knowledge given by rational nonempirical insight of fundamental substantive principles or of other matters of substance is simply ruled out from the beginning. As Hook puts it, "Naturalism as a philosophy is concerned only with those assertions about existence from which something empirically observable in the world follows that would not be the case if existence were denied" (Hook 1961a, 133–34). But that, Demos maintains, is, by methodological *stipulation*, simply to rule out any claim to a road to a priori rational insight into substantive matters not claiming to be governed by empirical testing. However, though this is not evident in his reply to Hook, Demos is not defending as a "final court of appeal" such rationalism (Demos 1945). He thinks, that is, that rationalism, as well as naturalism, or any other "First Philosophy," rests on faith (Demos 1953, 1961b).

What kind of case does he make for that and does the naturalist have an adequate rejoinder? Let us first look at how beyond bald assertion Demos tries to make a case for his claims. All these belief systems, Demos believes, rest on ultimate commitments; they all "are in the same boat, all floating on the infirm waters of faith" (Demos 1953, 72; 1961b). These commitments are usually unconscious and they apply as much to a belief "in the existence of independent physical objects" or to a belief in the reliability of memory or to a belief in the "existence of other people" as to belief in God or a belief that there is a material substratum or a belief that the fundamental constituents of reality are relations, qualities, and events or to the belief that the only sound way of fixing belief is through the scientific method or to the belief that there are synthetic a priori propositions known by rational, nonsensory intuition. They all are, Demos continues, "to a considerable extent, commitments as to what is a valid way of knowing. The air of important demonstration in science and philosophy is disputed as soon as we notice that both make basic assumptions as to what constitutes evidence; for instance as to the meaning and validity of 'experience,' as to the validity of memory, as to the criteria of valid theory—and so forth" (Demos 1953, 72). In saying all these beliefs rest on faith he means that they rest "on no evidence whatever, whether empirical or a priori" (Demos 1953, 71; 1961b).[22]

Naturalism and natural science itself have "an undemonstrated belief in something like the uniformity of nature—a belief, that is to say, that nature has the kind of structure which justifies our taking its behavior in the past as a clue to its behavior in the future" (Demos 1953, 74; 1961b). This, he has it, along with our belief in the reliability of our memory beliefs, rests on the sheer trust of faith: that is, they are beliefs which rest on no evidence whatever, whether empirical or a priori. Religious beliefs, including belief in God, are in the same boat. They all rest on sheer trust—on faith. It is just that we have different ultimate commitments. "Religious belief," Demos contends, "is no more of a faith than is the belief that nature is uniform" (Demos 1953, 74). They both not only go beyond evidence, but "up to a point, they go against the evidence" (Demos 1953, 74). Job says, "Though he slay me, yet will I trust him" and the scientist will say vis-à-vis his belief (Demos has it), "Somehow there is an explanation for everything that happens." It is one of his fundamental articles of faith. The scientist's attitude is "I will go on believing there is an explanation even though I cannot find one" (Demos 1953, 74).[23] He, Demos maintains, exhibits something very like the method of tenacity here. Christian philosophers base their philosophy (at least when push comes to shove) on the authority of the Bible. Naturalistic philosophers accept the premises and attitudes of natural science and simply systematize them and perspicuously represent them. According to Demos, "The naturalist's rules of evidence are the scientist's rules of evidence. Verification must be (sense-) empirical; also a concept has a meaning only to the extent that, in principle, it may be verified or falsified by sense-experience" (Demos 1953, 77). But the naturalist does not offer any arguments in support of these views about validation and meaning. He simply, Demos tells us, "borrows the practice of the natural scientist and erects it into a formal principle. His meta-scientific statements . . . are precisely personal declarations of faith, professions of belief, not assertions but expressions of the form 'I believe that p'" (Demos 1953, 77). And the Christian philosopher or theologian does exactly the same thing and is exactly in the same boat. This is not to imply that either belief-system makes false statements or at least that its central propositions are false. But they are not known to be true or false; they are not known or warrantedly believed to be knowledge or even justified beliefs.

I have described, and Demos has described, his account as claiming that these various belief-systems rest on ultimate commitments, rest on sheer faith. But in the middle of his 1953 article, Demos does an abrupt *volte-face* illustrating John Austin's claim about the penchant for philosophers first to say it and then to take it all back. Demos remarks

> [I do not] regard faith as the last word for either of these systems. Naturalism and theology are unself-criticized philosophies. I will call this level

Philosophy A. "True" philosophy (Philosophy B) begins with the Socratic query: why do I believe as I do?; with the Socratic knowledge, which is knowledge of one's ignorance—the awareness that one's beliefs rest on faith. Then there is Philosophy C, which (in the way of Plato's dialectic) criticizes, modifies, or justifies fundamental beliefs; or even adds wider speculations of its own. For myself, I take the basic beliefs of both science and religion to be "insights"—instances of knowledge in the sense in which Plato opposed knowledge to opinion. (Demos 1953, 77)

So in the end he avers Platonic rationalism as not just one belief-system among others but as *the really true belief-system* which will give us comprehensive nonfallibilistic knowledge of the way things are and must be and of how they hang together, and indeed must hang together, in a comprehensive unified system—a comprehensive system that will also be a distinctive *lebensphilosophie* yielding "the wisdom of living" (Demos 1945, 273; 1953, 77).

But again, doing another reversal, Demos takes it all back. He asks himself how he would justify such a system of belief while at the same time rejecting others. "There must," he remarks, "be an implicit reference to some fundamental criteria, but if so would not these criteria constitute but another set of premises, that is to say, of beliefs, and therefore of 'commitments'? Any attempt to justify premises would appear to be a self-defeating task. Perhaps then the very question is a pseudoquestion?" (Demos 1953, 77–78). So we are back to the acknowledgement that these different belief-systems rest on faith—on a trust with no grounds of any sort for our trust or our faith. The only new element is that Demos takes as his *particular personal expression of faith* that some form of Platonic rationalism—a "rationalism" which paradoxically, and unlike Brand Blanshard's sturdier rationalism, itself avowably rests on faith and so at least seemingly belies his claim that it is a rationalism.[24] ("Rationalism resting on faith" certainly sounds like an oxymoron.) But we also learn that Demos does not believe that premise-adopting is an arbitrary commitment for that very claim would be self-defeating—would constitute a pragmatic self-contradiction—for to claim that it is arbitrary would itself be to claim, as well, and inconsistently, that at least one premise-adopting claim was not arbitrary, namely that one (Demos 1953, 78).

VIII

Hook, in one brief paragraph, has responded to Demos's argument and C. J. Ducasse in more detail has responded as well and in a manner that Hook records he is in sympathy with (Hook 1961a, 239). I shall start with Hook's response. In saying, Hook remarks, that Demos's claim that science (or common sense) and religion rest equally on faith, the term "faith" is being used to cover two very different attitudes (Hook 1961a, 242). Consider the belief "Do not cross the road when there is a car coming in close proximity to you." If we want to continue living or at least not be hurt, and, if we are adults of normal mind, we will advert to that remark and keep out of the way of speeding cars. This is something that we can't help "believing" or having "faith" in. Our behavior shows this well enough. All of us, if we are even remotely normal, believe such things. And "if we want to die, we can't help but have 'faith' in the operation of other physical laws," among other things what stepping into the path of a speeding car will do to you (Hook 1961a, 242). There is no alternative for the person who is the least bit rational here. But people can and do live and die without having faith in God or in the resurrection of the body. That stepping into the path of a speeding car will kill or injure you is something, if you are near adult and normal, you cannot help but believe. It requires no act of will to have "faith" in the truth of that proposition. But it requires "an act of will to have religious faith" and many sane and reasonable people do not have that faith while all sane adults living in industrial societies in the twentieth century have such a "faith" (if that is the right word for it) about cars. Moreover, it requires no commitment, normative orientation, or act of will on their part.

There is plainly a difference here. Faith certainly does not come to the same thing in both cases and indeed there is little warrant for the claim that our common-sense, humdrum beliefs here rest on faith construed in the same or even a similar way to the way it is construed in religion and over religion. Indeed "faith" seems the wrong word here for such ordinary practically inescapable beliefs. Hook concludes, "Science is an elaboration and development of common-sense knowledge which because it is knowledge is not faith. If it is retorted that such knowledge rests on 'faith' and is therefore no more valid than religious knowledge which rests on 'faith,' what must first be established is that we have religious knowledge" (Hook 1961a, 243).

Perhaps this is reasonably decisive. At least it should lead us to be skeptical about whether common sense and science, on the one hand, and religion, on the other hand, should be taken to be in the same boat as both resting on faith in the same sense of "faith" or even in a relevantly similar sense. However, could not Demos, acknowledging that, respond that what he was concerned with was not certain practices, scientific or commonsensical, but whole belief-systems—philosophical *weltanschauungen* such as naturalism, idealism, Christian philosophy, Islamic theology, and the like? It is these that are essential for his case about belief-systems resting on faith. Demos could grant that there are some mundane commonsense beliefs and some routine scientific beliefs that are nearly uni-

versally believed that do not rest on faith and yield unproblematic
knowledge while claiming that the framework beliefs that infuse our
lives such as naturalism, idealism, Christian, Jewish, and Islamic philosophy as *weltanschauungen* do rest on faith and on faiths which are either
conflicting or incommensurable. And they all rest on "faith" in the same
sense of "faith," namely on faith as trust.

However, if he admits this, much of his account is vulnerable to
another very pragmatic argument of Hook's fully in the naturalistic
spirit. It goes like this: there are many common-sense beliefs and routine
scientific beliefs of which we can be more confident than we can of the
grand framework beliefs of naturalism, idealism, or of any of the religions. We do not doubt for a moment that fire burns, that ice is cold, that
water will run down hill, that the sun will come up tomorrow, that
someday we will die, that many of our beliefs rest on observation, that if
something is red then it is colored, that if Bill's house is to the right of
Jane's house and Jane's house is to the right of Mary's house then Bill's
house is to the right of Mary's house, that suffering without point is a bad
thing, that telling the truth is usually a good thing and that some of our
memory beliefs or sense-experiences are reliable. We are, and reasonably
so, much more confident of the soundness of these beliefs than we are or
even can be of any framework beliefs or philosophical principles—grand
systems of philosophical or even scientific thought (if such there be)—
that would deny them or put them in question. Even if these framework
beliefs rest on faith or are simply posited, we can either set them aside or
say those that are justified are those that are compatible with these firmly
validated ordinary beliefs, including ordinary scientific beliefs. They are
the beliefs to be appealed to when push comes to shove.

Naturalism is justified as the most systematic articulation and
Occam's-razor-respecting expression of what is involved in relying on
those unproblematic beliefs. When we come to see that these beliefs are
beliefs that can be justified by the use of the scientific method we will, or
at least should, see the reasonability of sticking with this method of fixing
belief for the more problematic ones, including more general ones, *of the
same type.* We have a reliable method for fixing belief at least in such
domains. Why not stick with it for more problematic cases? Many problematic scientific beliefs can be so fixed: turned from problematic beliefs
to validated ones by the resolute use of that method and many other
problematic ones falsified or at least infirmed by the use of that method.
And none of the religious ones can be so tested. This being so, we have,
at least *prima facie,* good reasons not to accept them for they are not validated by a widely used, consistently successful, and uncontroversially
acceptable method of fixing belief. And all of this can be done without
any appeal to "ultimate commitments," "metaphysical groundings of sci-

entific method," "validation of ultimate principles or premises," "defending the underlying presuppositions of scientific method," and the like. In short, we can reasonably accept them without any appeal to faith—any appeal to beliefs which rest on no evidence or no grounds whatever, whether empirical or a priori.

Let us now look at Ducasse's rather different arguments against Demos's claim that all belief-systems are equally faith rooted (Ducasse 1953). They are arguments compatible with the above arguments, but they are still distinct and independent of them. Since some might still think—though I am not clear on what grounds—that in some complicated way my above arguments are question-begging, Ducasse's arguments should be examined. They are arguments which are at a higher level of abstraction and thus might be thought by some people (not me) to be therefore less vulnerable than the previous ones to the charge that they are question-begging.

Demos, recall, claims that the basic beliefs of science are like those of religion: pure matters of faith; they "rest on no evidence whatsoever, of any kind; so that there is not the slightest reason to regard them as true rather than as false" (Ducasse 1953, 93). But in so introducing the term "evidence"—he could and with the same effect have used "ground" instead—we implicitly appeal to a contrast between beliefs which rest on evidence or grounds, and *thus* are candidates for knowledge, and those which do not. In saying that there are some beliefs which rest on no evidence or grounds whatsoever, we are implicitly acknowledging that there can be beliefs based on evidence or beliefs having grounds and so they are *not* and, indeed, since they are held in this way, cannot—logically speaking "cannot"—be matters of faith. But many scientific claims and some common-sense ones as well are beliefs for which there is evidence or grounds and thus they cannot rest on faith.

There are the rules of the game that go with the pursuit of knowledge and the linked rules of the games of seeking evidence or giving grounds. (I do not say they are the same thing.) They both contrast with the rules of the game of confessing faith. These are different games, different practices, with different postulations, rationales, and aims. They should not be confused with one another. The rules of the game of the pursuit of knowledge or justified belief and the rules which define its nature and differentiate this game from others are those called the rules of evidence and involve "rules of observational, experimental, inductive, deductive, circumstantial, and testimonial evidence" (Ducasse 1953, 94). Nobody, Ducasse remarks,

> is obligated to obey these rules, but whoever flouts them is automatically then playing a different game; and, if he nevertheless continues to

employ the words which have meaning only in terms of those rules—words, namely, such as "true," "false," "valid," "fallacious," "proof," "probability," "knowledge," etc.—then the game he is actually playing is that of cheating at the pursuit of knowledge; just as purporting to play chess but making the king move two steps instead of only one is not playing chess but cheating at chess. (Ducasse 1953, 94)

Philosopher-theologians who reason as Demos does are unconscious or unwitting cheaters (Ducasse 1953, 95). They intend to be playing the knowledge-producing game: "they intend their statements to *communicate* their thoughts; they intend their arguments to *prove* or *disprove* something; and intend their assertions to represent facts, not fictions" (Ducasse 1953, 95). But they fail to do so, their intentions to the contrary notwithstanding, for they do not use terms such as "true," "false," "valid," "fallacious," "proved," or "warranted" as they are used in the knowledge-producing game. What Demos calls "the basic beliefs of science *are really not beliefs at all*, but are the rules of the game of pursuit of knowledge; and that it is only *within* this game, i.e., in terms of its rules, that the question whether a given belief is erroneous or true, groundless or well-grounded, valid or invalid, has any meaning at all" (Ducasse 1953, 95). Rules and the definitions and postulates that go with them "are neither true nor false and neither believed nor disbelieved, but only respected or disregarded" (Ducasse 1953, 94). If we play the pursuit of knowledge game, we must play according to certain rules: we make hypotheses and carry out deductions elaborating the implications of our hypotheses or following these deductions out, construct (hopefully with imagination) still other hypotheses; we test hypotheses; we further elaborate from the observation sentences we have used in the testing and we seek to ascertain the coherence of these elements or where we do not find much in the way of coherence we seek to forge coherence making adjustments here and there.

This is very different from an appeal to faith which involves playing a very different game indeed. If the theologian or Christian philosopher "takes, as a starting point for his inferences of fact, assertions merely *known to be contained* in the Bible, instead of—as the rules [of the pursuit of knowledge game] require—assertions *known to be true* by observation," he cheats at the pursuit of knowledge game. That is not the way that game is played.[25]

So it is not that we have rival faiths clashing and competing for our allegiance—science versus theology or naturalism versus Christian philosophy—but conflicting sets of practices, different games with their distinctive rules and rationales. Science, and its extension naturalism, operates according to the rules of the pursuit of knowledge game; theology, Christian philosophy, and the religions that go with them do not. But then they cannot, Ducasse argues, yield knowledge or warranted or justified beliefs. Moreover, unless we had pursuit of knowledge games with their rules of evidence, we could not have the faith-game for that is a game in which by definition we have a system of beliefs which rest on no evidence whatever. But to know what this would be like, we must understand what it is like for there to be a system of beliefs which appeal to evidence and are governed by rules of evidence. But this is just what science is and if everything is said to rest on faith (including science) then nothing can. If everything is said to rest on faith there can be no faith at all, for there can only be systems of belief that rest on no evidence whatsoever if some systems of belief have some evidence that counts in their favor or at least that we have a conceptualization of an activity—a set of practices—where this could be so. We could not have practices constitutive of faith if we did not have practices which were not so constitutive. We need a nonvacuous contrast here. It is dramatic to say that everything rests on faith, but it is all the same an incoherent claim.

Demos, trying to take two steps backward in order to take one step forward, could amend his view in two ways in an attempt to escape Ducasse's criticism. First he could respond by saying that he should not have said that science and theology, naturalism and Christian philosophy, are belief-systems which rest entirely on faith, but only that their premises—their "ultimate premises"—rest on faith. But to this response there is the familiar pragmatist response that it is not such putative "ultimate premises" that are crucial but the system of beliefs taken holistically and fixed by the scientific method that is crucial and here, as we have seen above, and as Demos is now conceding, there we do not have an appeal to faith.

Secondly, and alternatively, Demos might respond that he should not have so appealed to faith at all, but to have stuck, like Murphy, with his argument that the naturalist's arguments are question-begging. When he saw, or thought he saw, that he no more than the naturalist knows how to validate his ultimate premises in a non–question-begging, noncircular way, he was led to say, we can now see mistakenly, that both his appeal to rational insight—to immediate a priori knowledge of the structure of the world—and the naturalist's appeal to the hypothetico-deductive observational method with its reliance on sense experience rested on faith. What he should have said instead, we are now making him say, is that there are these two methods: a rationalism resting on a priori insight—what Peirce called the a priori method—and the scientific method with its appeal to intersubjective observation and testing and that neither can establish itself in a non–question-begging way or, more cautiously, it has not been shown how this can be so for either of them. Neither has shown, that is, non–question-beggingly, how their way of fixing belief is the *only* justified, or the *only* "ultimately justified," way of doing so. The arguments that have been given for them have all been circular and indeed viciously circular.

Hook has defended methodological naturalism by denying there is a genuine circularity here and by arguing "that the appearance of circularity arises because the question of method is raised in the abstract, not in relation to a problem-solving context. Once we locate the class of problems we wish to solve, we can justify our choice of rational or scientific method by its fruitfulness in solving these problems" (Hook 1974, x–xi). An example may help here. There are diseases that are very persistent, hard to treat, and the results of treatment very problematic. But when a person has the disease—say, cancer—the reasonable thing to do is to chose medical practices (the most reliable ones the person can get) for treatment rather than to abandon scientific treatment and use instead some method of the laying on of hands or reciting certain prayers. Does making such a choice show that we are reasoning in a vicious circle? We would only be going in a vicious circle if we were "prepared to argue that the facts in the case are determined *only* by the theoretical assumptions we bring to them" (Hook 1974, xi, italics added). But this, Hook contends, is an absurd claim. Even though our observations are very theory dependent, they are not *completely* so. If they were *completely* theory dependent we would be going in such a circle, for no matter what method, with what categorial framework we adopted, no facts could conceivably refute any claim we make. Your friend gets cancer and refuses medical treatment and requests certain prayers instead, believing they will be the most efficacious method of cure. We so pray for him, but he dies anyway and in a very short time with considerable misery. People with this religious belief-system may not take this as a refutation of their "method," but will claim we did not pray hard enough or with enough sincerity. But all this means, Hook responds, is that we have adopted a method; and developed a conceptualization about the complete theory dependence of facts (something that Demos at one point commits himself to) that allows "no possibility of ever finding evidence that will disprove what one believes, thus generally opening the way to believing anything about anything" (Hook 1974, xi). By contrast, by using a scientific approach, by being methodological naturalists and using scientific method resolutely with respect to any particular problem, we at least have provided ourselves with a way of discovering where we have gone wrong, of making progress by eliminating error (Hook 1974, xi). Here we are playing the pursuit of knowledge game and we can, *fallibilistically to be sure*, sort out truth or warranted assertability from error. With the alternative "method" of facing medical problems there is no way of detecting error and so there is, as well, no way of detecting a correct treatment. And here, by sticking with the scientific method, we have nothing that is viciously circular: that just follows from the theory we adopt. How things fall out depend on the empirical consequences.

However, this does not get to the bottom of the matter. Methodological naturalism claims that the *only sound* method for fixing belief is the scientific method construed broadly as Hook and Nagel (and Dewey as well) construe it. The metaphysical a priori method, however, defended by Demos does not deny, what is obvious enough, that in limited empirical domains the scientific method is a legitimate method for fixing belief; what it denies is that it is the *sole* legitimate method in all domains for fixing belief. It denies that it can be extended, as Hook and Nagel wish to extend it, and as Dewey did as well, to moral domains and other normatively social domains or that it can be used as a critical tool for sorting out or elucidating metaphysical or religious claims or for eliminating them *en bloc* as incoherent. It could be said, and I would add reasonably said, that in the case of laying on hands to heal or the case of healing by prayer, religion was superstitiously being extended to matters that should be left to science. But that we should use scientific method there does not entail or justify the claim that we should, or even could, use it, as methodological naturalism prescribes, in all, or even most, moral, religious, or metaphysical domains. The claim that in all domains it is the only sound method stands in need of a sound non–question-begging argument.

Hook and Nagel would, in response, following Peirce's argument made in his seminal paper, "The Fixation of Belief," argue that only the scientific method sustains itself in practice. It is the only method that succeeds in solving problems so that the rub of doubt—actual, real life-doubts, not paper Cartesian doubts—actually gets, for a time, resolved (the irritation of doubt relieved) and a stable pattern of belief established leading to an informed consensus. Demos's a priori way, like Descartes's, with its appeal to rational insight, does not enable us to distinguish between what *we think or feel is agreeable to reason and what really is so.*

However as many critics, including Murphy but including as well some substantive naturalists (e.g., A. J. Ayer, Richard Robinson, J. L. Mackie, Axel Hägerström), have argued the scientific method cannot be extended to cover all moral issues and most particularly not to its most fundamental ones. This remains so whatever we may say about metaphysics, theology, or religion. It is plausible, of course, to believe that some moral issues can be so resolved, but that all can, including some very tormenting ones, is less obvious. Moreover, there are borderline, not easily classifiable questions—or at least matters taken by many people (including reflective and knowledgeable people) to be questions—such as "What are we to make of life?," "What are we to make of our own lives?," "What sense (if any) does life have?"—desperately vague as they are—which are still questions (putative questions) that many reflective people find pressing and unsettling (Rhees 1997). We can see that they are not biological, anthropological, or sociological questions and that none of these disciplines, nor history either, whether singly or together, can answer them, though this is not to deny that what we can learn from these sciences could be relevant to them or at least to some of them. But the idea that science could solve them is a plain naivete. Anyone who thinks so could not have thought about them very much. They are not that kind of question at all (Rhees 1997). They are not scientific questions and it seems completely unclear how the scientific method could be deployed to answer them. This is not to say that they are unscientific questions or antiscientific questions as distinct from being nonscientific questions.[26] One could say in a narrowly positivist fashion that they are pseudoquestions best set aside. Faced with them we just need to tighten our belts. Still, many reflective people (both naturalists and nonnaturalists) engaging themselves, sometimes intensely, try to make sense of them and see what could be said concerning them while realizing that, though they have an ethical dimension they are not just ethical questions (Rhees 1997). But it seems very problematical to regard them as problems that the careful use of the scientific method would yield answers to. What seems so obscure is the idea that what it is to live a life and how and why life is important are questions answerable by the resolute use or the imaginative application of the scientific method: that careful empirical inquiry, that the intelligent use of something like Dewey's theory of inquiry, would give us answers here seems very remote.

To have a feel for what is involved in these questions—putative questions so as not to beg the question—makes the idea of treating them as questions answerable by the scientific method seem at least absurd. Yet we can be intelligently reflective about them and some things we can say about them are better than others and some reflective endorsements seem at least to be better, more insightful, more reasonable than others. But *methodological* naturalism seems barren here though one could be a naturalist—like this naturalist—and still be concerned with these questions and believe that some responses are both more reasonable and run deeper than others. (See here chapter 4 of this volume.)

This, however, does not show à la Murphy and Demos that arguments for naturalism and theism (even a theistic rationalism) are stalemated in question-begging responses. It shows rather, if my above argument is on the mark, that methodological naturalism is a mistaken view and thus the form of naturalism advocated by Nagel and Hook is at least to that extent inadequate. But it does nothing to show that there is a mistake in their substantive conceptions of naturalism and that their critiques of supernaturalism and rationalism, where not rooted in methodological naturalism—what some would call their scientism—are not on the mark (Rorty 1991, 63–77). Moreover, naturalists could use, as I do, the method of wide reflective equilibrium in the domains (moral, political, and social) where the scientific method seems at least to limp, while remaining robustly substantive naturalists and atheists (Nielsen 1996, 12–19, 159–206). Indeed it is worth exploring whether the coherentist method of wide reflective equilibrium could not come to play more adequately the role that Dewey, Nagel, and Hook wished the scientific method to play in a naturalistic account of the world.

IX

There is one more inning to play in my examination of the issues between Nagel and Hook and their critics over the adequacy of the defense of naturalism given by Nagel and Hook. What is involved here comes to a head in Demos's 1960 essay and in a few passages of his 1953 essay. Demos could agree that a substantive naturalism, abandoning methodological naturalism and the scientism that goes with it, using instead a method of wide reflective equilibrium, could give morality a more adequate treatment than such a scientism, but it still, he could claim, would not yield a fully adequate treatment of morality or of values, something which only a theistic view of the world linked with a somewhat Platonic metaphysical rationalism could provide. In fleshing this out we will see how deeply Demos is committed to a Platonized Christian metaphysical religiosity with its metaphysically rooted morality. (See Hägerström 1964, 175–223 for a perceptive, devastatingly critical articulation of metaphysical religiosity.)

Has he done anything to show that this vision of things is more adequate than the through and through naturalist stance of Nagel and Hook? I shall argue, hardly surprisingly, that he has not and that how and why he has not is revealing (a) about the relation of naturalism to religion and (b) metaphysically. An examination of what is going on here does—or so I shall argue—something to show how inescapable naturalism in some form has become and with it a secularism all the way down (Nielsen 1998a; see also chapter 2, this volume). Moreover, it shows that it is not only inescapable but reasonably so.

I will go at what is involved here indirectly. Demos tells us that "the belief in God is equivalent to the view that things make 'moral' sense in the universe; that, although there is evil in nature, this evil will somehow be overcome by good" (Demos 1953, 74).[27] Forget, for starters, about what appears at least to be a Spinozatic reduction of God to the universe viewed somehow morally—the universe somehow being good itself. Some rationalistic theists, without intending anything so pantheistic, have tried to understand goodness—given the reality of God—as somehow for such a universe as either being rooted in it or somehow being constitutive of it. To take a theistic and religious point of view, for them, is to have a metaphysical conception of the universe in which *the universe itself is seen as being good*. Demos, who has such a view, wants to know whether "nature is hostile or indifferent or cooperative with man's wishes and ideals" (Demos 1960, 173–74). He concludes that if the universe is as naturalists depict it, moral striving and indeed life itself is without significance (Demos 1960, 173–76).[28] Naturalism, as Demos has it, sees human beings as a mere brief episode "in the course of nature, a very tiny minority in the huge cosmic population. His interests no more reflect those of the cosmos than the concerns of an ant do those of the very ground on which it creeps" (Demos 1960, 174). Human aspirations, he claims, will come to nothing if naturalism is true. Unless the naturalist manages to deeply deceive himself, he must recognize that if things are as he says they are "all hope is gone; there is only despair ennobled by Promethean defiance and mitigated by Stoic resignation. Since all achievements are doomed by extinction, why attempt to achieve anything? Whatever we build is nothing better than a child's sand castles which the tidal sea will wash away" (Demos 1960, 175).

With naturalism, we get a bleak morality not answering to our deepest aspirations and hopes about life and our destinies. By contrast religion and, Demos has it, particularly the Christian religion, answers to our aspirations. "Naturalism is unable to provide a basis for certain things we believe in: democracy, moral obligation, and dedication beyond self; and finally that life is worth living" (Demos 1960, 175).

By contrast:

1. "Religion is the view that the cosmos is friendly to values and that consequently there is a strong chance that man's nobler aspirations will be fulfilled" (Demos 1960, 175).
2. "To say that God exists is to hold that goodness is a ruling power in the universe" (Demos 1960, 175).
3. ". . . religion asserts the existence of a moral order in the universe" (Demos 1960, 175).
4. "To believe in God is to believe that things make moral sense in the universe" (Demos 1953, 79).

It seems to me that we have an embarrassment of confusions here, only some of which I will expose, and that, soberly viewed, we do not have much here in the way of a challenge to naturalism. But we do have an expression of a view that in our culture (more in North America than in Europe) is widely shared, so it is not without point critically to examine it to see if it is the bundle of confusions I take it to be.

I shall limit myself to challenging three things: (1) the above 1–4 cosmological-ethical claims, first concerning their very intelligibility and, then, even if they somehow pass that test, their plausibility as knowledge-candidates or justified-belief candidates; (2) the claim that without God the moral lot of human beings is hapless;[29] and (3) the claim that "naturalism is unable to provide a basis for certain things we believe in, i.e., democracy, moral obligation, and dedication beyond self and that life is worth living, and that the Christian religion does justify them" (Demos 1960, 175).

What is common to the above four cosmological-ethical propositions is the assertion (putative assertion) that the universe has a moral order: that the cosmos is friendly not hostile to values. Goodness is claimed to be a ruling power of the universe; there is a moral order in the universe and that all this is a very important part of what is meant by saying that God exists. It is, Demos avers, very important for us to ask "whether nature is hostile or indifferent or cooperative with man's wishes and ideals" (Demos 1960, 174). If, Demos goes on to tell us, the cosmos, being as powerful as it is, is hostile, our aspirations will inevitably be defeated. "If the cosmos is indifferent, then certainly there is no assurance whatever either that man will lose or that he will win. There is not even a reasonable hope that he may win" (Demos 1960, 174). But if God is in his heaven and is the God that Christians take him to be then the cosmos is friendly to our values and our highest aspirations can be met. Goodness is a ruling power in the universe. There is a moral order in the universe itself.

The trouble (more accurately, a trouble) is that that kind of talk makes no sense. It makes no sense to say that nature, the cosmos, the universe is hostile, friendly, indifferent, or cooperative. People or nations or institutions like the international monetary fund, the multinationals, or capitalism or socialism have such attributes, but not the universe or nature. Demos's kind of talk could make sense only if it is treated as some kind of metaphorical talk and then we need to be told what its metaphors are metaphors of. Metaphorical talk is inescapably parasitical on literal talk. Sentences like "The cosmos is friendly to values," "Goodness is a ruling power in the universe," or "There is a moral order in the universe" are, if we try to use them to assert propositions, lacking of both truth-conditions and assertability-conditions. We do not know what must be the case, what observable effects must obtain, for them either to be true or probably true or to be false or probably false. Thus we do not understand what we are asserting or denying when we employ them. In that very important way they are unintelligible. If we try to be literal minded we do not understand what we are talking about when we use them.

It could be retorted (mistakenly I think) that this is too verificationist—that here Hook and Nagel are too like Carnap and Hempel. Even factual intelligibility is not so constrained. Such sentences have a *use* in the language and *so* they have a *meaning*. Our very understanding of language is tied to use. And they have a use.

They have a use all right, it should in turn be retorted, but many people do not use such sentences and they feel about people who use them to try to make assertions what Michelet thought about theology, namely that it was "the art of befuddling oneself methodologically." These sentences have a use in the language, but a use where the engine is idling.

However, even if we do not want to assert, or even give to understand, that they are unintelligible or are devoid of "cognitive meaning," they are not good candidates for knowledge or warranted belief. They lack truth-conditions and assertability-conditions. That is to say, we have no understanding of the conditions under which we would be justified in asserting that they would be true or probably true or false or probably false.

Suppose we try to demythologize them and treat them as metaphors. To say "Goodness is a ruling power in the universe" is to say "God providentially orders things" or to say "There is a moral order in the universe" is to say that "There is an omnipotent, all-wise, all-good creator God who protects and loves His creation." Here we are on more familiar ground with sentences that do not have such a Platonic metaphysical ring. But they, when we try to use them to make assertions to say something that could be true, have the very same verificationist difficulties. They are without truth-conditions or assertability-conditions. Thus, if the pragmatist conception of meaningfulness is near the mark, we should say they lack *factual* or perhaps even cognitive intelligibility (Nielsen 1971, 420–37). If that is too strong—too verificationist as it is usually said—it remains the case that we have no idea of whether such claims are true (probably true) or false (probably false) or how we could go about ascertaining or determining whether they are true or false. We do not understand what we are trying to talk about here. Or to put it more modestly, we have at best a very scant idea of what we are talking about here.

Suppose we try to demythologize them still further in something like the fashion of William James (James 1967, 317–95). To say "Goodness is a ruling power of the universe" is to say "The best things are the more eternal things" or "Human beings will cooperate and come to have relations with each other such that human flourishing will be enhanced." But here we have something that is compatible with a thorough secularization all the way down. Many secularizers would think that that expresses too rosy a picture of life and so would not accept these propositions as *true*, or as even probable, but all the same, as they well realize, they make secular *sense*—they have factual intelligibility—and *make no nonnaturalistic claims*. So that is no way to save Demos's claims.

Let us turn now to Demos's all-hope-is-gone-if-naturalism-is-true thesis and that *au contraire* with Christianity there is hope for us. First we should see that arguments here are independent of what was argued above about his metaphysical religiosity. Even if it is not only intelligible but even true that there is a moral order in the universe and that God is author of it, that does not establish what Demos claims about our hopeless, utterly bleak moral condition in a naturalistic world. If we look at things on a cosmic scale we will see that we are but a very tiny and insignificant part of a huge cosmic population. We are fleeting inhabitants of a minor planet circling around a minor sun which is but a miniscule part of a vast universe. Our planet will eventually cool and human life and indeed probably all life will become extinct. As Bertrand Russell put it,

> Brief and powerless is man's life; on him and his race, the slow doom falls pitiless and dark. Blind to good and evil, reckless of destruction, omnipotent matter rolls on its relentless way; for Man condemned today to lose his dearest, tomorrow himself to pass through the gates of darkness, it remains only to cherish, ere yet the blow falls, the lofty thoughts that ennoble his little day . . . to sustain above, a weary but unyielding Atlas, the world that his own ideals have fashioned despite the trampling march of unconscious power. (Russell 1918, chapter 8)

When we look up at the starry skies and think about the cosmos it is not unnatural to have the feelings Bertrand Russell so eloquently expresses. But when we reflect again in a cool hour we should recognize that we need not, if we would be resolutely nonevasive, take that moral stance or think with Demos that this is what a consistently thought through atheism and naturalism leads to and that only with religion (presumably a theistic religion) is there hope for us. That our lives are short makes them more precious to us and our relations with others and theirs with us more precious. Human suffering, exploitation, and debasement are no less evil because we all must die and our lives count for nothing in *cosmic* terms. *The moral point of view is not the cosmic point of view*, even assuming (what surely should be questioned) that the very idea of "the cosmic point of view" makes sense. We care about our own lives and the lives of others close to us, fragile and replete with contingencies as our lives inescapably are, and if we are persons of moral integrity we will also cast a much wider net. We will care about people throughout the world and not only about the near and dear. That so many people unnecessarily starve or lead hellish lives of great impoverishment and not infrequently of degradation with little hope of a better life will anguish us as other forms of injustice will anguish us, embitter us, and strengthen our resolve to struggle against them. We will want a world where people respect each other, cooperate with each other, care about each other at least in the sense that caring relations will pervasively come to prevail and where human beings thought of collectively will flourish, just as we want a world where we as individuals can flourish. We want it to be a world where kindness, love, and mutual understanding prevail. We will want, as Brecht put it, to achieve conditions for the foundations of kindliness. These are key elements of the moral life that we will reflectively endorse if we are moral beings. That the sun will cool, our planet cool, that the human race is doomed to extinction, that we will have but a short hour upon the stage, has no effect on that at all. We will go on, and reasonably so, endorsing these things. That there is no God and we are not immortal and that every human thing will come to an end—will in time be gone without a trace—does not make human flourishing and a joy in life and a desire to have a moral community any the less valuable. Perhaps we should *not* even say with William James, with whatever metaphor, that the best things are the eternal things. Some of the very fleeting things may very well be the most precious. And recognizing them to be so fleeting sometimes makes them even more precious to us.

I now turn to Demos's claim that naturalism is unable to provide a basis for democracy, moral obligation, dedication beyond self, and a basis for regarding life as worth living. He tells us that he has "shown that naturalism is not, while religion is, compatible with moral obligation, democratic ideals, and valuation in general" (Demos 1960, 177). Now his only argument for that is his above argument that without religion there is no hope and that at best we could only, with Russell, have a morality of "despair enobled by Promethean defiance and mitigated by Stoic resignation" (Demos 1960, 175). But, if my above argument is even remotely on track, there are no good reasons at all for believing this. We start— atheists, agnostics, and believers alike—with considered convictions: common-sense ones (including common-sense moral convictions), for some of us, as well, with scientific ones and, for many of us, moral and political ones going beyond our common-sense convictions. Here, with a certain stress on this cluster, is where an element of my own naturalism enters that is distinct from Nagel's and Hook's naturalism, but is still compatible with the substantial side of theirs. (It was something that surfaced at the end of the last section.) The reasonable thing to do, giving considerable weight to our firmest considered convictions, is to forge them, together with other things (scientific, otherwise theoretical, otherwise practical and factual) that we have firm grounds for thinking we know to be so, into a consistent and coherent cluster of beliefs and convictions, pruning here, modifying there, adding elsewhere new things reflectively endorseable that come along, until we for a time obtain the most coherent package of beliefs and convictions that we can manage. We weave our beliefs, attitudes, and convictions into a coherent pattern. When we have done that we have got our beliefs into wide reflective equilibrium and we have a set of beliefs and convictions that is the most reasonable one that we can for the time gain. It will be just the opposite from what is arbitrary, whimsical, and dogmatic or even just postulatory.

We can get our beliefs in democracy, moral obligation, and the conviction that life is worth living into wide reflective equilibrium (Nielsen 1996, 12–19, 159–206).

Demos resists what he calls the secular gospel of humanism (Demos 1960, 163–69). He admits the obvious, namely that naturalists like Nagel and Hook are committed persons, committed democrats, with decent views about human beings and society. But naturalists, Demos avers, cannot reconcile their democratic idealism with their view of human beings. Their image of human beings is incompatible with their faith in human beings (Demos 1960, 170). He asks, "What is man that the naturalistic philosopher should be mindful of him?" He remarks that according to naturalists

> man is a collection of living cells like an animal or a plant, or an aggregate of atoms like a stone. We think it is right to use an animal as a beast of burden, a tree for lumber, and we exploit the earth for its resources. Why not use and exploit man also? What then becomes of the concept of the absolute worth of man, which is the cornerstone of democracy? Why should we relieve human suffering, comfort the sick and old people and take care of the feebleminded and the insane when there is no expectation of a social return in value? If man is nothing but a biological fact, then surely, since compassion is biologically inefficient, compassion is wrong. (Demos 1960, 169)

First, as we have already seen, human beings are, of course, biological beings, but they are not *just* biological beings but also *social* beings as well and with that carriers of a culture including deeply engrained considered convictions (Nielsen 1998a; see also chapter 2). So even *if* in good Darwinian fashion we come to see that compassion is inefficient, we would not be justified in ceasing to be compassionate persons and would still have reason to continue to see value in compassion. And there would be nothing irrational in so responding to things.[30] Efficiency is indeed something, but it is not everything. We sometimes make trade-offs between justice and efficiency and sometimes considerations of justice have the greater weight. And justice does not just come to Pareto optimality.

Secondly, that we should relieve suffering, comfort the sick and the like is due to the fact that they are among our deepest considered convictions (convictions that we reflectively continue to endorse) and they are considered convictions that we can get in wide reflective equilibrium with other considered convictions and other things we have good reason to believe. When Demos asks, rhetorically, "Why was Hitler wrong in enslaving the Jews and other non-Germans?" naturalists can, and do, answer in the same straightforward way that religious people can by saying, and truthfully, that doing that was a bestial act that degraded, destroyed, and caused incredible suffering to many, many innocent people and standardly as well degraded their murderers, that is, by their very actions they degraded themselves. Human beings were treated mercilessly as if they were something of no account (worse than brutes) and often sadistically as well—the Nazis were not just efficient killers—and in ways which turned those who committed such crimes into brutes—but brutes which unfortunately were often intelligent and knew what they were doing. In short it went against the deepest considered convictions of people in Western Civilization—I do not say only Western Civilization—including Germans. That ideologists of Nazism such as Goebbels could make it seem to some that their grim duty rested on a plain anthropological falsification of Jews as being members of a distinct and subhuman race that was destroying Western Civilization. That belief flies in the face of what we know, including what most educated Germans knew, so that such beliefs could never be gotten into wide reflective equilibrium even in the German culture of the Nazi period. They offend our deepest considered convictions and are irrational to boot. We can be more confident of the soundness of these convictions than we can of any theoretical, Christian or naturalist, account or set of abstract principles that we might trot out to support them or to question them or to raise issues of value nihilism. And they are just as compatible with naturalist views as with Christian, Islamic, or Jewish ones. We need not turn to God to save us from barbarism or a rejection of human rights or of democracy.

In the penultimate paragraph of his lecture "Naturalism and Values," Demos makes a set of remarks that makes him sound—though surely that is not his intent—like an ally of Nagel and Hook, and, as well, of Rawls and myself, as articulators and defenders of the method of wide reflective equilibrium. Demos remarks

> In any system of thought, there are immediate beliefs and then derived beliefs which are justified by the fact that they are presupposed by the immediate beliefs. I speak of immediate beliefs because we have to start somewhere; absolute doubt leads nowhere. Unless we are to abandon ourselves to complete skepticism, we must have some premises. Where shall we look for such basic propositions? Not in pure reason; abstract reflection, divorced of content, yields nothing. Then why not look for them in sense-experience, as is done in science? But sense-experience is only one selected portion of experience; moreover, whether sense-data are good and sufficient grounds for belief is precisely one of those matters which are in dispute. I propose, paradoxically enough, to start with beliefs bereft of reasons and unsensed by sense, beliefs of which one may say either that they are suspended in mid-air or that they support themselves. These are the immediate beliefs such as we find ourselves having,

beliefs which are inevitable and are involved in the tissue of our lives. From these beliefs as data, I propose to work back to their presuppositions, and so enlarge the scope of belief. Such immediate beliefs are those, for instance, of common sense: the belief that there is a world of hard physical objects surrounding us, and which we did not make. Then there is the system of scientific beliefs which is partly an enlargement but to a great extent a correction of common sense. When there is disparity between such basic systems, we should not be partial to one, rejecting the other, but should try to accommodate each to each. (Demos 1960, 177–78)

Demos goes on to add that "our moral beliefs are as basic, as unavoidable, as those of common sense and science" (Demos 1960, 178). These immediate beliefs—the moral beliefs he refers to—are what Rawls, Daniels, and I have called considered convictions—indeed among them our firmest considered convictions. We start with them and we need to get them, as Demos says, by mutual accommodation, into reflective equilibrium with our similarly basic common-sense beliefs and scientific beliefs. Here all of us are using a coherentist method. These immediate beliefs, what I have called considered convictions or considered judgments, in different domains are, as Demos puts it, "involved in the tissue of our lives" (Demos 1960, 177). Some of them, perhaps most of them, are practically speaking inescapable. And to have a reasonable and justified view of the world is to get these beliefs—taking them as data if you like—into reflective equilibrium. But this is something which is naturalism-friendly and perhaps, standing where we are now, knowing or reasonably believing what we know or so believe, it even requires naturalism (Nielsen 1996). Demos *au contraire* thinks that the basic values—the firm considered convictions—commit us to Christianity and that these moral beliefs roughly correspond "to the essential components of the Christian doctrine" (Demos 1960, 178). But he, as we have seen, has given us no good reasons for believing that. Perhaps we have good reasons for believing just the opposite, to wit that we cannot get Christian beliefs into wide reflective equilibrium. (I argue in detail that this is so in Nielsen 1996.) There are some things that Demos says that would incline us to think this. "For Christian thought," Demos has it, "human nature is radically evil; to bring about the good life means to be born again in a process which involves the shedding of natural man" (Demos 1960, 164). Naturalists like Hook and Nagel or like me would never say that human nature is either radically evil or wholly or radically or even basically good. Human beings are more malleable than that, capable of both good and evil—sometimes of great good as well as sometimes of great evil. We are a malleable and fluctuating mix and what this mix will be will depend in large measure on particular circumstances—something that Marx saw very clearly. Where, as Brecht powerfully shows us, the circumstances are favorable and the society is rich and stable and somewhat egalitarian, it is easier to be decent and more people behave decently than when the society is impoverished, corrupt, and inegalitarian. Compare Iceland and Kosovo. Humanists—Hook and Nagel for instance—certainly do not believe the opposite of what Christians or Jews believe, namely that we are basically good or that (*pace* Demos) naturalism could establish a paradise on earth (Demos 1960, 165). They would take—and rightly—any such belief to be silly. They think we are a fragile mixture of both—Pascal is right, man is a frail reed—and that fortunate circumstances can enhance our goodness and decrease the evil of which we certainly are capable. The Christian view espoused by Demos could not be gotten into wide reflective equilibrium while our naturalist view very well might. And this is a way of saying—indeed I think the most reliable way of saying—that it is a more reasonable, better justified view than such a Christian view. We have here no good reason to believe (*pace* Alvin Plantinga) that naturalism and Christian philosophy stand on *a par* and that we just have to commit ourselves one way or another, to say nothing of saying with Demos that we are justified in opting for Christianity as the best way for human beings to live their lives. That is, at best, just ethnocentric.[31]

NOTES

1. In our "Afterword: Whither Moral Philosophy?" (Couture and Nielsen 1995, 273–337), we have made a critique of Hampton's 1995 essay (pp. 278–90).

2. Is it so clear that this claim is really testable? What would we have to observe or fail to observe to see that it is false or probably false? I do not want to deny that it is testable, but I would like to see its test-conditions clearly set out. And I am not confident that it has any.

3. See also Nagel 1976.

4. But consider what was said in note 2.

5. For a skeptical examination of this see Murphy 1963, 1964, and 1993.

6. But he may be caught on Quinean grounds if Quine is right about analyticity. But this would not count against naturalism, but only against Nagel's argumentation here.

7. It is not so terribly clear that it could not be false. Bouwsma moves too quickly here.

8. I do not intend to give to understand above that only naturalistic philosophers have done this.

9. But note my remark in note 2.

10. Nagel's account is superior to Hook's here for it is less vulnerable to Hampton's criticisms.

11. This is something with which Peirce would have had considerable sympathy.

12. Paradoxically enough, Murphy, stressing his contextualism, argues in much the same way. See Murphy 1964, 285–317 and 318–54. See also Nielsen 2001. But Murphy is not an ethical naturalist or indeed any kind of naturalist.

13. But their conception of scientific method is a very general one. Dewey, for example, has remarked that the scientific method "is but systematic, extensive, and carefully controlled use of alert and unprejudiced observation and experimentation in collecting, arranging, and testing evidence" (Dewey 1944, 12).

14. Hook has argued a rather similar point against me. Like Bernard Russell, he thinks we have not been given enough evidence for the various "theistic hypotheses" while I think we do not know what it would be like to have evidence for the nonanthropomorphic ones. See Hook 1975. Waiting for evidence here is like waiting for Godot. For a discussion of this see chapter 7, part 3, this volume.

15. The categorial predicament is the claim that our categories set for us how we are to view things and indeed how we can view things and that there is no way, free from our categories, to assess their adequacy—to see if they fit the facts. There is no category-free ascertaining of what facts, events, or things there are or even determining what is to count as a "fact" or "event."

16. Hook must have in mind only claims that are substantively meaningful and not logical truths.

17. See here Rescher 1999.

18. The views of the philosophers mentioned above, of course, extensively differ. But there are features of their views sufficiently similar to raise problems about talking of claims being adequate to the facts of experience. I do not say these problems are insuperable. See also note 15.

19. Demos's use of "valid" here is neither standard nor clear. We know what it is like for an inference or an argument to be valid. It is unclear what it could be for an experience to be valid or invalid. I suppose Demos means reliable as opposed to being unreliable.

20. Certainly we can argue against them as Peirce does very effectively in his "The Fixation of Belief."

21. That they have been challenged does not, of course, mean that they have been successfully challenged.

22. "A priori evidence" is probably an oxymoron. It is at least an infelicitous and unclear way to talk or write.

23. It is a metaphysical and not a scientific attitude that there is an explanation for everything. The scientist's attitude is that where there are problematic situations she will look for *explanations*. That is part of her vocation as a scientist. She may have no belief at all that if investigations are pushed far enough an explanation must be found. She can remain completely agnostic about that. That some scientists have this metaphysical belief only shows that some scientists are *also* rationalist metaphysicians—something which has nothing to do with their being scientific.

24. On such a sturdier rationalism see Nagel 1955, 266–95 and Nielsen 1994, 113–40.

25. I think Ducasses's point is essentially right, but as it stands it is too strong. That is not the way the mathematical knowledge game or the moral knowledge game is played. Or at least not obviously so.

26. This seems at least to put scientism in jeopardy.

27. Strangely and unhappily enough the pragmatist William James said many of the same things. But he also saw how monstrous such a view is. James 1967, 317–45 and, on the monstrous side, 369–73.

28. By stark contrast see Nielsen 1981 and Nielsen 1996, 557–97.

29. See Nielsen 1990 and 1996, 203–10. And see chapters 2 and 4, this volume.

30. I am not giving to understand that a Darwinian outlook takes compassion to be inefficient.

31. I mean "enthnocentric" in the standard anthropological sense, not ethnocentric in Rorty's eccentric but in some ways useful sense. See Rorty 1991, 203–10.

BIBLIOGRAPHY

Bouwsma, O. K. 1965. *Philosophical Essays*. Lincoln: University of Nebraska Press.

Carnap, Rudolf. 1959. "The Elimination of Metaphysics through Logical Analysis of Language." In *Logical Positivism*, edited by A. J. Ayer, 60–81. Glencoe, Ill.: The Free Press.

Couture, Jocelyne, and Nielsen, Kai. 1995. "The Ages of Metaethics." In *On the Relevance of Metaethics*, edited by Jocelyne Couture and Kai Nielsen, 1–30. Calgary, Alb.: University of Calgary Press.

Daniels, Norman. 1996. *Justice and Justification: Reflective Equilibrium in Theory and Practice*. Cambridge: University of Cambridge Press.

Demos, Raphael. 1945. "Reply." *Philosophy and Phenomenological Research* 42: 264–92.

———. 1953. "Are Religious Dogmas Cognitive and Meaningful?" In *Academic Freedom, Logic and Religion*, edited by Morton White, 71–97. Philadelphia: University of Pennsylvania Press.

———. 1960. "Naturalism and Values." In *The Student Seeks an Answer: Ingraham Lectures in Philosophy and Religion, 1951–1959*, edited by John A. Clark, 161–80. Waterville, Maine: Colby College Press.

———. 1961a. "Religious Faith and Scientific Faith." *In Religious Experience and Truth*, edited by Sidney Hook, 130–36. New York: New York University Press.

———. 1961b. "Religious Symbols and/or Religious Beliefs." In *Religious Experience and Truth*, edited by Sidney Hook, 55–58. New York: New York University Press.

Dennes, William R. 1944. "The Categories of Naturalism." In *Naturalism and the Human Spirit*, edited by Yervant H. Krikorian, 270–94. New York: Columbia University Press.

———. 1960. *Some Dilemmas of Naturalism*. New York: Columbia University Press.

Dennett, Daniel. 1993. "Back from the Drawing Board." In *Dennett and His Critics*, edited by Bo Dahlbom, 203–35. Oxford: Blackwell Ltd.

Dewey, John. 1944. "Antinaturalism in Extremis." In *Naturalism and the Human Spirit*, edited by Yervant H. Krikorian, 1–16. New York: Columbia University Press.

Dewey, John, Hook, Sidney, and Nagel, Ernest. 1945. "Are Naturalists Materialists?" *Journal of Philosophy* 42 (September): 515–30.

Ducasse, C. J. 1953. "Are Religious Dogmas Cognitive and Meaningful?" In *Academic Freedom, Logic, and Religion*, edited by Morton White, 89–97. Philadelphia: University of Pennsylvania Press.

Feigl, Herbert. 1950. "De Principles Non Disputandum: On the Meaning and the Limits of Justification." In *Philosophical Analysis: A Collection of Essays*, edited by Max Black, 119–56. Ithaca, N.Y.: Cornell University Press.

Frankena, W. K. 1964. "Ethical Theory." In *Philosophy*, edited by Roderick M. Chisholm, et al., 347–461. Englewood Cliffs, N.J.: Prentice-Hall.

Hägerström, Axel. 1964. *Philosophy and Religion*. Translated by Robert T. Sandin. London: George Allen and Unwin Ltd.

Hall, E. W. 1960. *Philosophical Systems: A Categorial Analysis*. Chicago: University of Chicago Press.

Hampton, Jean. 1995. "Naturalism and Moral Reasons." In *On the Relevance of Metaethics*, edited by Jocelyne Couture and Kai Nielsen, 107–34. Calgary, Alb.: University of Calgary Press.

———. 1998. *The Authority of Reason*. Cambridge: University of Cambridge Press.

Hook, Sidney. 1944. "Naturalism and Democracy." In *Naturalism and the Human Spirit*, edited by Yervant H. Krikorian, 40–64. New York: Columbia University Press.

———. 1961a. *The Quest for Being and Other Studies in Naturalism and Humanism*. New York: St. Martin's Press.

———. 1961b. "The Atheism of Paul Tillich." In *Religious Experience and Truth*, edited by Sidney Hook, 59–64. New York: New York University Press.

———. 1974. *Pragmatism and the Tragic Sense of Life*. New York: Basic Books.

———. 1975. "For an Open Minded Naturalism." *Southern Journal of Philosophy* 13, no. 1: 127–36. See also chapter 7 of this volume.

James, William. 1967. *The Writings of William James*. Edited by John J. McDermott. Chicago: University of Chicago Press.

Misak, C. J. 1991. *Truth and the End of Inquiry: A Peircean Account of Truth*. Oxford: Clarendon Press.

———. 1995. *Verificationism: Its History and Prospects*. New York: Routledge.

Murphy, Arthur E. 1963. *Reason and the Common Good*. Englewood Cliffs, N.J.: Prentice-Hall.

———. 1964. *The Theory of Practical Reason*. La Salle, Ill.: Open Court.

———. 1993. "Pragmatism and the Context of Rationality." *Transactions of the Charles S. Peirce Society* 29, nos. 2, 3, and 4: 123–78, 331–68, 687–722.

Nagel, Ernest. 1955. *Sovereign Reason*. Glencoe, Ill.: The Free Press.

———. 1956. *Logic without Metaphysics*. Glencoe, Ill.: The Free Press.

———. 1976. "Philosophical Concepts of Atheism." In *Critiques of God*, edited by Peter Angeles, 3–18. Amherst, N.Y.: Prometheus Books.

Nielsen, Kai. 1971. *Reason and Practice*. New York: Harper and Row.

———. 1981. "Linguistic Philosophy and 'The Meaning of Life'." In *The Meaning of Life*, edited by E. D. Klemke, 177–204. New York: Oxford University Press. See also chapter 4.

———. 1990. *Ethics without God*. Amherst, N.Y.: Prometheus Books.

———. 1994. "Jolting the Career of Reason: Absolute Idealism and Other Rationalisms Reconsidered." *Journal of Speculative Philosophy* 8, no. 2, (new series): 113–40.

———. 1996. *Naturalism without Foundations*. Amherst, N.Y.: Prometheus Books.

———. 1998a. "On Being a Secularist All the Way Down." *Philo* 1, no. 2 (fall–winter): 6–20. See also chapter 2.

———. 1998b. "Liberal Reasonability a Critical Tool? Reflections after Rawls." *Dialogue* 37, no. 4: 739–59.

———. 1999. "Taking Rorty Seriously." *Dialogue* 38, no. 3: 503–18.

———. 2001. "Murphy, Arthur Edward (1901–1962)." In *Encyclopedia of Ethics*, 2d edition, edited by Lawrence C. Becker and Charlotte B. Becker. New York: Garland Publishing.

Putnam, Hilary. 1992. *Renewing Philosophy*. Cambridge, Mass.: Harvard University Press.

Quine, W. V. 1969. *Ontological Relativity and Other Essays*. New York: Columbia University Press.

———. 1990. "Let Me Accentuate the Positive." In *Reading Rorty*, edited by Alan Malchowski, 117–19. Oxford: Basil Blackwell.

Railton, Peter. 1995. "Made in the Shade: Moral Compatibilism and the Aims of Moral Theory." In *On the Relevance of Metaethics*, edited by Jocelyne Couture and Kai Nielsen, 79–106. Calgary, Alb.: University of Calgary Press.

Rawls, John. 1999. *Collected Papers*. Cambridge, Mass.: Harvard University Press.

Rescher, Nicholas. 1999. "Fallibilism." In *Routledge Encyclopedia of Philosophy*, edited by Edward Craig. New York: Routledge.

Rhees, Rush. 1997. *On Religion and Philosophy*, edited by D. Z. Phillips. Cambridge: Cambridge University Press.

Rorty, Richard. 1982. *Consequences of Pragmatism*. Minneapolis: University of Minnesota Press.

———. 1991. *Objectivity, Relativism and Truth*. Cambridge: Cambridge University Press.

Russell, Bertrand. 1918. *Mysticism and Logic*. New York: Longmans Green and Co.

Sellars, R. W. 1944. "Materialism and Human Knowing." In *Philosophy for the Future: The Quest of Modern Materialism*, edited by Roy Wood Sellars et al., 75–105. New York: Macmillan.

———. 1994; original 1944. "Reformed Materialism and Intrinsic Endurance." In *American Naturalism in the Twentieth Century*, edited by John Ryder, 79–101. Amherst, N.Y.: Prometheus Books.

Sellars, Wilfrid. 1963. *Science, Perception and Reality*. London: Routledge & Kegan Paul.

Waismann, F. 1968. *How I See Philosophy*, edited by R. Harré. London: Macmillan.

6

NATURALISM UNDER CHALLENGE

I

In our contemporary philosophical context naturalism (except some-times as a position in the philosophy of mind) is more often presup-posed than stated let alone articulated or defended. As a systematic or semisystematic working out of a nontheistic and thoroughly secular worldview it hardly captures the imagination or attention of many pre-sent-day philosophers. This was not so for the generation of philosophers working in the first half of the twentieth century. George Santayana, W. J. Woodbridge, John Dewey, and a host of lesser lights produced extended and systematic articulations and defenses of naturalism and, as we have seen in the last chapter, two important followers of Dewey, and distin-guished philosophers in their own right, Sidney Hook and Ernest Nagel, who were also influenced by the then rising tide of analytic philosophy, provided succinct and canonical articulations and defenses of naturalism. But this is no longer true. What was once stated, articulated, and defended is now pretty much an unstated and thus undefended view, in effect a background assumption, of many philosophers, including many of the most distinguished ones. Quine, Dennett, Davidson, Rorty, Putnam, Bernstein, McDowell, and Brandon are all naturalists. They, like Santayana, Woodbridge, Dewey, Hook, and Nagel before them, are not reductive naturalists, but, that notwithstanding, thoroughgoing naturalists they are. Their naturalism, like the naturalism of Hook and Nagel, is, cosmologically speaking, a modest and rather minimalist naturalism, but a firm naturalism, as is my naturalism as articulated in Part One of this volume and in my *Naturalism without Foundations*. What is distinctive about my own naturalism, along with Putnam's and Rorty's, is its firm break with scientism and its eschewal of any claimed hegemony for the scientific method. I am not, that is, a methodological naturalist. But I remain resolutely antimetaphysical and antiontological. I think philosophers are blathering when they talk about their ontological commitments. But I share with the philosophers mentioned above the determination to find a way of being a naturalist without being a reductive one and in regarding ideals and norms as having in some, I hope reasonable sense, a natural basis. Like Santayana and Dewey, I want a naturalism that accommodates art, morality, and religion while naturalizing them in the spirit of an uncompromising atheism. (By this I do not mean, of course, that you have to be an atheist to be moral.)

I am inclined (though somewhat ambivalently) to feel that the largely unarticulated assumption of a substantive naturalism by many of my contemporaries is as it should be. These battles have been fought and won and what is left, it is not unreasonable to believe, is a matter of fine tuning, avoiding scientism, and the avoiding of talk of ontological commitment. We are all, or at least should be, naturalists now; what the more exact design of our naturalism should be, or whether it should have an essentialist articulation, is another matter. But *perhaps* not a very pressing matter.

However, this might be thought to be a rather lazy dogmatism—too lazy to even get very assertive about. But still a way of making things easy—too easy—for myself. So I have in this work and in my *Naturalism without Foundations*, turned to the task of articulating and defending naturalism. In the spirit of this endeavor, I want in this chapter to face and examine a forceful and intelligent challenge to naturalism made by Jean Hampton—a challenge a nonevasive naturalist cannot afford to ignore (Hampton 1995, 1998).

As we secular humanists are up front about our atheism or in some instances agnosticism, Jean Hampton is someone, as she puts it, "who is committed" to being a Christian analytic philosopher and, like any atheist worth her or his salt, Hampton, speaking for herself, seeks for her proclaimed Christianity to construct sound arguments and perspicuous constructions answering to the expectations of rational and reasonable people (Hampton 1998, xii). However, in her case in "Naturalism and Moral Reasons" (1995) and more extensively in her *The Authority of Reason* (1998), it is principally nay-saying in which she engages. It is over such matters that her arguments and perspicuous articulations obtain. As a prolegomenon to making reflective space for Christianity (it surely has plenty of cultural and political space), she wants to show how broken-backed naturalism is. She remarks in her preface in *The Authority of Reason* that she has "aimed to write a book that does not so much attempt to persuade, as to dissuade . . . to shake readers loose from the grip of a conception of the world that threatens our ability to act both rationally and reasonably. . . . [She wishes to construct] a work that attempts to rattle those who read it" (Hampton 1998, xi).

She has not succeeded in dissuading me or even in rattling me. But then perhaps I am too deep in my dogmatic slumbers or am in some way self-deceived. That I do not feel that way—do not feel dissuaded or rattled or self-deceived—of course, proves nothing. But the arguments that follow might. She has, however, succeeded in making me realize that we need a better understanding and a better characterization of naturalism than we have at hand and that we should not so be complacent about our secularism—complacent about our secularism all the way down (see chapter 2). That doesn't at all mean or even suggest that we should abandon it, but it needs a clearer articulation and defense. So as part of this project I turn to her arguments.

II

I shall begin by setting out Hampton's critique of naturalism. She claims that we do not have a workable conception of "the natural" such that we can give a perspicuous articulation of naturalism (Hampton 1998, 14). Philosophers, she has it, both in defending naturalism and in criticizing it are working with a conception of nature that has not been precisely defined (Hampton 1998, 34). She argues vigorously and clearly that we have not succeeded in pinning down what naturalism is so that we can provide a plausible articulation and defense of it (Hampton 1998, 109). She goes on to add "to make matters worse, there is also no definitive argument showing that only the entities recognized in scientific theories can exist" (Hampton 1998, 109). Thus, even if "the 'natural' could be defined more precisely, naturalists lack a decisive argument showing that only the natural is real" (Hampton 1998, 109).

There are many influential naturalists (Hägerström, Carnap, Ayer, Robinson, Stevenson, Gibbard, Williams, Mackie, Harman, Blackburn) who are noncognitivists or something very like that in ethics. They argue that moral norms cannot pass scientific muster. However, to make their case, they must explain "what 'scientific muster' is supposed to be and why a theory is commonly thought to be disreputable unless it passes it" (Hampton 1998, 19). To examine, she claims, what makes "a theory either scientifically acceptable or scientifically disreputable, we should begin with the concept of the 'natural'" (Hampton 1998, 19). In starting there Hampton first distinguishes, roughly in the way I did in the previous chapter, between *methodological* naturalism and *substantive* naturalism (Hampton 1998, 20–21). But, unlike the naturalists discussed in the last chapter, Hampton takes substantive naturalism to be the more plausible form of naturalism of the two because, she has it, it clearly "accommodates the successful use of nonempirical methods of mathematics and logic within scientific practice" (Hampton 1998, 21).[1] Troubles, as we have noted Hampton claiming, start for any form of naturalism, but most acutely for substantive naturalism, over the fact that "the natural" that we are working with has not been precisely defined. Hampton argues that there are "two ways in which this term can be defined" (Hampton 1998, 35). The first is what Hampton calls a "science-based definition." On such a conception "the natural" "is that which is allowed and/or studied by science" (Hampton 1998, 35). As Hampton remarks, this "definition makes the current theories of science the ultimate arbiters of what counts as natural. In this view, science is not defined in terms of the natural, but rather the reverse" (Hampton 1998, 35).

The second way of spelling out what we are to take as "the natural" gives a substantive use to the term (Hampton 1998, 35). It does this by attempting to make clear how there is such a use for "natural" in our language-games. G. E. Moore and David Brink, among others, so define "natural." "Natural" on such a conception "denotes a kind of object or property that is the opposite of nonnatural" (Hampton 1998, 35). What is natural in this sense—something we are supposed to grasp intuitively—"is conceptually prior to our understanding of science and (at least in part) determinative of the subject matter of science" (Hampton 1994, 35). Hampton calls such a definitional stance "the 'substantive' definition" of "natural."

Both science-based definitions and the "substantive" definitions of "natural" have crippling difficulties according to Hampton (Hampton 1998, 34–43). Science-based definitions could not, on the one hand, be used to support atheism or agnosticism as over and against theism or deism or, on the other hand, to support naturalistically generated noncognitivisms such as Hägerström's, Ayer's, Stevenson's, or Gibbard's or any form of ethical naturalism as over and against rationalistic forms of ethical realism, even forms appealing to intuition. It is not at all clear that the "commitment of present-day science to things such as quarks or DNA preclude commitments to rights and obligations" or, for that matter, to God and the soul. But, even if it did, Hampton observes, this does nothing to sanction our saying "that we could *never* acknowledge that these objects and properties exist, since it would seem possible that science could evolve in a way that would require it to recognize their existence. All that we would be licensed to conclude is that [such entities, objects, or properties] seem queer from the present scientific point of view, but might one day be scientifically acceptable after all" (Hampton 1998, 36).

Such a science-based conception of the natural yields, Hampton has it, a conception with no teeth. It does nothing at all to help the cause of atheism, secularism, secular humanism, or, more generally, some robust naturalistic world perspective. If naturalism is to have any plausibility, she argues, it must yield a plausible substantive definition of what is natural.

However, Hampton also has it that substantive definitions are in trouble as well. Physics itself, she remarks, has "undermined in this century a popular and seemingly sensible conception of the natural that animated the thinking of many scientists and philosophers through the nineteenth century" (Hampton 1998, 36). What was this conception—a conception that yielded a sturdy substantive definition? It was a conception that thought of the world as being made up of solid, inert, impenetrable, and conserved matter—a matter that interacts deterministically and through contact. This naturalism—or materialism as it was then usually called—was robust and yielded a naturalism that was plainly substantive and carried a determinate naturalistic picture of the world. It was something that clearly contrasted with a theistic, supernaturalistic world-perspective. There was no need to be perplexed, with that conception, concerning what we are talking about in talking about nature. But the catch is that this picture no longer squares with contemporary physics. Twentieth-century physics, Hampton observes, "has posited entities—and interactions between these entities—that do not fit the materialist characterization of the real" (Hampton 1998, 36). Materialism's contemporary descendants, in the face of these firmly established elements of contemporary physics, have, understandably, lost their metaphysical nerve. They no longer try to limit the subject matter of physics a priori; they now take a more subservient attitude: "the empirical world, they claim, contains just what a true complete physical science would say it contains" (Crane and Mellor 1990, 186, quoted by Hampton 1998, 35). So we are back to a science-based definition of "the natural" and, from the point of view of naturalism at least, its disabling discontents. What the natural is becomes very obscure indeed.

Hampton, in a very important passage, which I shall quote in full, calls our attention to another difficulty with relying on physics to define what the natural can be.

It is understandable why physics would be the arbiter of the natural—
where the natural is supposed to cover all and only that which is real—
if we have a well-founded conception of what counts as natural, and
physics is understood to be designed to uncover and clarify all that is
natural, and thus all that is real. But without that conception, what
makes us think that the subject matter of physics, whatever it turns out
to be at any given time, is licensed to define what is real? The metaphysical authority of physics is puzzling if reality is defined in terms of
it, rather than vice versa. If it is true that the world is made up of all and
only the sorts of entities that physics studies, then what physics tells us
about the world should be authoritative for our beliefs. But if we don't
have any way of knowing, or even characterizing, what is real independent of any particular theory, then for any of our favorite theories (take
your pick), we have no particular reason to believe that (only) this
theory depicts the real. Who says it does? Why should we believe what
the physicists say is real (particularly when they keep changing their
minds) and not, say, the pope or the dalai lama? How do the former constitute a reliable authority about the world in the way that the latter do
not? (Hampton 1998, 37)

The first thing that comes to mind by way of response is the line of
argument developed by C. S. Peirce in his "Fixation of Belief," originally
published in 1877 (Peirce 1992a, 109–23). Science gains its authority
because of all the alternative methods of fixing belief on offer it is the
most successful in resolving doubt—real live doubts—and fixing belief.
Indeed the success of science in enabling us to build huge suspension
bridges, go to the moon, split the atom, discover and utilize DNA, and
the like gives us reason to treat it as an authority about the world. We can
see from this record of success why we take it seriously rather than
numerology or Cartesian or Aristotelian metaphysics. However,
Hampton counters, throughout history we have had various practices
and the theories centering around them—political, religious, and moral—
that have at various times enabled people in different cultures to do various things: things that have, in one way or another, enabled them to
cope. "But we do not think that this instrumental value is sufficient by
itself to make them [that is, all these practices and the theories that go
with them] accurate descriptive accounts of the world. So why does the
fact that our present-day theories have allowed us to make rockets,
mobile phones, and camcorders show that they are reliable indicators of
what reality contains?" (Hampton 1998, 38).[2]

Suppose, alternatively, we say, assuming quite tendentiously, that we
know what we are talking about here, that it is the very considerable predictive power of science that justifies our believing that it gives us the best
approximation there is to "the only true description of the world"

(Hampton 1998, 38). But "scientific theories are predictively successful with respect to certain aspects of the world (for example, micro particles, chemical events, biological species)" (Hampton 1998, 38). But, in telling us about globalization, how capitalism works, what national identity comes to, let alone what should be done about globalization and capitalism and the importance, or lack thereof, of a sense of national identity or (alternatively) of some other cultural identity and of the depth and nature of alienation in contemporary societies, its track record of predictive success has not been so great. Some people call themselves political *scientists*. But that is more of a boast than a reality. Some "political science" departments recognizing that have sensibly changed their names to "departments of political studies." In these domains we do not—at least for anything very significant—get much in the way of predictive success. Moreover, in thinking about globalization, capitalism, alienation, national identity, and the like, we are less concerned with predictive success than with trying (a) to get an accurate description of them—though a description which is always for some distinctive purposes—and (b) in trying to ascertain what we should reflectively endorse concerning them and what we should do in the light of those reflective endorsements. We have issues here where predictive success plays a marginal role. But are we not here still concerned with realities just as much, though differently, as when we are concerned with micro particles, chemical processes, or biological species? Various of us have different interests and as a result we concern ourselves with different things. A person may investigate whether or not it is the case that in any society for the society stably to sustain itself there must be some sense of religion—something of its felt importance—motivating most of the members of that society. A person carrying out that investigation is concerning herself just as much with what is real as is the person who is concerned to investigate whether or not the North Pole contains zinc or whether there is water on Mars. We have no good reason to believe that natural science alone investigates what is "really real." That is scientism pure and simple and it is an ideology and a distorting one as well (Habermas 1970, 81–122; Nielsen 1978, 131–47). Moreover, to talk about what is "really real" is arm waving. We have no coherent idea what we are talking about here. Hampton in a good antiscientistic manner asks "what justifies one in believing that all that exists is what science (at a given time) posits? This ontological faith is undefended, and difficult to know how to defend" (Hampton 1998, 39).

Hampton follows W. V. Quine, a committed naturalist if there ever was one, in ridiculing (though mostly by way of argument) the very "idea that there is some obvious correct naturalist ontology to which all scientifically inclined people are committed" (Hampton 1998, 39). Quine has worked out the semantics of existence claims. But his succinct "to be is to be the value of a bound variable" tests the conformity of a sentence to a prior standard. "We look," Quine remarks, "to bound variables in connection with ontology not to know what there is, but in order to know what a given remark or doctrine, ours or someone else's *says* there is; and this much is quite properly a problem involving language. But *what there is* is another question" (Quine 1980, 15–16, italics mine). To find out what there is we do indeed need to rely, Quine has it, on an ontological standard. But it is evident, he also has it, that this is just the start. After that we actually have to do some investigating to find out what there is. Something, he avers, which is the task of science. What we need the standard for is to tell us *what sort of entities* we should accept or reject: what sort of entities we can reasonably believe there are.

The ontological standard Quine relies on is *simplicity* both in accepting an ontology and in accepting a scientific theory. We, if we are being reasonable, will adopt the simplest account "into which the disordered fragments of raw experience can be fitted and arranged" (Quine 1980, 16). But the standard of simplicity, in Quine's view, doesn't yield a *unique* ontology. A physicalist (naturalist) ontology and a phenomenalist one are, Quine believes, equally simple. But on the latter, as Quine also has it, physical objects are regarded as myths. Just as physicalists (naturalists) dismiss classes or attributes as mythical Platonic entities, so phenomenalists dismiss physical objects as mythical Platonic entities. One person's myth is another person's reality. Moreover, simplicity doesn't settle matters here, for both ontologies, as we have just noted Quine averring, are equally simple. But then how can there be good reasons for believing that only explanations that use a naturalistic ontology are true or warranted or can be reasonably believed to depict the only actual entities there are? Or even the only entities we can reliably posit? It looks like for the naturalist we have groundless believing resting on an arbitrary posit.

Quine has gone on to argue that it is foolish to engage in ontological speculation, naturalistic or otherwise, about the *ultimate components* of the world (Quine 1981, 20). Suppose in trying to define "natural," and in articulating a naturalist ontology, we say the ultimate constituents of the universe are space-time regions. "We can," Quine points out, "represent these as classes of quadruples of numbers according to an arbitrarily adopted system of coordinates. But the numbers of these quadruples can be modeled using set theory, and if these sets can themselves be constructed from the null set, then the null set is the ultimate constituent of the universe" (Quine 1981, 17–18). But this, as he stresses, is an obvious *reductio* of a search for the ultimate constituents or components of the universe. But this is the fate of a naturalist account which is searching for "ultimate reality" and "the one true description of the world"—an account that searches for the ultimate constituents or components of the world. But this is at best a foolish enterprise and at worst (and very likely) an incoherent one (Putnam

1990, 3–29). (Wittgenstein, though arguing quite differently, comes to the same conclusion. Wittgenstein 1953, 21–24.) It will not give us an accept-able account of what is natural. However, we must hasten to add that not all naturalisms take that form—not Quine's own, not Putnam's, not Rorty's, not Dewey's, not Hook's, not mine, to mention a few.

Quine, however, holds out a straw to the naturalist so conceived. (Remember Quine is a charter member naturalist.) Ontological specula-tion, for at least the reasons we have canvassed above, about what the basic or ultimate components or constituents of the world are is foolish. However, it is not objects, Quine claims, that are essential to science and to a scientific naturalistic worldview. Perhaps we can instead define the natural with reference to the physical sciences by specifying the *authori-tative structure* that is "the hallmark of physical sciences" and thereby gain a characterization of the natural that will make sense of naturalism? What are these compelling, authoritative structures? Perhaps they are the laws of science? They are, if there are any such laws, not just accidental generalizations; they must sustain contrary-to-fact conditionals. But does not this presuppose some mysterious necessity—some modalities—in the world that is foreign to naturalism? A naturalism that is a "scientific empiricism," to use Sidney Hook's phrase, could never sanction that.

Suppose, alternatively, eschewing such rationalism, that we take a positivist turn, in trying to make clear what we are talking about when we as naturalists appeal to a distinction between what is natural and what is not? According to positivists a statement has factual significance—and thus can tell us about what is natural—only if it is at least in principle ver-ifiable (empirically testable, confirmable, or infirmable). What is at least in principle empirically testable is what we are talking about when we speak of nature or the natural. Something is a part of nature if it is so testable and is found, or would be found, after an appropriate investigation, to be what we have good grounds (i.e., directly or indirectly verifiable grounds) for asserting to be so. But it is also necessary to note that positivists held that for *single propositions* to be factually significant they must be individually verifiable; they held that unless what is alleged to be a proposition is itself verifiable it is not a genuine proposition with factual content. But, from a later probing of this criterion by the positivists themselves, a well as by Quine and others, it became evident that it is not single propositions that must be verifiable to be factually significant but a body of propositions taken together which must be verifiable (testable). Individual propositions in that verifiable body of propositions can be unverifiable and still be meaningful, cognitive, fact stating propositions in good order, standing as propositions of a scientific theory or of some other forms of life. Some of them, while not being verifiable themselves, still must, to be meaningful (to make sense), be a part of a system of propositions at least *some* of which are verifiable. So the factual and what is part of nature—that is, *here* particular factual claims—is not captured by what is (directly or indirectly) verifiable. On such a holistic account of verification religious and theological propositions making claims about the supernatural or the transcendent could be fact stating as long as they are part of a system of propositions *some* of which are verifiable. And that is easily achieved by religious belief-systems. So on such an account they could pass scientific muster. (I do mean to give to understand that religious believers should aspire to that for them. In my view they should be perfectly indifferent to such matters. See chapter 9.)

If, to preserve the positivist criterion of factual significance, we make things more restrictive, we end up chucking out not only religious and theological propositions but important, and sometimes uncontroversial, parts of science as well. So something which is a part of nature can be quite unverifiable, either directly or indirectly; that is, a proposition asserting it can itself be unverifiable and still be genuinely a factual statement asserting that (and perhaps correctly) something is a part of nature. It asserts, that is, and coherently, the existence of something that is part of nature. Being verifiable is not *the* or even *a* criterion of the natural.

We are, it appears, still without a substantive definition or characterization of nature. And we have nothing we can legitimately appeal to to determine what passes scientific muster. Hampton concludes that "there is no consensus at all in the philosophical community on any substantive conception of the natural, nor any consensus on what science is, such that this enterprise, so defined, could be taken to define the natural" (Hampton 1998, 111).

III

Does this give naturalism its quietus? I do not think so. But it should make naturalists run scared. Scientism is a distorting ideology expressing a mystified worldview. We have no good grounds for believing that physics—or more generally natural science—is the arbiter of the real.[3] When we probe our intuitions a bit in the light of contemporary natural science, we see that our conceptions of nature are quite obscure. To operationally define "the natural," as Hook does, in terms of whatever the natural science of the time takes to be nature or the natural, initially attractive as it may seem, will, as we have seen, not work. Hampton makes that plain. And philosophical conceptions of the natural—or so at least it seems—do not work either. Either they are reasonably clear, as was the older nineteenth-century materialist conception of nature, but clash with contemporary physics or they are obscure, giving us no adequate conceptualization of what we are talking about when we say, for example, that nature is all-pervasive or that there is nothing beyond nature or that nature is the marker of the real. Is there any escaping the mousetrap Hampton has set for us?

Let us see, trying for a substantive definition or characterization of "nature," if we can whittle down that obscurity a bit until we get something that is acceptable. "Natural" on substantive conceptions of natural will denote the kind of object or property of an object which is the opposite of nonnatural. So conceived, what is natural is, as Hampton puts it, "conceptually prior to our understanding of science, and (at least in part) determinative of the subject matter of science" (Hampton 1995, 121–22). But that distinction (putative distinction) is not very helpful for we do not understand the supposedly contrastive term "nonnatural." As discussion of G. E. Moore's gesturing at a use brought out, we do not know what a nonnatural property is or, in the relevant sense, what a "nonnatural object" is. We are caught with something like a *via negativa* here; we do not know, with that mystery term "nonnatural," what the relevant contrast with "natural" is. "Natural object" and even "natural property" can seem pleonastic. Of course, "natural" answers to a number of reasonably (in many contexts) unproblematic contrasts: natural/artificial, natural/conventional, natural/contrived, natural/social, or perhaps even, as in old-fashioned natural moral law discussions, natural/unnatural. But, for what is at issue in the naturalism discussion, none of the above contrasts and the distinctions that go with them is relevant. For naturalism, an artificial object is just as natural as a natural object. For what we are trying to capture with the conception of naturalism is that both rocks and cars are natural objects. But then it starts to look like "natural object" really is pleonastic. However, what we are trying to capture in speaking of naturalism is the distinction (putative distinction) between natural/supernatural where "supernatural" refers to core conceptions of theism, deism, idealism, and the like. A naturalist is someone who rejects such beliefs. She *may* even reject the conceptions that go with them, regarding them as somehow incoherent. Still, it is not clear how to be more complete about "the like" and "such" here. We seem just to have some examples. And even what we do list, as I shall show below, is a mixed bag. Moreover, "supernatural" when we reflect a bit may be as troublesome as "nonnatural." It seems wrong to classify the core conceptions of idealism as supernatural ones, though they are certainly not natural. J. M. E. McTaggart was as much of an idealist as they come, but he was also an atheist (McTaggart 1906). So we seem to have a mixed bag not yielding with our examples a determinate conception of things which are not natural.

It would, I believe, be helpful in trying to make sense of "naturalism" to turn away from thinking of physics and the so-called basic stuff or basic structure of the universe and to think instead of Darwin and biology and of human beings in Darwinian terms. We should, as John Dewey did, and after him as Daniel Dennett, Richard Rorty, and Donald Davidson do, look at human beings as complicated language-using animals whose minds should be thought of as a very large network of intentional states: states attributed to an organism with a behavior that is very complex. These intentional states are elements in a causal interaction of this organism with its environment. We are animals—albeit intelligent and reflective animals—that in certain respects are like and in certain respects different from the other animals. We differ from the other animals, as Hume stressed, in being language-using animals, capable of reflection and of forming and acting on moral conceptions. All of this is shown in how our behavior is in certain respects different than the behavior of the other animals. Our distinctive patterns of behavior, instantiating certain concepts distinctive of the human animal, are, for the most part, useful for animals like ourselves—animals capable of reflection—in coping with our environment. (See chapter 2.) In such a way we are complicated objects (macro objects) from the point of view of physics. But from a biological and social point of view we are culture-creating and sustaining organisms attuned— wired for, if you will, critically examining our behavior, thinking through our actions, and acting in the light of this. And this, of course, is another bit of very linguistically oriented behavior.

To so view human beings is to be the kind of nonreductive physicalist that Dennett, Rorty, and Davidson are (Rorty 1991, 113–25). And it is to be the kind of naturalist that Dewey was, as he Darwinized Hegelian conceptions, and that David Hume was still earlier. It is a thoroughly secularist way of viewing things eschewing *recherché* objects and transcendental conceptions. While Kant postulated a *noumenal* realm—something that is plainly nonnaturalistic—to square free agency with conceptions of science (something that many present-day Kantians find difficult to swallow), contemporary naturalists, as Hobbes, Spinoza, Hume, and Engels did before them, will defend or at least adopt some form of compatibilism. And unlike nonnaturalists such as Kant, Thomas Reid, or Richard Price, they will take acting from duty to be realizable by, and explainable of, as Peter Railton put it, "a being who is (among other things) a causal being situated in a causal world" (Railton 1995, 98).

The distinction between naturalism and nonnaturalism, between natural objects, properties, and conceptions, and nonnatural ones, comes out in the above contrasts. Naturalism takes human beings to be complicated, language-using animals (and thus objects) in causal interaction with other physical objects, and it will not postulate entities acceptable to, and in some instances required by, nonnaturalism, to wit, *noumenal* beings, God, gods, bodiless minds, minds as some private physically indescribable something mysteriously interacting with bodies or as remaining somehow distinct from but still parallel to bodies. *At most* a naturalism might accept a *property* dualism. So, after all, we do get, where the human animal and other animals are concerned, a natural/nonnatural contrast. Moreover, as can be seen from the above, it is a contrast which is nonvacuous, at least if we do not push too hard about the coherency of the nonnatural notions, e.g., *noumena*, God, spirits, and the like.[4] It is not the case (*pace* Hampton) that we cannot specify what the nonnatural is as distinct from the natural. And, though we appealed to Darwinian notions rather vaguely and generally, the specification of natural here is conceptually prior to our scientific understanding. Hume, whom Darwin read, put it, much as we have put it, commonsensically, but in a way which comports well with Darwinianism, but does not depend on it. It is fair enough to observe that this is a prescientific but not an antiscientific or even an unscientific way of talking about human beings without invoking any transcendental notions and while maintaining a tolerably clear contrast between what is natural and what is not. We have, that is, a conception of the natural that admits of a nonvacuous contrast.

In speaking of a substantive conception of what is natural, Hampton rightly observes,

> in the seventeenth century naturalists called themselves "materialists," insofar as they thought of the world as made up of "solid, inert, impenetrable, and conserved" matter that interacts deterministically and through contact. (Hampton 1995, 123)

Unfortunately for naturalists, as I have already noted her remarking, physics itself came to undermine in our century this "popular and seemingly sensible conception of the natural" (Hampton 1995, 123). Twentieth-century physics "posited entities, and interactions between these entities, that do not fit the materialist characterization of the real" (Hampton 1995, 123). But we do not need to consider microphysics when we are talking about macro particles (middle-sized objects like us). Whatever an ant, toad, or a human being "ultimately" is made up of, they are observationally identifiable and, their movements are quite deterministically predictable. And a biologically and socially oriented naturalism, centrally concerned with human and other animal behavior, is concerned with middle-sized objects, and there is no good reason not to think that something like a nonreductive materialism (a physicalism of a nonreductive sort), or at least a property dualism embedded in an overall naturalistic framework, is not quite in place here. Moreover, it is the complex behavior of just such objects—including their social behavior—in its interaction with their environment that is relevant to morals, but this does not require the specification of anything that cannot be specified in naturalistic terms. "Freedom ('counter-causal freedom') among the electrons," if indeed there is any, is quite irrelevant.

It may be responded that this is not a conception of a *complete* naturalism. A naturalism that is complete would be a specification of every kind of entity in the entire universe, showing that the universe—all of it—is made up only of micro particles and macro particles in space-time, though, of course, some things are more micro and some things are more macro than others.[5] The above Darwinian-Deweyan-Dennettian account does not show how everything in the universe, including micro entities, can be specified in naturalist (physicalistic) terms.

Why, it can be replied, should we find it important for our naturalism (the naturalism of secular humanists) to be *complete*, particularly when the very idea of a complete specification of what the entire universe is like—what, considering everything, the correct description of it is—is, to put it mildly, not a very lucid idea? (Putnam 1990, 3–29) What is important is to be able to talk of human beings and the environment in which they interact in naturalistic terms. And that we have done. Moreover, talk about the *nature* of micro particles—or indeed perhaps talk of the *nature* of anything else with its implicit commitment to essentialism—is a slippery business (Rorty 1999, 47–71). And if we think that is the way to get at "ultimate reality," then we should, in turn, respond to this with Quine's ridicule, shared by Hampton, concerning talk of the ultimate constituents of the universe. To this we should add, following J. L. Austin, how it is nonsense to speak, as Hampton does, of "the materialist characterization of *the real*" or of "the idealist characterization of *the real*" or "the theistic characterization of *the real*." No sense has been given to "the real" here, and it is unclear that any nontendentious sense can be given to it. It is as bad as talk of being or being as such or of the ground of being. We have something sensible when we talk of "real beer" as distinct from "beer without alcohol," or "real butter" as distinct from "margarine," or "real philosophy" as distinct from "the philosophy of sport," or a "real hike" as distinct from "a stroll." *Persuasive* definitions of "real" are, of course, at work here, but still we do have a genuine contrast and, not infrequently, a contrast with a point, a contrast that is clearly not arbitrary. Charles Stevenson, who, along with I. A. Richards, showed us so deftly how *persuasive* definitions work, was also concerned to stress that they were not *all* arbitrary and without a reasonable point (Stevenson 1944, 206–52). But when we just, *sans contexte*, speak of an investigation of, or reflection on, *the real*, there is no contrast with the unreal. What is the difference between a materialist characterization of the real and a materialist characterization of the unreal, unless the characterization we have in mind is to speak of trees, seas, lemurs, and human beings in contrast with gods, *noumena*, pure spirits, bodiless intellects, entelechies, the *élan vital*, and the like? (Note again the trouble—or at least the apparent trouble—with completing "the like.") But the latter cluster of terms in their comparison with trees, tables, etc. is of dubious, or at the very least problematic, intelligibility. It is not, for example, clear that we have said anything intelligible when we speak of pure spirits. It is not at all like comparing "real cream" and "nondairy creamer." But, if this is so, we are back with the familiar Darwinian-Deweyan-Dennettian position which was not thought to be a general enough specification of "natural" to identify it with "the real." But the crucial point here is that there is no sensible talk of "the real" except in a *determinate context for determinate purposes* (Hägerström 1964, 41–74, 313). The kind of naturalism relevant to a social understanding of *our* world is much more contextualist than such a vast speculative endeavor of dubious intelligibility as a putative investigation of or discovery of "the real," or as an attempt to define or describe "the real" *sans contexte*. Put otherwise, *contra* scientistic forms of naturalism, a nonanthropomorphic naturalism is for me at least both unwelcome and unnecessary. To try to go for it reflects the metaphysical compulsions of philosophers and some scientists (usually physicists or mathematicians nearing retirement) running out of control. It has all the ills of metaphysical realism (Putnam 1992a, 80–133; Rorty 1998, 43–97). Again language has gone on a holiday.

Hampton, as a self-proclaimed moral objectivist and moral realist, is in search of "the only true description of the world" but such a quest is incoherent (Putnam 1990, 1992a; Rorty 1991). There is, of course, a deep and persistent metaphysical temptation to try to speak of the way the world is just in itself or of how things just are anyway. But it is incoherent to speak of how the world is or of how things are independently of any choice of a vocabulary, independently, that is, of how it can be described by a particular language answering to determinate interests, or of how a vocabulary we have, or can come to adopt, characterizes the world or will come to characterize it. The metaphysical illusion is to have a picture of nature as having something like "her own language": to think (incoherently think) of nature, as speaking to us revealing just how things are (Putnam 1990, 301–302). The idea here is, of course, incoherent, but it is all the same possible, where our metaphysical craving to be able to grasp how the world is in itself—to finally get things right—is so very great that we will not recognize the incoherence. We will not see what is obvious to the person without such cravings. We blind ourselves here with a metaphysical picture. But, given what we want, to wit to know what the world is like in itself, it can be, humanly speaking, a compelling picture, but something which is incoherent all the same. It can be very difficult for some of us to free ourselves from the grip of such a picture.

It is terribly important to be careful how we put things here, for even the reference to "it" in "of how it can be described" in the previous paragraph can mislead. There is no "it" there to be identified, taking different specifications, but mysteriously somehow standing apart from *all* these descriptions making various specifications of something allegedly *independently* identifiable and knowable apart from these or any other specifications. It is pictured as "a something" of which an understanding is gainable without some language (Putnam 1990, 301–302). The picture—a metaphysical picture—is that we have some language-independent way of knowing or of understanding things.

This is not linguistic idealism for it does not suggest or in anyway imply absurdly that there were no stones or trees around before there were humans with their languages to describe them. But it does claim that that we cannot think about them or understand what they are and, of course, and trivially, talk about them without having a language. Similarly, though they exist quite independently of what we say or think, there would be no *truths* about them without a language. Truth is in this way language-dependent in the way most objects (e.g., stones or trees) are not. *There is no truth without language.* And relatedly, but still distinctly, we cannot without having a language know or understand anything about them or anything else.

In cold sobriety we need to recognize that it makes no sense to try to discover the way the world is apart from any linguistic description of it: linguistic descriptions which will vary from context to context, changing with our differing purposes, interests, and situations (Putnam 1990, 1994). Hampton cannot have her one true description of the world. There can be no such thing for such talk makes no sense (Putnam 1990, 1992a). Rather descriptions answer to human needs, interests, and purposes and are structured by them. They reflect the problems and resulting perspectives that people inherit or otherwise come to have. There is no intelligible "point of view from nowhere," "the point of view of the universe" or "an absolute conception of the world," that is, a point of view or a conception that is interest-free, particularly perspective-free, and could yield the one true description of the world, so that, free of some determinate human interests, scientific or otherwise, we could just say—describe how—the way the world is *anyway* quite apart from any human interests and resultant ways of describing and conceptualizing things. There is (*pace* Hampton) *no just finding out about reality so that we could discover whether, after all, it—Reality Itself—is really naturalistic or otherwise.* This need not at all to be to junk a naturalistic perspective. But it is to say that naturalism is not something that could just be discovered to be true and most particularly it could not just be discovered to be true by discovering "the only correct description of the universe."

Hampton takes Bernard Williams's conception of an absolute per-spective to be relatively unproblematic and claims that he has just arbi-trarily excluded moral properties and, as she puts it, "moral objects" from being a part of an absolute perspective. But this utterly misses the prob-lems, pressed by Putnam, Rorty, and myself concerning whether such a conception makes any sense, so that a coherent debate could be carried on between her and Williams over "moral realism" (Putnam 1992a, 80–107; Rorty 1991, 4–10, 48–61; Nielsen 1996, 418–24).

IV

I have found unpersuasive some of the things Hampton says in criticism of naturalism and I have found (or at least thought I have found) alternative naturalistic accounts that are not vulnerable to her acute criticisms of some forms of naturalism. But all that notwithstanding, it should be stressed that her tightly organized, and carefully reasoned, series of arguments are for-midable and deserve careful scrutiny, including skeptical sober second thoughts concerning the soundness of the above criticisms of her account. She has, at a minimum, put forms of *naturalism hostile to morality* (to adopt her not untendentious way of putting things) very much on the defensive. But she has not been similarly successful against the form of substantive naturalism I have defended above and I shall argue in this section that there are forms of ethical naturalism not hostile to morality that she has not undermined. Still all these arguments of hers are on her *nay*-saying side, the side that she is principally concerned with in her writings of 1995 and 1998. However, along the way, she also makes some positive claims and utilizes distinctive conceptions which are at least as vulnerable as the nat-uralistic claims and conceptions she finds problematic. She announces on the first page of her 1995 essay that she is a moral objectivist, as if, with that, we have anything even reasonably clear or unproblematic. Someone (John Rawls, for example) not at all tempted by moral skepticism or subjectivism might still well want to say that the very notion of objectivity, particularly in such domains, is elusive. Perhaps to speak of objectivity in such a con-text is only to speak of some form of rather full intersubjectivity or of what would be affirmed in *wide* and *general* reflective equilibrium (Rawls 1995, 140–41)? Yet some philosophers have wanted something more in the way of objectivity, but what that is, or whether they can have it or even coher-ently articulate it, is anything but clear. There have, in the history of our subject, been metaphysical cravings for all kinds of things, cravings that have, again and again, turned out to involve incoherent beliefs. What it is to be a moral objectivist does not wear its meaning on its sleeve. The same thing is true of moral realism, which Hampton also un–self-consciously avows. Even if J. L. Mackie's and Gilbert Harman's arguments do not go through, the very idea of moral realism remains thoroughly problematic. It seems to have all the difficulties of metaphysical realism plus the additional ones connected with normativity (Couture and Nielsen 1993, 365–87). Even noncognitivists can correctly say, and account for, the claim that moral utterances are either true or false, if they stick, as well they might, with a minimalist or deflationist account of truth (Ayer 1963, 231–32; Smith 1994, 1–12). If the moral realist claims a stronger substantive correspondence theory of truth, all the standard difficulties arise concerning whether we can make sense, in any domain (even the-cat-is-on-the-mat domain) of correspondence accounts of truth, beyond Tarski's "correspondence-platitudes," platitudes accepted by both minimalists and deflationists: philosophers who firmly reject correspondence theories of truth. We have Donald Davidson's point that the very "notion of fitting the facts, or of being true to the facts adds nothing intelligible to the simple concept of being true" (Davidson 1984, 193–94). Realism, moral or metaphysical (as distinct from Putnam's common-sense realism), has arguably an incoherent, or at least an unnecessary, conception of truth: more metaphysical baggage standing in the way of gaining a good understanding of morality (Rorty 1999, 23–46).

However, we need not, and indeed should not, flee to anti-realism or to irrealism either and adopt some form of noncognitivism or error-theory. We can perfectly well, not going beyond minimalism, say that moral utterances can be true, and, if they are, then there are moral facts again in the perfectly minimalist and uncontroversial sense that a fact—moral, mathematical, empirical, or whatever—is just what a true statement states. But that platitude (true all the same) does not take us to moral realism, metaphysical realism, or scientific realism, where there is a claim that truth is correspondence to facts, where, as Peter Strawson puts it ironically, facts are taken to be nonlinguistic, sentence-shaped objects: kinds of replicas of *that*-clauses—very queer kinds of objects indeed—somehow just there in the universe waiting to be passively recorded. But this is an obvious reification which neither nature nor the *noumenal* realm (if such there be) dictates by already containing in the natural world or in the *noumenal* world sentence-shaped objects, like *that*-clauses, simply, in a quasilanguage, revealing the way the world is (nature's own writ so to say), including the way the moral world is, that we can somehow just access in a passive way. We have here something very like the old copy theory of knowledge and understanding. The thought is that, if our language is to get things right, it must simply so record what we so passively access. But this is pure mystification. Yet Hampton quite unblushingly speaks of moral objects (a particularly fishy-sounding notion) and of moral facts to which we somehow have direct access.

I hope (and the hope seems reasonable) that Hampton's account could be demythologized into an ethical naturalism, say something like Peter Railton's, which is an ethical naturalism that *needs* (*pace* Railton) make no commitment either to moral realism or to moral antirealism or to a moral objectivism that involves anything other than wide and general reflective equilibrium (Daniels 1996; Nielsen 1996). (We can have objectivity without objectivism, to wit, a thoroughgoing and general intersubjectivity.) The funding theory Railton articulates squares with a scientific worldview—the Darwinian view I gestured at—unless we unrealistically mean by "scientific worldview"—a sparsely Galilean worldview—a view that would not in its account contain anything evaluative or normative, insisting on a normatively neutral vocabulary, again assuming problematically, given the infusion of the normative into our language, that anything like that even could obtain, i.e., be a coherent possibility (*contra* Putnam 1990, 135–78). But Railton does not believe that a scientific worldview should, or perhaps even could, be so sparsely Galilean. His is "a funding theory of morality that would enable us to see the compatibility of our moral categories and assumptions with going empirical theory" (Railton 1995, 82).

In coming to understand the strength of ethical naturalism, it is important to consider *supervenience* and specifically the supervenience of the normative on the factual. Railton says important and on the whole convincing things here. But it is well to start with a remark of Allan Gibbard's made in his "Reply to Railton" (Gibbard 1993, 52–59). "Norms," Gibbard remarks, "apply to types of possible circumstances. If they apply, then, to two possible circumstances differently, that must be because the circumstances are of different types. *No normative difference without a factual difference*: If what to do differs in two possible circumstances, the facts differ" (Gibbard 1993, 55; italics added). This notion is obviously naturalist-friendly, but nonnaturalistic cognitivists (if there still are any) and noncognitivists can also acknowledge it, as indeed they would have to if it really is, as Gibbard takes it to be, an a priori and necessary truth (in whatever sense we are going to make of that notion in these post-Quinean times) (Gibbard 1993, 55–56). I say it is naturalist-friendly for, as Railton puts it, without any identification (even *de facto* identification) of the moral with the natural or moral properties with natural properties, "the supervenience of moral properties upon natural properties brought an inevitable commitment to seeing morality as such that the natural world could support it" (Railton 1995, 162). That this is so, and how it is so, if it is so, Gibbard's remark makes plain. Railton comments that some take supervenience to be a metaphysical or a normative claim. But these are confusions, if Gibbard's claim is so, for the supervenience of the moral on the natural is a conceptual, in a broad sense a logical, claim rooted in our use of normative, including moral, language. It is, if Gibbard is right, a feature of what in the bad old days would have been called "the logic of moral discourse." But seen in this "clean" way, as Railton stresses, it "carries no presupposition of the existence of moral properties" (Railton 1995, 103–104). One is only constrained to believe, if one cares about consistency and intelligibility, that if two situations differ morally they must also be different in their (nonindexical) natural properties. "No moral difference without a factual difference" is not a moral or even metamoral imperative, or indeed any kind of imperative, but has the same status as "No bachelorhood without unmarriedness." We would not even understand moral talk, or other normative talk, unless we had at least an implicit recognition of supervenience. (It might with many, indeed, most, just be a knowing how rather than a knowing that.)

Two situations, to see rather more concretely what is involved here, cannot differ *solely* in their moral character. Sven and Erik are two adults similar in all relevant respects and relevantly similarly situated. We cannot intelligibly say that it was vile the way Sven was slashed, beaten, and strangled and go on to say that it was perfectly all right the way that Erik was slashed, beaten, and strangled when that way was the same and there are no relevant differences between Erik and Sven or in their circumstances (Nielsen 1985, 91–101). We are not here just making moral judgments from which someone might coherently dissent, but we are in effect reminding ourselves of how the moral language-game is played. Calling it "vile" is no doubt a strong moral response expressive of our moral emotions and tending to evoke similar emotions in others, but it is rooted in our seeing what happened to Sven and in knowing that, if the same thing happens to Erik and there is no relevant different between Sven and Erik or in their circumstances, we must—to be consistent, must—whether we feel the same emotion or not, believe the same thing about what happened to Erik. We can, of course, say that consistency is simply a hang-up of pedantic minds, but then we convict ourselves of irrationality. If, in turn, we respond "So what?," then it is not clear what more is to be said. But it is understandable that people will quickly lose interest in the discussion, if that is what it is to be called, if it takes that turn. We are held to a certain kind of consistency patterned upon the sameness of the facts in the case (the natural facts, if that is not pleonastic) (Stevenson 1983, 13–37).

Whenever something is good, right, just, fitting, suitable to the situation, and the like, it is so because of certain nonethical, factual characteristics. The noncognitivists may be right that to say that something is good, right, fitting, and the like is not to report or describe some natural state of affairs (let alone some "nonnatural" state of affairs), but to express a pro-attitude toward such states of affairs or to prescribe that such states of affairs obtain. Nonetheless, as Railton puts it, such moral judgments "have an intimate relation to such states of affairs—moral qualities are constituted by or grounded in natural qualities" (Railton 1995, 101). Moreover, this is a strong connection. It is not the claim that moral judgments merely correlate with or harmonize with such statements of fact. Rather, the naturalist claims, again in Railton's words, that if "moral judgment is ever in place it is in place because the world (apart from moral opinion) is such as to make it so" (Railton 1995, 101). But then questions about the way the world is (under some description, of course), questions about what explains what, questions about what might constitute what—"in short, questions raised by the development of empirical inquiry—can reach to the heart of morality" (Railton 1995, 101). Moreover, the supervenience of the moral on the factual is not a reciprocal supervenience, but an *asymmetrical* one: the factual must constitute or at least produce the moral, but surely not the other way around. We see here what Railton calls "a core truism of the moral realm—the dependence of the moral upon the natural" (Railton 1995, 102). Moreover, if Gibbard is right, "No normative difference without a factual difference," as distinct from "No factual difference without a normative difference," is a proposition that is "a priori and necessary: it holds independently of experience, and applies to all possible situations" (Gibbard 1993, 55–56). This core truism, if it really is that, if it could be successfully linked with compatibilism, would underwrite ethical naturalism. Moreover, it would be a nonreductive, *nondefinitional* ethical naturalism that need not be troubled by the *open-question argument*: the open question could remain *open* and still this naturalism could remain firmly in place. Moreover, it could, and indeed should, accept the expressiveness and prescriptivity stressed by noncognitivists as well as the essential action-guidingness, and, in that sense, the practicality of moral judgments also stressed by noncognitivists and, as well, by Kantians. Moral utterances could, in their very nature (if there is such a thing), be expressive-evocative and action-guiding and still asymmetric supervenience would obtain: with the factual producing the moral such that if someone claims that something is good, right, just, fitting, suitable to the situation and the like, it must (a) be because of certain natural facts about it and (b) that, as well, when the same situation obtains, or a relevantly similar situation obtains, including the sort of people involved being the same or relevantly similar, the same moral judgment must, in consistency, be made.

We only have *lebensraum* for moral argument here over whether the situation is relevantly similar (Nielsen 1985, 91–101). Moreover, as Railton also stresses, this nonreductive ethical naturalism is compatible with the acceptance of an "is"/"ought" gap. Natural facts can produce or even constitute values while it remains true that there is "a logical gap between any alleged fact and any conclusion expressed in moral terms" (Railton 1995, 104). We can begin to see that and how this is so, if we consider the fact that supervenience is compatible with Mackian-Blackburnian moral skepticism: "the possibility that our moral thought is massively in error" (Mackie 1946, 1977). If Hampton's and Sturgeon's arguments are on the mark, such an error theory is very problematical (Hampton 1998; Sturgeon 1995). But neither would claim, nor could they reasonably claim, to have decisively or conclusively disproved it. It still seems to be at least a logical possibility that our moral thought is massively in error. So the truth, indeed the logical truth, of the asymmetric supervenience of the moral on the factual does not guarantee that fixing the natural properties of the actual world a priori guarantees the presence of *any* moral properties. If an error theory is right, then there are no real oughts, not even *ought nots*. Facts produce or constitute oughts, *if there are any oughts*, so we cannot have a moral difference without a factual difference. If there is something we ought to do, it is, Railton argues, because the very idea of "ought or ought not to be doneness" is not illusory. It would, however, be illusory if there were no genuine ought, *neither oughts nor ought nots. If* there is nothing that we ought or ought not to do, the facts will show that too. But an appeal to the facts is not sufficient to *logically* guarantee *which situation actually obtains*, which situation is the case. This should hardly be surprising. It is a notion that Hume and Kant were onto as later Henri Poincaré and Max Weber were as well, and it was expressed forcefully by Moore and by the noncognitivists. The acceptance of asymmetric supervenience does not affect that. There still remains, even with the acceptance of an ethical naturalism like Railton's, something of the "is"/"ought" gap. We are not going to get anything normatively substantial that is *unconditional* either here or anywhere else. We are not going to find out by just looking at the facts or analyzing concepts that there is something we must do.

However, Railton argues, rightly it seems to me, that, though an ethical naturalist can and should accept that much of the autonomy of ethics (the "is"/"ought" gap), she also should be a good fallibilist—perhaps even a pragmatist-fallibilist—and, accepting the logical autonomy of ethics, deploy the method of wide and general reflective equilibrium, a method, as Railton puts it, that "knows of connections that are more than logical" (Railton 1995, 104–105). Someone deploying such a method will want to display the most plausible fit between our various moral judgments and our actual beliefs, including for us our reflective beliefs about the (for us now) best established "substantive and methodological elements of empirical science" (Railton 1995, 86). Moreover, wide and general reflective equilibrium will seek to show how we can have a cluster of moral beliefs that avoids "intolerable strains with the substantive and methodological elements of empirical science" (Railton 1995, 86).

Suppose—to run with this a bit—that Sturgeon and Hampton are right against Harman. Central moral notions (virtue, duty, and agency) play not only a *justificatory* role, but also an *explanatory* role, explaining in particular situations not only what we do, but what we believe we ought to do in those situations. Note, however, that to explain what we *believe* we ought to do is not *eo ipso* to explain what we ought to do. Still, if people are not worked up, not bombarded with ideology, and have good and accurate information concerning the situation in question, then, if they believe they ought to do something in that situation, then we have a very good reason to believe they ought to do it (Kumar 2000). There is, of course, no entailment, but, as we have noted Railton observing, people who work with reflective equilibrium routinely use connections that are weaker than entailments. It is reasonable for us to want to be compatibilists about this; if we can, we will want these explanatory roles we attribute to moral notions to square with whatever we know or reasonably believe about how the world operates. We are not, to repeat, looking for entailments, but to see how these notions can be compatible. How, if you will, they coherently hang together. How, for example, we can be free even if the universe, for macroscopic objects at least, is deterministic. "Showing compatibility is a way of promoting the autonomy of moral reasoning for it would show that we are not running afoul of our own convictions about the relation of the moral to the natural" (Railton 1995, 105). Given what we know, or at least plausibly think we know, about the world, including its continuing, though with ups and downs, demystification, we will not wish (if we are being clearheaded and reasonable) to postulate Kantian noumenal agency, contracausal freedom, a space of reasons holding independently of what has empirical warrant, a natural order of reasons, systematic error in all moral thought, complete lack of human freedom, and the like. We will eschew such notions, if we reasonably can. We will try to get a wide and general reflective equilibrium without such notions, a wide and general reflective equilibrium within an utterly naturalistic framework (no transcendental notions, no *élan vital*, no *noumena*) (Nielsen 1996, 12–19, 219–23). We want, and reasonably so, to be able to see, and to perspicuously represent, how things hang together in a way that makes sense of our moral convictions and, as well, of our scientific and common-sense knowledge of the world (common-sense knowledge that has good empirical backing). Error theory vis-à-vis morality is something we would reasonably accept only if all such attempts at wide reflective-equilibrium rationalization fail and fail after repeated and careful attempts.

So reasonability dictates a compatibilist strategy (a generalization from its original home in the freedom-determinism controversy), though it does not a priori, or in any other way, *guarantee* its truth. But that is no defect, for it is foolish to look for such guarantees. To quest for certainty is always a mistake. Reflective equilibrium sets us, instead, to the articulating of a naturalistic funding theory (if we need any theory at all) rooted in our ordinary reflective thinking about ethics, which will also be a theory that will ground our moral thought and practice in the natural world and, though some moral beliefs will no doubt be revised and some even abandoned, it will fund as well many of our most centrally embedded moral convictions, showing there can be a moral life that has a rationale and a point without our succumbing to illusions or to blinding ourselves to how our world is (Daniels 1996; Nielsen 1996).[6] Here, as we have seen, asymmetric supervenience is a crucial conception. Reflections on it, and on the plausibility of a general compatibilist strategy, make the case for a nonreductive, nondefinitional ethical naturalism (a synthetic ethical naturalism) very attractive (Couture and Nielsen 1995, 22–27). It is an ethical naturalism that leaves the open question *open*, and the "is"/"ought" gap in place. But note the sea change here. In the recent history of ethical theory it has often been taken to be a definitional truth, or at least an uncontroversial one, that to be an ethical naturalist one must deny that there is an "is"/"ought" gap and define "good" and other ethical terms in naturalistic terms (e.g., "good" as "answering to interests"). But this is both a very recent and a very tendentious history, for it would turn both Jeremy Bentham and John Stuart Mill into philosophers who were not ethical naturalists (Hall 1964, 106–32). It might even be maintained, though controversially, that, on that recently conceived typology of ethical theory, not even John Dewey would count as an ethical naturalist. Such considerations attest to the inadequacy of such a typology as well as to the inadequacy of definitional ethical naturalism and reductive ethical naturalism.

V

To what I have argued in the two previous sections Hampton could respond "It may be all very well to so defend ethical naturalism and perhaps even to, in such a broadly Darwinian fashion, regard human beings—beings purely of flesh, blood, bones, and with complicated nervous systems—as complex, language-using animals causally interacting with each other and with the rest of their environment. But this still does not meet my concern about the need for *completeness* for any naturalism worthy of the name." The claim, Hampton puts in the naturalist's mouth, is that he must, to be a thorough naturalist, claim, and to be able to make that claim stick, that *the natural covers all and only the real*. Or, alternatively phrased, so as to elude arguments about the incoherence of noncontextual talk about "the real," a naturalist must be able to claim, and make it stick, that *all that there is and can be is a part of nature*. (More minimally he must claim that all that there is is a part of nature.) My above defense at most shows that all macro objects are a part of nature and only a part of nature. They are, from the point of view of physics, including contemporary physics, solid determinate bits of conserved matter interacting deterministically and through contact. If I could show that all that there is is such then I would be naturalistically home and free. We would then understand what nature is, what a part of nature is: "the natural" would have a reasonably determinate denotation and connotation. But, alas, there is Hampton's point that contemporary physics is not so obliging. There are the queer little critters of micro physics that cannot—or at least all cannot—be *so* naturalistically characterized. Yet they are paradigmatic parts of physics and have as much a claim to be a part of what there is as anything else. (Some even think—incoherently, I believe—that they are "the ultimate constituents" of what there is.) But we have no substantive definition of "nature" or "the natural"—a definition that gives a conception of nature concerning everything contemporary physics accepts, while still being conceptually prior to science—that enables us, relatively unproblematically, to characterize these micro particles of physics, as well as the macro particles, as bits of nature without making it the case that we conceive of some bits of nature as being so weird that we have no grip on what it would be to say that they are parts of nature. Indeed, weird or not, they are very different from what we can unproblematically materialistically (physicalistically) characterize.

Is this so certain? Let us go back to the characterizations of nature or the natural given by Dennes, Hook, and Nagel discussed in the previous chapter, conceptions which comport well with Quine's views. When, for them, we speak of nature we speak of regions of space-time. What there is are the various events, processes, objects, and properties of objects (something having no distinct existence apart from the objects they are properties of) in space-time.[7] The queer little critters of micro physics are such objects, bizarre though they be, in space-time. Micro particles are not solid, inert, impenetrable, conserved matter and it *may* be that they do not interact deterministically with other particles. But they are also not *transcendent* realities. They are, just like rocks, ants, protozoa, flashes of lightning, chimps, and human beings, qualitied existents (to be pleonastic) in space-time. Queer critters indeed, but critters all the same. There is more in heaven and earth than was dreamt of in the philosophy of Holbach and Hobbes and nineteenth-century materialism. Still we have with micro particles invoked nothing that is transcendent or transcendental such as God or *noumenal* selves, pure spirits or the soul. All these make a contrast with nature and give a nonvacuous contrast— assuming (controversially) that they are in *some way* intelligible conceptions—between the natural and the supernatural. So, along the lines developed by Dennes, Hook, and Nagel, and explicated and defended in the last chapter, we have a substantive conception of nature that has at least a few teeth and has (*pace* Hampton) sufficient determinativeness and nonarbitrariness to yield a sound conception of naturalism.

A conception of nature limited to macro particles is plainly not a complete conception of nature. But with the above we have something more complete. And is it at all clear that we are asking for anything that is intelligible in asking for something that is still more complete? Recall Wittgenstein on the "ideal" of "complete clarity." Would not "utter completeness" or "full completeness," "complete completeness" (something as bad as "the really real") have the elusiveness and opacity that Wittgenstein finds in talk of "complete clarity" (Wittgenstein 1953, 21–24)? Talk of "completeness" and of "clarity" like talk of "real" only makes sense in determinate contexts. Isn't the Dennes-Hook-Nagel conception of qualitied-existents in space-time adequate for both macro particles and micro particles? And is that not complete enough to cover anything that there is that could intelligibly be said to be a part of nature? And is it not reasonable to say that nature, so conceived, is all that there is?

My claim is that the answer should be yes to all these questions, though the worry remains as to just what are these existents that are qualitied existents in space-time? (Whatever they are, isn't "qualitied existents" a pleonasm? And isn't it nonsense to speak of "bare existents"?) Some of these qualitied existents are very, very different than your standard bits of conserved matter (Austin's middle-sized dry goods); some of them are very strange critters indeed. Still none of these qualitied existents in space-time are transcendent existents (assuming such a notion makes sense). Such a conception of qualitied existents *may* let idealism in the door but not theism. But even idealism will have trouble with these existents being in *space*-time. Perhaps we have here a complete enough naturalism for our stormy times?

VI

I want as a kind of coda to this chapter to add some metaphilosophical comments. Hampton, for all her analytical sophistication, has a very traditionalist and uncritical conception of philosophy. She writes as if Wittgenstein or neopragmatists such as Hilary Putnam or Richard Rorty had never written. (She cites all of them, but neither confronts their thought where it might make difficulties for her nor utilizes their at least putative insights.) Here she has a metaphilosophical naïveté that is characteristic as well of most "scientific realists," metaphysical realists, and moral realists. (I refer here to philosophers such as Richard Boyd, Michael Devitt, Clark Glymour, and Nicholas Sturgeon.) This being so, even if my arguments in the previous section are not well-taken, her case against naturalism would, as I shall proceed to argue, still be defective. She speaks for example of physics being a claimed arbiter of the real or being the arbiter of the natural and of the natural covering all and only the real and argues that we have no reason to believe that any of these things are *true*. But she seems to think we understand what we are talking about when we say these things: that, though we know (she seems at least to assume) what it would be like for them to be true or false or warranted or unwarranted, we just do not know which they are for we do not have adequate evidence or grounds to assert that they are or that they are not so. She writes (like the naturalist Sidney Hook) as if the problem is that we simply lack evidence here, but that we still know well enough what it would be to have evidence concerning such matters (if that is the right word for such talk). But it is not just that we have no evidence or good grounds for believing that science is the arbiter of the real, we have no evidence or good grounds for believing *anything* is the arbiter of the real and *a fortiori* we have no good grounds for believing that science or nature is the arbiter of the real. We do not even understand what it would be like to have evidence or good grounds here. Since we have no good grounds for asserting or denying that anything is the arbiter of the real— indeed we do not even know what we are talking about here—it cannot be a defect of naturalism or of science that they are not arbiters of the real. "Arbiters of the real" has no determinate use in the language.

It is such considerations that seem at least to just bypass the understanding of Hampton. As we saw earlier, we have no understanding of "the real" apart from a determinate context, e.g., real cream or real golf as distinct from nondairy creamer or mini-golf. And even assuming counterfactually that we understand contextless talk of "the real," we are still unclear about the force of "arbiter" in "Science is the arbiter of the real." We understand what it is for someone or some group (say a court or a panel) to be the arbiter in a labor dispute, a tenure dispute, a trade dispute between nations, but we do not have any clear understanding of what it would be for someone, and even more plainly no understanding for what it would be for something, to be an arbiter of the real or of the natural. Again language seems at least to be idling.

Perhaps demythologized it comes to something like Peirce's claim that the scientific method is the best method for fixing belief. There it looks pretty good for claims about ascertaining empirical facts, but less good for claims about science (i.e., scientific method) being the—or even an— arbiter of real art, real religion, real friendship, real aesthetic sensitivity, real moral discrimination or integrity, real democracy, real cosmopolitanism, and the like. Even if we delete the "real" as something functioning persuasively, it is unclear that the use concerning such normative matters of scientific method is of much use for fixing belief concerning *such* normative matters. (That the employment of scientific method was the way to fix belief in all domains [methodological naturalism, that is] is something that Dewey, Hook, and Ernest Nagel thought to be so, but not Peirce. See Peirce 1992, 105–22, a lecture given in 1898, and Putnam's commentary on it, Putnam 1992b, 55–59.) So we better stop talking about "the real" and of the arbitrating of the real by science. It is plainly a metaphor and indeed sometimes metaphors are useful. But not here.

Does not that doom, if accepted, the attempt I made in the previous section to give a *general* characterization of naturalism? Perhaps. If we try to say that what there is are qualitied existents in space-time, we perhaps are in similar trouble, with talk about "what there is," as with talk about "the real"? We can sensibly ask what there is in the cupboard, the basement (meaning some determinate cupboard or basement) or what there is on Mars or at the center of the earth, but not just of what there is without qualification. We can't, that is, sensibly, *sans* context, just ask about what there is. Still to ask what there is in space-time *might* make a little more sense? But only a little, for to answer rocks, people, mountains, seas, planets, stars, neutrons, neutrinos, quarks is to just give a list and a list that can hardly be completed. Do we even understand what a "completed list" will come to in such a context? It is not like making a complete list of people in my apartment block. And, it is not like asking what there is in Grandmother's cupboard or even what there is at the bottom of Lake Constance. Moreover, talk of listing or counting all the objects that there are in a room, to say nothing of in the universe, is incoherent (Putnam 1992a, 80–133; Putnam 1994, 303–304).

To say very generally, in answer to the question "What is there?" that there are events, objects, processes, and properties of things in space-time may be true and firmly naturalistic or at least naturalist-friendly, but it is hardly to make an empirical claim like claiming there are only candies in Grandmother's cupboard or that there is only sand at the bottom of Lake Constance. They are plain enough empirical claims that are either true or false and determinately so. But the empirical status (or even the logical status) of "There is nothing other than nature and what nature consists of is all and only qualitied existents in space-time and thus there are only qualitied existents (events, objects, processes, properties of things in space-time)" is unclear. It looks like a correct if rather platitudinous thing to say. But it is unclear how, rather than stipulatively definitionally, we would go about determining its truth. And is there a way here to determine its truth or to determine whether it is warrantedly assertable, if those are different things? Just as Quine's remark about the semantics of existence—to be is to be the value of a bound variable—does not tell us what there is, but only what we can intelligibly say there is, so perhaps to be is to be a qualitied existent in space-time does much the same thing without saying or even giving to understand *what* there is and thus not even implicitly calling for an empirical investigation?

Given such considerations, there *may* not be much point in trying to say positively what nature is. Perhaps we instead should in good Wittgensteinian fashion proceed negatively by proceeding to show—less arrogantly trying to show—whenever someone tries to claim a "transcendental reality" or a "transcendent reality" (say a "supernatural reality")—whenever someone shows the ambition of transcendence—that no sense has been given to their talk and that when we make intelligible claims about *what* there is and not just about what we can coherently *say*—truly or falsely—there is, i.e., remarks about the semantics of existence, we are, for all we can tell, always talking about some qualitied existent in space-time, some event, process, object, or property of an object in space-time. When we are secure about what we are saying—when our claims have truth-conditions or assertability-conditions concerning what we take to be the case—such background conditions are in place.[8] We should, it can be reasonably argued, content ourselves with that and not to try to develop a *theory* or an *account* of "the natural" or of what "nature really is." We can justifiably turn our faces from Hampton's challenge as just one more metaphysical obsession that we can, and should, ignore.

These are contestable matters, matters involving a lot of contestable metaphilosophy; it surely would be a mistake to claim anything like definitiveness for the metaphilosophical arguments I have made above— or indeed for any metaphilosophical argument. Plausibility—greater plausibility than the alternatives—is all we can reasonably aspire to over such matters. But we can reasonably aspire to that and that perhaps is all we or anyone can aspire to concerning any significant philosophical consideration. A naturalist, and particularly a naturalist who is also a pragmatist, can even settle for a weaker claim. Whenever someone like Thomas Nagel or Richard Swinburne or Jean Hampton shows an ambition of transcendence, and tries to make a substantive claim which can only be transcendentally vindicated, it is enough to show or give very good reason to believe that nothing of the sort has been vindicated and that a negatively characterized naturalism stands there undefeated in accordance with science, critical common sense, and disciplined philosophical reflection. This is more piecemeal and nay-saying than my above more positive characterization. But that *may* be all that philosophy can reasonably aspire to. Certainly such a way of proceeding gives fewer hostages to fortune and would, if it can be repeatedly successfully so argued against the particular claims of what Rorty calls the new *myste-rians*, keep a naturalistic orientation to things in good order with minimal general claims. It can *seriatim* show the errors of claims of transcendence (claims concerning a "transcendent reality") and hint with considerable plausibility at the *hubris* of such ambitions of or to transcendence. Per-haps, if this kind of therapy is repeatedly successfully practiced, people will catch on that transcendental philosophy is a bad thing, something we can usefully dispense with.

Hampton being a Christian philosopher has, even more than Thomas Nagel, the ambition of transcendence, but in addition she has a commit-ment—as she makes explicit—to transcendence. Thomas Nagel, while keeping his ambition of transcendence, can still remain what he wants to be—an atheist (Nagel 1997, 130). But Hampton's actual work under con-sideration here has been devoted to naturalism-bashing (and thus atheism-bashing) albeit in a sophisticated argumentative way. If my argu-ments have been near to the mark, for all her very considerable resourceful efforts, Hampton's bashing has in crucial respects been unsuccessful. She has not shown that naturalism rests on a mistake or that it is just something arbitrarily or opaquely posited. But, even that aside, her Christian alternative has been left here not only undefended but utterly unexplicated. She tells us she is committed to being a Chris-tian analytic philosopher, but she tells us neither how nor why nor does she show us even a little bit of what this comes to, to say nothing of what difficulties might attend a Christian view. Given this, even if her case against naturalism is much stronger than I believe it to be, given the alter-natives, naturalism may very well, for anything Hampton has said, be the more plausible option of the options on offer. After all Christianity, for anything she has said or even hinted at, may be the scandal to the intel-lect that Kierkegaard thought and said that it was. Naturalism may have its problems, but what of the supernaturalist (theistic) or idealist alterna-tives? In deciding what shoes to wear for a hike, we need to know what the shoe options are for us. None of them may be so great, given what we have, but the reasonable thing is to choose the least unpalatable option. Why should it be different in philosophy?

Perhaps Hampton believes that it should be different for, unlike Peirce, Dewey, Carnap, Hempel, Quine, Davidson, Rorty, Bernstein, and Putnam, she is *not* willing to accept that fallibilism is the name of the game. Hampton repeatedly speaks of the need to get things precisely defined, to gain decisive or definitive arguments; she talks, as well, about the need to have a *complete* physical science or a *final* physical theory. For-getting John Rawls's distinction between justification and proof, she keeps asking for proof—strict proof—all along the line. But, if we have learned anything from the pragmatists or from Quine and Davidson or from Wittgenstein or Rawls, this is exactly what we are not going to get in philosophy or in any other nonformal domain. Plausible arguments and a reasonable case for our claims is all that we can sensibly even hope for (Passmore 1961; Smart 1966). But we can sometimes have them. Where we get things precisely defined, they will turn out to be what are in effect stipulative definitions made for limited purposes, not definitions that will do much philosophical work. (*Perhaps* definitions never do?) Decisive arguments in philosophy are as rare as hen's teeth. We should remember, and take to heart, Fredrich Waismann's irony about the number of theorems proved in philosophy (Waismann 1968, 1–3). And it is entirely unclear what it would be like to have a *complete* physical science or a *final* physical theory. Nothing in the history of thought—scientific or philosophical—should give us any hope to gain such certainty. Moreover, Hampton seems to be oblivious to the arguments of pragmatists that *fallibilism is not skepticism*, that "certain knowledge" is not a pleonasm—an argument made by Carnap as well—and that we can live with contingency and still make sense of our lives and our world (Carnap 1949, 119–27). Indeed, we better be able to for there is no living without it. Hampton looks for a power in philosophy that neither philosophy nor anything else has. Failing to find it in naturalism, she finds naturalism wanting. But on her part that is rationalism running wild: the irrational heart, as Waismann put it, of what, whatever Hampton's intentions, is in effect a rationalist philosophy.[9] And rationalism is philosophical fantasy. Hampton's tough-mindedness is an ersatz tough-mindedness.[10]

NOTES

1. However, as we saw in the last chapter, both Sidney Hook and Ernest Nagel characterize methodological naturalism in such a way that it accommodates logic and mathematics, activities (particularly mathematics) which are very much a part of most sciences. Hampton gives too narrow a characterization of methodological naturalism. This is evident if one compares her characterization of methodological naturalism with Peter Railton's where they stand almost cheek to jowl in their respective contributions to *On the Relevance of Metaethics* (Couture and Nielsen 1995, 79–133). Hampton characterizes methodological naturalism narrowly as "the view that philosophy, and indeed, any other intellectual discipline, must pursue knowledge via *empirical methods* exemplified by the sciences and not by a priori or nonempirical methods" (Hampton 1995, 108, italics added). Railton, in a manner similar to the characterizations given by Sidney Hook and Ernest Nagel, takes methodological naturalism to be "a commitment to employing norms and methods of inquiry characteristics of the developed empirical sciences" (Railton 1995, 86). Railton's characterization is a weaker one, and, just for that reason, is preferable, for it leaves both a less controversial place for

mathematical reasoning and a less controversial conception of mathematical reasoning, which, on any reasonable conception, is surely, in many of its deploy-
ments, a part of science. As Hampton characterizes methodological naturalism, a
methodological naturalist would have to rule out "logic and mathematics," and
the characteristic modes of reasoning that go with them, unless they could be
shown to be "empirical enterprises after all." But that, to state it conservatively, is
a very problematic position. Railton's conception of methodological naturalism
does not have that strong Quinean commitment and seems at least more plausible
as a conception of methodological naturalism, for, *if* our understanding of mathematical and logical reasoning, as it forms a part of science, requires an understanding of them as a priori forms of reasoning, we can still accommodate them
within a methodological naturalism as Railton (as well as Hook and Nagel) construe it: constructed, that is, as a commitment to "the methods of inquiry characteristic of developed empirical science." The claim is the pragmatist one that these
methods, as varied as they are, and these methods *alone*, enable us reliably to fix
belief. This conception of Railton's gives far fewer hostages to fortune than
Hampton's stronger characterization which also makes the same claim, a claim
common to *all* methodological naturalists, that *only* the scientific method reliably
fixes belief, but which, on Hampton's construal, requires in addition that we take
a Millian or Quinean position about the a priori, requiring it to be empirical in
character. To cease, that is, to be a priori. By contrast, Railton's characterization of
methodological naturalism is neutral in this respect. It does not affirm or deny the
Quinean thesis (Couture and Nielsen 1995, 278).

    2. Here she is just uncritically, and seemingly unconsciously, assuming rep-
resentationalism without as much as a nod at the powerful antirepresentationalist
arguments made by Donald Davidson and Richard Rorty.

    3. Later in this chapter I argue that such talk is of doubtful coherence.

    4. However, the worry remains that, if we press hard concerning such
notions, that we will not find anything that makes sense. Here again we have the
return of the repressed.

    5. Keeping in mind some of Putnam's arguments, it is not unreasonable to
wonder if that notion makes sense (Putnam 1992a, 120–23).

    6. This involves a rejection of the error theory of ethics (Mackie 1946, 1977). But
it, at least arguably, leaves the possibility, and perhaps even the plausibility, intact that
we could properly argue, as I try to in chapter 1, for an error theory of religion.

    7. To be sure as we can be that there are no nonnaturalistic residues about
properties (bringing up the ghost of Plato), we should, after the fashion of
Richard Rorty, go nominalist about properties and dispositions and generally
espouse an antiessentialism (Rorty 1999, 47–71).

    8. Perhaps Putnam is right that we cannot have one without the other
(Putnam 1994, 254–78). But I need not take sides on that issue here.

    9. Jean Hampton's philosophical career was, abruptly, tragically, and at a
considerable loss to the philosophical community, cut short by her premature
death in 1996. This fact gives me a somewhat queasy feeling about the very strong
criticisms I make of her work. I wish she were here to respond, if she would feel
inclined. I doubt very much that I have said the last word here and it is reason-

able to believe that she would have found resources to respond. I would have welcomed that response even if it would have shown me to be in some fundamental ways mistaken. If my general metaphilosophical view of things is near to the mark, we are unlikely to get, in any event, decisiveness over such issues, though we may get greater or lesser reasonability in philosophical arguments and articulations. Be that as it may, I very much doubt that she or any other philosopher of integrity would wish philosophers to hold their fire because of the death of the philosopher they would criticize. That would not advance philosophy or any other intellectual endeavor. What they, of course, would wish, for themselves and for others, is fair and accurate treatment. I have striven for that. Whether I have succeeded is for others to judge.

10. I would like to thank Jocelyne Couture for permission to use material (in section IV) that we once jointly authored, but which, as it appears here, is extensively transformed. But her input remains, though *perhaps* not always in a form she would assent to. See Couture and Nielsen 1995, 278–96.

BIBLIOGRAPHY

Ayer, A. J. 1963. *Philosophical Essays.* New York: St. Martin's Press. The essay I cited by Ayer was originally published in 1949.

Bowie, Norman, ed. 1983. *Ethical Theory in the Last Quarter of the Twentieth Century*, 13–37. Indianapolis, Ind.: Hackett Publishing Co.

Carnap, Rudolf. 1949. "Truth and Confirmation." In *Readings in Philosophical Analysis*, edited by Herbert Feigl and Wilfrid Sellars, 119–27. New York: Appleton-Century Crofts, Inc.

Couture, Jocelyne, and Nielsen, Kai, eds. 1993. *Métaphilosophie: Reconstructing Philosophy?* Calgary, Alb.: University of Calgary Press.

———. 1995. "Introduction: The Ages of Metaethics." In *On the Relevance of Metaethics*, 1–30. Calgary, Alb.: University of Calgary Press.

Crane, Tim, and Mellor, D. H. 1990. "There Is No Question of Physicalism," *Mind* 99 (April): 182–87.

Daniels, Norman. 1996. *Justice and Justification Reflective Equilibrium in Theory and Practice.* Cambridge: Cambridge University Press.

Davidson, Donald. 1984. *Inquiries into Truth and Interpretation.* Oxford: Clarendon Press.

Gibbard, Allan. 1993. "Reply to Railton." In *Naturalism and Normativity*, edited by Enrique Villanueva, 52–59. Atascadero, Calif.: Ridgeview.

Habermas, Jürgen. 1970. *Toward a Rational Society.* Translated by Jeremy J. Shapiro. Boston: Beacon Press.

Hägerström, Axel. 1964. *Philosophy and Religion.* Translated by Robert Sandin. London: George Allen & Unwin.

Hall, Everett W. 1964. *Categorial Analysis: Selected Essays of Everett W. Hall.* Edited E. M. Adams. Chapel Hill: University of North Carolina Press.

Hampton, Jean. 1995. "Naturalism and Moral Reasons." In *On the Relevance of Metaethics*, edited by Jocelyne Couture and Kai Nielsen, 107–33. Calgary, Alb.: University of Calgary Press.

———. 1998. *The Authority of Reason*. Cambridge: Cambridge University Press.

Kumar, Chandra K. 2000. *Power, Freedom, Ideology and Explanation: A Marxian View*. Unpublished Ph.D. dissertation, University of Toronto.

Mackie, J. L. 1946. "A Refutation of Morals." *Australasian Journal of Psychology and Philosophy* 64: 77–90.

———. 1977. *Ethics: Inventing Right and Wrong*. Harmondsworth, U.K.: Penguin Books.

McTaggart, J. M. E. 1906. *Some Dogmas of Religion*. London: Edward Arnold.

Nagel, Thomas. 1997. *The Last Word*. New York: Oxford University Press.

Nielsen, Kai. 1978. "Technology as Ideology." In *Research In Philosophy & Technology*, edited by Paul T. Durbin, 131–48. Greenwich, Conn.: JAI Press Inc.

———. 1985. "Universalizability and the Commitment to Impartiality." In *Morality and Universality*, edited by Nelson Potter and Mark Timmons, 91–101. Dordecht: D. Reidel.

———. 1996. *Naturalism without Foundations*. Amherst, N.Y.: Prometheus Books.

Passsmore, John. 1961. *Philosophical Reasoning*. London: Duckworth.

Peirce, Charles Sanders. 1992. *The Essential Peirce Vol. 1 (1867–1893)*. Edited by Nathan Houser and Christian Kloesel. Bloomington: Indiana University Press.

———. 1992. *Reasoning and the Logic of Things*. Edited by Kenneth Laine Ketner. Cambridge, Mass.: Harvard University Press.

Putnam, Hilary. 1990. *Realism with a Human Face*. Cambridge, Mass.: Harvard University Press.

———. 1992a. *Renewing Philosophy*. Cambridge, Mass.: Harvard University Press.

———. 1992b. "Comments on the Lectures." In *Reasoning and the Logic of Things*, by Charles Sanders Peirce. Edited by Kenneth Laine Ketner, 55–102. Cambridge, Mass.: Harvard University Press.

———. 1994. *Words and Life*. Cambridge, Mass.: Harvard University Press.

Quine, W. V. 1980. *From a Logical Point of View*, 2d edition. Cambridge, Mass.: Harvard University Press.

———. 1981. *Theories and Things*. Cambridge, Mass.: Harvard University Press.

Railton, Peter. 1995. "Made in the Shade: Moral Compatibilism and the Aims of Moral Theory." In *On the Relevance of Metaethics*, edited by Jocelyne Couture and Kai Nielsen, 79–107. Calgary, Alb.: University of Calgary Press.

Rawls, John. 1995. "Reply to Habermas." *Journal of Philosophy* 92, no. 3: 132–80.

Rorty, Richard. 1991. *Objectivity, Relativism, and Truth*. Cambridge: Cambridge University Press.

———. 1998. *Truth and Moral Progress*. Cambridge: Cambridge University Press.

———. 1999. *Philosophy and Social Hope*. London: Penguin Books.

Smart, J. J. C. 1966. "Philosophy and Scientific Plausibility." In *Mind, Matter and Method*, edited by Paul K. Feyerabend and Grover Maxwell, 377–90. Minneapolis: University of Minnesota Press.

Smith, Michael. 1994. "Why Expressivists about Value Should Love Minimalism about Truth." *Analysis* 54, no. 1: 1–11.

Stevenson, Charles. 1944. *Ethics and Language*. New Haven, Conn.: Yale University Press.

———. 1983. "Value-Judgements: Their Implicit Generality." In *Ethical Theory in the Last Quarter of the Twentieth Century*, edited by Norman Bowie, 13–37. Indianapolis, Ind.: Hackett Publishing Co.

Sturgeon, Nicholas. 1995. "Evil and Explanation." In *On the Relevance of Metaethics*, edited by Jocelyne Couture and Kai Nielsen, 155–86. Calgary, Alb.: University of Calgary Press.

Waismann, Frederich. 1968. *How I See Philosophy*. New York: St Martin's Press.

Wittgenstein, Ludwig. 1953. *Philosophical Investigations*. Translated by G. E. M. Anscombe. Oxford: Basil Blackwell.

—— *7* ——

AN EXCHANGE BETWEEN HOOK AND NIELSEN ON NATURALISM AND RELIGION

Kai Nielsen

**UNIVERSITY OF CALGARY
& CONCORDIA UNIVERSITY**

RELIGION AND NATURALISTIC HUMANISM

SOME REMARKS ON HOOK'S CRITIQUE OF RELIGION

SIDNEY Hook has given distinguished expression to a *Lebensphiloso-phie* which is humanistic and naturalistic. Though he once—perhaps partly in jest—called himself a "God-seeker," he has not "found God" and regards a belief in God—taken as a "cognitive belief"—as a "speculative hypothesis of an extremely low order of probability" (Hook 1961b, 100). While, for the reasons Renford Bambrough has aptly stated, I do not like to place myself behind the party banners of humanism and naturalism, I would regard myself as a plain old atheist, though neither (what in reality is a contradiction in terms) a "Christian atheist" nor a "Jewish atheist," and—tub-thumping aside—a naturalist and a humanist (Bambrough 1964, 64–67). While I regard the brunt of philosophical work to be conceptual analysis, I agree with Sidney Hook that our ultimate aim in doing philosophy should be the attainment of wisdom and the articu-

From *Sidney Hook and the Contemporary World*, edited by Paul Kurtz (New York: John Day, 1968), pp. 257–80. Reprinted by permission of Harper Collins Publishers; and *Southern Journal of Philosophy* 13, no. 1 (spring 1975): 115–21, 124–25.

lation of a *Lebensphilosophie*, the central segment of which consists in systematic critical normative inquiry. It is the problems of human beings, the problems of human conduct, the problems of morals in a broad sense, that are at the center of such a conception of philosophy.[1] If to say this is to be a traitor to the analytic cause then I am an analytic Aaron Burr.

Hook's writings measurably influenced me in my student days to adopt the attitudes toward humanism and naturalism that I now have. And if we take his remark about being a "God-seeker" as a hyperbolic statement to the effect that he will always remain open to all rational arguments vis-à-vis religion, then I can truly say that my attitudes toward religion are in large measure the same as his. But much water has gone over the dam since he wrote most of his essays about religion. Moreover, some have thought that Hook's account of religion is too rationalistic: that here he has hardly been a faithful pragmatist or empiricist. My aim is to reexamine some of Hook's crucial writings on religion and try to ascertain, polemics aside, how much of his central critique of religious belief can stand up to the canons of rational scrutiny of which he has been such a distinguished champion.

I

The word "God," even in its employment in a religious context, is used in several different ways. Hook, particularly in his "Modern Knowledge and the Concept of God" (reprinted in his *Quest for Being*), examines some of these ways. He rightly notes that religious humanists can (and some do), without saying anything incoherent or false, use "God" as a symbolic umbrella term for their most precious moral aspirations or man's deepest concerns. Yet he also notes that such secular conceptions of deity are highly misleading. Hook appropriately reminds us that there is such a thing as the ethics of words. To use the highly emotive word "God" to gloss over what in reality is an atheistic substance is to do violence to the ethics of words. We do not play such a language-game with "God" in the great religious traditions. To redefine "God"—a word with such deep normative overtones and cosmological associations—in such a persuasive manner muddies the waters of thought and feeling. Religious humanism aside, it is also true that *purely* immanent conceptions of God radically depart from Jewish and Christian orthodoxy and hardly provide adequate conceptions of religious worship; and, unlike humanistic conceptions of God, such immanent conceptions of God—Whitehead's for example—provide metaphysical stumbling blocks which are at least as perplexing as the metaphysical conceptions which seem to be embedded in orthodox Judaism, Christianity, or Islam. Thus neither naturalistic humanist nor purely immanentist reconstructions of the concept of God will do. To save a belief in God at all, we are forced back to the God of theism or at least to a conception of God in which (a) God is a worthy object of worship and (b) God is thought to be transcendent to the world. In fine, we are once more considering a transcendent deity: a God which is both the God of Abraham, Isaac, and Jacob and the God of Maimonides and Aquinas.

"This idea of God," Hook rightly remarks, has as an essential element the idea of "a transcendent power, independent of the world of nature and man" (Hook 1961b, 120). Such a transcendent God is conceived of in Judaism, Christianity, and Islam as the creator of the world. In developing a naturalistic critique of religion in the West, or in any critical examination of the concept of God, it is this conception of God that should be the center of our attention. Hook finds, as I find, this conception of God riddled with "insuperable intellectual difficulties." It is a conception of deity which is not simply difficult and hard to accept—after all God is by definition a mystery—but is, as Hook puts it, "intellectually unacceptable" (120). I also agree with Hook that Judaism, Christianity, and Islam viewed as institutions and ways of life are by and large morally debilitating and, as Feuerbach—to whom Hook is deeply indebted—would say, men to be whole men should set aside these myths and learn to live as free, responsible agents in a world without God. Religion is indeed—to speak metaphorically—the sigh of the human heart, but it is the sigh of men who in certain very central respects cannot become whole men. Whether men can someday live without the comfort of their religious illusions I do not know. But, as Feuerbach and Freud well saw—and Hook follows them here—some can, in spite of all the religious indoctrination to which they are subjected. Moreover, philosophers should be concerned with questions of meaning and truth and not with providing therapy or consolation for the masses. I grant that there is a sense in which philosophers should be concerned to articulate an ideology, but plainly it should not be simply to articulate an ideology they can successfully market to "irrational man"—an ideology which is comforting or soothing enough or simple-minded enough to win acceptance in the marketplace. If the Grand Inquisitor is right and most men cannot be "whole men"—cannot live in the white light of clarity and truth—then so be it, but the philosopher's task vis-à-vis religion is to display perspicuously the nature of religious claims and to assess critically the truth claims of religion. If the Grand Inquisitor is right, the philosopher in carrying through this task is indeed a tragic figure doomed to be ignored. If such be the situation, he, like Sisyphus, is, I repeat, a tragic figure and not like Quixote, a comic figure, for an ignored truth, an anxiety-arousing, agonizing truth, is still a truth (a significant tautology), and truth still has its distinctive human value even if it is ridden down by the forces of irrationality.[2]

II

While I agree with Hook that the transcendent God of theism, as well as Paul Tillich's rather different God, is not intellectually acceptable, and I side with Hook in rejecting such conceptions, I am troubled and perplexed over the rationale for his rejection. There is, I believe, a vacillation in Hook's own argument. Sometimes, like atheists coming out of the linguistic tradition, e.g., Antony Flew, Paul Edwards, or myself, he rejects the God of theism—the transcendent deity of Judaism and Christianity—because such theists "cannot give an intelligible account of the concept of God" (Hook 1961b, 120), but at other times he—and this fits better with his official program—plainly regards belief in God as intelligible, for he takes it that to believe in God is to accept "a speculative hypothesis of an extremely low order of probability" (Hook 1961b, 100).

It could be the case that there is no conflict in these two statements, for in the one Hook might be speaking of an anthropomorphic conception of God, in which to believe in God, like believing in Zeus, is to believe in something intelligible, for we know what it would be like to have evidence of a quite empirical sort, for and against his existence. Such an anthropomorphic conception of God is indeed testable on grounds acceptable to pragmatists and empiricists, but it is almost certainly the case that there is no such deity. Here to assert there is a God is to assert something which has the same semantical status as a speculative hypothesis of an extremely low order of probability. But where we speak of developed theism, the transcendent God of Maimonides and Aquinas, as well as of Luther and Pascal, we have, to speak crudely, an unverifiable and unfalsifiable God, but we also—or so I would argue—have a concept of God which is so incoherent that we should firmly claim that no intelligible account of such a God can be given. Thus, depending on how God is conceptualized, we have different grounds, but in both cases good grounds, for rejecting theistic belief. This is the tack I would take and I think Hook *should* take, but he does not. In fact he said at the New School Conference on Methods (Spring 1967), and he has said to me in conversation, that he does not regard the concept of God as meaningless or incoherent. Rather the central consideration is whether we have adequate evidence to warrant the claim that there is such a God.[3] We can, according to Hook, characterize God, but we have no good grounds for believing that what we have described actually exists. Such a starting point, Hook intelligibly claims, is methodologically preferable to an approach which would raise questions about the intelligibility of the concept of God, for if we start out by arguing about the intelligibility of God-talk, we run the risk of getting bogged down in complicated and controversial questions about the meaning of "meaning." I can understand Hook's reluctance to get involved in such intractable controversy. I even agree that at a certain level of apologetic argument Hook's strategy is the more effective, but, as I shall proceed to argue, over fundamental philosophical questions concerning religious belief, questions of meaning and coherence unavoidably arise. The dialectic of Hook's argument, as I shall attempt to establish, will not be effective against a sophisticated Jew or Christian, unless supplemented by effective arguments concerning these controversial questions of meaning. The arguments which we must be able to give, if our critique of religion is really to run deep and to refute effectively theistic claims, must establish either that the concept of an unverifiable transcendent God is incoherent or unintelligible, or that the claim that we can know or have reasonable grounds for believing in such a God is unjustified. But even the latter claim, I shall argue, cannot be successfully sustained, without the resolution of certain fundamental considerations about what it makes sense to say.

III

Hook argues that considering the powerful critical thrusts of such philosophers as Hume and Kant concerning the paucity of evidence for believing in God, the burden of proof is on the believer to provide some evidence for the truth of his assertion. If someone asserts that there are gremlins and it turns out upon investigation that there is considerable evidence that there are no gremlins but still no *conclusive* evidence that there are none, the burden of proof is plainly with the believer in gremlins. To the extent that the concept of God is a cognitive concept and "There is a God" is a factual statement the same logic must apply here. Here Hook seems at least to be on solid ground.

However, when we come to talk of the intelligibility or coherence of the putative concept of God or of our concept of knowing God, the burden of proof shifts to the religious skeptic. I would maintain this on the solid Wittgensteinian grounds that "God" has a regular use in our language—some God-talk is not linguistically deviant—and that God-talk is part of an ancient and venerated form of life. These facts create an *initial presumption* in favor of its intelligibility and coherence. (I don't go all the way with Wittgenstein. I deliberately said "initial presumption" and no more.[4]) Hook's own preface to *Religious Experience and Truth* would suggest that he is making a similar assumption. Given the fact that "God" and associated expressions have a settled use in the language, given the fact that we can operate *with* though perhaps not *upon* them, it becomes essential that the critic of religion provide good grounds for the claim that central segments of God-talk are unintelligible or incoherent, or that we can never know or have grounds for believing that there is such an "ultimate Reality." However, to see exactly what is involved here, we need to follow out the logic of some of Hook's central arguments against supernaturalism.

IV

In calling his philosophy a naturalistic humanism, Hook most essentially has in mind a methodological stance. Where "science" is construed broadly and with a due allowance for its systematic ambiguity and where it is taken to be continuous with, and a systematic and more precise extension of, nonmythical, nonmagical common-sense ways of dealing with the world, Hook, like Russell and Dewey, contends that "all knowledge men have is scientific knowledge" (Hook 1961b, 214). He does not take physics as his sole or preferred model for "scientific knowledge" but rather claims that to know anything or to have a warranted belief that anything is so, we must utilize "the pattern of hypothetico-deductive-experimental observation exhibited in the different sciences in different ways depending upon the specific subject matter" (Hook 1961b, 214). There is, Hook maintains, no essential conflict between science and common sense. Following Malinowski, Hook stresses in "Naturalism and First Principles" that the technological and more generally the secular knowledge of all cultures exhibits a universal pattern. Such common-sense ways of knowing rest on observation and experiment. Scientific method is a systematic extension of those ways of fixing belief. Here we find universally accepted and employed canons of rationality. Hook contends that "An analysis of the implicit logic of technology and the common-sense operations it involves, reveals that no hard and fast line of separation can be drawn between the general pattern of scientific method and reasonable procedures in the primary knowledge-getting activities of men struggling to control their environment" (Hook 1961b, 182).

Naturalism, in turn, is for Hook "the systematization of what is involved in the scientific method" (Hook 1961b, 173). One might call it the ideology (taking "ideology" in a quite nonpejorative manner) of those who employ the scientific method as the sole legitimate method for fixing belief.[5] The denial that there is a God or that there are disembodied spirits "generalizes the cumulative evidence won by the use of this method" (Hook 1961b, 173–74).

Such a naturalism is committed to the principle that there is nothing which could properly be said to exist which in principle cannot be explained scientifically in the broad sense of "science" characterized above. There is one method of explanation: the scientific method, and this method is continuous from domain to domain. There are indeed mysteries: there are things we do not understand, but there is nothing that is in principle unknowable. Moreover, whatever can be known, can be known by use of the scientific method.

To be a naturalist, on Hook's account, is not only to accept the scientific method as the sole legitimate method for fixing belief, but it is also to accept "the broad generalizations which are established by the use of it" and to articulate a conception of man. Such a naturalistic conception of man involves, as one might expect, the categorial commitment that man is to be regarded "as an integral but distinctive part of nature, as wholly a creature of natural origin and natural end" (Hook 1961b, 197). And as a humanistic philosophical anthropology it "offers an adequate and fruitful basis for the social reconstruction which is essential for the emergence of patterns of human dignity on a world-wide scale" (Hook 1961b, 197). In addition, Hook's naturalistic categorial commitments involve the claim that "the occurrence of all qualities or events depends upon the organization of a material system in space-time, and that their emergence, development, and disappearance are determined by changes in such organization" (Hook 1961b, 185–86). That is to say, everything which exists, exists within the spatio-temporal and the causal orders. This, however, is not to assert or to give one to understand "that only what can be observed exists, for many things may be legitimately inferred to exist (electrons, the expanding universe, the past, the other side of the moon) from what is observed" (Hook 1961b, 186). However, we cannot correctly claim to be able to know or to have good reasons for believing in "the existence of anything which does not rest upon some observed effects" (Hook 1961b, 186).

As a naturalist Hook treats God's existence in the same generic way that he treats "assertions about the existence of invisible stars or hidden motives or after images or extrasensory perception," for "naturalism as a philosophy is concerned only with those assertions about existence from which something empirically observable follows in the world that would not be the case if existence were denied" (Hook 1961b, 193–94). On this basis, in true-blue empiricist fashion, Hook concludes, as I have noted, that the evidence does not warrant belief in the existence of anything corresponding to the traditional conception of a transcendent God. The God of the Bible and of Maimonides and Aquinas is intelligible enough, Hook contends, but we have no good grounds for believing that such a God actually exists (Hook 1961b, 190). Applying the scientific method, the only reliable method for fixing belief, we find that we as rational persons should reject a belief in such a God. Hook, I repeat, is not maintaining that we cannot know what cannot be directly experienced, but he is main-

taining that our assertions, to be warranted assertions, must be empirically testable. To know p or to have grounds for believing p—that is, for
p to be knowable or believable—it must be possible to know what, among
the empirically identifiable states of affairs, would be the case if p were
true or probably true and if p were false or probably false. "God," as it is
used in standard Jewish and Christian contexts, is thought by believers to
be a genuine identifying or referring expression. But if this is so, Hook
stresses, it must have an intelligible opposite (Hook 1959, 164). We must
know what would be the case if there were no God. But in order to know
this we must know "something empirically observable in the world"
which would justify the assertion that there is no God.

V

Hook is very concerned, as we saw in chapter 5, to meet squarely and
adequately the criticism frequently voiced against naturalism that it rules
out a priori, by stipulative definition as it were, the very possibility of
asserting significantly the existence of any transcendent realities. The
very categories and methodology of a position like Hook's—it is
argued—make it a priori impossible to assert, or for that matter even significantly to deny, the existence of the transcendent God of Judaism,
Christianity, or Islam. In rejecting belief in God, naturalists in an arbitrary
fashion take the high a priori road.

The objection I have in mind is stated in a rather bald form by Father
Thomas Corbishley.[6] According to Corbishley the arbitrary and a priori
assumption of the naturalists and empiricists consists in their overly
narrow conception of what could count as a fact. They assume that
"unless facts are visible, audible, tangible, or some way observable by
sense-experimentation, they are not only ungetable: they just are not
facts" (Corbishley 1950–51, 11). But this rules out by definitional fiat its
being a fact that there is a God where "God" is conceived nonanthropomorphically. But why, Corbishley asks, accept such linguistic gerryman-
dering? Why accept such a narrow use of "fact"? It may well be thought
that to speak of facts as Corbishley does as either visible or invisible is to
commit some kind of category mistake. Facts are not things or processes
or events but what true statements state. But even so, Father Corbishley's
essential point can be put another way. Hook is operating under the
implicit and unjustified assumption that only what is observable can exist;
to be a genuine statement of fact, Hook assumes, the statement in question
must assert something which is directly or indirectly observable or experienceable. But this Corbishley in effect argues is to operate with an unjustified and a priori assumption about what one can significantly assert.

Hook takes considerable pains to meet objections of this type. He asserts, as we have seen, that naturalistic humanists do not believe that

> only what can be observed exists. Both in science and common life many things may be reasonably inferred to exist from what is observed, and then confirmed by further observations. It does hold that where there is no evidence drawn from observed or observable effects, existence cannot be responsibly attributed. Otherwise the distinction between fact and fantasy disappears. (Hook 1961b, 205; see also 186, 188, 192–94)

There is surely good sense in this remark, for it is absurd to assert that only what can be observed or perceived exists. Naturalists and empiricists have generally not denied the reality of electrons, photons, magnetic fields, and the like. But there is an ambiguity in Hook's remark that should be probed. Can anything—to use Hook's way of putting it—responsibly be said to exist in other than a purely conceptual manner, e.g., as a theoretical construct or number, if it is not at least *in principle* either directly or indirectly observable or in some way experienceable? It is not so clear either what Hook would say to this or what should be said. Surely we do not know what it would be like to observe or experience photons. Current physical theory, the theory in terms of which "photon" gets its use, makes no provision for seeing photons. In terms of that theory a photon is something that you couldn't see. Anyone who talked about "seeing photons" or "experiencing photons" would show by his very talk that he did not understand the theory in which photon-talk has its home. But unless, like "neutrino," a "photon" is treated as a theoretical construct, in which case no question about its reality can—logically can—arise, the *logical* possibility of its being observed cannot be ruled out. It is one thing to say we do not know what it would be like to observe a photon or even that physical theory tells us that it is on that theory or any foreseen extension of or revision of that theory *theoretically* impossible to observe it, it is another thing again to say it is *logically* impossible to observe it; i.e., "Photons can be observed" is a contradiction in terms.

Science is rightly not concerned with mere logical possibilities, but it would seem that to assert there really are photons, i.e., that they are actual nonconceptual realities in the series rocks, grains of sand, germs, microbes, genes, electrons, etc., is to give one to understand that we cannot preclude the *logical* possibility of their being observed. In this sense it is not so obvious that to say that x has something more than a purely conceptual existence is not to commit oneself to the claim that x is at least *in principle* directly or indirectly observable.

Moreover, if we say, as Hook does, that to responsibly assert the existence of anything, it must at least have observable effects, we are committed to the doctrine that if anything can be responsibly said to exist it is either directly or indirectly observable. But to say that something is indirectly observable logically commits us to the claim that it is at least *logically possible* to directly observe it as well. Otherwise "indirectly observe *x*" would have no significant opposite. In such a situation "indirectly" could not qualify "observe"; it could do no descriptive work at all, and thus "indirectly observable" would be without a use. So if we can observe the effects of *x* and thus indirectly observe *x*, it must also be *logically possible* directly to observe *x*.

Similarly to speak of causes and effects for a naturalist is to speak of occurrences within a spatio-temporal order. There can be, Hook tells us, "no evidence for the existence of anything which does not rest upon some observed effects" (186). But it only makes sense to assert that *y* is the effect of *x* where we can in principle observe (experience) that *y* and *x* are constantly conjoined.[7] But again this makes *x* observable (experienceable) in principle. Thus while it is indeed not true that Hook assumes that "only what can be observed (experienced) exists," it seems, from the way in which he argues, that he is assuming and must assume that "only what can at least *in principle* be observed (experienced) can sensibly be said to have a more than conceptual existence."

However, it will be and has been argued that this is simply an empiricist or naturalist dogma and it is a priori to boot. Some empiricists—though not Hook—would, so to speak, take their courage in their hands and be prepared to accept a conceptual scheme in which it would be impossible to significantly assert or deny the existence of "transcendent powers" or "transempirical entities" (Hägerström 1964).

What would be the justification for making such an assumption other than to make the verificationist claim that a statement describing a state of affairs, a statement which has factual significance, has this significance only if it is at least logically possible to indicate the conditions or set of conditions under which it could be confirmed or disconfirmed (infirmed) by some observation or experience? If such a criterion for factually significant discourse could be justified, Hook's position would indeed be justified; i.e., we could *not* responsibly assert that some things can exist even though it is logically impossible to observe (experience) them. But (1) Hook seems not to accept such a criterion of factual significance, and (2) he, as we have seen, does not want in his critique of religion to appeal to controversial questions of meaning; rather he wants to establish that belief in God is a "speculative hypothesis of an extremely low order of probability" (Hook 1961b, 100).[8] That is to say, he wants to rest his "criticisms of the belief in Deity" not "on semantic considerations but on the weight of scientific discovery" (Hook 1961b, 189). But it seems that to support his critique of theism against a really determined and philosophically sophisticated Jew or Christian, he would have to get involved in these controversial semantical issues which he wants to avoid.

Hook might reply that when he was speaking of "the responsible attribution of existence," he was *not* speaking of what it would make *sense* to assert exists or what could coherently be *said* to exist, but of what we would be *warranted* in believing exists. I do not think this would be a natural reading of his remark there, but assuming that it is we are now faced with a new difficulty (Hook 1961b, 205). Hook—and to my mind rightly—argues that if we assert the existence of anything we must also be able to say what empirically determinable state of affairs would obtain if its existence were denied (Hook 1961b, 194). Moreover, Hook believes that some descriptions of "God" can be given. That is to say, we understand what we are saying when we speak of such a Transcendent Reality, but we are not justified in asserting that such a Reality exists. But then, given what Hook says about the necessity of a nonvacuous contrast, we should be able to say what empirically determinable state of affairs would have to take place for it to be true or probably true that there is a transcendent God. But he nowhere gives us the slightest hint of what it is that we would have to find in order for it to be true or even probably true that there is such a deity. Hook calls himself a "skeptical God-seeker," who is "willing to go a long way, to the very ends of reason itself, to track down every least semblance of evidence or argument which promises fulfillment of the quest" (Hook 1961b, 115). He reports he has always come back empty-handed and so he remains a religious skeptic. But then on his own Peircean conception of doubt and on his own employment of the principle of nonvacuous contrast, he must have some idea of what he would have to find to dispel or at least assuage his skepticism. He should be able to tell us something about what kind of evidence we need so that we could all search for the Holy Grail. But Hook has never said what evidence we would need—he has never given us so much as a hint—and, all joking aside, it seems to be the impossibility of saying what would count as evidence, where God is conceived as "a transcendent reality," that leads many people to believe that such skepticism is an ersatz skepticism and that fundamental semantical questions are at issue here.[9]

VI

It will be replied that if such semantical issues are unavoidably on the dock and if, as it seems, Hook, whether he likes it or not, is committed to some version of the verifiability (testability) principle as a criterion of factual significance, then he indeed has unwittingly committed himself to a quite unjustified semantical dogma, and in terms of this semantical dogma he has ruled out any *possible* knowledge of God. On such a criterion it could not—logically could not—be a fact that God exists.

Let me flesh out how such an objection might develop. I will do it by setting forth some of Father F. C. Copleston's responses to some philosophical contentions made by Hook's fellow naturalists Axel Hägerström and Richard Robinson.[10] Copleston points out that "in Christianity, Judaism, and Islam, God is described in such a way that he cannot be perceived, and that anything which can be perceived is not a Deity" (Copleston 1964, 405). Here, I take it, Copleston is reminding us of what is involved in the *Sprachspiel* in which such religious people engage. Moreover, in these religions "God is conceived as a purely spiritual being" and hence he could not in any case be perceived. Furthermore, in these religions, it makes no sense to speak of finding "a god in the universe." God is not "a being" among the other beings which compose the world (Copleston 1964, 405). "God" in discourses of this type is not, like "Zeus" or "Apollo," described in such a way "that if they existed they would be perceptible in principle" (Copleston 1964, 406). With Zeus and Apollo, Hook's methodology works well, viz., "if they are never perceived and if the phenomena which they were supposed to explain can be explained otherwise, there is no good reason to assert their existence" (Copleston 1964, 406). But this is not the way the mainstream traditions in Christianity, Judaism, and Islam use "God." In such discourses "God" by definition is said to be transcendent and this is taken to mean that God is transcendent to the world, that he is Other than the world, and that he is pure spirit. This means, as Copleston stresses, that "the God of Christianity, Judaism, and Islam is not perceptible in principle" (Copleston 1964, 406). Hägerström tries to establish the logical incoherence of such a conception of God, and Robinson, like Hook, claims that it is a groundless claim, for there is no evidence for such a God. Copleston responds to them both, and presumably he would so respond to Hook, by arguing that they have in effect assumed (Hägerström's denials to the contrary notwithstanding) a metaphysics, which has an "initial, though concealed, assumption that everything which can be said to exist must be perceptible" (Copleston 1964, 406). Copleston then, sensibly enough, asks for the justification for such a claim.

If I have been correct in what I have said about Hook's argument this is indeed an unacknowledged, implicit, but leading assumption in his own critique of theism. In the very logic of God-talk of nonanthropomorphic theism there is a rejection of such an empiricist assumption; it is not and it cannot be an acceptable assumption in the *Sprachspiel* that Jewish and Christian theists play, That is to say, if we are going to talk of the God of such Jewish and Christian universes of discourse, we must be prepared to speak of a *kind* of reality which is not observable, not perceivable, and not encounterable or experienceable even in principle. But Hook, if my argument has been correct, assumes that everything which can be said to exist must be perceptible or experienceable in principle.

Given his assumption, Hook should say with Hägerström and Flew that to assert the existence of such a putative reality as a transcendent God is a mistake, for such a concept is a logically incoherent concept. But it is evident from the way Copleston argues that he would maintain that this would commit Hook, as he thinks it commits Hägerström, Ayer, Edwards, Flew, and Robinson, to a metaphysics. Ayer, Edwards, and Flew, at least, would counterargue that careful attention to the logic of our language—to such key terms as "understand," "know," "truth," "fact," and the like—would make it evident that their own key semantical assumptions are rationally unavoidable and that these assumptions do not at all commit them to a metaphysics. Hägerström argues that whatever we call it—call it a worldview if you like—there are no intelligible alternatives to it (Hägerström 1964, 299). Hook, in what *seems* to be a more modest and more tentative position, wishes to avoid such controversial semantical claims. But without them and without justifying or vindicating them—which is something else again—Hook's core case against theism seems at least to come a cropper: to be simply question-begging.

VII

It might be thought that I am ignoring the central argument of his "Naturalism and First Principles." There Hook devotes some considerable effort to the charge that naturalism is question-begging and circular. (See also chapter 5 of this volume.) He perceptively remarks

> Even if all philosophical positions are *au fond* question-begging, there would still remain the task, pursued by all philosophers, of determining which of all question-begging positions is more adequate to the facts of experience. Every philosopher who seriously attempts an answer does assume in fact that there is some common method of determining when a position is adequate to the facts of experience and when not. The contention of the naturalist is that this common method is in principle continuous with the method which we ordinarily use to hold individuals to responsible utterance about the existence of things in the world—a method which is pre-eminently illustrated in the ways in which men everywhere solve the problem of adaptation of material means to ends. (Hook 1961b, 177–78).

It is Hook's contention that in philosophy and in reasoning about religion, he is simply continuing to apply the method which both he and his critics use in science and everyday life.

However, as Arthur Danto has pointed out, such a contention is not adequate.[11] Critics of naturalism can respond that in philosophy and over fundamental questions of religion, the issues are different from the issues faced in science and everyday life, "and the continuity of method is exactly what is at issue" (Danto 1967, 450). Copleston, for example, maintains "that metaphysical philosophy begins, in a sense, where science leaves off" (Copleston and Ayer 1957, 727). He goes on to explain that by this he means that the philosopher "asks other questions than those asked by the scientist and pursues a different method" (Copleston and Ayer 1957, 727). As he makes evident in his debate with Ayer, Copleston does not deny the legitimacy or the autonomy of the scientific method to questions of empirical fact or in everyday questions of technology or factual investigation. There is no issue between him and Hook here. He would be as happy to accept Malinowski's conclusions as is Hook. But when we move from the secular to the sacred, when we make or attempt to make "positive descriptive statements about the Transcendent," the logic of our discourse is different and to validate or vindicate claims made in such a discourse, we cannot rely on the scientific method but we must have, Copleston contends, "an intellectual experience or intuition if you like— of being" (Copleston and Ayer 1957, 728, 755). We must not, Copleston maintains, identify "rational" with "scientific." We must not by definition rule that the scientific method is the only reliable method of fixing belief. To assert or deny the existence of a Transcendent Reality commits one, Copleston contends, whether one is aware of it or not, to certain metaphysical claims. And it is only by "intellectual reflection on experience" that one can come to know that certain metaphysical propositions are true (Copleston and Ayer 1957, 748). Moreover, while we could not understand them if we had no experiences at all, they are not scientifically or empirically testable. They could not be, Copleston points out, without their ceasing to be metaphysical statements (Copleston and Ayer 1957, 731).

It is certainly natural to object that now I am ignoring another side of Hook's work. In his central essay, "The Quest for 'Being,'" and again in "Modern Knowledge and the Concept of God," "Scientific Knowledge and Philosophical 'Knowledge,'" "Pragmatism and Existentialism," and "The Atheism of Paul Tillich," Hook has amply demonstrated the absurdity of metaphysical talk of being, whether Scholastic, Heideggerian, Tillichian, or in the less modish fashion of Nicolai Hartmann.[12] He has shown that metaphysical claims, construed as Copleston construes them and as they are typically construed, are incoherent. I agree, Hook has done just that; these essays should be required reading for all people who would be "shepherds of Being," whether of the disciplined sort like Father Copleston or Clarke or the intellectually flabby sort who follow in the footsteps of Tillich or Heidegger. Parenthetically, it should be noted that no refutation has been forthcoming of Hook's perceptive critique of such an appeal to Being. Those "hooked on Being," if they care to be intellectually responsible, should not shrug Hook's criticism off as shallow or Philistine, but they should produce some counterargument if they can.

However, reference to Hook's critique of Being and of traditional and existentialist metaphysics is not to the point in our present context, for in this critique Hook does not utilize his naturalistic methodology but produces linguistic and semantical arguments after the fashion of Flew, Ayer, or Hepburn. Where God-talk is elucidated in terms of Being-talk, Hook's criticism of Being shows that we do not have a genuinely coherent claim at all. If Judaism, Christianity, and Islam really involve a commitment to such a metaphysical base, Hook has given Judaism, Christianity, and Islam their *quietus*. But, as we have seen, when Hook defends his naturalistic approach to religion, he explicitly claims that he does not wish to rest his case on semantical points but on the claim that only the scientific method is an adequate method for fixing belief. But if he sticks to that method—even given his wide use of "scientific"—he seems only to beg the question with a theist like Copleston or Corbishley. To refute such a position—and it is a standard position among Jewish and Christian philosophers—Hook must instead enter into the semantical disputes he would like to avoid. And that is in fact what he does in the above-mentioned essays. There he makes certain semantical arguments which have become the stock and trade of many linguistic philosophers. *But his procedure there is not compatible with Hook's official naturalistic program vis-à-vis religion. His official program precludes his relying on such semantical claims but commits him to acknowledging that "God" is meaningful and that the concept of God is intelligible and coherent, and arguing from this assumption, to trying to establish that we do not know or have good grounds for believing there is such Divine Existence.* But Hook's method of argument here, as we have seen, exposes him to the charge that Copleston made against Richard Robinson, viz., that his conception of what would count as "knowledge" or "grounds for belief" makes it by stipulative redefinition impossible to have adequate grounds for believing that God exists.

VIII

It still might be contended that if Hook's claim is true, "that all human beings in their everyday experience are guided by the conception of knowledge as scientific knowledge," the burden of proof rests entirely upon those who assert that there exists "another kind of knowledge over and above technological, common-sense empirical knowledge which is an outgrowth and development of it" (Hook 1961b, 217). But against

Hook's claim here, it can be maintained that religious forms of life are ancient forms of life and that within these forms of life—and as an integral part—there are religious doctrines which purport to be true or false and give us cosmological knowledge. That is to say, in the sense referred to above, they have a metaphysical status. This, of course, isn't all that religion is but these cosmological claims remain an essential part of it. Whether such theistic metaphysical beliefs are but one set of quite unjustifiable Absolute Presuppositions that certain people at certain times make, or whether we can know they are true, such knowledge—if indeed there is any such—cannot be scientific knowledge. "Knowledge," it might be added, seems to be used in a systematically ambiguous way. Knowledge of logical truths, and the practical knowledge of what to do, is not the same as empirical or scientific knowledge. Why should it not be true that religious knowledge and religious belief are still different types of knowledge and belief? Given the systematic ambiguity of "knowledge," given the fact that religion as an ancient and venerated form of life is a *fait accompli*, and that many wise and reflective human beings have claimed that there are distinctive claims in religion, it is far from clear, if indeed it is even true at all, that the burden of proof rests on the religious believer to establish that there actually exists another kind of knowledge called "religious knowledge." Rather, it might well be argued that it is an assumption we are quite safe in making, unless some very good reason can be given for thinking there is no religious knowledge. Hook has only shown that knowledge of God is not scientific knowledge.

We seem to have a draw here. There are reasons for thinking that there could be such "religious knowledge" and there are reasons of the sort Hook deploys for doubting it. To break the deadlock we need a careful, semantic analysis of "knowledge," "belief," and "fact." Hook needs to be able to establish by such an analysis with all its controversial claims about what it makes sense to say, that, as he puts it, "knowing is a way of understanding, of interpreting and reorganizing our experiences in the world and making predictions about events" and that where knowledge of fact is concerned it must always be scientific knowledge (Hook 1959, 161). I happen to think—given his broad reading of "scientific"—that Hook may be right in making his last claim, but many able and careful philosophers disagree with him. And surely many would query or even outrightly reject his first claim. His contentions here need a careful justification if indeed such a justification can be given.

It will not suffice to say "that where knowledge of fact is claimed, evidence must rely directly or indirectly upon judgments gained by observation and upon such other judgments as may legitimately, or logically, be inferred from them" (Hook 1961b, 213). It will not suffice for two reasons. First, because to speak of "such other judgments as may legitimately be inferred from judgments gained by observation" is so vague, until what counts as "legitimate inference" in such a context is specified, it allows in almost anything, including Father Copleston's talk of "ontological entailment" (Copleston and Ayer 1957, 401). Second, it will not suffice because there are those who will deny, and give careful philosophical arguments for this denial, that "a testable statement of fact" is a pleonasm, even when all the "in principle" and "directly and indirectly" qualifications have been made. Statements with mixed quantifiers or contrary-to-fact conditionals, it will be claimed, are synthetic factual statements, yet they do not meet Hook's criterion, and no adequate reasons have been given for the claim that we can never know whether any of them are true.

I think Hook could make some effective counters here. But such counters need to be made; and they do involve those contested questions about what it makes sense to say that Hook would like to avoid.[13] Short of such a justification, his claims look like unjustified assumptions rather than assumptions that we should all make if we are to be reasonable.

IX

In sum, Hook's naturalistic critique of religion fails because its main logical force rests on certain contested semantical assumptions which many of Hook's theistic opponents do not accept and which he does not justify or vindicate. He tries by sturdy commonsensism to avoid a defense of such controversial issues, but he cannot, if his pragmatic naturalism is to serve as a thorough refutation of its ancient religious foes. A successful vindication of naturalism would involve the kind of critical commonsensism which would come to grips with these questions concerning the limits of intelligible discourse. I am of the opinion that naturalism can, like the phoenix, arise from the flames, for the minimal semantical assumptions it makes seem to me sound assumptions.[14] In summary form they are as follows:

1. To intelligibly function as a descriptive or identifying expression a term must have an intelligible opposite.
2. For something to count as an intelligible assertion of the existence of anything, it must be at least logically possible to characterize the state of affairs which would obtain if its existence were denied.
3. Only what can at least *in principle* be observed or experienced can be said to have a more than conceptual existence.
4. A statement has *factual* significance only if it is at least logically possible to indicate the conditions or set of conditions under which it

could be to some degree confirmed or disconfirmed, i.e., that it is logically possible to state some evidence for or against its truth.

I have maintained that Hook either wittingly or unwittingly assumes in his case for naturalism all four of the above claims. He has, as we have seen, explicitly committed himself to 1 and 2. I think he would disavow 3 and 4, but I have tried to establish that (a) in his actual arguments he assumes them and (b) without them his case for naturalism could not be made out. However, it might be maintained that he does not assume 3 or 4 but something weaker, which I shall list below as 5. It seems to me, however, that to defend 5 successfully one would have to appeal to 3 or 4, but, be that as it may, there are similar questions concerning undefended assumptions connected with 5.

5. To be a *warranted* factual assertion it must be at least logically possible to indicate the conditions or set of conditions under which it could be confirmed or disconfirmed.[15]

It is worthwhile to contrast 4 and 5. If Hook is only assuming 5 it could well be said that while the logical empiricists maintained that assertions in order to be factual assertions must be empirically testable in principle, Hook only maintains that factual assertions to be *warranted* factual assertions must be empirically testable in principle. To be committed to 5 rather than to 3 or 4 certainly seems to be committed to a more modest and plausible program.

However, this initial reaction requires inspection. Hook tells us, recall, that to distinguish between fact and fantasy we must make a claim such as 5. But this itself sounds like a categorial or conceptual remark—a remark Wittgenstein would call a "grammatical remark." Do we observe by means of the scientific method that nonveriflable claims are fanciful or is this part of the specification of the very meaning of the distinction between fact and fantasy?[16] It seems to me to be the latter. Whatever the origin of the matter, a person could not intelligibly claim for any objective state of affairs that it was as he said it was and still deny that it was in principle impossible to check what he said or that he himself had never had any evidence for it or experience of it.

There is also an important ambiguity in 5. How are we to take "warranted factual assertion"? Does it have the force of "genuine assertion" as distinct from "pseudofactual assertion"? If it does there is not much difference between 4 and 5. However, for Hook, I would think, it would have to mean "an assertion which we have reason to believe to be true." This would indeed make 4 and 5 quite distinct. Hook might defend this last reading of 5 by maintaining that it only makes sense to say that an assertion is warranted—that we have reason to believe it to be true—if we have evidence for its truth, as we can only have evidence for its truth if it asserts something which is either directly or indirectly observable or experienceable. We cannot know or warrantedly believe anything for which we have no evidence. But this in turn makes a semantical assumption that leads us back into the bog again. It assumes that we can only know or responsibly assert that for which we have evidence. It rejects all "knowledge without observation," not to mention still vaguer and more traditional claims to "intuitive knowledge." It assumes

6. To know *p*, where *p* is some proposition, is to be able to predict or retrodict what *p* asserts or to reorganize or interpret our experiences of what *p* stands for in the world.

This is far vaguer than the other semantical assumptions, but it does summarize what Hook means by "knowledge."[17] Furthermore, without assuming 3 or 4, some such restriction would be necessary in order to support the claim that all knowledge must be experiential or scientific. It is not enough to maintain that this method has been the most successful way of resolving everyday questions of fact about what goes on in the world. All parties can agree on this. *What must be done is to establish that scientific knowledge alone is genuine knowledge.* This has not been done, yet 6 is essential for the defense of 5, where 5 is not grounded on 3 or 4 or a variant of 4. But 6, to put it conservatively, is at least as much in need of defense as 3 or 4. And to give it an adequate defense would surely involve some thorny issues about the meaning of "knowledge," "understanding," and the like. Again we are led back to questions of meaning.

Hook wishes to avoid semantical issues in his defense of naturalism, but he cannot if he is to refute central theistic claims. I think 1, 2, 3, and 4 are all quite defensible and I believe they should be defended, but these assumptions are all extremely controversial. (But see my Postscript.) To cite one example, John Passmore, who certainly is no enemy of naturalism or defender of theism, sets up in the last three chapters of his *Philosophical Reasoning* some of the standard hurdles that would have to be hurdled.[18] And empiricists such as Quine and Feyerabend would regard such a defense as I am suggesting as a defense of a lost cause.

My own hunch is that if such semantical assumptions cannot be sustained, it is entirely unclear how naturalism can successfully be defended and a sophisticated theism rationally be rejected. Naturalists might say with reference to theism that they do not *want* to make such ontological commitments, play such language-games, hold such Absolute Presuppositions, adopt such theistic frameworks. But such a defense of pragmatic naturalism seems to provoke readily and justifiably the obvious retort from theists that they, on the other hand, *want* very much to make such ontological commitments, play such language-games, hold such Absolute Presuppositions, adopt such frameworks; and they see no reason why they shouldn't. After all, why should they want what the naturalists want vis-à-vis religion? If we are reduced to such a defense of "questions external to the framework" we will be on very thin ice indeed. But I think 1 through 5 are quite defensible and that we should return to a philosophical defense of them. To say that they are controversial is only to mark their philosophical nature. (But again note my Postscript.)

X

There are at least three specific points at which Hook would attempt a counter to some of my arguments.

1. Much of the force of my above critique of Hook comes from the claim that "God" is thought by believers to refer to something unique and that given this uniqueness it is impossible to describe God in terms which are applicable to other things. But Hook might reply that he has already met that objection. He pointed out against Father Copleston that we can describe unique things in terms applicable to other things of a quite mundane sort. "If there was a first man in the world, then by definition he is or was certainly unique. There couldn't be two first men. Nevertheless, we have a rather adequate understanding of what it would mean for anything to be the first man. But here Hook misses the point about uniqueness vis-à-vis God. The claim is that God, as a being with *aseity*, has a unique *kind* of existence. Some of the central problematic conditions associated with "God" are (1) that of being a completely independent being (a being who depends on no other being or group of beings), (2) being a being who has no sufficient conditions, (3) being a being upon whom all other beings are dependent, (4) being a being which is not a being among the other beings but an eternal, non–spatio-temporal, infinite Pure Spirit, and (5) being a being who is transcendent to the world. These are some of the central conditions associated with the mainstream Judeo-Christian conception of God. It is these conditions—conditions essentially associated with the concept of *aseity*—that give meaning to talk of God's necessary existence; it also gives us a contrast—in terms of its kind of existence—with finite and contingent existence (Hook 1961b, 117). If we allow the intelligibility such a characterization of *aseity*, as Hook appears to be willing to do, then we must admit that God has a distinctive uniqueness—as a *kind* of reality— and it is in this sense that God is said to be unique and not characterizable in the way we characterize ordinary objects. Moreover, vis-à-vis God, it is a category mistake, as Plantinga has shown, to ask (as both Hook and Rus-

sell do) for a causal explanation about why God exists. For God by definition can have no sufficient conditions.[19] If there is a God he is a completely independent being.

2. Hook, like Ayer, makes the by now familiar claim that if one maintains that the concept of God is meaningless, unintelligible, or incoherent,
this destroys atheism and religious skepticism along with religious belief.
After all if it makes no sense to assert that there is a God, then it makes
no sense to deny it either.[20] To make disbelief meaningful, we must keep
belief in supernatural and transcendent powers and entities an open
question. A naturalism such as Ayer's, Edwards's, Flew's, or Hägerström's would, on Hook's account, be in effect devastating to atheism, for
it would open it up to Duhem's counter that the categories of natural science make both atheism and theism meaningless (Hook 1961b, 217).

Here Hook betrays an overly narrow conception of atheism. For him
an atheist is someone who says that it is false or probably false that there
is a God. But a more adequate characterization of atheism would claim
that an atheist rejects belief in God for—*depending on how God is
conceived*—one of the following reasons: (1) because it is false or probably
false that there is a God, (2) because the concept of God is meaningless,
unintelligible, contradictory, or incoherent, or (3) because the concept of
God in question is such that it merely masks an atheistic substance, e.g.,
"God" is a symbolic term for moral ideals. I am an atheist and I take the
first tack toward an anthropomorphic God, like Thor or Zeus, the second
tack toward the various conceptions of God of mainstream Judaism and
Christianity, and the third tack against Dewey's, Hare's, and Braithwaite's
God. Given a more adequate characterization of atheism, Duhem's chal-
lenge is no challenge at all and Hook's difficulty here is an empty one.

Moreover, my above characterization of atheism fits better with the
psychological realities vis-à-vis the religious believer. As Susan Stebbing
pointed out years ago in reviewing *Language, Truth and Logic*, the religious
believer finds no greater comfort and no less confrontation in being told
that his beliefs are meaningless than in being told they are false (Stebbing
1936). In short, an atheist is anyone who rejects belief in God for any of
the above reasons. Thus it is perfectly possible for an atheist to reject the
very idea of "a 'timeless' God" at the outset because he thinks it contradictory, incoherent, meaningless, or unintelligible. He denies God's existence by rejecting the very category God for any of these reasons (Hook
1961b, 189). He may be muddled in making such a claim, but such a claim
is not inconsistent with atheism (Hook 1961, 193).

3. Indeed, as Hook remarks, if a Transcendent Concept of God "falls
outside the basic explanatory categories" of naturalism, then it "cannot
be recognized by naturalism." This is analytically true. Furthermore, any
meaningful conceptual scheme or set of categories will be restrictive in a

similar way "since a necessary condition of a meaningful statement is that it should be incompatible with its opposite."[21] Thus that naturalism is so restrictive it is no legitimate criticism of naturalism. Moreover, pragmatic naturalists are "not committed to any theory concerning which categorial terms are irreducible or basic in explanation" (Hook 1961b, 176). Rather, Hook has it, "what all naturalists agree on is the irreducibility of a certain method," the scientific method, which utilizes the same basic pattern of inquiry that is used universally in technology and in commonsense resolutions of questions of fact (Hook 1961b, 191). The central question, Hook claims, is not whether naturalism is restrictive but whether it is "narrowly restrictive, whether there are matters of knowledge in common experience which they [naturalists] exclude or whose existence they make unintelligible" (Hook 1961b, 182, 191).

The center of Hook's argument in "Naturalism and First Principles" is that such a naturalism is not overly restrictive. In defending naturalistic restrictions, Hook points out that we could not logically demonstrate the first principles of any such conceptual scheme or even establish them in indirectly. *Rather the interesting and significant question is whether we can give a proof of naturalism in the sense of vindicating naturalistic principles in a way analogous to the way in which Bentham and Mill tried to vindicate the principle of utility* (Hook 1961b, 176). Hook tries to do this by making his assumptions "reasonable to 'reasonable' men," where the "mark of a 'reasonable' man is his willingness to take responsibility for his actions, to explain why he proceeds to do one thing rather than another, and to recognize that it is his conduct, insofar as it is voluntary, which commits him to a principle or belief rather than any form of words where the two seem at odds with each other."[22]

However, as we have already seen, there is a catch here. It is manifest that there are reasonable believers and reasonable skeptics and atheists. Furthermore, believers can readily accept the naturalists' methodological restrictions for "matters of knowledge in common experience." In everyday matters both believers and skeptics should and indeed must, if they are reasonable, fix belief in this naturalistic fashion. There can be general agreement about this, but *in addition* Jews and Christians believe in a transcendent God. Yet in adhering to that belief *they can* be reasonable human beings, *according to Hook's own characterization of "reasonable human beings."* Hook can in turn perhaps convince them that he is being reasonable in his skepticism, for believers can also well believe what is plainly true, namely that there are reasonable skeptics as well as reasonable Jews and Christians. So what Hook needs to do to vindicate his naturalism and his critique of theism is not simply to make his assumptions reasonable to human beings, but to give reasonable persons adequate reasons for accepting naturalism and rejecting theism. But it is not evident that Hook has done that.

It may very well be true that there is for matters of determining questions of empirical fact "a universal pattern of intelligibility understood by everyone who grasps the problem which the tool or technical process is destined to solve" (Hook 1961b, 177). But again this does not show that there cannot be as well questions of nonempirical fact. We can accept Hook's contention about the ubiquity of the scientific method for questions of empirical fact and even for all mundane everyday matters and still not accept either the claim that (1) it is not a fact or (2) that it *cannot* be a fact that there are Transcendent Realities. Again it would be possible to accept Hook's claim about the pervasiveness of the scientific method concerning questions of everyday life and still consistently maintain either that Transcendent Realities are known in a quite different way or that belief in them à la fideism is legitimately fixed in a quite different way—that after the fashion of Pascal or Dostoevsky, there can be a pragmatic vindication for belief in God even when we cannot know or have rational grounds for believing that God exists.

That some forms of theistic institution have, as Hook documents, been vicious, morally debilitating, intellectually stultifying institutions does not mean that all must or that even that such institutions are prone to such wickedness and infantilism. So we are still left asking why accept a naturalistic *Lebensphilosophie* rather than a theistic one. Perhaps it is all a matter of "You pays your money, you takes your choice"?

We must, however, not neglect to note that following Levy-Bruhl, Goldensweiser, and Malinowski, Hook offers a reason which we have not yet discussed for rejecting theism and accepting naturalism. Hook points out that religious beliefs arise as emotional comforts or reliefs where our actual knowledge or ability to cope with life situations break down. "It is a safe generalization," Hook remarks, to "say that the depth of religious sense is inversely proportionate to the degree of reliable control man exercises over his environment and culture" (Hook 1961b, 179). Religions serve to reassure, to provide comfort and release anxiety, where knowledge and human control fail.

Even if this is an adequate account of the genesis and psychological function of religious belief, it would not in the absence of good reasons for thinking theistic beliefs groundless be a vindication of naturalism. As Hook himself has stressed repeatedly in other contexts, the validity of a belief is independent of its origin. Thus to note the origin and psychological function of these beliefs is not to discredit them. We are still looking for a vindication of a naturalism over theism. But recall chapter 1.)

Again a theist such as Aquinas or Maimonides (or in our time Copleston or Fachenheim) could well grant that we could appropriately use the scientific method for fixing belief concerning a god, a "supernatural power," having the same logical status as an electron or invisible star and still deny quite consistently that such a god was the God of their religious discourse (Hook 1961b, 180). After all, a believer in Transcendence could not accept such an anthropomorphic God. Though it is indeed true that he would—particularly if he were a Christian—have to contend that a divine life manifests itself in the universe while still insisting on the full transcendence of God. (Perhaps such a believer is making incompatible claims here. But if so, this is but another way of showing that his concept of God is incoherent.)

However, as we have seen, it is this concept of a Transcendent Deity, which even in principle can be neither directly nor indirectly encountered or experienced, that falls outside the scope of Hook's basic descriptive and explanatory categories and thus cannot be recognized, given his conceptual scheme. In short, such a Deity is ruled out a priori on Hook's account of religion. Hook indeed denies this but for his denial to be well taken he must be able to state what *conceivable* empirically indentifiable state of affairs would, if it were to obtain, justify asserting the existence of *such* a Deity. There would seem to be a logical or conceptual ban on confirming or disconfirming the existence of such a Deity for such a putative reality cannot even in principle be experienced. Hook must show that this is not so, that there is no such conceptual ban. If we are to be confident that he has grounds for denying that there is such a God, he must also be able to state what conceivable empirically indentifiable state of affairs would, if they were to obtain, justify asserting such a Divine Existence. But this has not been done and it would appear at least to be logically impossible for him to do so (Nelson 1965 and 1973).

Hook has given us no adequate grounds—his arguments from meaning aside—for assuming a conceptual scheme in which God is ruled out a priori rather than accepting a nonnaturalistic scheme which can say everything naturalists do—using naturalistic criteria for scientific and everyday explanations—and in addition speak of God in a quite nonnaturalistic way, using in the appropriate religious contexts nonnaturalistic criteria. Theists might even counter that we should abandon the exclusive use or even attempted exclusive use of scientific method for fixing belief, so as not to rule out by definitional fiat the possibility of acknowledging the existence of God. In order not to block inquiry here, one must reject claims to the omnicompetence of scientific method.

It is indeed true that Hook *wants* to keep God's existence an open question. Rather than ruling it out as an incoherent concept, he wants to establish that the weight of scientific evidence makes divine existence improbable. But the God of Aquinas and Maimonides is so conceived that his existence cannot be established or disestablished this way. As Father C. B. Daly has put it,

But if the theist's reason for asserting the existence of God is the finitude

or contingency of any and all finite being, then quite obviously the assertion is not open to empirical verification or falsification in the sense
intended and the proposed tests display an enormous *ignoratio elenchi*.
Flew's falsificatory occurrences occur in an already existing world
whose existence is taken for granted; the theist invokes God as the *Cause
of the existence* of the world. Nowell-Smith supposes that the "God-
hypothesis" will imply one kind of world; the "no-God hypothesis" a
different kind of world. But the theist's proposition is that on the "no-
God-hypothesis" there is *no* kind of a world. Father Corbishley, S.J., was
perfectly right in retorting to Flew "In reply to the question, 'What
would have to occur or to have occurred to constitute for you a disproof
of the love of, and of the existence of God?', the only thing to be said is,
quite literally, 'Nothing.'" The theist declares, if there is any kind of
world, God exists. His alternative is, either God or nothing. He invokes
God, not to explain why the world is "like this, and not like that," but to
explain how there can be a world at all. (Daly 1959, 103–104)[23]

XI

We have come full circle and again it might be argued that I am ignoring
Hook's arguments concerning the incoherence of such metaphysical talk.
I have neglected here such standard but effective purely conceptual argu-
ments as

> ... the great difference between God as an object of religious belief, and
> objects of scientific belief, is that assertions about the latter are controlled by
> familiar rules of discourse, understood by all other investigators, that they
> are related by logical steps to certain experimental consequences, and that
> these consequences can be described in such a way that we know roughly
> what counts as evidence for or against the truth of the assertions in question.
> Now this is not the case with respect to those statements which affirm the
> existence of God. Certain observable phenomena will sometimes be cited as
> evidence *for* the truth of the assertion, but it will not be shown how this evi-
> dence follows from God's existence; nor will there ever by any indication of
> what would constitute evidence *against* its truth. (Hook 1961b; 118–19)

Hook goes on to say that

> in fact those who talk about experimental evidence for the existence of
> God are obviously prepared to believe in him no matter what the evi-
> dence discloses. It is considered blasphemous in many quarters to put
> God to any kind of test. Truth or falsity as we use the terms in ordinary
> discourse about matters of fact or as synonyms for warranted or unwar-
> ranted assertions in science arc not really intended to apply in the same
> way to religious assertions. (Hook 1961b, 119)

Surely there is force in these remarks though they indeed do not meet head on remarks like Daly's. Coupled with his claim that every descriptive or designative term must have an intelligible opposite and his further claim that to make an intelligible assertion about existence we must be able in principle to say what empirically determinable state of affairs follows if we deny it we have a strong case against the coherence of God-talk (Hook 1961b, 119). I have, it might be continued, in my analysis of Hook's critique of religion neglected his arguments to establish that theists "cannot give an intelligible account of God," where God is conceived of as a transcendent reality.

I indeed have not forgotten his arguments here. They are standard arguments—they might have been made by any typical linguistic philosopher—and they seem to me for the most part well taken. But what I wish to stress again is that they clash with Hook's official naturalistic programme in which he insists that naturalistic criticisms "of the belief in Deity" are not "based on semantic considerations" but the weight of scientific evidence. I have been concerned to argue that along such lines Hook has not at all been able to meet the account of a believer in a Transcendent Deity, though his naturalistic arguments would render implausible the claims of an anthropomorphite. What I have been concerned to establish is that *without his semantical arguments about the incoherence of talk of Being, transcendent Causes, Necessary Existence, and a special "religious way of knowing"* his arguments are simply question-begging; they show that the scientific method is the most effective method for attaining knowledge of empirical fact and not that it is the only reliable method for fixing belief for all ranges of belief and in all domains.

It should also be stressed that Hook does not show that all knowledge is obtained by a single basic pattern of inquiry. Hook, following Dewey, states the basic problem thus: the procedure to follow in any intellectual inquiry is the following: "recognize the problem, state the hypothesis, draw the inferences, perform the experiment and make the observation" (Hook 1961b, 147, 194).[24] But his own very perceptive arguments against "shepherds of Being" and his distinctively philosophical arguments generally do not at all follow this pattern. This would lead one to question Hook's own conception of the continuity of method. Philosophical argument seems to have its own problems and its own techniques and no adequate reason has been given along *naturalistic lines* for rejecting the religionists' claim that religion too has its own techniques and its own way of knowing. If our denial that there is a God is based on the cumulative evidence won by the scientific method, it is not well based and by such arguments naturalism cannot (more modestly has not) established that it is more reasonable than at least some of the conceptual schemes alternative to it.

FOR AN OPEN-MINDED NATURALISM

SIDNEY HOOK
NEW YORK UNIVERSITY

I welcome Kai Nielsen's adhesion to the philosophy of naturalistic humanism although I have a premonition that his philosophical odyssey is still not complete. I am indebted to him for the attention he has given my views but confess that I am puzzled by the upshot of his analysis and somewhat repelled by the tone of his argument against those who believe in God. He is not content with refuting their beliefs in the existence of God but seems intent upon silencing them by his insistence that even to talk about the existence of God is plain or fancy nonsense.

I am puzzled because sometimes he seems to be agreeing with me, as when he endorses my criticisms of conceptions of God as a force, power, or principle that transcends experience. At other times, he expresses dissatisfaction with my position on the ground that I have not established my philosophical right to hold it, that, despite my denials, I am committed to my views in an a priori fashion, and that what is lacking is a more sophisticated defense, which he has supplied, that would establish in advance that all references to a transcendent God are ultimately incoherent, and that literally people who talk this way do not know what they are talking about, and that therefore "true" or "false" cannot intelligibly be predicated of what they say. Although I have been especially concerned with avoiding the charge of question-begging or legislating what exists in the universe, he taxes me with being guilty of the charge because of certain semantical assumptions I make. Yet if I have understood him properly—I am not sure that I have!—he himself is committed to these assumptions (1 to 6). The great difference between us, so it seems to me, is that he seeks to foreclose future discourse about transcendent conceptions of God while I am prepared on principle to listen and to modify my position if reason and evidence convince me. I have tried to show, and according to Nielsen himself I have sometimes succeeded, that many writers who talk or write about God do not do so intelligibly, but I would not on the basis of any semantic theory of meaning conclude that therefore everyone who talks about God must talk unintelligibly. And this for at least two reasons. Many who do talk about God, like most religious people I know, do talk intelligibly, and what they say seems to me to be clearly false or extremely improbable. Whatever my theory of meaning currently is, it is not a principle of logic but a proposal, justified by its fruitfulness, in furthering communication and in acquiring new knowl-

From *Southern Journal of Philosophy* 13, no. 1 (spring 1975): 127–36.

edge, and therefore modifiable in the light of further inquiry. That is to say, although I cannot establish the logical validity of my theory of meaning, I present it as a proposal and offer reasonable grounds for accepting it—among them, that it accounts better than any other theory of meaning for the truths that all human beings, religious or irreligious, theist or atheist, accept about the world, and especially that it helps us to advance the growth of knowledge about the world. I am pretty sure that this will always be the case, but I cannot be certain. What bothers Nielsen is that I am prepared to admit the logical possibility of the existence of God and other supernatural creatures and my refusal to assert that all theists are literally talking nonsense or gibberish. That is why although he regards himself as a naturalist, too, I feel that *Nichts trennt uns, nur der Abgrund* (Nothing separates us—only an abyss).

I

Almost every sentence in Nielsen's critique of my position invites extended commentary. However, I shall restrict myself to just a few comments in hopes of clarifying my views.

To begin with, some relatively minor points of nomenclature. Nielsen refers to my position as "agnostic atheism." I am puzzled by his adjective "agnostic." An agnostic is someone who claims that either we do not or we cannot know whether God exists or not. An atheist is one who denies that he exists and who asserts that in the light of all the available evidence, there is no more reason to believe that he exists than do the creatures of mythology. The fact that the atheist may possibly be mistaken does not make him an agnostic anymore than the fallibility of all our beliefs about matters of fact makes us agnostics about whatever we believe true or false.

Further, I distinguish between religion and belief in God. Although all theists are religious not all who are religious are theists. There are some religions (early Buddhism) that do not believe in God, and there are some religious philosophers like McTaggart who are atheists, who do not believe in God or Gods. The term "God," however is sometimes used in a way that has nothing whatsoever to do with theism, e.g., in the writings of Spinoza, Hegel, H. Spencer, S. Alexander, and Whitehead to name a few. I find the concept of God as defined in these and other metaphysical systems (the "One" of Plotinus) unintelligible. But I would regard it as extremely odd to say that because I am an atheist, I reject their belief in God. Nor would I say in their case that because their concepts are unintelligible to me that *therefore* I am an atheist. Yet at one point, Nielsen contends that he is perfectly justified in designating himself an atheist "because the concept of God is either meaningless, unintelligible, contradictory, or incoherent." In so doing it seems to me that he is arbitrarily extending the connotation of the term "atheism" and is guilty of violating what Peirce called "the ethics of words." He is using the word "atheist" as loosely as philosophers who are not theists use the term "God" in a cultural tradition in which that term normally has definite theistic implications. Atheism is the denial of the existence of God customarily regarded as a "self-existent, eternal Being, infinite in power and wisdom and perfect in holiness and goodness, the Master of Heaven and earth," etc. (the predicates of God vary with different theistic believers). Now I do not see by what right Nielsen can call himself an atheist; and go from the claim that those who talk about God do not do so intelligibly or coherently to the assertion that God does not exist. After all many of those who talk about God admit that what they say about him is stutteringly inadequate. They are not at all fazed by the discovery that ordinary usage doesn't apply to him. There are other analogies of experience in which men and women talk incoherently and unintelligibly about some person or occurrence. And it is risky—and sometimes downright dogmatic—on that ground *alone* to assert that what they are talking about does not exist. Sometimes despite the language of oxymoron, we can dimly discern the objectively existent reference of the discourse. Sometimes we have reason to deny the existence of what the incoherent language seems to be referring to. A man or a woman in a state of shock or hysteria can talk about an experience in such a way as to convince us, despite the disjointedness of their speech, that something dreadful really occurred. On the other hand, we may conclude that they are deluded or that they imagined or dreamed up the incident. It all depends upon the evidence available. To infer *merely* on the basis of discourse, that something is or is not present in the nature of things is extremely hazardous. The ontological *disproof* of the existence of God is no more valid than the ontological proof.

I am not an agnostic or skeptic about the existence of God any more than I am an agnostic or skeptic about the nourishing qualities of stories, the existence of elves and gremlins, or the Virgin Birth. I deny that stones nourish, that elves and gremlins live outside books of fairy tales, or that the Virgin Birth ever occurred. Nielsen wants me to say that no possible evidence would ever lead me to admit I was wrong. This I cannot and will not do. Professor Walter Stace once sardonically inquired, after I read a paper at the New York Philosophy Club, what account I would give of myself if I died and woke up in the presence of God. "My answer would be," I replied, "Oh! Lord, you didn't give me enough evidence!" At the time I thought the retort was original with me but since then several persons have claimed priority for it. One of them was Bertrand Russell.

Speaking of Russell, I vividly recall his remark about the matter at issue as we walked through New York's Washington Square Park in the lovely dusk of a rare autumnal day. I was organizing a meeting on Naturalism for the Conference on Methods in which he was to be pitted against Reinhold Niebuhr. I was briefing him about Niebuhr's odd views on God with which he was completely unfamiliar. In the course of our conversation, I asked him in a semihumorous vein under what circumstances, if ever, he would be prepared to believe in God. His reply, as I recall it, was "If I heard a voice come out of the sky, referring to something I, and I alone, knew, predicting some altogether unlikely event that no one else anticipated, and if that happened again and again, I would acknowledge the existence of God."

Russell was probably just as aware as Nielsen that *logically* the state of affairs he described that would bend his belief toward accepting God's existence is just as compatable with the nonexistence of God—i.e., an extraordinary world in which the belief in God was a belief in an illusion. There is nothing *logically* compelling one way or the other about these beliefs, in the sense that one conclusion is strictly necessary and the other contradictory or impossible.

The crucial point, however, and one it seems to me completely missed by Nielsen, is that we are not dealing with a question of pure logic but of existential probability of the same order as the question whether, in the face of certain special circumstances observable on earth, it would be more reasonable to believe that there were other intelligent creatures in outer space with powers of perception and control roughly as superior to our own as ours is to that of ants, than to believe that the pattern of continued observable effects was a matter of chance.

Given the situation Russell describes, after careful inquiry, in which I would bring in not only the most knowledgeable and critical scientists of all kinds but the Houdinis and other specialists on fraud, sound effects, etc., if I had to bet my life on my belief, I would bet with Russell. It would be a reasonable bet even if it turned out to be wrong. I have bet my life on evidence and considerations in the past that were not so strong. On Nielsen's position he could not bet at all. He could not even suspend judgment. He would simply insist that one of the options was unintelligible. In *practice*, however, I hazard the guess that he, too, would also, under the circumstances, bet the same way—not out of fear or weakness but as the vestigial expression of common sense. Peirce's warning against philosophical insincerity in his critique of Descartes's profession of universal doubt is apropos here. Let us not profess to doubt what in our hearts and minds we firmly believe—although we may very well be mistaken about that belief. That is to say that there is a reasonable habit of inference with respect to belief or disbelief about natural fact which we follow with respect to supernatural fact. And it is still a reasonable habit of belief despite the claim that the supernatural fact is of a different order. For however unique it is, it is still, in Santayana's phrase, a concretion in discourse and it is reasonable to extend the logic and ethics of discourse and inquiry to it. Some theists have concluded that they can only discourse about God in negative terms. The presupposition of an intelligible statement—about *what* a thing is not, is *that* it is which is precisely what an atheist denies upon reflection and inquiry after the theist affirms existence. If the theist, as some have, chooses silence, there is no issue but he must never be browbeaten into silence by any antecedently formulated theory of meaning. He must always be free and feel free to speak.

II

Nielsen seems to me to misconceive the strength of the naturalist's position with respect to what exists in the world, the furniture of heaven and earth. I need not repeat the detailed arguments in my *The Quest for Being*. Their gist has been stated by Nielsen and I have no quarrel with his summaries except with his view that I have begged all the questions at issue. He admits that everyone including believers in their secular behavior operate with the empirical methods of common sense and science. He admits that "all parties agree on this," that it has been "the most successful way of resolving everyday questions of fact about what goes on in the world." But he then asserts that this is not sufficient, that what I must do *"is to establish that scientific knowledge alone is genuine knowledge"* (his italics). I do not see the necessity of it. I do not know how to establish that scientific knowledge alone is genuine knowledge, for every attempt to establish it rests on assumptions about what constitutes knowledge. And one can always ask us to establish that these assumptions themselves are *alone* essential for the acquisition of genuine knowledge. Anyone can claim that he has a different or higher kind of knowledge that is incompatible with these assumptions, and accuse those who deny its possibility of vicious and stultifying circularity in their position.

I submit, however, that this is the wrong approach to the question whether or not God exists in the sense that something is present or, more pertinently, whether or not some*one* is present, and indeed, someone who is a Person or who possesses some essential traits of personality. The naturalist who is not a dogmatist simply asks: show me what difference there is between saying he exists and saying he doesn't exist? What different consequences ensue? Surely there must be different consequences, for if *all* the consequences of the affirmation and denial of the existence of God are the same, the two expressions would have the same meaning, and there would be no difference between the beliefs of the theists and those of atheists. But since the beliefs are asserted to be different, presumably the consequences will be different. The naturalist does not claim that the existence of God is logically impossible, and he rejects the view of some believers that his existence is logically necessary. But many things may exist which are not logically necessary; and God is among them, especially the God of the Judaic-Christian-Moslem faith.

However, and this is the simple but weighty point that Nielsen overlooks, whoever says that God exists must give reasons and evidence. *The burden of proof rests on him* in the same way that it rests on those who assert the factual existence of anything natural or supernatural. The naturalist, after carefully pondering the reasons and evidence offered by the believer, asserts that it is false to say God exists or that the statement is unwarranted. Nielsen regards the intellectual responsibility of the naturalist and supernaturalist as on the same plane, as if they were arguing a case on the basis of equally funded experience. But his admission that everyone including the supernaturalists recognizes the validity of the empirical, scientific approach shows that they are not on the same plane. They have different responsibilities in the quest to establish what is. We are not dealing with two conflicting hypotheses about *what* kind of God exists but with the question whether he exists. It rests with the supernaturalist to present the evidence that there is more in the world than is disclosed by our common empirical experience.

This appears too simplistic or unsophisticated to Nielsen. Since the supernaturalist's belief cannot be falsified, it is not common sense or scientific knowledge. If it has any meaning, it is not the meaning of an empirical fact. Let the naturalist therefore prove, Nielsen declares, that there can be no other kind of knowledge, that there can be none but empirical fact! And unless *he* can prove it, *he* is a question-begging a priorist, and we are back to square one with Murphy, Sheldon, and other critics of the naturalism of Dewey, Nagel, and Hook.

But here, too, the naturalist need undertake to do no such thing. Is there a different kind of knowledge that makes God an accessible object of knowledge in a manner inaccessible by the only reliable method we have so far successfully employed to establish truths about other facts? Are there other than empirical facts, say spiritual facts or transcendent facts? Show them to us. Is this knowledge by revelation? What about false revelations? How are they distinguished from true ones? After all, not all revelations can be true since so many of them conflict. If you can't tell the difference between the true and false until *after* the event, whatever it may be, what good is this knowledge by revelation? And if you can tell the difference between true and false revelation *before* the event, how do you do it without falling back upon empirical methods? What holds for claims of knowledge by revelation or authority holds for claims of knowledge by intuition.

Is there a method *discontinuous* with that of rational empirical method which will give us conclusions about what exists on earth or heaven, if there be such a place, concerning which all qualified inquirers agree? Tell us about it.

We must first agree, Nielsen seems to me to be saying, on what we mean by knowledge before we deny the theists' assertion on pain, once more, of obvious question-begging. I fail to understand why we must do so. Indeed such a strategy is intellectually disastrous. Before we attempt to discover what the proper analysis of "knowledge" is we must be able to identify pieces of knowledge or be in possession of some knowledge— just as before we can determine what the best or most adequate definition or analysis of "truth" is, we must know some truths. For the naturalist the paradigmatic instances of knowledge are those drawn from common-sense experience and science. There is nothing arbitrary about this, for we are not dealing with a skeptic who denies that we know anything, but with the supernaturalist *who in his secular life agrees with the naturalist* yet who maintains that beyond the natural order there is another, and that at the center of this order is God.

It is well known that in the history of thought the argument for theism has not always presupposed that the supernatural order is unrelated to the natural order, and that the methods of common sense and science are necessarily incompetent to establish the existence of God. Many have contended that the book of nature properly studied points to the existence of a Creator of nature. Many tracts have been written that are variations on themes of "the common sense of theism" (or of Christianity). The arguments of natural or rational theology do not presuppose a different conception of "knowledge" or the acceptance of a special method of discovering truths that go beyond the methods used by those unconverted and who have not yet seen the light. A whole library of literature exists written by scientists, especially some eminent English scientists, who have attempted to show by arguments that claim to be continuous with those employed in scientific inquiry that the nature of things is spiritual and that "all active mind" and "energizing Will" is operative throughout the universe. The considerations are of the same character as are those of physicists who have linked the jump of electrons from one orbit to another with freedom of the will—and with no greater validity. I do not think that it is unfair to say that only when the appeal to common-sense experience and the scientific knowledge of the time demonstrably fails to give a rational warrant for believing in the existence of God, or when it is realized that the invocation of such arguments and evidence makes God's existence problematic or unlikely, is there a resort to conceptions of God that allegedly would make the methods by which we ordinarily acquire knowledge incompetent or irrelevant.

Naturalistic humanism has developed in opposition to supernaturalism, and especially to theism. The term "God" sometimes appears in metaphysical systems designating categorial features of existence that have nothing to do with theism—for example, with the principle of creativity or concretion or totality. Even when it is innocent of theistic implications, its use causes confusion because readers import religious and theistic significance into its connotation. Although all naturalists reject metaphysical systems that involve transcendent terms, including systems that are atheistic (like Heidegger's), they differ among themselves about the nature and intellectual validity of metaphysics. Those who speak of a naturalistic metaphysics regard it as vaguely anticipatory of, or continuous with, science, which makes those who have denied that it has a distinctive subject matter, metaphysicians, too. Some regard it as devoid of any cognitive significance. These raise interesting problems but for present purposes they do not bear directly on the theological questions of the existence of God as theists understand it. The three great theistic religions, Judaism, Christianity, Mohammedanism, no matter how refined or sophisticated, assert the existence of a self-existent, eternal power, infinitely wise and good, who directs the destinies of the world and its creatures. Not every account of God is coherent or intelligible for by definition the attributes are possessed in a pre-eminent degree. But in all the variations offered of his nature, he appears as a Person—and if he did not, it would make pointless the rituals and practices of myriads of believers.

The naturalist denies that there is any convincing evidence or reason for believing in the existence of any person of this kind in the universe. It should be obvious—and it surprises me that Nielsen does not see this—that to the naturalist all belief in God—all theism—is either open or disguised anthropomorphism. He has read Feuerbach to little purpose if he does not see this. The great merit of Feuerbach's still unappreciated contribution is to show in detail that all the predicates of God are "anthropomorphisms," and therefore, that the belief in the existence of God is an anthropomorphism, too.

At this point I believe it is necessary to say that Nielsen, in characterizing "naturalisms like Hook's, Nagel's, or Dennis's," has a very crude notion of scientific method. He seems to think that the use of logical analysis is foreign to it and introduces a special philosophical or semantic method which is more fundamental or intellectually superior to scientific method, since it can sit in judgment, so to speak, on the relative merits of the scientific way of knowing and the religious way of knowing. But in formulating a hypothesis among various alternatives, in drawing their implications, a great deal of logical analysis may be involved. Hypotheses may be rejected because they are discovered to be too fuzzy or vague or question-begging or contradictory or seemingly paradoxical. A considerable amount of logical analysis is required to answer the question "What does it mean for two events to be simultaneous?" But the logical analysis helps us only to clarify: no amount of it will enable us by itself to deduce what actually exists in the world. If I understand Nielsen this is what he claims to be doing. On the one hand he castigates most naturalists on the ground that they have not properly rejected "the religionists' claim that religion too has its own techniques and its own way of knowing." On the other hand, he purposes to improve on these simple-minded naturalists who rely on empirical methods by fixing the limits of intelligible discourse *in advance* and ruling out the existence of God from the actual scheme of things. But in a world where some religionists say that they believe in God because existence is absurd and others proclaim that God is completely Other than man and human discourse necessarily inadequate in describing him, Nielsen's improved strategy betokens a naïveté profounder than any he criticizes.

How do the "simple-minded naturalists" deal with the religionists' claim that "religion too has its own techniques and its own way of knowing?" Presumably these techniques and ways of knowing result in assertions that certain events have occurred and that certain states of affairs exist. They not only ask for confirmable instances, for which they are still waiting, but they turn to the two thousand years war of religion against science which are replete with disconfirming instances—a history which is apparently irrelevant in Nielsen's view—as among the grounds for denying the validity of religious techniques and ways of knowing. They are not as dogmatic as Nielsen because some of them at least still have an open mind about the existence of God (or more likely the Devil) whereas nothing conceivable about what could happen in the universe would ever lead Nielsen to recognize him. Naturalists are well aware that there are difficulties in the concept of a Divine Person or of a disembodied consciousness but instead of ruling out references to them as meaningless or unintelligible, they ask what follows in the way of consequences from the statement that a Divine Person exists different from the statement that he does not exist? Nielsen contends that this does not meet Father Daly's retort to similar questions as to what would have to occur to constitute a disproof of the love or existence of God—viz. "quite literally 'Nothing.'" To the naturalist the retort is a compound of logical errors. For the alternatives "God or nothing" may be exclusive, they are obviously not exhaustive. In addition even if it makes sense to speak of the universe as contingent, as this argument implies, it would not establish that the existence of God, no less the existence of a loving God, was necessary. The God of Maimonides and Aquinas may not be the God of Abraham, Isaac, and Joseph implies Nielsen—which would certainly be news to Maimonides and Aquinas—but there is no more evidence of the existence of the God of the former than of the God of the latter.

One concluding observation. Nielsen asserts that according to me the distinction between fact and fantasy rests upon assumption 5 and that this assumption is itself "a categorial or conceptual remark" (or in Wittgenstein's language, a "grammatical remark"). "Do we observe by means of the scientific method," he asks, "that nonverifiable claims are fanciful or is this part of the specification of the very meaning of the distinction between fact and fantasy? It seems to me to be the latter." I find this very confusing, and unless I have radically misunderstood Nielsen another illustration of his tendency to determine what exists in the world and what does not exist by semantic or conceptual fiat. The distinction between fact and fantasy or reality and illusion rests upon the differences in their experiencable *effects*. The difference between the fire I truly perceive and the imaginary or illusory fire is that the first warms or burns me or others, and the second does not; the difference between the real feast and the Barmicidean feast is that, among other specifiable effects, the first nourishes me or gratifies my hunger while the second does not. Whether or not I declare something to be a fact or an illusion, in either case I am relying upon the *same* set of epistemological assumptions, whatever they may be, and therefore it is false to say that these assumptions enter into the specification of the very difference between fact and fantasy. And every theist when he is not talking about God knows and accepts this. He is at one with the naturalist. I am confident that most theists would find it as bewildering as I do to read that the truth of the statements "God exists" or "God created the heavens and the earth" is *au fond* a categorial or conceptual or grammatical remark. If he did, he would have to treat my denial that God exists, that the belief in him is a belief in an illusion, as another conceptual remark rather than as an impious, atheistic utterance. And although we may agree with Wittgenstein that it is sometimes difficult to draw the distinction between empirical and conceptual questions, as the history of the *empirical* sciences show, it no more bears on the question whether the atheistic conclusion of the naturalistic humanists is warranted by evidence and reason than that the actual length of any object although objectively relevant to other things, depends on whether it is described in yards or meters.

ON THE COMPLEXITIES
OF OPEN-MINDEDNESS:
A REPLY TO HOOK

KAI NIELSEN

I

Sidney Hook and I are both atheists and naturalistic humanists and that is unequivocally recognized by both of us of each other. But Hook, who thinks my views are in certain respects very mistaken and even arrogantly and a prioristically so, remarks, not unsurprisingly with his characteristic irony, that, fellow atheists and naturalists to the contrary notwithstanding, "Nothing separates us—only an abyss" (Hook 1975, 128). If my dear friend Sidney were only still with us, I would try to convince him that, though along with important substantial agreement, that concerning religion there are at least seemingly crucial substantive differences between us; and I would, not surprisingly, try to nudge him in my direction. And in doing so, also show him that there is not the abyss that he believes there to be. I believe that his so moving, if indeed he would have, would render his own position more coherent and would strengthen our common defense of naturalistic humanism and atheism. But alas he is not with us. But, I hope, I can do our common cause some service in sorting things out and in trying clearly to say something of what sort of atheists we atheists should be and why. And to show as well why this stand here—or so I shall argue—is not the question-begging one that it is often taken to be.

Hook remarks that "almost every sentence of Nielsen's critique of my position invites extended commentary" (Hook 1975, 128). But to engage in that detailed inspection, as we both realize, would, for most readers, at least, be tedious. I shall rather first try to clear the decks by specifying where we, to no good purpose, argue past each other. That out of the way, I will turn to a consideration of what crucially divides us. Finally, I will try to say something of where, after sorting out our dispute, things should stand for someone wishing to defend with sound reasons atheistic humanism. How, that is, should an atheist humanist conduct her case and how compelling is it.

The first bit of deck-clearing concerns a priorism and fallibilism. My view is every bit as fallibilist and devoid of a priori blockages to inquiry as is Hook's. He sees "the great difference between us in it being the case that I want 'to foreclose future discourse about transcendent conceptions of God' while he is prepared on principle to listen and to modify [his] position if reason and evidence convince [him]" (Hook 1975, 127). He thinks that I want to browbeat theists into silence on the basis of an "antecedently formulated theory of meaning" (Hook 1975, 130).[25] He takes me as seeking to fix "the limits of intelligible discourse in advance" and to be ruling out a priori, and in effect dogmatically, "the existence of God from the actual scheme of things" (Hook 1975, 134). He thinks, that is, that I am trying to determine "what exists in the world and what does not exist by semantic and conceptual fiat" (Hook 1975, 135).[26] And he remarks, perfectly correctly, than an "ontological disproof of the existence of God is no more valid than an ontological proof" (Hook 1975, 129).[27] It is here where we have the abyss. But Hook has badly misread me in attributing any of these things to me.

I am, as is plainly evident in this book, like Hook, a fallibilist through and through. I do argue, perhaps mistakenly, that where theists, as is generally the case with sophisticated ones, have a severely nonanthropomorphic conception of God, where God is said to be a purely Spiritual Person transcendent to the universe, that such a concept of God is incoherent and such conceptualizations of God make no sense (Hägerström 1964, 224–50). Believers when they say such things do not know—do not understand—what they are saying and those atheists or agnostics who ask for evidence for claims made by the use of such conceptualizations appealing to such a concept show they do not know what they are saying either. To ask for the evidence for the existence of a God so conceived— an utterly disembodied, omnipresent, infinite individual transcendent to the universe—makes no more sense than to ask for evidence for the claim that Thatcher sleeps faster than Pinochet or that the stones in my garden are conversing. There is disguised nonsense and plain nonsense, as Rudolf Carnap stressed (Carnap 1959). Such God-talk, I am arguing, is the former. That may be off-putting to Hook. There may be, he might think, too much Carnapian scorn in my tone and, of course, whatever my tone, I may be mistaken in thinking such talk nonsensical. But I am not a prioristically, or in any other way, laying down anything by conceptual fiat or simply ruling out anything. And surely I am not trying to make it the case that theists will not feel free to speak their minds (Hook 1975, 130–31). I am asking though in a challenging manner whether their God-talk makes sense. But that is a challenge to religious belief and plainly not an attempt to silence religious believers. It is no more true for such a claim than it is true for an argument that we have compelling evidence that God does not exist or for an attempted proof that he does not exist. What I say is empirical, though it is empirical concerning our linguistic behavior. I say to such believers and such atheists and agnostics "Look carefully at what you are saying and why, look at the language-games and social practices involved in your actual God-talk, when it is so severely nonanthropomorphic, and look as well and comparatively at your rather more secular talk (your more ordinary commerce with the world) and see, in the light of this, whether you can make sense of talk of 'an infinite individual transcendent to the world'; of 'a pure spirit' or of 'an omnipresent person.' Just try to think literally here." But no answer is dictated here and no a priori claim is made.

We have more plainly anthropomorphic talk of God—an anthropomorphic God—which may semantically speaking make sense, though the probability with such talk, as Hook argues, of saying anything that is warrantedly assertable is rather low. But—eschewing such anthropomorphism—theologians and theistic philosophers and some others as well in seeking transcendency (seeking to get beyond anthropomorphism), find themselves forced into using such strange utterances: utterances that will point to, in some way try to articulate, the transcendency of what they take (are trying to take) God to have. (Simone Weil is an extreme example of this. But she is a good example of what a person with a religious consciousness that is impassioned and reflective and contains a deep moral sensitivity can be driven to.) My claim is that, for all of the integrity of the best of these expressions of faith, they do not, and probably cannot, make sense. The believer, that is, cannot make sense of such talk of God as the "infinitely ineffable Other." Given what they are trying to say, they have not, I argue, shown how their putative assertions have either truth-conditions or assertability-conditions. They cannot specify what it would be like for them to have either truth-conditions or assertability-conditions. And thus, being the kinds of claims they purpose to be, they are good candidates for incoherence.

The present point vis-à-vis Hook is that my claim here, true or false, plausible or implausible, is an empirical claim about their use of language and is fallible like all empirical claims. I remain (*pace* what Hook says of me) perfectly open to counterargument and counterevidence about their use of language, about what their language-games are like, about how they work and what claims they make (try to make) as I am about the whole structure of my own argument. Hook doesn't trump me for openness here. (Indeed I would have taken this whole matter as something that just goes without saying about any properly conducted philosophical argument, but for the fact that Hook challenges me here.) When I claim that not only is there no evidence but that there could be none for such religious claims, I remain open to both counterarguments here that my claim is (a) false or alternatively that (b) it is itself incoherent. I am, that is, perfectly willing to play my own game with my own account. Hook has no grounds for claiming that I am taking a high, or even a low, a priori road or trying to lay down the law or to intimidate believers. (The latter, I think, is an absurd claim.)

Now to clear another part of the deck. It has to do with how atheism is to be characterized. First, a retraction. I was mistaken in characterizing Hook as an agnostic atheist. That is a confused notion for the reasons that Hook gives. I should have said he was a fallibilistic atheist. But there is nothing either unusual or wrong with that. So am I a fallibilistic atheist and so are all reasonable atheists (Nielsen 1996, 509–56). I would hope in time that "fallibilistic atheist" would become a pleonasm.

Hook thinks—and now we go to a different matter where I will not be so concessive—that I extend "the connotation of the term 'atheism' and am guilty of violating what Peirce called 'the ethics of words'" (Hook 1975, 128). I think, on the contrary, that he uses the term 'atheism' too narrowly. This results in it being the case that not everything that a reflective atheist will want to consider as atheistic will come under Hook's net.[28] I will try to sort this out. (This is also something I did, though not with reference to Hook, in the first part of chapter 2.) Instead of simply saying that someone is an atheist if she believes "that it is false or probably false that there is a God," a more adequate characterization of atheism, not at all violating the ethics of words, would be that an atheist is someone who rejects belief in God for the following reasons, where the specific reason operative in a particular case will depend on the claim being made by the believer. The reasons are (1) if an anthropomorphic God is what is at issue, the atheist rejects belief in God because it is false or probably false that there is such a God; (2) if it be a nonanthropomorphic conception of God (e.g., the God of Luther and Calvin, Maimonides, Aquinas and Averroes) that is at issue, an atheist (on my conception) rejects belief in that God because such a conception of God is, depending on the details of the particular conceptualization, either meaningless, unintelligible, contradictory, incomprehensible, or incoherent; (3) an atheist (again on my conception) rejects belief in God because the conception of God in question is such that it merely masks an atheistic substance, e.g., "God" so conceived is just another name for love or simply a symbolic term for moral ideals (Nielsen 1985, 20–21). (Here such an atheist feels believers are being shortchanged and secularists misled.) In (3) we speak of God, as portrayed by some modern or contemporary theologians and philosophers. Premise (1) captures Hook's conception of the believer's God and Hook's account provides the proper grounds for an atheist's rejection of God so conceived. But "God" is not always so construed and (2) and (3) show that and how this is so and what it would be for an atheist to reject such a conception and the belief which it captures. On Hook's narrow conceptualization of 'atheism' an atheist (so conceived) is left without resources relevantly to respond to someone who conceptualizes God as in (2) or (3). My characterization by contrast captures everything Hook's conception of atheism does while capturing other matters that are relevant to the dialectic of belief versus unbelief that Hook's conception does not address or at least not adequately. But I should add that this last claim of mine is contestable. Whether (*pace* what I believe) Hook's manner of argumentation is successful for God as conceived in (2) and (3) is one of the genuine matters at issue between us that I will turn to after I have finished clearing the decks.

To continue with the clearing of the decks, Hook says that in pushing him for his grounds of atheism I am, like A. E. Murphy, in effect saying that we must "first agree . . . on what we mean by knowledge before we deny the theist's assertion on pain . . . of obvious question-begging" (Hook 1975, 132).[29] Hook rightly remarks that "such a strategy" would be "intellectually disastrous. Before we attempt to discover what the proper analysis of 'knowledge' is we must be in possession of some knowledge—just as before we can determine what is the best or most adequate definition or analysis of 'truth' is we must have some truths" (Hook 1975, 132). This is exactly right and that I agree with Hook here is clear from what I argue in discussing his views in chapter 5.[30] Such a rejection of what Kierkegaard called Socratism is common to pragmatism, G. E. Moore, Wittgenstein, and ordinary language philosophy. I have repeatedly either argued for it or assumed it. (See, for example, Nielsen 1995.)

One final bit of deck clearing and then we can get to what really matters, where Hook and I, or at least not so obviously, are not speaking past each other and where our views really do conflict. Hook remarks that I have "a very crude notion of scientific method. He [Nielsen] seems to think that the use of logical analysis is foreign to it and introduces a special philosophical or semantic method which is more fundamental or intellectually superior to scientific method, since it sits in judgment, so to speak, on the relative merits of the scientific way of knowing and the religious way of knowing" (Hook 1975, 134). I certainly do not think that logical analysis is foreign to scientific analysis or scientific method and I have never even suggested such a thing. But I have stressed, as does Hook, that it is an integral part of scientific method. If my notion of scientific method is very crude, then so is Hook's and Ernest Nagel's as well, for our conceptions of scientific method are very similar. But more importantly, like the classical pragmatists, like Hook and Ernest Nagel, like Quine, like neopragmatists such as Richard Rorty and Hilary Putnam and like the logical positivists, I have consistently and repeatedly rejected any special philosophical way of knowing or any epistemological or metaphysical perch—anything like a First Philosophy—to be set in judgment of scientific method, religion, morals, science, politics, or anything else (Nielsen 1995). Here I am one with Hook and he has no reason to think otherwise.

I do think we human beings—we big-brained, language-using, self-interpreting animals—reasoning together, with whatever tools come in handy, can and do assess our forms of life and decide, in a way that repeatedly gets revised (repairing the ship at sea), what it is reasonable to do and to believe. But this is not to invoke any special philosophical skyhook or any other kind of skyhook or a special philosophical method (Nielsen 1996, 12–19). Any such Archimedian point (to switch the metaphor) is as mythical as Hook and I agree that religious skyhooks are.

II

Where then are the real issues that divide us? First, and perhaps most importantly, it is over the role of evidence vis-à-vis religious beliefs. Hook thinks that at least the centrally crucially important ones are false or very probably false. We simply, he believes, do not have enough evidence for them for us justifiably to assert that we have any grounds for believing them to be true or even probably true. I believe this is true enough, as I argued, among other places, in the first chapter, concerning the religious beliefs of believers with Zeus-like, Wotan-like, anthropomorphic conceptions of God (a conception of God that is in much, but not all, of the Bible, where it is taken at face value) but not for the core religious beliefs of developed Judaism, Christianity, and Islam, the conceptions of God in common to Maimonides, Aquinas, Averroes (Ibn Rushd), Luther, and Calvin.[31] These philosopher-theologians seek transcendence both with the concept of God that is theirs and with many of the various conceptions emerging around the concept. The conceptions, reflective, philosophically disciplined, and sophisticated as they often are, are transcendental claims about an infinite individual transcendent to the universe yet still everywhere and all-knowing and all-good. This infinite individual is said to have created the universe out of nothing. These are, I argue, incoherent claims without truth-conditions or assertability-conditions, the very kind of conditions that Hook also requires for intelligibility. (See my arguments in chapter 6.) It is senseless to talk about waiting for evidence for God so conceived. We have nothing here for which we understand what it would be like to have evidence. We literally do not understand what we are trying to assert when we say such things and the "we" here ranges over believers and nonbelievers alike. And this is not an a priori claim or the laying down of "a meaning rule." It is rather, as I argued in the previous section, an empirical claim about our use of language. To repeat a method of challenge I used earlier: carefully inspect and reflect on what is being uttered and see if you understand it. See if you know how to use such utterances to make a truth-claim. Religious believers, ubiquitously I believe, have a conception of things that their background metabeliefs about religious belief commit them to having. It is that their religious beliefs commit them to a mysterious, utterly nonnaturalistic conception of transcendency. That their religious talk embodies such a claim is an *expectation* that reasonably orthodox believers have about their God-talk and that many of us (believers and nonbelievers alike) have (perhaps mistakenly) about the uses of certain religious utterances that believers take to be essential for belief (Nielsen 1962 and see my remarks about the error theory of religion in chapter 1).[32]

Hook all the same thinks this is a prioristic dogmatism on my part and puts forth the following considerations against it. Hook relates a story very similar to one given independently by Bertrand Russell.[33] Walter Stace, Hook reports, once sardonically asked him what account he would give of himself if he died and woke up in the presence of God. Hook said that his answer would be, "Oh! Lord, you didn't give me enough evidence" (Hook 1975, 129). I think—unless it is just taken as a joke with no philosophical or religious point—that this is an utterly superficial story, even though philosophers as distinguished as Hook and Russell did so remark and concerning which John Searle has voiced his approval (Searle 1998, 37). It reveals that these three philosophers have a very crude conception of God—some kind of Zeus-like empirical or quasiempirical entity that we might somehow see, stand in the presence of, converse with, and form empirical hypotheses about. They, of course, do not think that there is such an entity, but that is how they conceive of God. As I argued long ago against John Hick concerning "eschatological verification," if we do not understand what it would be like to stand in the presence of God now or how to individuate God so that we can gain some understanding of what "God" refers to, dying and waking up in heaven will not help us one bit (Hick 1960; Nielsen 1963a; Nielsen 1971a, 73–79). (We also need to understand something of what kind of "place" this heaven is. Again language may be idling.) Moreover, Hook just assumes he understands what it would be like to die and then wake up— with his "resurrection body" or as a disembodied being or a pure spirit— in heaven and then see or at least hear God and talk to Him and get a reply. (See chapter 3.)[34] But it is just the intelligibility of this very talk that is at issue. It—or some of it—perhaps is intelligible, if it gets anthropomorphic enough. (We could then *pace* Wittgenstein and/or actual God-talk ask about God's eyebrows, the color of his eyes, and about how loud he speaks.) Hook with his newly fitted out resurrection body newly arrived in heaven talks to an embodied God sitting on his throne. All of that is verifiable in principle and we know what it would be like to have evidence for it. When believers and nonbelievers alike have such very anthropomorphic pictures, we understand such talk so construed. It is intelligible enough, but it plainly gives expression to beliefs which are superstitions and are widely regarded as such by many believers and nonbelievers alike. But to avoid something plainly false—there is no such God or heavenly throne—we seek a less anthropomorphic conception of God—we take God, for example, to be Pure Spirit. We have a conception, that is, that does not have an anthropomorphic picture of God. But then our picture would have to be a very abstract "picture"—indeed so abstract that it would not be a picture at all. We seem at least to be without an understanding of what an "abstract picture" or a "nonanthropomorphic picture" of God would be, though we, of course, understand the idea of abstract painting. Again language is being pulled apart here. If we think for a minute, we will realize that we are at sea over what a "nonanthropomorphic picture" of God would be. To put it conservatively, we have something here whose sense is very problematical and concerning which the very idea of evidence for such a God loses its bite and very probably its sense.

Hook's Russell story also comes a cropper. Hook reports asking Russell "if ever he would be prepared to believe in God" (Hook 1975, 129). Hook continues, "His reply, as I recall it, was, 'If I heard a voice come out of the sky, referring to something I, and I alone, knew predicting some altogether unlikely event that no one else anticipated, and if that happened again and again, I would acknowledge the existence of God'" (Hook 1975, 129–30). This is something like the example I once had thrust at me when I was being pressed as Russell was. Suppose, it was put to me, that I was standing in the dark looking up at the starry heavens on a clear night and suddenly the stars rearranged themselves to spell out clearly GOD EXISTS. Would not this be evidence for the existence of God? And would it not be even stronger evidence if it started happening repeatedly and it was the case that very many people saw these occurrences and no one who was in a position to observe what was going on denied that that was what occurred. If that happened would not this be fairly conclusive evidence for the existence of God such that it would be unreasonable to continue being an atheist or even an agnostic in such a circumstance? And shouldn't a similar thing be said for the Russell case, though, since my case has a social dimension and his does not, mine is even a stronger case of being able to say what it would be like to have very good evidence indeed for the existence of God? But would not both of them if they occurred provide strong evidence for the existence of God?

From such considerations Hook concludes that it is fair enough to say that we know what it would be like to have evidence for the existence of God: even evidence for the allegedly utterly nonanthropomorphic God of The Tradition. The relevant point, and indeed the telling point, for atheism (Hook has it) is that we plainly do not have any such evidence or indeed any evidence at all for the existence of God. But the above cases show us that logically speaking we could have. I am just being dogmatic in denying that the existence of God is at least verifiable in principle. And, as Hook also argues, and as has been repeatedly argued, that since there is, as a matter of fact, no empirical evidence giving us good grounds for believing that God exists, we should conclude that it is probably the case that God does not exist. That is, if we are to be consistent scientific empiricists (indeed pragmatic naturalists), we should then conclude, as Hook does, that we have good empirical grounds for believing that God does not exist. Indeed, if the situation is as he describes it, should we not conclude that God does not exist? I am just, Hook has it, being a dogmatic a priorist in denying a priori that we could have such evidence for the nonexistence of God. It is simply not true that we do not know what it would be like to have evidence for or against the existence of even a nonanthropomorphic God. We as a matter of fact do not have that evidence, but we could have. And if we did, we would have evidence for the existence of God. I have, to repeat, just been given some plain instances of what it would be like to have such evidence. Here we have a head-on and important conflict between Hook and myself.

I am, Hook to the contrary notwithstanding, not being such a dogmatist. Let me come at this indirectly. We should first note that such things, as it is agreed on all sides, do not happen. Moreover, we do not have the slightest reason to think they could as a matter of fact happen. What has been described is "consistently thinkable," but then so is "I ran around the world in ten seconds." Logical possibilities count for very little here. However, if things like the stars so rearranging themselves were to happen, my world and the world of others, including that of many believers, perhaps all believers, would be shattered. What I, and they, reasonably and without question, expect not to be possible ("empirically possible" of course) would have inexplicably turned out actually to have happened. It would upset everything—or almost everything—we have learned from our common life and from science. But, if I could bring myself in such a circumstance to look at matters calmly and not think I had gone mad (something which in such a circumstance would be the reasonable thing to believe) I would still have to conclude that if I—and we (my cultural peers)—do not understand what is meant by something being "a pure spirit" or "an infinite individual, omnipresent but still transcendent to the world" or by "an immaterial person whose existence is metaphysically necessary," we will not be any better off from observing such startling phenomena. It will not enable us to understand such talk. We will still draw a blank about God. All we can conclude is that there is something very, very strange going on that we do not understand at all—something that is so bizarre that it has shattered our world. I, in such a circumstance, would not know how to think about things anymore. Still these bizarre occurrences will not help us understand such religious phrases and without some understanding of them we cannot form sentences with them to make statements having truth-conditions or assertability-conditions. We are no better off with the stars in the heavens spelling out GOD EXISTS than with their spelling out PROCRASTINA-TION DRINKS MELANCHOLY. We know that something has shaken our world, but we know not what; we know—or think we know, how could we tell which it was in such a circumstance?—that we heard a voice coming out of the sky and we know—or again think that we know—that the stars rearranged themselves right before our eyes and on several occasions to spell out GOD EXISTS. But are we wiser by observing this about what "God" refers to or what a pure disembodied spirit transcendent to the universe is or could be? At most we might think that maybe those religious people have something—something we know not what—going for them. But we also might think it was some kind of big trick or some mass delusion. The point is that we wouldn't know what to think.

Hook misses all that. Hook says—it seems to me bizarrely and incorrectly—that we are dealing in the above cases with something "of existential probability of the same order as the question whether, in the face of certain circumstances observable on earth, it would be more reasonable to believe that there were other intelligent creatures in outer space with powers of perception and control roughly as superior to our own as ours is to that of ants, than to believe that the pattern of continued effects was a matter of chance" (Hook 1975, 130). But the cases are markedly, relevantly and crucially different. We know what it would be like for there to be intelligent embodied creatures in outer space with greater powers of intelligence than our own and we even understand their having such greater powers, though certainly not in detail. But we are there still talking about physical entities—dynamic material beings—with different powers than ours, but still powers of the same kind only greater. Everything here is identifiable in a relevantly straightforward way. But the same is not true of a nonanthropomorphic God, e.g., the God of Aquinas and Calvin. And there is the rub.

The term "God" in the metaphysical systems of Spinoza, Alexander, and Whitehead, Hook correctly points out, is used nontheistically as it also is in the theological system of the Christian theologian Paul Tillich. Hook remarks that he finds "the concept of God as defined in these and other metaphysical systems . . . unintelligible" (Hook 1975, 128). It is completely baffling to me that he does not then also find the concept of God in the metaphysical religiosities (to use Hägerström's phrase) of the developed religious belief systems—systems which are also metaphysical systems, though not just metaphysical systems—unintelligible rather than giving rise to statements which are false or probably false (Hägerström 1964, 175–223). All these metaphysical systems have similar kinds of difficulties from the point of view of a scientific empiricist like Hook. And I would say similar kinds of difficulties period. If one is unintelligible why not the other and for much the same reasons? Why is Spinoza unintelligible in his talk of God and Aquinas not?

For reasons noted above the concept of God of Calvin, Luther, the Catholic Church, Judaism, and Islam (as they have developed) is very problematic with a plethora of metaphysical danglers. If intelligibility and incoherence (as I believe it can) can admit of degrees, it would seem that Spinoza's and Whitehead's conceptions of God—or at least Spinoza's—are not as unintelligible as the conceptions of Aquinas or Maimonides. Is it anything more than that their strange remarks are more familiar than those of Spinoza and especially of Whitehead? But is familiar nonsense—to put it tendentiously—less nonsensical than unfamiliar nonsense? Perhaps it is if what is unintelligible and what is not just comes down to what is familiar and what is not. But that itself (*pace* Richard Rorty) is a very problematic view. Assuming it is not just a matter of that, I put it to us: reflect on the fact that when we read of the religious conceptions of primitive tribes that they often—indeed typically—seem to us fantastically absurd, often even unintelligible, while it takes a certain kind of cultivation, a certain kind of taking thought, to so view the religious conceptions of our own tribe. Yet, if we can bring ourselves to look at them with a cold, clear eye, and, abstracting from the soothing effects of their familiarity, are they not just as absurd, not just as good candidates for unintelligibility, as those of primitive societies? It seems to me that it is plain that they are. I think, moreover, that there is relevant analogy here with the comparison of the conceptions of God of Aquinas and Spinoza. Isn't it just the greater familiarity of the conceptions of Aquinas that carries the day with many people? And is that not an illusory carrying?

However, be that as it may, the basic question remains why say that the concept of God of any one of these metaphysical systems is unintelligible but not the other? Is it just that the Judeo-Christian-Islamic ones are more familiar and had an earlier home in anthropomorphic concepts of God—concepts we do, more or less, understand? But the developed forms of these religions do make an unqualified claim to transcendence and with that they seem at least to break the bounds of human understanding. So the reason that they had such an anthropomorphic origin and familiar home is no reason to claim that they, functioning as they do now, are intelligible and that the Spinozistic-Whiteheadian ones are not. With respect to their intelligibility/unintelligibility, they seem at least to be on a par. If they all are unintelligible it seems to me that we have only room to argue about their comparative degree of unintelligibility. Here Spinoza would seem clearly to come off better than Aquinas. But the central issue is whether they both are, as I think, unintelligible. The degree of unintelligibility is comparatively unimportant.

It seems to me that Hook should, shifting his views, say of both of them that they are unintelligible because in neither case does "God" stand for anything either identifiable or introducible intralinguistically by definite descriptions. "God" is not introducible be definite descriptions because in these alleged definite descriptions some terms occur whose referents (e.g., "Creator of the universe") similarly cannot be secured. That is we do not understand what we are talking about in speaking of them. If Hook resists taking that route then he should say that they both are intelligible, but both reasonably to be judged to be false because we have no evidence for the claims made by the use of either of them. What is a complete muddle, given their similar logical status, is to say one is unintelligible and the other false. But that is exactly what Hook does.

Furthermore, it should be noted that the key bits of God-talk of such belief-systems are not verifiable even in principle. "God is our loving celestial father," "God is a wholly other all good and all knowing being" or "God created the heavens and the earth out of nothing" are not verifiable even in principle.[35] We (believers and nonbelievers alike) do not know how to go about establishing (even probabilistically) their truth or falsity. We cannot show what evidence even in principle could establish, or even make probable, their truth or their falsity. We do not understand what it even would be like for them to be either true or false or warrantedly assertable or not so. We are at a loss to say how or that they could be true. And if they cannot be true (logical falsities apart) they cannot be false either.

This could be attacked for being too verificationist. But that is not a line Hook will take for he is at least as verificationist as I am. (We both accept my propositions 1–6. See the first essay in this chapter.) God, for Hook, is some kind of supernatural bodiless Person. Hook asks, in good verificationist fettle, "Show me what difference there is between saying he exists and saying he doesn't exist. What different consequences ensue? Surely there must be different consequences for if all consequences of the affirmation and denial of the existence of God are the same, the two expressions would have the same meaning, and there would be no difference between the beliefs of the theists and those of atheists. But since the beliefs are asserted to be different, presumably the consequences will be different" (Hook 1975, 131).

It would not be adequate just to come to rest with the above, for, even if the consequences of the use of the two expressions were the same, the atheist could appeal to Occam's razor as a reason for sticking with his account. But I think Hook could reasonably reply that we must be sophisticated with our conceptualizations of consequences and count considerations of simplicity as a part of the consequences here too.

I have considerable sympathy, as my writing in this volume as well as in others attests, for this way of going about things in sorting out what it makes sense to assert as true or false claims about what is to be the case if a certain state of affairs is said to obtain—if things (under some description) are to stand in one way or another and we are going to be able to ascertain that that is so. Hook's way of going about things here is roughly the way we should sort out merely putative factual claims from genuine ones (true or false). We further agree that all even somewhat religiously orthodox believers take such religious claims, as have been mentioned above, e.g., "We are in God's providential care," as at least putatively factual claims (Nielsen 1962, 110–37). The believer, of course, believes that they are not just putatively factual propositions but are actually factual propositions (true or false) and that beyond that they are as a matter of fact true. Where Hook and I differ is (1) that I take the nonanthropomorphic ones to be *putatively* factual *only* and to have failed to make genuinely factual claims either true or false and (2) I do not take the nonanthropomorphic ones to be utterances which tolerably Orthodox religious believers would take to be even putatively empirical hypotheses. But neither of us needs to, or should, dogmatize about these matters. It is not a place where we should dig in our heels, though which position is the more adequate is of very considerable moment for our respective accounts. (But perhaps practically speaking less so for the secular humanist movement.) Either or both of our claims could be false or even incoherent. Or, as on Quine's account, it could be that it does not make much difference whether we say they are unassailably false or incoherent. In trying to ascertain what should be said here we have to attend to our language-games and social practices, neither of which, of course, is our private affair, and see what we can reasonably reflectively endorse. We will never get anything like certainty in such discussions. Nothing like an algorithm will settle matters here.

III

Hook will resist what I have been saying in two ways at least. I shall consider these two. First about what I say about anthropomorphism and nonanthropomorphism, he will say that I have neglected his argument that "all belief in God—all theism—is either open or disguised anthropomorphism" (Hook 1975, 134). Nielsen has read, he continues, "Feuerbach to little purpose" if he does not recognize that this is what Feuerbach compellingly argues. Feuerbach shows "in detail that the predicates of God are 'anthropomorphisms' and therefore that the belief in the existence of God is an anthropomorphism, too" (Hook 1975, 134). The idea that developed forms of theism have a nonanthropomorphic conception of God, Hook claims, is false. But Hook misunderstands what Feuerbach is saying here and misunderstands its import as well. Feuerbach is not saying that such believers do not think that what they speak of in speaking of God is something which transcends anthropomorphism. Of course they do and it is essential for the socio-psychological effectiveness of their belief—their orthodox Christian belief, say—that they continue to think that. Feuerbach is saying, like a good error theorist, though believers are trying to say more, that all that they are really justified in believing and saying is something anthropomorphic. That is all their religious concepts really mean though they mistakenly think otherwise. Feuerbach says that the subject matter of theology is really anthropology. Believers, though they think they are talking about a transcendent God, are in reality talking about, and only talking about, a projected image of idealized human beings—of human beings at their best. Moreover, that is all they can be talking about. They think otherwise, but they are in error. (See chapter 1.)

When Feuerbach says these things (these reductive things) he is aware that a believer could not believe them and *remain a believer*. His task, being normative, and not just descriptive-explanatory, he did not want them to remain so fixated. He, like Marx, wants to change their lives. He is not primarily concerned to analyze the believer's use of religious language, but, taking it to be the case that such talk taken straightforwardly is unintelligible, he wants to show from an atheistic point of view—the point of view that he takes to be the realistic, tough-minded point of view—what its real import is. He is concerned to show that "the real essence of religion" is something different from what believers take it to be. It is something purely secular and moral. Feuerbach's contemporaries correctly saw that for all his concern with religion he was a resolute atheist secularizer. Recognizing that, they made it impossible for him, in a severely religious society, to attain a teaching position. He was, and I think very powerfully, not trying to elucidate God-talk, but, with a deeply, and in this case profoundly, reductive account, trying to show religion's real function in the lives of human beings. What he says about anthropomorphism does not at all gainsay my claim that in Judaism, Christianity, and Islam, as we have them now with their claims to transcendence, we have the attempted postulation—and as a necessity—of a nonanthropomorphic conception of God. It is essential for developed theistic belief-systems that the anthropomorphism remain disguised, for if religious beliefs were recognized by the faithful to be just anthropomorphic, the very belief-system would self-destruct (Nielsen 1962). We would move with Feuerbach from a religion of God to a religion of man, from theism to secular humanism.[36]

Secondly, Hook maintains that my above arguments miss the fact that though sometimes people "talk incoherently and unintelligibly about some person or occurrence" yet sometimes what they are talking about is all the same real (Hook 1975, 129). "Sometimes despite the language of oxymoron, we can dimly discern the objectively existent reference of what the incoherent language seems to be referring to" (Hook 1975, 129). That is perfectly true, but we can only be justified in believing this for some particular utterance or cluster of utterances when on some other basis we know that what they say is so or at least could be so or when we have good reasons to believe that it is so or could be so. Someone must be able to articulate in intelligible language what it is that the persons in unintelligible speech were trying to say.[37] Feuerbach's reductive account attempts to do this and I think with considerable success. But, as we have seen, it will not be an account which believers will accept or indeed can accept and remain believers. What is required instead to yield what Hook is claiming is an account which will say intelligibly in language believers can accept, while still remaining believers, what the believer, speaking disjointedly and inchoately, was trying to gesture at. With my arguments about unintelligibility, I argue that this has not been done in a way that would meet his religious expectations and it looks very unlikely that it can be done. We—that is, we players of our language-games—have not been able to give an account of religious discourse which both meets religious believers' expectations and makes sense. We can give reductive accounts like Feuerbach's, Freud's, and Durkheim's which make sense. (See chapter 1.) But they will not meet the expectations of religious believers. My argument is that this is so because the believers' expectations are incoherent and their speech expressive of their expectations is incoherent (Nielsen 1962).

IV

I return to Hook's own line of argument for an open-minded naturalism. I am confident that Hook was well aware that religious believers (and others as well) will have the following counters to his verifiability proposal: (1) Such a stress on verifiability point by point for all individual purportedly factual statements leads not only to affirming the senselessness of key religious and metaphysical claims but to claiming the senselessness of some well-established scientific claims as well. But that certainly looks like a *reductio* of verificationism. (2) Many moral beliefs and other beliefs about what to do or to be are not verifiable. They are too much like imperatives for that. Moreover, in their very logic (use), they, since they are beliefs about what to do or to be, do not even purport to be factual claims, true or false, in the way factual claims are true or false.[38] (3) Language—the language-games of the forms of life that are our forms of language—have many uses other than to be factually informative and to make claims about what there is and what there must be. To put religious belief and conviction on such a verificationist grid (perhaps "grill" would be the better word?) is problematical at best. Many religious believers will claim that such verificationist talk is simply irrelevant to religious belief. They will claim that if we attend carefully to our religious practices with the language-games that go with them, that it will become evident that there the question of the existence of God is not at all treated as a hypothesis for which there even could be evidence. God is not conceived of as a reality that is to be put to such a test. No question sensibly arises from a religious point of view about religious utterances needing to pass scientific muster. To think anything like that is to fail to understand our religious language-games and practices.

I think that we atheists and naturalists must face up to such considerations and I have taxed Hook with not having faced them or at least for not having adequately faced them. But if (1), (2), and (3) are not met, both Hook's verificationism and methodological naturalism (the view that in all domains we must pursue warranted belief via the empirical-cum-logical methods exemplified by the sciences) become problematical. To meet this challenge Hook would need at least to show that scientific knowledge (where this includes mathematics and logic) and scientific knowledge alone is genuine knowledge. Hook remarks that "I do not know how to establish that scientific knowledge *alone* is genuine knowledge, for every attempt to establish it rests on assumptions about what constitutes knowledge. And one can always ask to establish that these assumptions themselves are alone essential for the acquisition of *genuine* knowledge" (Hook 1975, 131, first italics mine). And so we go on a merry-go-round with no evident natural why-stoppers, no evident "natural order of reasons."

However, Hook believes that there is no necessity to meet such a demand. His verificationist proposal for sorting out both sense from nonsense and what is reasonable to believe from what is unreasonable offers us a good account of what all of us (believers and nonbelievers alike) do in practice in our ordinary interactions with the world where, in various actual problematic situations we try to sort out what is warranted and what is not, what is fact and what is fiction. Hook argues that religious persons—or at least reasonable ones—as well as secularists use this method (this pragmatically characterized, broadly conceived scientific method) in ascertaining fact and making practical decisions about practical matters. The scientific method, broadly construed, as believer and nonbeliever alike (at least in practice) acknowledge, is accepted as a reliable method for fixing belief. If we go on to say, as Hook does, that it is the sole reliable method for fixing belief, then, if Hook is right here, C. S. Peirce's "The Fixation of Belief" is vindicated, where he wanted it vindicated, namely in practice.[39]

However, that there is a consensus (if there is) about this, important as it is, does not show—or even let us just go on assuming reasonably—that scientific knowledge (even broadly conceived) is the only genuine form of knowledge or the only reasonable way of fixing belief. People not accepting that scientistic conception could, however, accept that it is the way to fix belief and sort out either or both (a) what it makes sense to say in many contexts but not all and (b) to determine what we are justified in believing in many contexts but not in all. They could add, however, that (*pace* Hook and Dewey) in either or both respects it does not work in certain normative contexts, including in certain moral contexts, and that its failure to work there, in either respect, is not sufficient to render moral belief groundless, arbitrary, something that is inescapably in error, or as something that is senseless.

Ethical naturalism could counter this and perhaps John Dewey or Hook himself have adequately worked this counter out. And we have seen in chapter 6 how Peter Railton has made a strong case for ethical naturalism. Still that ethical naturalism has won the day is, while arguable, still very problematical. And what is there to stop people, who play religious language-games, engage (and seriously) in a cluster of religious practices, from resisting the claim that their beliefs must be verifiable to be intelligible or to be true or false or even to be warrantable? Do we know that only beliefs sanctioned by the scientific method are warrantable or are something we can reasonably and reflectively endorse? Suppose I contend with someone that his life is not, as he thinks it is, senseless, just one damn thing after another. If the considerations I bring to him have any force must this force come to a warrant established by scientific method? This, to put it minimally, seems dubious. Or why should religious believers accept the claim that there is no religious knowledge, or acceptable religious belief, unless these religious beliefs can be shown to be scientific beliefs or beliefs grounded on scientific beliefs? What if they say that that is just a dogmatically asserted scientism?

To take the atheistic humanist line that both Hook and I take is not a matter of getting back to some knowledge claims that make no assumptions or that cannot be contested. Here I agree with Hook. No such foundationalism—or indeed any foundationalism—is involved (Nielsen 1995). But it is—or so at last it is plausible to argue—necessary to show, or to make it reasonable to believe, that our religious talk, and the beliefs that go with our religious practices, cannot be reasonably acceptable unless such talk and such beliefs can be shown to be grounded in the logico-empirical method characteristic of our scientific practices. But have we done anything like that?

Hook makes, and not unreasonably, a burden of proof argument here. He maintains that "it rests with the supernaturalist to present the evidence that there is more in the world than is disclosed by our common empirical experience" (Hook 1975, 132). But suppose a religious believer remarks that he is not interested in showing anything like that and that he does not know that or how it could be done, even if he tried. He hasn't, he candidly remarks, the foggiest idea about that. But, he replies, he does not care about that. He simply takes belief in God on trust and is not trying to prove or to warrant anything, but simply (with or without warrant) to orient his life. Why shouldn't he do this? And what warrant do we have to say that in so acting he is being irrational or unreasonable? And what justification do we have for saying that he is being irrational if he doesn't argue for so taking things on trust or seek out evidences for his belief? He just believes on trust and (suppose being a good liberal, as well as a believer) that he doesn't tell others what to do or believe. Suppose he (being rather unorthodox) doesn't even accept that there is some authoritative order which should tell them that. What, if he is thoroughly so oriented, is wrong with his so fixing his religious beliefs? On what grounds can we rightly say he is mistaken or being unreasonable? It looks at least like we secular humanists have something to face up to here.

In facing this it is important to recognize that such a believer is making no claim to knowledge or to warranted or justified belief. But suppose all the same she avers "I know that my Savior liveth," as it would be natural for her to do as an expression of her faith, taken by her on trust. Then, whatever her intentions, she has in effect made a knowledge claim—or so it is not unnatural to take her remark—and it would seem at least that the burden is clearly on her, or on people speaking for her—the people she takes as spiritual guides—to show that that utterance can in some way be warranted or vindicated or at least be shown to be not unreasonable.[40] Even more minimally, it would seem that it would at least be necessary for *someone* to give us good reasons for believing that such utterances are intelligible. But then Hook's battery of verificationist arguments seem at least to come into play. Hook, in resolute naturalist fashion, asks, "Is there a different kind of knowledge that makes God an accessible object of knowledge in a manner inaccessible by the only reliable method we have so far successfully employed to establish truths about other facts? Are there other empirical facts, say spiritual facts or transcendent facts? Show them to us" (Hook 1975, 132). (Note that here Hook just assumes that spiritual facts or transcendent facts are some kind of empirical fact. But, reasonably orthodox believers would assert that this is just what they cannot be. The language-games of theistic religions are not played like that.)

If the believer appeals to some putative revelation here, then the answer is that the number of putative revelations are legend and not infrequently conflicting. He plainly, without vicious circularity, cannot use a claimed revelation to sort out which of the putative revelations are the genuine ones. The same thing also obtains for appeals to authority or to intuition. Hook, maintaining his pragmatically oriented naturalism, presses this method of challenge: "Is there a method discontinuous with that of the rational empirical method which will give us conclusions about what exists on earth or heaven, if there is such a place, concerning which all qualified inquirers agree? Tell us about it" (Hook 1975, 132).

Believers—or at least sophisticated ones who have some understanding of their religion and of what it is to be religious—will reply that while this way of fixing belief is certainly appropriate in mundane domains, scientific ones and perhaps even in some social domains, it is not in most religious domains and it is particularly not so in the crucial religious domains. "God is our heavenly Father," "God loves us," "Nothing can really harm us," "God is infinite being," "God is transcendent to the universe and is the creator and sustainer of it" and the like are central claims in Jewish, Christian, and Islamic religious life. They are an essential part of the warp and woof of those religious practices. But their truth is not establishable by the use of scientific method. And most believers do not seek—I would say vainly seek, if they seek—to make them so. Indeed a believer who tried to do this would thereby attest to his confusion about religious belief. To ask for an empirical warrant, for empirical evidence, (a pleonasm) for these beliefs is to show that you do not understand them. We cannot verify the above religious utterances and utterances like them. And this, as Hook well understands, means we cannot show them to be false either. To ask to fix religious beliefs by the method of science, where they are nonanthropomorphic, is to treat them as if they were beliefs about empirical realities, but that is exactly what they are not or at least believers cannot take them as such, by some reductionist move, and still remain believers—or at least believers who are even remotely orthodox (Nielsen 1962). And, if we assert, "Empirical realities are the only kind of realities there are," the question immediately faces us, how do we know this to be so? Or do we know or have reasonable grounds for believing it to be so? Do we establish it, if there is any way of establishing it at all, by the use of the scientific method?

If Hook replies that if their beliefs are not so warrantable then their beliefs are thereby "beyond knowledge," they are not something that could be known to be true, a fideist believer, at least, could bite that bullet and say that they are taken just on trust, just on faith. If Hook retorts that such trust is irrational if not supportable somewhere along the line by evidence, then the believer can in turn respond, "But that is just what it is to take them on trust, on faith. That is the risk of faith. And what is irrational about that? Must we have evidence or grounds for everything? You, Hook, whatever your intentions, are in effect simply ruling out faith."

So we seem, at least if we take Hook's way, to be at an impasse. If, on the other hand, I am right and these religious utterances are unintelligible, I can agree with the believer that they are not verifiable. (And this does not commit either of us to saying that the meaning of a proposition is its method of verification.) But if I am right and they are unintelligible, then we cannot (logically cannot) take them on trust or just on faith, for while we can take on trust something that we cannot prove or have no evidence for, we cannot take on trust or on faith what we literally do not understand. I can take it on trust that a classless society is possible. I cannot take it on trust that procrastination drinks melancholy or that Clinton sleeps faster than Blair is possible. We have to able to answer the question "What is it that I am supposed to take on trust?" Without at least that very minimal understanding, we are not able to take something on trust, no matter how much we want to, for we do not understand what that something is. We can take an obscure, even a desperately obscure, belief on trust, though even here where it slides in the direction of unintelligibility there is, for us and for others, the problem of understanding what it is we are supposed to take on trust. But where we have something that is plainly unintelligible, e.g., "Being transmigrates redly," there is no possibility of taking it on trust (Nielsen 1963b, 1965).

V

To sum up: putting aside our arguing at cross-purposes discussed in the first section and keeping firmly in mind that we are discussing the nonanthropomorphic conceptions of God embedded in developed forms of Judaism, Christianity, and Islam, Sidney Hook and I differ most fundamentally over whether such God-talk is unintelligible or simply false. Making either claim commits us to being atheists, but our grounds for atheism will differ depending on which claim we make. Hook thinks the fundamental beliefs of these religions are false or very probably false. I think they are unintelligible. Hook thinks they are false or probably false because we do not have sufficient evidence for them to make them warrantedly assertable. We have, he believes, strong disconfirming evidence against them. I think *au contraire* that we do not even have any kind of reasonable sense of what it would be like for them to either be true or false. We do not understand what would confirm them or disconfirm them or even confirm them or infirm them. They have a use in our language-games all right, but a use that conflicts with many of our other very central uses such that, if we consider them in relation to the other language-games of our language and the social practices that go with them, they threaten to inject incoherencies into that language by making our language-games in certain areas conflicting, e.g., we have a use for "infinite" and for "individual" but, given these uses, "infinite individual" does not make sense. Yet that is a key part of our religious language-games and without it our concept of God would be undermined. But it is undermined, given how we use "infinite" and how we use "individual," for we cannot coherently speak of an "infinite individual." But our God-talk commits us to trying to so conceptualize things. But, that notwithstanding, Hook continues to wait for evidence and declines to believe because we do not have that evidence. I say (though surely not as an a priori claim) that coming to have evidence—now or "hereafter"—is not in the cards (Nielsen 1963a, 1971a). Waiting for it is a waiting for Godot. As important as their religious beliefs are to believers and as crucial in our lives as religion has been, and for some people still is, we should conclude, if they and we are to be nonevasive, that these beliefs are unintelligible and that the forms of life in which they are embedded are fantasies, but humanly freighted fantasies nonetheless carrying profound and persistent human hopes, fantasies that are deep in our culture and carry with them intense feelings and intense commitments on the part of some people: people who are tying their hopes for a human life to these incoherent beliefs (Nielsen 1996, 467–507). We atheists cannot—and indeed should not—deny that intense feelings and commitments are often involved here. Indeed I am inclined to think that to the extent in which religious beliefs are genuine that this must be so. (Here, as in many other places, Kierkegaard was on to something.) Still what we have are fantasies all the same, bound up with incoherent beliefs.

Hook will agree that they are fantasies, but not, he thinks, because key parts of religious narratives are unintelligible or incoherent, but because the key claims in these narratives have not been confirmed. I think it is simply incredible to think that they might be confirmed or to think that they are even confirmable. And I think here as well as elsewhere I have given sound reasons for that belief (Nielsen 1971a; 1973b; 1982, 17–42 and 140–89). But I am not laying it down as a priori dictum or a positivist dogma. Perhaps I am mistaken in my claims about what it makes sense to say here. Still Hook has done nothing to show that I am mistaken. But, if I am mistaken, and we have to rest here with Hook's position, a position that is essentially Ernest Nagel's as well, atheistic humanism is rendered vulnerable by being caught with asking for evidence where believers see—and see with a good internal understanding of their religion—no need for evidence or (some of them) no possibility of having evidence and do not so conceptualize their religion such that it must pass muster against such a method for fixing belief. That is not, they claim, the way religious language-games are played; to ask for such a grounding here is to ask that religion cease to be religion. It is like criticizing logical reasoning for not being empirical reasoning or induction for not being deduction.

It is true that believers (like everyone else) in their ordinary commerce with the world reason much in the way Hook and Nagel say they do and perhaps this is true for all their scientific beliefs as well. But their using that method in those domains, and with the success Hook claims for it, does not justify the claim that to be reasonable they must, or even can, use it in religious domains as well, given what religious claims are and a recognition of their distinctness and the role they play in the lives of religious people. Perhaps my contentions and the arguments used in support of secular humanism will not fare any better than Hook's. But, be that as it may, Hook's in many ways powerful and reasonable traditional defense of secular humanism will not adequately do the job it sets out to do.

NOTES

1. In the opening pages of his presidential address Sidney Hook has given a convincing statement of this conception of philosophy. See Hook, 1967.

2. In a panel discussion Richard Rubenstein—the "God-is-dead rabbi"—maintained against me, and such an argument would apply to Hook as well, that such critiques of religion don't matter. Philosophers, he remarked, can establish the falsity or incoherence of belief in God quite conclusively and people will go on believing anyway. Such philosophical arguments won't make any difference to belief. If "won't make any difference to belief" means in this context "won't bring to an end Judaism, Christianity, or Islam" then no doubt Rubenstein is right, though, particularly among the better educated, philosophic criticism since the Enlightenment seems to have diminished their ranks. But while atheists cannot be as optimistic about this as was Engels—there is a point to Rubenstein's remarks—we should also not forget that there is a large and growing class of non-believers who feel no need for such tribal affiliations. But what is more deeply at issue between, on the one hand, someone like Rubenstein and, on the other hand, someone like Hook or Flew, is hidden in "doesn't matter." The force of it for Rubenstein is that of "won't change the world much" while I—and I think Hook and Flew as well—would take "doesn't matter" to be linked with truth. What is the truth about religion is important, for truth itself is important, even if only a few souls—and they *need* not be lonely or anguished—can bear it.

3. He remarks in his methodological essay "Naturalism and First Principles" (Hook 1961b, 189) that naturalism's "criticisms of the belief in Deity have not been based on semantic considerations but on what it presumed to be the weight of scientific discovery."

4. Part of my reasons will be found in my "Wittgensteinian Fideism" (1967).

5. I use "ideology" here as E. A. Gellner does, to signify "A propagated general outlook which consciously incorporates certain values, and aims at an alteration of human life and society." I further agree with Gellner that this is an important part of philosophy and is crucially related to the more technical aspects of philosophy. See Gellner 1964.

6. Corbishley's arguments are actually directed at Flew, but they can be readily applied to Hook as well.

7. For an argument for this where applied to discourse about God see my "God-Talk" (1964).

8. On page xii of his preface to *Religious Experience and Truth*, Hook speaks as if he would not accept such a criterion of factual significance.

9. John Wilson, I. M. Crombie, and John Hick provide the most determined and careful attempts with which I am acquainted to show what it would be like to have evidence here. I have attempted to show that they fail in my "Christian Positivism and the Appeal to Religious Experience" (1962a), "On Fixing the Reference Range of 'God'" (1966), and "Exchatological Verification" (1962b). But Hook makes no such an attempt.

10. See his reviews of Axel Hägerström's *Philosophy and Religion* and Richard Robinson's *An Atheist's Values* (Copleston 1966 and 1964, respectively).

11. See Danto 1967.

12. The last-mentioned work is Hook's own contribution to Hook 1961b.

13. Some further hurdles to be hurdled are set up in Plantinga 1963. I have tried to meet these counters in Nielsen 1971a chapter 4 and 1971b, 393–476.

14. I indeed do not mean all naturalism, but I have in mind philosophical positions like Hook's, Nagel's, or Dennes's, and I only have in mind their general statements of naturalistic principles. I should also remark here on my use of "semantical." Following Hook's practice, I do not use it in any severely technical sense, but only use it as a general term for considerations about what it makes sense to say. I prefer it to "linguistic" to make it evident that I am not merely concerned about the usage of a given natural language.

15. This obviously could be no more than a necessary and plainly not a sufficient condition for an assertion's being a warranted factual assertion.

16. Wittgenstein in his brilliant final notes about knowledge and certainty makes us aware of how difficult it is sometimes to draw this distinction. There is in our language no pellucid division between empirical and conceptual questions. If I ask "Are eyes the only organs of human sight?" or "Can an inner experience show me that I know something?" it is not clear, special circumstances apart, which kind of question I am asking.

17. Hook has remarked: "Knowing is a way of understanding, of interpreting and reorganizing our experiences in the world and making predictions about events." See Hook 1959, 161.

18. How far he is from being "a friend of theism" can be seen from his important "Christianity and Positivism" (1957).

19. For statements of this conception of *aseity* see John Hick 1961b and Clarke 1966. I have criticized such accounts in my "God and Factual Necessity," Nielsen 1974.

20. See Plantinga 1964. Contrast Hook 1961b, 226. Plantinga's account has been soundly criticized by Daher 1970.

21. See here Nielsen 1967, 1972, and 1973a.

22. E. W. Hall brilliantly shows how Bentham and Mill so argued in his *Categorial Analysis* (1964), pp. 106–32.

23. This is not only done by traditional theologians like Copleston or Mas-

call, operating with traditionalist philosophical methodology, but also by such Christian philosophers as R. F. Holland and J. M. Cameron. Operating with a basically Wittgensteinian methodology, both—their differences notwithstanding—reject, as a category mistake, trying to treat God as a quasiscientific object or "There is a God" or "God created the heavens and the earth" as experimental or experiential hypotheses. See Holland 1956, Cameron 1956.

24. However, there are challengable assumptions here. I have tried to locate them precisely and show that they are justified in my *Reason and Practice*, pp. 423–35 and 448–72.

25. Something similar was at issue between Rodger Beehler and me. See Hendrik Hart, et al., eds., *Walking the Tightrope of Faith*, chapters 1 and 3 (Beehler) and (Nielsen) chapters 2 and 6. Like Wittgenstein, Putnam, Cavell, and Rorty, I make it abundantly clear that I am not concerned to give a theory of meaning. We can ascertain what it makes sense to say and what is unintelligible without that. Indeed, if we could not, we could never construct a theory of meaning. Here is another place where Hook and I speak past each other or, better put, where Hook fails to understand me.

26. I argue against any such ontological establishment or disestablishment in Nielsen 1971b, 146–67 and 227–40.

27. A well-known and powerfully argued example of the former is J. N. Findlay's "Can God's Existence be Disproved?" (Findlay 1948). He sensibly and interestingly recanted in Findlay 1964.

28. See my characterization of atheism in Nielsen 1985, 20–22. Susan Stebbing, in her critical notice of A. J. Ayer's *Language, Truth and Logic* (Stebbing 1936), makes some similar remarks about atheism as does Paul Edwards. Here Hook is similarly at odds with Edwards over the characterization of atheism (Stebbing 1936, 264; Edwards 1967, 175–77; Hook 1969, 4–7).

29. I discuss Murphy's critique of Hook in chapter 5.

30. Again, see chapter 5 and more generally Nielsen 1995.

31. Hook makes sport of my distinguishing between the conceptions of God in Maimonides and Aquinas, on the one hand, and Abraham, Isaac, and Joseph, on the other (Hook 1975, 135). But while the conception of God of both Maimonides and Aquinas is rooted in the Holy Texts, Maimonides and Aquinas had philosophically refined and nonanthropomorphic conceptions of God while Abraham and Isaac did not.

32. Of course we, as Wittgenstein forced on our recognition, may be so dominated by a picture that we cannot see the discourse for what it is. But Wittgenstein also stressed that (a) we almost always have some kind of a picture affecting how we see things, (b) that pictures are very important, and (c) that it is not the case that all pictures mislead. But still we have to be very aware of distorting pictures here—pictures that nonetheless can come to seem very compelling particularly when we do philosophy (Conant 1994 and Putnam 1994, 276–77).

33. John Searle recounts the story about Russell in Searle 1998, 36–37.

34. It would be comforting to think that they would regard such talk as metaphorical talk and not as making claims about what is or what could be. But the philosophical purposes for which they put their commentaries on such talk to

work will not allow such a charitable reading. They are, of course, talking about things which they obviously think do not happen, but still they are thought by them to be "consistently thinkable," perfectly intelligible things which, as far as clear logical possibilities are concerned, could happen.

35. Some might argue that my claim here is far too strong. The above religious propositions are verifiable but not *conclusively* verifiable. But then little is. We would have to toss out most of science if such a strong claim for verifiability were to be made. But, the claim goes, if we do not assume conclusive or decisive verification, such God-talk is verifiable. Suffering counts against "God is our loving celestial father"; extensive kindliness in the world and reasonable relations between human beings counts for it. Of course such evidence is compatible (and equally so) with atheism as well and perhaps atheism is preferable on grounds of simplicity. But that does not show that such God-talk is not verifiable. The response should be that pragmatists think that what makes no difference in practice is no difference. If there is no conceivable empirical difference, even the *conceivable* empirical consequences being the same, between "God is our loving celestial father" and its denial, then there is no difference. When we look to the empirical consequences of this and other religious utterances we see that there is no *experiential* difference between them and their denials. In that very straightforward way there is no verifiable difference between them and it is because of this that I say that nonanthropomorphic God-talk is not even verifiable in principle.

36. I would not call it "a religion of man," though Feuerbach does, but a "secular humanist view of the world."

37. This entails that in some very minimal sense they must have some intelligibility. Otherwise the interpreter could not give an account of what they were trying unsuccessfully to say. This minimal sense is that the utterance has some use in some language-game. See my discussion of Wittgenstein in Part Three.

38. This assumes—or at least seems to—some substantial account of truth. A minimalist account of truth such as Quine's, Rorty's, or Horwich's can quite properly speak of moral utterances or mathematical ones being true without any assumption of correspondence or claim of substance. That is why Rorty argues that truth is not a very important notion, but justification is. In the light of that technical distinction, I would have to alter the vocabulary of my last sentence in note 2 of this chapter to speak of "justifiability" rather than "truth." But nothing of substance would change.

39. This was the Peirce of "The Fixation of Belief" and it became characteristic of the thought of the Classical Pragmatists and most particularly of John Dewey. But Peirce changed his mind and in the first lecture of his *Reasoning and the Logic of Things*, entitled "Philosophy and the Conduct of Life," Peirce argued that over vital questions concerning the conduct of life the scientific method was of no avail (Peirce 1992, 105–122).

40. Though it might be said—though this seems to be stretching things a little—that to say what I have just said is to confuse surface grammar with depth grammar—to fail, that is, to catch the actual use of the language. "I know that my Savior liveth" should be taken as an avowal expressive of one's faith (trust) and not as any kind of knowledge claim. It is in certain ways like "I know that I am in pain."

BIBLIOGRAPHY

Bambrough, Renford, et al. 1964. *Religion and Humanism*. London: Reading and Fakenham.

Cameron, J. M. 1956. "Holland on Religious and Theological Discourse." *Australasian Journal of Philosophy* 34, no. 3 (December): 223–28.

Carnap, Rudolf. 1959. "The Elimination of Metaphysics through Logical Analysis of Language." In *Logical Positivism*, edited by A. J. Ayer, 6–81,Glencoe, Ill.: The Free Press. Original in German 1932.

Clarke, Norris. 1973. "Analytic Philosophy and Language about God." In *A Secular Culture*, edited by George F. McClean, O.M.I., 390–44. Staten Island, N.Y.: Alba House.

Conant, James. 1994. "Introduction." In *Words & Life*, by Hilary Putnam, xi–xxvi. Cambridge, Mass.: Harvard University Press.

Copleston, F. C. 1957. Review of *An Atheist's Values*, by Richard Robinson. *Heythrop Journal* 5: 70–74.

———. 1965. "Commentary on 'The Five Ways' of Aquinas." In *A Modern Introduction to Philosophy*, 2d ed., edited by Arthur Pap and Paul Edwards, 475–82. New York: The Free Press.

———. 1966. Review of *Philosophy of Religion*, by Axel Hägerström. *Heythrop Journal* 7: 234–38.

Copleston, F. C., and Ayer, A. J. 1957. "Logical Positivism—A Debate." In *A Modern Introduction to Philosophy*, 1st ed., edited by Arthur Pap and Paul Edwards, 586–618. New York: The Free Press.

Corbishley, Thomas, S.J. 1950–51. "Theology and Falsification." *University* 1: 8–12.

Daher, Adel. 1970. "God and Factual Necessity." *Religious Studies* 6: 315–21.

Daly, C. B. 1959. "The Knowableness of God." *Philosophical Studies* 9 (December): 103–104.

Danto, Arthur. 1967. "Naturalism." *Encyclopedia of Philosophy*, edited by Paul Edwards, vol. 5, 448–50. New York: Macmillan.

Edwards, Paul. 1967. "Atheism." *Encyclopedia of Philosophy*, edited by Paul Edwards, vol. 1, 174–89. New York: Macmillan and the Free Press.

———. 1968. "Difficulties in the Idea of God." In *The Idea of God*, edited by Edward H. Madden et al., 43–77, 93–97. Springfield, Ill.: Charles C. Thomas

Findlay, J. N. 1948. "Can God's Existence be Disproved?" *Mind* 57: 176–83.

———. 1964. "Some Reflections on Necessary Existence." In *Process and Divinity*, edited by William L. Reese and Eugene Freeman, 516–27. Lasalle, Ill.: Open Court Publishing.

Hägerström, Axel. 1964. *Philosophy and Religion*. Translated by Robert T. Sandin. London: George Allen & Unwin, Ltd.

Gellner, E. A. 1964. "French Eighteenth-century Materialism." In *A Critical History of Western Philosophy*, edited by D. J. O'Connor, 275–95. London: Collier-Macmillan Ltd.

Hall, E. W. 1964. *Categorial Analysis*. Chapel Hill: University of North Carolina Press.

Hart, Hendrik, et al., eds. 1999. *Walking the Tightrope of Faith*. Amsterdam: Editions Rodopi.

Hick, John. 1960. "Theology and Verification." *Theology Today* 1: 437–51.
———. 1961a. "God and Necessary Being." *Journal of Philosophy* 58: 725–54.
———. 1961b. "Necessary Being." *Scottish Journal of Theology* 14: 353–69.
———. 1966. *Faith and Knowledge*, 2nd edition. Ithaca, N.Y.: Cornell University Press.
Holland, R. F. 1956. "Religious Discourse and Theological Discourse." *Australasian Journal of Philosophy* 34, no. 3 (December): 210–22.
Hook, Sidney. 1959. "Pragmatism and Existentialism." *Antioch Review* 19 (summer): 151–68.
———. 1961a. "The Atheism of Paul Tillich." In *Religious Experience and Truth*, 59–64. New York: New York University Press.
———. 1961b. *The Quest for Being*. New York: St. Martin's Press.
———. 1961c. "Preface." In *Religious Experience and Truth*, xi–xiii. New York: New York University Press.
———. 1967. "Pragmatism and the Tragic Sense of Life." In *Moderns on Tragedy*, edited by Lionel Abel, 227–49. Greenwich, Conn.: Fawcett.
———. 1969. "Some Reflections on the Encylopedia of Philosophy," *Religious Humanism* 3: 4–7.
———. 1975. "For an Open Minded Naturalism." *Southern Journal of Philosophy* 3, no. 1: 127–36.
Nielsen, Kai. 1962a. "Christian Positivism and the Appeal to Religious Experience." *Journal of Religion* 42 (October): 246–66.
———. 1962b. "Eschatological Verification." *Canadian Journal of Theology* 9: 271–81.
———. 1962c. "*On Speaking of God.*" *Theoria* 28: 110–37.
———. 1963b. "Can Faith Validate God-Talk?" *Theology Today* 20: 173–84.
———. 1964. "God-Talk." *Sophia* 111 (October): 15–19.
———. 1965. "Religious Perplexity and Faith." *Crane Review* 8, no. 1 (fall): 1–17.
———. 1966. "On Fixing the Reference Range of 'God.'" *Religious Studies* 2, no. 3 (October): 13–39.
———. 1967a. "Atheism." *Encyclopedia Britannica*, vol. 1. New York: Macmillan.
———. 1967b. "Wittgensteinian Fideism." *Philosophy* 42 (July): 191–201.
———. 1971a. *Contemporary Critiques of Religion*. London: Macmillan Press.
———. 1971b. *Reason and Practice*. New York: Harper & Row.
———. 1972. "Religion and Commitment." In *Problems of Religious Knowledge and Language*, edited by W. T. Blackstone and R. H. Ayers, 18–43. Athens: University of Georgia Press.
———. 1973a. "Agnosticism." *Dictionary of the History of Ideas*, vol. 1, edited by Phillip P. Wiener. New York: Charles Scribner's Sons.
———. 1973. *Scepticism*. New York: St Martin's Press.
———. 1974. "God and Factual Necessity." *Scottish Journal of Theology* 27, no. 3: 230–37.
———. 1975. "Secularism and Theology: Remarks on a Form of Naturalistic Humanism." *Southern Journal of Philosophy* 13, no. 1: 109–26.
———. 1982. *An Introduction to the Philosophy of Religion*. London: Macmillan Press.
———. 1985. *Philosophy and Atheism: In Defense of Atheism*. Amherst, N.Y.: Prometheus Books.
———. 1995. *On Transforming Philosophy: A Metaphilosophical Inquiry*. Boulder, Colo.: Westview Press.

————. 1996. *Naturalism without Foundations*. Amherst, N.Y.: Prometheus Books.

Passmore, John. 1957. "Christianity and Positivism." *Australasian Journal of Philosophy* 35, no. 2 (August): 204–10.

Peirce, Charles Sanders. 1992. *Reasoning and the Logic of Things*. Cambridge, Mass.: Harvard University Press. Based on lectures given in 1898.

Plantinga, Alvin. 1963. "Analytic Philosophy and Christianity." *Christianity Today* (October 25): 75–78.

————. 1964. "Necessary Being." In *Faith and Philosophy*, 97–108. Grand Rapids, Mich.: Eerdmans.

Putnam, Hilary. 1994. *Words & Life*. Edited by James Conant. Cambridge, Mass.: Harvard University Press.

Searle, John. 1998. *Mind, Language and Society*. New York: Basic Books.

Stebbing, Susan. 1936. "Critical Notice of Language, Truth and Logic." *Mind*, new series 45: 260–70.

---- *8* ----

ANTONY FLEW
ON ATHEISTIC HUMANISM

I

Antony Flew's *Atheistic Humanism* is divided into four parts. Part One, "Fundamentals of Unbelief," is his Prometheus Lectures delivered in November 1991 at the State University of Buffalo. It carefully characterizes what he takes to be a cogent form of atheism and then provides a defense for that atheism both by showing its positive attractions and by a sustained critique of the claims of theism. Part Two discusses knowledge and responsibility. Part Three discusses what Flew takes to be the myth of scientific socialism. Part Four is on applied philosophy with discussions of the right to death, mental health, racism, freedom, and human nature. Flew writes in a spirited fashion with a remarkable aptitude for the perfect quotation or a striking capsule account of what he is writing about. He writes in a way which is designed to provoke—and *Atheistic Humanism* will, in a variety of areas, certainly provoke. I shall limit my remarks to his actual Prometheus Lectures, "Fundamentals of

Unbelief," and his striking essay, "Must Naturalism Self-Destruct?" for it is in these contexts, where the issue of atheism is front and center, that Flew is at his strongest and where, along with his studies of Hume, he makes his most distinctive contribution.

Flew writes, correctly I believe, of David Hume (who is clearly a hero for Flew): "Hume . . . was a complete unbeliever, the first major thinker of the modern period to be through and through secular, this worldly and man centered." This through and through secularism and unbelief characterizes Flew as well. *Atheistic Humanism* articulates a powerful critique of theistic belief, a defense of a negative atheism that "constitutes no more than a defeasible presumption" but, when carefully examined, is a strong presumption all the same. And *Authentic Humanism* provides, as well, an elucidation and defense of a non*scientistic* naturalism. Flew works over again, amazingly not showing the slightest ennui, the standard attempts to demonstrate the existence of God or to, as in the argument to Design, provide an inductive basis for belief in God. In the process of doing this he exposes a not inconsiderable amount of nonsense about physical cosmology proceeding from certain readings of the Big Bang theory: absurd claims that this theory has given us good reasons for believing in God. He also, turning to more traditional grounds, aptly criticizes both claims that religious experience yields religious knowledge and claims that we have good reasons to believe in the miracles of any religion, including "the miracle" of the Resurrection. He, as well, argues that, even with the free will defense, Christians and other such theists have not provided a satisfactory response to the problem of evil. The Thomist conception of God as the Supreme Being who is perfectly good comes to praising "a supreme goodness that simply is no more, nor less, nor other than supreme, absolute, total power" (Flew 1993, 54). The free will defense, he argues, cannot show how God—the Mosaic God of Judaism, Christianity, and Islam—can be merciful and just though still with the power to move our wills. This God, of his own free will, has made us proper subjects of damnation. These things, Flew argues, just do not coherently go together. Finally Flew in chapter 4 produces a carefully reasoned argument for the rejection of any belief in disembodied existence. This argument, if sound, shows not only that neither we nor anyone else can exist as bodiless persons and thus that we cannot survive bodily death, but also that we have another reason, indeed a decisive reason, if his argument is sound, for believing there is no God—indeed that there can be no God—for the God of traditional theism is conceived of as a bodiless person. There can be no bodiless person and so, if that is so, there plainly can be no God. There, so to say, Flew hits two birds with one stone.

Flew, for the most part following in the footsteps of Hume, has given us very good reasons for being atheists. I am, hardly unsurprisingly, largely sympathetic with Flew here, but I shall argue in what follows that there are two places where Flew's arguments, if they are to be established as sound, need further support—support which may not be forthcoming. I shall conclude with an argument to the effect that there is an important place where Flew's overall account of philosophy and philosophical method definitely needs modification. And I shall sketch that modification.

II

Flew's nonscientistic naturalism stresses, following Locke here and not Hume, (a) the importance of agency, of having, that is, the personal power to do or forebear from doing, certain things and (b) the distinction between *evidencing* reasons and *motivating* reasons. Scientistic forms of naturalism ignore agency and regard, he has it, motivating reasons as illusory. Moreover, over social matters, the "psychologizing and sociologizing of believers thus replaces the rational examination of beliefs" (Flew 1993, 112). Flew agrees with Locke against Hume "that we all have the most direct and the most inexpungably certain experience: not only of both physical (as opposed to logical) necessity and physical (as opposed to logical) impossibility," but also of sometimes being able—possessing the personal power—to do other than we do and of sometimes being unable—"lacking power (personal) to behave in any other way then that in which we are behaving" (Flew 1993, 130). I go, for example, to the top of a rickety ladder to pick some apples. I am quite aware that I could have done otherwise: that I have the power and opportunity to so act or to forbear from so acting. When I am on top of it and the ladder collapses and I fall to the ground, I am there directly aware of a physical necessity. I am also aware of the physical impossibility of my being able to just levitate and so avoid falling to the ground. Suppose I try to climb the apple tree instead of using the ladder, but, in trying to do so, I come to realize that I cannot climb it. I have the opportunity but I lack the ability to do so. We are, Flew stresses, directly aware of our own agency here and we recognize that we could not—logically could not—even be *agents* unless we had such a direct awareness of our being able to do otherwise. This being so, Flew concludes, universal determinism cannot be true. Not every event has a cause because there are agents in the world who could do other than what they do.

What baffles me here is that Flew simply abandons his earlier compatibilism. Hume's form of it is flawed, but there are sophisticated contemporary forms of compatibilism that accept full-bodied agency and with it the realization that such beings—human beings with such agency—sometimes can do other than what they do without abandoning determinism. Compatibilism *may* be mistaken, but it is not so easily and obviously shown to be mistaken as Flew takes it to be. Indeed, it may not be implausible to think that some form of it must be so. It may well be the case that we can, and reasonably so, be nonscientistic naturalists, fully acknowledging our rationality, and capacity, to act on motivating reasons, while still being determinists (though, like Hume, Hobbes, Spinoza, and Engels compatibilist determinists). Flew's sober naturalism leads him to say, commonsensically and rightly, I believe, that "human beings are organisms, creatures of flesh, blood, and bones, and other sorts of stuff and nothing else besides" (Flew 1993, 135). Whatever we want to say about micro-particles and determinism it is reasonable to believe that there are causal and deterministic explanations (accounts) of why these particular organisms (e.g., trees, beavers, as well as us human beings) are as they are and not otherwise. But it is equally reasonable to believe that some of these middle-sized organisms are agents who can make things happen and are able to choose between alternative possible courses of action. They are persons who not infrequently could have done otherwise than what they in fact did. To make sense of these two things, neither of which is plausibly deniable, we need to work out some form of compatibilism. Plausible versions exist, but Flew simply turns a blind eye on an alternative he once accepted and in doing so is saddled with the paradoxes of libertarian freedom (Flew 1993, 136). But he has not shown that compatibilism (soft determinism) is false, incoherent, or even implausible.

III

I shall turn now to some comments about the problem of evil. Flew remarks, following Hume, that without trying to rely on revelation, the expectations of natural reason, given what we can discover of our world, must surely be that such a Creator God, if there is one, "would be as detached and uninvolved as the gods of Epicurus" (Flew 1993, 57). But Jewish, Christian, and Islamic believers would respond that, after all, we have revelation and that that is what makes all the difference. *Revelation* tells us that God is perfectly good, his goodness is unlimited, and he is, as well, omniscient and omnipotent. But how then can we explain or justify the evil that we find in the world? Theodicies wrestle with this problem. Christian revelation, but certainly not our unaided reason, insists that God is perfectly good, all powerful, and all knowing. How can we, or can we, square this with the reality of evil?

Flew, in a vigorously written, and for the most part at least, cogently argued account, argues that no theodicies succeed in justifying God's ways to man. Not even the free will defense strategies do so. What the

Book of Job shows us, what Augustine, Aquinas, and Luther show us, is not God's infinite goodness but the morally outrageous use of, absent revelation, his power. If we just use our brains and common experience without trying to rely on revelation, that is what we should make of the Mosaic God, if we can make anything of him at all. That, of course, was not their intent. But that is what, according to Flew, they actually succeed in showing us. Flew cites, in this context, telling passages where they condemn themselves out of their own mouths (Flew 1993, 53–66).

His writing here, as he is well aware, is surely going to provoke indignation and protest. But all the same, we need to ask, are not his arguments and accompanying narrative compelling? It should be said straight off that mildly revisionist forms of Judaism and Christianity are not so ferocious as Augustine, Aquinas, Calvin, and Luther. Damnation, hell, eternal punishment are not in the repertoire of all current theisms, though the current (1996) Church of England has resurrected a reductive form of hell as utter nonbeing. Still, should not God, even on such a revisionist conception, because he is the ultimate cause of our being what we are and of our making of the choices that we make, be blamed for the evil in the world? Could that be something that a perfectly good God who was also omnipotent and omniscient would allow? Here is where the so-called free will defense comes in. God in his merciful foresight doesn't make our choices for us. God created us as human agents, but to be agents we must be creatures who can choose, who can do otherwise than what we do. And even God cannot do what is *logically* impossible—that is, make us both agents and nonchoosers. Explicating this position, Flew remarks that this argument necessarily implies the possibility of doing evil as well as good, that is to say that there would be "a contradiction in speaking of creatures with freedom to choose good or evil, but not able to choose evil—which, no blame to God, is what creatures so often do" (Flew 1993, 58). So, if this argument is sound, it is logically impossible for God or anyone else to create agents who could not do evil. If they sometimes do that, that is, do evil things, that, the claim goes, is no ground for denying the unlimited goodness of God. So God should not be held responsible for evil since he could not—logically could not—have created free agents who could do no evil. But being free agents is essential to our being moral persons and is essential to our very humanness. God is not responsible for our choices. He cannot do what is logically impossible: both make us free agents and also be the cause of all our thoughts and actions. (We can see in this very argument the rejection of compatabilism.)

To this familiar free will defense it could be responded that from the fact that God could not create free agents who could not do evil, it does not follow that he could not have created agents who were able to do evil but *in fact never do so*. It is one thing to have the ability or the capacity for doing something; it is a quite different thing again to actually exercise that ability or capacity. Why could not God have given us the ability but also have made us such that we never in fact act on that ability? Recall that God is supposed to be omnipotent and omniscient.

However, even if the Theodicist can supply an adequate response to this, there is still the further problem that even if God, given that he is to create agents at all, cannot stop some evil from occurring, why does he have to allow *so much evil*? It doesn't take a cynic to see that our world is full of the most diverse kinds of blatant evil. It is, to put it mildly, far from a pretty place. Our century (and other centuries as well) has simply wallowed, and indeed continues to wallow, in evil (e.g., genocide and other forms of gross and irrational beastiality). Why could not God have created *agents* who were less evil and more reasonable than the ones he did in fact create? Why did he have to create so many brutes who devote so much of their time and energy, and sometimes so effectively, to such brutalities? Moreover, and not touched by the free will defense, there are the facts of physical evil, e.g., lightning strikes in a forest and a fawn burns up, suffering horribly. There is an enormous amount of suffering in the world linked to the actions of human beings, but there is also an enormous amount that is not. Indeed there was a lot of suffering that existed before human beings even existed. But God is the ultimate cause of that. How does he get off the hook for that?

There appears, at least, to be no answer to these questions—no way of justifying God's ways to human beings or other creatures or of explaining his ways to us so as to make them morally acceptable to our moral reflection. God (an all-powerful, all-knowing creator, and sustainer of the world out of nothing), if he exists, or even could exist, looks more like a moral monster than a loving, perfectly good creator of us all. Again, absent revelation, the Mosaic God does not commend himself to our honest, nonevasive moral reflection.

IV

Alvin Plantinga, a well-known Reform Philosopher/Theologian, in what I think is one of his best stretches of writing (a place where he does not obfuscate things with the unnecessary use of modal logic), has produced a thoughtful response to such questions (Plantinga 1993). Plantinga grants that, as far as we can see, there are many cases of evil that are apparently pointless. Indeed there are many cases of such evils where we have no idea at all what reason God (if there is such a person) could have for permitting such evils. But, Plantinga remarks, from granting these things it does not follow that "an omnipotent and omniscient God, if he existed, would not have a reason for permitting them" (Plantinga 1993, 400). From the fact that we can see no reason at all for God to permit those evils, we cannot legitimately infer that God has no reason to allow such evils. It is not just, Plantinga continues, "obvious or apparent that God could have no reason for permitting them. The most we can sensibly say is that we can't think of any good reason why he would permit them" (Plantinga 1993, 400). But on "the theistic conception of our cognitive powers, as opposed to God's, ours are a bit slim" (Plantinga 1993, 400). This being so, it is *hubris* on our part to think that "if God did have a reason for permitting such evils, we would be likely to have some insight into what it is" (Plantinga 1993, 400–401). We have, Plantinga claims, no "good reason to think that we would be privy to God's reasons for permitting evil" (Plantinga 1993, 401). Job, a through and through good man, is tormented by God. Terrible afflictions are brought on him by God, for, as far as Job can see, no reason. This being so he wants to go to court with God. Since he cannot "see any reason why God should allow him to be afflicted as he is, he concludes unthinkingly," Plantinga has it, "that God doesn't have a reason" (Plantinga 1993, 401). But, as we readers of the Old Testament see in the narrative, Job does not see that God does have a reason for permitting him to suffer. What we need to realize, Plantinga maintains, "is that the reason for Job's sufferings is something entirely beyond his ken, so that the fact he can't see what sort of reason God might have for permitting his suffering doesn't at all tend to show that God has no reason" (Plantinga 1993, 401). When God, speaking out of the whirlwind, "answers" Job with a series of condemnations and questions such as "Where were you when I laid the foundations of the earth?" Hobbes and Flew take it, and I had always taken it before reading Plantinga on this, that God only reveals to Job his awesome power, his omnipotence—he does nothing at all to reveal the justice or the rightness of his actions or his goodness. Indeed God does just the opposite: he— this Mosaic God—appears to us more like a cruel, oriental despot magnified many times over.

However, I am now convinced that Plantinga has, all things considered, given us a more adequate reading than this traditional atheological reading of the text, though, as we shall see, he does add a wrinkle that makes things more complicated. That is to say that even on his reading we are not free and clear of the problem of evil. God does not, on Plantinga's account, *just* induce Job to shut up, to bear and obey, and to come to realize that neither he nor any other creature is in, or can be in, a position "to question or challenge the absolute, infinite power of the despot" (Flew 1993, 55). God does induce Job to shut up all right, to allow himself to be instructed by God and to recognize to the full God's incredible power. But what Plantinga nicely shows is that God does more than that, and that to grasp this more is vital both for understanding the text and for understanding the problem of evil. God also shows Job how little he knows, or can come to know, compared with God. He not only shows his greater power but reminds Job of his greater wisdom and, reminding Job of the kind of being God actually is, "attacks Job's unthinking assumption that if he can't imagine what reason God might have, then probably God doesn't have a reason at all" (Plantinga 1993, 401). "Tell me," God asks Job, "How the universe was created and why the sons of God shouted with joy upon its creation?" Job sees the point. He sees not only that God's power is far greater than his, but he also sees that so is God's knowledge and understanding and Job desists from questioning God further, remarking, "I have spoken of great things which I have not understood, things too wonderful for me to know" (Job 42:2).

So we should conclude—or so Plantinga has it—that evil is sometimes inscrutable. It is inscrutable when we can't think of any reason God could have for permitting it. Moreover, that seems at least to be massively the case, though Plantinga does not stress that. But, Plantinga concludes, even with this widespread inscrutable evil, nothing much follows from that fact, for "if theism is true, we would expect that there would be inscrutable evil. Indeed, it is only *hubris* which would tempt us to believe that we could so much as grasp God's plans here, even if he proposed to divulge them to us" (Plantinga 1993, 402).

V

Is this response of Plantinga's adequate? Does it enable us to square a nonevasive recognition of the vast amount of evil in the world with a belief in the perfect and unlimited goodness of a God who is also omnipotent and omniscient? Believers (including Plantinga and Alasdair MacIntyre) and unbelievers alike have been perplexed and troubled by the problem of evil. Should we go the way of Plantinga or should we, like Flew, and Wallace Matson and Paul Edwards as well, indignantly lay the evil at God's door and claim that there is, because of this evil, good reason to believe that the God of the Jewish, Christian, and Islamic traditions could not exist? If some god exists it is not *that* god. Or is there some other alternative?

I think for Plantinga's solution (if that is what we should call it) to be satisfactory, a very heavy reliance will have to be made on Jewish, Christian, and Islamic revelation, namely that it has been *revealed* to us that God is perfectly good. Then, with that revelation in hand, we could perhaps get that belief in the perfect goodness of God to square with the other things Christians believe in in the way Plantinga indicates. But this runs up against the problem that there just are all the often very different religions of the world with their extensive diversity of *claimed*, often conflicting, revelations. Why should we think either the Jewish or Christian or Islamic *putative revelation* is the genuine revelation rather than the Zoroastrian one or some other putative revelation, say Buddhist or Hindu revelation? Why should we think that one putative revelation rather than another has a corner on the truth? This is particularly pressing when we realize that in trying to decide this all we can appeal to is one or another *putative* revelation.

If we try to stand free from this—that is, do not appeal to the putative revelations of Judaism, Christianity, or Islam—and do not just assume God's perfect goodness but take it as something our theodicy must establish, are we not back with Hume and, following him, Flew, with Flew's recognition that, looking at the world we know, seeing things by our own lights—the only light we can have to go on anyway—we would never reasonably conclude that it was even at all likely that this world of ours was created by a being who was perfectly good, all powerful, and with perfect knowledge? As far as we can see, if there really is an omnipotent and omniscient being, that being is a cruel being, inflicting pointless suffering on human beings and other sentient beings alike. Going by our own lights, without the aid of revelation (something that somehow is supposed to allow us to dispense with or transcend even our best own lights), such a belief seems at least rationally inescapable. Surely Plantinga is right if such a being as the Mosaic God exists. He could know things we do not know and have reasons we do not understand. But looking at the world we live in and absent revelation why should we think it at all plausible that such a god exists?

Going *internal* to a Christian framework, where this question about other claimed revelations is blocked, we will still have trouble squaring God's ways to humans with our conception of his loving goodness. We can only see by our own lights and no matter how superior God's knowledge is to ours, we cannot see things by his lights, but must, logically must, see things by our own lights. The Book of Job shows us both how God's power and how God's understanding transcends ours. But nonetheless we are stuck, and inescapably, with our own understanding. Job still does not see why God permits him to be afflicted and we still do not understand *why* God permits the evil he does. Plantinga has shown us how we can understand that a perfectly good God, if there is one, could possibly permit such evil. And we also see that plainly and massively God does. But *why* he does is entirely beyond our ken. By our own lights it still seems like a morally arbitrary and indeed a brutal and inhumane use of power. We do not see that God is a just or a good God at all, though, accepting Christian revelation, we are simply told that he is. And we, if we accept Jewish or Christian revelation, see that we must just accept that and we realize, as well, that God may have reasons that we do not understand. Indeed, if we accept *that* revelation, we will believe that God *will* have reasons for doing what he does that we do not understand. Still, we do not see *what* this reason is. It still looks like, by our own lights, an evil exercise of power. So seeing things is not *hubris* but a recognition of our inescapable finitude.

As Plantinga goes out of his way, and correctly so, to remind us, God, when he "replies to Job . . . doesn't tell him the reason for his suffering (perhaps Job couldn't so much as grasp or comprehend God's reason)" (Plantinga 193, 401). But in the Book of Job itself, God's reason for allowing Job's suffering isn't very complicated. We readers of the book, unlike Job, see it very well. God made a bet with the Devil about how Job would behave under torment. So to win his bet God had to put Job to the test—to set him on the rack—something that itself, at least on the face of it, is not, to understate it, very morally elevating. The Old Testament, at times, seems at least to be a very morally crude document. But that aside, given that the evil is so manifest and given the conception of God of Christianity and the other theistic religious that evil is inscrutable to us and given that we can only grasp things by our own lights, why does not God in his mercy explain why he does what he does and allows things to happen as he does? Being omnipotent and omniscient, he can make things simpler for us so that we could understand. At least he could give us some of the story such that something of what goes on could make some sense to us. But that God does not do. Much of the massive evil in the world remains, in relation to God and his ways, utterly inscrutable. God could have a reason—Plantinga is right about that—but why does he have to be so secretive about it? To remind us, Plantinga might respond, of the utter arrogance of our presuming to question God or his ways, or, like Job, trying to take God to court. Who are we to challenge God? More utter *hubris* again! But that Plantingaean response will not do, for, where we cannot rely on a claimed revelation (as we cannot, given the many often conflicting putative revelations), we need a reason to conclude that God, all appearances to the contrary notwithstanding, is merciful and good. But that we have not been given. We have not been given the slightest reason to even *trust* here. *Sans* revelation we should conclude that God, if there is one, is anything but merciful and loving. Perhaps the idea is to make our faith just an arbitrary leap in the dark. We really show the depth of our trust and our faith if we can bring ourselves to so crucify our intellects—to believe what seems to us absurd and utterly morally repugnant.

VI

It might be responded, as a kind of metaremark, that this still assumes that if we cannot think of a reason for God not to so act, and his not so acting seems to us morally arbitrary, that it still does not follow that it *actually is morally arbitrary*. Again things may be beyond our comprehension. Given what God is taken to be, and given Jewish-Christian-Islamic conceptualizations of him, that is exactly what we should expect.

However, this seems at least to rely on putting, or trying to put, a whole lot of things beyond our understanding. (See here chapter 11.) We do not understand why God permits evil. It doesn't seem to be compatible with his goodness at all. In fact, it looks more like, if he exists and is all powerful and all knowing, that then he is more likely to be evil. However, we see that all the same he *might possibly be*, as Jewish, Christian, and Islamic religions say he is, perfectly good. But we cannot see *that* he is. The Mosaic God looks, to understate it, petty, unjust, and cruel to us. We are asked, in the face of this, as children of faith, to stick with a belief in what we see to be some kind of *possibility*, namely that God is, after all, appearances to the contrary notwithstanding, perfectly good. But this in effect just asks us to stick with the Christian faith—similar things could be said for Judaism and Islam—even when we do not understand the ways of God to man. But this looks like just a straight appeal to faith against reason (i.e., what by our lights seems the most reasonable). But why opt for faith when by the use of our brains (including our moral reflection) we would conclude otherwise and there are so many different, sometimes conflicting faiths on offer? (Is this intellectualism running wild? See chapter 10.)

VII

I now want to argue, tying it in (though rather indirectly) to what was said above, that Flew's sober, nonscientistic naturalism would be significantly improved if it were less Popperian and more of a pragmatist naturalism, a naturalism that is also a nonscientistic naturalism more in the general manner of John Dewey, Sidney Hook, and Ernest Nagel (Nielsen 1996). In particular it would be much improved if it would take on board Peirce's critical commonsensism with its subtle link with a stress on verifiability and more generally with his stress on the use of scientific method (Nielsen 1996).

Flew remarks:

> The aim of all theoretical science is truth. If that is what we are sincerely seeking, then we have to adopt what Popper calls the critical approach.

For people who truly want to discover the truth, like knights who with pure hearts and single minds seek the Holy Grail, cannot and will not embrace unexamined candidates. They must and will be ever ready to test and test, and test again. (Flew 1993, 124–25)

He also follows Karl Popper's stress, in engaging in this critical approach, on the making of bold conjectures: "conjectures apparently fitting all available facts while also carrying extensive implications of what else must be the case if these bold conjectures are correct" (Flew 1993, 125). What scientists are to do then, according to Flew, following Popper, is to try and try again and again to falsify their conjectures. We, of course, want our own hypotheses to be true—to be so—but, as truth-seekers using the critical approach, scientists and critical intellectuals must tenaciously seek to ascertain whether "all theories and hypotheses proposed—most especially their own—are after all false" (Flew 1993, 125). No matter what happens as a result of this repeated and rigorous testing, Flew claims, we, and science, are the gainers. Suppose that a hypothesis, a conjecture, a theory for the time, survives "the most rigorous and comprehensive criticism," then it can best be taken for true as things stand now as far as we can understand. (Something, of course, can be taken for true, and reasonably so, and still turn out to be false.) And, as well, science and human reasonability have been advanced. If, on the other hand, the theory or hypothesis is falsified, then we will know that "the strenuous testing culminating in this conclusion most surely here advanced research" (Flew 1993, 125). The successor theory, taking note of the failure here, may very well take us closer to the truth.

The notion of *the* truth is not here or anywhere very clear, but what is involved here can, I think, be demythologized (Rorty 1984). More important is the recognition that such a stress on criticism—on repeated and relentless testing and falsifying—may actually impede what Flew and Popper take to be the aim of science, i.e., the attainment of truth. If scientists so busied themselves in continuously and relentlessly testing, they would have little time for theory construction, for elaborating theories and making discoveries and giving them a perspicuous representation. Still I think such a Popperian-Flewian account, properly reduced, remains an important conception. The stress on the central role of claims, hypotheses, and theories which are testable, and indeed repeatedly tested, is important and the use of conjectures, together with their elaboration and testing, is a vital way of pushing science forward. But it is not the only thing involved in science and a too exclusive fixation on it can hinder our scientific understanding.

What I think is a more important lacunae is Flew's failure to recognize that this testing and falsification can only take place against the background of a massive and routine acceptance of certain common-sense beliefs—Peircean acritical beliefs if you will—such as the earth has existed for many years, water quenches thirst, plants require water to survive, snow is cold, water is wet, people die, get born, have desires, beliefs, form intentions, and the like. (We saw in chapter 5 how Sidney Hook deployed such acritical beliefs.) There are, as C. S. Peirce stressed and Donald Davidson stressed again after him, a great mass of such beliefs which must be assumed for any testing to take place and, while we need not deny that it is logically possible that some circumstance might arise where some one or another of them would need to be tested, most of them would have to stand fast for any such testing, or indeed any testing at all, to take place (Davidson 1984, 183–98). "That things do not just disappear without cause," "Water is wet," "People have beliefs" are anomalous with respect to either falsification or verification. To take a critical attitude toward them, to seek to falsify them would be utterly crazy. Indeed it is not clear what it would be to take a critical attitude toward them, as if they were reasonably up for doubt (Peirce 1934; Nielsen 1996, 295–328). There are a host of such utterly unproblematical background beliefs, most of which must be taken for true, for any investigation to proceed at all. Socrates taught us the importance of doubting while Wittgenstein taught us the importance of seeing that sometimes it is *unreasonable* to doubt or to engage in a search for truth (Wittgenstein 1969). We should keep in mind Sidney Morgenbesser's quip that while the unexamined life may not be worth living the over-examined life is no bargain either. This is not, on the one hand, relativism or subjectivism or, on the other hand, dogmatism. It is just the recognition that, unless for one or another of our acritical beliefs the situation *actually* becomes problematic concerning them, there is no point, or holus-bolus even possibility, of doubting them or of trying to establish their truth. Rather than relativism or dogmatism here, we just have a sturdy common sense that is not gulled by philosophical extravagance (Peirce 1934).

Peirce, valuably, by showing us the contexts in which we need to engage in testing, turns a commonsensism into a *critical* commonsensism (Peirce 1934, 346–75). But he also, as do Wittgenstein and Davidson, and even Hume, on some readings, shows us the absurdity of universal methodological doubt, of seeking to test everything, in a craze for falsification and of our not seeing that many things will never be even in the slightest degree doubtful and that there is no reason, or perhaps sometimes even sense, in trying to doubt them (Peirce 1934, 223–47). Such Popperian-Flewian falsificationism is too Cartesian. Flew's sober and rather puritanical naturalism would be more fully and realistically sober if it were a pragmatic naturalism.

However, I do not want to end this examination of Flew's defense of atheism on such a negative note. Flew, without abandoning his naturalism, could go, without losing anything of his critique of religious faith, in a much more Deweyan than Popperian way. He could, and I believe should, become much closer in intellectual orientation to Sidney Hook, whom he resembles in many ways, without abandoning anything of his atheism.

VIII

I want in this last section to bring out a distinctive feature of his atheism that, though Flew over the years has stressed it over and over again, still gets inadequate notice. It is his argument about the burden of proof and it is something that Reform Philosophers and theologians in particular need to take to heart. In a pluralistic world awash with different and often conflicting faiths as well as some utterly secular orientations, the burden of proof should be on the Mosaic Theist and not on the religious skeptic. Imagine, for example, that the theist was talking with Chinese students who have not been enculturated into a form of life in which conceptions of this Mosaic God are embedded. In such a context the theist (*pace* Plantinga) should introduce and defend his proposed concept of God into such a real environment and to provide sufficient reason for believing that this concept does in fact have application—that the term "God" answers to something. Against such a background, he should articulate it, show that it makes sense, and show how "God" really denotes; that is, has genuine application.

It is in this perspective, Flew argues, that we should view the arguments made by theists. We should see theists as attempting to defeat the defeasable presumption of atheism because, if we so proceed,

> then our inquiries begin by considering how the concept of God would have to be explained to a person who, though entirely rational and scientifically well informed, had nevertheless never previously come across this concept. The consideration of the concept itself, and all subsequent questions about possible evidencing reasons for believing that it does in fact have an application, are bound to look very different to a person so paradigmatically unprejudiced. (Flew 1995, 4)

People who have been immersed in Jewish, Christian, or Islamic forms of life, even when they react fideistically, agnostically, or atheistically to them, are not in a very good position to see them with an unprejudiced eye as, say, someone from China or someone brought up in an utterly Buddhist culture. We need to be able to view them as, or at least as near to as possible as, we view very different religious concepts of some distant culture that anthropologists might tell us about.

Flew translates this into the concrete by remarking of the Chinese students he taught at the Institute for Foreign Philosophy in Beijing. He remarks

> Unlike us these Chinese students were not raised in a culture in which generations of parents and pedagogues, of priests and ayatollahs, had been providing everyone with confidently authoritative assurance of the existence and constant activity of (the Mosaic) God. So if asked to suggest what might have been the first initiating cause of our Universe such unprejudiced, rational people naturally look for a physicist's sort of cause for the Big Bang. (Flew 1995, 5)

So considering things—so thinking from the perspective of people who stand outside of our cultural circle—we would find no credibility at all in Plantinga's claim (following Calvin) that "if not for the existence of sin . . . human beings would believe in God to the same degree and with the same natural spontaneity that we believe in other persons, an external world, or the past" (Plantinga 1974, 120). What Plantinga confidently affirms human beings would spontaneously believe at best only indicates what people socialized into certain ways of life would believe—the belief would appear to them to be spontaneous when it in fact was the result of a distinctive socialization. Plantinga confuses being enculturated in a certain way—indeed in a way to which there are historical alternatives—with what any nonsinful human being would believe. The attaining of an unprejudiced view here—being neither indoctrinated into theism or into atheism—is very important if we are to gain a clear understanding of what is going on. It is important for us, if we can, to try to simulate such a perspective in order to see in such a way what kind of concept the concept of God is.

Flew stresses both in *Atheistic Humanism* and in his "The Presumption of Atheism" that

> The effects of parochial prejudice are most clearly seen in the tendency of even the ablest and most careful thinkers to assume without sufficient or even any reason given that anything possessing any of the defining characteristics of God must possess some if not all the others. (Flew 1995, 6)

It is only by making such an assumption that anyone would assume that if he had established that the "Universe was produced by an omnipotent Designer" that he should then conclude that this "Designer is a righteous judge." As we have seen, there is not only no reason to assume that, but very good reasons for believing that to be false. As Flew puts it, what Islam calls "people of the book" just assume we have a unitary concept here—where being all powerful, all knowing, and perfectly good just naturally go together. But there is no reason at all, the happenstance of a distinctive enculturation apart, to assume or believe anything like that.

A response to Flew's arguments here comes trippingly on the tongue. In arguing as he does, the response goes, Flew forgets a very important thing we have learned from Wittgenstein. The forms of language are the forms of life or, to use a more anthropological idiom, language and culture are intimately and indissolvably linked. There is no private language, conceptually unlinked to, and not parasitic on, some public language (a language that is part of some culture) in virtue of which some solitary agent, wholly free of his culture, can see the world rightly and, free of his or any culture, give the one true description of the world (Putnam 1992; Rorty 1991). There is no such thing and there is no such private language. In the cultures of the West, cultures that Flew, like the present writer, are soaked in, talk of God, and more generally religious talk, is pervasive and with, as the culture has developed (though not on nearly such a massive scale), antireligious talk or religiously skeptical talk as well. These things just are a part of those cultures. And it is important to remember that, even with the antireligious talk, we get certain elements of its central conceptualization from religious talk. It is, in short, and not unsurprisingly, in some ways parasitic upon it. We are not, and cannot be, like Flew's Chinese students. In learning thoroughly English, French, Italian, Swedish, German, Hebrew, Arabic, and the like, the concept of, though not necessarily the belief in, the Mosaic God gets socialized into the very way we conceptualize the world. We cannot attain the innocence that Flew asks of us.

We can, and should, however, to a certain extent, *simulate* it and that, I believe, is sufficient for Flew's purposes or for anyone's purposes in defending atheism. In learning English, Hebrew, Arabic, French, and the like we normally, among other things, learn about the Mosaic God or something closely similar and come to conceptualize God and related concepts in a distinctively Jewish-Christian-Islamic way. (They, of course, are not exactly the same ways, but they are very similar.) Our forms of language and forms of life go together here. And it is at least plausible to believe that we would have little or no understanding of the concept of the Mosaic God absent such socialization, or the coming to gain such an understanding as an anthropologist does when he, becoming a kind of participant observer, masters the language, and with it, something of the culture, of another culture. (Though here he typically also has a distance that the actual participants lack.) But we also should realize—and Wittgenstein would not for a moment deny that—that language is not a seamless web. Conceptualizations that are at one time part of it drop out or come to be rejected without the rest of it collapsing. Indeed in modifying, setting aside, or rejecting the conceptualizations of a given part we use other parts. We never stand free of our language. The very idea of such a thing is unintelligible. But that is no imprisonment, conceptual or otherwise. Again the famous Neurathian metaphor of rebuilding the ship at sea is useful. Once talk of ghosts and fairies was a firm part of English but now most speakers of English, working well with their language and learning more about the world, have come to understand that such notions do not make sense. Talk of God and immortality are more deeply embedded, but Flew is offering us a technique——and I think a good technique—for critiquing and rejecting such conceptualizations as something that should be normative in our lives. And this he does, whether he is aware of it or not, without having to reject a Wittgensteinian way of viewing our language and our lives. Indeed, it is by using it that we can see the full force of Flew's critique, his intransigent rationalism to the contrary notwithstanding.

BIBLIOGRAPHY

Davidson, Donald. 1984: *Inquiries into Truth and Interpretation*. Oxford: Clarendon Press.

Flew, Antony. 1993: *Atheistic Humanism*. Amherst, N.Y.: Prometheus Books.

——— 1995. "The Presumption of Atheism." *New Zealand Humanist*, 3–15.

Nielsen, Kai. 1996. *Naturalism without Foundations*. Amherst, N.Y.: Prometheus Books.

Peirce, C. S. 1934. *Collected Papers of Charles Sanders Peirce*, vol. V. Cambridge, Mass.: Harvard University Press.

Plantinga, Alvin. 1974. *God, Freedom and Evil*. Grand Rapids, Mich.: Eerdmans.

———. 1993. "Belief in God." In *Perspectives in Philosophy*, edited by Michael Boylan, 389–406. Fort Worth, Tex.: Harcourt Brace Jovanovich.

Putnam, Hilary. 1992. *Renewing Philosophy*. Cambridge, Mass.: Harvard University Press.

Rorty, Richard. 1984. "Life at the End of Inquiry." *London Review of Books* 2 (August): 6–7.

———. 1991. *Objectivity, Relativism and Truth*. New York: Cambridge University Press.

Wittgenstein, Ludwig. 1969. *On Certainty*. Oxford: Basil Blackwell.

Part Three

THE CHALLENGE
OF WITTGENSTEIN

9

WITTGENSTEIN AND
WITTGENSTEINIANS
ON RELIGION

I

Wittgenstein once remarked, "I am not a religious man: but I
cannot help seeing every problem from a religious point of
view" (Rhees 1984, 79). Though he wrote very little about either religion
or ethics, it is true that a sensibility to and concern for broadly speaking
ethical and religious matters is pervasive in almost all of his work. He
wrote extensively about language, meaning, intentionality, mind, consciousness, the self, logic, mathematics, and necessity, but woven into all
these considerations, which have been central to the main historical tradition of philosophy, is a religious and ethical concern. Perhaps it is better
characterized as an intense ethico-religious concern, for when he speaks
of ethics it is always in a distinctively religious way. But this would be
badly understood if it were taken, after the fashion of Richard Braithwaite and R. M. Hare, to be a reductive view of religion in which religion
is viewed as morality touched with emotion associated with certain tra-

ditional narratives which may or not be believed (Braithwaite 1975; Hare 1973). Wittgenstein linked ethics and religion tightly. But, as we shall see, his thinking here was very different from that of the reductive, basically straightforwardly ethical accounts of religion of Braithwaite and Hare.

It should also be noted that Wittgenstein did not write treatises or even articles on either ethics or religion and that he did not even discuss the topics that moral philosophers normally consider. Moreover, it is clear that he would have regarded both philosophy of religion and ethical theory with great suspicion and even with disdain. John Hyman rightly observes that "Wittgenstein's influence in the philosophy of religion is due to scattered remarks, marginalia, and students' notes. He never intended to publish any material on the subject, and never wrote about it systematically" (Hyman 1997, 156). But all of that, as I will try to make plain, does not gainsay the import of my opening quotation from him.

In understanding what Ludwig Wittgenstein has to say about religion or indeed about anything else, it is crucial to understand how Wittgenstein proceeded in philosophy and why he proceeded in that way. Here we must see that and how Wittgenstein was remarkable in generating and carrying out two revolutions in philosophy, the latter one dismantling the philosophical practices, techniques, and conceptions of the former while keeping a very similar metaphilosophical conception of the aim of philosophical activity.[1] It is not an exaggeration to say, as P. M. S. Hacker does, that "Ludwig Wittgenstein . . . was the leading analytical philosopher of the twentieth century. His two philosophical masterpieces, the *Tractatus Logico-philosophicus* (1921) and his posthumous *Philosophical Investigations* (1953), changed the course of the subject" (Hacker 1999, 538). Hacker goes on to observe that "the first was the primary origin of the 'linguistic turn' in philosophy, and inspired both logical positivism and Cambridge analysis in the interwar years. The second shifted analytic philosophy away from the paradigm of depth-analysis defended in the *Tractatus* and cultivated by logical positivists . . . and Cambridge analysts toward the different conception of 'connective analysis,' which was a primary inspiration of Oxford analytic philosophy" (Hacker 1999, 538). However, this remark of Hacker's while saying something importantly on the mark is also in a way misleading, for not only in tone and attitude, but in method and aim Wittgenstein was very different from Rudolf Carnap or Hans Reichenbach (positivists) on the one hand and Gilbert Ryle or Peter Strawson (Oxford analysts) on the other. Wittgenstein would have rejected the "scientific philosophy" of Carnap and Reichenbach and the "descriptive metaphysics" (more descriptive than metaphysical) of Strawson as well as the avuncular complacently confident tone of Ryle's ordinary language philosophy. Both positivism and Oxford analysis would have struck him as scientistic—though Carnap's and Reichenbach's plainly more overtly so. Moreover, the system-building of Carnap and Strawson would have been regarded by him as impossible (more "houses of cards") and, even if possible, unnecessary and indeed harmful.

Through both revolutionary turns, Wittgenstein held a therapeutic and antiscientistic conception of philosophy with a deep underlying ethico-religious intent. (Hence the word "harmful" in the previous sentence.) But it is important that we do not misunderstand Wittgenstein here. It is not at all that he wanted to replace logic, metaphysics, epistemology, or semantical analysis with moral philosophy, reformist moralizing, or some *lebensphilosophie*. Nothing could be further from his intent. Rather he thought *philosophy itself*, as a particularly bad species of intellectualizing, was bad for human beings since it stands in the way of our coming to grips with our lives. This coming to grips with our lives—something which he took to be supremely important—had, in his view, as well as in Kierkegaard's, nothing to do with philosophy. Philosophy just gets in our way here. Philosophical perplexities, both traditional and those arising in contemporary "scientific philosophy," arise from the often obsessively gripping but still misleading pictures of the workings of our language that we come to have when we reflect on it, though often we do not recognize that it is certain pictures of our language that are generating our perplexities. And it is where that happens that we get in philosophical trouble: we catch the philosophical disease. We do not command a sufficiently clear view of the workings of our language when we try to think about (for example) consciousness, thought, sensations, truth, warrantability, intentionality, and the like. The idea is not to provide some general descriptive account of our language (Strawson) or some formal scientific account of the semantics of our language (Carnap), but to provide, at our conceptual trouble spots, where we are experiencing mental cramps, a sufficiently clear representation of how our language works to break that perplexity. It will not, of course, cure all perplexities forever, but it might cure the particular one that is befuddling us and so we proceed on from case to case. In this way philosophy is to be therapeutic. It does not (*pace* Carnap or Strawson) yield a theory of any kind—the search for one is perhaps *the* philosophical illusion—but is an activity which, where successfully pursued, yields a sufficient understanding of the workings of our language and with that of our practices and forms of life to break the spell that a misleading picture of the workings of our language at some particular spot exerts on us. Philosophy is taken by Wittgenstein to be an activity and not something which constructs some theory to explain our language or the forms of life in which our language is embedded.

There has been a tradition in philosophy (extending even to Gottlieb Frege and Bertrand Russell) which regards philosophy, in contrast with the empirical sciences, which investigate the domain of contingent truth, as the a priori science which investigates the domain of necessity. Wittgenstein argues in the *Tractatus* that this "view" is nonsensical. The propositions of logic are either tautologies or contradictions. They are not in any sense descriptions or characterizations of anything substantive. They neither (*pace* Frege) describe timeless relations between abstract objects (meanings) nor (*pace* Russell) do they describe the most general features of the world. Both Frege and Russell failed to see a crucial radical difference between the propositions of logic and empirical propositions. They thought that the propositions of logic, like empirical propositions, *say* something. Logical propositions, they thought, say very different kinds of things than what empirical science does, but they still say something. Wittgenstein denied this. The propositions of logic (tautologies or contradictions) say absolutely nothing and thus are degenerate propositions. They give no information whatsoever about the world or "the structure of the world" or about some "*noumenal* world" (assuming such a notion is even intelligible). So-called logical truths are simply tautologies. Wittgenstein remarks in the *Tractatus*, "I know nothing about the weather when I know that it is either raining or not raining. . . . All propositions of logic say the same thing, to wit nothing" (Wittgenstein 1921, 4.461, 5.43). Neither tautologies nor contradictions are bipolar (capable of being true and capable of being false). They have no truth-conditions or assertability-conditions. Tautologies are "unconditionally true" and contradictions "unconditionally false." A tautology is true under every possible assignment of truth so it excludes no possibility. A contradiction, by contrast, is false under every possible assignment of truth and thus it excludes every possibility. They both have zero sense and say nothing at all. But this vacuous logical necessity is the only a priori necessity that we have. There is no argument at all for a claim common to Descartes, Wolff, Kant, Husserl, and many other traditional philosophers that while the empirical sciences investigate the domain of contingent truth philosophy, by contrast, is an a priori science or a priori theory which investigates the domain of necessity. Pure reason cannot attain knowledge about reality, for to know the truth of a tautology is not to know anything about how things are or how things stand in reality or even about how in some substantive sense things must be. (There is no substantive a priori necessity.) In the philosophy of religion it is sometimes claimed we can obtain such a knowledge of God—that there are some necessary but still substantive religious propositions (Copleston 1956, 1957, 1975). But that belief rests on an illusion.

Wittgenstein famously in the *Tractatus* asserted that "what can be said can be said clearly, and what we cannot talk about we must pass over in silence" (Wittgenstein 1921, 3). He went so far as to assert that "the whole sense of the book might be summed up" in those words (Wittgenstein 1921, 3). Propositions according to what is *Tractarian* doctrine (assuming for the nonce that he was serious about there being such doctrine and not purposefully for therapeutic purposes leading us down the garden path) can only describe facts, neither philosophy nor anything else can be used to explain how sentences must be related to the states of affairs they represent, for to do so is to try to do more with words than merely describe the facts (Wittgenstein 1921, 4.12). But when we try to do so—that is, when we try to do philosophy—we end up talking nonsense. Wittgenstein recognized that this claim entails that his own philosophical propositions in the *Tractatus* are nonsensical. But here he bites the bullet and remarks in a famous passage at the end of the *Tractatus*: "The correct method in philosophy would really be the following: to say nothing except what can be said . . . and then, whenever someone wanted to say something metaphysical to demonstrate to him that he had failed to give a meaning to certain signs in his propositions" (Wittgenstein 1921, 6.53). And then Wittgenstein goes on to say, "My propositions serve as elucidations in the following way: anyone who understands me eventually recognizes them as nonsensical, when he has used them—as steps to climb up beyond them. (He must, so to speak, throw away the ladder after he has climbed up it.)" (Wittgenstein 1921, 6.54). Moreover, it is not just philosophy and metaphysics that are nonsensical, but religion, talk about the meaning of life, talk about making sense of life, talk about the meaning of the world, talk about God, ethics, and aesthetics. All such talk is nonsense—lacking in all propositional content—having no cognitive force. Such talk, Wittgenstein has it, belongs to "the mystical" and that is also something which is nonsensical.

On the standard reading of Wittgenstein, such talk—something identified with the meaning of life, which Wittgenstein understood as the meaning of the world—could not be just plain old nonsense, but must be deep nonsense hinting at *unsayable ineffable truths*. Something, that is, that can be *shown* but not *said*. It was, so this reading has it, Wittgenstein's belief at the time of the *Tractatus*—and before and way down to and through his "Lectures on Ethics" (1929–1930)—that all such talk—talk vital to our sense of life—could not be put into intelligible form. (Think, to feel the force of this, that "intelligible talk" should be pleonastic.) Nothing that touches on matters of value can be captured by words. People, of course, try to do so, but they end up, though unwittingly, talking nonsense. Any attempt to even articulate, let alone answer, "the problems of life" must be in vain. All thought, including philosophical thought, is useless here. And when "the answer cannot be put into words [then] neither can the question be put into words" (Wittgenstein 1921, 6.5).

Most straightforwardly understood we have here—once we take

away the rhetoric about *das Mystische*—what James Conant has called a "collapse into positivism," though (*pace* Hilary Putnam) it is not at all evident that *here* this is a bad thing (Conant 1989; Putnam 1995). That is to say, the importance we attach to religion, along with aesthetic experience, ethics, and metaphysics, is the result of an illusion. Hard as it is to face, we have, when we cut through the disguised nonsense, just plain nonsense. And, as Frank Ramsey famously said, if it can't be said it can't be said and it can't be whistled either. Wittgenstein quite unequivocally said such talk was nonsensical, but he would paradoxically just as clearly not say that religion and ethics were of no importance. For him they were of supreme importance though not as bits of philosophy or intellectualizing. He was very far from being a secularizer. So where are we here? It looks at least like we are in a very bad muddle.

The (as I mentioned) standard and pervasive interpretation of the Tractarian Wittgenstein (one I subsequently will resist) has it that the idea that we have nonsense full stop is not at all what Wittgenstein thought. Not even in that respect would he make one with positivism. Talk of a collapse into positivism here is off the mark. Rather, it is typically thought, what Wittgenstein felt was that what can be said—what can be put into words—is piddling by comparison with what cannot—*with what can only be shown*. Wittgenstein himself in a letter written to a friend in 1919 says of the *Tractatus* that it "consists of two parts: of that which is under consideration here and of all that I have not written. And it is precisely this second part that is the important one" (Luckhardt 1979, 94). The claim—certainly paradoxical—is that Wittgenstein believed during the *Tractatus* period, and at least up to 1929, that there are things that *can be shown that cannot be said*. As Hacker, for example, reads Wittgenstein, "What is shown by a notation cannot be said. Truths of metaphysics are ineffable and so too are truths for ethics, aesthetics, and religion. Just as Kant circumscribed the bounds of language in order to make room for faith, Wittgenstein circumscribed the bounds of language in order to make room for ineffable metaphysics" (Hacker 1999, 344).

Pace positivists, this standard reading goes, there are truths here and presumably sometimes insight into these truths. They are things that, though only with heroic difficulty, can be grasped but not said. They show themselves to us if we have insight. Among them (on such a reading) are the "ineffable truths" of religion that, Wittgenstein has it, for people who are genuinely attuned, form a passionately grasped system of reference. Still, given the traditional interpretation of Wittgenstein, these truths are ineffable and what the system of reference is is unsayable. But, for all of that, the traditional interpretation goes, they are of powerful significance.

Wittgenstein did indeed remark in the *Tractatus* "How things are in the world is of complete indifference for what is higher. God does not reveal himself *in* the world" (Wittgenstein 1921, 6.432). In the very next sentence Wittgenstein goes on to remark, "It is not how things are in the world that is mystical, but *that it* exists" (Wittgenstein 1921, 6.44). But he ends up—or so it seems—with another "unsayability" here. For, as he also says, "the fact" that the world exists is "the fact" that "there is what there is" (Wittgenstein 1961, 86). But "there is what there is," unless "is" in its two occurrences is used equivocally, is a tautology, so there is no fact at all and we have something on Wittgenstein's own Tractarian conception that is impossible to state. Remember that Wittgenstein stresses that tautologies say nothing. Yet the standard interpretation has it that Wittgenstein also believes that here is another supposed showable but not stateable something that reveals to us, in a way that cannot be said, a deep but ineffable truth. If the "is" in its first occurrence in "There is what there is" is used differently than the "is" in the second occurrence, then we also have something that is nonsensical. We simply have no understanding of what we are saying: nothing can be made of such remarks. Either way, it is here, *if* this is how we are to understand Wittgenstein, where, for all his concern with clarity, the charge of obscurantism seems at least to have force. He appears at least to be trying to say—or to gesture at—that there is something of which we must say that we can only show it but not say it. But trivially we cannot say what the "it" is that we are supposed to understand. But what then can understanding come to here? And how can "There is what there is" be the least bit significant? But then again what can understanding possibly come to here? How can there be an it which we are supposed to understand if we can't *say* what this *it* is? It would surely appear to be—against the standard interpretation—*nothing*. But nothing is not a strange kind of something. We just do not understand what we are talking about—or trying to think—here. Put even more strongly, we cannot know or understand what we are talking about or trying to think here for there is no *what* or *this* for us to be talking about or to somehow conceptualize or grasp as an ineffable something we know not what. It is better—shows more integrity and clarity of thought—to say that we have just plain nonsense here on Wittgenstein's Tractarian conception of language and not some "deep nonsense" taking us to some profound "ineffable truths" about the meaning of life, fate, and the meaning of the world itself (Wittgenstein 1961, 73).

There is a persistent tendency in our thought, both philosophical and religious, to believe that language cannot capture our deepest thoughts and feelings (Ambrose 1950). But that is nonsense and indeed Wittgenstein in his arguments in effect establishes this or, put more cautiously, at least gives us reason to question this claim of depth. We should just, without vacillation, acknowledge that Wittgenstein shows that it is nonsense full stop and that there is an end on it.

Still this doctrine of the unsayable but somehow showable with its supposed deep significance is the standard reading of Wittgenstein of the period of the *Tractatus*. And with *that interpretation* goes the not unfounded charge of obscurantism. But there is a minority view concerning Wittgenstein, with which my last remark in the last paragraph is attuned, represented powerfully by Cora Diamond and James Conant which sees things differently (Diamond 1991; Conant 1989, 1990). On this interpretation, Wittgenstein is not even giving one to understand or hinting at obliquely in indirect discourse, let alone trying (but failing) to assert, that there are things that can be shown that cannot be said, including the claim that what is shown by a notation cannot be said in that notation. And that among these "unsayables" there are deep "ineffable truths" that cannot be said, but, ineffable though they be, can still be known or at least grasped. Wittgenstein indeed does say that such remarks are nonsense. Any interpretation of Wittgenstein will acknowledge that. But in addition this minority view denies that the gnomic remarks in the *Tractatus* that get highlighted by Wittgenstein as nonsensical are "deep nonsense" pointing at something profound but unsayable. Rather they are just plain old nonsense—gibberish, though gibberish that tends to be disguised from us. And further, the claim is, Wittgenstein so regarded them. But the very conceptual work that Wittgenstein does should enable us to see that. That we typically do not understand that that is so is due to the fact "that we do not *command a clear view* of the use of our words—our grammar is lacking this sort of perspicuity" (Wittgenstein 1951, 122).

My aim here is not to try to adjudicate which reading most accurately represents Wittgenstein's thought. My hunches are with the second one and a principle of interpretive charity would push us, I believe, in that direction. But I will not try to argue that. However, I will argue that if Wittgenstein did not take that latter way he should have. This way of reading him saves him from obscurantism and, as I shall attempt to show, it still allows him to take the respectful attitude toward religion, or rather some parts of it, that he was so concerned to take.[2]

James Conant, in a subtle though somewhat overblown article, probes carefully what needs to be said here (Conant 1989). The standard interpretation, as we have seen, takes it that Wittgenstein is telling us— and some of his interpreters think that that is something very profound on Wittgenstein's part—that there are things he cannot say but which he can and is gesturing at. There are some particular things, some of them very crucial to our lives, that can be shown but cannot be said. Conant, *au contraire*, argues that Wittgenstein is giving us to understand, and rightly so, that "there is no particular thing that cannot be said. The 'what' in 'what cannot be said' refers to nothing" (Conant 1989, 244). The *Tractatus* ends as it does because of Wittgenstein's understanding that "beyond what can be said there is nothing more to say or offer except more silence" (Conant 1989, 244). But at least some of the standard interpreters would respond in alarm that, so read, "Wittgenstein would become indistinguishable from Carnap" (Conant 1989, 244). On the standard view "Wittgenstein only agrees with Carnap insofar as he holds that the positions of ethics and religion are nonsense. However, [the standard view has it] they are supposed to be deep and significant forms of nonsense whereas for positivism they are void of any cognitive content whatsoever" (Conant 1989, 244). Conant, in a fine fit of reasonable common sense, wants to reject such a claim both as a correct reading of Wittgenstein and as an important bit of philosophy in its own right. And I want to reject it too for at least the last reason. If this is what it is to be Carnapian then we should all in that respect be Carnapians. It makes no sense to speak of something being "nonsensical yet significant" or "meaningless but *not* void of cognitive content." Those conjunctions are unintelligible. They could only be *made* intelligible by some arbitrary stipulative *redefinition* of some of the constitutive terms. They are not intelligible as they stand. And the arbitrary stipulative definitions are just that.

However, as Conant worries out, what, if we do not resort to bald assertion, are we to say to a standard interpreter who retorts "What kind of sense do you wish to make here?" Conant remarks, "They are willing only to concede that these conjunctions were, strictly speaking, nonsensical. Nevertheless, they would say, they were *not* incoherent, admittedly they could not be coherently expressed, but they are not unintelligible. Indeed, for these commentators, it was the possibility of making such conjunctions intelligible that was the singular achievement of such works as the *Postscript* and the *Tractatus* to have delimited" (Conant 1989, 245). Both Conant and I wish to dig in our heels here and reject this as good philosophy, good sense, good thinking about religion, and as a way to make the maximal sense out of Wittgenstein.

What argument can be made for such a digging in of one's heels? I will proceed indirectly by first intensifying our sense of what is at issue here. The standard interpreters maintain that for the *Tractatus* the propositions of ethics and religion—as well as all the important propositions of the *Tractatus* itself—are both nonsensical *and* deeply significant. They seem to lack cognitive content and still in some mysterious way have cognitive content, though an "ineffable cognitive content." Their significance is reputed to lie either in the fact that they do, or at least attempt to, *show the unsayable, exhibit in some unsayable way the ineffable.* This, Conant remarks,

> requires a conception of language as possessing capacities for exhibiting meaning over and beyond its ordinary capacities for conveying the sense of a proposition. Such a conception is required even if one only

wants to maintain that Wittgenstein's deeply nonsensical propositions are only *trying* (but failing) to say something that cannot be said. For one needs an account of how one can so much as recognize what it is that a piece of nonsense is even just trying to say. (Conant 1989, 248)

The standard commentators wish to claim that there are *kinds* of nonsense leading to a *hierarchy* of nonsense. It is not only that we need to distinguish between intelligible nonsense as opposed to gibberish or gobbledygook, but we must go further and attribute to Wittgenstein the view that there are certain forms of intelligible nonsense, culminating at the top of the hierarchy of kinds of nonsense, in something which consists in certain ways of transgressing the syntax of our language which are ways that are "deeply revelatory of the nature of certain matters that lie beyond the scope of language" (Conant 1989, 246). In the case of religion, the deep nonsense at the top of the hierarchy of nonsense—the "profound intelligible nonsense"—is (in its generalized form) the claim that the deepest ineffable truths are revealed in mystical experience—the very paradigm of the (so-called) unsayable and inexpressible but still revelatory of "ultimate reality."

In his *A Study in Wittgenstein's Tractatus*, Alexander Maslow remarks that "mysticism is an important part of Wittgenstein's view. Mysticism becomes the last refuge for the most cherished things in life, in fact for all values, for all that cannot be discussed and yet is of the utmost importance to us" (Maslow 1961, 160). Commenting on this passage, Conant remarks "that Wittgenstein views mysticism as some form of 'last refuge' and that he has the greatest respect for the impulse to seek such refuge, both strike me as correct perceptions" (Conant 1989, 276). But he adds significantly that the claim that Wittgenstein wishes to condone mysticism as a refuge is without textual support. Wittgenstein says in the *Tractatus* that "the feeling of the world as a limited whole is the mystical feeling" (Wittgenstein 1921, 6.45). Wittgenstein wished to give a diagnosis of the source of that feeling. What he wished to diagnose was the claim that mystical experience, as it is understood by William James and others, is experienced as something utterly ineffable and yet seems to those who have had such an experience that it has (a) a distinctive *noetic* quality but is also (b) felt by them not to be identical with pure states of feeling. They are, or seem to be, states of feeling *and* states that seem to those "who experience them to be also states of knowledge unplumbed by the discursive intellect" (James 1935, 380). This is a rather standard characterization of mystical experience. Wittgenstein was not concerned to reject such descriptions of how things *seem* to the mystic, but was concerned to diagnose it: to diagnose, that is, what James, who gave a careful account of it, took mystics to be trying to say of their experience. But in doing that Wittgenstein was not at all acknowledging that there was or even could be such knowledge or understanding.

A crucial error in the traditional interpretation is "to mistake the views that are under scrutiny in the *Tractatus* for the views the author wishes to espouse" (Conant 1989, 248). Wittgenstein's diagnosis of our situation is as follows. The only alternatives to silence are (1) plain ordinary effable speech including scientific extensions of it; (2) *actually* unintelligible though *apparently* in some way intelligible talk; and (3) mere gibberish. Conant remarks, correctly, that (2) and (3) "differ only in their psychological import: one offers the illusion of sense where the other does not. Cognitively, they are equally vacuous" (Conant 1989, 249). There is, he goes on to say, no fourth alternative, as the standard interpretation would have it, namely the possibility of speech that lacks sense but still yields deep, unsayable, ineffable truths (Nielsen 1973). That, when we take away the obscurantist rhetoric, is just the contradictory claim that these mystical utterances both—and in the same respect—are void of cognitive content *and* somehow have it. When we inspect with an unclouded eye these oracular utterances, we go from an obscurity to a contradiction. Sometimes we are conceptually confused and *mistakenly* think a sentence has cognitive content—makes sense—when it does not. Here Wittgensteinian philosophical therapy can sometimes help. "The only distinction between deep nonsense and mere nonsense . . . that the *Tractatus* allows is between pieces of gibberish that *appear* to have sense and those that don't. In neither case does the book countenance the possibility of a piece of irreducible nonsense" (Conant 1989, 268).

This is not gainsaid by the famous ending of Wittgenstein's "Lecture on Ethics"—still very much in the Tractarian mode—where he says that religion "springs from the desire to say something about the ultimate meaning of life. . . . What it says does not add to our knowledge in any sense. But it is a document of a tendency in the human mind which I personally cannot help respecting deeply and I would not for my life ridicule it" (Wittgenstein 1993, 44). This shows clearly enough Wittgenstein's respect for human beings and his sense of what deep needs such religious utterances and the experiences that go with them answer to, but it does nothing to show that there is any error in our claim that, on his Tractarian account, religious conceptions—what Wittgenstein regards as *das mystiche*—must be just nonsense: straightforward nonsense. Seen clearly, that is, they are seen to be what they are, namely just nonsense though where seen through a glass darkly—seen confusedly—they remain *disguised* nonsense. But disguised nonsense is all the same nonsense and not something obscurely pointing to some deep "ineffable truth," some deep reality we cannot otherwise grasp. We never have "intelligible nonsense" or "ineffable knowledge" for there is and can be no such thing.

Conant *might* be thought to be blurring the austerity of the above conclusion when he says that the "*Tractatus* . . . does hold that we can always breathe life into a piece of language by finding a use for it in our lives" (Conant 1989, 260). However, we cannot do this without engaging in arbitrary stipulative redefinition of the religious utterances that Wittgenstein is most concerned with—the supposedly "deep foundational ones" that he has in mind, the ones that on his view make religion religion. They *have* no sense and the sense that we can *give* them in an attempt to breathe life into them renders them into empirical trivialities or at least empirical utterances that no longer meet religious needs—that no longer could serve as a last refuge for people with religious impulses.

Take, for example, what Wittgenstein in "The Lecture on Ethics" regards as the key paradigm religious experience. It is the experience a person has when he wonders at the very existence of the world—at *that* the world is, not *how* it is. It is the experience people have when it strikes them "how extraordinary that the world should exist" (Wittgenstein 1993, 41). Wittgenstein flat out says that the verbal expression "we give to these experiences is nonsense" (Wittgenstein 1993, 44). He remarks

> If I say "I wonder at the existence of the world" I am misusing language. Let me explain this: It has a perfectly good and clear sense to say that I wonder at something being the case, we all understand what it means to say I wonder at the size of a dog which is bigger than any one I have ever seen before or at anything which, in the common sense of the word, is extraordinary. In every such case I wonder at something being the case which I *could* conceive *not* to be the case. I wonder at the size of this dog because I could conceive of a dog of another, namely the ordinary size, at which I should not wonder. To say, "*I wonder at such and such being the case has only sense if I can imagine it not being the case. . . .*" But it is nonsense to say that I wonder at the existence of the world, because I cannot imagine it not existing. I could of course wonder at the world round me being as it is. If for instance I had this experience while looking into the blue sky, I could wonder at the sky being blue as opposed to the case when it's clouded. But that's not what I mean. I am wondering at the sky *whatever* it is. One might be tempted to say that what I am wondering is a tautology, namely at the sky being blue or not blue. But then it's just nonsense to say that one is wondering at a tautology. (Wittgenstein 1993, 41–42)

Suppose we say instead that in wondering (thinking one wonders) not *how* the world is but *that* it is we are still wondering about something that is the case, namely *that* the world is, and in doing that I am all the same making a nonvacuous contrast. I am wondering instead why there is not instead nothing. In wondering at that, I am wondering in every case at something actually being the case which I *could* conceive not to be the case. I can wonder in every particular case that could possibly be brought to my attention why it could not be the case and I understand clearly that, as far as logical possibilities are concerned, it could not be the case. In wondering at the existence of the world I am wondering why there is not nothing rather than anything at all. Why could not all *empirical* existential statements be false and, if they were, then there would be nothing. But some empirical statements must be true for it even to be *possible* for us to know this or understand what is being said. And this makes the statement itself nonsense. Moreover, "nothing" does not stand for a something that might be the case but just doesn't happen to be. It is, to put it mildly, an opaque notion to try to conceptualize what it would be like for all empirical existential statements to be false at once. What we could say distributively of each statement taken by itself entails nothing of what we could collectively be taken to be saying about them. Wondering—trying to wonder—about why there isn't nothing is nonsense. It is like trying to say there might be nothing which is also some kind of something. It would be like saying "There is an is which is an isn't."

We might give, following Conant's instructions, "I wonder at the existence of the world" a sense by saying it is equivalent to "I wonder why people must die." But now we have turned a pseudoquestion into an obvious empirical triviality. If we are wondering why people must die there are empirical answers to that. We have given—rather far-fetchedly—the religious pseudoproposition a use by turning it into a straightforward, perfectly secular, perfectly empirical remark. We have given it a use all right, but not a religious use or even a use which has much in the way of a religious significance.[3]

Suppose we say instead, in saying "I wonder why people must die," I mean "Why could people not be made of such a hard metal that they would never wear out and thus never die?" But again there are, to the extent that we can make sense of that, as perhaps we can in some science-fiction way, empirical answers to it and, even if there were not, what we have said, in so speaking, has no religious significance. It is not a reasonable candidate for giving a use to "I wonder at the existence of the world."

Suppose we say that in wondering why people wear out—don't just have endless duration—we are wondering why they are not immortal, why they do not have life eternal. But to have life eternal is not just to have endless duration, but to have a life such that the question of our dying cannot arise. Here we have a question that is religious all right, but we have simply substituted one form of nonsense for another (Nielsen 1989b and chapter 3). (Remember that "endless duration" is one thing, "eternity" is another [Malcolm 1960].)

II

I turn now from an examination of the so-called saying/showing distinction and remarks about *das mystische* in the work of the early Wittgenstein and its relevance for his and our thinking about religion to what I take to be more fruitful and more interesting considerations for religion emerging from Wittgenstein's later work, work which again, now for the second time in contemporary history, revolutionized philosophy. In my view, a view I share with Conant and Diamond, Wittgenstein continued to view philosophy as conceptual therapy, but his method for dissolving conceptual confusions—centrally the metaphysical confusions that stand in the way of our understanding—radically changed. In this way there was in his later work a radical dismantling of the *Tractatus* along with a continuity in his conception of the role of philosophy. I think this shift in method leads to a much more valuable way of doing philosophy and yields a much more adequate account of religion. (The fascination with— I'm inclined to say fixation on—the work of the early Wittgenstein rather than the later reflects for many philosophers a continued hang-up with metaphysics. They see the *Tractatus* for all its antimetaphysical thrust as the last great work, Wittgenstein's intentions to the contrary notwithstanding, of metaphysics.)

I shall very briefly say a bit more about what Wittgenstein's second revolution consists in and then turn to a detailed consideration of what it comes to for religion. Again there is a paucity of material directly on religion; during this later period, as well as in the earlier, Wittgenstein wrote nothing for publication specifically and in detail about religion. But there are many things, though often only indirectly, that are very suggestive for thinking about religion in quite different ways than has traditionally been done—in ways which I think cut through or rightly bypass much of the cackle that goes for "the philosophy of religion." Fortunately, as far as texts go, we have in a recent work written by a former student, close friend, and well known interpreter of Wittgenstein, Norman Malcolm, a work (*Wittgenstein: A Religious Point of View?*) which provides a detailed collection of remarks on religion made by Wittgenstein along with an analysis by Malcolm of those remarks followed by a substantial critique of Malcolm's account by Peter Winch. In this account of Wittgenstein on religion by two prominent Wittgensteinians, who are also philosophers of importance themselves, we have a perceptive and faithful account of Wittgenstein's views on religion, plus, particularly on Winch's part, the beginnings of a probing critique of them. (Winch is less of an uncritical disciple than Malcolm is.) I shall build on this material seeking to etch out (a) a portrayal of Wittgenstein on religion in his later philosophy and (b) an account of some Wittgensteinian emendations provided by Wittgensteinians (principally Winch) that will not only bring out the force of Wittgenstein's later account, but will, pointing to its vulnerabilities, enable us better to assess its soundness and import, both in its pristine form and in its critical Wittgensteinian reformulations. Here we can hopefully examine Wittgenstein's account of religion at its full strength. I shall attempt to do something of this.

But first a thumbnail general account of what the later Wittgenstein was up to. In *Philosophical Investigations* (1953), the central work of his later philosophy, as well as in work beginning as early as 1930 and in work following *Philosophical Investigations*, and most particularly in his last work, *On Certainty* (1969), Wittgenstein articulates his changed conception of how to proceed in philosophy and applies it to a range of philosophical problems. Propositions are no longer construed as having a fixed logical form and, more generally, language is no longer construed as having a fixed and timeless structure, but is viewed as changeable, and not infrequently changing, in which these forms of language are now seen as our historically and culturally contingent forms of life. The picture account of meaning is completely abandoned in his later work. The conception that words stand for simple objects that are their meanings is now regarded by Wittgenstein as a bit of incoherent philosophy. (On the Diamond-Conant reading of the *Tractatus* that was true of it too.) Instead the notions of language-games and practices are introduced. In being socialized—in learning, as we all must if we are at all to navigate in the world, to be human—we come to have practices in which words and actions are interwoven. In this activity, in learning to play these language-games, we come to understand words by coming to know their uses in the stream of life, and with this we come to know how to use words in the course of our various practice-embedded activities.

With this Wittgenstein abandoned his earlier formalist Tractarian demand that language, if coherence is our goal, requires determinacy and exactness and that the sole function of language is to describe. Rather language is seen as an activity that has many different functions, is embedded in different practices which answer to and structure our different needs, interests, or purposes. For someone to understand a word it is not sufficient to bring the learner face to face with its putative referent while repeating the word. In many cases nothing like this is possible and in all cases, or at least almost all cases, the learner must come to understand what *kind* of word he is being taught; to grasp this an extensive training needs to have taken place in which the learner comes to be at home with the everyday activities—the social practices—of which remarks using the word are a part. As Wittgenstein put it in an oft quoted remark from his *Philosophical Investigations*, "For a large class of cases—though not for all—

in which we employ the word 'meaning' it can be defined thus: the meaning of a word is its use in language" (Wittgenstein 1953, 43).

There is on Wittgenstein's account no standing free of our practices and forms of life or escaping the context, including the historical contexts, in which they are embedded. Both the Tractarian (on the traditional reading) and metaphysical realist conception of an independently articulated world are incoherent on Wittgenstein's later account. We have no coherent conception of a world that we can describe by accurately copying it or mirroring it or even representing it in our thought. There are no referents "out there" that simply force our concepts on us. We rather understand our concepts by coming to understand their use in our life activities. Concepts are aspects of our forms of life. They are not items forced on us by the world. To understand a concept is to understand the use of words expressing it as they function in our language and in our lives. And these will be various things, depending on the particular concept, as part of the varied contexts and the various purposes we have. These varied activities and ways in which we talk form our practices and they build together into our forms of life. We have no concepts or conceptions which stand independently of them.

Wittgenstein's earlier views—more accurately his metaviews—on religion, at least on the standard interpretation of the *Tractatus*, could not withstand his changed conceptions about language. As I have noted the idea of a general propositional form is illusory. There is no common property or set of common properties that all and only propositions have. There are many different kinds of structures that we call propositions. As P. M. S. Hacker has put it, many things count as "propositions":

> avowals of experience (such as "I have a pain" or "It hurts"), avowals of intent, ordinary empirical propositions, hypotheses, expressions of laws of nature, logical and mathematical propositions, "grammatical propositions" (in Wittgenstein's idiosyncratic use of this term) which are expressions of rules (such as "red is a color" or "the chess king moves one square at a time"), ethical and aesthetic and so on. (Hacker 1999, 545–46)

In the regimented, austere conception of *The Tractatus*, religious utterances are pseudopropositions lacking bipolarity. They are, that is, not capable of being true or capable of being false. They on that conception describe nothing, are without any cognitive content at all, and thus are nonsensical. By contrast, given Wittgenstein's later philosophy, they are not, at least on these grounds, nonsensical. On Wittgenstein's later, more relaxed and more realistic conception of propositions many of them are propositions. "Bipolarity is a feature of an important member of the family, but not a defining property of propositions as such" (Hacker 1999,

546). Moreover, Wittgenstein's earlier conception that it was the sole function of a proposition to describe is mistaken and importantly so. The "roles of many kinds of propositions, such as logical propositions and mathematical propositions are not to describe" (Hacker 1999, 546).[4] Yet for all of that, they are in order. We cannot take such a short way with dissenters and simply rule out religious utterances *carte blanche* as expressions of pseudopropositions and thus nonsensical because they fail to have the general form of a proposition. The shoe is on the other foot. The error—the illusion—is to believe that there is such a general propositional form: that there is something that propositions essentially are.

Wittgenstein continues, the above notwithstanding, to believe that religious beliefs are very different from factual beliefs. Surface appearances to the contrary, quite ordinary religious propositions are unlike factual propositions. They function very differently. But they are not, Wittgenstein now has it, any the worse for all of that. They are not therefore nonsensical.

A pervasive and, Wittgenstein believes, a pernicious error of our scientistic culture is to try to assimilate key uses of religious language (e.g., declarative sentences such as "God created the world.") to those of hypotheses, predictions, or theoretical explanations. To do that, he has it, is to completely misunderstand their use. It is to be fettered by one kind of use of language and to try to read it into other uses. When, for example, a religious person says "I believe that there will be a last judgment," it is a complete mistake, according to Wittgenstein, to take that utterance to be making a prediction. That is not the use, or even anything like the use, it has in religious language-games. In believing in the last judgment a person is not, Wittgenstein maintains, thinking that there will be, or even that it is probable that there will be, a certain kind of extraordinary event which will occur sometime in the future. The religious person—or at least Wittgenstein's religious person—is not thinking any such thing (Nielsen 1982, 43–64). He is not trying to make any kind of prediction at all (Wittgenstein 1969, 56). Rather, Wittgenstein equates having religious beliefs with (a) using affirmatively certain religious concepts and (b) having the emotions and attitudes that go with these concepts. He remarks, as we have seen, "that a religious belief could only be something like a passionate commitment to a system of reference" (Wittgenstein 1980, 64). But these beliefs—beliefs such as a belief in the meaning of life or the meaning of the world—can be neither true nor false. The question of their truth or falsity cannot even meaningfully arise. Moreover, they are beliefs which are neither reasonable nor unreasonable. But what Wittgenstein does regard as unreasonable are apologists either for or against religion who assume that religious beliefs can in any way be tested: can be shown to be either true or probably true or false or probably false by evidence or by argument or "grasped by reason" to be so. Views like that he regards as ludicrous (Wittgenstein 1969, 58).

Now with something of Wittgenstein's later conception of how to proceed in philosophy before us, I shall turn to an examination of *Wittgenstein: A Religious Point of View* starting with some central considerations by Norman Malcolm. They consist in a rather orthodox but still well thought out articulation of a Wittgensteinian point of view.

A *leitmotif* of Malcolm's discussion of Wittgenstein on religion is Wittgenstein's remarks in his *Philosophical Investigations* that "philosophy simply puts everything before us, and neither explains nor deduces anything" (Wittgenstein 1953, 126). Concerning this Malcolm remarks

> Wittgenstein is here proposing a radical change in our conception of what philosophy should be doing. To say that philosophy does not seek to explain anything is certainly not a true description of philosophy as it has been, and still is, practiced. Many philosophers would be dumbfounded or outraged by the suggestion that they should not be seeking explanations. The traditional aim of philosophy has been to explain the essential nature of justice, right and wrong, duty, the good, beauty, art, language, rules, thought. A philosopher may well ask: "What am I supposed to do if not explain?"
>
> In Wittgenstein's later thinking there is an answer. The task of philosophy is to *describe*. Describe *what*? Describe *concepts*. How does one describe a concept? By describing the use of the word, or of those words, that express the concept, that is what philosophy should "put before us." (Malcolm 1994, 74)[5]

There is no language-independent access to concepts, Wittgenstein is at pains to maintain in *Philosophical Investigations*, and Malcolm follows him here. Malcolm continues, "The description of the use of a word is called by Wittgenstein describing the 'language-game' with that word" (Malcolm 1994, 74). Then, without highlighting the therapeutic side of Wittgenstein's conception of philosophy, but in effect remaining faithful to it all the same, Malcolm remarks that it is not the task of philosophy to describe the use of a word in its *totality*, as if we had an understanding of what it would be like to do that, but only those features of the word that in certain determinate contexts give rise to philosophical perplexity. We assemble reminders to break a certain perplexity where we have mental cramps concerning the workings of our language. (Here again we see how very different Wittgenstein is from Strawson.) Describing the use of an expression is called, rather eccentrically but harmlessly by Wittgenstein, describing the grammar of the expression. But this, as by now should be evident, is not just giving an account of sentence-construction or syntax. The point of speaking of language-games is to bring into focus, and clear prominence, "the fact that the *speaking* of a language is part of an activity or a form of life" (Wittgenstein 1953, 23). Malcolm, uncontroversially and rightly, takes this to mean "that in describing the language-game, or some part of the language-game with a word, one is describing how the word is embedded in actions and reactions—in human behavior" (Malcolm 1994, 75). "Words," Wittgenstein remarks in his *Zettel*, "have meaning only in the flow of thought and life" (Wittgenstein 1967, 173). "Our talk," he adds in *On Certainty*, "gets its sense from the rest of our actions" (Wittgenstein 1969, 229). Our language-games embedded as they are in forms of life provide us a place for explanations, for giving reasons and for justifications inside the framework of these language-games or forms of life. But there is, *Malcolm* has it that Wittgenstein has it, neither explanation nor justification for the existence of these forms of language or language-games themselves.

Illustrating the way language-games work and their links with forms of life, Malcolm comments on our use of "motive." We not infrequently wonder about the motives of people. Normally the quickest and surest way to find out is to ask them. "Now of course he may not reveal it: perhaps he himself does not understand it, or perhaps he misrepresents it both to himself and to others" (Malcolm 1994, 76). But then Malcolm goes on to observe, "what is highly interesting is that if he does disclose his motive, typically his acknowledgement of it will not be based on any *inference* from the situation, or from his own behavior or previous actions—as would be the conjecture of others. He *tells* us his motive *without* inference" (Malcolm 1994, 76, first italics added).

We can, when we reflect about how this language-game works, just be struck by its sheer existence and contingency. And this is true not only with the language-games we play with "motive" but also with "intention" or with any other language-game (Malcolm 1994, 75–77). We have contingency here, not necessity. Gone are the supposed necessities of the *Tractatus* and indeed of the whole philosophical tradition. Reflecting on how Wittgenstein is reasoning and how Wittgenstein thinks we should reason if we would be realistic, Malcolm remarks, we "cannot explain why this use of language exists. All we can do is describe it—and *behold* it" (Malcolm 1994, 76). He quotes from *On Certainty* where Wittgenstein makes a general comment about language-games. "You must bear in mind that the language game is, so to speak, something unforeseeable. I mean it is not based on grounds. Not reasonable (or unreasonable). It stands there like our life" (Wittgenstein 1969, 559).

Religions, that is Judaism, Christianity, Islam, Hinduism, Buddhism, etc., etc., are ancient and complex forms of life, that over time change in a myriad of ways with their distinctive but purely contingent language-games.[6]

Within these language-games there can be the giving of reasons, explanations, and justifications, but for the language-games and forms of life themselves, as we have noted, there can be no explanations or justification and no foundations for them either. They are human activities that are just there and religious forms of life like other forms of life are neither reasonable nor unreasonable. They do not rest on some deeper metaphysical or theological foundations or any kind of grounding theory. They neither have some foundationalist epistemological grounding nor any other kind of grounding nor do they stand in need of such grounding, rationalization, or theorizing. They are, Wittgenstein argues, in order just as they are. They are just there, as we have already noted Wittgenstein saying, like our lives. There can, and indeed sometimes should, be *internal* criticisms within religious language-games. Some expressions of faith are less adequate than others, less adequately capture the aspirations of a particular religion, but there can be, Wittgenstein has it, no intelligible standing outside these forms of life and assessing them. Justification comes to an end when we come up against them. This is true for all forms of life, religion included. As Malcolm puts it, giving what he takes to be Wittgenstein's account, "Wittgenstein regarded the language-games, and their associated forms of life, as beyond explanation. The inescapable logic of this conception is that the terms 'explanation,' 'reason,' 'justification' have a use exclusively *within* the various language-games" (Malcolm 1994, 77, italics added). Or again, "An explanation is *internal* to a particular language-game. There is no explanation that *arises above* our language-games and explains *them*. This would be a super-concept of explanation—which means that it is an ill-conceived fantasy" (Malcolm 1994, 78). What we can and should do as philosophers is observe and describe language-games; and, with hard work and luck, we will come to see more clearly, by a perspicuous representation, the use of the terms of our language-games and the role they play in our lives. Philosophy, the kind of therapeutic philosophy that Wittgenstein, Conant, Diamond, Malcolm, Rhees, and Winch practice, enters when we become entangled in our concepts—the use of our terms. There in such particular situations philosophy can, by assembling reminders for a particular purpose, enable us to command a clearer view of our use of these terms and it can dispel our confusions about them. Philosophy, Wittgenstein has it, as do neopragmatists as well, "cannot explain why anything happens or exists" and "it cannot reveal the essential nature of anything" for there are no such essential natures. Its way of proceeding is descriptive and elucidatory, elucidatory in the service of dispelling the confusion we almost invariably fall into when we reflect on our concepts. We normally can operate *with* them without difficulties, but we often fall into confusions—suffer from mental cramps—when we try to operate *upon* them.

All of this, of course, applies to our religious concepts, as much as to any other concepts. When the engine isn't idling; when we work with them—operate *with* them rather than *upon* them—we understand them,

Wittgenstein gives us to understand, well enough, if we have been enculturated into such forms of life, but when we think about them, as when
we think about other concepts as well, we almost irresistibly fall into confusion about them. The task of philosophers, for themselves as well as for
others, is to dispel such confusions by providing *in situto* a perspicuous
representation of these concepts. We move about, usually effortlessly, in
our grammar, in our everyday practices. But in thinking *about* what we
do with words we not infrequently fall into perplexity. In order to remove
our misconceptions, Malcolm has it, no *theorizing* is called for, neither scientific nor philosophical. What is required is only that we *look* carefully at
the grammar which is at our command. We can think with it even if we
stumble, while still thinking with it, when we try to think about it. But in
doing this Wittgenstein's counsel is, "Don't think, but look!" (Wittgenstein 1953, 66; Malcolm 1994, 79–80).

Philosophy, that is good philosophy, should replace our age-old
metaphysical theorizing and its ersatz scientific replacements in a so-
called scientific philosophy bent on formulating theories about the nature
of meaning, thinking, reference, belief, knowledge, mind, good, and God.
By contrast, good philosophy—therapeutic philosophy practiced after
the fashion of Wittgenstein—cannot interfere with the actual use of language. For it *elucidation* comes to accurate description in the service of
dispelling confusions *about* our use of language. We have a mastery of
our language—of the use of our terms—but we fall into confusion when
we try to think about them; when we reflect about our use and try to
grasp "the essence" of our concepts expressed by these terms. Wittgenstein remarked in his *Philosophical Investigations* that our "mistake is to
look for an explanation where we should see the facts as 'primary phenomena [*Urphänomene*].' That is, where we should say: *this language-game
is played*" (Wittgenstein 1953, 176). Or again, "The question is not one of
explaining a language-game by our experiences, but of observing a language-game" (Wittgenstein 1953, 176).

A language-game, as Malcolm well puts it, "is an employment of language that is embedded in one of the innumerable patterns of human life"
(Malcolm 1994, 81). *Some* forms of life are forms of life that not all people in
all cultures share (Malcolm 1994, 82). We cannot, Malcolm has it, explain
why this is so: that is why some people have them and others do not. He
remarks, "Neither philosophy nor science can explain this. What philosophy
can do is to correct our inclination to assume, because of superficial similar-
ities, that different language-games and forms of life are really the same"
(Malcolm 1994, 82). Some words refer to or stand for something. They have
a reference. But "Hans," "blue," "2," "the Empire State Building," "grace,"
and "God" do not all refer in the same way. We must, in particular, not
assume that "God" refers like "Hans" or "the Empire State Building."

Wittgenstein, and, for that matter, Norman Malcolm and Peter Winch both following Wittgenstein, are as much set against the idea that there could be a one true description of the world or some ultimate explanation which would show us what reality really is as are neopragmatists such as Richard Rorty and Hilary Putnam. Such notions, they all believe, are without sense. Natural theology and natural atheology, as much as metaphysical realism, are incoherent. We can have no such knowledge and we do not need it. Religious beliefs neither can have any backing from metaphysics or natural theology or science, nor do they need it. (Here there is no difference between the earlier and the later philosophy of Wittgenstein.) But, by parity, atheological metaphysical theories or so-called scientific theories of a so-called scientific philosophy or a "scientific worldview," which are really metaphysical theories in disguise, are also incoherent and can provide no intelligible ground or basis for *rejecting* or *criticizing* religion. Such activities—theology and atheology—take in each other's dirty linen. Both should be set aside as houses of cards.

However, Malcolm is quick to remind us that Wittgenstein's account is not a form of irrationalism or nihilism which says goodbye to reason or reasonableness, though Wittgenstein, as much as does Paul Feyerabend, says farewell to Philosophical Reason or Scientific Reason. (So-called Philosophical Reason or Scientific Reason would be more apt.) But to be against Reason is not to be against reasoning and justification *within* language-games and to the reflective effort to make sense of our lives and to be reasonable. And that reasons, falsifications, explanations come to an end "does not mean that there are no reasons, justifications, explanations for anything" (Malcolm 1994, 82).

Within many of our language-games, when we are operating with them, and reasoning and reflecting inside their parameters, reasons, justifications, explanations often can be given and often are perfectly in place. What, however, Wittgenstein does stoutly claim, and Malcolm and Winch follow him here, is that the giving of reasons, justifications, and explanations come to an end *somewhere*.

> Where is that? It is at the existence of the language-games and the associated forms of life. There is where explanation has reached its limit. There reasons stop. In philosophy we can only notice the language-games, describe them, and sometimes wonder at them. (Malcolm 1994, 82)

There we see what has been called Wittgenstein's *quietism*. Quietism or not, for us here it is a key question whether, and if so how, it applies to religion—to Christianity, Hinduism, Islam, Judaism, and the like. What is at least initially unsettling in this context in thinking about Wittgenstein and Wittgensteinians such as Malcolm and Winch is that it seems that, if their way of characterizing how to proceed in philosophy is correct, this means that no philosophical or any other kind of reasonable criticism, or for that matter defense, is possible of forms of life or indeed any form of life, including Hinduism, Christianity, and the like.[7] Is this where we are? Is this the end of the line?

III

It can be responded to such Wittgensteinianism that religions, and most strikingly Christianity with which Wittgenstein and Malcolm are most concerned, are *inescapably in part metaphysical religiosities* (Hägerström 1964). Moreover, the part that is metaphysical cannot be excised from the rest leaving the rest intact. Without a metaphysical part as a settled element (component) in that form of life, the form of life will not even be recognizable as Christianity, Hinduism, Judaism, or Islam. There are no doctrineless or creedless religions. Religion is indeed a doing, a committing yourself to act or try to act in a certain way, but it is not *only* that. In Christianity, for example, God is said to be the ultimate spiritual being—the very ground of the world—transcendent to the world and, in being so, is eternal and beyond space and time. And it is an essential part of that very religion to believe that human beings have immortal souls such that they—that is we—will not perish or at least will not perish forever when we die: when, that is, we lose our earthly life. And in addition there is what Kierkegaard called the scandal of the Trinity, but still, he believed, a scandal to be accepted trustingly on faith. These are central beliefs for Christianity and without them Christianity would not be Christianity. It, of course, is not *only* a belief-system. It is also, as Wittgenstein and Kierkegaard stress, a demanding way of life that requires of believers— genuine believers—a reorientation of their lives. But it is also, and inescapably, a belief-system with a set of doctrines.

This belief-system is a metaphysical belief-system and Christianity integrally is a metaphysical religiosity. It simply comes with the religion. But, if what Wittgenstein, Malcolm, Winch, and the neopragmatists say is so, metaphysical belief-systems are all incoherent: "houses of cards," as Wittgenstein said. But then that very form of life, *metaphysically infused as it is*, should be said by Wittgenstein and Wittgensteinians to be incoherent. But that is not at all what they say.

Still, that antimetaphysical strain is central to their accounts. But, on another equally central part of Wittgenstein's account, Christianity can't be incoherent, for Christianity, as other religions as well, consists in a more or less integrated cluster of distinctive language-games—employments of language embedded in a pattern of human life—and thus a form of life. But forms of life and language-games cannot on Wittgenstein's account be incoherent or illusory or even in any central or crucial way in error. Such notions have no application with respect to forms of life. So we can see here that something has to give. Two central points of Wittgenstein's account—or so at least it seems—are incompatible with each other. Religions are metaphysical schemes and metaphysical schemes are incoherent, but religions are forms of life and it makes no sense to say of a form of life that it is incoherent.

Wittgenstein, I think, would respond, and here I think Kierkegaard would respond in the same or a similar manner as well, that these doctrinal elements—these metaphysical or metaphysical-theological beliefs as important as they have *historically* been to Christianity and other religions as well—are nonetheless incoherent and should be set aside while still keeping other elements which are vitally important to those religious. These religious metaphysical beliefs are not what is really important in religion and religiously sensitive people have—though sometimes inchoately—always recognized that.

What Wittgenstein saw as important in religion is that, if one could have faith—if one could trust in God—that that will turn around one's life enabling one to be a decent person and to without vanity or arrogance do good in the world. He took *faith without works* to be utterly vain. Indeed it should not, as he saw it, properly speaking even be called "faith." Moreover, as he says in his *Notebooks* of 1916, "to pray is to think about the meaning of life" and that "to believe in God means to see that life has a meaning" (Wittgenstein 1961, 73; Malcolm 1994, 10). These remarks are, against most of the philosophical temper of Wittgenstein, utterly reductionistic. If what they say is so, it would make, by implicit stipulative redefinition, many reflective and sensitive atheists into believers in God. By verbal magic all sensitive, reflective, caring people become religious believers. It is to take what may very well be a *necessary* condition for genuine religious belief and turn it into a *sufficient* one. Is this the end of the matter? Perhaps not quite. Let me proceed indirectly by first recording some of Wittgenstein's specific comments about religion. Moreover, it is important to keep in mind the fact that historically religions have changed over time and that there is no reason to believe "history has come to end" and to think that they will not continue to change.

Wittgenstein had, as I have remarked, scant patience with philosophical theology or the philosophy of religion, but throughout his life he read and reread the gospels, thought at one time seriously about becoming a priest, and was deeply taken by the ancient liturgical prayers of the Latin rite and their translation in the Anglican prayer book, remarking that they "read as if they had been soaked in centuries of worship" (Malcolm 1994, 17). Speaking to his close friend, Maurice Drury, who had formed the intention to be ordained as a priest, Wittgenstein remarked

Just think, Drury, what it would mean to have to preach a sermon every week. You couldn't do it. I would be afraid that you would try and give some sort of philosophical justification for Christian beliefs, as if some proof was needed. The symbolisms of Catholicism are wonderful beyond words. But any attempt to make it into a philosophical system is offensive. (Malcolm 1994, 11)

It was the *activist*, life-orientation involving *not* the speculative-cosmological side of Christianity that appealed to Wittgenstein. What gripped him was Christianity's call to radically alter the manner of one's life—to be just and caring with one another, to clearly see what a wretched person one was, to atone for one's sins, and to struggle to be a decent human being.

The influence of Kierkegaard on Wittgenstein was very deep. It shows itself in the above remarks about guilt and sin and, again quite differently, in his attitude toward the historical claims of Christianity and in what he thought philosophy could achieve vis-à-vis religion. Wittgenstein (echoing Kierkegaard) wrote, "Christianity is not based on a historical truth; rather it gives us a (historical) narrative and says: now believe! But not, believe this narrative with the belief appropriate to a historical narrative—rather believe, through thick and thin, and you can do that only as the result of a life" (Wittgenstein 1980, 32; Malcolm 1994, 32). Wittgenstein, again like Kierkegaard, saw religion not only as something that makes extreme demands on one, but as something which answers to the needs of genuinely religious people—people who not only see themselves to be extremely imperfect but as wretched. "Any halfway decent man," Wittgenstein wrote, "will think himself extremely imperfect, but a religious man believes himself *wretched*" (Wittgenstein 1980, 45; Malcolm 1994, 17). Somewhat earlier in his *Miscellaneous Remarks*, Wittgenstein wrote "faith is faith in what my heart, my soul needs, not my speculative intelligence. For it is my soul, with its passions, as it were with its flesh and blood, that must be saved, not my abstract mind" (Wittgenstein 1980, 33; Malcolm 1994, 17).

He, given his sense of what religion really is, is fully, intellectually speaking, on the fideist side coming down to us from Tertullian, Pascal, Hamann, and, most fully, from Kierkegaard. But in his very conceptualization of fideism there was also for religious persons an intense activist side very distinct from his Quietism in *philosophy*. This comes out strikingly in a remark he made in 1946:

One of the things Christianity says, I think, is that all sound doctrines are of no avail. One must change one's *life*. (Or the *direction* of one's life.)

That all wisdom is cold; and that one can no more use it to bring one's life into order than one can forge *cold* iron.

A sound doctrine does not have to *catch hold* of one; one can follow it like a doctor's prescription.—But here something must grasp one and turn one around.—(This is how I understand it.) Once turned around, one must stay turned around.

Wisdom is passionless. In contrast faith is what Kierkegaard calls a *passion*. (Wittgenstein 1980, 53)

For Wittgenstein, as for Tertullian, Pascal, Hamann, and Kierkegaard, religion was not a question of proving anything or even the articulating of doctrine, even a doctrine that orders one's life.

[Wittgenstein] objected to the idea that Christianity is a "doctrine," i.e., a theory about what has happened and will happen to the human soul. Instead, it is a description of actual occurrences in the lives of some people—of "consciousness of sin," of despair, of salvation through faith. For Wittgenstein the emphasis in religious belief had to be on doing—on "amending one's ways," "turning one's life around." (Malcolm 1994, 19)

He came to have, mixed together with this striving to turn his life around and his realizing that this was what religion was about, an intense desire for purity together with an equally intense sense of his own impurity, his sinfulness and guilt, his standing under Divine judgment, his need for redemption and forgiveness. He had a keen sense of a judging and redeeming God, but the conception of a creator was foreign to him and, as Malcolm put it, "any cosmological conception of a Deity derived from the notion of cause or of infinity would be repugnant to him" (Malcolm 1994, 10).

In spite of Wittgenstein's statement that "I am not a religious man," I think that it is, as Malcolm puts it, "surely right to say that Wittgenstein's mature life was strongly marked by religious thought and feeling" (Malcolm 1994, 21). Kierkegaard has percipiently shown how difficult it is to be religious, how many people are deceived in thinking they are religious when they are not, and that some people who would honestly say they are not, and even some—say, some militant atheists—who would vehemently assert that they are not, are nonetheless religious and indeed deeply so. It is also the case that with his clarity of intellect, together with his deep religious sensitivity, Wittgenstein is likely to have had a keen sense of what a religious form of life is. I have claimed, as have many others, that there is no doctrineless religion and that religion inescapably involves making cosmological (metaphysical) claims (Nielsen 1989a, 1999). Wittgenstein firmly rejects this. Is he right to do so?

IV

Concerning what we discussed in III and what we shall continue to discuss here, it will be necessary, as Winch reminds us, "to observe the distinction between Wittgenstein's own religious reflections and his philosophical comments on religious discourse" (Winch 1994, 133). I shall be concerned centrally with the latter and shall show concern with the former principally to help us, if it can, to gain a purchase on how we should think and feel about religion. I want to try to see what kind of form of life it involves, what kinds of language-games are integral to it, what role it can and should play in our lives, and what philosophically we are justified in saying about these matters.

Pursuant to this I should say something about Peter Winch's discussion of Wittgenstein on religion and about his reservations concerning Malcolm's account. Malcolm's account of how Wittgenstein understands religion and how he understands philosophy in relation to religion is an important one. That notwithstanding, Winch, I believe, has brought out some key ways in which Malcolm's account is flawed. I want to highlight them and then comment on them.

1. As we have seen, Malcolm claims, and claims for Wittgenstein, that there is no explanation for the existence of language-games or forms of life. Winch says that this is misleading. I think he actually shows something stronger, namely, that, taken straightforwardly, the claim is just false. Still, though false, taken straightforwardly, we can give it a very specialized reading in which it is not false and, so understood, it makes an important point that is frequently lost sight of in thinking about what religion is.

Winch does not disagree with the general understanding that Wittgenstein firmly maintained that explanation has an end and that explanatory theories are inappropriate in philosophy (Winch 1994, 100). Good philosophy, he agrees, should be descriptive in the way Malcolm, following Wittgenstein, characterizes. That is not at all in dispute between them or between me and them as being something that Wittgenstein firmly maintained. Moreover, Winch, like Malcolm, thought that Wittgenstein was right about this. But Malcolm overlooks, Winch has it, "the very different issues that are at stake in various of the contexts in which Wittgenstein insists that 'explanation has an end' " (Winch 1994, 100). Winch writes that it "is misleading to say that 'Wittgenstein regarded the language-games and thus associated forms of life, as beyond explanation.' Language-games are not a phenomenon that Wittgenstein had discovered with the peculiar property that their existence cannot be explained!" (Winch 1994, 104–105). Malcolm maintains that neither the "hard" sciences nor the "soft" sciences can explain why various practices exist. But, as Winch points out, that is simply false. There are many cases, he observes, "in which historians, anthropologists, or linguists give well founded explanations of the existence of this or that practice. Why ever not! The important question for us [that is for we philosophers] to ask is:

what relevance would such explanations have to the resolution of philo-sophical difficulties?" (Winch 1994, 106). What Winch takes it that (*pace* Malcolm) we should *not* maintain is that language-games are *intrinsically* beyond the power of these sciences to provide explanations of, but rather what we should say is that any explanation they might offer would turn out to be quite uninteresting, and useless *as far as the philosopher's charac-teristic puzzlement is concerned* (Winch 1994, 106).

Wittgenstein, Winch has it—and it seems to me correctly as a bit of Wittgenstein interpretation—was not concerned to deny that there was any reasonable sense in which explanations of practices could be given. He was concerned, rather, "with the peculiar pseudosense in which philosophers seek 'explanations.' " Spinoza, for example, thought, as Winch remarks, "that because explanations have come to an end there must be something which has no further explanation, a *causa sui*" (Winch 1994, 104, quoting Spinoza). Wittgenstein was concerned to combat that, to show that that kind of rationalism is senseless: that it makes no sense to say that there is some-thing beyond explanation—something intrinsically unexplainable—on which all ordinary explanations depend or that there is, if we push matters resolutely, some *ultimate explanation*—some super-explanation as it were—which finally explains everything and brings inquiry to an end. Wittgenstein does not think, Winch observes, "that explanations come to an end with something that is intrinsically beyond further explanation. They come to an end for a variety of quite contingent and pragmatic reasons, perhaps because of a practical need for action, perhaps because the puzzlement which origi-nally prompted the search for explanation has evaporated (for one reason or another)" (Winch 1994, 104). There are many situations, perhaps most situa-tions, in which we have no need "at all" to explain a practice. The practice seems to us—and sometimes rightly so—unproblematic. But then, as C. S. Peirce and John Dewey stressed, circumstances might arise in which we need, or at least want, an explanation for one or another specific pragmatic purpose—political, moral, sociological, or some combination of them or per-haps because the practice does not seem for some reasonably specific reasons to be working so well and indeed might not be working well. Such situations do arise and there is no reason to think such explanations, answering to such problematic situations, are impossible, always or even generally undesirable, or that they will invariably, or even standardly, degenerate into philosophical pseudoexplanations. Moreover, we do not have good textual grounds for thinking that Wittgenstein thought that.

Suppose, however, we stop talking about explanation and talk of *jus-tification* instead. Wittgenstein also famously said that justification must come to an end or it would not be justification. Malcolm has stressed as a view which is both Wittgenstein's and right "that reasons, justifications, explanations, reach a terminus in the language-games and their internally related forms of human life." Let us set aside explanation and just concentrate on the giving of reasons and the justifying (if such is in order) of a form of life. Winch takes it, correctly, as a bit of Wittgenstein exegesis, "that the expression of religious belief is itself a language-game for which it makes no sense to ask for . . . rational justification" (Winch 1994, 111). *Within* a form of life, a justification of particular beliefs or particular conceptions in accordance with the constitutive norms and conceptions of that form of life can sometimes be given. But a request for a justification of the constitutive norms and conceptions—the very framework beliefs of a religious form of life—is another matter. Wittgenstein has it that to ask for justification here is senseless. Job's seeking to require God to answer to him is seen to rest on a mistake for one who has faith. The showing of why God's will is sovereign and should never be questioned—the challenging of the whole framework—is, given Wittgenstein's conceptions, out of place. Indeed, not simply out of place, but incoherent. Malcolm had remarked, Winch reminds us, that even in this technological and materialistic age, there are people who are inside the practices, the language-games of, say Christianity or Judaism, who pray

> to God for help, asking him for forgiveness, thanking him for the blessings of this life—and who thereby gain comfort and strength, hope and cheerfulness. Many of these people would have no understanding of what it would *mean* to provide rational justification for their religious belief—nor do they feel a need for it. (Malcolm 1994, 84)

And indeed Wittgenstein has it—and here both Malcolm and Winch follow him—justification here is not possible and, moreover, even if it were, there is no need for it. Asking for it is not only obtuse but is wrong, morally wrong.

There are at least three issues here. First, it seems fair enough to say that a plain, untutored person—say a minimally educated person living in an isolated community of believers—is being reasonable—or at least not unreasonable—in so believing. Moreover, it would, in most circumstances, be sadistic to challenge such a person's faith—a faith that that person regards as an undeserved *gift* from God. It would be unnecessary and pointless cruelty causing, if it was at all psychologically effective, unnecessary and pointless suffering. *Second*, there is the question that, if that person began to feel—say quite without wishing it—the irritation of doubt, whether (a) there are considerations available to an honest, reflective person sufficient to still, without subterfuge or self-deception, those doubts or (b) whether this is even an intelligible or legitimate possibility: whether it makes sense to have such doubts? They *may* themselves rest on philosophical confusions. Moreover, perhaps concerning something so basic—something so much a part of the life of some people—we have something which does not admit of such rationalization, such a reasoning out of things? *Third*, whether, that isolated person aside, for anyone in our modern cultures there are considerations which that person, or several persons reasoning together and sensitively feeling through the matter, could articulate which would show that such beliefs were not only coherent but not unreasonable? Or to come to the opposite conclusion? Are these, as it seems Wittgenstein and Wittgensteinians believe—*must* believe?—bad questions? But if that is claimed, it seems to be in order for us to ask just *why* are these bad questions. Or are they really bad questions? Do we just have, in maintaining they are, Wittgensteinian dogma here?

I think any Wittgensteinian would respond to this last query and the second one as well by rejecting them out of hand. It is *practices* which give the intelligibility and coherence to talk—words as they are used in their living contexts, in this case the context of a living engaged faith. *If theorizing, he would say, makes the talk seem incoherent or unreasonable, then so much the worse for the theorizing.* Moreover, and in addition, religion is something special for it is not a matter, except peripherally, of the intellect but of the heart. The intellect in this context can only dispel bad philosophical reasoning that gets in the way of faith. There is in such fideistic reasoning a great distance between the confident doing of natural theology by Aquinas and Scotus and the fideistic reasoning of Kierkegaard and Wittgenstein: between the confident claim that if we reason carefully and attend to the facts we can see that it is irrational not to believe in God, to the acceptance of God simply on faith—on a faith, or a trust, that eschews all search for or recognition of the appropriateness or even the very possibility of justification, except in the purely negative sense of showing the mistakes of those who would say that without justification your faith is in vain. For to say that—to demand justification here—is not only unjustified but unjustifiable. Philosophical clarity, Wittgensteinians will argue, shows such argumentation is at best mistaken. If Wittgenstein and Wittgensteinians such as Norman Malcolm, D. Z. Phillips, Rush Rhees, Peter Winch, Stanley Cavell, and James Conant and neopragmatists such as Hilary Putnam and Richard Rorty are right about the incoherence of metaphysics and foundational epistemology, then the rationalistic arguments of the philosophy of religion or natural theology or atheology cannot get off the ground. Then isn't the conclusion we should come to about religion such a Wittgensteinian one? Though this, of course, does not mean that we ourselves should become religious, but that we should desist from making philosophical claims about religious belief resting on a mistake. That is itself, they would argue, a mistake—a very big philosophical mistake. We might continue perfectly appropriately, if we are, to remain atheists. But we should not engage in atheology—philosophical arguments for atheism. Philosophy has nothing to say here either for or against religious belief. Isn't this the conclusion we should be drawn to?

2. Perhaps what has been said above should be sufficient to put such matters to rest, to lead us, if we would be reasonable, to react and view things in such a manner. Still such an equilibrium is seldom the case in philosophy over something so fundamental. So let us look at things from another angle. Malcolm, correctly catching something that Wittgenstein stresses, remarks that what for Wittgenstein is "most fundamental in a religious life is not the affirming of creeds, nor even prayer and worship—but rather, doing *good deeds*—helping others in concrete ways, treating their needs as equal to one's own, opening one's heart to them, not being cold or contemptuous, but loving" (Malcolm 1994, 92). Surely someone with any religious sensitivity—or indeed with just plain human sensitivity—will feel the force of that. That said, Winch's cautionary remarks are very important here. Winch says that the link between faith and works "is by no means as straightforward as Malcolm's discussion may suggest" (Winch 1994, 121). There are people with just the doings and feelings described above—people having exactly those attitudes— who lack religious sensibility who, as Malcolm himself in his seventh chapter reminds us, "take a serious view of religion, but regard it as a harmful influence, an obstacle to the fullest and best development of humanity" (Winch 1994, 121). Are we, to return to something mentioned earlier, to turn them into religious believers—people with religious faith—by *stipulative redefinition*? Wittgenstein remarked to Drury that it was his belief "that only if you try to be helpful to other people will you in the end find your way to God" (Malcolm 1994, chapter 1). Winch tersely and correctly remarks,

> It is important because Wittgenstein did *not* say that being helpful to other people *is* finding one's way to God, nor that it is a *sufficient condition* of doing so. He said it is a *necessary condition* of doing so. One cannot live a godly life *without* "good works"; but all the same there is more to the godly life than that. (Winch 1994, 121)

Moreover, as Winch also stresses, we cannot, as Malcolm sometimes seems to think, understand the "works" Wittgenstein stresses—understand the role they play in the believer's life—independently of their connections "with a particular faith on the part of the doer" (Winch 1994, 124). The doing of good, the being loving and humble, are for the religious believer *internally* connected to the "use of the language of faith in the life of the believer" (Winch 1994, 124). This seems to me, but *perhaps* not to Winch, to imply that such ways of being cannot in the thought and actions of a believer be disconnected from certain doctrinal strands and the creedal expressions of a particular religion. But this at least seems to run against Wittgenstein's own setting of doctrines aside as not being what religion is or anything essential to religion.

It is not difficult to surmise how Wittgenstein, and Kierkegaard as well, would respond. "There you go again," they would no doubt snort, "with your stubborn and even arrogant intellectualism, turning religion into a *theory*—failing to see what is there before your eyes that gives religion its importance. It is not doctrines or creeds that count but commitment and concern turned into action on yourself, though at the same time with a certain inwardness, and *for* others. Religion is ultimate commitment and concern. Brush aside all this sterile intellectualism. Theorizing about religion is not the way to God: thinking of great intellectual mansions while you live in a little moral shack" (Kierkegaard's comment on Schelling and Hegel).

Theorizing about religion is, indeed, not the way to God, if there is a way to God. The way is in your action on yourself and for others, but, if it is done religiously, it is embedded in words integral to a form of life that would not be the form of life it is without the doctrines and the creeds. Religions are for the sake of life—for the very things Wittgenstein stresses—but genuine religious believers, immersed in those forms of life, see and feel their commitments and concerns and deeds in terms of these very forms containing, and inescapably, these doctrines and creeds. *They do not have religious feelings which swing loose from religious concepts.* Both their very understanding and deepest reactions are tied up (internally linked) with doctrines and creeds and the distinctive concepts that go with them. And their reactions and understanding here cannot be split apart (as if there were a "cognitive" and a "noncognitive" side to them). *There is no religious understanding without the reactions and no reactions which are intelligibly religious without that understanding.*

To try to reduce religion and religious belief to some basic deep commitment and a concern to be a decent human being, to really care about others and do good, even if we add—probably with very little understanding—"ultimate" to "commitment" and "concern," just takes what, as we have already observed, is a *necessary* condition for being genuinely religious (note the implicit *persuasive* definition here) and turns it into a *sufficient* condition. On such a view of things Marx, Engels, Luxembourg, Durkheim, Freud, Dewey, Weber, Gramsci all become religious. But that is a *reductio*.

3. Wittgenstein, under the influence of William James's *Varieties of Religious Experience*, came to recognize that the way in which people express their religious beliefs differs enormously (Winch 1994, 108). Even within a given confessional community there are "vastly diverse forms of religious sensibility. And these different forms of diversity criss-cross in bewilderingly complex ways" (Winch 1994, 109). Even if we avoid any attempt to so define "religion" such that it captures all and only the great

historic religions and those group activities and beliefs anthropologists firmly regard as religious activities of recognizable religions, e.g., the religion of the Dinka or the Neur, and concentrate only on those religions— Christianity and Judaism—in which Wittgenstein took the most interest, we still get very diverse forms of religious sensibility and conceptualization and interpretation of doctrine and even doctrine itself.

Wittgenstein saw life as a "gift" from God for which one should be grateful, but life, he firmly believed, was something that also imposes inescapable obligations. He also thought in his work and in his life he required help. Some "light" from above, as he put it. These attitudes, Winch observes, unlinked as they are with specific confessional commitments, are from the "point of a developed theological doctrine" inchoate (Winch 1994, 109). But this, as Winch is perfectly aware, would not have bothered Wittgenstein one bit. He set himself, as we have seen, against theological and religious *doctrine*. More worrisomely, from Wittgenstein's point of view, there are considering the above attitudes—the above expressions of religious sensibility—some serious and reflective people whose very seriousness manifests itself in opposition to such attitudes (Winch 1994, 110). Some people will have an attitude that accepts "one's fate as 'the will of God,' an attitude which neither pretends to provide any explanation of that fate nor seeks to find one" (Winch 1994, 110). This attitude characteristically goes along "with an attitude of *gratitude* for life" (Winch 1994, 113). But Wittgenstein remarks, commenting on the expression of a very different attitude,

> We might speak of the *world* as malicious; we could easily imagine the Devil had created the world, or part of it. And it is *not* necessary to imagine the evil spirit intervening in particular situations; everything can happen "according to the laws of nature"; it is just the whole scheme of things will be aimed at evil from the very start. (Wittgenstein 1980, 71)

But the reference to the Devil here is, of course, no more an explanation— nor does Wittgenstein think that it is—than is a reference to the will of God. Either viewed as attempts at an explanation would be what Wittgenstein called an unnecessary and stupid anthropomorphism (Wittgenstein 1980, 71). But faced with all the horrible contingencies of life, the suffering, cruelty, indifference, pain, jealousy, hatred, failures of integrity, the breaking of trust—the whole bloody lot—some would speak of neither God nor the Devil or of the goodness, in spite of it all, of the world or of the malignancy or maliciousness of the world. Indeed they would think (*pace* William James) that such talk makes no sense. Some would say, as I would, " 'That's how things are' without reference to God or the Devil" (Winch 1994, 114). I think (to abandon for a moment a Wittgensteinian commitment to description and to speak normatively) this austere approach is a more proper frame of mind. We see that the plague is always with us, though sometimes rather dormant but at other times raging, and always as something that will return and we resolve to fight the plague. (Recall this was Albert Camus's figure of speech and his resolve as well.) But again this expression of attitude makes no more an attempt at an explanation than the expression of attitude that goes with speaking of God's will does or of the Devil having created the world does. Winch remarks perceptively that one "might want to single out the reference to the will of God as the only one that expresses a religious attitude; or one might want to single out 'that's just how things are' as the only attitude among these particular attitudes genuinely 'free of all superstition'" (Winch 1994, 114). Our language-games and forms of life, he observes, let us do either. And people, of course, do either. People, including reflective people of integrity, often differ here. And, as Hilary Putnam stresses, this is something to take to heart (Putnam 1995, 27–56). Moreover, it is not at all evident, to put it minimally, that there would be anything even approaching a consensus about which attitudes are the more appropriate or which run the deepest. Indeed not a few will think there is no answer to such "questions" and indeed no genuine questions either. And others would think that, even if in some sense there were, it would be inappropriate to ask them.

"It's God's Will," "It's the work of the Devil," and "That's how things are" are all nonexplanatory and in some language-games are where not only explanation stops, but where, Wittgensteinians would have it, justification and the giving of reasons stops as well. I think myself "That's how things are" is by far the more adequate way of viewing things. It is cleaner with less mystification and comes closer to—or so I think—telling it like it is. However, it should be immediately skeptically queried: how can I consistently say anything even remotely within that ball park, given my pragmatist and Wittgensteinian perspectivism and contextualism with its rejection of the idea that there can be a one true description of the world and my arguments to the effect that it makes no sense to say that one vocabulary is closer to reality than another or that we can coherently speak of standing outside all our practices and assessing them or that there is some unifying comprehensive practice that, like the Absolute, encompasses everything? (Putnam 1992, 80–107). I could say that for certain purposes "That's how things are" is the more adequate response and for other purposes the other ways are better, but I could not consistently, it is natural to respond, flat out say "That's how things are" is the more adequate conception. I could not say this because some noncontextualist conception of "That is how things are" is unintelligible. And, even more plainly and less controversially, I cannot even consistently say that that is so because it comes closer to telling things like they are and is less mysti-ficatory and obfuscating. There is no way things are *überhaupt* or even if there is, even if such talk somehow makes sense, we have no way of knowing or even plausibly conjecturing when this is so. So we are back with my pragmatic contextualism and how Wittgenstein sees things.

I think I can consistently have my pragmatist perspectivism *and* my claim about the greater adequacy of what I call my more austere "That's how things are" way of viewing things. I will now argue that this is so: that it is not a case of having my cake and eating it too. We have genuine descriptions and explanatory-practices which are nonconflicting alterna-tives to each other. For example, the giving of a physiological description of bodily movements or a description in terms of actions and intentions. Or, to take another, the giving of a common sense description of tables, bits of mud, water flowing, the moon being pink on a given night, in con-trast to giving a scientific physical description where we will say different things about solidity, color, and the like. These are alternative descriptive and explanatory-practices utilized for different purposes. But none of these descriptions are "closer to reality" or more adequate *sans phrase* than any other. We can only say that for different purposes one is more adequate than another; not that one is a more adequate or a better telling it like it is than another *period*. There the story about my perspectivism and contextualism is perfectly in place. It is also the account that Richard Rorty and Hilary Putnam would give of things.

To say (1) "That's God's will," (2) "That's the Devil's work," (3) "That's how things are" do we not also have, in a way similar to describing things in terms of bodily movements and describing things in terms of human actions, different perspectives answering to different interests with none of them being in some general, "perspective neutral" sense, more adequate? We can and should retort by remarking that with "That's God's will" or "That's the Devil's work" we have *metaphysical* utterances penetrating into our common life. They are metaphysical conceptions. And they, being meta-physical conceptions, are nonsensical, as Wittgenstein, and both Malcolm and Winch following him, contend, and, as we neopragmatists do as well. They are, when expressed, utterances which, in being metaphysical utter-ances, are incoherent, yielding pseudodescriptions and pseudoperspectives from which no intelligible descriptions, interpretations, or explanations could flow. Premises (1) and (2) but not (3) yield nonsense, but not "intelli-gible nonsense" somehow conveying "cognitive depth" as traditionalist interpretations of the *Tractatus* claim Wittgenstein obliquely hints at. If Wittgenstein, the Wittgensteinians, and the neopragmatists are right in seeing metaphysical claims as houses of cards that require philosophical therapy to break their spell, we do not have three alternative perspectives here but only one (a) in effect summarizing a bunch of empirical observations and more or less concrete moral observations and (b) making a morally freighted generalization about them and two expressions of metaphysical fantasies that have crept into the language-games of *some* people. These metaphysical fantasies are, as Wittgenstein puts it in other contexts, wheels that turn no machinery, conceptions that do no work in these practices, and the people who use such phrases are only under the illusion that they have some understanding of what they are saying and that these metaphysical conceptions are functioning parts of our social practices with their embedded language-games. There are no metaphysical forms of life. (If it is replied they do rhetorical work this is in effect to concede the point.) And there are no metaphysical language-games, rule-governed social practices. The above cases are not like saying that we use physiological descriptions for certain purposes and action-intention descriptions for other purposes and that both can be perfectly in place for their own purposes but no one is just telling it the way things are. The three allegedly alternative characterizations under discussion consist in one actual characterization and two pseudocharacterizations and, of course, if this is so, we can, and should, say the one genuine one is more adequate. But that is not at all to say that it gestures at "the one true description of the world." There is no such thing.

Some (including Wittgenstein) might deny that "It's God's will" or "It's the work of the Devil" are metaphysical utterances. And if "God" and "the Devil" are taken to denote Zeus-like empirical entities then these utterances are not metaphysical. They are implicit, very vague empirical hypotheses. They are just crude, plainly false empirical propositions plainly disconfirmed. *Such* religious beliefs are superstitions and Wittgenstein was keenly aware of that and rejected *such* religious beliefs and such a way of looking at religion with disdain. But it is very unlikely that now—or even for a long time—many Christians, Jews, or Moslems so superstitiously conceive of God and the Devil. Indeed by now most of them do not. And where they do, Wittgenstein would have no sympathy at all with that. Where, alternatively, "God" is construed as an infinite individual transcendent to the universe, we plainly do have a metaphysical claim—and a very esoteric one at that—and as such it is held to be nonsensical not just by positivists but by Wittgensteinians and neopragmatists such as Putnam, Rorty, and myself as well (Nielsen 1982, 1985, 1989a). If to that it is said that is not how to construe "God" either, then it is difficult to know, unless we want to go back to the crude anthropomorphic construal or to a purely symbolic construal, how we are in some nonmetaphysical way to construe "God." Just what is this non-Zeus like, nonpurely symbolic, nonmetaphysical construal of "God"? Do we really have any understanding of what we are talking about here?

If instead it is said, "That's how things are" is itself a metaphysical statement this should be denied for it functions as a summarizing, somewhat moralizingly emotive, but all the same empirical, proposition standing in for (a) a lot more particular propositions such as people suffer, the wicked often flourish, starvation and malnutrition are pervasive, droughts and devastating earthquakes occur, people are struck down in their prime, alienation is pervasive, tyranny often goes unchecked, and the like and (b) the comment that this goes on at all times and in all places without much in the way of abatement. This—(b) in particular—*may* be an exaggeration, but that surely does not make it a metaphysical statement.

Suppose someone retorts that Jews and Christians do not have to treat "That's God's will" or "That's the Devil's work" in either the superstitious or the metaphysical way I attributed to them. Keep in mind, the response goes, that *practice* gives words their sense. Some mathematicians, when they speak of numbers, say they are abstract entities: real things but abstract things. And with this they become entangled in metaphysics. Indeed we have the shadow of Plato here. But they could, and most do, legitimately refuse to *so* theorize and just go on proving theorems, setting up axiomatic systems, or, as applied mathematicians, grinding out calculations for particular purposes and the like. Why cannot Jews, Christians, and Moslems do a similar thing? Why could they not, and indeed why should they not, just stick with their practices in saying and thinking the things about God that their language-games allow them to say? They need no more theorize *about* God than mathematicians *need* theorize *about* numbers. Indeed it is not only that they *need* not theorize, Wittgenstein and Kierkegaard would insist, but that they *should* not theorize. That is destructive of faith. It is my *intellectualism* again—and here I am a token of a familiar type—that is leading me down the garden path, that is making me mistakenly think that practices which actually are not unreasonable—indeed are compelling for the people who engage in them—are unreasonable and irrational.

It should be responded in turn that there are at least two disanalogies between the language-games of mathematics and the language-games of religion. First we know, without any metamathematics, without any theory of numbers, at least if we are mathematicians, how to establish truth-claims, or at least assertability-claims, in mathematics. Mathematics is a theory-structured practice and mathematicians in doing mathematics cannot but use theory and in that way theorize. We need not theorize *about* mathematics, but we, not infrequently, theorize, often to good effect, *with* it. Secondly, we have in mathematics some ability to say what we are talking about. We often talk nonsense in talking *about* mathematics but not always. But actual mathematical talk is another matter. We have no such ability with our talk of God, the Devil, or the soul. It is not just the metatalk that is troubling.[8]

Suppose, it is in turn responded, that this only shows some of the differences between the language-games of mathematics and those of religion. We understand, if we are religious, that God is a *mystery* and—or so Wittgensteinians have it—that the very demand to be able to warrant our religious claims shows that we, in making that demand, do not understand them or understand what *faith* requires, including what it is to believe in God. Anything that we could warrant—establish the truth of—wouldn't be a genuine religious claim. To make such a rationalistic demand shows, Wittgenstein *et al.* would have it, that we do not understand religious language-games and that we are not operating from inside them. It would be like in logic to demand that an inductive argument be deductively valid. It would show that we understand neither what induction is nor what deduction is. We are just senselessly asking for induction to be deduction.

If this is what religious language-games are like, would it *not* be better *not* to engage in them? We do not know what counts for truth or falsity or in being reasonable or unreasonable here; indeed we do not even understand what we are saying. We are just in a fog. Nonsense engulfs us. Isn't talk of mystery just a high-fallutin' way of saying that? Once we see this clearly should we not desist—close up shop, so to say? Moreover, it is not just that we do not understand, we are forced, if we would play that language-game, to say things that we, if we reflect a bit, would not wish to say. Consider again Wittgenstein's remark in *Culture and Value* that we "might speak of the world as malicious" or "easily imagine the Devil created the world, or part of it" or that "the whole scheme of things will be aimed at evil from the very start." We not only *cannot (pace* Wittgenstein) easily imagine these things; we do not understand these utterances. We only, if we do not think, have the illusion of understanding them by extension from some familiar utterances we do understand. We understand what it is for a person to be malicious or an action or attitude to be malicious. We have truth-conditions or assertability-conditions for such claims. But for the *world* to be malicious? We can't intelligibly impute *intentions* to the world. That makes no sense at all. Speaking of the world being malicious is but a misleading way of making the perfectly secular utterance "Many people are malicious and this maliciousness is pervasive in our lives." Similarly while we understand "Sven created a new recipe" or "Jane created a more efficient electric car," we do not understand "The Devil created the world" or, for that matter, "God created the world." The former two sentences have truth-conditions or assertability-conditions. The latter two do not. Similarly language has gone on a holiday with "The whole scheme of things will be aimed at evil from the very start." Aside from not understanding what "the very start" comes to here, more importantly, we are, with such a remark, again imputing intentions and aims to what it makes no sense to say has or can have intentions or aims. To say Shakespeare's Richard III aimed at evil or the Nazi regime or the Reagan regime aimed at evil makes sense, but the whole scheme of things, no more than the world, cannot be intelligibly said to *aim* at things either for good or for evil. A scheme of things or a world cannot have aims, form intentions, have desires, goals, and the like. There is and can be no such teleology of nature. There is no such functional language-game. Language is idle here. In support of this, we have supplied what Wittgenstein has called grammatical remarks. But would not Wittgenstein, of all people, perfectly well realize that? That is the way he repeatedly reasons. And the grammatical remarks I have assembled above seem to be plainly so. It looks like Wittgenstein, or anyone who tries to so reason, is in a double bind.

Of course Wittgenstein is right, as he says in the sentence following the one quoted above, that "things break, slide about, cause every imaginable mischief." But that, minimally hyperbolic though it is, is a purely secular utterance. We have not even the hint of a *religious* language-game here. *If* that is what we "*really* are saying in saying that the whole scheme of things will be aimed at evil," we have turned it, by stipulative redefinition, into an utterly secular platitude without a whiff of religion or religious sensibility. Where we understand what we are saying we do not have a religious language-game at all; where we have one we do not—the superstitious anthropomorphic ones aside—understand what is said and thus cannot understand what it is for something to be, for example, God's will and thus we cannot do God's will or fail to do God's will.

Suppose someone says that that is a philosopher's hat trick. People do God's will. People, following God's will, make pilgrimages to Lourdes, go to confession, give up philosophy, lead a life of celibacy, go to the Congo or Haiti to alleviate suffering, etc., etc. But to this, it in turn can be responded, that this—this doing of God's will—is but to do things that some people take to be obligatory, the right thing to do, desirable to do, and the like and that some of them associate these moral commitments with their *avowals* that that is doing God's will without understanding what God is or what his will is or how one could ascertain what it is to do God's will. It is just a formula they recite with, if they are genuinely theistically religious, great conviction and sometimes with intensity of feeling. But that does not, and cannot, turn it into sense, into an intelligible utterance.

Your intellectualism continues to get in the way, some will respond or at least think. The aim in speaking of religion, as Kierkegaard and Wittgenstein do, is to expose the roots of the intellectual's compulsion in approaching religion "always to reflect upon the task of living (a certain sort of life) rather than to attend to the task itself" (Conant 1993, 207). The thing to do is to go to church, to pray, to confess, to sing songs in praise of God, to alter your life by becoming more open and loving, to fight against your arrogance and pride, and above all help your fellow humans by engaging with them in their life struggles. Don't think, act! Thinking will never lead you to faith. To think that it can is a grand illusion of much of the philosophy of religion business. Philosophy will not lead us to God or help us in our religious endeavors or even our religious understanding.

There is, both Wittgenstein and Kierkegaard have it, no summing "up the sense of a religion in philosophical or theological doctrines" (Winch 1994, 128). Kierkegaard stressed that religious belief stands at a very great distance from philosophical clarity. Such clarity is of no avail in coming to a religious life or, for that matter, in turning away from it and combating it. Wittgenstein, as we have seen, had scant use for religious doctrine, theology, or the philosophy of religion. He took it that one of the things that Christianity teaches us is that *even sound* doctrines are useless. The thing is to change your life or the direction of your life. Even achieving wisdom, if indeed we could do this, is of little value. Wisdom is cold and does not connect to your passions, does not grip your life, as religion does by taking hold of you and turning your life around (Wittgenstein 1990, 53). Wittgenstein, in a deeply anti-intellectualistic way, wrote, as we have already noted, that "Wisdom is cold and to that extent stupid. (Faith, on the other hand, is a passion.) It might also be said: Wisdom merely *conceals* life from you. Wisdom is like grey ash, covering up the glowing embers" (Wittgenstein 1990, 56). Religious faith is a passion yielding a trust that grips your life and turns it around. Trying to be intellectual about religion—trying to rationalize religion—will never get you anywhere. People who are gripped by religious forms of life will not try to show how the religious life is reasonable, though they need not say it is unreasonable either. They will see all argument and attempts at reasoning here either on the part of the believer or the skeptic as utterly pointless.

V

Is this the end of the line? Should we, vis-à-vis religion, take some such anti-intellectualist stance and claim that philosophical thinking, or any kind of thinking, only stands in the way of coming to grips with religion whether by way of faith or by rejection of religious faith? Perhaps one way—a somewhat indirect way—of coming to grips with things here is to contrast Pascal, and the world he lived in, with that of Kierkegaard or Wittgenstein and the worlds they lived in. Pascal was as much of a fideist as Kierkegaard or Wittgenstein, though I now think it is better to say Wittgenstein was a passionate friend of fideism rather than a fideist. Pascal says very much what we have noted Wittgenstein and Kierkegaard saying above about religion and passion and about doing rather than thinking and about the role of faith. Yet for Pascal, in a way that is at a very great distance from both Kierkegaard and Wittgenstein, there "was only one true religion, Christianity; only one true form of Christianity, Catholicism; only one true expression of Catholicism, Port Royal" (Winch 1994, 108). Kierkegaard was a Protestant, but, unlike Calvin and Luther who believed Protestant versions of what Pascal believed, Kierkegaard would never for a moment have believed anything like that. The confessional group that is Lutheranism could not have had such a standing for him. Indeed he thought little of the possibility of being a Christian in Danish Christendom. The times, we should note, they are a-changing. Kierkegaard's cultural life, and even more so Wittgenstein's, is very different than Pascal's. And our cultural conditions are not Wittgenstein's. Today someone with deep religious sensibilities and something like a university education could not, without self-deception and irrationality, respond as Pascal did, though the latter's religious sensibilities are as deep as they go and he certainly had a fine education and a keen intelligence. To respond in a manner similar to Pascal's would now be perceived as fanaticism, by intellectuals, and indeed be, fanaticism or at least blind dogmatism. Wittgenstein was a person passionate about religion and while he did not regard himself as a religious person, he had the deeply embedded "ultimate" concerns and sensibilities of an intensely religious person. In that way he was a passionately religious person, if anyone ever was, but knowing what he does about religion, about the great diversity of religious responses, including in that diversity, deep religious responses and with them deep antireligious *religious* responses, he could never attach his faith—his, if you will, "infinite passion"—to any doctrine in the way that Pascal quite naturally did and as Luther and Calvin did. What was natural for Pascal's time and for Luther's is quite unthinkable for Kierkegaard's and Wittgenstein's (or for that matter for William James's). And for us the demystification of the world has gone even further. To repeat, "the times they are a-changing."

As we have seen, Wittgenstein wanted to eject all doctrine from the religious life or at least to regard it as of no importance. He, brought up a Catholic as he was, tended to use the vocabulary of Catholic Christianity; but it was clear enough that he attached little importance to the particular words that were used or, to be more specific and accurate, to the particular *doctrinal* formulae. Words used in prayer, words used in hymns and in rituals were—in just the form they took—very important to him. But while remaining intense about religious commitment and ambivalent but intense about the Catholic faith, still, as he saw things, the doctrinal content of that faith was not, to understate it, very important. Indeed for faith to be genuinely faith, it must for the person *in* the faith (though not at every moment of his or her waking life) be a matter of intense passion.

But, as Wittgenstein saw it, the content of that faith could, all the same, be very diffuse. Religious responses and religious conceptualizing vary greatly even within particular religious groups—say, Anglicanism, Presbyterianism, Reformed Judaism, Catholicism, Lutheranism. And, as things go on—as we stumble into our Brave New World—the diversity, and our sense of it, increases.

Wittgenstein was neither a believer nor a secularist, but there can be, and are, atheistical friends of religion and, what is something very different, even people who are antireligious *religious* persons. We can be, as I think it is plain that Wittgenstein was, firm friends of fideism, believing that fideism is the only acceptable religious response, the only religious game in town, yet be quite unable and, perhaps even if able, unwilling to believe. Still, he was firmly convinced, if one is to be religious, one should be a fideist.[9] In this rather extended sense only was Wittgenstein a fideist. Here he differs from Kierkegaard and Pascal.

Atheists—or through and through secularizers if the word "atheist" puts you off—come in various shapes and colors (Nielsen 1996, 427–50, 509–56). I am thinking of such different people as d'Holbach, Hume, Feuerbach, Marx, Gramsci, Santayana, Russell, Weber, Freud, Dewey, and Rorty. Many atheists are passionately antagonistic to religion and could never be thought of as atheistical friends of religion. I am thinking classically of d'Holbach and Diderot and among contemporary philosophers of Paul Edwards and Antony Flew. They see religion as a tissue of metaphysical errors and superstitions that yield no sound arguments for the existence of God at all and as being utterly incapable of in any reasonable way meeting the problem of evil or making sense of miracles or immortality. They see it as a groundless and pointless bunch of beliefs and practices that do more harm than good. Christianity, Judaism, and Islam are irrational and immoral belief-systems and practices. Religion, they have it, just leads us down the garden path. For them it is little better than superstition and a superstition with largely evil results. Here the conflict with Wittgenstein or Wittgensteinians is (to understate it) in tone and over what belief in God comes to. Wittgensteinians could say to such an atheist that, as you conceive of God and religion, it consists principally in a crude form of metaphysics that we have been as concerned as you to reject. Indeed such religion is ridiculous and religiously offensive; it is a superstitious set of beliefs. But Wittgensteinians will insist that religion isn't that. Religiously sensitive people would not so conceive of it, though they also stress that *some* people who are "minimally religious" (what Wittgenstein and Kierkegaard would regard as not genuinely religious at all) and even some who vociferously claim to be religious are religious in this superstitious and Neanderthal way. Some Wittgensteinians believe that "religious Neanderthals" and the d'Holbachians complement each other, they take in, that is, each other's dirty linen.

Atheistical friends of religion will, however, agree with rationalistic atheists—the d'Holbach-Flew sort described above—that sometimes religion integrally involves such crude metaphysics and they will believe, as well, that even in its genuinely religiously nuanced forms religion will contain cosmological elements that indeed are in error. Indeed they may think for *Tractarian* reasons that they are cognitively unintelligible. But with Wittgenstein they will agree that the cosmological side is not what is important about religion or what gives religion life. What gives it life is pretty much what Wittgenstein says it is, namely that religion helps us face and accept our tangled lives. They remain atheists because, setting cosmological conceptions aside as (to be pleonastic) bad metaphysics, as Wittgenstein does, what is left, as they reflectively sense these things, is inwardness and a certain kind of morality rooted in passion and the practices which are constitutive of religion. That, they agree, is all fine, but its substance, they point out, is *utterly secular*. Religious symbolism, however humanly important, is just that—*symbolism*. The substance is just that broadly moral substance and indeed it, given the incoherence of metaphysical concepts and most particularly supernaturalistic ones, cannot be anything but that. But unlike rationalistic atheists (the d'Holbach-Flew sort) they think this particular moral substance—this sense of what our lives and our values should be—is terribly important. Wittgenstein, and Kierkegaard as well, articulate for us, these atheistical friends of religion believe, a deep and compelling sense of what a really human life should be. So here we have what I have called atheistical friends of religion and *some* of them are even atheistic friends of fideism. George Santayana is a good example of such an atheist friend of religion.

What of what I have, not unparadoxically, called antireligious *religious* persons? Where do they stand in such a conversation? Like the atheistical friends of religion, they agree that Wittgenstein and Wittgensteinians with finely attuned religious sensitivity capture something that is deeply important in human life concerning which rationalistic atheists have a tin ear. This religious sensibility, they stress, is something that should not be lost. They see it in its strongest forms as a deep, humanly important response to life. Because of this stress, I have called them antireligious *religious* persons. Perhaps, less provocatively, they should be called instead intense religiously sensitive people—people such as Ludwig Feuerbach or George Elliot—but not literally religious persons, for, though they are sensitively attuned to religion, they passionately combat and reject religion. In this way they are not like the atheist friends of religion. (Contrast here Feuerbach and Santayana.) They believe that such finely tuned religious sensibilities should not be lost, while still believing that religious belief and practice should be firmly rejected, only kept in mind for what these beliefs and practices have been for some people—and not just for what they have done to people—but still not to be lived, taken to be part of the repertoire of our affective and cognitive existence. The doctrines, many of the particular religious moral beliefs, religious stances, many of the attitudes toward life of religious persons and the institutional structures of religions should, they believe, drift, but not without continued remembrance, into obsolescence. In that they importantly differ from atheistic friends of religion. They actively—though, of course, without force—want to see Christianity, Judaism, Islam, Hinduism, and the like come to an end (quietly fade away) and a genuinely secular age come into being. But they also differ from such genial and bemused dismissers of religion as Bertrand Russell and W. V. Quine who could hardly be bothered to think very much about it. (When Russell, for example, did think a bit about it he stayed very much on the surface.) Feuerbach and Nietzsche, by contrast, passionately reject it, and not *just* because of its metaphysical nonsense, but for the human harm—or what they take to be the human harm—religion does and not just, as it were accidentally, but just in being what it is. Contemporary antireligious *religious* people (me, for example), if they were to study Wittgenstein, would recognize insights in Wittgenstein's understanding of what morality demands of people, but they (we) also see it as one-sided, and, if stressed, just as Wittgenstein stresses it, it does not yield the fullest kind of human flourishing of which we human beings are capable. Such a conception of the moral life feeds too much on a one-sided diet.

Such matters need long pondering and careful dialectical examination and I am not confident that there are the resources within Wittgenstein's conception of what philosophy sensibly can be to come to grips with such issues. (But *perhaps* we deceive ourselves in thinking there is any intellectually oriented way of coming to grips with them?) Remember that for him good philosophical work, work with a therapeutic intent, is an activity and not an articulation of a theory of any kind or the taking of any kind of moral or otherwise normative position or stance. He is bent solely on elucidation, though elucidation for a particular purpose. And this comes to giving a perspicuous representation through clear description—leaving all explanation, normative *theorizing* and criticism aside—of those stretches of language (which also, remember, are parts of our forms of life) that we get confused about when we think about them. Though we typically do not see that, it is so being entangled in our language that generates the urge to do philosophy in the bad metaphysical sense that Wittgenstein would theraphize away. However, remember that for him it is a therapy which, as he sees it, will never end and will yield (and then only sometimes) only small temporary victories where we in some particular areas come, perhaps, only for a time, to command a clear or a clearer view (though always for a particular purpose) of the workings of our language and thus of the forms of our life. Though we should also recognize that Wittgenstein thought of his elucidations as having, in a very broad sense of "ethical," an ethical point. But, be this as it may, this clear or clearer view is given by attentive description, a description which shows that everything is there before us, that nothing is hidden. There is, that is, nothing somehow revealing fleetingly in its hiddenness some essence or fundamental underlying structure there to be unearthed or something deep and unstateable that cannot be said, not even indirectly, but can only be shown to us as some unsayable deep something, some "ineffable truth" (Malcolm 1986). There is nothing like this and there is no logical form of the world or of language or of thought. There are rather our practices there plainly to be seen, if only we will look, and, if we become perplexed about them, to be clearly described. What Wittgenstein calls for is description, though (*pace* Strawson), always for therapeutic purposes and not for theory-construction or for criticism. It is not even to be systematic description for its own sake. It is this that has been taken to be Wittgenstein's *quietism* or *neutralism*. But this—or so it at least seems—leaves us without the resources to come to grips with the issues mentioned in the previous paragraph.

There *may* be something more here that can be said, and of a *philosophical* sort, something that Wittgenstein's very way of construing philosophy *may* block. It will perhaps surface if we contrast Wittgenstein's way of construing philosophy with Rorty's or with a Deweyian pragmatism. Consider Rorty's remarks concerning the distinction he draws between *Philosophy* and *philosophy* (Rorty 1982, xiii–xlvii). Wittgenstein's conception of philosophy, as therapeutic conceptual elucidation, should be located *as part of, but not the whole of*, what Rorty calls *philosophy*. *Philosophy*, by contrast, has been a central part of the tradition from Plato and Aristotle down to Edmund Husserl and Brand Blanshard.[10] This tradition of *Philosophy* has many variants. But they all claim to yield, and as part of a *discipline*, distinctive philosophical knowledge: some a priori knowledge that the *Philosopher* can grasp, utilizing some specialized philosophical technique, that cannot be gained from common sense reflection and inquiry or from empirical inquiry. *Philosophy* is the attempt either in the grand metaphysical tradition or in the tradition of foundationalist epistemology or in the philosophy of logic or language to construct a systematic a priori theory which, as part of an *autonomous* discipline, would in one way or another found or ground the various forms of life and critique or at least clarify our ordinary and scientific beliefs, as well as our nonordinary religious, moral, and aesthetic beliefs and responses, showing what their real nature and import is. Wittgenstein and Wittgensteinians as well as neopragmatists such as Putnam, Rorty, and myself, take *Philosophy*, in all of its various forms, to be houses of cards: as something, root and branch to be exposed as incoherent. It takes in some difficult cases the genius of Wittgenstein's probing to enable us to see how some bit of disguised nonsense is really plain nonsense and nothing more (Conant 1989). The very idea of having any such Philosophical knowledge or understanding makes no sense. We have only the illusion of understanding here and there is nothing with such Philosophy that we could build on to make sense of our lives or to understand our world more adequately. This is common ground between Wittgensteinians and neopragmatists including, of course, someone like Putnam, who seems to be a Wittgensteinian pragmatist (Putnam 1995, 27–56).[11]

However, Rorty argues, there is a contrasting activity he calls philosophy which, unlike Philosophy, he takes to be unproblematical. Wittgensteinian therapeutics is a part of this, but by no means the whole of it. I follow Rorty here in articulating such an activity, though I am less confident than he is that it is so entirely unproblematical (Williams 1986, 21–24). But surely, if not securely unproblematical, it is not nearly as problematical as Philosophy is. Rorty, following Wilfrid Sellars, construes philosophy to be the attempt to see how things, in the broadest sense of the term, hang together in the broadest sense of the term. Doing philosophy in this sense requires no specialized knowledge (no expertise in metaphysics, epistemology, logic, semantics, linguistics, or anything of the sort) and it is not something that has a disciplinary matrix and it is as old as the hills: people at all times and places have engaged in it. No matter what happens to Philosophy, philosophy, like Old Man River, keeps right on rolling along, as an attempt, common to critical intellectuals—but not limited to them—to see how things hang together.[12] Giving up any claim to Philosophical knowledge or expertise, philosophers are general all-purpose critical intellectuals (among other things critics of society) including, as I put it in my *Naturalism without Foundations*, "in their ranks all sorts of scientists (from both the natural and human sciences), historians, scholars in cultural studies and religious studies, former Philosophers (reformed into philosophers), novelists, poets, dramatists, literary critics, literary theorists, legal theorists, and the like" (Nielsen 1996, 540). Anyone can join in; it is not a prerogative of the "experts," though no doubt, as an utterly contingent matter, some people, given what they have learned, have come in how they have lived their lives—including what they have been able to do with their leisure—to be a little better at forging a coherent conception of how things hang together and of understanding how they are to live their lives than others. (They may, of course, be better at *understanding* it while still being hopelessly inept at living it, a point not lost on Kierkegaard.) But there is here, as elsewhere, no a priori knowledge gained from the Philosophical tradition, no "esoteric knowledge" or any kind of any privileged knowledge and there are no overall experts in seeing how things hang together. Foundationalist epistemologists as cultural overseers are out of business. In that important way there has been a demise of Philosophy (Nielsen 1991, 1995).

I added the following in *Naturalism without Foundations*:

> So construed *p*hilosophy is not an a priori purely conceptual investigation. It will be broadly empirical and historicist and rooted in a consideration of the problems of the epoch in which the *p*hilosopher *p*hilosophizes. In doing *p*hilosophy, such all-purpose critical intellectuals (*p*hilosophers), coming from all over the place, with a heterogeneous bunch of skills, notions, and sensibilities, will be starting with their traditions, their own preconceptions, and their considered convictions. Some of them will, as well, sometimes use, in a pragmatic manner, certain Philosophical notions or conceptual analyses, where *p*hilosophy, now as conceptual elucidation, functions purely as an elucidatory second-order discourse. But these things will be used with caution by the *p*hilosopher and only where they have a chance of working. And in being so used pragmatically, they will not be taken as contributing to or as presupposing a foundational theory or any kind of a priori theory or perhaps any theory at all. They will just be something which such *p*hilosophers (critical intellectuals) use in their attempts to see how things hang together and in looking with a critical eye for a conception of how things might better hang together. These *p*hilosophers—these critical intellectuals—will try to see how things hang together and they will, in doing so, and quite properly, ask critical questions concerning religion or any other practice, including *p*hilosophy itself. (That is why we have such a thing as metaphilosophy.) They will most particularly ask questions about how these beliefs fit together with our other beliefs, if indeed they do. Repairing the ship at sea, including sometimes throwing overboard some rotten planks, they will try for a time, but only for a time, and thoroughly fallibilistically, to see how things hang together. In doing so, the *p*hilosopher will not infrequently reject certain beliefs and conceptions—and indeed sometimes, though rarely, very fundamental ones—as not being conducive to our being able to forge a coherent picture of how things hang together and thus to a gaining of a better understanding of our lives and perhaps, as well, to a coming to understand a little more adequately how we might best live our lives both together and as individuals.

What I characterized in section III.5 of this chapter, with my use of wide reflective equilibrium, was just such an attempt to articulate how to do that and something of a conception of what this would come to. It was not an attempt to articulate a foundational theory or indeed any kind of theory. And it most certainly was not an attempt to articulate an autonomous Philosophical theory. But it was an attempt to do *p*hilosophy. It pragmatically used a few Philosophical notions coming principally from positivist and other analytical traditions, but, in my utilization, they were not systematically tied to those traditions or to any Philosophical view. Like any good carpenter, pragmatists use whatever tools and materials that come in handy for the problem at hand. There is, in such work, a Deweyan pragmatist philosophy and a roughly Wittgenstein therapeutic metaphilosophy. The latter has the purely negative task of making the world safe from Philosophy. It is in this contextualist way in which we, without the "aid" of some superdiscipline, can critically appraise our practices, including sometimes showing that certain ones should be put out to pasture as in the past we put out to pasture our astrological and magical practices. (Nielsen 1996, 540–41)

I think Wittgenstein would resist much of this. He would be skeptical that with or without Philosophy we can get very far with seeing how things hang together. I think *au contraire* that this is only true if we think, as I guess Wittgenstein supposes, that we would only be satisfied if we got something that was "completely clear" and "completely certain" and this, of course, as he has powerfully contended, is impossible. We, as the *Philosophical Investigations* well argues, do not even have any criterion for, or conception of, what is to count as "complete clarity." He seems to think in going on this quest for being able to understand how things hang together, we could not help but be driven into being Philosophers and thus be taken down the garden path. People with the Philosophical itch— and there will always be such people—will never stop being compelled to do Philosophy and/or to exorcise such ghosts. *Perhaps* this is one with a common religious impulse? Be that as it may, there will never (*pace* Habermas) be, if Wittgenstein is near to the mark, a post-Philosophical age. But we—that is "we" as individuals—need not be such Don Quixotes. Sometimes the therapy has worked. Moreover, there have been all kinds of attempts at coherence that make no such extravagant claims. Dewey's is a prominent one. And philosophers and other intellectuals can sometimes profit from Wittgensteinians' therapeutic accounts and no longer be a prey to such conceptual obsessions. Rorty is a very good example. Wittgensteinian therapy worked on him and, turning away from the obsessions of and about Philosophy, he seeks to articulate a more adequate conception of life and of society, using wide reflective equilibrium (Rorty 1991, 175–96). By looking carefully and reflectively at our practices, seeing how they fit together, sometimes seeking to forge a better fit, sensing the historicity of things and the contingency of our various fittings, but also seeing that some of them answer better to our needs (including, of course, our intellectual needs) than others, we will—particularly if we sense the impossibility of meeting some of the more esoteric of them—gradually lose the need, in our attempts to see how things fit together, to have some metaphysical backing or irreducibly metaphysical religious orientation—some grounding of our practices and language-games. Wittgensteinian therapy, on a metalevel can, and should, go hand in glove with a Deweyan-Rawlsian broadly historicist and contextualist forging of a wide and general reflective equilibrium.

We should also be more *holist* than Wittgenstein or most Wittgensteinians are prepared to be. We should not take distinctive language-games to be autonomous, yielding their own wholly distinctive criteria of what it makes sense to say, what is justified, what is acceptable, and the like. We need repeatedly to attend to how our various language-games and practices relate, criss-cross and effect, or would effect, each other, if we saw with any clarity how they are related. Though no doubt, without any clarifying articulation, these different practices just do affect each other. But with a clearer understanding of how they relate and affect or could affect each other, we may gain a more adequate understanding of how things hang together and of the import of it. This may not happen, but it is not impossible that it could and it is worth struggling to attain. Here there should be no *quietism*. Such a struggle is both reasonable and worth the candle.

If we look at our religious practices, including those containing rather well firmed-up secular knowledge claims, we can come to see without any theory at all that certain religious notions make such a bad fit with other things that are very pervasive in our culture and important to us, that, in coming to understand that, we will come to see that there is very little, if any, sense in these religious notions. With respect to that it is surely right to tell us not to be so sure of ourselves and to look again to see if we are being blind to a fit that is there before our eyes which we simply do not see (Rhees 1997). (Perhaps we are ideologically blinkered here?) Wittgenstein has given us reason to believe, over the language-games he agonizes over, how often this is the case. But it is also possible that there is no fit—just clashing irreconcilable beliefs (sometimes just attempts at belief) and conceptions—or that a better fit can be made of the various things we know, reasonably believe, and care about, by jettisoning religious beliefs and practices; setting them aside so that they, though no doubt this takes time, will no longer play a part in our thought and behavior and in our conception of how we should guide our lives. It may be the case that there is a severe strain and indeed even a clash between different elements in our forms of life and that the religious element will, if we really press things with integrity, be the odd man out. It may be that, in the attempt to overcome the tension by making our religious beliefs and conceptions fit with the rest of our beliefs and conceptions, we will have to resort to increasingly *ad hoc* assumptions or esoteric readings of our religious beliefs and conceptions. It seems to me that something like this is actually happening and indeed has been happening for some considerable time (Nielsen 1996, 79–155).

Holistic description here also can serve as criticism. Philosophy, little p *p*hilosophy, utilizing the method of wide reflective equilibrium, need not, and sometimes should not, leave everything as it is. A critical *p*hilosophy will utilize Wittgensteinian elucidation principally to break the picture that certain *P*hilosophical conceptions seek to impose on us, but it will also engage in critical assessments—engaging with our lives as well as just with our cogitations—that pass without metaphysical extravagance or any other kind of extravagance beyond Wittgensteinian philosophical *quietism* and *neutralism*. This is done without trying to have some "ultimate vocabulary" or some ultimate point of reference or to claim that there is one and only one true description capturing how the world just is anyway. Indeed such talk makes no more sense than William James's talk of an "ultimate datum."

Wittgenstein well shows us the incoherence of such conceptions. But we have seen how we can, and sometimes should, criticize practices, and not just stop with the reminder that this language-game is played. But our criticism will itself rest on other practices. There is no Archimedean point, *independent of all practices*, from which to criticize any of them. But from this—to make a good Peircean point—it does not follow that *any* practice is immune from or beyond criticism. We can't criticize them all *at once* or stand free of all of them and criticize them. But where there is a clash among the practices or the irritation of doubt is at work—real live Peircean doubt, not what Peirce well called Cartesian paper doubt—concerning any one, or of several, of our practices, criticism is possible and in order. So we can see how a pragmatist need not, and should not, acquiesce in *quietism* (philosophical or any other kind). And we can see also how we can be pragmatists and consistently say that the Christian faith or any other faith or any set of beliefs and responses embedded in practices can rest on a mistake or (*pace* Putnam) be in deep and massive error (Putnam 1995). And this holds true not only for religious forms of life, but for *any* practice or form of life. We start with practices and it is important to see that and how many of them are crucial for our understanding and our lives and are irreplaceable. There is no place else for us to be than to start with practices and to remain with practices. Moreover, *taking them together*, we are stuck with them. There is no perspective outside of or beyond our practices as a whole. There is, that is, no leaping out of our skins, but for any one or several or for particular clusters of practices, where for *specific reasons* we come to have trouble with some specific practice or specific cluster of practices, it or they can either be reformed (sometimes deeply reformed) or sometimes even set aside. There is, to repeat, no practice which is immune from criticism. And the same is true, at least in principle, of clusters of particular practices. So we can repeatedly, relevantly, and intelligently criticize our very practices and the beliefs and attitudes that are a part of them. This includes our faiths—that is, our trustings. It is just that (1) we cannot criticize *them all at once* or stand free of all of our practices and (2) that in criticizing a practice or a cluster of practices we must also be using practices. Thus we have Peircean *fallibilism* and Peircean critical commonsensism—something that was fully incorporated into the texture of Dewey's philosophical practice (Peirce 1935, 293–304, 354–67; Nielsen 1996, 295–328). With this, and without falling into Philosophy and the conceptual confusions Wittgenstein was concerned to dispel, we can do something critical concerning our forms of life. We can reasonably engage in an activity here for which Wittgenstein did not make space and indeed did not envisage.[13] With his feeling for a religious sense of life he would probably have thought it all *hubris*. But need it be?[14]

NOTES

1. Wittgenstein rejected the idea of "metaphilosophy" for he thought, and rightly so, so-called metaphilosophy was itself philosophy. What has come to be called "metaphilosophy" is indeed itself philosophy. It is (among other things) philosophical thinking about what we are doing, can intelligibly be doing, should be doing, and the point(s) of our doing it when we philosophize (Couture and Nielsen, 1993).

2. Andrew Lugg has remarked (*pace* Conant) that it is hard to avoid the impression in reading the *Tractatus* that Wittgenstein is putting forward views. Indeed, Lugg continues, he says as much in the so-called framing remarks. That impression is indeed hard to resist and hence the pervasiveness of the traditional interpretation. But this would saddle Wittgenstein with either or both an atomistic metaphysics and a doctrine of ineffability. The former would not sit well with his own conception of what he is doing and the latter is obscurantist. To make maximal sense of Wittgenstein it seems as if we are driven to something like the Conant/Diamond reading.

3. Andrew Lugg, who knows a lot more about the *Tractatus* than I do, says he would argue that what Conant says here has no basis in Wittgenstein's text. Even if that is so, it has a basis in Wittgenstein's "Lecture on Ethics" and has a considerable interest in its own right. Moreover, the "Lecture on Ethics" remains in the *Tractarian* spirit.

4. It is not that Wittgenstein came to have a new view about the kind of propositions logical and mathematical are. He never thought they described anything or were in anyway informative, but he came to have a new view about how they as nonrepresentational are to be understood. Again I am indebted to Andrew Lugg.

5. It might be argued that Malcolm's appeal to concepts as well as my own in the last few sentences is more Platonic than Wittgensteinian. But I do not reify or objectify the notion. I stick with *uses* of words, but I speak of concepts as a convenient way of noting I am, though I talk about the uses of words, not just talking about the uses of words in a *particular* language. Wittgenstein most of the time

wrote in German and he has been translated into French and English (among other languages). What he calls, rather eccentrically, "grammatical remarks" in the English translation carries over into the French and German texts. It is to make plain that "carrying over" that I speak of concepts.

6. I do not mean to suggest that religion or Judaism or Christianity are language-games. That is neither Wittgenstein's view nor my own. However, Judaism and Christianity contain language-games embedded in their practices and are not understandable without reference to them.

7. It could be said that Wittgenstein should be understood as only denying that it is possible to give reasonable *philosophical* criticisms or defenses of a form of life, but that he is not ruling out the possibility of giving any kind of reasonable criticism or defense of a form of life. But, given Wittgenstein's way of going about things, it is unclear what kind of criticism or defense of a form of life would be reasonable or that engaging in it would be a coherent activity. See more on this in Section V of this chapter.

8. One reader has remarked that the parallel with mathematics seems to beg the question. Many, he claims, of the same issues crop up in mathematics. And is it clear that all of the troubling issues can be shunted off to the metalevel? Why not say that metaphysics is intertwined in the practices of mathematics? Mathematics and religion run parallel here. I say in response that we can do mathematics, engage in the practices of mathematics, reason mathematically without ever raising the kinds of issues that Plato, Frege, Russell, and Quine raise. We cannot, however, escape metaphysics when it comes to religious belief and practice. It is right there in our very first-order religious beliefs and discourse.

9. What I have in mind here in saying he was a "friend of fideism" rather than a fideist is explained two paragraphs after the paragraph in which I signaled the occurrence of this note. I have in the past (Nielsen 1982, 43–64) thought of Wittgenstein as a fideist. My remarks in my present text indicate a correction. But Wittgensteinian fideism is alive and well and paradigmatically exemplified in the work of D. Z. Phillips (Phillips 1970; Nielsen 1982, 65–139).

10. Rorty would say "Rudolf Carnap and Hans Reichenbach" where I said "Husserl and Blanshard." Perhaps, as is frequently said, Carnap and Reichenbach were unwittingly entangled in metaphysics, that is, they did metaphysics in being antimetaphysical. Their critique of metaphysics, the claim goes, rests on metaphysical premises. But that that is so is not so evident as it is usually assumed. After all, they did not think there was any a priori *philosophical* knowledge. And it is not evident that they in effect assumed any.

11. Putnam's attitude toward metaphysics is somewhat different than Rorty's or my own. He agrees that metaphysical utterances are nonsensical, yet he thinks we need to acknowledge and keep firmly in mind the importance they have had in the history of human thought and that they continue to have in philosophical thought. I am less willing to genuflect before the tradition and would seek a more thorough transformation of philosophy (Nielsen 1991, 1995).

12. Remarking on the last few pages above, Lugg comments: "This seems to suggest there is one correct view and one right vocabulary, contrary to what you said earlier." *If* what I said in the past few pages, or anywhere else, commits me

to that I would immediately retract it and go back to the drawing board. Neither my antirepresentationalism, perspectivism, or fallibilism fits with this. And, though I deploy the method of wide-reflective equilibrium, I also argue that the very idea, *sans* particular context, of the widest or broadest equilibrium does not have a coherent sense. One reflective equilibrium can be wider or broader than another one at a given time and in a distinct context. At least in certain respects and in a determinate context one equilibrium might reasonably be thought to be the widest and broadest on offer, but we have no idea of what the widest possible reflective equilibrium would be. Wide reflective equilibrium is at home in assessing accounts of justice, morality, law, and science. I also use it to apply to worldviews. There it is *somewhat* problematical, but not, I believe, impossibly so. But it is certainly not unreasonable to be skeptical about it in that context. But even this application of wide reflective equilibrium does not commit me to the idea of the one true description of the world or to speaking of the way the world is in itself. What it does commit me to is to the possibility that we can gain a coherent account of how and why our practices just happen to hang together and to how it may be possible to forge an even more adequate way for them to hang together. But there is no reaching for the Absolute or for a conception of the way things just are anyway or of the one correct view or right vocabulary. Such notions are at best mythical.

13. Perhaps I am too harsh on Wittgenstein here. He did not engage in critical social inquiry into social and moral issues in anything like the way in which Dewey did and Rorty does. I do not think Wittgenstein would have thought that was a philosophical activity at all. But Lugg may be right in saying that Wittgenstein leaves plenty of room for critical discussion of our forms of life. He only rejects the idea that this can be done in some sort of an a priori philosophical way. But it would have been useful if he had done some of this nonphilosophical criticism or have shown how he thought we should go about doing it.

14. I want to thank Stanley French and Andrew Lugg for their perceptive criticisms of an earlier version of this chapter. Their comments helped me very much. Sometimes, in the face of their criticisms, I have remained stubborn and did not budge. I hope that is not pigheadedness on my part.

BIBLIOGRAPHY

Ambrose, Alice. 1950. "The Problem of Linguistic Inadequacy." In *Philosophical Analysis: A Collection of Essays,* edited by Max Black 15–37. Ithaca, N.Y.: Cornell University Press.

Braithwaite, Richard. 1975. "An Empiricist's View of the Nature of Religious Belief." In *The Logic of God,* edited by Malcolm L. Diamond and Thomas V. Litzenberg Jr. 127–47. Indianapolis, Ind.: Bobbs-Merrill.

Copleston, Frederick. 1956. *Contemporary Philosophy.* London: Burns and Oates.

Copleston, Frederick, and A. J. Ayer. 1957. "Logical Positivism—A Debate." In *A Modern Introduction to Philosophy,* 1st ed., edited by Paul Edwards, 586–618. Glencoe, Ill.: The Free Press.

Copleston, Frederick, and Bertrand Russell. 1975. "The Existence of God—A Debate." In *A Modern Introduction to Philosophy*, 3d ed., edited by Paul Edwards and Arthur Pap, 473–90. New York: The Free Press.

Conant, James. 1989. "Must We Show What We Cannot Say?" In *The Senses of Stanley Cavell*, edited by Richard Fleming and Michael Payne, 242–83. Bucknell, Pa.: Bucknell University Press.

———. 1990. "Throwing Away the Top of the Ladder." *Yale Review* 79, 328–64.

———. 1993. "Kierkegaard, Wittgenstein and Nonsense." In *Pursuits of Reason*, edited by T. Cohen et al., 195–224. Lubbock: Texas Tech University Press.

Couture, Jocelyne, and Nielsen, Kai, eds. 1993. *Mèta-philosophie/Reconstructing Philosophy*. Calgary, Alb.: University of Calgary Press.

Diamond, Cora. 1991. *The Realistic Spirit*. Cambridge, Mass.: MIT Press.

Hacker, P. M. S. 1999. "Wittgenstein." In *A Companion to the Philosophers*, edited by Robert L. Arrington, 538–50. Oxford: Blackwell, Ltd.

Hägerström, Axel. 1964. *Philosophy and Religion*. Translated by Robert T. Sandin. London: Allen & Unwin.

Hare, R. M. 1973. "The Simple Believer." In *Religion and Morality*, edited by Gene Outkan and John R. Reeder Jr., 393–427. New York: Anchor Press.

Hyman, John. 1997. "Wittgensteinianism." In *A Companion to Philosophy of Religion*, edited by Phillip L. Quinn and Charles Taliaferro, 150–57. Oxford: Blackwell Publishers.

James, William. 1935. *Varieties of Religious Experience*. New York: The Modern Library.

Luckhardt, C. G., ed. 1979. *Wittgenstein: Sources and Perspectives*. Ithaca, N.Y.: Cornell University Press.

Malcolm, Norman. 1960. "Anselm's Ontological Arguments." *Philosophical Review* 69: 378–90.

———. 1986. *Nothing Is Hidden: Wittgenstein's Criticism of His Early Thought*. Oxford: Blackwell.

———. 1994. *Wittgenstein: A Religious Point of View?* Ithaca, N.Y.: Cornell University Press.

Maslow, Alexander. 1961. *A Study in Wittgenstein's Tractatus*. Berkeley: University of California Press.

Nielsen, Kai. 1973. *Scepticism*. London: Macmillan.

———. 1982. *An Introduction to the Philosophy of Religion*. London: Macmillan.

———. 1985. *Philosophy and Atheism*. Amherst, N.Y.: Prometheus Books.

———. 1989a. *God, Scepticism and Modernity*. Ottawa: University of Ottawa Press.

———. 1989b. "The Faces of Immortality." In *Death and Afterlife*, edited by Stephen T. Davis, 1–30. London: Macmillan.

———. 1991. *After the Demise of the Tradition*. Boulder, Colo.: Westview Press.

———. 1995. *On Transforming Philosophy*. Boulder, Colo.: Westview Press.

———. 1996. *Naturalism without Foundations*. Amherst, N.Y.: Prometheus Books.

———. 1999. "Atheism without Anger or Tears." In *Walking the Tightrope of Faith*, edited by Hendrik Hart et al., 82–127. Amsterdam: Rodolpi.

Peirce, Charles. 1935. *Collected Papers, Vols. V and VI*, edited by Charles Hartshorne and Paul Weiss. Cambridge, Mass.: Harvard University Press.

Phillips, D. Z. 1970. *Faith and Philosophical Inquiry*. London: Routledge and Kegan Paul.

Putnam, Hilary. 1992. *Renewing Philosophy*. Cambridge, Mass.: Harvard University Press.

———. 1995. *Pragmatism*. Oxford: Blackwell.

———. 1997. "God and the Philosophers," *Midwest Studies in Philosophy* 21: 175–87.

Rhees, Rush, ed. 1984. *Ludwig Wittgenstein, Personal Recollections*. Oxford: Oxford University Press.

Rhees, Rush. 1997. *Rush Rhees on Religion and Philosophy*. Edited by D. Z. Phillips. Cambridge: Cambridge University Press.

Rorty, Richard. 1982. *Consequences of Pragmatism*. Minneapolis: University of Minnesota Press.

———. 1991. *Objectivity, Relativism, and Truth*. Cambridge: Cambridge University Press.

Williams, Michael. 1986. "The Elimination of Metaphysics." In *Fact, Science and Morality*, edited by Graham Macdonald and Crispin Wright, 9–25. Oxford: Blackwell.

Winch, Peter. 1994. "Discussion of Malcolm's Essay." In *Wittgenstein: A Religious Point of View?* 95–135. Ithaca, N.Y.: Cornell University Press.

Wittgenstein, Ludwig. 1921. *Tractatus Logico-Philosophicus*. Translated by D. F. Pears and B. F. McGuinness. London: Routledge and Kegan Paul.

———. 1953. *Philosophical Investigations*. Translated by G. E. M. Anscombe. Oxford: Blackwell.

———. 1961. *Notebooks, 1914–1916*. Translated by G. E. M. Anscombe. Oxford: Blackwell.

———. 1966. *Lectures and Conversations on Aesthetics, Psychology and Religious Belief*. Edited by Cyril Barrett. Oxford: Blackwell.

———. 1967. *Zettel*. Edited by G. E. M. Anscombe and G. H. von Wright. Translated by G. E. M. Anscombe. Oxford: Blackwell.

———. 1969. *On Certainty*. Translated by Denis Paul and G. E. M Anscombe. Oxford: Blackwell.

———. 1978. *Remarks on the Foundations of Mathematics*. Edited by G. E. M. Anscombe, et al. Cambridge, Mass.: MIT Press.

———. 1980. *Vermischte Bermerkungen*. Edited by G. H. von Wright. Translated by Peter Winch under the title *Culture and Value*. Oxford: Blackwell.

———. 1993. "A Lecture on Ethics." In *Ludwig Wittgenstein, Philosophical Occasions, 1912–1951*, edited by James Klagge and Alfred Nordman, 36–45. Indianapolis, Ind.: Hackett.

———. 1993. "Remarks on Frazer's Golden Bough." In *Ludwig Wittgenstein Philosophical Occasions, 1912–1951*, edited by James Klagge and Alfred Nordman, 119–55. Indianapolis, Ind.: Hackett.

1 O

THE HARD FACE OF RELATIVISM
Wittgenstein and Putnam
on Religion and Relativism

I

For Hilary Putnam the project of an absolute conception of the world, the project of describing "the things in themselves" and of dividing our common world into what is "really there" and what is "only a projection" have all collapsed (Putnam 1994). What, if anything, does this portend for what philosophy should say about religion? Putnam, in a good pragmatist spirit, to obliquely come at this question, wants to "point the way toward and exemplify the possibility of philosophical reflection on our lives and language that is neither frivolously skeptical nor absurdly metaphysical" (Putnam 1992, 141; Putnam 1997). He wants to engage in "serious and fundamentally honest reflection" on the deepest problems of human life. He starts, understandably enough, by talking about religion, and he takes Ludwig Wittgenstein's *Lectures and Conversations on Aesthetics, Psychology and Religious Belief* (lectures given in 1938) as a text to examine for its own sake as a powerful example of such probing and, as well, as a springboard for his own wrestling with the problems of human life. We do not have the full text of these lectures of Wittgenstein's, but rather extensive notes taken by one of the students present at the lectures (Putnam 1992, 142). That notwithstanding, Putnam takes them as important texts in an attempt to think coherently about religious language and religious belief and to gain an understanding of what Wittgenstein thought about these matters (Putnam 1992, 142). It is interesting to note that neither Norman Malcolm nor Peter Winch, in talking about Wittgenstein on religion, pays attention to these texts (Malcolm 1994; Winch 1994).

In these lectures Wittgenstein speaks of the Last Judgment and the afterlife. Putnam starts his discussion of Wittgenstein's lectures by pointing out their paradoxical nature.

> Wittgenstein imagines someone asking him if he believes in a Last Judgment, and on the first page of the published notes Wittgenstein says, "Suppose I say that the body will rot, and another says, 'No. Particles will rejoin in a thousand years, and there will be a Resurrection of you.' " Wittgenstein's comment is "If someone said: 'Wittgenstein, do you believe in this?' I'd say: 'No.' 'Do you contradict the man?' I'd say: 'No.' . . . Would you say: 'I believe the opposite,' or 'There is no reason to suppose such a thing'? I'd say neither." In short—and perhaps this is the only thing that is absolutely clear about these lectures—Wittgenstein believes that the religious man and the atheist talk past one another. (Putnam 1992, 143)

We normally would think that if a believer says "I believe there is a God" and the atheist says "I don't believe there is a God" that they respectively affirm and deny the same thing. But they have such different conceptions in mind, Wittgenstein claims, that it is not the case, as it appears to be on the surface, that the believer is making a claim and the atheist asserts its negation. Rather—or so Wittgenstein's claim seems to go—their views are *incommensurable*. By this we should mean, according to Putnam, that two speakers or two groups are not able to communicate because their words have different meanings (Putnam 1992, 152).

To see what is involved in this obscure claim about believing or not believing in God, consider an example Wittgenstein uses. Suppose A says "There is a German airplane overhead" and B says "Possibly, I'm not sure." Their views are close and they are plainly commensurable. Both have a good idea of what evidence they would need to decide what is probably the case and how to move to a position where they both could be practically certain that it was a German airplane that was overhead. But suppose A says "I believe in the Last Judgment" and B retorts "Well, I am not sure. Possibly." We should realize, Wittgenstein has it, that there is an enormous gulf here between them. Their views, it is not unnatural to believe, are incommensurable. For a Christian believer of a tolerably orthodox sort, Wittgenstein tells us, his belief in the Last Judgment, as all his religious beliefs, is *unshakable*. It isn't a matter of inquiry, or gaining of evidence, of a maybe or a probably. The believer does not at all entertain his belief in that way while in contrast for a typical atheist the Last Judgment isn't even a possibility or if it is, it is something of a very low order—vanishingly small—of probability. The believer and the atheist do not at all think alike here. Or so Wittgenstein believes. Their views appear to be incommensurable (Putnam 1992, 144).

The atheist, Putnam has it that Wittgenstein has it, will regard belief in God, the afterlife, the Last Judgment as beliefs which are part of a discourse of a prescientific or primitive culture "which has somehow strangely—due to human folly and superstition—managed to survive into the age of the digital computer and the neutron bomb" (Putnam 1992, 143). The concept of God, for such an atheist, is like some kind of quasiempirical concept and sentences such as "God will judge mankind" or "God governs the world" are treated like hypotheses open to confirmation or disconfirmation.[1] They are taken by him to be falsifiable beliefs that have indeed been falsified. (See Putnam on Bernard Williams in Putnam 1997.) This as we have seen is Sidney Hook's view. But this is not at all how the believer views God. His way of conceptualizing God is very different. His belief in God, God's providence, the Last Judgment are for the believer unshakeable beliefs. Belief in the Last Judgment and belief in the afterlife show themselves "not by reasoning or by appeal to ordinary grounds for belief, but rather by regulating . . . all his life" (Wittgenstein 1966, 54). We see here, the claim goes, a deep incommensurability between the believer's and the atheist's perspectives. They are, Putnam thinks, blindly speaking past each other.

I do not think it shows that at all. Rather, what is the case is that there are crude forms of very anthropomorphic theisms that are quite parallel to crude atheisms which treat religious belief as a superstitious belief-system with a Zeus-like concept of God. Here these religious and these atheistic beliefs are quite commensurable: the one denying what the other asserts. But then there is the less primitive, more nuanced beliefs of developed Judaism, Christianity, and Islam—the religious belief of which Wittgenstein speaks—in which God is said to be some mysterious ineffable Other without spatial and temporal location and utterly transcendent to the world (Hägerström 1964, 224–59; Carnap 1959, 65–67; Nielsen 1982). But there is a parallel commensurable atheistic conception that does not conceive of God as an empirical Zeus-like entity of empirical belief, but (though, of course, it is not seen this way by believers) as the attempt, caught in incoherence, to give expression to a belief in, and expressing, as well, an unshakeable commitment to, what is taken by such a believer to be an utterly spiritual ultimate reality—beyond space and time—and transcendent to the world (Hägerström 1964; Nielsen 1962). Such a religious belief is not a superstitious belief, but is a belief which some reflective, sophisticated, and intelligent people are driven to in spite of the fact that some of them—quite possibly many of them—fear their belief may be unintelligible. But, that notwithstanding, they are driven to these beliefs for deep religious reasons. The parallel type atheist takes Kierkegaard's point that intense religious conviction and doubt, even deep skepticism, are not incompatible. Again we have forms of religious belief and forms of atheism that are commensurable (Nielsen 1982).

If there is an incommensurability, it is between, on the one hand, the crudely anthropomorphic conception of God of both some atheists and some superstitious believers and, on the other, the nonanthropomorphic or the radically less anthropomorphic beliefs and conceptions of developed forms of Judaism, Christianity, and Islam and of an atheism that so understands religious belief, and does not take it, where it is genuine, to be a crude Zeus-like anthropomorphism. What possibly could be an incommensurability cut (if the very notion of incommensurability makes sense) is not between belief and atheism, but between anthropomorphic and nonanthropomorphic understandings of religion (Hägerström 1964, 224–59).

II

Putnam also stresses that when Wittgenstein thinks religious persons and nonreligious persons "think entirely differently" this need not be expressed in different beliefs—beliefs may play an absolutely minor role—but in their organizing their lives around very different *pictures* which are deeply important for their lives. The believer and the atheist, where they are nonsuperstitious, do not, Wittgenstein and Putnam have it, contradict each other. Indeed Wittgenstein thinks they can't *contradict each other*. It is just that the atheist hasn't got the thoughts or anything that hangs together with them that the believer has. And the nonscientistic atheist, attuned to, though rejecting, religion, fully recognizes this and takes it to heart. This has led Putnam to speak of incommensurability here between "belief and unbelief": to say, as we have seen, that they are not able to communicate because their words have different meanings (Putnam 1992, 152). But Putnam also shows deftly and perceptively that and why Wittgenstein pulls back from such a claim.

It is certainly true that in these lectures "Wittgenstein is concerned to deny any continuity at all between what he considers to be religious belief and scientific belief" (Putnam 1992, 150). The role of reasoning is

very different in the different cases. Religious persons in believing in the
Last Judgment are not looking for evidence and basing their belief on the
degree of evidence. It speaks of the Last Judgment in their sacred scriptures and that is enough for them and they hold onto their belief through
thick and thin. They think, Wittgenstein has it, and Putnam seems at least
to go along with Wittgenstein, in entirely different ways here than the
secularist. Their beliefs—what they subscribe to themselves—for both the
believer and the secularist, are *sui generis*. But this to me (*pace* Putnam)
continues to sound like a claim of incommensurability.

Putnam, however, argues that, the above notwithstanding, Wittgenstein does *not* treat these beliefs as incommensurable and, moreover, that
he is right in not doing so. Such a notion, at least in the context of discussing religious belief, is, Putnam claims, useless (Putnam 1992, 148).
The philosophical doctrine of incommensurability does not at all help us
to understand what religious discourse is really like (Putnam 1992, 153).
But why not? Again I will come at this indirectly. What Wittgenstein is
saying (in company with Kierkegaard) is "that religious discourse can be
understood in any depth only by understanding the form of life to which
it belongs" (Putnam 1992, 156). Someone, Wittgenstein remarks, who
tries to give an emotive or otherwise noncognitive analysis or elucidation
of religious discourse would thereby show she doesn't understand it. To
say "We are in God's providential care" is not *just* to express the attitude
that one feels safe no matter what happens and to urge others to feel like-
wise. "God" does not just mean "Yippee" and "the Devil" does not just
mean "Ugh." And "God created the world" does not mean "Take an
agapeistic attitude toward life" or anything of the kind (Nielsen 1989,
172–89). *Religious language, as all language, means just what it says and not
something else.* Why on earth should it mean something else? Why should
it, or even can it, be translatable or paraphraseable into some other form
of discourse? One is suffering from a metaphysical mystification if one
thinks this *must* be so. It is just the old *reductionist* urge that is so strong
and persistent in philosophy, but has repeatedly led us astray. Still, and
this is another side of the matter, we can learn the words of these language-games perfectly well and still not—the claim goes—understand
them. I, with very little preparing, could play the part of a pastor or a
priest in a film or a play. A person, Kierkegaard stresses, in a way with
which Wittgenstein would surely agree, "may think and say all the right
words and be living a thoroughly nonreligious life" and "a person may
think he or she is worshipping God and really be worshipping an idol"
and be without a clue as to what religion and religious belief and devo-
tion really are (Putnam 1992, 154). That that is so is evident; the difficult
thing is to understand how it can be so.

All that to the contrary notwithstanding, when we are considering religious language-games and forms of life, we need to keep firmly in mind, Putnam claims, that what "characterizes that form of life is not the expressions of belief that accompany it, but a way—a way that includes words and pictures, but is far from consisting in just words and pictures—of living one's life, of regulating one's decisions" (Putnam 1992, 154). Putnam stresses that what "Kierkegaard and Wittgenstein have in common is the idea that understanding the words of a religious person properly . . . is inseparable from understanding a religious form of life, and this is not a matter of 'semantic theory,' but a matter of understanding a human person" (Putnam 1992, 154). Still, one might say, to live religiously attuned to such a form of life is one thing, to understand what it is to live religiously, to understand what one is doing when one lives religiously, is another. It is in something like this way in which the religious person herself may feel deeply buffeted. She may feel—and feel intensely—religiously attuned but be at a loss concerning what this comes to.[2]

Putnam stresses something that neither Malcolm nor Winch stressed in speaking of Wittgenstein on religion. Putnam adverts to the fact that in his lectures on religion Wittgenstein says that a religious person uses *a picture*. Wittgenstein takes this to be something very important to the religious life and to our understanding of religion. In understanding religious language-games and the form of life in which they are embedded, we notice that pictures play a large part. Religious "people do employ pictures [and] . . . they draw certain consequences from them, but not the same consequences that [nonbelievers] draw when they use similar pictures in *other* contexts" (Putnam 1992, 156, italics mine). If we speak of Jones as having blue eyes we will also normally be prepared to speak of his eyebrows. But if we speak of the Eye of God being upon us we are not prepared to speak of God's eyebrows or ask what color his eyes are. When religious people talk of God speaking to the faithful, they do not take it as pertinent, or indeed even sensible, to speak of what language or languages he uses. Does he speak them all—all the several thousands of them—all at once or select one or another of them depending on whom he is talking to? Religious people believe that all things are possible for God. But they think nothing like the above about how God talks and this is not thought to limit God's powers in any way. It is just something that does not go with how religious people think and speak of God anymore than God is thought to be limited because he doesn't have ears. People who talk in the above way about how God speaks—wonder what language or languages he uses—show they have no understanding of God-talk. Religious people have a picture of the Eye of God being upon them or of God speaking to them, but religious people draw very different consequences from these religious pictures than secularists not attuned to religion do—or indeed that religious people themselves do—from similar pictures used in *other contexts*. (Remember Rilke's quip, "Does God speak Chinese, too?")

Wittgenstein, in his *Post-Tractarian* writings, is often said to be against pictures and indeed in practicing his philosophical therapy he does attack philosophers for being in the grip of a picture. But, as Putnam points out, "Wittgenstein in his lectures during the 1930s repeatedly praises pictures in two ways: he praises them as good ways of explaining the meaning of words . . . and, moreover, he speaks of pictures as having 'weight' or of pictures being 'at the root of all one's thinking'" (Putnam 1992, 156). So it is plain that Wittgenstein at that period of his life at least is assuming there are good and bad pictures. The bad ones—the ones that people, when they philosophize in the usual way, are often in the grip of and need to be liberated from—are metaphysical pictures that, unintelligible as they are, could not be at the root of all of one's thinking and of one's life. But the good ones somehow are metaphysics-free and guide our understanding (Putnam 1990, 42 and 1994, 276–77; Diamond 1991, 59–71; Conant 1994, xlvi–lviii). But it would be useful to have some criteria, or if not criteria, some way of distinguishing which are which. Do we just have to rely on our linguistic ear and our enculturation into the relevant forms of life? There is something that needs sorting out here. Are the good pictures—or at least some of them—after all also in some way metaphysical pictures? Putnam likes to stress how the rejection of metaphysics is often the expression of another metaphysics. He thinks, for example, that this was the case with logical positivism and he surely would have thought that about Axel Hägerström and about Hägerströmists. If that is so, and if that is also how Wittgenstein views things, is Wittgenstein telling us there is good and bad metaphysics? That, to put it mildly, doesn't sound like Wittgenstein! A central thrust of Wittgenstein's thought is to have it that "good metaphysics" is an oxymoron.

However, to return to the central point Putnam is making about religion—his point about forms of life and the importance of pictures—note the following passage:

> Pictures are important in life. The whole weight of a form of life may lie in the pictures that that form of life uses. In his own notes, some of which are republished in the collection *Culture and Value*, Wittgenstein says "It is true that we can compare a picture that is firmly rooted in us to a superstition, but it is equally true that we always eventually have to reach some firm ground, either a picture or something else, so that a picture which is at the root of all our thinking is to be respected and not treated as superstition." (Putnam 1992, 156)

Is religion, everywhere, at the root of our thinking? Is it at the root of the thinking of all human beings or at the root of thinking of all sensitive and reflective human beings? It seems at least not to be so now for many people with what Max Weber called the relentless disenchantment of the world in full sway. They are not in the grip of any *such* pictures. Indeed such pictures are quite foreign to them and for some of them being free of them and of the thoughts and feelings that go with them is experienced as a kind of liberation (Levine 1996). Moreover, and quite distinctly, if the "whole weight of a form of life may lie in the pictures that that form of life uses" and if the "may" becomes an "is" for some form of life—say, religion—is not that to give to understand that the discourse of that form of life is somehow *noncognitive* or *purely symbolic*? This is a conclusion Wittgenstein wishes to avoid. When, during his lectures discussed above, one of his students raised the issue of whether that might be so, Wittgenstein tersely said, "Rubbish." But can he avoid that conclusion, given what he says about pictures? Most logical positivists thought that religious discourse, like moral discourse, and metaphysical discourse, should be understood not as fact-stating discourse or any kind of cognitive discourse but as emotive forms of discourse used to express and evoke feelings: discourse without *cognitive* content or with only incidental cognitive content. In talk of such discourse—particularly in the context of metaphysics and religion—they spoke of users of that discourse having different *picture preferences* from nonbelievers and thought of such picture preferences as having no relation to truth or what is warrantedly assertable—to anything that could be justified or be seen as something we could have any obligation to accept (Carnap 1959). Isn't Wittgenstein more obscurely saying much the same thing? (Wittgenstein 1993, 38–43, a talk given in 1929) But surely that is not his intention as Putnam is fully aware (Putnam 1992).

III

Putnam asks trenchantly, "Has Wittgenstein simply immunized religion from all criticism? Has Wittgenstein made it impossible to be an atheist?" (Putnam 1992, 165). I think Putnam, as well as Malcolm, Winch, and Rush Rhees, would say that Wittgenstein has given us a persuasive case for having made religion safe from both metaphysical and antimetaphysical criticism. But that is not to say that they believe that Wittgenstein has made it immune from all criticism, though they *may* think he has made it immune from all *philosophical* criticism (Rhees 1997).[3] They also believe that Wittgenstein has shown that religious belief is neither in part nor in whole metaphysical. The above views are in common to all four of them. Winch, I believe, though I am not terribly confident of this, would also say that inside religious language-games, there is space for both relevant atheistic criticism and religious countercriticism, but that that, however important, is not a *philosophical* matter (Winch 1994). Philosophy, he has it, in good Wittgensteinian fashion, can only describe what is at issue here and in doing so hopefully perspicuously to represent what is involved and reveal the confusions involved when either side tries to go *metaphysical*. Here we see again Wittgenstein's, or at least Wittgensteinian, *philosophical quietism*.[4] Putnam remarks enigmatically that Wittgenstein has "not entirely" made it impossible to be an atheist (Putnam 1992, 169). And it is not clear that, unlike Winch, that Putnam does not think, and for Wittgenstein as well as for himself, that this could properly be a philosophical issue. After all this may be where his pragmatism is showing (Putnam 1995). Be that as it may, Putnam makes it plain that, while Wittgenstein found talk of the Last Judgment very significant, Wittgenstein "himself would never say that he believes that there will be a Last Judgment. . . . Indeed Wittgenstein says . . . that he doesn't even know whether to say he *understands* the man who says that he believes there will be a Last Judgment" (Putnam 1992, 169).

Wittgenstein is very respectful of religion, intensely concerned with it as a form of life, but at the same time in a certain way distant from it (Wittgenstein 1993, 38–44). He is not confident that he understands it or even what it would take for him to come to understand it, though certainly he believes he would not be helped here by the study of theology, philosophy, history, or linguistics or by any academic study. Indeed he seems to despise such inquiries into religion. While Rudolf Carnap and Hans Reichenbach were scornful of religion, Wittgenstein was scornful of most academic study of religion.[5] There are for him exceptions. Kierkegaard's and Karl Barth's work are powerful examples of what he took to be the right way of going about things in this domain. But still it looks like, after all, Wittgenstein has so construed things that he has immunized—tried to immunize—religious discourse from all relevant *secular* criticism.

IV

Wittgenstein criticizes anthropologists of a previous era—James Frazer is his main target—for failing to see how very different primitive language-games are from ours and for, in a patronizing, supercilious, self-congratulatory, and ethnocentric manner, just seeing primitive language-games and forms of life as inferior versions of our own or, even worse, as just crude approximations of science (Wittgenstein 1993, 118–55). They see crude blunders and superstitious mistakes where there are very different purposes, with a different rationale, answering to different interests in a different setting.

However, and that notwithstanding, Wittgenstein does *not* say "we can never criticize a primitive culture" (Putnam 1992, 170). He says that sometimes we should combat another culture, though in the same breath he speaks of the difficulty of giving reasons why we should combat another culture. Here we have, lurking in the background, the specter of cultural or conceptual relativism. It is clear that we don't and can't choose our forms of life. We are just born into the world at a determinate time and place and are enculturated into a given culture. Wittgenstein in his later work adverts to the deep and pervasive power of socialization (Wittgenstein 1969). Where we are situated in life intellectually, morally, religiously, politically, indeed in every way, is historically and culturally accidental. Some few of us, within some severely limited constraints, can to some degree move around in some few not too dissimilar cultures, but our ability to do that is itself plainly in considerable measure the effect of certain kinds of previous enculturation. We, relatively well educated people in the rich capitalist democracies, are in a rather different position than someone in the jungles of Central Africa or South America. And we, in the more advantaged, including more educated, strata in our own society, are in a rather different position than someone who is very much poorer and has little education.

Even with such luck (if that is the correct word for it) in our circumstances, we do not have, if Wittgenstein is on the mark, much of a toehold to set ourselves, except in certain limited and distinctive ways, against the pervasive thrust of our enculturation. Where we do shake things up in certain ways, as Nietzsche well understood, even the direction of that reflects our culture and our distinctive enculturation. "Perhaps Wittgenstein," Putnam observes, "just thinks that there are a variety of different possible language-games, or variety of possible human forms of life, and there is nothing to be said about the rightness or wrongness of one as opposed to another" (Putnam 1993, 171). Putnam cites a famous series of passages from Wittgenstein's last work, *On Certainty*, that have often been thought to, in effect, if not in intention, support this relativistic interpretation of Wittgenstein. There Wittgenstein remarks:

> '608: Is it wrong for me to be guided in my actions by the propositions of physics? Am I to say that I have no good grounds for doing so? Isn't it precisely this that we call a "good ground"?

> '609: Suppose that we met people who did not regard this as a good ground, and who did not regard that as a telling reason. Now how do we imagine this? Instead of the physicist, they consult an oracle. And for that we consider them primitive.
>
> Is it wrong for them to consult an oracle and be guided by it?—If we call this "wrong," aren't we using our language game as a base from which to *combat* theirs?

> '610: And are we right or wrong to combat it? Of course there are all sorts of slogans which will be used to support our proceedings.

'611: Where two principles really do meet which cannot be reconciled with one another, then each man declares the other a fool and a heretic.

'612: I said I would "combat" the other man—but wouldn't I give him *reasons*? Certainly, but how far do they go? At the end of reasons comes *persuasion*. (Think what happens when missionaries convert natives.) (Wittgenstein 1969, 80–81)

Putnam remarks that this certainly sounds like relativism and adds how dismayed he was when he first encountered those paragraphs (Putnam 1992, 171). However, he believes a closer examination of them makes the standard relativist interpretation of them look less plausible (Putnam 1992, 171). It is clear that Wittgenstein himself is not being a neutral onlooker here, but asserts that he, Wittgenstein, would combat the other person in the other culture who appeals to oracles or the practice of reaching a verdict on anything through an ordeal by fire. But he also makes it plain that we have no place to stand in doing so but within our language-games. There is no standing free from our forms of life—from all our language-games and all our forms of life—and then criticizing them. That very idea is incoherent. But standing as we must within our language-games, we think—indeed we are utterly firm here—that it is absurd to consult oracles or settle questions through ordeal by fire. But, that notwithstanding, we are a particular "we." Heirs to a particular tradition. There are other "We's" and other traditions. Something like a relativism returns like the repressed.

However, when we recognize there are others, and sometimes with well worked-out rationales, who think in very different and sometimes conflicting ways, how can we not but feel, responding as we do, that we are, and inescapably, being in some ways ethnocentric? Faced, say, with the Azande, there are times when we cannot find reasons that are also reasons for them: the worldviews—ours and the Azande's—are so deeply different that we would find—or at least sometimes could find—that in a discussion "with an intelligent Azande we cannot resort to ordinary argument based on premises that we share with the Azande but have to resort to persuasion" (Putnam 1992, 172).

Both Wittgenstein and Putnam seem to think that here we have a situation in which very deep underlying assumptions and principles clash and that we cannot reconcile them. This being so, we end up, having no other resources, and, given the strong emotional pressures here, just declaring the person we are in such an irreconcilable conflict with a fool and a heretic—or something to that effect. We, that is, if we say anything at all, end by simply exchanging at worst insults and at best slogans.

I think Putnam is right in thinking Wittgenstein regards such sloganeering and brute condemnation with distaste. And it is, of course, something that Putnam thinks, as a good wet liberal, that we should avoid if at all possible. And indeed do we not, if we are reflective persons seeking to be impartial and fair, feel the same way ourselves? (But before we conclude that things are so straightforward think of our discussing matters with a dedicated Nazi.) Putnam remarks:

> If I am right in reading the *Lectures on Religious Belief* in juxtaposition with Wittgenstein's notes on Frazer's *Golden Bough*, then Wittgenstein wants us to stop and think about *when* we should combat a religious language game or a primitive language game which is not ours or our culture's. If we view other language games as simply stupid or ignorant forms of our own language games, we will be constantly combating and we will be constantly failing to *see*. If we see more accurately, we may find that there are fewer language games that we want to combat. But even when we do combat, and Wittgenstein does sometimes join us in combating, we don't have to scream "Fool!" and "Heretic!" (Putnam 1992, 173)

And note Putnam's further remarks:

> Elizabeth Anscombe once asked Ludwig Wittgenstein what he would do if a friend of his believed in faith healing; would he try to talk him out of it? And Wittgenstein replied that he would, but he didn't know why. (In conversation, Saul Kripke once cited this to me as clear evidence that Wittgenstein was a relativist.) I take it that Wittgenstein did not mean, by what he said to Elizabeth Anscombe, that he does not know that sulfa drugs or penicillin are more effective in treating bacterial pneumonia than faith healing is. The point is rather that this is a perfectly useless thing to say to the man who believes in faith healing (it is a premise he doesn't share), and Wittgenstein was, I think, recoiling from using *allerlei Schlagworten*. Slogans may be part of our language games, but they are by no means the best or the noblest part. (Putnam 1992, 173)

V

Surely we will agree with Putnam that we do not want, and should not in such a context (*perhaps* in any context), want to, scream or say or even think anything like "Fool!" or "Heretic!" (But would we not want to say of and to a Nazi that what he is committed to is vile and beastly? And could not that remark be backed up with reasons? Is there no justified place for such talk? There is such a thing as being too wet. But still see Wittgenstein 1969, 81, on the giving of reasons.) Still, while we realize that such sloganeering is a part of our language-games, it is not a part that we, if we are at all reflective and reasonable, welcome. We would like to have circumstances in the world where we could just excise it. We would very much like it to be the case that no circumstances would or even could arise where we would have to so speak and act.

However, all this quite plainly does not get us very far and it is possible to wonder if we can go further. How can we be justified in saying that using *in such contexts* these slogans is not the noblest or best part of our language-games? How can we, except as rhetoric, even speak of "the highest or noblest part of our language-games"? Such sloganeering uses are, after all, an established part of our language; they are well ingrained practices which have been around for a long time and these practices have clear functions in our social lives. On Wittgenstein's practice-oriented account of things what grounds could we have here for rejecting the playing of such language-games? How do we nonarbitrarily rule out such *Allerlei Schlagworten*?

I think we can legitimately take an end-run around such problems. Our practices, the Azande practices and the practices of any other tribe as well, are not balkanized practices. Our talk of God and the Azande consulting of oracles are both part of a larger interlocking cluster of practices. And "cluster" is the right word here and not "system." Between us and the Azande it isn't that we have different belief-systems—some closed worldviews analogous to axiomatic systems such that the two worldviews are isomorphic or cut off from each other so that we are inescapably reasoning and conceptualizing things internal to a framework and that we do not, nay cannot, even understanding things in some radically different framework. Nothing like this either on Wittgenstein's view or in actuality is the case or even could be the case. The whole picture is wrong—and not wrong because it is a picture—but wrong because it is the wrong picture.

We have a bunch of practices serving different purposes—a bunch of language-games that answer to different interests. Other peoples, often in many respects, though not in all, very different peoples, have their more or less distinctive practices and language-games too. They in certain places overlap with ours while in certain respects it is still the case that they are very different from ours, but where they do not overlap with ours, their very different language-games overlap with other language-games of theirs which in turn overlap with language-games of ours. So there is always a bridge which allows us and the Azande (or any other culture) to gain some common understanding. We are never so conceptually imprisoned that there are no bridges in our practices and language-games linking them and us. Indeed if this were so, as Donald Davidson well argues, we would never be able to discover it or notice it (Davidson 1984, 183–98). This being so, it makes no sense to speak of *such* differences. Language is idling here; we are in the grip of an incoherent metaphysical picture.

As strikingly, and sometimes unsettlingly, different others sometimes are from us, we are never just in "other worlds" where there is no *possibility* of understanding each other, of discoursing together and of arguing with or reasoning with each other. It is indeed true that sometimes we do just shout slogans or turn from each other with contempt, anger, or, keeping it cool, just respond in a patronizingly superior manner not caring what the other has to say. (It is difficult to resist this with a view we think is very wrongheaded and harmful as well. We see this happening in philosophy all the time and what happens in philosophy happens perhaps even more frequently in what is our common lives.) But still we need not so react; such ways of reacting are not forced on us; we are not driven to them by the inexorable logic involved in there being different cultural clusters of beliefs, attitudes, ways of conceiving and doing things. There are no such *ubiquitously* different conceptual systems, as Donald Davidson has well argued (Davidson 1984, 183–98). And this is not rationalism, but just being realistic and literal about our language-games and practices (Diamond 1991). It is more of what Cora Diamond calls the realistic spirit—something which has nothing to do with metaphysical realism or scientific realism.

VI

There is still a different but related way of thinking, not alien to Wittgenstein's way of thinking, which we should use in resisting that *apparent* relativism in his thought. We end with practices and forms of life when we try (really try) to gain our bearings in thinking about—though these are not the only cases—the problems of life that thrust themselves upon us. There we, not infrequently, and perhaps always when we resolutely and nonevasively push ourselves, are morally and religiously at sea as to what to say, to think and sometimes at sea as well over what to do and how to live: how to order our lives (Rhees 1999). Any nonevasive person should acknowledge that. There is perhaps no "natural order of reasons." Perhaps Richard Rorty is right that the very notion does not make sense. Here, Wittgenstein has it, we need to really come acutely to sense what our forms of life, and the practices embedded in them, are and how they structure our lives. But in doing this we do not need to end by simply recognizing that *this language-game is played*. We need not, quietistically, simply to acquiesce in that fact. Our language-games and practices are indeed primitive for us, that is, they are bedrock. There is no sense (*pace* Hägerström) to the idea of in some wholesale way getting back of them and finding the ground on which they lie. There is no funding theory that will ground them (Bjarup 1999). Wittgenstein, and Putnam with him, are right in recognizing that the very idea of having such a place to stand here is incoherent. But, while we cannot dispense with all our practices at once, we can, using other of our practices, and, never standing free of all practices, relevantly criticize any of our practices or any determinate cluster of our practices. Practices we can criticize include crucially practices interconnected with other practices we rely on in doing our critiquing. We are bootstrapping all the way along. We sometimes even discover, as we do this, a cluster of them—a family of practices—to be problematic. They can even be crucial, but still problematic practices, practices we may well come in time, sometimes with pain and ambivalence, to turn away from—set aside. (Religious practices are paradigms of such practices.) We can, always using some of our practices, and with no possibility of standing all at once free of all of them, critique any practice. As nothing is hidden; similarly nothing need be unquestionably sacred. Conceivably, just as a bare logical possibility, we might over time *seriatim* reject all of them, replacing them, as we go along, with other practices (modified from the old ones or by quite different others that replace them). But we cannot—logically "cannot"—reject them all at once standing there comprehending and acting with no practices. What we can do, and indeed sometimes we actually do, is, reasoning in accordance with some of our practices, criticize and sometimes modify or even reject a particular practice or even a range of determinate kinds of practice. (Whether we should call that a philosophical endeavor or not is comparatively unimportant.)

Our practices are interconnected and sometimes a practice or cluster of practices may conflict with other practices. If we are thoughtful and have a concern to have ways of living that will be as reasonable and as conducive to human flourishing as can be had, we will try to see if we can forge a conception of how these practices consistently and coherently hang together; and, indeed, where they do not hang together very well, we will seek ways to achieve a world in which they hang together better—at least as much as a reasonable forging can achieve. And indeed such forging, such constructing, is always possible, though it often may be unsuccessful.

Where one practice or cluster of practices (say some type of practice) conflicts with the great mass of our other practices, most of which are unproblematic for us, and where they conflict as well as with other practices which are problematical but still less problematical than the first cluster of practices, then we have good reasons, internal to our language-games and practices, for altering or sometimes even jettisoning these conflicting strongly problematical language-games and practices.[6]

We should not acquiesce in the idea that this language-game is played, thinking the buck stops there. And in refusing to so acquiesce, we do not have to attain some impossible—indeed inconceivable—perch, some sky-hook, "beyond all language-games and practices." That idea is incoherent.

So reasoning, it is intelligible to critique Azande belief in oracles and on grounds that the Azande could, at least in principle, come to recognize and accept; and we can in a similar manner criticize, and perhaps set aside, some, and perhaps all, of our own religious beliefs and practices. We are not trapped in a relativism, conceptual or otherwise; we need not in so viewing things be ethnocentric and we do not need to try to break free from a rock-bottom appeal to forms of language seen as, what they are, forms of life.[7]

VII

Let us return to our general consideration of Wittgenstein on religious belief from a different angle. Suppose someone resists the line of argument we have just developed and continues to react to what they take to be the inescapable relativism of such a Wittgensteinian approach. We are, as they see it, on Wittgenstein's approach, just stuck with language-games and forms of life being "simply irrational arbitrary facts of nature" (Putnam 1992, 174). Indeed, such a philosopher might support his claim from another famous passage from *On Certainty*. There Wittgenstein remarks that "you must bear in mind that the language-game is so to say unpredictable. I mean it is not based on grounds. It is not reasonable (or unreasonable). It is there—like our life" (Putnam 1992, 174; Wittgenstein 1969, 73). In this passage Wittgenstein, in saying the language-game is not reasonable or unreasonable, is asserting that it is not based on reasons. But he is suggesting something else as well which is obscured in the English translation. The word for "reasonable" in German is *"vernünftig"* and it suggests a historical philosophical reference that the perfectly proper English translation does not suggest. Putnam puts it as follows: "In German the word *vernünftig* connects with *vernunft*, and this particular notion of Reason was given pride of place by Kant, who contrasted Reason in that sense with mere understanding, *vernunft* with *verstand*" (Putnam 1992, 174). In saying that a language-game is like our life in that neither is based on *vernunft*, we get a firm rejection by Wittgenstein of the heart of Kant's philosophy and indeed as well of the whole rationalistic tradition from Plato to Spinoza. Kant attributed to human beings *vernunft* which he took to be a unique transcendental capacity. Wittgenstein utterly rejects anything like that. He does not deny that we understand things and have reasons, but these he construes naturalistically, but not reductively (Putnam 1992, 174–75). "We are," as Putnam puts it, "not mere animals, but our capacities for understanding and for reasoning are capacities which grow out of more primitive capacities which we share with animals" (Putnam 1992, 175).[8] Language does not emerge from or as some kind of ratiocination. It is important that we understand things here in Darwinian terms. "Human life is not the empirical manifestation of the transcendental capacity to reason" (Putnam 1992, 175).

So much for transcendental philosophy. But we should, Kant aside, keep in mind that "*vernünftig*" in colloquial use is very close to the English word "reasonable." And are not our language-games, or at least many of them (say, the language-games of physics or biology) reasonable given our goals? That is plainly so and, so as not to be or even sound scientistic, so are our language-games about being hungry or thirsty. They are also plainly reasonable given our goals. And there are *some* language-games we, wired as we are, being the biological and social creatures we are, as a matter of fact, could not but have. Moreover, in saying generally that they are not reasonable (or *unreasonable*), Wittgenstein is clearly giving to understand that they are not *irrational*, for they are *not unreasonable*. And, given that they answer to certain interests and goals of ours, some of which are obvious and unproblematic, it is hardly plausible to say that they are arbitrary. Relativism here does not raise its ugly head. They are just not based on *vernunft*. But Kant's transcendental capacity is mythological anyway. We can have here what Putnam calls a "sane naturalism"—something which is identical to my social naturalism (Putnam, 1994, 279–94; Conant 1994, ixiii–ixiv).

Some will argue that Wittgenstein is all the same trapped in a relativism or ethnocentrism because we just have, as a plain matter of fact, these diverse and often either conflicting or (perhaps) incommensurable language-games. Moreover, the argument goes, in speaking in such contexts of what is warranted, reasonable or true, all that Wittgenstein can consistently say is that physics, for example, makes claims that are taken to be true claims by people using our language-games, but the Azande appealing to oracles can also make claims that are taken by the Azande (using their language) to be true claims and there—or so it seems—is no way of justifying that something is true or false *period*. We make our claims and the Azande make theirs and there appears at least to be no non–question-begging way, when the claims are conflicting or incommensurable, of determining which claims are true or have the more adequate warrant. For *us* it is just obvious that ours are. What the Azande believe cannot be true. But they, with an equally strong sense of what is obvious, will return the compliment. And it looks like we have no relevant perch—no Archimedian point—from which to adjudicate matters. We can only intelligibly say that something is taken to be warranted by people having our language-games, but not taken to be warranted by people who have different language-games or that something is taken to be reasonable by people having our language-games, but not by people having different language-games. Canons of justification are always to some degree local and time dependent. There we are, after all, caught, some say, in an utter relativism or ethnocentrism. Or at least we are in a culturally variable lingua-centric predicament (Hall 1960, 1961, 64).

However, even taken at face value, we have to be careful how these matters are put. The notion of *something being true (warranted, reasonable) in our language-game*, Putnam sides with Richard Rorty in arguing, is an incoherent idea. "The thought that everything we believe is, at best, only 'true in our language game' isn't even a coherent thought: Is the very existence of our language then only 'true in our language game'? So our language game is a fiction?" (Putnam 1992, 177). Putnam argues that Wittgenstein cannot be saying this.

> The reason that this cannot be what Wittgenstein is saying is that to say that it is true in my language game that you are reading this book is not to say that you are reading this book; to say that it's true in my language game that I am eating dinner is not to say that I am eating dinner; and Wittgenstein was obviously aware of this. To say something is true in a language game is to stand outside of that language game and make a comment; that is not what it is to play a language game. Whatever it is that makes us want to replace moves like saying "it's true" or "it's reasonable" or "it's warrantable" by "it's true in my language game" or "it's reasonable in my language game" or "it's warranted in my language game" (or makes us want to do this when we see that the language game itself is not grounded on Reason) is something that makes us want to *distance* ourselves from our own language game. It is as if the recognition that our language game does not have a transcendental justification made us want to handle it with kid gloves, or to handle it from a metalanguage. But why is the metalanguage any more secure? (Putnam 1992, 176)

If we try to take "true in a language game" not as a metalinguistic remark—a plainly *second-order* remark—but try instead to speak of "true in a language-game" of sentences made in the object-language in a language-game, we are caught in the impossible situation of trying to be inside and outside the language-game at *the same time* and in the same respect. We are at one and the same time with the very same sentence trying to make a metalinguistic remark about the language and a first-order assertion in the language (using the language to make claims which are not about the language). Moreover, the word "true" in the above metalinguistic sentence is not meant to apply just within a language-game. When I say "The robins have returned to the botanical gardens" I am not saying—or trying to say—that that is true in my language, but that it is true because of what occurred in the botanical gardens. But if I didn't use language-games—if I were not a speaker of some language—I could not have asserted this and if there were no language-games there would be no such *truths* or indeed any truths to be asserted or denied. But that is not to say that it is true in my language-game that the robins have returned to the botanical gardens. If there were no such language-games there would be no such *truth* (e.g., that the robins have returned to the botanical gardens), but that does not mean that the robins would not have returned to the botanical gardens if there were no such truths (Putnam 1990, 301–302). What the robins will or will not do does not depend on our ability to say something, including saying what they will do. But *truth* does. Putnam has it that we should say that "some things are true and some things are warranted and some things are reasonable, but, of course, we can only *say* so if we have an appropriate language. But we do have the language, and we can and do say so, even though that language does not itself rest on any metaphysical guarantee like Reason" (Putnam 1992, 177). What then does it rest on? Wittgenstein says quite simply and shockingly to us with our *rationalistic* penchants—something that just goes with being a philosopher—that *it rests on trust*.

This we find hard to swallow and "we wriggle and turn in search of a transcendental guarantee or a skeptical escape" (Putnam 1992, 177). But this wriggling shows that we are still trapped in the fly bottle. We will either have a grand metaphysical solution or we will have nothing: that is to say we will be skeptics on a grand scale. The conceptual ill from which we need a Wittgensteinian conceptual cure is our inability really to acknowledge the world and other people without these supposedly robust *metaphysical* guarantees. "Something in us craves more for than we can possibly have and flees from even the certainty that we do have" (Putnam 1992, 178). And even if we continue to balk at Wittgenstein's remark that our language and our language-games rest on trust, we can say instead, in what I think is a genuinely Wittgensteinian spirit, that there is no intelligible idea of our language or our language-games resting on—being founded on—anything or, for that matter, of their needing to. They are just there, as we have seen Wittgenstein putting it, like our lives. If we acknowledge this and take it to heart, we will have broken the spell of looking for metaphysical comfort and have done so in Wittgenstein's realistic spirit (Diamond 1991). Wittgenstein, that is, in giving us a realistic and clear look at our forms of life and their roles in our lives, seeks to free us from the irrational obsession of looking for a foundation of or for language or, for that matter, a *foundation* of or for life. He wants to lead us away from philosophical fantasies to the reflective common sense of our common life with full nonevasiveness concerning our finitude, but with, as well, our having some primitive certainties that can never be undermined by philosophical or scientific theorizing or require some philosophical backup. Neither absolutism nor skepticism nor relativism nor subjectivism is in order.

VIII

Let us now set aside considering how we might or might not adjudicate matters between the Azande and us and consider a dispute—or failure of understanding—within "our own tribe," namely between, on the one hand, Jews, Christians, Moslems and, on the other hand, secularists (atheists, agnostics, and secular humanists). There are, of course, Neanderthals and/or fanatics on both sides of the divide (which for short I shall call the divide between believers and secularists), but there are reasonable and informed people on either side: people who are anything but fanatics. And this poses a problem, at least for a secularist, and no doubt for a certain kind of believer as well. Putnam (1997) considers this as does Thomas Nagel (1998, 130–34). Nagel, an atheist, remarks that while religion seems to him fantastic, thoroughly unreal, there are also people whom he esteems (including philosophers) who are, perplexing and unsettling as he finds this, firm believers. The unsettling part aside, I feel exactly the same way. There are friends of mine, able philosophers, reflective intellectuals, knowledgeable and fair-minded people, who are believers. There are even philosophers of science—and very good ones too—who are believers. Hilary Putnam and Bas C. van Fraassen, for example, are believers. They have forgotten more about science and the philosophy of science than I know and they are careful, imaginative, sophisticated philosophers or philosopher-scientists pushing very deeply into their subject. Yet believers they are. That frankly boggles my mind. I want to say "How could they?" Yet there we are. They are believers. It is not hard for me to believe that of someone indoctrinated with scholastic philosophy or Straussian metaphysics or with a severe Orthodox Jewish background, e.g., Saul Kripke. But Bas van Fraassen, and even more so, Hilary Putnam, a red-diaper baby, a doctoral student of Hans Reichenbach's, a colleague of Quine's, a very distinguished logician and philosopher in his own right—that is hard to believe. But again there it is.

What should secularists make of such things? What attitude should they (we) take to that? Here, *this* secularist will speak in his own voice, perhaps only for himself. As James Conant has made us aware, it is a tricky business in intellectual matters when to speak in one's own voice. *Perhaps* in *philosophy* we should never so speak? But it seems to me that in trying nonevasively to think about moral, religious, and, I think, political matters, there comes a time when we should so speak. At least I am resolved here—I hope reasonably—to so speak. And, philosophy not being the name of a natural kind, I am not terribly concerned whether it is philosophy or not. What I am concerned about is whether I can be honest with myself where self-deception and what Kierkegaard called double-mindedness are easy to unwittingly succumb to; and to, hopefully escaping that, be clear about such matters as the subject matter will admit.

When I come across believers who are disciplined and knowledgeable intellectuals and particularly when they are philosophers with both an analytical training and an understanding of science, I find it (I repeat) mind boggling that they could be believers, and most particularly rather fundamentalist believers. It seems to me their fundamentalist beliefs are plainly either false or incoherent and that they should, without much effort, see that. What is at issue here does not, it seems to me, rest on very arcane considerations. Yet they believe. I tend to look for a *causal* sociological explanation for their belief. They can't, it seems to me, have reasons for believing that they themselves cannot see through or would not see through themselves in a cool hour when, if they think about such matters at all, their thought—discourse, if you will—is not distorted. So I tend to look for psycho-sociological *causes* of their belief. But I fully realize that they can as well, with as much relevance or as little relevance, as the case may be, play that game against me or any other secularist. So where are we?

One thing is firmly in place. I respect these people not *just* as persons (ends in themselves)—though I do that too—but I both respect and esteem them as thoughtful and knowledgeable people of integrity who are at least my intellectual peers. And I think Thomas Nagel had a similar thing in mind when he made the remark mentioned above. How, I ask myself, can I, if I am being reasonable, be so sure that I have a corner on the truth concerning these matters or indeed any matters? Of course I cannot. But the same goes for the believer as well. (Think of Alvin Plantinga's or on the other side Antony Flew's confident proclaiming. Something they can hardly be entitled to.) Yet I honestly believe the believer's beliefs are incoherent and that they are plainly so. Standing where we are now—knowing and understanding what we know and understand—religious belief should, I believe, be impossible and this seems to me obviously so.

This has led me to say that it is irrational for a contemporary person who is both philosophically and scientifically sophisticated to believe in God or even to believe that God exists (Nielsen 1985, 1989, 1999). That, understandably, has caused offense even after I have explained that I am certainly not claiming that these *believers* are irrational, but, on the contrary, acknowledging that they are typically plainly rational and reasonable, I am claiming instead that their key religious beliefs are irrational and that it is irrational to have such beliefs. But, even after I have been quick to point out that reasonable people often, perhaps even always, have *some* irrational beliefs and that it is the *belief and the sticking with that belief, not the people that have them, that I am saying is irrational.* They are being irrational in having such beliefs and acting on them, but reasonable people can have *some* irrational beliefs and act on them. Even the most reasonable among us are not creatures of "Pure Reason." But even after saying that I still provoke and what I say seems to many people—surprisingly to me—to be itself unreasonable. Some people just tune out when I say things like that. The argument is not attended to.

For those who are shocked or irritated enough to respond, something like this will typically be said: "Where do you get off saying that? Is it not *hubris*, arrogance, and dogmatism on your part—a kind of antireligious fanaticism?" To this I respond by pointing out that I put forward my argument in a fallibilistic, impartial, and tolerant manner. I am not claiming, absurdly, that my argument must be right and that anyone who disagrees with me is either being blind or stupid or suffering from some neurosis. I am not engaging in *allerlie schlagworten*. I do not say or give to understand or think anything like that. Yet I remain utterly flabbergasted that reflective, intelligent, and informed people—people with keen analytical minds—such as Putnam, van Fraassen, Jean Hampton, Hendrik Hart, Terence Penelhum, Charles Taylor, and Alasdair MacIntyre can be believers. I, as I remarked, go on feeling "How could they?" But, I also ask myself, is there something I understand that they do not? Well, I do not see that they have faced, at least publicly, in any thorough way the considerations that I and other similar secularizers have brought against belief. But I am also acutely aware that there may well be things they know or have good reason to believe that I do not know or, perhaps, seeing through a glass darkly, I have not seen the need to face. They may, and *perhaps* rightly, not feel at all threatened or challenged by such critiques of religion. But why not?[9] But they in turn may think that people like me have not faced things they have and they may well ask themselves why not?

So where should we stand here? What is to be done? Surely not to shout "fool" or "heretic" or push causal hypotheses about how one or another of us got socialized and, as a result of this, live under an illusion. Though some such hypotheses may be true, I do not even consider them, let alone appeal to them.

The first part about how to respond is easy. We must practice fully tolerance at least in the political sense that John Rawls has so powerfully pursued in his *Political Liberalism*. Within the public sphere, within the domain of Public Reason, we must just acknowledge the public acceptability of all religious, nonreligious, and antireligious orientations, no matter what comprehensive conceptions of the good (if any) they have, as long as they accept and act in accordance with the political principles of justice, with its built in doctrine of tolerance, of political liberalism. (They do not, of course, have to be Rawls's principles but principles within that general family, e.g., Brian Barry's.) Furthermore, we must also regard any of these conceptions of the good, with their distinctive religious or secular orientations, as, in a *political and social* sense, reasonable if the people with these conceptions of the good (comprehensive or noncomprehensive) act in accordance with the political principles of justice of political liberalism. From the vantage point of Public Reason they are reasonable; and a decent and just society will be tolerant of these various beliefs and ways of living: religious, nonreligious, and antireligious. On a personal level, this is just what it is to be tolerant persons and to be committed to a politically liberal society, which, as Rawls and Brian Barry recognize, could be a socialist society. This political understanding and acceptance of tolerance must be firmly in place in such a society. In *this way* we must all be good wet liberals.

However, as Rawls also recognizes, beliefs which, in a political sense and in terms of Public Reason, must be accepted as reasonable may not in another sense and from another vantage point be accepted as reasonable and, we may be justified in arguing about whether they are reasonable or not in *that sense* as long as we refrain from carrying whatever judgments we come to here over to the public sphere of political argument and social exclusion (Rawls 1993, 60).[10]

In accordance with this, I have argued, though in a thoroughly fallibilistic and tolerant spirit, that religious beliefs, and most plainly theistic ones, are beliefs that philosophers and other such intellectuals, living at the present time under conditions of modernity, who are reasonably sophisticated about philosophy and science, should find to be irrational and they should conclude that, everything considered, it is unreasonable for people so placed to hold them. But this for the Rawlsian reasons given above cannot be a matter of Public Reason. In terms of *Public Reason* we cannot say that they are unreasonable beliefs to hold and that people are being unreasonable in holding them and, of course, we cannot tolerate the attempt to shut up people who have such beliefs. (This, of course, goes for atheists—even militant atheists—who are themselves tolerant.) But not all talk of unreasonablity is from that point of view. Still people making such judgments of unreasonablity, and indeed any justified judgments of reasonability, can tolerate no coercion of the unreasonable at least as long as the unreasonable continue to act in accordance with the principles of justice of Political Liberalism. They may even tolerate them when these people with the unreasonable beliefs are not themselves tolerant *where* their unreasonablity and intolerance will not result in harm to other people or the violation of their rights. Of course, they not infrequently will and then their intolerance cannot be tolerated.

Sophisticated believers (as well as unsophisticated ones), *perhaps* Kierkegaardians aside, will, of course, not agree that it is unreasonable to have religious beliefs if you are scientifically and philosophically sophisticated and living in our cultural ambiance. And they may be right. I can't for the life of me see how they could be. But then perhaps I am blinded in this respect. I would not be the first or the last person to be blinded over such deep matters of the heart. (I do not say they are just matters of the heart.) But, of course, the same thing applies to believers as well. My particular arguments or thoughts (not everything, even in philosophy, is a matter of argument) concerning religion (or for that matter everything else philosophical), like everyone else's, are, of course, most surely flawed. (If only I knew where!) What philosophical arguments are not? Though, of course, some more so than others. But I would maintain that the cumulative arguments and considerations—including philosophical arguments—of modernity count heavily, even decisively, against religious belief (Nielsen 1999, 32–48, 82–127). But religious believers—think of Charles Taylor here—will contest that. And so the dialectic goes on.

What reasonable intellectuals can and should do—this should be a platitude—is continue the argument or discussion in as open-minded a spirit as possible with a recognition that some of their most cherished presuppositions will be challenged and that they should attend to those challenges as open-mindedly and reflectively as possible. But we need also to realize here that we are not just playing a little philosophical game. Matters of the heart, and deep and persistent matters of the heart, and not *just* matters of the head, are at stake. Both kinds of consideration are at issue and we cannot, if we would be nonevasive, ignore either. So we just must go on, as reflectively and honestly as possible, and see where the court of history will take us. But I am sufficiently Marxian to say that if our circumstances are not propitious—if the springs of social wealth do not flow reasonably freely and fully—we should not, if we can help it, give, at least in the short run, the court of history the last word. It is not very likely that we—that is "we" as various peoples, even peoples in liberal societies—will, in any socially pervasive way, be tolerant and impartial—that a Deweyian creative intelligence will guide our actions—when life bites hard and conditions for education are not abundant among the masses of people.

How does all this stand concerning "Wittgensteinian" worries about a relativism built into our diverse forms of language with their diverse forms of life? As we have seen, there is, a not infrequent claim goes, just an incommensurability between believers with their language-games and secularists with theirs. They not only do, but they must, argue past each other. But, as we have also seen, this is neither Wittgenstein nor right. Language-games are not balkanized and believers and secularists are not hermetically sealed off from each other. Language, as Wittgenstein tells us, is like an ancient city criss-crossed, involuted, and extensively unpatterned with many roads leading off in all directions and in an unfinished way, but not in such a way that religious language-games and other language-games as well do not make contact so that there are not the resources for discussion, critical reasoning, the operation of creative intelligence, and reflective endorsement of which I have spoken. Reflectiveness about the reasonableness, or lack thereof, of religious belief, on the one hand, and of an utterly secular orientation, on the other, is difficult both intellectually and emotionally, but not impossible. The reflectiveness about reason-ability I speak of here is about the reasonableness of one life-orientation over another or about whether what should be concluded is that there is nothing to be concluded here about what is the more reasonable or the better path to take. But whatever we conclude here there is no good reason to believe that arguments and discussions here are essentially contestable. (Perhaps nothing is essentially contestable?) Such arguments will invariably be messy, open-ended, and most of the time inconclusive. But, it could be, for all of that, that some arguments, everything considered, will have more force and a greater plausibility than others.

All the above notwithstanding, and not in anyway taking any of it back, my atheism remains a hard, unyielding atheism. And, like Sartre, I want an atheism that consistently faces up to itself, to its own implications and consequences and is in no way evasive. For people who have been lucky enough to have a good education, belief in God, I say, should be rejected. And Judaism, Christianity, and Islam should, in a world of abundance with well-educated people, become merely cultural-historical artifacts. Respected, as such, for what they brought that was good for humanity and criticized for the ill that they have also brought. But in my heart and mind there is not a trace of nostalgia for religion or any doubt about the general cumulative thrust of secular arguments—what Max Weber calls the disenchantment of the world—that has been going on since the dawn of the Enlightenment and which has slowly evolved into an intellectually and morally powerful secular culture—a culture without God at the center or even at the periphery.

I have, of course, no such assurance about *my own particular* arguments about atheism. No particular philosophical arguments of any considerable scope even get near to getting it exactly right. There are no decisive arguments *in philosophy*—and most strikingly about philosophical arguments concerning belief and unbelief—though some arguments and some narratives are better than others. Fallibilism, as I like to say, is the name of the game. So I am confident that my own arguments are in some ways mistaken, though, of course, I do not now know where or how or I would correct them. And recognizing that, even with corrections, they always in turn will need to be corrected again, I still can and do *hope* (though without much confidence) that they cumulatively will add up to something that will push our reflective thought along a little bit. But generally about atheism—the work of many minds over long periods of time—I have no doubts at all. Mine, to repeat, is a hard and unyielding atheism.

It may be insisted that this still is dogmatism on my part with a little touch of fanaticism as well. I am, some might think, forgetting about my fallibilism here. Wittgenstein said that for religious persons their beliefs are unshakeable. This was a mark of the religious. But are not my atheistic beliefs unshakeable? Yes they are. But then does it not make them religious? No it doesn't. I am not appealing to faith here or to trust. I am saying (perhaps mistakenly) that the cumulative arguments for atheism, looking at the whole development of the Enlightenment (including, if you will, postmodern developments against Enlightenment *rationalism*), are overwhelming and there is no room (beyond general fallibilism) for doubt. But does not this renege on your fallibilism? No it doesn't, first because, as Charles Saunders Peirce taught us, fallibilism is not skepticism and secondly because I put forth my claim for the unshakeability— a firm belief in the truth of atheism—in a fallibilistic spirit. I can, reflecting in that spirit, see no grounds at all for doubts about atheism, but I recognize that it is perfectly open to reasonable doubt whether the general argument for that, or indeed for any general argument of substance, is in all respects, or even possibly in any respect, established beyond peradventure. Moreover, a consistent fallibilist will treat fallibilism itself as being fallible—as being open to doubt. There is no quest for certainty anywhere along the line and no claim of self-evidence. But Peircean critical-commonsensism does come into play. There are plenty of beliefs that could in principle be doubted that we do not actually have any reason to doubt. I am maintaining, plainly controversially and conjecturally, that for contemporary disciplined intellectuals atheism is one of them, or at least in time (given abundance and high levels of education) will become one of them. (I would, as a fall-back position, assert that, even if in time, given high levels of education and abundance, atheism does not become common sense, that it *should* become so. But here the basis for my "should" becomes *somewhat* wobbly.)

Before it is said that my atheism is fanatical or even dogmatic (as distinct from perhaps being mistaken), we should consider the spirit in which it is put forward. And here the earlier arguments made in this section should be recalled. The hardness of my atheism to the contrary notwithstanding, I am completely—though perhaps a little paternalistically—tolerant of all those who will themselves be tolerant, even when I think their religious beliefs are irrational. I do not at all share Lenin's belief that religion is not something to be discussed but to be denounced and, if possible, eradicated. It is perfectly true that I am completely out of sympathy—but then so was Kierkegaard and Wittgenstein, people with acute religious sensibilities—with the philosophy of religion business. When people come up with new arguments for design or a new argument for the existence of God from the big bang, I have a feeling of utter *déjà vu*. We have been over these things so often, and sometimes (or so it seems to me) reasonably decisively, that I cannot get excited about them or consider them with anything more than a bored sense of duty. It all seems to me very tedious. But I do not, of course, say that such work should not be published, read, or studied, though I do argue—not just proclaim—that there are matters needing to be discussed vis-à-vis religion that are of far greater human moment. And I do believe and hope that people, religious and secular, with an insight into what religion is, will (pedagogical and combative purposes aside) ignore them. And I am certainly glad (for pedagogical and combative purposes) that I have secular humanist colleagues who do get excited about them and set out, I hope carefully and impartially, to examine and refute them, if they have sound reasons for doing so. (One can and should do that while still remaining combative.) And my fallibilism will not allow me to say that these arguments of such philosopher-theologians *must* be wrong, though I am quite confident that they are. Similar considerations apply to the careful analytical defenses of metaphysical religiosity of someone like Hugo Meynell, Alvin Plantinga, and Richard Swinburne. All these orthodox bits of the philosophy of religion business seem to me utterly wrongheaded and a great waste of time and energy. But again I suspect they would return the compliment. And, again—and, of course—I fully realize that I and the philosophers and other intellectuals I find as allies may be wrong. And I recognize that there are philosophers, including analytical atheist philosophers—Richard Gale and Keith Parsons, for example—who think that such work (e.g., Plantinga's, Adams's, or Swinburne's) is of considerable moment: that that is where it is at in the discussion of religion. They think that it is there where we have to argue out Belief versus Unbelief, while I think that it is just such discussions which lead us away from a penetrating and serious discussion of religion. But even if I am thoroughly mistaken and wrongheaded here, it does not at all make me fanatical or dogmatic or in any way intolerant. Moreover, it is not all writings from a religious point of view that so bore me and seem to me so pointless and even lacking religious attunement. When Rush Rhees's *On Religion and Philosophy* came into my hands I read it avidly with a realization that he had pushed much deeper, in thinking about religion and philosophy, than I had ever managed to and that he had gone very much, and with deep reflectiveness, to the heart of the matter.[11] And while I do not get nearly as excited about the books of Alasdair MacIntyre and Charles Taylor I read them with interest and pleasure and I learn from them and I am very glad that they are out there in the public domain to be carefully studied and reflected on. They enrich our intellectual life and I feel called upon—and not just out of a sense of duty—to respond to them. So it is not all books written from a religious point of view that seem to me so much dross.

To bring to an end this perhaps self-indulgent *apologia pro vita sua*, even if my temperament concerning the different works mentioned above is leading me in the right direction, what things, if any, of a general philosophical nature can be garnered from that? The following: It is a waste of time to rehearse arguments about the proofs or evidences for God or immortality. There are no grounds—or at least no such grounds—for belief in God or belief that God exists and/or that we are immortal. Hume and Kant (perhaps with a little rational reconstruction from philosophers like J. L. Mackie and Wallace Matson) pretty much settled that. Such matters have been thoroughly thrashed out and there is no point of raking over the dead coals. Philosophers who return to them are being thoroughly retrograde. (To see that I have not always treated such matters in such a high-handed and dismissive way, read Nielsen 1971, 135–257.) We should not always be going back to Philosophy One.

Similar things should be said for an appeal to Revelation or Scripture. Even without philosophical analysis, a cursory study of anthropology or the history of religions should disabuse us of that. Putative revelations and holy books or holy legends are many and conflicting. There is no way by an appeal to any putative Revelation or Scripture to establish or to know which, if any, is, or even could be, "the genuine Revelation"—*The* Truth and *The* Way—and to return to natural theology, philosophy, or historical inquiry to establish which one is the genuine one is to abandon the appeal to Revelation or Scripture as our ultimate court of appeal and to appeal to something else instead to ascertain genuine Revelation from counterfeit. If we try to say "Well, they are all genuine!" then we are just left with a conflicting mess of different appeals—sometimes with radically different and conflicting or perhaps upon occasion incommensurable conceptions.

Another standard, but also discredited, move is to say that morals must be based on religious belief. Without God morality is groundless. But by now it is recognized on all sides that there are both through and through decent believers and nonbelievers who are reflective persons of moral principle and that both of them often have reasons for being such. They both live in accordance with moral practices they reflectively endorse. To the retort that only believers, and then only believers of a certain sort, e.g., Christians, have ultimate grounds for their moral commitments, it should in turn be responded that (a) it is very doubtful that religious believers have made out their case for having ultimate grounds (Nielsen 1990, 1991, 1996, 557–97) and (b) that it is equally questionable that to have a reasonable morality we need, or even can have, anything like a moral philosophy of *ultimate* principles. Appeal to "ultimate principles" may block the road to proper and effective moral deliberation and justification (Hook 1961; Murphy 1964; Rorty 1999).

The above is all nay-saying—the things, in my view, we ought to set aside in thinking seriously about religion and in thinking seriously about its relation to secularism. What then do I think we should take seriously? It is a cluster of considerations turning around questions—desperately vague yet humanly pressing questions—such as these: What is it to live a life? What is it to live a human life? What significance (if any) can there be to our lives? What sense (if any) does life have? How are we to live our lives together? What kind of community, if any kind of genuine community, can we find, sustain, or create? Can we, if we are secularists all the way down, without religious traditions and a religious community, find, sustain, or create the social bonds to help keep our lives from being fragmented and alienating—from being just one damn thing after another? Where religion once gave us that social glue can any form of secular humanism, in the ambiance of the disenchantment of the world, afford us sufficient orientation so that we human beings (particularly if we are reasonably clearheaded) can have a community in which we can flourish? Historically, religions with their traditions have provided the medium, the context, in which we could respond to, if not answer, questions such as what is it to live a life, what significance can life have, how are we to relate to each other and the like. Are there purely secular ways of so responding that can be adequate or must we, if we are consistent secularists, say these are meaningless or incoherent questions (Ayer 1990)? "Questions" just to be resolutely set aside.

MacIntyre and Taylor have claimed against we secularists that only societies with religious traditions can yield and sustain the social bonds sufficient to make a genuine community possible, where we human beings, without fragmentation and alienation, can flourish to the fullest extent. Do we have good responses to them? It seems to me that we do and that John Dewey (not only him but prominently him) has offered us a reasonable account of how in a genuine community of secularists, secularists all the way down, could have a flourishing life and indeed a more stable flourishing life than anything that could be found, given conditions of modernity or postmodernity, in religious traditions. It is revealing that in all their extensive writings MacIntyre and Taylor have not come to grips with Dewey. That omission is telling. But still they might be right, their unfortunate neglect of Dewey to the contrary notwithstanding, about the need for a religious tradition. There *may* in secularism be no such anchor and nothing to steer by. Perhaps religion can somehow yield something distinctive and compelling here even for people who are clear-sighted and nonevasive? But perhaps nothing can and the only nonevasive stance is some kind of value nihilism or Mackian moral skepticism? I am not trying to answer or respond to these questions here, but to point to the yea-saying side of the dialogue between Belief and Unbelief. I am giving to understand that we should be discussing, and carefully, these live issues. They are the live issues worthy of coming to grips with. These, that is, are the issues that we believers and secularists alike should be discussing and not what we should conclude religiously or nonreligiously from the big bang or whether contemporary science gives us the base for a new design argument or whether there is, after all, some sound form of the "ontological" argument or of the argument from contingency to necessity. Here we stand in debt to Wittgenstein and Kierkegaard.

NOTES

1. Note that, given the way that he conducts his case against me, it must be something like this that Sidney Hook is assuming when he conceptualizes God. See the exchange between Hook and me, chapter 7, this volume.

2. *Contra* the above, could one be religiously attuned, could one live religiously, without at all understanding that one was so living and something of what that constituted? One might not understand the *analysis* of "what it was to live religiously," but that is another matter.

3. Andrew Lugg has alerted me to this kind of consideration.

4. We should not go from that *philosophical* quietism to a broader quietism. We should not think for a moment that Wittgenstein thought that everything is all right as it is and that there is no need to be critical of how things are or go. To think that is utterly to fail to understand Wittgenstein. Think, for example, of the way he detested and was critical of what he took to be the scientism of our age.

5. The work of William James in his *Varieties of Religious Experience* was an exception.

6. Still there is the lingering issue how do we decide which of the practices are *problematic*? We say those practices are problematic which fit badly with the great mass of the others. But is that all we have to go on and is that enough? I am not giving to understand that it is or it is not. My *hunch* here is that it is. But at present that is little more than a hunch.

7. To be "ethnocentric" in the standard anthropological usage is to believe that the way one's own culture views things must be the correct way to view things and that the ways other cultures view things, to the extent that they differ from one's own, must be mistaken—must be the wrong way to view things. The ethnocentric person unreflectively believes that the way of viewing things in his or her own culture is the right way to view things and that it carries with it the proper way of behaving and living; any way of viewing things, of behaving or living, that differs from their way, is gravely wrong and in error. Strangers, if they are to do things rightly, must learn from them. A perfect exemplification of this was the Greenlander's belief that strangers came to Greenland to learn virtue

from the Greenlanders. Richard Rorty, at first sight paradoxically, defends ethnocentrism. But the paradox is resolved at least in part when it becomes clear that his use of "ethnocentric" is not the standard one. He thinks it important to distinguish, on the one hand, between ethnocentrism as *an inescapable condition*—we cannot stand outside, in any very extensive way, of our own acculturation—where ethnocentrism is "roughly synonymous with human finitude" and, on the other hand, talk of ethnocentrism "as a reference to a particular ethnos." Rorty remarks "our acculturation is what makes certain options live, or momentous, or forced, while leaving others dead, or trivial, or optional. We can only hope to transcend our acculturation," and, I would add, then only in part, "if our culture contains (or, thanks to disruptions from outside or internal revolt, comes to contain) splits which supply toeholds for new initiatives. Without such splits—without tensions which make people listen to unfamiliar ideas in the hope of finding means of overcoming these tensions—there is no such hope. . . . So our best chance for transcending our acculturation is to be brought up in a culture which prides itself on not being monolithic—on its tolerance for a plurality of subcultures and its willingness to listen to neighboring cultures" (Rorty 1991, 13–14). Rorty, and rightly, defends such a culture and in *that sense* is being ethnocentric, though, in my view, to good effect.

8. It should be noted *here* how Putnam, and indeed Wittgenstein himself, are like John Dewey.

9. It is interesting—and perhaps revealing—that none of these "philosophical big guns" have provided arguments for their faith or even, except sometimes obliquely, responded to their critics on the subject of religion. They have left that to lesser philosophical lights. Why is this so? Is it because they feel that such defenses cannot be provided? Is it because they think that doing so would be all too easy? That does not seem to fit with their attitudes toward religion. Is it because they think there would be so much speaking past each other that there would be no point in their responding? But we do not know whether that would be so until we have tried. Maybe they think that the whole thing is just too unspeakably vulgar? But need it be? Are they just assuming their secularist critics are fanatics who are wildly *parti-pris*? Some are but others are not. It looks like we need something like a defense of theistic faith (or some subset of it) from at least some of these philosophical big guns.

10. Rawls remarks, "Certainly, comprehensive doctrines [of the good] will themselves, as they present their case in the background culture, urge far tighter standards of reasonableness and truth [than argued for in the public sphere]. *Within that culture we may regard many doctrines as plainly unreasonable or untrue*, that we think it correct to count as reasonable by the criterion in the text [a criterion for political justice in a liberal society]. That criterion we should see as giving rather minimal conditions appropriate for the aims of political liberalism" (Rawls 1993, 60. Italics added.)

11. I shall someday write about Rhees. I shall try to sort things out with him. But I say for the record his is the most powerful example we have of a Wittgensteinian account of religion (Rhees 1999).

BIBLIOGRAPHY

Ayer, A. J. 1990. *The Meaning of Life.* New York: Charles Scribner's Sons.

Bjarup, Jes. 1999. "Scandinavian Legal Realism." In *The Philosophy of Law: An Encyclopedia,* vol. II, edited by Christopher Berry Gray, 773–77. New York: Garland.

Carnap, Rudolf. 1959. "The Elimination of Metaphysics Through Logical Analysis of Language." In *Logical Positivism,* edited by A. J. Ayer, 60–81. Glencoe, Ill.: The Free Press. Originally published in German 1932.

Conant, James. 1990. "Introduction" to Hilary Putnam, *Realism with a Human Face,* xv–lxiv. Cambridge, Mass.: Harvard University Press.

———. 1994. "Introduction" to Hilary Putnam, *Words and Life,* xi–lxxvi. Cambridge, Mass.: Harvard University Press.

———. 1995. "Putting Two and Two Together: Kierkegaard, Wittgenstein and the Point of View for Their Work as Authors." In *Philosophy and the Grammar of Religious Belief,* edited by Timothy Tessin and Mario von der Ruhr, 248–331. London: Macmillan Press Ltd.

Davidson, Donald. 1989. *Inquiries into Truth and Interpretation.* Oxford: Clarendon Press.

———. 1989. "The Myth of the Subjective." In *Relativism: Interpretation and Confrontation,* edited by Michael Krausz, 159–72. Notre Dame, Ind.: University of Notre Dame Press.

Diamond, Cora. 1991. *The Realistic Spirit Wittgenstein, Philosophy and the Mind.* Cambridge, Mass.: MIT Press.

Hägerström, Axel. 1964. *Philosophy and Religion.* Translated from Swedish by Robert T. Sandin. London: George Allen & Unwin Ltd.

Hall, Everett W. 1960. *Philosophical Systems: A Categorial Analysis.* Chicago: University of Chicago Press.

———. 1961. *Our Knowledge of Fact and Value.* Chapel Hill: University of North Carolina Press.

Hook, Sidney. 1961. *The Quest for Being.* New York: St. Martin's Press.

Kumar, Chandra K. 2000. *Power, Freedom, Ideology and Explanation: A Marxian View.* Unpublished Ph.D. dissertation, University of Toronto.

Levine, Andrew. 1996. "Just Nationalism: The Future of an Illusion." In *Rethinking Nationalism,* edited by Jocelyne Couture, Kai Nielsen, and Michel Seymour, 345–63. Calgary, Alb.: University of Calgary Press.

Malcolm, Norman. 1994. *Wittgenstein: A Religious Point of View?* Ithaca, N.Y.: Cornell University Press.

Murphy, Arthur Edward. 1994. *The Theory of Practical Reason.* Edited by A. I. Melden. La Salle, Ill.: Open Court.

Nagel, Thomas. 1997. *The Last Word.* New York: Oxford University Press.

Nielsen, Kai. 1962. "On Speaking of God." *Theoria* 27–28: 110–37.

———. 1971. *Reason and Practice: A Modern Introduction to Philosophy.* New York: Harper & Row.

———. 1982. *An Introduction to the Philosophy of Religion.* London: Macmillan.

———. 1985. *Philosophy and Atheism: In Defense of Atheism.* Amherst, N.Y.: Prometheus Books.

———. 1989. *God, Skepticism and Modernity.* Ottawa, Ont.: University of Ottawa Press.

———. 1990. *Ethics Without God,* rev. ed. Amherst, N.Y.: Prometheus Books.

———. 1991. *God and the Grounding of Morality.* Ottawa, Ont.: University of Ottawa Press.

———. 1996. *Naturalism without Foundations.* Amherst, N.Y.: Prometheus Books

———. 1999a. "Atheism Without Anger or Tears." In *Walking the Tightrope of Faith,* edited by Hendrik Hart et al., 82–127. Amsterdam: Rodolpi.

———. 1999b. "God and the Crisis of Modernity. In *Walking the Tightrope of Faith,* edited by Hendrik Hart et al., 32–48. Amsterdam: Rodolpi.

———. 1999c. "Hounding Heaven Again." In *Walking the Tightrope of Faith,* edited by Hendrik Hart et al., 159–89. Amsterdam: Rodolpi.

Putnam, Hilary. 1990. *Realism with a Human Face.* Edited by James Conant. Cambridge, Mass.: Harvard University Press.

———. 1992. *Renewing Philosophy.* Cambridge, Mass.: Harvard University Press.

———. 1994. *Words and Life.* Edited by James Conant. Cambridge, Mass.: Harvard University Press.

———. 1995. *Pragmatism.* Oxford: Blackwell.

———. 1997. "God and the Philosophers." *Midwest Studies in Philosophy* 21: 175–78.

Rawls, John. 1993. *Political Liberalism.* New York: Columbia University Press.

Rhees, Rush. 1999. *Rush Rhees On Religion and Philosophy.* Edited by D. Z. Phillips. Cambridge: Cambridge University Press.

Rorty, Richard. 1991. *Objectivity, Relativism, and Truth.* Cambridge: Cambridge University Press.

———. 1999. *Philosophy and Social Hope.* Harmondsworth, Middlesex, England: Penguin Books.

Winch, Peter. 1994. "Discussion of Malcolm's Essay." In *Wittgenstein: A Religious Point of View?* edited by Norman Malcolm, 95–135. Ithaca, N.Y.: Cornell University Press.

Wittgenstein, Ludwig. 1953. *Philosophical Investigations.* Translated by G. E. M. Anscombe. Oxford: Blackwell.

———. 1966. *Lectures and Conversations on Aesthetics, Psychology and Religious Belief.* Edited by Cyril Barrett. Oxford: Blackwell.

———. 1969. *On Certainty.* Translated by Denis Paul and G. E. M. Anscombe. Oxford: Blackwell.

———. 1980. *Culture and Value.* Edited by G. H. von Wright. Translated by Peter Winch. Oxford: Blackwell.

———. 1993. "A Lecture on Ethics." In *Ludwig Wittgenstein Philosophical Occasions 1912–1951,* edited by James Klagge and Alfred Nordham, 36–45. Indianapolis, Ind.: Hackett. (Lecture given in 1929.)

———. 1993. "Remarks on Frazer's Golden Bough." In *Ludwig Wittgenstein Philosophical Occasions 1912–1951,* edited by James Klagge and Alfred Nordham, 119–55. Indianapolis, Ind.: Hackett.

---

1 1

CAN ANYTHING BE BEYOND
HUMAN UNDERSTANDING?

I

The answer to the question of my title, if anything could reasonably count as an answer, depends in large part on how we take "can" and "beyond understanding." I will come to this. But my discussion also takes place against the background of D. Z. Phillips's remarks about "the vicissitudes of human life being beyond human understanding" and about the "limits of human existence." All, in turn, take place against the background of thinking about religions in a nonrationalistic Wittgensteinian manner. I will argue that there are senses in which Phillips is right in his claim that there are vicissitudes in human life which are beyond human understanding, but that these senses are of little philosophical interest. In the senses that might deliver philosophical gold, the claim is at best false.

Phillips is a charter member of the club which I have called Wittgensteinian fideists.[1] I am still inclined to believe that my criticisms of Wittgensteinian fideism were essentially correct. That notwithstanding, I have considerable sympathy with what Phillips says about theodicies and toward what he takes to be the key division in the philosophy of religion: a division not between believers and unbelievers, but between rationalistic believers and unbelievers, on the one hand, and nonrationalistic believers and unbelievers on the other. The rationalists think it important to formulate theodicies or antitheodicies, to examine what "miracles" can show, and to examine the proofs for the existence of God with an eye to determining whether any of them could after all be sound. By contrast, a nonrationalist approach takes such rationalistic philosophical questions as questions which tend to distract us from serious thinking about religion. Here, as the previous two chapters should make evident, I am in agreement with Phillips. But for reasons I will make clear in this chapter, I do not wish to characterize the nonrationalists (whether believers or not) as people "who recognize that the limits of human existence are beyond human understanding" (Phillips 1993b, 153).

It should be noted, however, that the *Weltgeist* has gone against both of us. I had hoped twenty years ago that the discussion of religion—including the deliberations between belief and unbelief—would take a broadly Wittgensteinian/Kierkegaardian/Feuerbachian/Barthian turn. Instead, such nonrationalism was short-lived, going along with the rise and fall of Oxford linguistic philosophy. The dominant trend is now toward the pre-Wittgensteinian and pre-Kierkegaardian issues and questions: toward a kind of religiosity which discusses the traditional metaphysical questions of natural theology making use of analytical philosophy and modal logic, but still proceeding as if only Alston, Geach, Dummett, and Kripke—but not Wittgenstein, Quine, Putnam, Davidson, and Rorty ever existed. We get foundationalist arguments for or against realism rather than a sense that the dispute between realists and antirealists is a pseudoissue better dissolved than resolved. Rather than leaving such metaphysical issues to benign neglect, most analytical philosophers of religion rush in to take either a staunch metaphysical realist stance, as in the case of William Alston, or, with Michael Dummett, they adopt a firm antirealist stance. Insisting on "ontological seriousness," they take such metaphysical theses at face value and try to resolve them. Davidson, Putnam, and Rorty have, by contrast, shown us the way to go here; and more generally, they have set aside metaphysical issues as unanswerable without falling into positivist dogma. With Putnam there is from time to time a nostalgic looking back, but there is also a firm understanding that metaphysics is a house of cards which neither requires nor stands in need of answers. But contemporary analytic philosophy of religion, seemingly unaware of these developments, is deep in the metaphysical mud. Phillips sets his face against this as firmly as I do. This is all to the good. But he unwittingly tangles himself in some metaphysical issues which stand in the way of a perspicuous understanding of our forms of life, and with this, of our lives.

II

Phillips has written voluminously on what I should characterize as a Wittgensteinian approach to the philosophy of religion. In years past I have come to grips with roughly the first half of Phillips's corpus on this broad topic. As I remarked initially, I have not changed my views in any essential respects about what I called Wittgensteinian fideism. But in the last decade my disinterest in the philosophy of religion has become so great that I have read very little of the literature, and except for the following two essays I have not studied Phillips's later work at all. Here I shall concentrate on two recent essays germane to my topic: his "On Not Understanding God" and "From Coffee to Carmelites." I shall argue that in these essays Phillips surely wants to get out of the fly bottle, but that he has not succeeded and that this failure carries a salutary lesson.

III

I now turn to his arguments and to his narrative. Phillips claims that in philosophy, and in our Enlightenment culture generally, there is a reluctance—rooted, he believes, in prejudice, or at least in confusion—to admit "that there is anything which passes beyond human understanding" (Phillips 1993a, 131).[2] There are many things, of course, that we do not understand—ignorance and self-deception are widespread. Even when we work at them in a careful and disciplined way—as scientists, logicians, or philosophers—there are things we fail to understand. There is wide cultural agreement about this.

However, this is still something which just happens to be the case. It does not at all mean, or even suggest, that what we fail to understand "is something which is beyond understanding." What we fail to understand remains in principle, the orthodox claim goes, within the reach of human understanding. There is nothing that is *necessarily* beyond human understanding. "That something could be necessarily beyond human understanding seems to be an intolerable thought, the denial of a philosophical vocation" (Phillips 1993b, 153). Phillips takes the belief that this is so to be a pervasive philosophical prejudice flying in the face "of what is platitudinously obvious: that there is much that passes beyond human under-standing" (Phillips 1993a, 131). He believes that a philosopher might, and that a fully perceptive philosopher will, come to understand that there is something—*necessarily*—beyond human understanding. And a crucial bit of this is "that the limits of human existence are beyond human under-standing" (Phillips 1993a, 131). It is surely evident that if accepted this would give consolation both to the Kierkegaardian knight of faith and to the Camusian-Sartrean existentialist atheist. But this is not a fine, brash, philosophical thesis to be affirmed or denied, but a philosophical muddle which rests on a failure to command a clear view of our language. It is a claim which should be up for dissolution rather than resolution.

Let me turn now to an explanation of why I say this. What is it to say that when "one is reacting to the vicissitudes of human life . . . one is reacting to something which is beyond human understanding" (Phillips 1993b, 160)? And what does it mean to say, as it is standardly said by reli-gious people, that "the ways of God are beyond human understanding" (Phillips 1993b, 163)? Put otherwise, the ways of God are said to be inscrutable. If, as I think, it is a right move in philosophy to begin think-ing about God by exploring "the grammar of talk about the ways of God, given in our language, instead of assuming *ab initio* standards by which such talk *must* be assessed," then we will start our exploration by simply acknowledging that religious people say that God is inscrutable and that his ways are beyond human understanding. That is just how we play, if we play such language-games at all, the language-game of Christian, Jewish, and Islamic God-talk.

So why does Phillips say "that there is something, necessarily beyond human understanding" (Phillips 1993b, 168)? According to Phillips, what is crucial here is to recognize that we are up against, not *limitations* to human understanding which might be overcome, but the very *limits* of human understanding. Whether your reaction to a recognition of the limits, rather than the limitations, of human understanding is religious or nonreligious, if it is not confused, it will be a recognition that *there is nothing to be understood*, nothing to be put right by understanding or action (Phillips 1993b, 168). Samuel Beckett says it, with a succinct trans-lation into the concrete, when he has his character Hamm say, "You're on earth: there's no cure for that" (Phillips 1993b, 168; Beckett 1976, 37).

What sorts of things does Phillips say are necessarily beyond human understanding and can take no relevant explanation, for there is nothing to understand? He tells us that there are certain facts of human existence which can typically be given mundane causal explanations, but where our *reactions* to them show us, if we reflect, that even when perfectly correct these explanations are plainly not to the point. They are, that is, not what is to the point when we react to these facts of human existence: facts of what Phillips obscurely calls the limits of human existence. Here we are talking about the vicissitudes of human life. As I noted, in some ways they are explainable, or at least in principle could be, but in an important respect they are still necessarily beyond human understanding. (I would think, since in the relevant respect they are not a matter of understanding or knowledge at all, they would be beyond superhuman understanding, if such there be, as well. They would be beyond God's understanding as well as ours, and since there is nothing to be known, that would be no limitation on God's omniscience or omnipotence.) The characteristic facts in question are the "blind forces of nature, the unpredictable visitations of disease and death, the transitoriness of fame, treason by friends and kin . . . [and] the limitations of time and place" (Phillips 1993b, 161).

Suppose a writer, caring much about her work and struggling against odds to achieve something of merit and insight, is, unknown to herself, about to receive the Nobel Prize for literature. But the day before the announcement was to come to her, she suddenly and unexpectedly has a heart attack and dies without ever knowing that she has received the award. It is natural in such circumstances to lament "Why did it have to happen to her just then, on just that day?" As Stephen Toulmin has noted with his conception of a limiting question, this "Why?" is not a request for an explanation but a verbal expression of a cry of anguish (Toulmin 1950, 202–21).[3] We characteristically ask it when we have good causal explanations of why it happened. We are not looking for more information; indeed, unless we are metaphysically befuddled, we are not asking for any bit of knowledge or any explanation at all. We recognize, causally explainable though it is, that we are just up against one of those brute contingencies that happen for no rhyme or reason. There is no justifying it or blaming anyone, unless it be God, for its happening; we are here outside the domain of what is justifiable and what is not. (If it cannot be justified, it makes no sense to say it is unjustified either. Such normative terms have no hold or application here.) Why it happened, *looking at it normatively*, is beyond understanding. And it is a plain example of things that happen again and again and are to be contrasted with a child's death from starvation—one of the thirty-five thousand that so die every day—or people dying of AIDS brought about by a transfusion of tainted blood. These latter things could, with care and commitment, be prevented. They are things for which certain people are responsible, and they are unjustifiable in that wrongs are done to people that can and should be prevented. But the writer dying just then, dismaying as it is, is nothing that is up before the bar of moral or otherwise normative assessment, criticism, or deliberation; it is not the sort of thing that with foresight and resolute action could have been prevented or ameliorated. Neither questions of justification nor exculpation are in order; there is nothing normatively relevant to be known.

While it is at least plausible to believe that in the order of causes a principle of sufficient reason is at work, it is altogether implausible to believe that such a principle is at work in the domain of good and bad such that there is a justifying or excusing reason for every bad or good thing that happens. Some bad and some good things happen to us for no reason, and where they are horrendous enough we may cry out against them. What is puzzling is not that these things happen but that Phillips makes such a hue and cry about them. If we like we can talk about the "limits of human existence," "the limits of understanding," of something being necessarily beyond knowledge or understanding. But this is just a grandiloquent way of saying what could be expressed more prosaically and less misleadingly by saying that these matters are important to us, and that they are not matters of knowing or failing to know, of understanding or failing to understand, of reason or lack of reason, but things to which the notions of knowing and understanding, for God or man, are not applicable.

IV

To sum up: the vicissitudes of human life are often understood well enough, in the sense that we know their causes. We also know that they happen for no rhyme or reason; and because of this the notion of justifying them, or failing to justify them, makes no sense. But there is no need to make a *mystery* out of that. There is no intolerable thought here, making mish-mash out of the "life of reason," that something is, or even could be, necessarily beyond human understanding in that sense. It is simply the case that in the domain of the normative the principle of sufficient reason does not apply. Horrible things happen for no reason, with no one to blame, with no injustice being done.

Is there, however, perhaps some more significant sense in which something could be said to be *necessarily* beyond human understanding? We—meaning people who are likely to read this book and people from a similar social stratum who share, in general way, a similar way of life—find certain other cultures utterly alien to us such that we cannot, or so we believe, understand them. These other people live in "an alien society" which we cannot understand from within the mode of understanding we possess. There is sometimes, to circumscribe the claim further, a radical *incommensurability* between two societies (Phillips 1993a, 133). Phillips accepts, plausibly enough it seems to me, the Wittgensteinian point that "language gets its sense from the way it enters human life" (Phillips 1993a, 132). But when people have radically different lives there will "be as many differences in their languages as there are in their lives" (Phillips 1993a, 132). As a result, they do not just fail to understand each other; they *cannot* understand one another.

This is H. O. Mounce's view, which Phillips is criticizing in part, but also partially endorsing—though not very plainly. It appears, that is, that Phillips is endorsing the claim of radical incommensurability just characterized. Sometimes there are societies, say A and B, in which there are some things in A which the people in B cannot understand: they necessarily pass beyond understanding for them. This, Phillips seems to agree, can and does sometimes happen.

But such an incommensurability claim misses the quite different, though mutually supporting, points made against it by Donald Davidson, Isaac Levi, and Charles Taylor (Davidson 1982, 1984; Levi 1981, 1992; Taylor 1985). If in saying that the beliefs, conceptions, and concepts of society A are incommensurable with those of society B, we are saying that there are beliefs, conceptions, and concepts expressible in the language of B which are untranslatable into the language of A, then we have said something which is at best false. Where we treat meaning *holophrastically* and go moderately holistic, as do Quine and Davidson, there is no indeterminacy of translation. There are, as a matter of fact, no languages which are mutually untranslatable (Putnam 1986; Quine 1986, 1990). This is true even of the radically different languages of radically different cultures. (This was even stressed, paradoxically, by the articulators of what came to be called "the Whorf-Sapir hypothesis.") Moreover, given the resources for mutual comprehensibility between radically different languages of radically different cultures, there are no good reasons, if we go holophrastic, to think that there are even terms in one language that cannot be understood in the terms of the other language. Where the one culture is very alien to the other, and where it is very difficult to understand a concept in the language of the one culture by utilizing the resources of the other, there is a temptation to speak of incommensurability. We cannot reasonably ask for term-by-term translation. We need to go holophrastic, and moderately holistic, and still we will make mistake after mistake, and perhaps never *in fact* get the translation of the alien language just right. Marcel Proust, for example, has been translated into English a number of times.

A good example of what I am contending is that of E. E. Evans-Pritchard's and Peter Winch's treatment of the Azande concept of witchcraft, a concept which certainly does not, to put it minimally, match our own (Evans-Pritchard 1939; Winch 1967). But Winch, in correcting Evans-Pritchard's errors and at the same time building on him, gave us an understanding of the Azande concept. Moreover, if we *necessarily* could have no understanding of the concept, such that in principle no attempt to characterize or elucidate it in our language or any other language could succeed, then for reasons Davidson has forcefully argued we could never know whether or not that was so (Davidson 1984, 183–98; Ramberg

1984, 116–40; Evine 1991, 134–71). We would understand nothing at all here. But that is very different from saying there is some belief, concept, conception, term, sentence, or truth which passes beyond understanding. We would at least have to know enough about it to understand what it was that passes beyond our understanding. Let us imagine some language and suppose there is in that language a term "uzad." Suppose I master the language but still do not understand "uzad." All my efforts to get a grip on it fail. But to say that it is logically impossible for me, starting from my native tongue, to translate or understand it, as distinct from saying that so far all attempts at translation have failed, makes no sense. At least to know that "uzad" is part of the language in question, I must understand it as a word, a phrase, or perhaps a sentence in that language. I see that it fits or fails to fit with other grammatical sentences in the language. I catch something of its syntax. If I do not understand anything like that, then I am in no position to say that there is a term, concept, conception, or belief in the language of that culture that I cannot— necessarily cannot—understand. The thesis that there are concepts of an alien culture that *necessarily* pass the understanding of the people of another culture is an incoherent conception, probably a product of the Kantian scheme/content dogma criticized so effectively by Davidson.

We can escape these difficulties by dropping talk of "necessarily" or "necessity." Doing so leaves us with the banality that it is often difficult in certain particular respects to understand others both within our own culture and, even more obviously, in different cultures.[5] Sometimes they have notions we do not understand very well at all, notions that thoroughly baffle us. Moreover, it is not only the people in New Guinea that I have a hard time understanding. The skinhead with the shaved head with a red stripe painted across it, his arms and chest almost completely tattooed, with long earrings and a strange gait, is nearly as strange to me. I observe him as he gets on the same bus as I do and then the same subway, and I wonder what he is thinking, what ambitions, hopes, and fears he has, what sense of himself he has and why it is that he so decks himself out. I feel at a considerable distance from such a person: his life seems, and no doubt is, alien to me; and mine to him, no doubt. But there are also all the familiar ways in which I could learn about the life of such a person. There is no logical or otherwise conceptual barrier of incommensurability here, or, as far as we can discover, anywhere else either, which justifies, or even gives sense to, the belief that there are, for a person in a given culture, other people in the same or in another culture, with conceptions so alien to this person that they are necessarily incommensurable, that is, untranslatable, such that this person can have no understanding of what they mean when the others speak: each being immersed in a different conceptual scheme such that both are conceptually imprisoned in their own perspective with no possible understanding of the other.

Suppose we say (*pace* Davidson) that incommensurability should not come to untranslatability but either to noncomparability or to the lack of shared standards of rationality, making common acceptance and assessment impossible. The response to this should be that once untranslatability is abandoned, there is no reason to believe that comparability is impossible or that we have so little common toehold in rationality that some sharing in understanding and common acceptance of what is rational and what is not is even in principle impossible. Of course, people, over time and place, will have different standards of rationality.[6] But to say, as Phillips does, that there is no common rationality which people can appeal to, is to say more than that standards of rationality differ. To establish this claim, we would need to know not only that standards differ, but also that they have no central features in common. The platitudinous truth is that in some respects they differ and in some respects they are the same. With that sameness, even if it is rather thin, we have some common starting-point from which we could reason and deliberate about our differences, using something like what John Rawls and Norman Daniels have called the method of reflective equilibrium (Rawls 1971; Rawls 1974–1975, 7–10; Daniels 1979; Daniels 1991, 90–109; Nielsen 1991a, 195–248; Nielsen 1991c, 67–93). To think, as did Lucien Lévy-Bruhl, that there is something like a primitive mentality that leads primitive people to think utterly differently than we do, is at best a groundless claim. Our wiring is very similar and with our large brains (something cutting across cultures) we can, if other things do not go too badly, think. Moreover, we all have beliefs, desires, intentions, and plans. We wish to realize our desires, to see whether our beliefs and desires fit, or fail to fit, reasonably well, and the like. And if they hang together reasonably well, we will seek a better fit. (If this is folk psychology, make the most of it.) With these capacities and resources we can, and do, deliberate about what it is reasonable to think and do. It is not plausible, perhaps not even intelligible, to think that we will run up against points where what we take to be reasonable to believe or think is *so different* from what people in other cultures take to be reasonable, that it is *necessarily* the case that any cross-cultural deliberations and comparisons will be fruitless, or will break down, revealing a radical incommensurability of perspective. It is more plausible to believe that than to believe in incommensurability as untranslatability. And if there are common resources of rationality, there will also be common resources for comparability. To put the point more modestly, if such deliberation and such comparisons are necessarily impossible across cultures, such that the disputants even in theory cannot understand one another or deliberate together, then (a) give some evidence for that, and more fundamentally, (b) show how it is that we can know, or even coherently believe, that this is so. There is the empirical fact that understanding, fruitful argument, agreement, and so on, across cultures, and even within cultures, is difficult. But we must not, if we wish to remain relatively clear-headed and reasonable, slip from that fact to the claim that they and we are conceptually imprisoned in utterly incommensurable frameworks. There is no good reason to believe that mutual incomprehension and bewilderment are so intractable and so deep.

V

So the fact that there are cultures alien to each other, and that even within a single culture there are very different people with very different perspectives (say a Hamann and a d'Holbach, a de Maistre and a Condorcet), gives us no toehold for a belief in a radical incommensurability whereby some people necessarily pass beyond the understanding of some other people. But Phillips also considers, critically following Mounce, whether "there are things which pass beyond the understanding of *all* human beings: things which human beings can never come to understand" (Phillips 1993a, 136; italics mine). The kinds of cases Mounce presents, and Phillips considers, are our trying to understand the condition of a dog, what it is like to be a bat, or whether fish can feel pain. Mounce works with these examples in order to "illustrate the difference between that which we fail to understand and that which passes beyond human understanding" (Phillips 1993a, 131). Phillips argues, cogently I believe, that the bat, the dog, or the fish cases do not show us that "there are things which pass beyond the understanding of all human beings; things which human beings can never come to understand" (Phillips 1993a, 136–41).

There are also, it is claimed, things that one class of human beings can never understand about another class. The rich, Mounce has it, can never know what it is like to be poor, to live on the dole for example. But (*pace* Mounce) the rich can see, indeed observe rather systematically (travel with their eyes open, as de Beauvoir and Sartre did); they can read social scientists' accounts of poverty, extend their understanding by the reading of imaginative literature, and the like. Like George Orwell they can even live and work with the poor, taking jobs the poor take, living with the poor as the poor live. But Mounce would say "that no matter how much understanding of the poor the rich have, they do not know *exactly* what it is like to be poor" (Phillips 1993a, 141–42). Even Orwell could not know what it is like to be poor, even after living and working with them and writing *Down and Out in Paris and London*, for he was not poor and did not have the same inescapable vulnerability as the poor. On Mounce's account, to really know what it is to be poor comes to saying that you must be poor. Since the rich do not have to live with poverty, they do not know, and cannot—really—know, what it is like to be poor. But this is to turn something by means of an implicit, persuasive definition into a tautology that on normal readings or understandings is not. It is very likely true that most of the time the poor know more about poverty than the nonpoor. But the nonpoor can know a great deal about poverty; and in some cases someone like Orwell, who acutely observed and reflected on what he saw, might very well come to know more about poverty and being poor than do many of the poor. At least we cannot rule this out by conceptual fiat. Similar things can, and should, be said about paranoia and schizophrenia. Harry Stack Sullivan probably knew more about what it is like to be schizophrenic than most, perhaps all, schizophrenics. We cannot justifiably identify "understanding a way of life" with "living a way of life." These examples do not show that there are some things for some human beings which necessarily pass beyond their understanding (Ambrose 1950).

The dog, bat, and fish cases may seem to show that there are some things which pass beyond the understanding of all human beings. But I think Phillips shows that those familiar claims are mistaken. I do not know whether fish feel pain or not; but by studying carefully their nervous system and the like, and watching carefully their behavior, I, and others, could come to a reasonable understanding of what is likely the case here. Similar things obtain for understanding what it is like to be a bat or a dog. A dog to which you are very close and know very well might, when you look at him reflectively, come to seem enigmatic to you. You wonder what is going on in his head, how he perceives the world. And this is even more so with bats, with whom most of us do not live in very close contact. Phillips shows how we could come to understand such animals reasonably well. There is not some conceptual gulf between what they are and how they react such that we could not understand them at all. What Mounce, and in this case Thomas Nagel as well, show is that we can never know from the inside, as it were, what it is like to be a dog or a bat, but this is only, again by the use of an implicit persuasive definition, to identify knowing what it is like to be a bat or a dog with being a bat or a dog. But this works no better for these cases than for the others. Dog trainers and some dog lovers know a great deal about dogs without being dogs, and bat specialists can know a great deal about bats without being bats. In general, to understand or know x is not the same thing as being x or even, in some tendentious sense, experiencing x (Ambrose 1950). We have no plausible or even firmly coherent model for saying that there are some things—a bat, a dog, a god, God, a Martian, a computer, or whatnot—that human beings *necessarily* cannot know so that these things are beyond human understanding. And this is not *hubris*, but a reasonable grasp of how our language-games are played.

VI

Mystical experience, and mystical awareness of the inscrutable, God in particular, is sometimes used as an example of what few special people who have had that experience can know, and that others cannot understand—necessarily cannot understand. Those of us who have not had mystical experiences cannot understand what the mystic can. It is sometimes claimed that this religious case will yield a genuine example of understanding something that for most people passes beyond understanding.

There are, of course, problems about the very intelligibility of talk of mystical experience, for the mystic as well as nonmystic. But that aside, there is, at least on the face of it, much that can be learned about mystical experience from those who have not had it but have carefully studied and reflected on it. William James, W. T. Stace, and Ninian Smart have, without having had mystical experience, written about it with care, and sometimes insight; and some people have, to some extent at least, understood them (James 1902; Stace 1960; Smart 1959). To say that what such writers and readers understand is not really to understand mystical experience, for to understand the experience it is necessary to have it, is to make the unjustified claim of identifying understanding *x* with having *x*. (See also Ambrose 1950.) We have already seen that there is no justification for that claim. Thus it cannot be correct to say that the mystical experiences, spiritual exercises, and more generally contemplative practices must pass beyond our understanding if we have not had mystical experience. Mystics were not, of course, born mystics. They came, typically after rigorous self-discipline, to experience something which at one time was beyond their understanding. Phillips claims that what they came to experience came about as the result of a transformation, not an extension, of their prior understanding. The claim is that only by such a transformation of the understanding can such experiences be understood (Phillips 1993a, 143).

Suppose it is claimed that reading these accounts of mystical experience, including the writings of someone like St. John of the Cross, will not convey real understanding until the reader has had the experience itself. Those readers who have not had mystical experience, the argument goes, are to St. John's reports like the blind are to the sighted. To this we should respond that the analogy is apt. The blind can understand what sight is; they just cannot see. The mystical experience case seems to be fully analogous. Moreover, even if the understanding requires a transformation of experience, the transformation is rooted in something we already have and is familiar to us, and we could not have such a transformation, with the changed perspective on life it brings, without it. It is a necessary background condition for the transformation. Indeed, extension and transformation slide into one another. In those ways the stress on a sharp contrast between extension and transformation is in error.

St. John of the Cross thought that what he was saying would only be fully understood by those specially prepared to receive it. But this "being specially prepared" was to have received a certain spiritual training; and this is, as Phillips remarks, "a matter of building on, extending, ordinary religious practices" (Phillips 1993a, 146). There is a transformation which takes place in mystical experience, but it is a transformation which is essentially connected with the religious practices and conceptions which preceded it. Mystical experience does not come about as a result of some unmediated initiation. The belief that it does, Phillips writes, is itself "a magical view of mysticism" (Phillips 1993a, 146). So mystical experience is not inherently inexpressible, the mystic's claims are not self-authenticating, and they are not something that can be understood only by someone who has them. Again we have nothing that goes beyond understanding.

VII

It has not been shown that it is the case, or even can be the case, that the experiences or understanding some people have *necessarily* pass beyond the understanding of all other human beings. Contingently, of course, there are many things that some people know and others do not and cannot know. Children, to say nothing of infants, do not know many things that normal adults do. Primitive peoples know some things that we do not know and we know some things they do not. In both cases some things *contingently* pass beyond the understanding of some people. These things are the merest truisms, but true for all that. They are only worth reminding ourselves of because of certain philosophical confusions.[7]

It is only slightly less truistic to say that if there are gods, or if God or intelligent Martians exist, these beings (if that is what God is) will know things that no human being as a matter of fact can know. But this is like saying that human beings cannot hear certain sounds that dogs can; as when we blow a whistle that we do not hear ourselves but dogs do. There is no conceptual, or logical, ban on our hearing these sounds; it is just the case that, as a matter of fact, we cannot hear them. But what the Martians or gods, if such there be, and what God, if he is even possible, can know that we cannot is just like that. This, however, is not the kind of "failing to understand" in which Phillips is interested. It is not the model he wants for trying to understand what "passing beyond one's understanding" amounts to. Moreover, philosophers, like everyone else, have not been at all reluctant to admit that things can and sometimes do pass beyond our understanding in these—philosophically speaking—trivial ways. However, where we stick with "in principle" and "of necessity" in trying to model the understanding of something passing beyond human understanding, we run into trouble teasing out a coherent sense for these claims. If a Martian can understand it, why is it *logically* impossible for us to do so? If an adult can understand it, why is it logically impossible for a child? If God understands it, why is it logically impossible for us to understand it? There seems to be no answer to these questions. At the very least Phillips has suggested none.

Suppose we drop the qualification "human" and say instead, including even God in our scope, that "there may be something beyond understanding; not something accidentally or temporarily beyond it, but something necessarily beyond understanding." It is a tautology to say that if something is not a matter of knowledge or understanding, so that there is nothing to understand or fail to understand, then it cannot be understood. But it is extravagant rhetoric to say that we have here something which passes beyond understanding. This is more like bad poetry than philosophical description and analysis. To say that we understand something which it makes no sense to understand is a contradiction; to say that we should not try to understand what in principle is not a matter of understanding is a truism—though it is perfectly true that as a *second-order* matter we can come to understand that some things are not matters of understanding or knowledge at all. But, as we have seen, we get into trouble when, as Phillips does, we add "human" to qualify "understanding." If understanding is logically impossible, then it is logically impossible, period. Bringing God in will not make the slightest difference. What we have seen is that in a trivial, philosophically uninteresting sense, Mounce is right that it is "platitudinously obvious that there is much that passes beyond human understanding," but that in the philosophically interesting ways of construing that claim it is at best thoroughly problematic.

We talk in an inflated and obscurantist way when we talk of the limits of human existence or the limits of understanding. In both instances, if it means anything, it means, as Phillips shows, that in certain situations there is nothing to understand: not for us, for Martians, for computers, or for God. So if there is nothing to understand then there is no object of, or proper occasion for, wonder or perplexity over the fact that there is something which passes beyond understanding that we could not set right by understanding. That is about as evident as anything can be. Consider an example. People age and sometimes their powers— physical, intellectual, and on occasion even moral—fail. There are reasonable causal explanations of why this happens. But there is no mystery here, nothing to wonder at or be perplexed about, or to reflect on with an eye to making sense of it. It is just a brute fact of the world, one of the contingencies of the world which matters to us. It does not pass beyond understanding in the sense that we do not know *why* it happens; neither does it pass beyond understanding in the sense that God or a Martian could see the justification for it while we cannot. There is no justification for it: not because it is unjustified, but because it could be neither justified nor unjustified. Such normative notions have no hold here. (Not seeing this is, in part, what is the matter with theodicies.) In that sense they are not a matter of knowledge. Suppose a great poet grows senile and comes to write drivel. Faced with this we may say "Oh, why did it have to happen to him? Why? Why?!" This is our old friend the limiting question again, expressing our lament and anguish and our sense of regret that the world is such. The "Why?" does not ask for an explanation, for more knowledge, for a rationale, excuse, or justification to be supplied, or anything like that. It gives vent to our feelings. It is an expressive use of language. To say that it points to something which passes beyond understanding is misleading at best, for it suggests that something like understanding is at issue, when what is at issue are human reactions and deliberations in the light of these brute facts on what are the more appropriate reactions in such circumstances, if this can ever be reasoned out or reasoned *and* felt out. (That we can in some instances deliberate on what are the most appropriate feelings does not mean that feelings themselves are a form of cognition or a form of knowledge or understanding.)

VIII

What has all this to do with Divine Inscrutability? Phillips, wanting to avoid theodicies, wants as a "philosopher . . . to understand what is meant by saying that God's ways are beyond human understanding." What he has perhaps succeeded in showing us, or at least given us some understanding of, is what can sensibly be meant by "God's ways are beyond understanding *sans phrase*." But then he has in effect also shown us that there is nothing to be understood except that the whole matter should be set aside. Moreover, even if we do somehow get, against what I have argued, some appropriate understanding of what it is for God's ways to be beyond human understanding, this does not mean, as Phillips is quick to point out, that we understand God (Phillips 1993b, 168–69). But we then fall into still other difficulties. The hope was that by coming to some understanding of "the place that the belief that God's ways are beyond understanding has in the lives of believers," we could gain a foothold on what it is to believe in God and what it would be to encounter God (Phillips 1993b, 149; Phillips 1993a, 169). But if this does not help us to understand God, then, we should ask, what does? It seems that the very concept of God, in developed forms of Judeo-Christianity and Islam, is incoherent. The idea of

God as an "infinite individual transcendent to the universe" has at least the appearance of a contradiction; and the definite descriptions used to teach the meaning of "God," where these descriptions are supposed to specify a nonanthropomorphic reality, all seem so problematic as to yield no tolerably firm sense of what we are talking about. We seem to have no more than human reactions to a something, we understand not what. Divine Inscrutability is so inscrutable that we do not even have a sense of what it is to scrutinize here.[8] If God is utterly beyond human understanding, then there is nothing to be said, nothing to be thought, nothing to be perplexed about, nothing to wonder at. Accounts of encounters with God, of coming to know and love God, of living or standing in the presence of God, of sensing or feeling the grace of God, are what Axel Hägerström called "empty phrases" without sense.

Phillips claims that the mystics do not give reports, flawed or otherwise, "or descriptions which fall short of the mark, but gave expressions of their encounter with God" (Phillips 1993a, 149). He also says that this encounter with God, if genuine, must be an experience which passes beyond all human understanding (Phillips 1993a, 149). Given the other things he says, it must be an experience which necessarily, and not just contingently, passes beyond human understanding. But we have seen that this is an incoherent notion, and this being so, that the very notion of an encounter with God, at least on this reading, must also be incoherent.

Phillips might respond, as he does to Mounce, that like most philosophers I place too much weight on *understanding*. I worry about the coherence or truth of the belief that, where God is concerned, we need to understand that it is something which passes beyond our understanding, "at least while we are on earth"; and, over-intellectualizing things, I try to see if any coherent sense can be made of that. Phillips remarks that "religious reactions . . . are very different. When they speak of that which passes beyond understanding, they invite us to consider the possibility of reacting to human life in a way other than by understanding" (Phillips 1993a, 149). One reaction that Phillips takes to be religious, and appropriately so, is that of wonder. But it is to wonder in such a way that we can think of the grace of God. It is not the speculative wonder of the Greek philosophers. Phillips thinks that this is a natural way for wonder to go for the person of faith. But we—including in the "we" the person of faith—need some understanding of "God," to see how the "gifts of nature can be seen as gifts of grace," God's grace (Phillips 1993a, 150). But then we cannot just be reacting to human life in a way other than by understanding. The very possibility of so reacting requires some understanding, and we cannot have that if God is necessarily beyond human understanding.

Phillips might respond that the language of the mystic, like religious language more generally, is in our midst and "language gets its sense from the way it enters human life"; so that "the language of walking with God, meeting God, gets its sense, if it does anywhere, from the way this language entered the life of St. John of the Cross" (Phillips 1993a, 151). That language, which is one paradigmatic strand of religious language, involves talk of God being beyond human understanding as well as talk of the importance in the religious life of "dying to the understanding." Phillips would no doubt claim that in saying that such talk is incoherent, that it does not make sense, I must be importing standards of rationality or intelligibility from outside the religious language-games actually played; and it is unclear where these standards could come from, what authority they could have, why we should appeal to them, or why the religious person, or anyone else, should pay any heed at all. They seem, Phillips could say, like news from nowhere, arbitrary impositions from out of the blue.

I agree with Phillips that language gets its sense from the way it enters human life. This is a lesson we have rightly taken from Wittgenstein. But language must be taken more holistically than Phillips takes it. We must not take one language-game or linguistic practice, or even a localized cluster of them, standing by themselves. It is not enough to say, "This language-game is played." We need to look at the language more broadly and try to gain a perspicuous representation of how various language-games in various domains of our talk and thought, of our discoursing with each other, go, or fail to go, together. Thus we might come to recognize that religious talk ("God-talk" as I call it, as distinct from other religious talk such as the Buddhist might engage in) could have the grammar—the logic, in Phillips's extended sense of "logic"—that he says it has and still be incoherent because of the way it stands with other parts of our talk. That something like this is the case is what I think to be so. But I can think that, while still taking it that language gets its sense from the way it enters human life, because I look at language more holistically than does Phillips—thinking that a moderate holism, such as we find in Donald Davidson and Richard Rorty, squares better with how our language and thinking works than any balkanized or molecular view of language.

I think, and indeed hope, that God-talk, and religious discourse more generally, is, or at least should be, dying out in the West, or more generally in a world that has felt the force of a Weberian disenchantment of the world. This sense that religious convictions are no longer a live option is something which people who think of themselves as either modernists or postmodernists very often tend to have. It may even be partly definitive of being such a person. For Alasdair MacIntyre, and presumably for Phillips as well, this is a distressing, or at least a saddening, matter. For me, firmly modernist as I am, it is a hopeful sign. As Richard Rorty puts it, perhaps we can at last get the Enlightenment without the Enlightenment's *rationalism*. Among the intelligentsia such attitudes of disenchantment are widespread; and these attitudes, given a moderate amount of security and wealth, can reasonably be expected to trickle slowly down to the rest of society. The view from North America is that the view has not trickled down extensively to the population more generally. (Recall here my Introduction.) There has, however, been a lot of such trickling down in the securer, more prosperous, and better educated Scandinavian societies.

This Weberian and Habermasian sense of how modernity can be expected to evolve under conditions of security and abundance could go with a view like Phillips's that language gets its sense from the way it enters human life. Simon Blackburn has stated, though rather as an aside, what many philosophers who have been touched by modernity or post-modernity think, including such Wittgensteinians as Richard Rorty. Blackburn remarks

> Practice alone rules whether the choice of a mathematical or physical or psychological or modal or moral or religious language stands us in good stead. The philosopher may, as a lucky amateur, make a contribution to recognizing the excellence or the infirmity of some discourse, but there is no profession of being lucky. And when a discourse or way of life dies, as the religious way has effectively done in the West, this is never because it could not stand the scrutiny of Minerva, but because the consolations and promises it offered eventually lost their power to animate us. The philosopher can only ride the hearse declaiming that he thought the patient dead before the rest did. (Blackburn 1993)[9]

There is a little hyperbole here, but not much. It seems to me that this is the situation we are in. Perhaps this is a superficial way of looking at or reacting to religion, a way that has not looked at it carefully enough, sympathetically enough, or long enough; but then again, perhaps not. Phillips tries to exhibit sources of animation, but he has in reality afforded more of a reason for thinking that the discourse is, or at least should be, dead. He has tried, by assembling reminders, to show us that there are some sources in our lives and language that will reveal how the consolations and promises of Christianity, and religion more broadly, still have the power to animate us. But he has, I think, failed. It is time, if we have an impulse to do any declaiming at all, to ride the hearse.

NOTES

1. The original article, "Wittgensteinian Fideism," appears in a somewhat expanded form and with a follow-up chapter, in my *An Introduction to the Philosophy of Religion* (1982), along with my direct discussion of Wittgenstein on religion. I pursue the twistings and turnings of Wittgensteinian fideism in my *God,*

Skepticism and Modernity; chapters 5–11 in my *Skepticism* (1973); in my *Contempo-rary Critiques of Religion* (1971); and in my *Philosophy and Atheism* (1985). See, as well, Michael Martin, "Wittgenstein's Lectures on Religious Belief" (1991).

2. See H. O. Mounce, "The Aroma of Coffee." This essay is the object of Phillips's attention in "From Coffee to Carmelites."

3. I discuss limiting questions in Nielsen 1955, 1959, 1979. See here, as well, Coburn 1963.

4. If there is a verificationist streak here so be it. Not everything in verifica-tionism is wrong, not every application mistaken. See the Postscript.

5. See Rorty 1982 and 1991 on the import of dropping talk of necessity.

6. Charles Taylor and Isaiah Berlin (his talk of incommensurability notwith-standing) make it clear why in spite of different standards of rationality we still have overlapping criteria of both rationality and what is taken to be humanly acceptable (Taylor 1985, 116–33; Berlin 1992, 557–60). Taylor goes on to show, in ways that mesh with the method of wide reflective equilibrium, how we can reason our way out of ethnocentric traps.

7. Anthony Kenny cites Wittgenstein as remarking in an unpublished man-uscript, "A common-sense person, when he reads earlier philosophers thinks—quite rightly—'Sheer nonsense.' When he listens to me, he thinks—rightly again 'Nothing but stale truisms.' That is how the image of philosophy has changed" (Kenny 1982, 22).

8. This claim about the incoherence of the concept of God in the developed forms of Judeo-Christianity and Islam is articulated in the works of mine cited in note 1. David Ray Griffin, in a clearly formulated and fairminded review of my *God, Skepticism and Modernity*, has succinctly stated the core of my account, setting it out usefully in the form of seven propositions. He then argues that both my argument against theism and for atheism are incomplete. I argue that nonanthro-pomorphic conceptions of God are incoherent (E), anthropomorphic conceptions of God may be coherent, but they are superstitious and plainly involve false beliefs (F), and that conceptions of God that are neither incoherent nor anthropomorphic are essentially atheistic (G). My case against theism is not exhaustive, Griffin has it, because the conceptions of God referred to in the above theses (E, F, and G) would have to be exhaustive but they are not. The nonanthropomorphic concep-tions of God of *traditional* theism are, Griffin seems at least to agree, incoherent, but I fail to consider subtler forms of anthropomorphism in nontraditional theisms such as Tennant's or Whitehead's, which also reject the conceptions of God of tra-ditional theism as incoherent without falling into a *crude* anthropomorphism or into atheism. Hence my case against theism is incomplete. I agree that it is not complete and that a complete case would have to consider such accounts and no doubt others as well. My suspicions here are (for now, they are no more than that) that if I did consider them I would find that (a) the God of such philosophers was at a very considerable distance from the God of Judeo-Christianity and Islam, (b) that where their views are coherent they will reveal (as Spinoza's conception of God does) an atheistic substance, and (c) that their distinctively metaphysical strands are, as all such speculative philosophy, at least as incoherent as traditional nonanthropomorphic theism. It is just such metaphysical thinking that we need, à

la Rorty (a former Whiteheadean), to get rid of. Arthur Murphy's "Whitehead and the Method of Speculative Philosophy" (Murphy 1941) is insightful here. Set it, as well, alongside his "Moore's 'Defense of Common Sense' " (Murphy 1942), and his "Can Speculative Philosophy Be Defended?" (Murphy 1943). My case for atheism is also incomplete, Griffin contends, for I do not argue but simply assert that nontheistic accounts of the world are adequate. But that is not true for I do argue for their adequacy in my *Equality and Liberty: A Defense of Radical Egalitarianism* (Nielsen 1985a), my *Reason and Practice* (Nielsen 1971), my *Why Be Moral?* (Nielsen 1989b), my *Ethics without God* (Nielsen 1990), and in my *God and the Grounding of Morality* (Nielsen 1991b). In *Reason and Practice, pace* Griffin, I also argue that the efforts of natural theology have failed. See part III and, more indirectly, but still crucially, part VI, chapters 31, 36, 37, and 38. See also in this connection Martin 1990. My arguments, no doubt, are in one way or another defective. That is not surprising in any event, but it seems to me that in the last three centuries there have been varied and *cumulatively* very strong arguments for the adequacy of nontheistic (i.e., naturalistic) accounts. Taken together they present a very formidable case. It is little wonder that so much of the defense of religion has turned fideistic. Moreover, and vitally, what is reasonably taken to be "adequate" or not varies with what the alternatives are (what the live options are). If the God of traditional theism is incoherent, Wittgensteinian fideism is at best obscurantist; the God of crude anthropomorphism is something yielding beliefs which are just plainly false and noncrude anthropomorphism is (where nonatheistic) metaphysical moonshine. There is, if these things are really true, little in the way of an alternative to a pragmatic, thoroughly nonmetaphysical naturalism such as that articulated (though differently) by John Dewey, Jürgen Habermas, and Richard Rorty. I have also turned my hand to that in my *After the Demise of the Tradition* (Nielsen 1989a) and I have, as well, a bit in the tradition of Murphy and a bit in the tradition of Rorty, sought, without reliance on positivist assumptions, to undermine the claims of metaphysics (most particularly revisionary metaphysics in Nelson 1995). If metaphysics is a nonstarter, then the very theological enterprises which rely on it, such as Paul Tillich's or Reinhold Niebuhr's or that (to quote Griffin) of such "nontraditional theists, such as Pfleiderer, James, Tennant, Whitehead, and Hartshorne," cannot, relying as they do on the constructions of speculative metaphysics, get off the ground. If I am right about the impossibility of metaphysics, there is little point in looking at the details of such views which are plainly metaphysical constructions. That is to say, key parts of their accounts rely on such constructions. I have argued for the impossibility of metaphysics in my "What Is Philosophy?" (1993), "Reconsidering the Platonic Conception of Philosophy" (1994b), "Jolting the Career of Reason: Absolute Idealism and Other Rationalisms Reconsidered" (1994a), and in "God, Skepticism and Modernity" (1992). In this setting aside of metaphysics (to return to the beginning of this chapter) Phillips and I, and Wittgensteinians generally, are one, though Wittgensteinians are usually loath to put things so bluntly. But Phillips, while abandoning metaphysics, and still seeking to keep the God of Christianity, or any other God for that matter, has only left us something akin to morality touched with emotion and obscurity.

9. The exaggeration there that needs questioning is that the scrutiny of Min-

erva can have no causal impute. It cannot have the grand causal impute that philosophers are self-deceived into assuming. But that it has none at all would take a lot of showing. I doubt that Blackburn really wants to make such a strong claim.

BIBLIOGRAPHY

Ambrose, Alice. 1950. "The Problem of Linguistic Inadequacy." In *Philosophical Analysis: A Collection of Essays*, edited by Max Black, 15–37. Ithaca, N.Y.: Cornell University Press.

Beckett, Samuel. 1976. *Endgame*. New York: Faber and Faber.

Berlin, Isaiah. 1992. "Reply to Ronald H. McKinney, 'Toward a Postmodern Ethics.'" *Journal of Value Inquiry* 26: 557–60.

Blackburn, Simon. 1993. "Can Philosophy Exist?" In *Reconstructing Philosophy? New Essays in Metàphilosophe*, edited by Jocelyne Couture and Kai Nielsen. Calgary, Alb.: University of Calgary Press.

Coburn, Robert C. 1963. "A Neglected Use of Theological Language." *Mind* 72.

Daniels, Norman. 1979. "Wide Reflective Equilibrium and Theory Acceptance in Ethics." *Journal of Philosophy* 76: 256–82.

———. "Reflective Equilibrium and Archimedean Points." In *Equality and Liberty*, edited by J. Angelo Corbett, 90–109. London: Macmillan.

Davidson, Donald. 1984. *Inquiries into Truth and Interpretation*. Oxford: Clarendon Press.

———. 1989. "The Myth of the Subjective." In *Relativism*, edited by Michael Krausz, 159–81. Notre Dame, Ind.: University of Notre Dame Press.

Evans-Pritchard, E. E. 1939. *Witchcraft, Oracles and Magic among the Azande*. Oxford: Oxford University Press.

Evine, Simon. 1991. *Donald Davidson*. Stanford, Calif.: Stanford University Press.

Hägerström, Axel. 1964. *Philosophy and Religion*. Translated by Robert T. Sandin. London: Allen & Unwin.

James, William. 1902. *The Varieties of Religious Experience*. New York: Paul R. Reynolds. Lectures XVI, XVII, and XX.

Kenny, Anthony. 1982. "Wittgenstein on the Nature of Philosophy." In *Wittgenstein and His Times*, edited by Brian McGuinness. Oxford: Basil Blackwell.

Levi, Isaac. 1981. "Escape from Boredom: Edification According to Rorty." *Canadian Journal of Philosophy* 11, no. 4 (December): 37–59.

———. 1992. "Conflict and Inquiry." *Ethics* 102 (July): 314–34.

Martin, Michael. 1990. *Atheism*. Philadelphia: Temple University Press.

———. 1991. "Wittgenstein's Lectures on Religious Belief." *Heythrop Journal* 32: 369–82.

Mounce, H. O. 1991. "The Aroma of Coffee." *Philosophy* 64, no. 248: 159–73.

Murphy, Arthur. 1941. "Whitehead and the Method of Speculative Philosophy." In *The Philosophy of Alfred North Whitehead*, edited by Paul Arthur Schilpp, 351–80. New York: Tudor.

———. 1942. "Moore's 'Defense of Common Sense.'" In *The Philosophy of G.E. Moore*, edited by Paul Arthur Schilpp, 299–317. New York: Tudor.

———. 1943. "Can Speculative Philosophy be Defended?" *Philosophical Review* 52: 135–43.

Nielsen, Kai. 1955. *Justification and Morals*. Unpublished Ph.D. diss., Duke University.

———. 1959. "The 'Good Reasons Approach' and 'Ontological Justifications' of Morality." *Philosophical Quarterly* 9, no. 35 (April): 2–16.

———. 1967. "Wittgensteinian Fideism." *Philosophy* 42, no. 161 (July): 191–209.

———. 1971a. *Contemporary Critiques of Religion*. New York: Herder and Herder.

———. 1971b. *Reason and Practice*. New York: Harper & Row.

———. 1973. *Skepticism*. New York: St. Martin's Press.

———. 1979. "Religion, Science and Limiting Questions." *Studies in Religion* 8, no. 3: 259–65.

———. 1982. *An Introduction to the Philosophy of Religion*. London: Macmillan.

———. 1985a. *Equality and Liberty: A Defense of Radical Egalitarianism*. Totowa, N.J.: Rowman & Allanheld.

———. 1985b. *Philosophy and Atheism*. Amherst, N.Y.: Prometheus Books.

———. 1989a. *God, Scepticism and Modernity*. Ottawa, Ont.: University of Ottawa Press.

———. 1989b. *Why Be Moral?* Amherst, N.Y.: Prometheus Books.

———. 1990. *Ethics without God*, rev. ed. Amherst, N.Y.: Prometheus Books.

———. 1991a. *After the Demise of the Tradition*. Boulder, Colo.: Westview Press.

———. 1991b. *God and the Grounding of Morality*. Ottawa, Ont.: University of Ottawa Press.

———. 1991c. "Rawls and the Socratic Ideal." *Analyse & Kritik* 13, no. 1: 67–93.

———. 1992. "God, Skepticism and Modernity." *Journal of the American Academy of Religion* 59, no. 1: 189–90.

———. 1993. "What Is Philosophy?" *History of Philosophy Quarterly* 10, no. 4: 389–404.

———. 1994a. "Jolting the Career of Reason: Absolute Idealism and Other Rationalisms Reconsidered." *Journal of Speculative Philosophy* 8, no. 2: 113–40.

———. 1994b. "Reconsidering the Platonic Conception of Philosophy." *International Studies in Philosophy* 26, no. 2: 51–71.

———. 1995. *On Transforming Philosophy: A Metaphilosophical Inquiry*. Boulder, Colo.: Waterview Press.

Phillips, D. Z. 1993a. "From Coffee to Carmelites." In *Wittgenstein and Religion*. New York: Macmillan and St. Martin's Press.

———. 1993b. "On Not Understanding God." In *Wittgenstein and Religion*. New York: Macmillan and St. Martin's Press.

Putnam, Hilary. 1986. "Meaning Holism." In *The Philosophy of W. V. Quine*, edited by Lewis Edwin Hahn and Paul Arthur Schilpp, 405–32. La Salle, Ill.: Open Court.

Quine, W. V. 1986. "Reply to Putnam." In *The Philosophy of W. V. Quine*, edited by Lewis Edwin Hahn and Paul Arthur Schilpp, 405–32. La Salle, Ill.: Open Court.

———. 1990. *Pursuit of Truth*. Cambridge, Mass.: Harvard University Press.

Ramberg, Bjorn T. 1989. *Donald Davidson's Philosophy of Language*. Oxford: Basil Blackwell.

Rawls, John. 1971. *A Theory of Justice*. Cambridge, Mass.: Harvard University Press.

————. 1974–1975. "The Independence of Moral Theory." *Proceedings and Addresses of the American Philosophical Association* 47: 7–10.

Rorty, Richard. 1982. *Consequences of Pragmatism*. Minneapolis: University of Minnesota Press.

————. 1991. *Objectivism, Relativism and Truth*. Cambridge: Cambridge University Press.

Smart, Ninian. 1959. *Reasons and Faiths*. London: Routledge & Kegan Paul.

Stace, W. T. 1960. *Mysticism and Philosophy*. Philadelphia: Lippincott.

Taylor, Charles. 1985. *Philosophy and the Human Sciences*. Cambridge: Cambridge University Press.

Toulmin, Stephen. 1950. *An Examination of the Place of Reason in Ethics*. Cambridge: Cambridge University Press.

Winch, Peter. 1967. "Understanding a Primitive Society." In *Religion and Understanding*, edited by D. Z. Phillips, 9–42. Oxford: Basil Blackwell.

—————— Postscript ——————

THE GATHERING
OF THE FUGITIVES

INTRODUCTION

Philosophers not infrequently seek closure even when they know—or at least strongly suspect—that is something they can get only as a result of arbitrariness somewhere along the line. Still it is reasonable, indeed part of the very vocation of an intellectual, to seek as much coherence and adequacy as can be gained standing where we are now, the only place we can stand. So, as I read over what I have written trying to meet that *desideratum*, I can see places of vulnerability or loose ends where more needs to be said—perhaps more than I can muster—to get something for the time which somewhat resembles closure and which as much as possible responds to what needs to be responded to and does not hide away vulnerabilities. I think I know I cannot succeed in that—certainly not fully succeed—but I want to approximate it as much as I can. So here I shall gather together some of the fugitives—the ones that press most in on me. The ones that I am not aware of—and I am confident that they are there—

I can't do anything about until they are brought to my attention or my own reflectiveness brings them to my attention and maybe not even then.

WITTGENSTEIN AGAIN

Most of the fugitives come from sources internal to my reflections, from reading and discussing, but one concerning Wittgenstein comes from a direct and perceptive critique by Robert Arrington (Arrington 2001).[1] Arrington finds what he takes to be an important lacunae in my account of Wittgenstein on religion. It is that I "do not take sufficiently to heart and mind the idea of theology as grammar. . . . [I] do not perceive that religious assertions are made against the background of a distinctive system of reference or representation, whose rules are expressed in numerous grammatical propositions" (Arrington 2001, 172).

In the *Philosophical Investigations* Wittgenstein said, "Grammar tells what kind of object anything is." And then immediately he added gnomically and in parentheses, "(theology as grammar)" (Wittgenstein 1953, 116). Arrington, in his " 'Theology as Grammar': Wittgenstein and Some Critics," explicates what this means and argues that I and some other critics of Wittgenstein on religion have not grasped what it means let alone grasped its import. If we had we would have seen our criticisms— or at least some central ones—of Wittgenstein were off the mark.

Let us see what is at issue here and in doing so let's see how Arrington conducts his case. He does not deny that Wittgenstein takes metaphysical utterances to be nonsensical. But he argues that I have missed Wittgenstein's most characteristic reason for asserting this to be so. Arrington, with several important quotations from Wittgenstein, remarks

> . . . Wittgenstein claims that metaphysicians misinterpret their assertions as *factual* propositions when in reality they are *conceptual* ones. "Philosophical investigations: conceptual investigations. The essential thing about metaphysics: it obliterates the distinction between factual and conceptual investigations" (*Zettel* § 458). Many of the houses of cards Wittgenstein wishes to destroy (*Philosophical Investigations* § 118) are metaphysical statements which are confused because the metaphysician attributes to them the properties of both factual and conceptual propositions. They are viewed by the metaphysician as being *about the world* (factual) and also as *necessarily true* (conceptual). (Arrington 2001, 169)

He illustrates Wittgenstein's distinction as follows. "Red is a color" is a conceptual remark. "There is a red car in our backyard" is an empirical factual remark. The first comes to much the same thing as saying " *'Red'* is a color word." Similarly "Red exists," though less clearly so, is also a conceptual remark while "On my desk there is a red book" is an empirical factual claim. If we try to take "Red exists" as a factual claim we produce nonsense. So taken it is not clear what use (sense), if any, "Red exists" has. But if it has a use it would be that of a conceptual remark used to license the use of the term "red" in the way we speak.

Similarly, and somewhat more interestingly, if a metaphysical realist asserts "There are physical objects" as a putative factual claim, claiming it to be factually true, his remark is nonsensical. If we try to take it as an empirical proposition, we should come to see (if we examine it) that it is not, for no empirical evidence (a pleonasm) will prove it or disprove it or to come near to doing so. Just what would have to be the case for "There are physical objects" to be false or probably false? We cannot say. But then it is not used to make a factual claim. People very frequently take it to be a factual proposition but it is not. Where we try to so take it we end up unwittingly making a metaphysical claim, to wit a claim that its asserters take to be some kind of factual or otherwise substantive utterance, but where it actually is not. It instead is a conceptual remark parading falsely as a factual claim. That makes it, from the point of view of the asserter, a disguised metaphysical remark.[2]

Instead "There are physical objects" is a rather awkwardly expressed conceptual remark. To see that is so note the following: suppose I were to try to prove that there are physical objects by pointing to a rock and saying "This is a physical object." But "A rock is a physical object" is clearly a conceptual utterance. It is a piece of instruction given to a person who doesn't understand what "physical object" means. It helps teach him the use of "physical object." It is an instruction about the use of words and "physical object" is a *grammatical category*. "A rock is a physical object" or even "That rock is a physical object" is not used to describe something in the world but to instruct someone in the use of a word or a phrase (in this instance, e.g., "physical object"). Such utterances are nonsense when taken as statements of fact about the world, but they are meaningful as a way of expressing a rule about what a word or phrase means or about the use of a word or phrase. A philosopher who took (tried to take) "That rock is a physical object" as an empirical proof of "There are physical objects" would be unwittingly going metaphysical: *confusing a conceptual utterance with a factual one.* "There are physical objects" is a grammatical remark, to wit, a remark used to explain the use of certain terms. As Arrington puts it, " 'There are physical objects' really means something like 'It makes sense to speak of objects having place, motion, weight, etc.' " (Arrington 2001, 170).

Arrington applies this conceptual/factual distinction to such paradigmatic theological statements (as he calls them) as "God exists," "God is omnipotent, omniscient, and eternal," "God is love," "God exists and is our creator," and the like.[3] They should, Arrington has it, not be understood as factual utterances or metaphysical utterances trying in some sense to be factual and failing, but as grammatical remarks. They are not about a being called God who is either in the world or "beyond the world" or about the transcendent ground of being and meaning. They are rather "grammatical remarks expressing rules for the use of theological terms in everyday religious discourse. These rules constitute or create the language of religious belief" (Arrington 2001, 173).

Wittgenstein speaks of theology as grammar "precisely because it consists of a set of rules for the proper employment of religious terms" (Arrington 2001, 173). And there is nothing philosophically awry with that, anymore than there is anything *philosophically* awry with any actual language-game with its built-in rules for the proper employment of the terms used in that language-game. Things would only go wrong if, concerning such theological propositions, we go metaphysical and claim, with such propositions, to be making true factual claims about God and in doing so fall into the usual metaphysical confusion of grammatical and factual investigations: the incoherent taking of a proposition at one and the same time to be both conceptual and factual. What I fail to do, Arrington has it, in critiquing as nonsensical metaphysical religiosity is to take "the next step and acknowledge that the senseless metaphysical proposition 'God exists,' etc. hides a grammatical proposition which is far from meaningless" (Arrington 2001, 173).

As religious believers of even a remotely orthodox sort found Richard Braithwaite's and R. M. Hare's *expressivist* account of religion as very distant from what they believe—they did not find it recognizable (for example) as an account of Christian belief, but as Alasdair MacIntyre did, as atheism in disguise—so such believers would find Wittgenstein's account as Arrington reads him very distant from what they believe (Braithwaite 1975; Hare 1973; Nielsen 1989, 172–89; MacIntyre 1956). When believers assert things like the following: "God really does exist," "There is a purely spiritual transcendent being who is omnipotent, omniscient, and eternal," "There is a living being, in some way a person (though still a timeless, eternal being), in whose providential care I am secure," "There is a pure spirit transcendent to the universe who created the universe out of nothing and all the things in it," and then they are told that they are in so speaking making grammatical remarks concerning how they as religious believers are to talk and conceptualize things, that would come as a great shock to their religious belief-system, to their (in Wittgenstein's terms) passionate system of reference. This is not what they *think* they are doing when they are engaging in such God-talk. They believe in (have a passionate commitment to) and also believe that there is an infinite mysterious, awesome, and fearsome power in whom they trust and upon whom they are utterly dependent who created the world and everything in it out of nothing (Hägerström 1964, 224–59). This infinite being is a Pure Spirit transcendent to the world who is omniscient, omnipotent, and perfectly good and who acts in the world. This, of course, tells Jews, Christians, and Moslems something—an important something—about what they mean by God, but it is also taken by them (incoherently I believe) to be a deep factual or in some way otherwise substantive truth—some kind of "necessary fact"—about what there is (about what the universe and life is like and about what sustains it). Believers, if they are even remotely orthodox, do not *think* they differ from secularists simply in having a different vocabulary with different moral implications—as simply being attuned to a different cluster of categorial terms in accordance with which they conceptualize things and live their lives while atheists are just attuned to a different vocabulary, to a different cluster of categorial terms, and have a partially different moral outlook. Believers are so attuned, but they also believe that the above theological statement is true—is a fact (perhaps even a "necessary fact"), a mysterious cosmological truth—about our condition and what the world is like. It is not, as they see it, for them just a grammatical expression in a language-game they choose to play or (more commonly) were socialized into playing without much in the way of choice in a world where other alternative language-games and grammar rules are on offer.

For a Christian, for example, "Christ is the Truth and the Way" doesn't just mean "Talk Christian, conceptualize Christian, and act Christian." It indeed admonishes them to do certain things. But it also gives to understand that there is a person—an individual—Christ who is (somehow) both God and human who shows us how to live our lives. So "Christ is the Truth and the Way" will not be taken by them to be just a further grammatical remark. They are not prepared to take it just as a rule about how they are to talk and conceptualize things.

Wittgenstein was trying in his remarks about religious belief to give us a perspicuous representation of the use of religious terms and sentences. He was trying to show us how religious language-games are played and something of the point in playing them. And that is indeed different from arguing against or for religion. But language-games partially constitute social practices and, for Wittgenstein, the forms of language are the forms of life and forms of life, among other things, contain beliefs about how things are. Christianity is a form of life and it, like all forms of life, contains such doctrines which I maintain are characteristically taken as expressions of such belief, while actually being incoherent attempts at expressing belief. They are not just, if at all, grammatical remarks in Wittgenstein's or anyone else's sense of "grammatical remarks." In saying "God loves me and protects me so that no harm can come to me" I am not saying, though I may be presupposing, something about what kind of grammatical categories there are. I am rather asserting something which I believe is true about my condition and about what the world is like. If Wittgenstein is to be read in Arrington's way, Wittgenstein, with his conception of theology as grammar, is deeply *revisionist* about religious discourse, thought, and belief. But normally that is the last thing Wittgenstein wants to be. He would not wish to propose new or partly modified religious language-games, but rather to clearly describe for therapeutic purposes the ones we have. Theology as grammar, at least understood as Arrington understands it, does not do that, though it tries to. It may be true that the only use (coherent use?) such theological utterances have is that of grammatical remarks, but the believer on pain of losing his faith cannot take them in that way—he has to have, as I argued in a different context in the first chapter, a different metabelief about them—for he must see them as mysterious and profound cosmological claims about the order of the world, claims which he regards as crucial in giving his life meaning. He has metabeliefs which get expressed as mysterious metaphysical remarks in just the sense that Arrington specifies: they confuse factual with conceptual considerations, but such a confusion is essential for *believers* and it is, of course, also essential that they do not see it as a confusion or the life-string of their faith will be cut (Nielsen 1962; Hägerström 1964, 224–59).[4] (See also chapter 1 on the error theory of religion.)

NATURALISM AGAIN

I claimed in section I of chapter 5 that, unlike the generation of philosophers before ours, with us naturalism is very often not argued for but just assumed with the *déjà vu* reaction "So what else is new?" This is true of what I have called cosmological naturalism, but it has never been true of what I have called methodological naturalism. Methodological naturalism always was and still is controversial. It was strenuously argued for by Dewey, Hook, and Nagel and was resisted by Josiah Royce, Arthur Murphy, and Roderick Chisholm among others. What has been called "The New Naturalism" (Dedrick 1993), while just assuming cosmological naturalism (what else could be reasonable?), has once again strenuously argued for (though usually not under that label) methodological naturalism. There has been a passion in the last little while, in a way that would have dismayed Gottlieb Frege, G. E. Moore, and Wittgenstein, for naturalizing everything: epistemology, logic, philosophy of mind, ethics and ethical theory, rationality, normativity, and even philosophy. Quine is the exemplar here, but many, though with critical variations on his theme, have followed him (Armstrong 1999, 1996; Kitcher 1992; Sober 1999).[5] Indeed naturalizing things has become a growth industry in philosophy (Kitcher 1992).

I have resisted methodological naturalism as has Hilary Putnam, John McDowell, and Richard Rorty, among others. However, the case for the New Naturalism in the hands of philosophers such as Philip Kitcher, Peter Railton, Richard Miller, Michael Friedman, and Elliot Sober has been forcefully articulated, and in doing so they have defended methodological naturalism. I will return to this topic later in this section, but first I want to turn to an issue about cosmological naturalism since that issue is more central to my own project in this volume. Only if it were the case that the falsity of methodological naturalism entailed the falsity of cosmological naturalism or weakened the plausibility of cosmological naturalism would methodological naturalism be center stage in my presentation and defense of a naturalistic outlook vis-à-vis religion. I have argued that it does not. But since some New Naturalists have thought otherwise, and not unperceptively so, I shall later in this section return briefly to considering again methodological naturalism in the light of the New Naturalism. (I shall also there give a characterization of the New Naturalism.)

So first to cosmological naturalism and what might be a conflict in my own account. "Naturalism," as I say in the first sentence of the first chapter, "denies that there are any spiritual or supernatural realities transcendent to the world or at least that we have sound grounds for believing that there are such realities or perhaps even for believing that there could be such realities." So far as *naturalism* is concerned, we are on safe grounds. Anyone who is a substantive (cosmological) naturalist would avow that and the religious or idealist opposition understands what they are opposing, what the naturalist is, in one way or another, denying and something of what is at issue. The substantive—that is, cosmological—naturalist, to put it crudely but accurately, is asserting that *nature is all*. There is nothing that exists that is not a part of nature and there is nothing beyond nature. But we have seen Jean Hampton pressing us for how we determine what is natural or what is nature (see chapter 6). Well, the above tells us that what is natural is not supernatural or spiritual or just mental. Still that does not tell us very much. As Barry Stroud well puts it, we need carefully to consider "what is and what is not to be included in one's conception of 'nature.' That is the real question and that is what leads to deep disagreements" (Stroud 1996, 43). In chapters 5 and 6, following roughly Hook, Nagel, Dennes, and Quine, I gave a conception of nature which was reasonably determinate and met, or so I argued, the critique of Jean Hampton and the earlier critics of Hook and Nagel.

A view very close to that—but metaphysically bolder—has been articulated and defended by David Armstrong, who might well be included among New Naturalists (Armstrong 1995, 1999). He conceptualizes cosmological naturalism as the view "that the world, the totality of being, all there is, is the spatio-temporal system" (Armstrong 1999, 77). The claim is that "the whole of being is constituted by the space-time world" (Armstrong 1999, 84), that "over and above space-time, there is nothing further that exists" (Armstrong 1999, 86).

I uphold, properly interpreted, such a naturalism. But how does it fit—or does it fit?—with my conception of a nonscientistic, nonreductionist *social* naturalism? As I remark in section I of chapter 2, my social naturalism is one which regards human beings as not *just* biological beings, let alone machine-like beings. It takes the human animal to be a self-interpreting social animal. "Social relations are partly constitutive of what it is to be a human being. They are not just danglers that might be snipped off to reveal the *purely* biological nature of what it is to be human." But how is this compatible with saying that all there is is a part of the space-time world? That sounds scientistic and reductionistic while my social naturalism is not. It looks like I want to have my cake and eat it, too.

I will now try to persuade you that I do not. Rorty, jibing at Putnam and John McDowell, likes to go around enthusing for "a picture of human beings as just complicated animals" (Rorty 1991, 133). But Rorty is not a reductionist and, as one can see from his critique of Hook, he is not a methodological naturalist either (Rorty 1991, 113–25, 63–77). In fleshing out what he means by human beings being complicated animals, Rorty stresses the usual thing that they are language-using animals and that with that there goes the ability to think, to reflect, to be self-interpretive, to make critical and reflective endorsements—all the conceptual reflectiveness that McDowell takes to be essential to his relaxed naturalism or what Putnam calls a sane naturalism (McDowell 1998; Bernstein 1995). It is also what is involved in my social naturalism. Only putting it as Rorty does unequivocally (and in my view rightly) clearly ties it to the space-time world. Complicated language-using animals are still animals, macroscopic objects, part of the space-time world. Still reason—it is no longer viewed as Reason—has been naturalized without losing its normativity. One *can* be scientistic *and* assert what Armstrong and Quine, Dennes, Hook, and Nagel do, but one need not be and in my view one should not be. There is no conflict between my social naturalism and anti-scientism, on the one hand, and my regarding, on the other hand, "that over and above the space-time world, there is nothing further that exists" (Armstrong 1999, 86).

However, why should we believe that cosmological naturalism is true? Why, that is, should we say "the whole of being is constituted by the space-time world"? Hook, recall, argued in response to Murphy that he knew of no way that he could prove it, but took it as a claim better fitting the ways we actually go about things in science and in our ordinary interactions with each other than any of the alternatives. Armstrong is bolder. He takes it as a plausible *hypothesis* that best fits with our total science. He is not only a naturalist—but as rationalistic as he sounds—he is also an empiricist though not an empiricist like the traditional empiricists (e.g., the British Empiricists) who "make immediate observation not merely the first but the last word about the nature of reality" (Armstrong 1995, 43). He is an empiricist more in the way, in spite of his distance from their pragmatism, Dewey, Hook, and Nagel are empiricists. Sharing this common commitment are naturalists, materialists, and nominalists (the doctrine that nothing exists except particulars) as well as upholders, such as Armstrong, of a basically Aristotelian conception of universals as being generals (as Peirce called them) "that are instantiated (at some time)" (Armstrong 1995, 50). This common commitment to empiricism comes to accepting

> the method of observation and experiment, the method of the natural sciences, as opposed to the attempt to gain knowledge by a priori reasoning. The central methodological postulate of natural science is that knowledge is not to be gained a priori. As Popper has insisted, scientific *hypotheses* need not be suggested by experience. But the testing and verification of hypotheses demands experience, observation, and a submission to the facts as found. Since contemporary if not past Materialism claims to spring out of scientific results and plausible speculations, it is committed to Empiricism. (Armstrong 1995, 43)

But how is (if indeed it is) this cosmological naturalism—this "ontological naturalism" as Armstrong puts it—testable (confirmable or infirmable)? How do we test "The whole of being is constituted by the space-time world"? What would falsify it or even count toward its falsity? What would we have to observe or fail to observe (understanding what it would be like to observe it) for it to be false or probably false? Armstrong claims the truth of Berkelian Idealism complete with a Christian God would do the trick. But we have nothing, either directly or indirectly, observable here. Some philosophers may try to assert that there are only ideas (mental representations) or that God (an infinite individual transcendent to the world) exists. But we have no understanding of what it would be like to confirm or infirm such claims, so we have not been given—and indeed we do not understand what it would be like to be given—even a possible falsification or even an infirming instance of the naturalist "hypothesis." What would it be to observe, directly or indirectly, a thing, a being, a process, which was not spatio-temporal? Armstrong, not unsurprisingly, does not tell us. He, of course, does not think we make such observations, but he seems to think that it is just obvious what it would be like to make them—that we have no difficulty in *understanding* here. But if we just think a little, if we try to gain something like Peirce's third level of clarity in trying to make our ideas clear, we will realize that we are in the fog here. It looks like "the whole of being is constituted by the space-time world" lacks truth-conditions or assertability-conditions. And it is not analytic nor would Armstrong take it to be or want it to be. And he, as a good empiricist, quite rightly makes no claim to have an a priori knowledge or some kind of "intuitive knowledge" of it or of any substantive matter. It appears at least that it is what logical empiricists called a pseudoproposition.

Dropping the idea of its being a hypothesis and not raising any question of its logical status, it does, as Armstrong remarks, still have hurdles that need to be met. *Perhaps* they might even by some stretch of the imagination be regarded as putative disconfirming instances. It is not only religious people affirming God and the soul, but that some philosophers, religious and nonreligious, "postulate all sorts of entities that are 'distinct existences' from the spatio-temporal world" (Armstrong 1995, 86). Various philosophers have proposed different ones, the list is familiar: "There are Platonic Ideas or Forms, there are universals, there are mathematical and logical objects, there are other possible worlds realistically construed, there are . . . classes" (Armstrong 1995, 86). In addition there are claims concerning moral norms, colors, norms of rationality, reasons, and the very "objective reality" of normativity itself. Armstrong thinks that these are matters we must as naturalists take seriously for they *prima facie* at least threaten the truth of cosmological naturalism. Armstrong's strategy is to *naturalize these matters*, to, as he puts it, develop a naturalist policy; in every case where these "philosophical postulations seem of value, to attempt to bring them down to space-time" (Armstrong 1999, 87).

Sometimes this is only done indirectly. With Platonic Forms, for example, we can show that naturalistically explicable Aristotelian universals can replace Platonic universals and, with greater ontological economy, do all the work they do. This is one way, he claims, of bringing the philosophical postulation of universals down to space-time. "To claim," Armstrong observes, "there are universals is no more than the claim that different things, different natural things, can have the very same properties and relations, with 'same' used in a perfectly strict sense. A special realm of universals is not required" (Armstrong 1999, 87).

He proceeds in the same way about mathematics. Only here, matters, he avers, are more tricky. Set theory and the account, due to Cantor, of natural numbers pose a difficulty for naturalism. Natural numbers exist, "the number of natural numbers, the greater infinite number of the continuum, and so on without end. Can we bring them down to space time?" (Armstrong 1999, 87). Armstrong hopes so, but remarks this has not been established yet. He takes doing so to be a naturalistic research program. It seems to me, however, that the matter can be handled in a much simpler way. We should not reify and objectify by talking in a Platonic idiom of mathematical and logical objects or speak of numbers—of any kind— as existing or not existing. We have mathematicians reasoning in a certain way, proving theorems and the like. They are playing certain distinctive language-games (engaging in certain practices) with certain distinctive rules. Armstrong believes that we should

> adopt a radically deflationary attitude to what the word "existence" means inside mathematics (and logic). When Cantor reasoning a priori, mathematically proves to us by the beautiful diagonal argument that there is an infinity of infinite numbers, what has he shown? Only, I suggest, that these mathematical structures involve no contradiction. They might exist, they are possible. What mathematical structures are actually to be found in reality is for the natural sciences, if they can, to decide. (Armstrong 1995, 87)

This does something all right to bring mathematics down to space-time. But it has not been nearly radical enough in its deflationary approach. We still have the idea of mathematical structures and talk of the possibility of their existing or not existing. Fantastically, Armstrong speaks of these structures as something there to be *discovered* by natural science. What we should do is drop all talk of existence and of structures that might or might not exist or to be found in reality. What we have is mathematical language-games, mathematical practices, with their characteristic rules, language-games that can sometimes be creatively and imaginatively extended or developed into partially new language-games. One central feature of these language-games is to display, perhaps forge, logical connections that will lead to the proof of theorems. But again we have nothing we need to reify. We have here an *activity* that people engage in using words and signs to establish certain logical truths. Even before we move from pure mathematics to applied, this way of viewing things is naturalist-friendly invoking no mathematical objects or structures that might exist or fail to exist. No such reification is necessary to make sense of what mathematicians do when they are not on holiday engaging in philosophy.

Another hurdle—or what some people (e.g., Stroud 1996, 49–50) have thought to be a hurdle—for naturalism are colors and more generally so-called secondary qualities (colors, smells, tastes, sounds, felt warmth) as distinct (supposedly distinct) from primary qualities (e.g., solidity, shape, size, and motion of objects). Colors, for example, are thought to pose a problem not because like Platonic Forms or God they are thought to be transcendent to the natural order but because they are thought to be purely mental and subjective. Scientific naturalists (so-called) or metaphysical realists believe that things as they actually are in the world of nature are not colored. There are perhaps round tables in the world of nature but not brown tables or green tables. My car is a part of the space-time world. But my *red* car, is not, strictly speaking, a part of the space-time world. Colors are not part of the causal order of the world and do not figure in a scientific account of what is so. So a robust "scientific naturalism" such as Armstrong's, Quine's, or J. J. C. Smart's must exclude them. Color, like taste, is an immediate, sensory quality and is not one of the fundamental explanatory properties of things. It is not part of the spatio-temporal order so it does not on Armstrong's account of cosmological naturalism count as an objective reality. Qualities such as colors are not scientifically tractable; they do not pass strict scientific muster. From a properly scientific perspective colors (along with tastes, smells, and sounds) cannot be thought of as real or objective properties of things existing independently of sentience (of people or other animals sensing them).

The standard response to this, to save appearances and to save "scientific naturalism" from what is at least paradox, runs like this: reminiscent of the error theories of ethics and religion, "scientific naturalists" will acknowledge that those illusory perceptions of colors and at best false beliefs about colors—claims that colors are part of the fabric of the universe—are themselves a part of nature. As Stroud puts it, a "naturalistic investigator must somehow make sense of them as the psychological phenomena they are" (Stroud 1996, 49). But, given the "scientific naturalist's" account of what there is, she cannot specify the contents of such perceptions and beliefs in terms of any conditions—any spatio-temporal realities—that she believes actually hold in the world. After all, it is one of her central tenets that there are no colored things in the world.

The "scientific naturalist" trying to save appearances will argue (correctly I believe) that there is no systematic error in our beliefs about the color of things. We have considerable intersubjective consensus concerning colors and we have scientific color theories explaining why we have that consensus. Beliefs about the colors of objects, when they are correct beliefs, are beliefs "about certain dispositions which those objects have to produce perceptions of certain kinds in certain kinds of perceivers in certain kinds of circumstances. *Objects in nature really do have those dispositions.* So the beliefs are preserved as largely true. The color of an object depends on what kinds of perceptions it is disposed to produce" (Stroud 1996, 49, italics mine). So colors are tied to the world after all. This is a hurdle that "scientific naturalists" can jump.

Stroud in an argument that somewhat baffles me contends that such a dispositional account will not do; such a plain reliance on common sense and science will not do. We, he has it, must push deeper than that to gain "a correct account of our beliefs about the colors of things" (Stroud 1996, 50). To be successful, he claims, there must be some way of identifying the color of things independently of the object's disposition to produce them. Stroud concludes that colors "must be identified only in terms of some so-called intrinsic quality they have. Not a quality that the perception is a perception of, but simply a quality of the perception itself" (Stroud 1996, 50).[6] In real life, he adds, he doubts that we can

> make the right kind of sense of perceptions of color in this [dispositional] way [described above. Moreover he doubts] that any dispositional theory can give a correct account of the contents of our beliefs about the colors of things. The way we do it in real life, I [Stroud] believe, is to identify the contents of perceptions of color by means of the colors of the objects they are typically perceptions of. It is only because we can make intelligible nondispositional ascriptions of colors to objects that we can acknowledge and identify perceptions as perceptions of this or that color. But if that is so, it requires our accepting the fact that objects in the world are colored, and that is what the restrictive naturalist who denies the reality or the objectivity of color cannot do. (Stroud 1996, 50)

Still, if I have rented a green Toyota and am looking for it in the car rental parking lot, I can in most circumstances easily, if I am of normal sight, pick out the green one from the red, yellow, or black ones. And the green one, in contrast, say, to the red one, has the color it has rather than the color red because of certain features of the green one—the physical object that is the car in question—that produces that visual appearance. And that is scientifically establishable and indeed established. A person unsighted from birth can study the chemistry of color and be able to determine, without any perception of color at all, or ever having any perception of color at all, which one is the green one and which one is the red one and be able to give an objective physical account of why it is that these two cars have different colors. That we—that is most human beings—*start* from color perceptions does not mean we must *end* there. Bootstrapping ourselves—using color perceptions to get us going—we can come to explain in a perfectly naturalistic fashion—rooting our explanations in space-time entities—why we make different color discriminations. There is no need for discontent with naturalism—even "scientific naturalism" here.

Still, without taking any of this back, we should say that our world is replete with colors. Almost all the things we see—except unstained glass, pure water, pure vodka, and the like—are colored things and we pretty much agree about the colors of those things. If we have (and quite properly) a physicist's or chemist's way of conceiving things and if for some reason in a certain context we are playing that language-game (engaging in that activity) and if we are not interested in the color of things, then we may hold that things as they are in the world of nature are not really colored.[7] But that does not mean that in the art world or our common-sense human world of our everyday and sometimes not so everyday life that our world here is not full of colors.[8] I sit here writing this in my garden with various flowers of different colors around me, the red brick floor, the Virginia creepers, and the green wall enclosing the garden and I see all kinds of colored things and they do not disappear when I go inside to get a cup of coffee, though I, of course, no longer see them while I am inside. There are in physical objects real powers and real dispositions that exist quite independently of me, though, if there were no animals with the proper sensory apparatus there would, of course, have been no awareness of this. That we (that is in general we human beings) start with some initial sensory awareness as a general capacity that most human animals have and in this way get color-talk in place in the first place, does not gainsay that with such talk in place (as it surely is) unsighted human animals (even unsighted ones since birth) with the proper scientific savvy can confirm or disconfirm claims made about color.

Analogously, I say the sun will set at 8:30 tonight and rise at 5:30 in the morning. Some pedant or metaphysician might say the sun doesn't set or rise but as the earth turns relative to the sun it becomes light in certain parts of the earth and dark in others. And of course something like this is true as the correct scientific account. But, in a way that does not at all conflict with the scientific account, in our everyday trafficking with the world, it is perfectly in order to say things like "The sun set at 8:30," "That was a glorious sunset," "It is wonderful to be up when the sun rises in the morning." All these remarks are perfectly in order in such contexts and at least the first one is true or false and is empirically verifiable as true or false. The same thing obtains for colors. "The hollyhocks are pink," "The wall is green," "The table is brown" are perfectly in order and can be empirically verified as true or false. And in our common sense way of conceiving things, in our ordinary language-games, such remarks are in place just as it is in order to say the sun is setting. This color-talk is perfectly proper, perfectly intelligible, in no way mythical. (Though, of course, it is possible to have mythical beliefs *about* how this is so.) There is with us now, in a way that has not always been true, a physical theory which in terms of the powers or dispositions of things will explain why it is that certain things have certain colors and would be seen to have those colors if there are any animals about with the proper sensory apparatus. But the justifiable color ascriptions we make concerning our seeing green Toyotas or yellow school buses does not wait on some scientific theory for their validation. Indeed it is only because we can make such everyday claims concerning color that we can develop and validate any color theory.

In the art world and in the everyday world of human interaction—my talking about my garden, for example—we normally do not at all need to concern ourselves with such matters as a scientific theory of colors. And in playing these language-games with colors, it is not that we are being subjective while in physics and chemistry we are being objective. In both cases we have an extensive intersubjective consensus relying on (though not only relying on) empirically confirmable statements and ideally we can get our beliefs and perceptions (expressed as beliefs) in both of these cases into wide reflective equilibrium. This is what objectivity comes to and when push comes to shove this is the objectivity that natural scientists gain when they are lucky.

This is where my perspectivism comes in as well as my contextualism and my nonscientism. My social naturalism is not a "scientific naturalism" though it certainly is not an unscientific or antiscientific naturalism, but is a naturalism akin to what Putnam calls a sane naturalism or McDowell a relaxed naturalism (Putnam 1990; McDowell 1998, 167–97). There is on such an account no one true description of the world, no one way we must look at the world or one way the world must look or one correct account of the world. Taking a leaf from Wittgenstein and such neopragmatists as Putnam and Rorty, I have argued that there are various accounts embedded in different practices answering to different interests and needs none of which are "closer to reality" or more of a telling it like it is than the others. What should be thought and said depends on the context and what interests are at issue. What is apposite to believe depends on the context.

I have also been at pains to argue—particularly in chapter 2 and in the sections of this book where I discuss Wittgenstein and Wittgensteinians—that this in no way implies any form of relativism, subjectivism, idealism (linguistic or otherwise), and that that relaxed naturalism is indeed what Putnam calls a *common-sense realism*—a realism that is in the realistic spirit, a spirit that is distant from metaphysical realism (Putnam 1999; see also Diamond 1991). Like Armstrong, I appeal to Moorean knowledge, but unlike him I do not try to supplement it or find a still firmer ground for it with a realist metaphysic or any metaphysics or ontology at all.

It might be responded that I can't have my perspectivistic, contextualistic naturalism and my cosmological naturalism too. I cannot consistently or coherently say what I have just been saying and have repeatedly said about there being no one true description of the world, about the ubiquity of perspectivism and contextualism, and still say with Armstrong, as I do, that the world, the totality of being, all there is, is the spatio-temporal system. Put otherwise, I cannot have my Quine and my Wittgenstein too.

I feel stuck here. I want to say both—I want to have my Quine and my Wittgenstein too—and I am not confident that I reasonably can. I follow Armstrong (and with minor modifications Hook, Nagel, and Quine) in my characterization of cosmological naturalism, the claim which takes space-time to be all that there is (Armstrong 1995, 50).[9] Where I do not follow Armstrong is in his attempt to articulate a First Philosophy—"the theory of the most general categories of all" (Armstrong 1995, 43)—which, as he takes the categories, will yield an account of properties and relations which are objective realities. The properties and relations he wishes to "uphold are relatively few in number and are *the real joints of the world*" (Armstrong 1995, 50). I definitely do not follow him here. That very idea, I have argued, is incoherent. We have no coherent, nonmetaphorical, metaphysical or scientific characterization of what that could even mean. We have no idea of whether any given characterization would truly or falsely characterize "the real joints of the world." There is understandably enough a deep metaphysical, or more broadly philosophical, urge to say such things. It is not only Armstrong, but a host of others, including David Lewis, C. B. Martin, and J. J. C. Smart, who have such a passion. Indeed, more significantly people with a speculative itch have been trying to say such things at least since the Greeks. Some of the most primitive things that drove many, though not all, of us to philosophy in the first place are rooted in this urge—the urge to get "to the bottom of things" finally to get things right. But here is the rub: we have only an inchoate understanding of what we are asking for when we ask for these things. What is meant by "the real joints of the world"? What is it a metaphor of? Perhaps of "The real underlying structure of the world"? But that is also a metaphor and what is it a metaphor of? The "real *basis* of the world"? More metaphor, metaphor built on metaphor.[10] And metaphor or not, why should we think *the world has a basis or a foundation*? I think language and thought are idling here. And why should properties and relations rather than the things the properties are properties of and that have the relations between them they have be the real joints of the world? Armstrong tells us that the properties and relations he wishes to give such categorial status are few in number. But he also says that they are things there to be *discovered*. But how? Insofar as, he further tells us, they can be discovered, they must be "discovered a posteriori, on the basis of our best science" (Armstrong 1995, 50). That is the only way, as far as he is concerned, they can be discovered, because, as he makes plain on the first page of "Naturalism, Materialism and First Philosophy," he is not only a naturalist but an empiricist as well and, as such, he rejects the whole conception of "establishing anything about the world by a priori argumentation" (Armstrong 1995, 35).

If there is anything of this sort to be discovered and if we have any coherent idea of what we are looking for here, then he is right in saying it is up to natural science to discover it. But the prior question here is, do we have an understanding of what we are looking for here or talking about here? Do either philosophers or physicists have a sufficient understanding here so that they would understand how to go on that quest? That there is such an understanding is thoroughly problematic.

How then do I get off agreeing with Armstrong "that reality consists of nothing but a single, all-embracing, spatio-temporal system" (Armstrong 1995, 35) or, as he puts it at the end of his 1995 essay, "Space-time, all that there is, if Naturalism is upheld, will be analyzed as, identified with, a vast interconnected assemblage of states of affairs" (Armstrong 1995, 50)—where "states of affairs" is his label for facts?[11] And, if I accept those claims, should I (or still stronger must I, if I am to be consistent) accept his further scientistic sounding claim that "the best guide we have to the nature of reality is provided by natural science" (Armstrong 1995, 45)?

I will start with the second question in the belief that it will provide the key to answering the first question which goes to the heart of the at least apparent incompatibility between my perspectivism and contextualism and my cosmological naturalism. Taken just as it stands, the claim that the best guide we have to the nature of reality is provided by the natural sciences is a piece of unreflective scientistic dogma. Indeed it is something that is almost certainly false. Anthropologists study kinship and cultural patterns, sociologists study social structure, political scientists voting patterns and procedures. Are they not studying reality? When Max Weber studied Japanese religion was he not studying reality? When Emile Durkheim studied suicide was he not studying reality? When Marx studied classes and class conflict was he not studying reality? When Freud studied infantile sexuality and psychosexual development was he not studying reality? *Perhaps* they all did it badly and we need a new way of doing these diverse things to do them well. But they were still dealing with "the nature of reality" though not the reality the natural sciences are interested in but with considerations which are nonetheless real, and just as real, as what scientistic naturalists such as Armstrong are interested in. And we do not expect physicists or chemists to tell us about these realities, though *sometimes* something of what they are saying may be relevant to these matters.

Outside of what is at least arguably science do not novelists like Turgenev, Balzac, Dostoevsky, Tolstoy, Melville, Zola, Sinclair, and even Joyce, Proust, and Wolf (directly or indirectly) tell us something about "the nature of reality" as well as dramatists and poets? Do we not learn a lot about certain psychologically very destructive ways, including self-destructive ways, humans sometimes behave from Eugene O'Neill and August Strindberg? And there are films, though not the usual junk, that give us a good sense of what is going on with us. Even art and, to a lesser extent, music do so as well. Moreover, in political and social struggle, in moral reflection and engagement and accounts reflecting on them or in critiquing what goes on there, we sometimes learn something about the nature of reality. Armstrong, like Quine, being scientistically blinkered, unwittingly makes a completely arbitrary persuasive definition of "the nature of reality" (Stevenson 1944). He gives us a narrow scientistic account that brings naturalism and materialism into disrepute.

Things would have been different, though certainly less controversial, if Armstrong had added the little word "physical" to his characterization and had said "The best guide we have to the nature of *physical* reality is provided by natural science." He would then have said something truistic though still true. And something worth saying (recall Hook here) when metaphysicians and some other philosophers, sober theologians, and New Age sillies try to intrude by denying this. That is something that is not scientistic at all, but it is very different from the dogmatic, unfounded, grand metaphysical claim that he actually made. One little word here makes all the difference, turning metaphysical extravagance into what is in most circumstances a truism. (Remember, even truisms can be true.)

How does this get me off the hook or does it get me off the hook? Like very many other people, I agree (what else is new?) with Armstrong that the best guide to coming to know about the structure of the physical world is through our best natural science. For us standing where we are now that just seems to me to be a bit of sound common sense. And, as my critique in chapter 6 of Jean Hampton brought out, there is no sense in talking about reality *full stop*. There is no intelligible investigation into reality as such for "reality as such" is nonsense. Contextless talk about "the nature of reality" is vapid. So my claim in arguing for cosmological naturalism is that in thinking about the structure of the physical world (the only kind of world, in the relevant sense of "world" *here*, there is) that we are thinking about a spatio-temporal system which we take to be, perhaps mistakenly, a single all-embracing spatio-temporal system.[12] In thinking about the structure of the physical world we are now—for this was not the way earlier physicists thought—thinking about a spatio-temporal system. And when we are speaking of physical realities space-time is all there is.[13] This says nothing about the art world, the world of human affairs, moral realities, political realities—the things that lead me to speak of a *social* naturalism. But it is a social *naturalism* in part because these social realities are not taken to be independent of physical ones and there would be none of these realities if there were not physical-realities—space-time entities.

In saying that, in talking about the structure of the physical world, we are talking about this all embracing space-time system and we are giving to understand, as Armstrong puts it, that "over and above the space-time world, there is nothing further that exists" (Armstrong 1999, 86). I am denying that there are—with the "over and above"—any supernatural realities, Platonic Forms, Pure Spirits, immaterial worlds, or transcendental realities (whatever that means). I am arguing that at least traditional metaphysics and theism rest on a mistake.[14] Indeed I have made the stronger argument that such talk is incoherent. But it is enough for me, in this context in company with Hook, to say that they rest on a mistake. But this is not to give to understand, let alone to assert, that there is a one true description of the world. There are many descriptions of the world made for different purposes, many of them with a quite legitimate rationale. And to assert this is not to imply that there is a single account of reality which tells us what reality is really like. ("Really," as it typically is, is telltale here. Stevenson 1944, 206–26.) There is no such an account for there is no sensible talk about what reality is like where it is not specified what *kind* of reality we are talking about (Hägerström 1964). Moreover, there are many accounts of our various realities made for quite different, often quite reasonable, purposes. What I am rejecting is that there is, or, as far as we can make out, even could be, any of the metaphysical realities claimed by theism, Platonism, and idealism. There are no well-formed (i.e., stably socially embedded) metaphysical language-games. There is nothing there to challenge or provide a coherent alternative to or a replacement of or even a supplement to the natural sciences or to provide their "metaphysical foundations." Moreover, there is no need for such (or any) metaphysical systems. I have been at pains to argue that their claims are at best false. But this is not at all to deny or in any way downgrade the social and human realities I talked about or to step away from my perspectivism and contextualism. To talk about these social realities is not to say anything metaphysical.

I want to return to the claim about the logical or semantical status of the principal thesis of cosmological naturalism. Let us put it as Armstrong did, though keeping my above clarifications and amendments in mind. It is the claim "that the world, the totality of being, all there is, is the spatio-temporal system." Let us use Hume's and the logical positivist's test. Is it an analytic proposition, something that is true in virtue of its meaning alone or is it an empirical proposition whose truth or falsity depends crucially on observation and experiment? If it is neither, Hume said to commit it to the flames. More cautious contemporary empiricists would say put it on the back burner (Sober 1999). But whatever we want to say about flames or back burners, these two means (experiment and logical connection) are standard measures of proposition accreditation (Berlin 1980, vii–viii, 1–11, 143–72; Couture and Nielsen 1993, 1–41).

The cosmological naturalist thesis surely does not appear to be analytically true nor would naturalists wish it to be, for we want it—or so it would at least appear—to be a substantive thesis. And, as empiricists, as well as naturalists, we are not going to appeal to what is arm waving anyway, namely to synthetic a priori propositions or to intuitions.

Armstrong, as we have seen, takes it to be a *hypothesis*—however conjectural—and thus an empirical proposition and thus verifiable or testable.[15] But there is trouble here for we do not have any understanding of what would disconfirm it or even infirm it. Moreover, it does not meet the requirements that Elliot Sober has carefully set out for the testability of a hypothesis, which is to say that it doesn't behave like a genuine hypothesis behaves (Sober 1999).

While not being a hypothesis with empirical observations that would falsify it, we have examined considerations that, if they yield true propositions of the type these considerations involve, would show that cosmological naturalism is false. By "considerations" here I refer to Platonic forms, mathematical objects, and to colors. (I do not say these are the only such considerations there are.) I have argued here that they do not undermine cosmological naturalism. But they would if there really were Platonic forms, mathematical objects, colors with a queer logical status. But, as we have seen, these very notions are so very problematical that they could not disconfirm or invalidate anything, including Armstrong's thesis.

Yet, all that notwithstanding, cosmological naturalism remains a strange thesis. The cosmological naturalist says (1) "The space-time world exists and it alone exists" or (more commonsensically cashing in physical objects as space-time entities), (2) "Physical objects and physical objects alone exist." But I want now to focus on the weaker proposition "Physical objects exist." Armstrong seems to think it is a straightforward factual statement, indeed an empirical hypothesis, but that is far from clear (Wittgenstein 1969, §35). What empirical evidence could prove or disprove it? Do we have any understanding at all of what it would be like for there to be no physical objects? Perhaps there could only be sense-data? But we cannot even identify a sense-datum statement without reference somewhere in the background to physical-object statements (Marhenke 1950). And we have as well Wittgenstein's point, discussed in the first section of this postscript, that if we look to the actual use of "A stone is a physical object" or "That is a physical object" we will realize that these propositions are pieces of instruction—linguistic teaching in the use of words for someone who does not understand what "stone" means or "physical object" means. We have here not factual propositions or empirical hypotheses about the world, but instruction in the use of words. "Physical object" is what Wittgenstein would call a grammatical category. "A stone is a physical object" can be given a use, but this use is not one of describing something in the world to be discovered or assumed, but of instructing someone in the use of a word or phrase. It is not an intelligible description of fact or substantive claim, but a way of expressing a rule about how a word is used. "This is a physical object" therefore is not a factual or an empirical proposition, but what Wittgenstein calls a grammatical remark (Wittgenstein 1969, §36). "Physical objects exist" is either nonsense or an obscure and constipated way of making a grammatical remark. And "Physical objects exist and physical objects alone exist," "The space-time world exists and it alone exists," and "The space-time world does not exist, only ideas exist" are either nonsense or are still more such constipated grammatical remarks. They are not (*pace* Armstrong and metaphysical realists more generally) grand "factual metaphysical" claims—hypotheses of incredible scope—that are either empirically true or false.

Taking Wittgenstein's remarks about "grammatical remarks" here we can carry it over into something Rudolf Carnap and Hebert Feigl say about proposals (Carnap 1956, 205–21; Feigl 1950). Consider first Group A: (1) "There are physical objects," (2) "The space-time system alone exists," (3) "Nature is constituted by the ensemble of the space-time system and there is nothing beyond it or other than nature." Or consider the less contentious Group B: (4) "The structure of the physical world is that of a single, all-embracing spatio-temporal system," (5) "When we are speaking of physical realities space-time is all there is," (6) "All physical realities are space-time realities," (7) "All that is substantively factual are physical or social realities; there are no purely spiritual realities, purely mental realities not dependent on physical realities."

As we have seen how "Physical objects exist" or "There are physical objects" can be treated as grammatical remarks so the idea is to treat all these seven propositions as in Wittgenstein's somewhat eccentric use as "grammatical remarks." ("Conceptual remarks" I think would be more felicitous, though these conceptual remarks need not be taken as analytic. But they show the use of language in some language-game.) It is not clear that all of them would most naturally be taken as grammatical remarks. And some of them—(2) for example—might best be taken as *stipulating* a use. But that too takes the form of a grammatical remark and it gives it a clear license for being a proposal, though, as I have argued here, a rather arbitrary one without considerable additional specification and qualification. Someone might try—as the language of physics has developed—to construe (4) and (6), particularly (6), as analytic, but many, perhaps most, would not. (Whether the very idea of "being analytic" is sufficiently clear to be useful is, of course, also an issue here.) And indeed some might construe (4) as well as (5) as empirical hypotheses. The truth of Newtonian physics would disconfirm (5). But others would say the systems (Newtonian physics and modern physics) are so disparate that it is better to speak instead of conceptual revolution. The short of it is that none of these seven propositions are clearly either analytic or high level empirical hypotheses and they all can be reasonably construed as grammatical (conceptual) propositions.

So the resolve of a naturalist with an empiricist bent is, taking them as having that grammatical status, to construe them as proposals—as distinctive ways to conceive and talk about things (Carnap 1956, 205–21; Feigl 1950).

Some will no doubt say that that is a desperate arbitrary move. We can talk Thomist, Aristotelian, theist, idealist, Platonist too. Why talk naturalist? We can ferret out grammatical remarks from those systems or by stipulation produce grammatical remarks for these systems too and make proposals using them. But how do—or can—we justify making such proposals? Carnap and Feigl say we justify them by appealing to their utility, where "utility" is taken in a broad sense. I shall argue for a naturalistic proposal in just that way. That, in effect, was what I was doing in parts of chapter 1, extensively in chapter 2, and when I argued for a naturalist outlook against Demos in chapter 5. I shall now argue for the greater utility of cosmological naturalism and the worldview that goes with it over any of the alternative worldviews on offer. I shall argue for treating propositions (1) through (7) as grammatical propositions and then go on to argue for them as grammatical propositions. Most particularly I shall argue for the propositions in part B taken as proposals about how best to conceive of things.

To so conceive of things naturalistically saves us from crucifying our intellects. We no longer have to uphold propositions that we can barely understand, propositions so problematical that we are anything but confident that we understand them. We no longer have to try to make sense of and try to believe that there is an infinite purely spiritual person transcendent to the universe, yet somehow acting in it. We no longer have to try to understand and believe that there is a supersensible World of Forms—the only fully real world there is—to which we can have an intuitive or a priori access. We no longer have to make out that only mental things really exist—perhaps Absolute Mind. These are at best difficult notions. Indeed it is understandable, in spite of the fact that he did not follow a principle of interpretive clarity, that the Greek dramatist Aristophanes lampooned such ideas in his *The Clouds*. We can in good conscience stick with a naturalistic outlook yielding a systematic and plausible view of the world without such wild metaphysical extravagances; there is considerable utility here.

Some will say—Kierkegaard, Martin Buber, and Karl Barth for example—that a naturalistic outlook may be coherent, even be more coherent, than any religious one, but it can't adequately cope with the existential problems of life. Without a belief in God, no matter how absurd that belief is, we must, unless we are deeply self-deceived, despair. There is no meaning to life or adequate moral orientation without belief in God. Some less extreme religious believers—John Hick and Terence Penelhum, for example—will recognize that a naturalist can, without self-deception, make sense of life and that there can be an utterly secularist moral outlook that is reasonable and well argued, but, they go on to say, that no secular outlook can match the goodness and hope that can be ours if the Christian message is true (Hick 1959; Penelhum 1992). I have tried to counter the more extreme fideist challenge in chapters 2 and 4 and the more moderate Hick–Penelhum challenge in chapter 4 of my *Ethics without God* and in chapter 17 of *Naturalism without Foundations*. Briefly here, a naturalist in all kinds of ways can give and even find meaning in life by the ways she deals with her aloneness, in her relations with others, in things she takes pleasure in doing and appreciating, in caring for others, in her work (if she is lucky enough to have creative, fulfilling work), in efforts at self-perfection, in realizing her life-plans, in political struggle, and in gaining a clear understanding of what she is doing and how she is living and (if this is so and it could be) in coming to understand the point or points of doing it or alternatively to see that it has little point and, taking that to heart, to be able, in the light of that, in some ways to alter her ways of living. (See chapter 4 of this volume for a further articulation of this.)

These things, in varying degrees, can be done and as much by the secularist as by the religious person. That we were not created for a purpose or that there is no purpose *to* life does not at all mean that there can be no purposes *in* life and some fairly encompassing ones at that that are both demanding and bring satisfaction and human fulfillment (see chapter 4). God or no God, there are things worth having and doing and certain ways of being that are deeply significant. Some of these things do not come easily, but that makes them all the more significant. And they are as available to the secularist with a thoroughly naturalistic outlook as they are to the religious person. And for the secularist, whose access here has nothing to do with any belief in God (except perhaps historically speaking: perhaps such ideas got into her culture by way of religious beliefs), she has access to them without any affront to her intelligence. But that is not so for the religious person (see chapter 2). So again naturalistic proposals have considerable utility—they help give sense to the lives of even the most tough-minded—and in that way trump their religious alternatives.

Similar considerations hold for morality and its demands. God or no God, there are certain moral truisms that are shared by secularist and believer alike and by anyone who would take anything like a moral point of view (Nielsen 1999). I have in mind such things as "Causing harm is wrong," "Unnecessary suffering is to be avoided," "Truthfulness and integrity is a good thing," "Truth is to be told," "Promises are to be kept," "Impartiality is a good thing," "Cooperation is desirable," "Needs are to be met," "Sensitivity to the needs and wants of others is desirable," "Care for one's children is obligatory," "Enslavement and exploitation are evil," "Self-determination is a good thing," and so on. These moral truisms—these considered judgments—are a crucial part of anything that is recognizable as a morality (Nielsen 1999). They are vague, *and usefully so* (like Peirce's acritical beliefs). And they do not always hold. *Sometimes*—though not very frequently—one must lie. Not to do so in those circumstances would be very wrong. And even more obviously, what one must sometimes do is break a promise (chapter 2). But it is *always prima facie* wrong (defeasibly wrong) not to act and live in accordance with these moral truisms. Without it being the case that most of the time most of us act in accordance with them, there would be no recognizable morality at all. Human cooperation and some mutual concern is necessary to keep life from being nasty, brutish, and short. And there are some plain and horrendous evils, as Stuart Hampshire compellingly depicts, that are always, or at least almost always, to be resisted. We human beings need a morality at least for those reasons and these moral truisms must be part of the content of any such morality (Nielsen 1999; Hampshire 2000, 43).

These moral truisms will sometimes conflict and there the coherentist method of wide reflective equilibrium will come into play with its inclusion of moral practices and principles, the inclusion of moral decision procedures as well as their results, the inclusion of reflective endorsements rooted in, though not just a reflection of, all kinds of empirical facts, empirical social theories, and normative social and moral theories. Considering such things, and seeking to get them, as part of a coherent package, into wide reflective equilibrium, we should set out to get our considered convictions, as well as less firmly held moral convictions along with the other matters mentioned above, into a consistent and coherent arrangement, jettisoning those moral convictions that do not fit. So proceeding will yield a rationale for which moral truisms in which situations will override others and which moral beliefs will be winnowed out in what can be an increasingly more adequate understanding of our human condition. The method of wide reflective equilibrium is a key instrument in that. Still there may remain *some* situations where we just will have to choose what in some limited domain to do or what to try to be, but this, to be a proper moral decision, will have to be a reflective endorsement or, where a quick decision must be made, something that after the fact would be sustained by reflective endorsement. Here the agent's point of view is inescapable. But we need also to recognize that we cannot make ourselves over from scratch.

However, in all of the above it is important to see that God need not come into the picture. His absence here is no loss. If the agent facing one of these difficult decisions says she will do God's will that—to do God's will—unavoidably remains *her* decision, not God's decision. Even assuming (what is to assume a lot) she can understand, even through a glass darkly, what God's will is, it is still *her* decision to act in accordance with it. And that is just a matter of what a decision is. If somehow she was just forced or compelled to do God's will or could not help but do God's will, it would not be her *decision* let alone a *moral* decision. Indeed it would not be a decision at all as far as she is concerned, though it could be someone else's decision about how she is to be treated. Moreover, for it to be a *moral* decision of hers it must not just be something she decides, but something she would reflectively endorse as well.

Secularism and a naturalistic outlook cut very deeply into morality. In all the above, things that both secularists and religious persons must acknowledge, if they would be reasonable, religious beliefs need not come into it. It looks like, here at least, God is dispensable and that we have still another reason for believing that the naturalist proposal has the greater utility.

So far—up until that last remark—Hick and Penelhum could—and I believe would—agree with me. But they do not think that that is the end of the matter. I want to examine why they would not, in spite of the above, take up my naturalist proposal and to consider whether their reasons are good reasons, sufficient for their cause (if that is the right word for it).

They agree that if we had no understanding of "good"—an understanding that is not *logically* tied to any conception of God—we could have no understanding of "God" or the demands of Christian morality. *In that way* religion is dependent on morality without the reverse being also the case. But they also believe—and consistently with that—that only a God-centered morality could satisfy our most persistent and deepest moral hopes and expectations. In that way they are like Raphael Demos (see chapter 5). Hick in particular stresses, in a way a naturalist would surely applaud, that considerations concerning our human nature—our actual desires and needs—are of enormous importance in morality. Hick stresses that human beings—nearly all or perhaps all human beings—desire happiness and would continue to desire happiness on reflection. It is of fundamental importance to us. The attaining of it is something that we not only desire, but we would reflectively endorse as well. Here he is one with Aristotle and Mill. But what we need to see, as well, and secular moralists (he has it) fail to see, is that only in communion with God can we find the deepest and most lasting happiness. The attainment of this goal, Hick has it, is the ultimate goal for all human beings (Hick 1959).

Christians, both Hick and Penelhum believe, look on life as something in which their ultimate end or purpose—the true source of their lasting happiness—is set by God. This is something unavailable to secularists for unfailing happiness, they claim, is only to be found in becoming the sort of person who is able to enter into final union with God.

This very way of talking seems utterly foreign to me. I find it incredible that educated human beings living now, understanding what we understand, could so conceptualize things. Hick and Penelhum would say in response that this shows that Christians, Jews, and Moslems, educated or not, conceive of things—see the world—very differently than naturalists do. We have what Rudolf Carnap calls different frameworks. Moreover, whatever we say about deriving an ought from an is, we (believers and nonbelievers alike) appeal in making moral judgments to the facts—to how we think the world is and to how we conceive of ourselves. Jews, Christians, and Moslems believe—take it on trust—that there is a God who created them and who acts in the world for their good while being, as they have it, "out of" or "beyond" the world. With this conception of how the world is, Christians, for example, will come to have in certain important ways, a radically different way of life from secularists, rooted in a very different conception of how things are from that of secularists. Christian morality would be uprooted and lack an intelligible rationale if it came to lack a distinctively Christian conception of the nature of things. In that crucial way it is tied to distinctively Christian beliefs, including cosmological beliefs. To be a Christian in Christendom is to have certain distinctive general aims and to believe that human beings are creatures in God's providential care, created by God, with a God-given purpose. The acceptance of Christian morality involves accepting the central tenets of the Christian religion including what in effect are its cosmological claims, e.g., that God created the heavens and the earth.

Penelhum illustrates this by showing the kind of morality that the Synoptic Gospels commits Christians to. Jesus, as depicted in those Gospels, tells us that the Kingdom of God is near at hand and he "clearly seeks to bring about changes in the moral objectives and attitudes of his hearers; and he does this in order to make them prepare themselves for the coming of the Kingdom of God" (Penelhum 1992, 108). Jesus stresses the need for inner purity—purity of heart and of intention. (Recall how much Wittgenstein was taken by that.) He also teaches that we must free ourselves from hatred and a desire for revenge. And we must do this without making this love conditional on how others are to us. We must come to love our enemies. We should so love our fellow creatures, the Synoptic Gospels tell us, because God is like that and he wants us to be like that as well and because we should want what God wants.

To the claim that we are vulnerable and that it would be foolish—turning the other cheek—to act as if there were no enemies out there, as if there were no people, who, sometimes in brutal ways, will harm us if we are not on guard, the proper response from this Christian point of view is that without God it would, of course, be wildly unreasonable to act as the Jesus of these Gospels advocates. But in a world where God actually exists and cares for us in such a way that no harm can befall us, it is perfectly reasonable to act as Jesus calls on us to act: to, so unstintingly and uncalculatingly love our neighbors (including our enemies) no matter what they are like. As Penelhum puts it, if people "really understood that, they would not worry about any risks that moral regeneration brought with it, they would enjoy the peace that comes with the knowledge that whatever the appearances, their real needs would be met by God" (Penelhum 1992, 110). In a very real sense, because of God, they are not vulnerable. They will, with such an understanding and faith rooted in that understanding, live completely without anxiety knowing that God will care for them. Understanding the world in such a way, so living would be reasonable and not an irrational leap of faith. What is wildly unreasonable in a Godless world would not be unreasonable where we live in God's providential care as it is conceived of in the Gospels (Penelhum 1992). Here between secularists and Christians we have radically clashing pictures of the facts (of what things are like in the world). And how it is reasonable to live depends on which picture of the facts seem to us right or at least the closest approximation we can get to that.

Penelhum, and Hick implicitly as well, seek to display the teachings that underlie the moral life of Christians (Penelhum 1992, 117). Both have done that clearly and have shown how a Christian morality is very different from a secular one and how what is reasonable, given Christian doctrinal assumptions, is thoroughly unreasonable given naturalistic ones. This does not mean that their use of "reasonable" or their conception of reasonability differs from that of secularists or that "reasonable" is an essentially contested concept or anything like that, anymore than what it is reasonable to do if we have no safe drinking water is one thing and what it is reasonable to do when there is such water in plentiful abundance is another without the use of "reasonable" or the concept of reasonability changing one whit (Nielsen 1996, 432–49). But what these articulations of what a Christian morality is like inadvertently bring out is how, given what we know now, absurd they are. These Christian conceptions are not conceptions that we critical intellectuals, standing where we are now in culture and history, should accept if we can be reasonable about such matters (Nielsen 1996, 578–83). Given that Christian doctrinal beliefs such as Christ is both man and God, that God is utterly beyond and distinct from the universe, but still acts in it, that God is an *infinite individual* utterly transcendent to the world, that God is Pure Spirit utterly bodiless yet active in the world, are beliefs of very dubious coherence or intelligibility, it is very unreasonable for present-day educated people to accept such Christian doctrines which are an essential background for the plausibility or reasonability of Christian morality. And even if we can somehow set aside the question of their intelligibility and coherence, we still have no reason at all for believing they are true or even anything like being plausible or even reasonable. This is a hard saying in our liberal culture where we are, and with good reason, committed to tolerance concerning religious matters. Yet it is true. (Here is where Kierkegaardians have one up on such moderates as Hick and Penelhum.)

If, trying to escape such a bind, we appeal to revelation, we are stuck with just irrationally plugging for one *putative* revelation among many not infrequently conflicting putative revelations. Unless, sticking our heads in the sand, we stick with utterly arbitrary assertion, to say the Christian one alone is the only genuine revelation, even setting questions of ethnocentricity aside, requires us to go outside of the appeal to revelation for the "true revelation" and then we are back in the fog again about grounds for faith. And what applies here to Christianity applies with equal force to Judaism and Islam.

With the reasonability of such belief such a nonstarter, it might still remain legitimate for an individual knight of faith to, like Kierkegaard, take such an utter leap in the dark and to subscribe for himself to such a way of life as Christian morality prescribes: here the way of life set forth in the Synoptic Gospels. But it is irresponsible and indeed immoral for him to teach it to his children or to others, for, if they come really to believe it, they will almost surely be gravely harmed if they follow the moral precepts of the morality of the Gospels. (Fortunately few, if any, Christians do.) They will as a result be cruelly exploited, brutalized, and be defenseless. Such indiscriminate love of our enemies or to see no one as our enemy can only lead to grave harm to us. Indeed in certain circumstances it can lead to our destruction. It is in effect to teach people to willingly let themselves be set up to be suckers. To so live is to set oneself up as a sucker and to talk others into such a morality is to sucker them: to set them up for abuse and exploitation by others. Cooperation and mutual reciprocity are crucial in morality. But our cooperation should be *conditional* on others so acting as well. Where they are predators rather than cooperators, we should protect ourselves and others who are also willing to be cooperators. We should fairly cooperate with cooperators, but not with those who will not genuinely cooperate. Morality requires a genuine reciprocity, not unrationalized selflessness.

Religious persons would no doubt respond that that is a narrow, calculating way of living that dehumanizes us all and that we should respond to others no matter what they are like with uncalculating love because God is like that and he wants us to be like that too and that we must do what God wants. But this places unreasonable demands on us that would harm us very gravely indeed, for we, unlike God, are vulnerable and very liable to harm.

A Christian response would be, as we see in the writings of both Penelhum and D. Z. Phillips, that in a world where God actually exists he will care for us and no harm can befall us. Given such a God-structured world, they claim, it is perfectly reasonable to act as the Gospels advocate. But, unless we play fancy free with the use of "harm" and what are plainly the facts, that belief itself is so unreasonable as to be thoroughly irrational. It fits with nothing that our experience of life or our knowledge of history and the world attests to. Are we to say that when the Romans threw Christians to the lions they were not harmed? Are we to say no one was harmed during the Crusades, the Thirty Years War, the slave trade, the First World War, the Second World War, the wars in Vietnam or in Kosovo? Are we to say that in our world, a world replete with genocide, that no one is harmed? When the Nazis not only exterminated Jews, Gypsies, and Communists, but sometimes sadistically tormented them or "experimented" with them before they killed them was no one harmed and should the victims love their tormentors? When priests and brothers sexually molest young boys in their charge should we say no one was harmed? When a father rapes his teenage daughter should we say no one was harmed? When sadistic people torture others should we say no one was harmed? When a professor does his best to demean his students should we say no one was harmed? When vast numbers of people starve each year or suffer from debilitating malnutrition or are infected with HIV and do not have available to them anything like adequate treatment should we say no one was harmed? We could easily go on and on, and it is plain that these questions are self-answering. It is grotesque to even ask them. The whole thing is horribly absurd. To say no harm can befall us is not only to say something which is absurdly false, but is, morally speaking, criminally irresponsible. I do not know how to find my feet with anyone who really believes that. Again I say something hard here, the sort of thing that is usually not said in academic discussion. But, all the same, isn't what I say here plainly true? Can it be that I am preaching or gratuitously moralizing here?

Someone taking this Christian stance might respond "Exactly so! In a way Wittgenstein understood so well, Christians and secularists talk past each other and unavoidably so: their beliefs are incommensurable. Conceptualizing things in radically different ways, they see the world differently." But such a Christian response is an evasion. "See the world differently" or not, the Christian claiming no harm can befall us either misuses the word "harm" or fails to take cognizance of a multitude of plain facts that no talk of "seeing the world differently" or "alternative frameworks" can conjure away. The naturalist has very good reason to stick with his proposal. Talk and conceive naturalist rather than Christian or theistic for that way of talking and conceiving of things clearly answers better to human needs and interests, fitting more adequately together our beliefs than a Christian, Jewish, or Islamic way of talking and conceiving of things (Nielsen 1996, 79–153). In this crucially important way such a naturalistic way of viewing things is more useful and humanly desirable. And to say this is a superficial way of viewing things is mere arm waving.

Some might say here that I am being unfair and a little fanatical as well. Hick and Penelhum are humane, decent, and reasonable persons as sensitive to human ills as I am. We detest many of the same things and certainly Dietrich Bonhoeffer, Karl Barth, Beyers Naudé, and Thomas Munzer were firm fighters against the kinds of ills of which I have just spoken. That is all true. I respond by saying that their *practice* was (is) better than their theory or way of conceptualizing things. Moreover, that *practice* hardly differs from that of a sensitive secular humanist. That is why Naudé and Marxists could together hand in hand fight apartheid. But it is this Christian *account* of morality that I am opposing. It rests on empirical and metaphysical claims that are at best false as well as on absurd—and dangerously so—moral beliefs. Moral beliefs which are not so arcane that their defects are not readily detectable. I have given arguments against them—indeed rather obvious ones. Show me where these arguments have been wrong or even uncharitable. Show me where I have been unreasonable or fanatical.

I turn now—radically shifting gears—to methodological naturalism and the New Naturalism. Methodological naturalism, as we have seen, is the view that science or any intellectual discipline (including philosophy) must fix belief via the basically empirical methods exemplified by the empirical sciences. One could be, as I am and Putnam and Rorty are, cosmological naturalists without being methodological naturalists and one could be, as Charles Saunders Peirce was for most of his life a methodological naturalist without being a cosmological naturalist. But while there is no entailment between cosmological naturalism and methodological naturalism, they tend to go together. As we have seen in chapter 5, Dewey, Dennes, Hook, and Nagel all were both methodological naturalists and cosmological naturalists.

I want now to consider how the New Naturalists developed methodological naturalism (they more or less took cosmological naturalism for granted), consider in what ways (if any) the New Naturalism is an advance over Dewey, Dennes, Hook, and Nagel and to consider a way in which I think my alternative appeal to considered judgments in wide reflective equilibrium is superior to their way of going about things. I wish to show without being antiscientific or unscientific how and why it is a mistake to claim that using the scientific method intelligently and resolutely is the *only* way, or always in all domains the best way, to fix belief, to attain an understanding of ourselves and our world.

I shall first set out, mainly following Philip Kitcher's masterful review essay "The Naturalist's Return" (Kitcher 1992), something of what this new naturalism has powerfully come to challenge and in some considerable measure replace, namely the once reigning antinaturalist orthodoxy in analytic philosophy epitomized by Gottlieb Frege and Michael Dummett, where in philosophy conceptual analysis replaced psychological and experimental procedures in which something like Dewey's naturalistic procedures are eschewed as a way of doing philosophy. Epistemological naturalism, the way Locke, Hume, Mill, Peirce, and Dewey proceeded in examining knowledge, was "scorned by Frege and labeled as illicit by Wittgenstein" (Kitcher 1992, 55).

Wittgenstein famously said in the *Tractatus*:

4.111   Philosophy is not one of the natural sciences.

4.112   Philosophy aims at the clarification of thoughts. . . .

4.1121 Psychology is no more closely related to philosophy than any other natural science. . . .

4.1122 Darwin's theory has no more to do with philosophy than any other hypothesis in natural science.

The New Naturalists come in several flavors, but, like the classical pragmatists, they "all share an opposition to the Frege-Wittgenstein conception of a pure philosophy above (or below?) the special disciplines" (Kitcher 1992, 55). They see the a prioristic movement "Frege inaugurated as an odd blip in the history of philosophy's proper task and proper roots" (Kitcher 1992, 56). (This, note, takes the traditional reading of Wittgenstein I opposed in discussing his views on religion.)

The what that is to be naturalized that Kitcher focuses on is epistemology and the philosophy of science. But much the same considerations obtain for the naturalizing of ethics as carried out by Peter Railton and Richard Miller. I would not, as Kitcher, Quine, and Goldman do, speak of epistemology but speak instead, as Peirce and Dewey do, of inquiry, associating, as I do, epistemology with the old a prioristic foundational enterprises that both the classical pragmatists and the New Naturalists set aside. But that is a matter of terminological felicity and I shall put that aside here, adopting for the nonce Kitcher's way of talking: a way of talking that has had wide currency since Quine. But nothing substantive turns on that terminological move.

Traditional analytic epistemological enterprises, following in Frege's wake, have two fundamental presuppositions both challenged by naturalistic epistemologists. The traditional, and until recently, the dominant tradition in analytical philosophy pursued "epistemological questions in an apsychologistic way—logic, not psychology, is the proper idiom for epistemological discussion" (Kitcher 1992, 57). The second presupposition is that these post-Fregean analytical epistemologists (e.g., A. J. Ayer, Rudolf Carnap, and Peter Strawson) "conceive of the products of philosophical reflection as a priori—such knowledge is to be given a 'logical analysis,' skepticism is to be diagnosed as subtly inconsistent, the improvement of methodology consists in formulating the logic of science" (Kitcher 1992, 58). Naturalistic epistemologists and methodological naturalists (where they are clear about what they are doing) are committed to rejecting both of these presuppositions of the classical analytic tradition. Kitcher sees this as a crucial segment, on the part of the naturalists, of a broader vision.

> Drawing on the deliverances of the sciences, naturalists view members of our species as highly fallible cognitive systems, products of a lengthy evolutionary process. How could our psychological understanding of ourselves—or our reflections on the history of the sciences—support the notion that answers to skepticism and organons of methodology (or, indeed, anything very much) could be generated a priori? (Kitcher 1992, 58)

There is not only the rejection of the a priori and philosophy as conceptual analysis (though characteristically some room is still left for conceptual analysis), they also, in line with that, do not take philosophy to be an autonomous discipline or activity apart from science but as a part of science or as thoroughly entangled with science. Unlike Rudolf Carnap, they did not regard it as philosophy's task to depict "the logic of science." On their view there is no such thing. Unlike Carnap they did not take philosophy to be *Wissenschaftslogik*. Not standing free from their time—fundamentally the actual state of science, the social conditions of our lives, and working with empirical materials—epistemological naturalists attempt to understand the growth of scientific knowledge, the goal(s) of inquiry, the task(s) and functions of science and to give an account of our cognitive performance. This involves understanding "the epistemic quality of human cognitive performance," and specifying "specific strategies, through whose use human beings can improve their cognitive states" (Kitcher 1992, 74–75). The task is the Peircean one of fixing belief by utilizing the best scientific canons, procedures, and knowledge of our time. And, unlike Descartes and Husserl, epistemological naturalists do not seek, in fixing belief, to start from scratch. Like Peirce and Dewey, they are contextual methodological naturalists. In attempting to give rationales for the improvement of our cognitive performance the New Naturalists have absorbed "the Quine-Kuhn idea that we are ineluctably dependent on the past" (Kitcher 1992, 75).

There is, however, no interest on their part on the stress common to

Dewey and Hook that philosophy recovers and transforms itself by directing its activities away from the problems of philosophers to the problems of human beings and, as well, to articulating a *lebensphilosophie*. The New Naturalists show no interest in that. They are much more like Quine and like Peirce. (Not Pierce the speculative metaphysician but Peirce the methodologist of science.) And with that they provoke the charge of scientism. (Remember Quine's quip that "philosophy of science is philosophy enough.")

With many of them, they have taken on board important lessons from Kuhn and Feyerabend and some of these threaten, or at least seem to, methodological naturalism. Methodological naturalists stress (as we have seen) that, in attaining a reliable understanding of ourselves and our world, we must rely exclusively on the scientific method: we must, that is, rely on the empirical-*cum* logical methods exemplified by the empirical sciences. But Kuhn would have it that there is no such thing as the scientific method. A belief in the scientific method is an unrealistic objectification. The history of the sciences and an examination of various present-day sciences makes it difficult to deny that instead of something called "the scientific method," we have a diverse lot of procedures, methods, and scientific practices answering to a very diverse lot of interests and problems. There is no nonplatitudinous core that could be justifiably called "the scientific method."

All the classical pragmatists, as well as Hook and Nagel, thought that, coming with the continued application of what they took to be the scientific method, there would be a continued growth in scientific knowledge, yielding growing predictive power and control (the ability to shape nature to our ends) and a greater understanding of nature (including, of course, of human beings). We would, by the repeated use of the scientific method, come to have a growing (but never completed) understanding of the causal structure of the world and a unified vision of it. Methodological naturalism, in that way, will deliver the goods: the repeated and intelligent use of the scientific method will yield extensive objective knowledge in a way that no other method for fixing belief can. Kuhn's account challenges this at least in the way that the growth of science is supposed to be tied to a determinate thing called "the scientific method."

Moreover, from different directions there are problems about accounts of the growth of knowledge and the attainment of objectivity that call into question claims common to Peirce, Dewey, Hook, and Nagel about what the creative use of the scientific method can yield. They stem in various ways from such different fellow naturalists as Quine, Kuhn, and Paul Feyerabend. The challenge comes from claims like the following: (1) There is no agreed on single conception of the aims of inquiry that holds across all periods and all contexts. (2) The methodological principle of total evidence rests on a myth; we cannot even deploy its first approximation, namely the requirement "that all available evidence be considered in forming belief" (Kitcher 1992, 86). (3) High-level scientific theory sometimes can be—and arguably should be—preserved in the face of recalcitrant evidence by jettisoning the putative observational evidence. What Pierre Duhem called *bons sens* (scientific judgment), guides the acceptance and rejection of data. But this at least seems to have a relativistic or subjective spin (Duhem 1974, 216–18). Science is not as evidentialist as the standard picture would lead us to believe. (4) Methodological naturalists have stressed that science, with its distinctive method, is self-correcting. But a response is that that is not true, for a study of decision making in science reveals that at many times there are alternative ways of modifying scientific belief, "each of which might with equal justice have been adopted" (Kitcher 1992, 93). We can see here the basis for several possible histories of science whose protagonists retrospectively praise their past decisions as self-correcting. Commenting on that, Kitcher remarks that because nothing distinguishes the actual course of events from those potential histories, there is no basis for concluding that the actual evolution of science is self-correcting while the others are not. "The history of science comes to resemble a random walk, not a unidirectional process" (Kitcher 1992, 31; Kuhn 1970, chapter 13). (5) Belief is underdetermined in our encounters with nature. As Quine put it, there is the possibility of alternative scientific systems (or any other kind of system) each fully consistent with all possible stimuli. Or at least there is in science, as Kuhn argued, the phenomena of scientists deciding between different systems none of which are fully in accord with the stimuli available. (6) In science there are frequently shifting standards and as a result alternatives are defended by weighing problems and accomplishments differently (Doppelt 1978, 1990). (7) Theoretical disagreements in science and elsewhere are sometimes unresolvable because the people involved report the evidence in the vocabulary of their preferred theories. This shows how theory-laden our observations are (Feyerabend 1975). (8) Science, even natural science, is socially embedded such that conclusions "about nature and about how to investigate nature are at least partly shaped by views about the proper social order" (Kitcher 1992, 95. See his note 107). (9) There is *contra* our standard Enlightenment picture an implicit appeal to *authority* in science. Heterodox scientific views are usually set aside. They only have a small chance of acceptance or transmission because of the force of reliance on authority within the scientific community (Feyerabend 1978, 1987). (See here, as well, Kitcher 1992, 79–80, 86, 92–95.)

These claims challenge the Peircean claim of methodological naturalism to have a method which will fix belief in a firmly objective way. If most of these criticisms are on the mark, or even near to the mark, that central claim of the classical pragmatists and epistemological naturalists such as Kitcher, Richard Miller, Richard Boyd, and Alvin Goldman cannot be sustained. If this is so skepticism and relativism run deeper than usually believed. Moreover, these objections to methodological naturalism and naturalistic epistemology (or at least a naturalistic epistemology such as Kitcher's or Goldman's which also makes normative claims) are quite different than the a priori skepticism of the philosophical tradition. They rest, as Kitcher points out, "on detailed analyses of individual episodes in the history of science, purporting to show that these features are present and also the mechanisms that might more readily be understood as constituents of a self-correcting process are either absent or too weak to generate 'decisions'" (Kitcher 1992, 95). If these kinds of skepticisms are to be met by methodological naturalists or anyone else, they must be based on a serious examination of the relevant historical, sociological, and psychological material. Here methodological naturalism is attacked on its own ground with arguments the relevance of which naturalists will recognize.

It should, however, be noted—though at some distance from the naturalistic tradition (Hume apart)—even *such* a skepticism is a naturalism, only it is what Kitcher calls a *radical* naturalism. Both Paul Feyerabend and Richard Rorty are such naturalists. Radical naturalists either abandon the normative project of epistemology (as does Rorty) "or honor it only insofar as it is explicitly relativized to frameworks, paradigms, sets of conventions or 'forms of life'" (Kitcher 1992, 96). They have argued that there is no such thing as *the* scientific method; rather there is in science a considerable number of often diverse methods deployed in different contexts for different purposes. Many of them are particular-discipline-specific and even within a discipline sometimes quite different methods are deployed. In any event, there is no super-scientific "scientific method" or underlying encompassing method that rationalizes all of them or shows they have an underlying rationale and aim. There is (*pace* Dewey) no general method of inquiry.

Such a radical naturalist relativizer could still be a methodological naturalist *of sorts*. She could say that the only reliable ways of fixing belief are these various scientific ways that fix these beliefs in these various contexts and domains. She might even add that all the knowledge we have is scientific knowledge, but scientific knowledge garnered in these diverse ways where sometimes diverse connections of science are at play. No a priori, speculative, purely rational method, or any other kind of method will work. In this limited way she could be one with Peirce. This is a recognizable methodological naturalism, even a scientistic one, but not the objective one that motivated classical naturalism and motivates New Naturalists such as Boyd, Miller, Kitcher, and Goldman.

Kitcher in the later sections of "The Naturalist's Return" gives, against radical naturalism, a sophisticated, careful, and forceful defense of a *normative epistemological naturalism* with a similar kind of claim to objectivity that the classical pragmatists made. However, it explicitly takes on board the kind of historicism that I have defended (Nielsen 1996, 28–29), stressing that an adequate epistemology and philosophy of science must be diachronic. Naturalism and historicism go nicely together. We cannot, if we are to know anything or reasonably believe anything, start from scratch. We cannot gain or assume a Cartesian perch. We must, though in a way that is compatible with fallibilism, rely on the beliefs and conceptions of others, among them, others from times previous to ours and from places and cultures distinct from ours. We are all and inescapably on Otto Neurath's boat. But, as I have stressed in various places, historicism is not relativism and Kitcher well recognizes that we can bootstrap ourselves into more adequate positions even where we inescapably start from a less adequate one. Relativism is quite different. It says that wherever you start, whatever views you have, they are as adequate as any other views: neither less so nor more so. Historicism, by contrast, says that it is impossible to stand free of all historical influences and just neutrally, apart from all influences, see the world as it is in itself. We are inescapably ethnocentric in Rorty's eccentric sense that we cannot help but see things by our own lights. (That comes close to being a tautology.) We cannot, standing free of all cultural and historical influences, just see things as they are in themselves. But that is not to say, or to give to understand, that "all seeing by their own lights" is equally valuable or "equally true" or "equally sound" or that we cannot, starting inescapably from our own lights, come to understand the lights of others and come, not standing entirely free of our own lights, to judge that some of the ways that our tribe—even our big Western tribe—does things, or at least certain of the ways it does some of the things it does, are in need of alteration or sometimes even of abandonment in the light of the ways others do things or in the light of what we discover when these diverse views clash. We have the resources, starting always and inescapably from where we are, to come to recognize that the ways of others are sometimes better than our ways. We can also sometimes see, in the light of that review, that we have good reasons to stick with our own ways. Relativism—probably an incoherent view—hobbles objectivity, historicism does not (Brandon 2000, 156–83; Rorty 2000, 183–90; Rorty 1998).

We could have a radical methodological naturalism or the more traditional kind that I have principally been concerned with in this volume. And both are compatible with, but do not require, cosmological naturalism. The New Naturalism, as we have seen, is a methodological naturalism. It could be radical or the more traditional kind advocated by

Kitcher, Miller, and Goldman among others. In either form is it an advance over the methodological naturalism of the classical pragmatists and over that of Hook and Nagel? In certain ways it is. It sees and takes into account more fully the inescapability of historicism, the complexity of science and—keeping in mind the often very different sciences—the various procedures, ways of conceptualizing things, and diverse methods actually deployed by the sciences and the inadequacy of just talking rather uncritically and broadly about the scientific method (the hypothetico-deductive-observational method). Here is an advance where the diverse influences of Kuhn, Quine, and Feyerabend are evident. But not all in *The New Naturalism* is an unequivocal advance. Dewey and Hook, as Rorty and Putnam among us now, have a well articulated sense of transforming philosophy to concern itself with the problems of life (Nielsen 1995, 245–53). And Dewey and Hook articulated a *lebensphilosophie* as an integral part of their naturalism and pragmatism. Such things, as I have noted, are for the most part absent from *The New Naturalism*. Indeed among many of them—perhaps most of them—such things, they believe, should be deliberately eschewed as not being in keeping with the "scientific status" of good philosophy. This is a *scientistic* posture and something that impoverishes philosophy. Dewey and Hook, and Rorty and Putnam, have a more adequate sense of things. Philosophy shouldn't just be professional business as usual. But this is not to deny that the rigor and good understanding of the history of science of the New Naturalists is an important advance. The methodological naturalism of Dewey, Hook, and Nagel could be replaced by the more sophisticated and more scientifically attuned methodological naturalism of the New Naturalists while keeping the stress of Dewey and Hook on *lebensphilosophie* and on the actual problems of human beings. There is no incompatibility here. But that notwithstanding, there is the issue of whether we can articulate and put to use anything not platitudinous that we might call a general theory of inquiry.

I now want to turn again to my claim, argued in various places in this book, and in my *Naturalism without Foundations*, that we should reject methodological naturalism whether it takes its traditional form that *the* scientific method is the *only* legitimate way—the only way, as Peirce stressed during one period of his life that will effectively work—of fixing belief or the radical form that there are many scientific methods utilized in different scientific disciplines and sometimes even in the same discipline, but that it is these diverse scientific methods, and these methods alone, that can justify beliefs: adequately fix belief. The latter would seem at least on the face of it to be less plausible, for the purposes à la Pierce of giving us a general standard for fixing belief, for once we acknowledge such a diversity of scientific methods the line between what is a scientific method and what is not is not so clearly drawn, or perhaps not drawn at all, and because of that there is less motivation for being a methodological naturalist. We will have no grounds for a confidence like that of Peirce in his classic essay "The Fixation of Belief." But it, all the same, may be a more adequate understanding of things even if, in effect, methodological naturalism is to some considerable extent eviscerated.

Be these considerations as they may, I wish to argue that, while remaining cosmological naturalists, we should reject methodological naturalism in any form. This is clearly done by philosophers such as Hägerström, Ayer, Mackie, and Williams while maintaining an overall naturalistic lookout. Moral values for them are not in any way part of the fabric of the universe and we cannot establish fundamental moral claims scientifically. But while ethical naturalists such as Dewey and Hook are also methodological naturalists, one could be an ethical naturalist like Peter Railton and (*as he does not*) reject methodological naturalism. He happens to be a methodological naturalist as well, but his ethical naturalism, unlike Hook's, stands—or at the very least, seems to stand—free of that.

Let us see how this could go. Moral values (and other values and norms) apply to types of circumstance, including types of possible circumstance. If they apply to two possible circumstances differently that must be because the circumstances are of different types. There can be no moral difference without a factual difference. If what we are to do differs in two possible circumstances the facts must differ. This is not an empirical claim or a metaphysical claim, but a conceptual one—or what Wittgenstein would call a grammatical remark. This is ethical naturalist-friendly, but being a conceptual claim it does not require ethical naturalism or any other substantive position. But it plainly anchors moral values in the natural world (Couture and Nielsen 1993, 290–94). Without any identification (even *de facto* identification) of the moral with the natural or moral properties with natural properties, the asymmetrical supervenience of moral properties upon natural properties brings an inescapable commitment to recognizing that morality is such that the natural world could support it. "Two situations can differ in their moral qualities just in case they also differ in some natural qualities" (Railton 1995, 100).

It is fair enough to call this a form of ethical naturalism. The connection between moral judgments and states (conditions) in the empirical world is very strong. As Railton puts it, if "moral judgment is ever in place, it is in place because the world (apart from moral opinion) is such as to make it so" (Railton 1995, 100).

However, when we try to make moral reasoning, even with such a way of conceptualizing morality, fit with scientific method (the hypothetico-deductive-observational method), it is anything but obvious that this can be done. Suppose we say "Doing good deeds is morally required of us" and someone replies "Not if it conflicts with our drive for self-perfection." Both remarks require (vis-à-vis supervenience) certain types of factual situation or possible types of situation for their very intelligibility. Certain empirical states of affairs must obtain for us to be able coherently to assert them. Thus to assert "Doing good deeds is morally required of us" we must be able to say something like this: "Doing good deeds is morally required of us because it reduces suffering." No moral difference without a factual difference. But it does not have to be just that factual difference. It could be instead "Because it contributes to the stability of society," "Because it contributes to the self-perfection of the doer," or "Because it makes the doer feel good." Most of us, I hope, would not appeal to those reasons, but they meet the requirement of no moral difference without a factual difference. The asymmetric supervenience which is involved need not—and often does not—pick out a determinate difference agreed on by all or even by all competent or impartial observers.

How are we to use the scientific method (assuming there is such a thing) to pick out whether it is because it reduces suffering or because it contributes to the stability of society or because of something else that "Doing good deeds is morally required of us" is true? What would we have to observe or fail to observe to be justified in asserting that it is "Because it reduces suffering" that it is true? How can we by observation and experiment determine whether the obtaining of it or of any of the other candidate empirical state of affairs establishes its truth or probable truth? Compare "MacIntosh apples are reddish in color." There we know what we would have to observe to establish its truth. Or compare "Sugar is sweet but salt is not." There we know exactly what we have to do to observationally establish that. Here, take this bit of sugar and taste it and now taste the salt. Carry out that experiment and we will observe that "Sugar is sweet and salt is not" is true. But no such unequivocal relation obtains between doing good and reducing suffering. Someone could still say that it is not that it reduces suffering that justifies doing the good deeds, but that, whether it reduces suffering or not, because it contributes to the moral perfection of the doer. That indeed sounds far-fetched to me and indeed it is far-fetched, revealing an impoverished moral understanding. But still we do not have something that is observationally and experimentally establishable—empirically establishable as in the apple case or the salt and sugar case.

Consider now another example where the scientific method for fixing belief does not seem to have a grip. Suppose we are thinking about theories of justice and we come up against two major contenders: John Rawls's egalitarian justice as fairness account and Robert Nozick's antiegalitarian justice as entitlement account. Rawls's theory tells us that, where the conditions necessary for sustaining equal liberty are met, an equal distribution of economic goods is to be carried out until the worst off are as well off as they can be compatible with no others being made even worse off than the worst off. The only justified inequalities are those that are left when such a procedure has been carried out. Nozick thinks that this is fundamentally wrong. Justice is not about distributions but about entitlements. No matter what distributional patterns obtain we have a just society when the legitimate entitlements of everyone in the society are respected. Resources, on Rawls's account, should be redistributed to the poor (the worst off strata in the society) until no different distribution of resources could be made without making the worst off strata of the society still worse off or at least no better off than they would be with any other distribution. Nozick, like Nietzsche, regards this as the very termination of justice. No resources can be justifiably or rightly redistributed which violate people's entitlements. People should have what they are *entitled* to, no matter what distributive patterns obtain. As far as *justice* is concerned, Nozick has it, people can starve in the streets, if they lack the proper entitlements.

I am not saying there is no argument that can be made here. In fact I have argued at length that Rawls's theory is clearly superior to Nozick's (Nielsen 1985). But what is relevant here is whether we could use *the scientific method* or scientific methods to confirm one theory and disconfirm the other or to establish what I have just asserted. What observations, deductions from observations, or confirmations or disconfirmations would count for the truth of one account and against the truth of the other? As far as I can see nothing so counts there or at least has anything remotely like a decisive weight. We reason and argue about such matters and sometimes effectively and rationally. But we do not use the scientific method or at least do not use it in any central way in doing so.

Let me proffer one more case, a case I have adverted to before, in arguing against methodological naturalism. Sometimes some of us reflectively and honestly ask such desperately vague questions as "What is it to have a life?" "What sense (if any) do our lives have?" "What is the meaning of life?" We can say they are meaningless questions, but they certainly are not like "What is the color of sound?" or "What is the language of rocks?" or (unless one is a Mormon) "How much does God weigh?" Some scientifically and philosophically informed persons, knowing full well how problematic such questions concerning the significance of life are, ask them anyway, sometimes repeatedly, even obsessively, reflecting on them. They, unless they remain silent, end up saying certain very indeterminate and indecisive things about them. But reflectively they dwell on them and in doing so some people carefully think about them. And sometimes in the light of some reflections they make some reflective endorsements. Whatever they are doing in doing that, they are not using, at least in any central way, the scientific method or scientific methods to try to figure out what to think concerning such questions. To say that then they are not genuine questions at all is to be very *parti-prís*. It reveals a considerable scientistic obtuseness to claim that if they cannot be scientifically answered then there is nothing we can reasonably say concerning them. And to think that does not require an abandonment of secularism (see chapter 4 and Rhees 1997).

In this section I have revisited naturalism seeking to push it forward a bit and to clarify what I have argued for in the main body of the text and in my *Naturalism without Foundations*. I further explicated and developed what I have called cosmological naturalism, distancing it from metaphysical realism or any metaphysical or ontological thesis; and I have considered again its relation to religion. I then reconsidered methodological naturalism and argued for its rejection as the method for fixing belief in all domains of life and inquiry. (Here I depart rather fundamentally from Dewey, Hook, and Nagel.) I also examined the views in the domains of epistemology and philosophy of science, of what has been called the New Naturalism (Dedrick 1993) considering it as a further development and sophistication of methodological naturalism. I tentatively concluded that *if* we need, and can intelligibly have, a general theory of inquiry or an epistemology that remained (*pace* Quine) both normative and naturalistic, as well as historicist and contextual, as in Kitcher's account, that such a development of methodological naturalism is plausible. But in criticizing methodological naturalism I argued that the belief that we have or can forge such a general theory of inquiry, rooted in such a general application of scientific method, is very problematic.

I argued that a radical naturalism (e.g., Rorty and Feyerabend), challenging that position (what Kitcher calls traditional naturalism), is a far stronger position than most traditional naturalists are willing to acknowledge. I think it is a thoroughly open question whether naturalism should go in a direction resembling Rorty's or in a direction resembling Kitcher's. Only with the latter is there much hope for methodological naturalism in the domains of philosophy of science or epistemology or for that matter in the philosophy of mind. But even here there is the alternative possibility of a method of wide reflective equilibrium replacing methodological naturalism.

In passing, I discussed ethical naturalism again and took it to be (as we see in Railton's account) a very live option for the best way to think about morality, where it is not linked, as it is in Dewey and Hook, to methodological naturalism as being hegemonic in all domains. Such versions of ethical naturalism may be but need not be committed to methodological naturalism. My view is that it is better for it cut free of methodological naturalism.

Finally, I want to highlight something I have said before: when we are thinking about naturalism in relation to religion it is *cosmological* naturalism that is front and center. One cannot, if one has any concern for consistency, be a theist and a cosmological naturalist and that is why a Jewish, Christian, or Islamic world outlook and such a naturalistic world outlook stand opposed. There is no reconciling them. But there can be, and indeed there have been, consistent *ethical* naturalists who are theists (e.g., Jacques Maritain and Reinhold Niebuhr) and there can be, and have been, consistent methodological naturalists—Charles Saunders Peirce, for example, for most of his active philosophical life—who are theists. But there can be no consistent cosmological naturalists who are theists. That is why it is so central to a naturalistic world outlook. To limit oneself, as most New Naturalists do, to some form of methodological naturalism reveals, it might be thought, a foreshortened vision or at least a poor historical sense. But it might signify instead (*pace* Jean Hampton and Alvin Plantinga) a barely articulated, but still rather deeply embedded, conviction—a conviction it seems to me not unrealistic to have—namely the conviction that it has become patently obvious that cosmological naturalism has no reasonable opposite. This being so, there is no point in going around asserting the obvious.

VERIFIABILITY

Early and late in all my writings concerning religion (writings spanning more than thirty years) I have again and again been accused of the sin of verificationism until I am almost beginning to feel sinful. What is at issue here and what should be said about it? David Armstrong has said—and this is typical of metaphysical realists and rationalistically oriented analytical philosophers of religion—that "contemporary analytic philosophers are deeply affected by the justified reaction against positivism" (Armstrong 1995, 39). And he goes on to add "Like all contemporary analytic philosophers I reject the verification principle" (Armstrong 1995, 40).

In the first paragraph of his Presidential Address to the American Philosophical Association entitled "Testability," Elliot Sober makes a much more nuanced and judicious remark:

> That some propositions are testable, while others are not, was a fundamental idea in the philosophical program known as logical empiricism. That program is now widely thought to be defunct. Quine's . . . "Two Dogmas of Empiricism" and Hempel's . . . "Problems and Changes in the Empiricist Criterion of Meaning" are among its most notable epitaphs. Yet, as we know from Mark Twain's comment on an obituary that he once had the pleasure of reading about himself, the report of a death can be an exaggeration. The research program that began in Vienna and Berlin continues, even though many of the specific formulations that came out of those circles are flawed and need to be replaced. (Sober 1999, 47)

Certainly logical empiricism (logical positivism) in the terms set out by the Vienna Circle and Berlin Circle is a thing of the past. Its leading exponents, Rudolf Carnap and particularly Carl Hempel, both articulators of the most sophisticated forms of the verifiability (testability) principle, came to abandon it as *general* criterion to sort out sense from nonsense or even as a criterion of what has cognitive meaning as distinct from what has noncognitive meaning, though they continue to see the force of its import. Hempel's transformation was particularly notable. Under the influence of Otto Neurath and Thomas Kuhn, and influenced in certain ways by Quine, he moved to a naturalistic, historicized, moderately holistic form of pragmatism not very dissimilar to the approach I have developed here and in my *Naturalism without Foundations*. Hempel, however, kept crucial elements of verificationism (Hempel 2000, 181–228, 253–87, 295–364). Armstrong is completely off-track and stands in ignorance of important work in his own discipline when he says that all contemporary analytic philosophers reject verifiability (testability) principles. All he could informedly and reasonably mean is that all contemporary analytic philosophers reject the verifiability principle in the forms it took in the heyday of logical empiricism. But that is a trivial remark which in effect gives us to understand that analytic philosophers have not been asleep. Among contemporary analytic philosophers who, in one way or another, are verificationists can be counted Michael Dummett, Elliot Sober, Bas van Fraassen, Hilary Putnam, Michael Martin, W. V. O. Quine, Richard Rorty, David Wiggins, Christopher Peacocke, and C. J. Misak (Misak 1995). They, of course, differ very extensively about how to articulate the verifiability principle or even over whether (as in Rorty's case) it needs or can have a useful articulation and they differ over the uses to which it is to be put. Take Martin, Misak, and Rorty. Among all three of them there is a world of difference. Still most verificationists try to articulate some form of a verifiability (testability) principle or at least something bearing a family resemblance to it. They all seek a criterion of legitimacy which in some crucial domains separates the wheat from the chaff, which gives us a handle on what we can sensibly and responsibly assert and what we cannot. They all accept the premise—a preanalytical, intuitive premise—*that experience is the sole legitimate source of information about the world*. In that broad sense they are all empiricists. And in the light of that they try to state a correct or at least a rationally persuasive form of the verifiability principle. I, not unsurprisingly, share that empiricist premise, though, like Dewey, Hook, and Nagel, I take "experience" in a broad, genuinely empirical sense—what common sense takes to be experience—and not in the narrow sense-data or sense-stimulation sense of the British Empiricists and of Quine (Dewey 1981, 58–97). But I claim, like Quine, that finally any claim to knowledge must justify itself before the tribunal of experience. But I do not take experience to be direct acquaintance with sense data or to be just sensory stimulation.

The taking of a proposition to have cognitive or literal meaning if and only if it is either true or false and to have factual meaning (significance) if and only if it is either directly or indirectly, empirically verifiable (confirmable or infirmable) at least in principle, posed a verificationist challenge for theists. Plainly anthropomorphic (Zeus-like) religious claims are obviously false (but they are verifiable or falsifiable). But in the developed forms of Judaism, Islam, and Christianity nonmetaphorical religious utterances are not used anthropomorphically, unless indirectly and probably unwittingly they are given some metaphorical spin. And these religious utterances do not *appear* to be verifiable. Yet religious believers, at least of a reasonably orthodox stripe, take it to be a fact—and it is crucial for their faith that they so take things—that God created the world and orders it providentially. (This could not, without their faith being undermined, be taken as being *just* symbolic.) But, or so verificationists claim, these claims, to be genuinely factual and cognitive, must be at least verifiable in principle. But they appear at least not to be. Given that believers (or at least reasonably orthodox ones) take their key religious claims to be factual claims, the verificationist challenge puts it to believers to show what evidence (what experience) would count for or against the truth of their religious beliefs. What would we have to experience to be justified in asserting "My Savior liveth" or to experience to be justified in denying it? If it is impossible to answer that, then, the claim goes, "My Savior liveth" lacks cognitive and factual significance. It is not a proper candidate for our being able to say of it that it is either true or false. It lacks all factual significance. But without factual significance religious belief crumbles for theistic believers (*pace* Wittgenstein) believe— and will not back off from that belief—that it is a fact that God exists and that he created and sustains the world and is the source of human happiness. But since these claims are unverifiable—they do not stand up before the tribunal of experience—they cannot—or so the logical empiricist claim goes—be genuinely factual claims. A common response is that *this just assumes verificationism*: the correctness of some form of the verifiability principle. But there are, the response continues, no sound reasons for accepting that principle.

I tried years ago in my *Reason and Practice* to defend a form of the verifiability principle that was robust enough to do the work set out for it above (Nielsen 1971a, 393–502). I think now that nothing as strong as that can be maintained and there is no sound form of the verification principle that *by itself* will do what I once thought it could. Though I still think, in a way I shall explain in this section, verificationism to be on the mark and to have a point, I also think (like almost everyone else) that there can be no appeal to theory-neutral experience to test alternative theories, hypotheses, or claims. I think, as well, in a way I will also explain, that a verificationist account should be much more historicized and less molecularist than the way I took it in my formulations in 1971 and the way it was formulated in its then canonical form by most of the logical empiricists (Misak 1995, 144–62; Hempel 2000, 76–79, 181–228, 253–88, 295–304). My earliest discussions of religion relied heavily, though even then not exclusively, on such verificationism (Nielsen 1971a).

Coming to realize that I was swimming against the current of what is at least philosophical fashion (and very likely not just that), I sought and found other arguments concerning religion matching with my preanalytic sense of things which—or so I believe—do not rely on verificationism in any form. These arguments my critics have ignored just honing in on what they take to be the errors of my verificationism. I shall here, in this concluding section, (1) briefly restate some of those at least putatively nonverificationist (though not antiverificationist) arguments, (2) examine whether any of them (contrary to what I think) in some oblique way presuppose verificationism, and (3) consider what if anything might be a sound verificationism and (if such there be) what its import is vis-à-vis religion.

Consider now some nonverificationist arguments. I have looked at some very central aspects of theistic religious conceptualization and have asked (verificationism aside) if they are not incoherent. Take for starters an example to which I am partial: Given how God is conceptualized in developed Judeo-Christian-Islamic discourses, he is said to be an infinite, purely spiritual individual transcendent to the world. But verificationist considerations aside, it is contradictory to speak of an "infinite individual" (or, though a little less clearly, of an "infinite person"). Consider just what it means to be an individual. Something could not be an *individual* unless she or it were differentiated from other individuals or things. But something that is infinite cannot (logically cannot) be so differentiated. She or it cannot, being infinite, be an individual distinct from other individuals, for something which is infinite is not bounded, is not, and cannot be, differentiated from other things in the way an individual can be. So "infinite individual" is self-contradictory: the idea does not make sense. "Infinite" and "individual" just do not go together. Moreover, God is said not only to be an infinite individual, but to be a purely spiritual individual. But "purely spiritual individual" or "purely spiritual being" is also incoherent because there is no way of establishing identity without appeal to bodily identity. We cannot otherwise identify an individual (a person or being). (See chapter 3.) Without a bodily criterion of identity a purely spiritual individual or being could not (again logically could not) be identified so that we could say what its identity is, so that in turn we could have some reason for believing it had an identity or even understand what that identity could be. Where what we are talking about does not have a body or is not otherwise a space-time entity, we do not understand what it means for it to have an identity and we have no idea of how we might proceed to find out. We have no criteria or criterion here.

Consider now what it is for an individual to be transcendent to the world (universe). What does or could "transcendent to the universe" mean? Perhaps being "beyond the universe"? But how could that be other than just more universe? Alternatively, if you do not want to say that, try—thinking carefully about the sense of "beyond"—to get a handle on "going beyond the universe." Isn't language idling here? Perhaps we should speak instead of being "independent of the world"? But what does that come to? We can know what it is like for Joan to be independent of Jim. That means, among other things, that Joan is not financially or emotionally or legally or physically dependent on or tied to Jim. And to say "Britain is independent of Germany but Bermuda is not independent of Britain" is at least to say that Britain has its own sovereignty; it is legally speaking not in the control of Germany while Bermuda is not sovereign; it is a colony of Britain, in certain respects in the control of Britain. But to say something is independent of the world has no such reasonably clear sense or—or so at least it seems—any sense. How do we identify that something is independent of the world? "Identifying something independent of the world" seems at least to make no sense at all. Try to think literally about what it is to identify something and, to make matters worse, take it that that something is supposed to be an individual—not some abstraction like a number, but an individual person. But for that we require bodily or some other space-time identity and that gives us something which is a part of the world.

These considerations show that what we have in that theological sentence ("There is an infinite, purely spiritual individual transcendent to the universe")—a crucial sentence in a theistic framework—is a collection of words that do not fit together, that are logically incongruent, so that we do not have anything there which could be either true or false. This being so, we do not have anything we can use to make an intelligible claim. It is like saying "Yellow colorless ideas transcend diaphanous axiomaticity." The only significant difference is that one is a familiar string of words and the other isn't.

Consider another example: "God, our loving Father, made us and all the rest of the world out of nothing, sustains us, and understands and guides our every thought, word, and deed." We do not understand "made out of nothing." That at least sounds like a contradiction in terms. To make something, even a tune, to say nothing of a pie, a ship, or a proof, is to make it out of something. Even the composer (*pace* Peter Geach) does not make a tune out of nothing. And that familiar difficulty aside, we have the additional difficulty of making sense out of "made the world." The world (the universe) is not some big, bounded thing that could be made. The universe, that is everything there is, except perhaps God (if such talk makes sense), could not be made. Or at least we have no understanding of what that could mean. Only a part of the universe could be made and then out of other parts of the universe by agents who are themselves parts of the universe. If part of the universe came into existence by a big bang that only means part of the universe came into existence from another part. We have no understanding of the universe, as distinct form a part of it, coming into existence, let alone coming to existence from nothing or out of nothing. That means we would have to be able to understand (apart from metaphor) something coming from nothing and that we do not understand. Here also, as in the first example, we have to be able to understand that something being transcendent to the world—something out of the universe—is interacting with the world (with persons, things, processes in the world). But again such talk is contradictory. If x is transcendent to the world and interacts with y in the world then x is thereby not transcendent to the world, but is a part of the world. Here we do not even have to rely on the familiar Humean doctrine about what causal connections come to, but simply to attend to the logic of our language. To say something *out of the world interacts with something in the world* is of the same logical order as to say that something red is not colored.

These examples—central "theoretical" claims of our religious life—could easily be added to. They all would have the effect of manifesting the incoherence of nonanthropomorphic God-talk. As we have seen in earlier chapters, it is tempting to say that this talk is in some way metaphorical talk and so free from such strictures of incoherence. But if the talk is metaphorical talk, we have to be able to say—in principle at least it must be possible for us to say—what these allegedly metaphorical sentences are metaphors of. Metaphorical talk to be metaphorical must be anchored in nonmetaphorical talk. But then we would be back with the difficulty of trying to talk literally of a creating, but uncreated, caring power transcendent to the universe.[16] The problems about the coherence of these propositions would then start all over again.

Now let us turn to our second issue. I have claimed that the above incoherencies can be made manifest by attention to the logic of our language—to how we can intelligibly put words together—without any appeal to verificationism. But is this actually so for all or even any of the above arguments?

Consider first two of the theistic sentences examined above. There are elements in them which consist in phrases which are self-contradictory. This being so we do not have to ask about their verifiability. Being self-contradictory they of course cannot be verified: no question of their verifiability can intelligibly arise. We only have to know about them that there is nothing more in this respect to know than that being self-contradictory they cannot be verified. I refer to "infinite individual," "out of the world yet acts in the world," and "made out of nothing." They are like "colorless yellow" and "round square." The following, unless taken metaphorically, are incoherent because they are contradictory:

1. "There are round squares in the museum in Caligari."
2. "There are colorless green leaves in Ontario."

No verificationist considerations are apposite, though of course 1 and 2 are unverifiable. But we recognize their incoherence, their unintelligibility, in recognizing their contradictoriness. Verifiability does not come in. There is no logical possibility here of such a thing. The same thing is true of 3 and 4.

3. "An infinite individual guides our destiny."
4. "God, utterly transcendent to the universe, made us out of nothing."

However, it is not so evident in other of my "nonverificationist" arguments given above that they do not presuppose verificationism. Consider the claim that there is a purely spiritual being is incoherent. I said it was incoherent because there are no criteria of identity for "a purely spiritual being." But on what grounds do I assert that? I say our criteria of identity for persons is bodily or otherwise space-time identity. But how do I know that and how do I know that whatever has a body is part of the world? There may, some say, be resurrection bodies in a resurrection world. (See chapter 3.) Perhaps such talk is contradictory, but it isn't just obviously so. Moreover, when we say that a purely spiritual being could not be identified, we are likely to back this up by saying that we do not know or understand what it would be like to identify a purely spiritual person. But this sounds very much like we do not know what would count as having evidence for its existence or against its existence and that is surely verificationist. Moreover, if we go on to say, as I surely would be tempted to, that if we could not say what its identity is (that is, if that is not even logically possible) then it could not have an identity. But then we have also said something that sounds at least to be verificationist.

Similarly, to say "God is transcendent to the universe" is to say something that is incoherent because there is no possible way to identify something which transcends the universe. If we do not understand what it would be like to identify God—a being or being transcendent to the world—then we cannot, even vaguely, say *what* "God" refers to and thus we cannot say what God is. Indeed we cannot say anything about what God is and if we cannot say anything about what God is we cannot say *that* God is either. To be able to say *that* something is presupposes *some* understanding of *what* that something is.

Is this verificationist too? Perhaps, but not evidently so—if at all. In the following way it sounds verificationist: to say we do not know what it would be like to identify God sounds like we do not know what we would have to see or in any way observe, directly or indirectly, to be able to identify God and that is verificationist. It sounds like we are saying something analogous to saying that we do not know what it would be like to identify a neutrino because we do not understand what it would be like to, directly or indirectly, observe a neutrino.

However, the God-as-transcendent claim gives to understand that we understand the word "God" (where it is used nonanthropomorphically)— and in understanding "God" we understand that God is in some sense a person, a distinct being—and that means that "God" is taken to be a referring expression. But then it must be possible to have some idea of what "God" refers to. We must in some way be able to identify God. But for any *x*—including God—that transcends the universe there could, *logically could*, be no way of identifying that *x*—think here of what identifying comes to— and this means that we could (again logically "could") have no understanding of God. The referent of "God" could not (logically could not) be identified by ostension and it could not be identified by definite description either, for some of the words in the definite description could not themselves be identified by ostension, e.g., "The uncaused cause of the universe." Properly nonanthropomorphic God-talk is incoherent. But all along the line here the arguments are nonverificationist and do not depend on verificationism.

So what should be said for the above at least putatively nonverificationist arguments is that some of them are clearly genuinely nonverificationist and some only arguably so. But enough has been said to show that I have central arguments against the coherence (intelligibility, factual significance, or factual meaningfulness) of nonanthropomorphic God-talk that do not presuppose verificationism.

I want to turn now to what can be said for verificationism. The standard answer would be very little. I shall resist by arguing "Quite a lot" once it is seen—what by now is hardly news—that some of the old answers given by logical empiricists will not work just as they stand. It is important to see that it was in large measure the logical empiricists themselves (particularly Carl Hempel) who brought about the demise of a once canonical form of verifiability while at the same time pointing to some important ways in which verificationism still, though in a partly transformed form, remained arguably sound.

First, I want to point to some things in the earliest, rather crudely iconoclastic, programmatic statements and programs of the logical empiricists and like-minded philosophers. They were things that horrified traditionalists. C. E. M. Joad, I believe it was, spoke of Ayer fiddling while Rome burns. What distressed traditionalists favorably touched a chord in many naturalistically and empirically minded people of my generation (myself included) when we first encountered logical empiricism as we first began to study philosophy; they, for me at least, when I reread them now, even after all the water that has gone over the dam, still continue to touch a chord, even when I know the ways in which they are mistaken. Perhaps it is a bit of nostalgia, but it is hard not to wish that things could not be simpler than they are. We, of course, should not fool ourselves here. That notwithstanding, there is a baby here which should not be thrown out with the bath water.

I shall first indicate, in trying to get a grip on verificationism, something of what was so appealing about it to many of us and then move, by steps, to what I hope is a sound account of verificationism, showing, as I go along, how and why the crude and programmatic versions had to be abandoned and finally showing what remains that is arguably sound and important, and what this involves for verificationism and religion. The programmatic empiricist claims I shall first be adverting to are the claims made in the heyday of the Vienna Circle, the Berlin Circle in the first two decades before the Second World War and even earlier, though in a somewhat different form, by a group of philosophers, social scientists, and legal theorists in Scandinavia centered around the Swedish philosopher Axel Hägerström (Hägerström 1964). These various empiricists and naturalists (naturalistic empiricists) would all have whole-heartedly accepted Bas van Fraassen's preanalytic empiricist premise, attitude, and conviction, previously partially quoted, "that experience is the sole legitimate source of information about the world" (van Fraassen 1985, 258). They would also have recognized, as van Fraassen does, an important difference *in attitude* between themselves and rationalistically inclined philosophers. As van Fraassen puts it, with empiricists, by contrast with rationalists, there will be a "disdain for opinions inflated beyond what can run the gauntlet of experience" (van Fraassen 1985, 258). Vienna Circle logical empiricists such as Rudolf Carnap and Otto Neurath, Berlin Circle "scientific empiricists" such as Hans Reichenbach and Kurt Grelling and Scandinavians such as Axel Hägerström and Ingemar Hedenius had such disdain and expressed it forcefully and set out briskly its rationale. They all claim, following Hume, that our beliefs, if they are justified, are justified by the data of experience. Sentences are cognitively, but not necessarily emotively, meaningless if they lack evidential connection with the world as we experience it—the only world we can possibly know and the only world we can reasonably judge not to be a metaphysically conjured fiction. We can, attaining Peirce's second level of clarity, define words in terms of other words whose uses are understood, but to attain genuine understanding—to go to Peirce's third level of clarity—we must break out of the circle of words, where words are interdefinable, to words whose meaning can only be understood by ostension; that is, by pointing at that to which the term refers. As C. J. Misak puts it in expounding classical logical empiricism,

> Terms and sentences must be about something—language must refer to what is given or to what can be pointed to in experience. If it is impossible to trace an expression to experience, then that is a way of showing that it has no meaning or content. (Misak 1995, 60)

This appeal to experience took different forms. For Moritz Schlick, A. J. Ayer, and the early Carnap, it took the phenomenalist form of referring to private sensory experience, that is, to sense-data. By contrast, experience for Neurath, Hempel, and Hägerström was taken as public experience and was understood physicalistically or materialistically or, as in contrast with phenomenalism, realistically as it was sometimes said. As Hägerström forcefully and iconoclastically put it, we must aim "to destroy metaphysics, if we ever wish to pierce through the mist of words which has arisen out of feelings and associations and to proceed 'from sounds to things'" (quoted in Bjarup 1999, 73). Hägerström went on to say that "only what can be seen or touched is to be admitted as real" (quoted in Bjurup 1999, 774). What we experience on such a materialist account is not normally sense impressions, but the facts, events, and processes of the world. But for all these philosophers, phenomenalists and physicalists alike, "science is the only form of knowledge" (Bjurup 1999, 774). Moreover, they contended, that "there is nothing in the world beyond what can in principle be scientifically known [and] that metaphysics is nonsense which must be eliminated" (Bjurup 1999, 774). The Scandinavians, as well as Carnap and Neurath, thought that ridding the world of metaphysics not only achieves good intellectual hygiene, but it would break the hold of religion on people, rooted as it is in metaphysical religiosity, and, as well, would break the spell of illusory religiously inspired moral and legal conceptions. In doing these things, it would liberate people, enabling them to respond to the world rationally and realistically. There was, that is, a strong emancipatory project in these scientifically oriented empiricist philosophers, perhaps most forcefully articulated by Otto Neurath, who was both a logical empiricist and what now would be called an analytical Marxist.

So much for the programmatic iconoclastic stance, but how did the argument for verificationism go for logical empiricists? Analytic uses of sentences aside, which being analytical, cannot be used to assert anything but merely explicate the uses of words or show logical connections between sentences, all statements must, directly or indirectly, be connected to experience: that is, for these statements to be intelligible, there must be some experience that they accord with and some experience that is incompatible with them. If this is not so the "statement" in question will be empty and thus devoid of substantive content. Carnap illustrated this as follows in 1932, when logical empiricism was a rising powerful antimetaphysical movement:

> suppose . . .that someone invented the new word "teavy" and maintained that there are things which are teavy and things which are not teavy. . . .How is one to ascertain in a concrete case whether a given thing is teavy or not? Let us suppose to begin with that we get no answer from him: there are no empirical signs of teavyness, he says. In that case we would deny the legitimacy of using this word. If the person who uses the word says that all the same there are things which are teavy and things which are not teavy, only it remains for the weak, finite intellect of man an eternal secret which things are teavy and which are not, we shall regard this as empty verbiage. (Carnap 1959, 63–64)

Here we have the procedure for slaying metaphysical monsters (e.g., God, the soul, the Absolute, Ego, the Infinite, transcendental entities, the thing-in-itself, and the like). That is, we can show, the claim went, that language using such notions is cognitively meaningless (Misak 1995, 63).

On the basis of such considerations logical empiricists articulated the verification principle as a criterion to sort out meaningful from meaningless utterances, sentences propositions, statements, thoughts, beliefs, and the like. We would have something analogous to a litmus test for which propositions (say) were genuinely scientific or commonsensically empirical ones and which were not (e.g., "There is a frog in my fish pond" as distinct from "An ineffable being inhabits my fish pond but is utterly undetectable"). We would have a way of sorting out genuine propositions from metaphysical and religious pseudopropositions by showing which could stand before the tribunal of experience, which could yield information about the world. With that litmus test we could show why the scientific and common-sense empirical statements made sense and the religious and metaphysical ones did not; why, cognitively speaking, the metaphysical and religious ones were nonsense, why they were pseudopropositions masquerading as propositions. They were, and are, pseudo because they could not possibly be true or false.

However, the earlier formulations of the verifiability principle, in ruling out, as an unintended effect, plainly meaningful propositions, hoisted themselves by their own petard as is by now well known. Among other things, the verifiability principle is itself neither analytic nor verifiable. But that aside, taking it as a proposal justified by its utility and, as such something without "cognitive status," other plain difficulties remain. I shall first consider such articulations of the verifiability principle and show why their attractiveness notwithstanding they are mistaken and then, moving by stages, from the rather plainly inadequate, but still intuitively attractive ones, to more adequate ones show something of what a sound form of verificationism might look like.

1. A proposition (belief, statement, declarative sentence, or utterance) is meaningful if and only if it is empirically verifiable.[17]

But 1 cannot possibly be correct for at least two reasons. First, it would render an a priori proposition such as "5 + 7 = 12" or "All biological sisters are siblings" meaningless, for they are a priori and thus plainly not verifiable. They do not even purport to be. No one who understands them will try to verify them. Perhaps for Quinean reasons, we might come to abandon any claim about their a priori status, but we would still not seek to verify or falsify them. Moreover, the logical empiricists (unlike Quine or Rorty) were very keen to keep these analyticities.[18] They saw rightly what Hook and Nagel also saw (and as we saw in chapter 5), that the utilization of logic and mathematics, with their at least arguably a priori (analytic a priori, of course) standing, is a key part of science. Second, 1, if adopted, would lead to its being the case that some plainly factual and empirical statements about the past would have to be said to be meaningless because unverifiable. We understand, and take it to be meaningful (intelligible), though rather pointless to utter, "There were only ten swans on Block Island in 15 B.C.E." or "George Washington belched two hundred times during his life." But these propositions are now unverifiable. We understand them, but we know, or at least have overwhelming good reason to believe, that they are now unverifiable. Nothing verifies them or probably even could verify them. To correct the second difficulty we, in the spirit of practically all of the logical empiricists, amend 1 to the following:

2. A proposition is meaningful if and only if it is at least in principle empirically verifiable, i.e., if it is logically possible to verify it.

This enables us to correctly say that those propositions about the past are verifiable for if there had been someone there at the time—and there could have been—then she could have made the observations necessary to verify those propositions.[19] But the first problem about the a priori remains. So we amend 2 to 3:

3. A nonanalytic proposition is meaningful if and only if it is at least empirically verifiable in principle.

With 3 we already no longer have a *general* criterion of meaning, but, that aside, we still have, causing trouble for 3, normative propositions like "Deliberately causing suffering to innocent people is evil" and "The rule of law is essential in any decent society." They appear at least not to be empirically verifiable, but, whether empirically verifiable or not, they are plainly meaningful. We have no trouble understanding them. This led from 3 to 4:

4. A nonanalytic proposition is *cognitively* meaningful if it is at least verifiable in principle.

Such normative sentences, as those given above, are said by most logical empiricists to be noncognitively meaningful. Logical empiricists (Carnap, Reichenbach, Ayer, for example) thought they had emotive meaning, that is, they are used expressively and evocatively. Others, alternatively, thought that even declarative normative utterances are disguised imperatives, prescriptions, or subscriptions. Their real meaning (use) is noncognitive or at least nondescriptive for they have no truth-conditions or assertability-conditions. However, these various claims about noncognitivity are very controversial and it appears at least as if they are implicitly assuming a rather arbitrary persuasive definition of "cognitive meaning" more expressive of logical empiricists' underlying scientism than anything that could withstand critical examination. If we stick to a minimalist Tarskian disquotational account of truth and do not try to extend it into a correspondence theory, a theory which is metaphysical in exactly the sense that logical empiricists objected to, we can quite unexceptionally speak of moral truths and legal truths as well as mathematical and logical truths. (Perhaps we can even speak of religious truths?) To limit the cognitively meaningful to what are factual truths or falsities seems arbitrary. So we move from 4 to 5:

5. A proposition is factually meaningful (has factual meaning) if and only if it is at least in principle verifiable.

This captures, I believe, the central intent of logical empiricists. They wanted a criterion—something analogous to a litmus test—which would enable us to decide which of the many utterances floating about in our cultural life made genuine claims about (to be pleonastic) the physical or social world, which told us what it is like, which gave us the empirical facts about what the world is like. They wanted a criterion to distinguish factual propositions from pseudofactual propositions—the metaphysical monsters—and 5, they thought (and initially it was not implausible to think so), yields that.

However, not quite as it stands at least. Premise 5 is claiming that to be factually meaningful there must be some evidential statements (expressed by some observation sentences) which, if true, would establish the truth—would verify—a proposition. If we have verified a proposition we then have grounds for thinking it true. If we have tried and failed to verify it we have grounds for believing it to be false. If we have no understanding of what would verify it or falsify it we do not understand what we are trying to assert or deny. But to say that such evidence—or any evidence—would constitute *conclusive* or *decisive* verification is something which we cannot say for some perfectly meaningful scientific propositions, including all scientific laws (Hempel 2000, 279). Indeed this is true for any universal generalization. Suppose I assert "All robins in Quebec migrate south in the fall"? No amount of observation of the behavior of robins in Quebec will verify the truth of that statement, will, that is, establish *conclusively* its truth, though some possible observations would count for its truth and some against it. But we cannot conclusively establish the truth of that statement or any other empirical generalization. A nonmigrating robin might always turn up and that would falsify the proposition. Such a proposition is falsifiable, but not verifiable, i.e., we cannot conclusively verify it.

This led to the proposal of a falsifiability criterion rather than a verifiability criterion of factual significance or meaning.

6. A proposition is factually meaningful (has factual meaning) if and only if it is at least in principle falsifiable.

That *perhaps* works fine for general statements—laws of nature and the like—but it clearly does not work for existential propositions like "There is at least one rattlesnake in Quebec." We can verify it—seeing one in a zoo or in our neighbor's backyard—but we cannot falsify it. No amount of observation will definitely establish it to be false. Some things, of course, will count toward its falsity but no amount of observation will conclusively establish its falsity. A superscrupulous and systematic search for rattlesnakes may be made and none might be found. Still a rattlesnake might turn up in Quebec.

The above considerations might well lead us to propose this:

7. A proposition is factually meaningful (has factual meaning) if and only if it is either at least in principle verifiable or at least in principle falsifiable.

But this won't work either, for as Hempel has pointed out—and for the same reasons as given above concerning the verifiability and falsifiability criteria—"Every substance has some solvent" is neither conclusively verifiable nor falsifiable even in principle.

The above familiar line of argument shows that a strong empiricist verifiability or falsifiability criterion of meaning, even of factual meaning or factual intelligibility or factual significance, will not work. It rules out too much of what we preanalytically and securely know to be meaningful and intelligible, including a lot of our most secure scientific and common-sense empirical beliefs. No such formulations, as we have given above, will do as a criterion of significance for an empiricist or naturalist outlook. They all rule out the metaphysical monsters all right, but they rule out too much of science and common sense along with it.

It was not only the critics of logical empiricism (e.g., A. C. Ewing and Fredrick Copleston) who pushed such objections, but principally the logical empiricists themselves, in this clear-minded fashion, as they sought to develop an ever more carefully articulated empiricist (naturalist) outlook. (Carnap and Hempel were exemplary in this.) They came to realize what Neurath had stressed all along, that strong verificationism in attempting to get conclusive or decisive verification or falsification was not in accordance with the fallibilistic spirit of science. We are not going to get in scientific inquiry—or anywhere else where matters of substance are at issue—certainty or conclusiveness. The most that we can hope for is to go on gaining ever more adequate scientific accounts and better philosophical explications or accounts of science. This realization led in the first instance to a *liberalization* of the so-called verifiability criterion. The talk now was of testability: confirmability or infirmability in principle (Carnap 1936, 1937; Hempel 1959, 1951).

A problem, though not the only problem, with the liberalized versions was not that they excluded too much, but that they were too inclusive. They didn't end up having grudgingly to grant that on that criterion well established science or common-sense empirical beliefs were nonsense, but it came to seem at least that liberalized versions let back in metaphysical and theological monsters. A logical empiricism, developing toward greater empirical and logical adequacy, seemed at least to lose all its old antimetaphysical bite. As an exact and exacting program to free the world of metaphysical and religious illusions (and the kind of moral and political notions held in thrall by them), it seems at least to have lost its way. It, of course, remained committed to clarity—and that is a good thing in itself—but it became increasingly unclear what the clarity was for. And they, and it seems to me rightly, were too programmatic to acquiesce in J. L. Austin's remark that we will be in a position to know whether we have clarity enough, or what we want clarity for, when we have a tolerable amount of clarity. Something, Austin thought, we do not have now.

I want to do a little to see if things are really as dismal as that and whether the logical empiricist commitment to clear thinking does lead to the demise of verificationism. Consider this:

8. A proposition is factually meaningful (has factual meaning) if and only if it is either at least in principle confirmable or in principle infirmable.

This means that there must be empirical observations that we could make—that it is at least logically possible for us to make—which would count either for or against any proposition that could count as a factually meaningful proposition. A proposition—to be factually meaningful—must not be equally compatible with everything and anything that it would be logically possible to observe either directly or indirectly. It must be the case that some things if observed would count for a factual proposition (for anything that could count as a factual proposition) and some things if observed would count against it. If that is not the case we do not have a factually meaningful, factually significant proposition. We have instead a proposition which is compatible with any and all observations we could make so that we have either an analytic proposition or a nonanalytic proposition also empty of content and thus (since it is not analytic) a pseudoproposition.

It would perhaps be somewhat more helpful to state 8 as 8':

8'. A proposition is factually meaningful (has factual significance) if and only if there is some observational statement that could count for or against it.[20]

But both 8 and 8' seem at least to let in metaphysical monsters. Someone who accepts the proposition "God is our loving Father" could on this basis take his proposition to have on the confirmability/infirmability criterion—say 8 or 8'—factual meaning. Human suffering counts against the above proposition and human well-being counts for it. To the remark that the very same evidence is compatible (and indeed equally so) with utterly atheistic views of the world, views which are articulated more economically and with fewer problematical assumptions, a believer should, if he is reasonable, agree. It, he could then add, is not infrequently the case in both science and in common life that the empirical evidence is compatible, even equally so as far as we can ascertain, with several different accounts of the evidence. And this does not mean that then the theories all have the same meaning or are equivalent for other matters come into play in theory choice: simplicity, fit with other theories, clarity, perspicuous representation, and the like. But it does show that the religious and allegedly metaphysical proposition is confirmable or infirmable (but not verifiable or falsifiable) and thus is, on this criterion, factually meaningful. So we have a central religious proposition which is confirmable or infirmable—which squares with 8 and 8'—and there is no reason to think that that could not be generalized to some other religious and metaphysical propositions. They are not all like "God is the ineffable Other." The liberalized empiricist criterion of factual meaningfulness lets in too much for we naturalistic empiricists to take such a liberalized criterion as providing a basis for the critique of religion. It will not do the work that Carnap, Reichenbach, Hägerström, and Hempel at least initially wanted it to do. It might even be thought that liberalized criteria (such as deployed in 8 and 8') are in effect, though surely not in intent, undermining (though clearly not decisively so) of a naturalist-empiricist outlook.

They are not. What they are undermining of is the use of verificationism to critique religion *without some considerable supplement from non-verificationist arguments* such as the ones I have made or at least some other nonverificationist supplement.[21] The verificationist challenge to religion was a good starter. It puts, as the classical 1955 discussion of "Theology and Falsification" did, believers on their toes.[22] It makes them see that they cannot make responsible religious claims without attention to evidence or without at least being willing to say what counts for and against their beliefs or to say, after facing the issues, in a deeply fideist mood, that nothing could count against or (given certain forms of fideism) either could or should count for religious beliefs. But she can also answer that something counts for and against some of them in a way that meets a liberalized—8 and 8'—criterion for factual significance. But this in itself does not show her religious claims are true or even plausible and it does not show that her claims are not incoherent or that they have factual meaning for there are, as we have seen in this volume perhaps *ad nauseum*, nonverificationist arguments for the meaninglessness, or better put, the incoherency of nonanthropomorphic God-talk.

What it does show is that once we liberalize verificationism sufficiently so as to not rule out secure parts of science and empirical common-sense belief, we will no longer have the strong criterion—the litmus test—logical empiricists thought they had to slay metaphysical monsters, including the metaphysical monsters of what Hägerström calls metaphysical religiosity (an inescapable feature of religion) (Hägerström 1964, 175–223). What we need to see, and what I for a long time did not see, is that the verificationist arguments do not play the central role in the critique of religion that I, and many others, took them to play (Feigl 1957).[23] They remain in a subsidiary role cautioning against religious extravagance and obscurantism. But it is the nonverificationist arguments for incoherence that have the central weight and that I did not initially see. I tried to milk more out of verificationism than could be milked.

None of this counts against verificationism, but only against the strength of verificationism (unsupplemented) as a tool for critique of religion. We have seen how a religious believer can legitimately make a liberalized verificationist appeal. And, whether she does or not, we can see how religion can accommodate itself to liberalized verificationism. Does this show that I should abandon verificationism? I think not. What it shows is that I should have been more circumspect than I was in my first writings about religion about its role in religious critique. But in the holistic ways—sometimes modest holistic ways—in which Neurath, Hempel, Quine, Peirce, Dewey, and Rorty are verificationists, and in which Misak has carefully described its history as well as defended it, verificationism seems very plausible indeed (Misak 1991, 1995). We need to follow Duhem and Quine in stressing holism, albeit, in the light of Dummett's strictures, a modest holism (Dummett 1973, 598–99; Misak 1991, 147). As Hempel said in characterizing their views, "single statements are, in general, not testable by observation at all" (Hempel 2000, 281). Still, hypotheses, to be hypotheses, must be testable. But as Hempel put it, in expounding the Duhem-Quine thesis,

> A single scientific hypothesis does not normally imply any observation statements by which it could be tested. In order to derive observation statements or experimental results from a singular hypothesis, one has to use many so-called auxiliary hypotheses—among them, for example, the assumptions that no malfunction in the experimental apparatus occurred and that the theoretical assumptions on which the use of the experimental apparatus is based are correct. Accordingly, all these auxiliary hypotheses are additional premises that allow one to derive predictions about experimental findings from the given hypothesis. If a predicted experimental finding is not obtained (i.e., if the derived observation statement has been shown to be false), then this shows only that at least one of the premises used in the derivation has to be false. But by no means is this required to be the hypothesis under investigation; it might also be the case that one of the auxiliary hypotheses is false. The history of science provides us with many examples of this latter scenario.
>
> When an observation sentence that has been derived from a given hypothesis turns out to be false, this does not show that we have to reject the hypothesis as falsified. What it shows is only that somewhere in the whole system of hypotheses that was used in the derivation, some appropriate changes have to be made. But purely logical considerations cannot determine which sentences of that system have to be changed. (Hempel 2000, 282)

Hempel adds, bringing out the holism of that view and showing his closeness to Quine and distance from Dummett, "Empirical content is ascribable only to the whole system of hypotheses, and the decision about whether to accept such a system does not depend *only* on observational findings but to a large extent also on holistic properties of the system in question"

(Hempel 2000, 282, emphasis added). But that not *only* observational findings are involved still gives us to understand that observations and testing remain essential. Without it, as Quine stresses, we would not have a scientific system. Quine, and Hempel too, remain verificationist only now in a holistic and naturalistic manner and, for Hempel, under the influence of Kuhn in a historicist manner as well (Hempel 2000, 281–83). We first get holism in Quine and then holism and historicism in Hempel.[24] He has traveled a long way from his initial logical empiricism.

Hempel and Quine's verificationism which rejects the myth of the given, stresses the theory-dependent nature of observation and with that rejects any foundationalist postulation of a basis for intersubjective agreement—the only kind of objectivity we can get or need—in "a basis of theoretically neutral observation sentences common to all humans."[25] Here we have a historicized and pragmatic turn alien to (Neurath apart) the Vienna Circle and to what Kitcher characterized as the a priorism of Frege and the antinaturalistic analytical philosophy influenced by Frege, e.g., Austin, Ayer, Carnap, Grice, and Strawson. Quine, Hempel (late in his life), Rorty, Davidson, Dennett, Levi, Feyerabend, and the naturalistic epistemologists (what Kitcher calls traditional naturalism) all rejected, though with different emphases, the central idea of the Vienna Circle that "the theory-neutral findings of observations can ground all empirical knowledge" (Hempel 2000, 287). We cannot just turn, shuffling off theoretical and cultural assumptions, to "the raw data of experience." Things are too deeply interconnected for that. That kind of atomistic empiricism is mythological. Theories and beliefs must meet the tribunal of experience to be acceptable, but not in that way. But a rejection of classical empiricism as well as a rejection of sentence by sentence testing of individual statements and a rejection of atomistic or molecular verificationism and some of (perhaps all of) the specific formulations of the verifiability or testability principle and the uses of it made by the logical empiricists does not require or naturally lead to a rejection of verificationism. All of the philosophers just mentioned, with the possible exception of Davidson, are verificationists, as was Wittgenstein, only verificationists not in the Vienna Circle mode but more in the naturalist, holistic, pragmatist mode we inherited from John Dewey.[26]

NOTES

1. Robert Arrington's essay " 'Theology as Grammar': Wittgenstein and Some Critics" will appear in *Wittgenstein and the Philosophy of Religion*, edited by Robert Arrington and Mark Addis, 167–83. London: Routledge, 2001.

2. I characterized such metaphysical propositions, following Gustav

Bergmann, as ideological propositions (Nielsen 1962). This was a rather stipulative, but still I believe useful, definition of "ideological." It is not the same as the Marxian use I now employ, but there are significant relations between the two uses.

3. I have not challenged the dichotomy conceptual/factual appealed to here. It is well known that Quine, Davidson, and Rorty have deeply challenged such dichotomies. Analytic/synthetic, scheme/content are very dubious distinctions and my predilection is to junk them. But it is not entirely evident that Wittgenstein's grammatical/factual distinction comes to the same thing as the dichotomies Quine, Davidson, and Rorty reject. But it is a testament to Wittgenstein's vagueness here that it is not evident that they do not either. In any event there does seem to be the distinction Arrington points to between "Red is a color" and "There is a red car in the driveway." Quine, however, it should be remembered, does not deny there are such truistic distinctions (Quine 1991).

4. The mention of "coherent use" above is deliberate. It is doubtful that it is a configuration of words that has a use on Wittgenstein's account, because, for him, anything that has a use in a language-game cannot be incoherent. Thus for him "coherent" does not add anything in "coherent use." Yet it still is a phrase we are—or at least I am—tempted to use. It indeed sounds very un-Wittgensteinian. But is it without reason? Does it not answer to anything that is reasonable? "Ineffable, unsayable truth" has a use in the language-games of some. But is it really a coherent thing to say?

5. Audi (2000) discusses the New Naturalism as does Dedrick (1993). Friedman (1997) provides a penetrating critique of a philosophical naturalism that rejects, à la Quine and Kitcher, any appeal to the a priori. See note 20. Kitcher's references are full and indispensable in giving the *dramatis personae* involved here.

6. This assumes that we understand what we are talking about when we speak of "intrinsic qualities" or "intrinsic properties." But this is very doubtful. It is tied up with a discredited essentialism. The more plausible thing is to take all properties as being relational (Rorty 1999, 47–71).

7. Note how this relies on an appearance/reality distinction that, deprived of any specific context, is a very dubious notion. Richard Rorty in his criticism—perhaps "deconstruction" would be the better word—has been very effective (Rorty 1998, 1999).

8. I am not reifying worlds here creating them with linguistic playfulness. There is but one world, namely our space-time material world, what we ordinarily call "nature." But speaking of the art world or the business world is a useful *façon du parler* for referring to certain extended and systematic activities that standardly some or sometimes, for some of them, even all human beings engage in.

9. This sounds funny. Are there not rabbits, rocks, and roses, too? Yes, of course, but they are all space-time entities. Do we have here a grammatical remark?

10. If something is a metaphor it must at least in principle be possible (logically possible) to say what it is a metaphor of. At some point we need something like literal speech.

11. Armstrong is completely insensitive here to what Davidson and Rorty say about such an appeal to facts (Davidson 1980; Rorty 1998, 1999).

12. In speaking of "a single, all-embracing, spatio-temporal system" am I assuming or presupposing some conception of *reality full stop*, a notion which I have rejected as incoherent? I think not. I do not identify "reality" with the system of the spatio-temporal world. I am simply saying that in thinking about the structure of the physical world, this, given what we know now, is the best way to think about it.

13. See notes 8, 10, and 12.

14. Some might respond by saying my antimetaphysical remark here is itself metaphysical. I am making—or trying to make—a substantive a priori claim about what there isn't. But the remark is not a priori, but an empirical, and falsifiable, claim about what, when we examine these remarks, it makes sense to say. It could be—but I argue it isn't—empirically false to say that such talk about pure spirits, supernatural realities or Platonic forms is incoherent. Just like it could be false—but isn't—to say "John sleeps faster than Joan" is incoherent.

15. But he makes it very clear that he rejects anything like a verifiability account of meaning (Armstrong 1995, 40).

16. For not thinking that the doctrine of analogy is an alternative here, see my discussion of this in Nielsen 1989, 190–209.

17. I put all these alternatives for there are things—though I think not crucial things—problematic about all of these notions. Some will say "We have no good understanding of what a proposition is." Others will say "It is not sentences or utterances that are verifiable or even true or false but statements." Others will say "We have no more idea of what a statement is than we have of what a proposition is. Both are reifications." Still others will say "If we do not employ them in our formulations, but employ sentences of utterances instead, we will have something which is particular language relative." I think, though I shall not argue it here, the problems raised here are unreal. I use "proposition" as *perhaps* the least problematical term. But, if you prefer, substitute sentence, belief, thought.

18. Michael Friedman shows clearly the rationale for their being so keen on analyticities. On Carnap's account particularly, Friedman persuasively argues, we have an account which is not in conflict with the Duhen-Quine thesis about holism, and does not accept or inadvertently require philosophy to be either above or under science so as to provide a basis for a critique of it or to provide a foundation for it. Moreover, in appealing to the a priori Carnap makes no claims to certainty or unrevisability. He is as fallibilist as Dewey or Quine. His conception of the a priori is a constitutive one. In all of this, except for his appeal to a priori considerations, he is one with Quine and the New Naturalists. Where he differs from them is in continuing to regard logic and mathematics as a priori (constitutive a priori) and in seeing the logical and mathematical side of science as confronting the tribunal of experience very differently than experimental science with logic and mathematics being a very different mode of reasoning than that of experimental science. Going with that, Carnap had a different conception of philosophy than Quine and the New Naturalists. Philosophy for Carnap is a priori. It was the formal articulation of *the logic of science*. It was for Carnap, as it was for Russell, logic, but it was for him *Wissenschaftelogik*. New Naturalists would instead say that even if some plausible conception of the a priori can be

articulated, it does not, artificial as it is, help very much in our understanding of science. Even if, they would argue, *Wissenschaftelogik* is not mythological, it is a dead end. Be that as it may, Carnap no more leads us into philosophical *extravagance* than Quine, though he may lead us into philosophical *irrelevance*. And he has perhaps captured with his defense of analyticity something we preanalytically see, namely that there is something more than a difference in degree between saying "All red things are colored things" and saying "There are red berries in the garden"—the distinction Wittgenstein aimed at with his distinction between grammatical remarks and empirical remarks. But matters are complicated here. I have hardly even begun to stir the pot. But I think that Friedman in arguing on behalf of Carnap, and Reichenbach as well, *may* have put in question the New Naturalist claim that there is only one way of knowing, the empirical way—that is the basis of science—so that there is no a priori knowledge. If Friedman is right, *methodological naturalism* as Quine formulates it and as Hampton does (only to oppose it) would be mistaken. But that would not touch methodological naturalism as formulated by Hook, Nagel, and Railton which takes it that one part of scientific method itself is a priori, namely its essential and integrated utilization of logic and mathematics in science, as something crucial to its method. And, in this way, Carnap would be free and clear as well, for that was his position. But it is important to note that none of this calls in question cosmological naturalism. All the conflicting players here could be and probably are cosmological naturalists (Friedman 1997).

19. This appeals to counterfactuals and Quine of course would not like that. But it seems to me that we can use them quite innocently but still effectively as Peirce does. And we can do so without making any metaphysical claims for modalities. But we need to be circumspect in their use and that requires what Duhem called *bon sens*.

20. See here Martin 1997. Martin, I should add, has clearly and succinctly stated my verificationist arguments, shown something of their force, and carried these matters forward to some issues that I did not consider.

21. It might be reasonably thought the supplement goes the other way. The nonverificationist arguments stand on their own without reference to the verificationist ones. The verificationist ones at best supplement the nonverificationist ones. With such a weight on the nonverificationist ones are we not once more getting an attempted ontological disproof of the existence of God? No, we are not, for the claims about the logic of our language themselves rest on contingent empirical premises about the use of words. There is no attempt to transcend fallibilism or gain a transcendental perch.

22. See Flew and MacIntyre (1955, 95–113). For further such argument see Mitchell (1957, particularly 31–83) and Diamond and Litzenberg (1975). The Diamond and Litzenberg collection is the most adequate collection of the crucial essays on this topic.

23. Herbert Feigl's short article—an article in the form of a dialogue—presents clearly central and obvious reasons that led logical empiricists to reject the cognitive significance of religious talk (Feigl 1957).

24. It is no accident that in a perceptive discussion of Quine's views Hilary

Putnam should have entitled his article "The Greatest Logical Positivist." Putnam writes, in reviewing Quine's collection of essays *Quidilities*, that he is, the adoration he inspires among scientific realists notwithstanding, "inclined to class Quine as the last and the greatest of the logical positivists [what I have called, following Carnap's preferred usage, 'logical empiricists']" (Putnam 1990, 269).

25. A remark of Misak's about Quine seems to me apposite here. She says "For him, logic and mathematics are genuine branches of knowledge because they are a part (the very core) of our web of belief or system of knowledge. And having a place in that effort to make sense of what James called the booming buzzing confusion of experience is, on Quine's view, all that legitimacy or objectivity amounts to" (Misak 1995, 148).

26. I end this section on verifiability and verificationism ambivalently. Not because I have grave doubts about what I say here—beyond the doubts that any person if she will be honest and reasonable cannot but feel about almost any philosophical claim—but with a feeling that I have only scratched the surface here for there are all kinds of things that I have not said or even hinted at that need to be said. We need, I believe, a new gathering of new fugitives or at least I need to make one. I hope to do something of that in my *From Classical Pragmatism to Neo-Pragmatism* (forthcoming). I only hope that what I say in this section—a backing off in certain respects from my earlier claims about verificationism—will suffice for what needs to be said on this score vis-à-vis religion.

BIBLIOGRAPHY

Armstrong, David. 1995. "Naturalism, Materialism, and First Philosophy." In *Contemporary Materialism: A Reader*, edited by Paul K. Moser and J. D. Trout, 35–50. London: Routledge.

———. 1999. "A Naturalist Program: Epistemology and Ontology." *Proceedings and Addresses of the American Philosophical Association* 73, no. 3: 77–89.

Arrington, Robert. 2001. " 'Theology as Grammar': Wittgenstein and Some Critics." In *Wittgenstein and the Philosophy of Religion*, edited by Robert Arrington and Mark Addis, 167–83. London: Routledge.

Audi, Robert. 2000. "Philosophical Naturalism at the Turn of the Century." *Journal of Philosophical Research* 25: 29–45.

Berlin, Isaiah. 1980. *Concepts and Categories*. Oxford: Oxford University Press.

Bernstein, Richard. 1995. "Whatever Happened to Naturalism?" *Proceedings and Addresses of the American Philosophical Association* 69, no. 2: 57–76.

Bjarup, Jes. 1999. "Scandinavian Legal Realism." In *The Philosophy of Law. An Encyclopedia*, vol. 2, edited by Christopher Berry Gray, 773–76. New York: Garland.

Braithwaite, Richard. 1975. "An Empiricist's View of the Nature of Religious Belief." In *The Logic of God*, edited by Malcolm L. Diamond and Thomas V. Litzenberg, 127–47. Indianapolis, Ind.: Bobbs-Merrill.

Brandon, Robert. 1994. *Making It Explicit*. Cambridge, Mass.: Harvard University Press.

Brandon, Robert, ed. 2000. *Rorty and His Critics*. Oxford: Blackwell.

Carnap, Rudolf. 1936 and 1937. "Testability and Meaning." *Philosophy of Science* 3 (1936): 419–31 and 4 (1937): 1–40.

———. 1956. *Meaning and Necessity*, 205–21. Chicago: University of Chicago Press.

———. 1959; first published in 1932. "The Elimination of Metaphysics through Logical Analysis of Language." In *Logical Positivism*, edited by A. J. Ayer, 60–81. Glencoe, Ill.: The Free Press.

Couture, Jocelyne, and Nielsen, Kai, eds. 1993. *Mèta-philosophie/Reconstructing Philosophy*. Calgary, Alb.: University of Calgary Press.

Davidson, Donald. 1980. *Inquiries into Truth and Interpretation*. Oxford: Oxford University Press.

Dedrick, Don. 1993. "The New Naturalism." *Metaphilosophy* 24, no. 4: 390–99.

Dewey, John. 1981. *The Philosophy of John Dewey*. Edited by John J. McDermott. Chicago: University of Chicago Press.

Diamond, Cora. 1991. *The Realistic Spirit*. Cambridge, Mass.: The MIT Press.

Diamond, Macolm L., and Thomas V. Litzenberg Jr. 1975. *The Logic of God/Theology and Verification*. Indianapolis, Ind.: Bobbs-Merrill.

Doppelt, Gerald. 1978. "Kuhn's Epistemological Relativism: An Interpretation and Defense." *Inquiry* 21: 33–86.

———. 1990. "The Naturalistic Conception of Methodological Standards in Science: A Critique." *Philosophy of Science* 57: 1–19.

Duhem, Pierre. 1974. *The Aim and Structure of Physical Theory*. Translated by Phillip Wiener. New York: Atheneum.

Dummett, Michael. 1973. *Frege: Philosophy of Language*. London: Duckworth.

Feigl, Herbert. 1950. *"De Principus Non Disputandum . . . ?* On the Meaning and the Limits of Justification." In *Philosophical Analyses: A Collection of Essays*, edited by Max Black, 119–56. Ithaca, N.Y.: Cornell University Press.

———. 1957. "Empiricism versus Theology." In *A Modern Introduction to Philosophy*, 1st ed., edited by Paul Edwards and Arthur Pap. Glencoe, Ill.: The Free Press.

Feyerabend, Paul. 1975. *Against Method*. London: Verso.

———. 1978. *Science in a Free Society*. London: New Left Books.

———. 1987. *Farewell to Reason*. London: Verso.

Flew, Antony, and MacIntyre, Alasdair. 1955. *New Essays for Philosophical Theology*. New York: Macmillan.

Friedman, Michael. 1997. "Philosophical Naturalism." *Proceedings and Addresses of the American Philosophical Association* 71, no. 2: 7–21.

Hägerström, Axel. 1964. *Philosophy and Religion*. Translated by Robert T. Sandin. London: Allen and Unwin, Ltd.

Hampshire, Stuart. 2000. *Justice is Conflict*. Princeton, N.J.: Princeton University Press.

Hare, R. M. 1973. "The Simple Believer." In *Religion and Morality*, edited by Gene Outka and John R. Reeder Jr., 393–427. New York: Anchor Press.

Hempel, G. Carl. 1951. "The Concept of Cognitive Significance." *Proceedings of American Academy of Arts and Sciences* 80, no. 1: 61–77.

———. 1959; first published in 1950. "The Empiricist Criterion of Meaning." In *Logical Positivism*, edited by A. J. Ayer, 108–29. Glencoe, Ill.: The Free Press.

———. 2000. *Selected Philosophical Essays*. Edited by Richard Jeffrey. Cambridge: Cambridge University Press.

Hick, John. 1959. "Belief and Life: The Fundamental Nature of the Christian Ethic." *Encounter* 20, no. 4: 494–516.

Kitcher, Philip. 1992. "The Naturalist's Return." *Philosophical Review* 101, no. 1: 53–114.

Kuhn, Thomas. 1962. *The Structure of Scientific Revolutions.* Chicago: University of Chicago Press.

———. 1970. *The Structure of Scientific Revolutions.* 2d ed. Chicago: University of Chicago Press.

MacIntyre, Alasdair. 1956. *Difficulties in Christian Belief.* London: SCM Press.

Marhenke, Paul. 1959. "Phenomenalism." In *Philosophical Analyses: A Collection of Essays,* edited by Max Black, 299–322. Ithaca, N.Y.: Cornell University Press.

Martin, Michael. 1997. "The Verificationist Challenge." In *A Companion to Philosophy of Religion,* edited by Philip L. Quinn and Charles Taliaferro, 204–12. Oxford: Blackwell.

McDowell, John. 1994. *Mind and World.* Cambridge, Mass.: Harvard University Press.

———. 1998. *Mind, Value and Reality.* Cambridge, Mass.: Harvard University Press.

Misak, C. J. 1991. *Truth and the End of Inquiry: A Peircean Account of Truth.* Oxford: Clarendon Press.

———. 1995. *Verificationism: Its History and Prospects.* London: Routledge.

Mitchell, Basil, ed. 1957. *Faith and Logic.* London: Allen and Unwin Ltd.

Nielsen, Kai. 1962. "On Speaking of God." *Theoria* 28: 110–37.

———. 1971a. *Reason and Practice.* New York: Harper and Row.

———. 1971b. *Contemporary Critiques of Religion.* New York: Herder and Herder.

———. 1973. *Scepticism.* London: Macmillan.

———. 1982. *Introduction to the Philosophy of Religion.* London: Macmillan.

———. 1985. *Equality and Liberty: A Defense of Radical Egalitarianism.* Totowa, N.J.: Rowman and Allanheld.

———. 1989. *God, Scepticism and Modernity.* Ottawa, Ont.: University of Ottawa Press.

———. 1995. *On Transforming Philosophy.* Boulder, Colo.: Westview Pres.

———. 1996. *Naturalism without Foundations.* Amherst, N.Y.: Prometheus Books.

———. 1999. "Moral Point of View Theories." *Critica* 93: 105–16.

Penelhum, Terence. 1992. "Ethics with God and Ethics Without." In *On the Track of Reason,* edited by Rodger Beehler et al., 107–18. Boulder, Colo.: Westview Press.

Putnam, Hilary. 1990: *Realism with a Human Face.* Cambridge, Mass.: Harvard University Press.

———. 1995. *Pragmatism.* Oxford: Blackwell.

———. 1999. *The Threefold Cord.* New York: Columbia Universitiy Press.

Quine, W. V. 1991. "Two Dogmas in Retrospect." *Canadian Journal of Philosophy* 21, no. 3: 265–74.

Railton, Peter. 1995. "Made in the Shade: Moral Compatibilism and the Aims of Moral Theory." In *On the Relevance of Metaethics,* edited by Jocelyne Couture and Kai Nielsen, 79–106. Calgary, Alb.: University of Calgary Press.

Rhees, Rush. 1997. *Rush Rhees on Religion and Philosophy.* Edited by D. Z. Phillips. Cambridge: Cambridge University Press.

Rorty, Richard. 1991. *Objectivity, Relativism, and Truth.* Cambridge: Cambridge University Press.

———. 1998. *Truth and Progress.* Cambridge: Cambridge University Press.

———. 1999. *Philosophy and Social Hope*. London: Penguin Books.

———. 2000. "Response to Robert Brandon." In *Rorty and His Critics*, edited by Robert Brandon, 183–90. Oxford: Blackwell.

Sober, Elliott. 1999. "Testability." *Proceedings and Addresses of the American Philosophical Association* 73, no. 3: 47–76.

Stevenson, Charles. 1944. *Ethics and Language*. New Haven, Conn.: Yale University Press.

Stroud, Barry. 1996. "The Charm of Naturalism." *Proceedings and Addresses of the American Philosophical Association* 70, no. 2: 43–55.

Van Fraassen, Bas C. 1985. "Empiricism in the Philosophy of Science." In *Images of Science: Essays on Realism and Empiricism with a Reply from Bas C. van Fraassen*, edited by P. M. Churchland and C. A. Hooker, 230–70. Chicago: University of Chicago Press.

Wittgenstein, Ludwig. 1953. *Philosophical Investigations*. Translated by G. E. M. Anscombe. Oxford: Blackwell.

———. 1969. *On Certainty*. Translated by Denis Paul and G. E. M. Anscombe. Oxford: Blackwell.

INDEX